Extending Intelligence
Enhancement and New Constructs

The Educational Psychology Series
Robert J. Sternberg and Wendy M. Williams, Series Editors

For additional information on titles in **The Educational Psychology Series**
visit www.routledge.com <http://www.routledge.com/>

Extending Intelligence
Enhancement and New Constructs

Edited by

Patrick C. Kyllonen
Richard D. Roberts
Lazar Stankov

Routledge
Taylor & Francis Group

NEW YORK AND LONDON

Routledge
Taylor & Francis Group
270 Madison Ave,
New York, NY 10016

Routledge
Taylor & Francis Group
2 Park Square
Milton Park, Abingdon
Oxon OX14 4RN

First Published by

© 2008 by Taylor & Francis Group, LLC
Routledge is an imprint of Taylor & Francis Group, an Informa business

Transferred to Digital Printing 2009

International Standard Book Number-13: 978-0-8058-4504-4 (Hardcover)

Library of Congress Cataloging-in-Publication Data

Extending intelligence : enhancement and new constructs/edited by Patrick C. Kyllonen, Richard D. Roberts, Lazar Stankov.
    p. cm. — (The educational psychology series)
Consists of papers presented at a seminar held in 2001 at the University of Sydney.
Includes bibliographical references and index.
ISBN 0-8058-4504-6 (alk. paper)
    1. Learning, Psychology of—Congresses. 2. Intellect—Congresses. 3. Cognitive learning—Congresses. 4. Intelligence tests—Congresses. I. Kyllonen, Patrick C. II. Roberts, Richard D. III. Stankov, Lazar. IV. Series

LB1060.E97 2006
370.15'29—dc22
    2005054159

ISBN10: 0-805-84504-6 (hbk)
ISBN10: 0-415-87780-6 (pbk)

ISBN13: 978-0-805-84504-4 (hbk)
ISBN13: 978-0-415-87780-0 (pbk)

Visit the Taylor & Francis Web site at
http://www.taylorandfrancis.com

Contents

VII   Conclusions   361

Foreword

Sidney Irvine

When I organized the first Spearman Seminar at the University of Plymouth in the summer of 1993, it was an attempt to review what was known about the nature and measurement of human abilities after almost a century of research following the publication of Spearman's landmark paper in 1904. John B. Carroll was the first to be invited to give the Spearman Lecture. In accepting, he was able to bring conceptions of intelligence into a framework that in summary reveals that all abilities have the potential to become general, but that some abilities are more general than others. In that view, he was able to reconcile Thurstone with Spearman, by way of Godfrey Thomson, whose work and approach he so admired. Apart from Carroll's work, the authors in *Human Abilities, Their Nature and Measurement* show how Spearman's construct of general intelligence g, had at last begun to lose its status as a logical primitive that could not be further explained and described. Kyllonen's chapter on the empirical redefinition of g in terms of working memory provides a key to the theoretical construction of test items that measure intelligence. Before this approach, there was only an ostensive definition of items by pointing them out in tests of general intelligence. Building upon the contributions of Baddeley and Hitch in the measurement of working memory, Kyllonen's work implicitly bridges the gap between experimental and individual differences psychology described by Lee J. Cronbach in 1957 and perhaps never adequately addressed until the last decade.

Four years later the Seminar was once more held at Plymouth. It was conceived by the late Sam Messick at my request, and organized jointly by Educational Testing Service and the university. Hans Eysenck was to give the Spearman Lecture on that occasion. The focus had shifted from abilities and the concept of intelligence to how the domains of personality and intelligence could be said to coexist. Eysenck was unable to attend because of what turned out to be a terminal illness. Arthur Jensen was able to provide the keynote with his work on biometric measures. The Seminar proceedings were produced under the title *Intelligence and Personality*. The contributors reflected Messick's deep understanding of the issues and his choice of those who could best address them. Only John Berry, David Lohman, and Robert Sternberg, apart from Messick himself, appear as authors in the 1993 and 1997 proceedings. The concept of intelligence was enriched by the diversity of approaches and viewpoints of a new generation of contributors.

Perhaps to describe Messick's volume as illustrating hybrid vigor might be misinterpreted as harboring a fundamentalist view of intelligence. The location of the 2001 Seminar in the University of Sydney and the theme of new constructs are a tribute to the quest for better understanding of the effect of rapid social change on the environment of tests and measurements. In my view, the diversity and quality of the chapters in this volume have reached a standard that will be hard to follow and difficult to emulate. I commend this work for its insights, methods, scope, and, of course, intelligence. Spearman would, I believe, have been glad to contribute, to acknowledge the rehabilitation of the construct so ably demonstrated in the work of its authors, and perhaps preeminently illustrated in the career publications of the Spearman Lecturer for 2001, Robert J. Sternberg.

Acknowledgments

This book is based on a conference "Extending Intelligence: Enhancement and New Constructs" held at Sydney University, Sydney, Australia, November 28 to 30, 2001. The conference was the third of the ETS-sponsored Spearman Seminar Series, the previous two having been held at the University of Plymouth, in Plymouth, England, and hosted by Professor Sidney Irvine.

Each Spearman Seminar is based on a current interest topic in the field of human intelligence. The first Seminar, in 1993, had the theme of intelligence and information processing, the second, in 1997, intelligence and personality. For this third Seminar we combined two themes—enhancement and new constructs—both of which represent ways to extend intelligence.

Educational Testing Service's Research & Development Division along with Sydney University's Department of Psychology provided funding for the Conference and preparation of the book. In particular, we thank Dr. Drew Gitomer, who at the time of the conference was ETS R&D Vice President; and Sydney University's Professors Beryl Hesketh, Dean of Sciences, and Ian Curthoys, Psychology Department, Head. Support for preparation of the book was continued under the leadership of Dr. Ida Lawrence, the current ETS R&D Vice President.

The conference Organizing Committee consisted of Patrick Kyllonen from ETS, Richard Roberts and Lazar Stankov, then from the Psychology Department of Sydney University (now at ETS), Ian Dennis (Psychology Department, Plymouth University), and Sidney Irvine (Plymouth University, Emeritus). The ideas, themes, and discussions emerging from committee meetings, overseas long-distance telephone calls, and e-mail exchanges shaped the conference and are reflected in the book.

Many people contributed to the success of the conference. We thank Kathy Howell for her assistance in making travel, payment, and other conference arrangements. We thank Gerry Pallier for his help in making venue and hotel arrangements, and for a spirited performance in his role as impromptu Master of Ceremonies at the conference dinner in the Great Hall. Many Sydney University psychology students deserve a special thanks for donating their time in assisting with the program, conference logistics, transportation, and other on-the-ground activities. These include Fadi "Mr. Magic" Anjoul, David Bowman, Andrew Cartwright, Vanessa Danthiir, Christina Donatti, Jason Gallate, Alicia Garcia, Andrew J. Hawkins, Tim "Reptilio" Iken, Lisa Karlov, Sabina Kleitman, Heidi Krause, Pippa Markham, Kirstin O'Brien, Jane "Ms. Dependable" Rouse, Kath Ryan, Joel Werner, Laura Whitfield, and a good many others that we regretfully (and with deepest and sincere apologies) have probably failed to mention. (In truth, we can't wait until the enhancement aids described by Bradley Rhodes, at the conference and later in this volume, become widely available.)

By tradition, Spearman Seminars recognize special invited speeches. Robert J. Sternberg gave the "Spearman Lecture," James P. Comer gave the "Spearman Public Service Lecture," and Sidney Irvine gave the "Spearman Opening Address." Finally, we were treated to an inspired lecture on various political and social issues in the Great Hall by the Hon. Dr. Carmen Lawrence, MP, Shadow Ministry for Industry, Innovation, and Technology, and Shadow Ministry for the Status of Women, and Federal Member for Fremantle, Australia. Being a psychologist by training, Dr. Lawrence expressed an informed and optimistic view about the possibility of enhancement and stressed the importance of research in this area of the behavioral sciences. Although not part of the current volume, her talk pointed to the possibility that research reported here may have broader implications and contribute to the improvement of the human condition.

Finally, although the compilation of this volume was made complicated by two of the editors leaving for the shores of the United States, we have several people to thank for bringing this to fruition. Again, Kathy Howell was fastidious in ensuring that the manuscript was just that, while various people gave of their time in editing, commenting, or otherwise assisting in the production process, including Susan Martin, Ralf Schulze, and many of the staff at Lawrence Erlbaum Associates. Thanks too for the support of various family and friends both during the conference and the writing phase—you have been patient, supportive, and above all, understanding.

—Patrick C. Kyllonen
Richard D. Roberts
Lazar Stankov

David Benton
University of Wales Swansea
Wales, United Kingdom

April Bleske-Rechepk
Vanderbuilt University
Nashville, Tennessee

Nathan Brody
Wesleyan University
Middletown, Connecticut

Margaret Burchinal
Frank Porter Graham Child Development Institute
University of North Carolina at Chapel Hill
Chapel Hill, North Carolina

Frances A. Campbell
Frank Porter Graham Child Development Institute
University of North Carolina at Chapel Hill
Chapel Hill, North Carolina

David R. Caruso
Work-Life Strategies
New Canaan, Connecticut

James P. Comer
Child Study Center
Yale University
New Haven, Connecticut

David F. Dinges
University of Pennsylvania
School of Medicine
Philadelphia, Pennsylvania

James R. Flynn
University of Otago
Auckland, New Zealand

Elena L. Grigorenko
Yale University
New Haven, Connecticut

Jan-Eric Gustafson
Goteborg University

Gothenburg, Sweden

Diane F. Halpern
Berger Institute for Work, Family, and Children
Claremont McKenna College
Claremont, California

John L. Horn
Deceased
University of Southern California
Los Angeles, California

Earl B. Hunt
University of Washington
Seattle, Washington

Linda Jarvin
Yale University
New Haven, Connecticut

Reinhold Kliegl
University of Potsdam
Potsdam, Germany

David Lubinski
Vanderbilt University
Nashville, Tennessee

John J. McArdle
University of Southern California
Los Angeles, California

John D. Mayer
University of New Hampshire
Durham, New Hampshire

Weihua Niu
Yale University
New Haven, Connecticut

David Preiss
Yale University
New Haven, Connecticut

Doris Philipp
University of Potsdam
Potsdam, Germany

Bradley Rhodes
Ricoh Innovations
Menlo Park, California

List of Contributors

Naomi Rogers
University of Pennsylvania School of Medicine
Philadelphia, Pennsylvania

Peter Salovey
Yale University
New Haven Connecticut

Robert J. Sternberg
Yale University
New Haven, Connecticut

I
▼▼▼▼▼▼▼

GENERAL BACKGROUND

1

▼▼▼▼▼▼▼

Enhancement and New Constructs: Overview and Rationale

Patrick C. Kyllonen[1]
Lazar Stankov
Richard D. Roberts
Educational Testing Service

This book is the third in a series commemorating the contributions of Charles Spearman, one of the pioneers of the study of human individual differences and the statistical technique of factor analysis. The previous two books in the series covered advances in modeling cognitive abilities (Dennis & Tapsfield, 1996) and the role of personality and cognitive styles in shaping the directions of intellect (Collis & Messick, 2001). In each instance, the books derived from a related conference, the Spearman Seminar. The goal of the present book, as well as the conference from which it originated, was to bring together diverse perspectives on the enhancement of human cognitive abilities and to challenge the premise that intelligence is destiny. Coverage of new constructs sought to broaden what might be considered the domain of human cognitive abilities even further. We consider the twin themes of intellectual enhancement and new constructs to be timely, for several reasons.

First, despite the potentially enormous societal and economic benefits that could be realized from addressing the questions of whether intelligence can be increased (and how), intellectual enhancement has not been given enough attention in the scientific literature. Much, if not most, of the scientific research on the topic of human cognitive abilities has focused on the issue of what intelligence is, not whether it can be increased.[2]

Can intelligence be increased? The answer is not simple. On the one hand, the stability of individual differences of scores on intelligence tests, from fairly early ages to later adulthood, is well established (e.g., Deary, Whalley, Lemmon, Crawford, & Starr, 2000). On the other

---

[1]The ideas expressed in this paper are those of the authors and not necessarily of the Educational Testing Service.
[2]This is not to suggest that ours is the first book-length treatment of the topic, rather we contend that research has not proportionately addressed intellectual enhancement, an issue that we take up further in the chapter. Witness too that, to the best of our knowledge, it is more than decades since the last book on this topic (see Detterman & Sternberg, 1982).

hand, this stability of intelligence test scores, even if high, does not imply that intelligence is immutable (e.g., Neisser, 1998). The findings of increases in cognitive test performance as a result of cognitive skill training interventions—the Carolina Abecedarian project (Ramey, Campbell, & Ramey, 1999), Venezuela's Project Intelligence (Herrnstein, Nickerson, de Sanchez, & Swets, 1986), coaching for the SAT (Powers & Rock, 1999), to name a few—are not inconsistent with the high stability of individual differences observed with intelligence. Nor is the well-documented increase in mean intelligence test scores over the past century, the so-called "Flynn effect" (Flynn, 1999).

An important question to address is what features of these phenomena and interventions are responsible for the increase in test scores. Several kinds of possibilities have been raised in research on different kinds of interventions. Project Intelligence data (Herrnstein et al., 1986) suggested a large teaching effect, but left open the question of what teaching methods or teacher qualities were responsible for it. The Abecedarian project (Ramey et al., 1999) and Head Start[3] (2000) focus on early childhood: How important are the age at the time of intervention and other individual characteristics for intellectual enhancement? Research reviewed by Powers and Rock (1999) on adolescent participants showed that coaching was especially effective as a remedial strategy, in that those with relatively low math scores showed greater coaching benefit than those with higher scores. Can these findings be generalized to and across age groups, other subpopulations, variants of interventions, measures of intelligence, and time? It would especially be useful to systematically identify and analyze intervention features that contribute to enhancement. Are some intervention strategies broadly generalizable? Or are there particular qualities and features associated with effective interventions?

A second reason for considering intellectual enhancement is that although it is a generally important phenomenon, it is perhaps particularly important when targeted to underperforming segments of the population. It is a reflection of this point of view that the preponderance of major intellectual enhancement programs—the Abecedarian project, Project Intelligence, Head Start—have been directed toward minorities and the poor, groups that have typically performed relatively less well on intelligence and achievement measures. This fact reflects a continuing interest in understanding, and attempting to close, *achievement* or *score gaps*, persistent differences in average test scores between African American and Hispanic students on the one hand and Whites and Asians on the other (e.g., Jencks & Phillips, 1998; Zernicke, 2000).

These differences are, of course, of serious concern for many reasons, including the desire to improve social justice and race relations, to eliminate the pernicious effects of racial stereotypes, and to improve early education and other social, employment, and educational policies and practices. Given the importance and the apparent stability of the score gap, a key question is what accounts for it. Many individual and social factors have been examined, including early childhood development such as weight at birth, lead poisoning, nutrition; differential expectations for individual achievement; parental education; educational opportunity; school safety; student mobility; class size; parent participation; and the effects of stereotyping on intellectual performance (see, e.g., Barton, 2003; Jencks & Phillips, 1998). Many of these variables are related to academic performance in mathematics and reading that are currently assessed for the purpose of Adequate Yearly Progress Reports under the No Child Left Behind Act in the United States, and some are known to contribute to the observed score differences.

---

[3]Information on Head Start Research may be found at the following www site: http://www.acf.hhs.gov/programs/opre/index.html

A third reason for considering intellectual enhancement is that there has been a clamor to consider intelligence from a wider perspective. Most of the attention in examining intellectual enhancement, and in accounting for and closing the test score gap, has focused on general cognitive ability. But there has been a growing sentiment that there is more to intellectual functioning than general cognitive ability as measured by standard intelligence tests. Practical intelligence (Sternberg & Wagner, 1986) and emotional intelligence (Mayer, Salovey, & Caruso, 2000) are examples of concepts reflecting this growing belief. Certainly, practical and emotional intelligences are rather disparate concepts. But a characteristic of the literature on them is that enhancement is a central concern. Are there general principles beginning to emerge from these "new intelligence" literatures? How do people become practically intelligent? How about emotionally intelligent? Are there findings and emerging principles that might be applied to understanding the score gap issue? Might these lead to more effective intellectual interventions?

To address these issues we organized the contributions to this volume into categories representing ways in which enhancement might occur: via direct instruction, via cognitive development, and over the passage of time. To these we added firstly a new constructs section that addressed the issue of how new conceptions of intelligence might be amenable to enhancement and secondly, a section exploring technological and biological attempts to enhance cognition, which are very much future-orientated. To provide the reader with our perspective on various issues raised by the contributors, a final section reviews each chapter and attempts to place these within an overarching framework that includes suggestions for future, systematic research.

Enhancement via Instruction

Chapters in this section review a variety of instructional strategies for enhancing intelligence. These include advances in computerized instructional methods, such as interactive model-based assessments (Hunt, chap. 2, this volume; see also Hunt, 2001; Hunt & Minstrell, 1994) and early childhood intervention strategies, such as Head Start and the Abecedarian project (Campbell, chap. 4, this volume; see also Ramey et al., 1999). There also is discussion concerning the development of cognitive ability that results from schooling (Gustafsson, chap. 3, this volume; see also Härnqvist, Gustafsson, Muthén, & Nelson, 1994). Themes are the identification of pertinent factors that have led to successful enhancement, and speculations about whether these factors might be applied in other contexts, such as with young adults, and for what kinds of instructional and training domains. To give a flavor both to consensus and controversies in this domain, Brody (chap. 5, this volume), who has written extensively about the relative effectiveness of various instructional intervention strategies on intellectual enhancement (Brody, 1992), discussed the chapters in this section.

Enhancement via Development (Over the Life Cycle)

Chapters in this section concern the intellectual enhancing effects of cognitive development. The focus is predominantly on interventions to enhance those changes, such as comprehensive assessment to increase self-awareness and to allow individuals to focus on observed strengths (Lubinski & Bleske-Rechek, chap. 7, this volume; see also Lubinski & Benbow, 2000) and the Comer School Development Program (Comer, chap. 6, this volume; see also Comer, 1998). We also included here applications of sophisticated growth models to help quantify the effects of various interventions (McArdle, chap. 8, this volume; see also McArdle, Prescott, Hamagami, & Horn, 1998), and a discussion of the role standardized testing can play in promoting intellectual development across four different countries (Grigorenko, Jarvin, Niu, & Preiss, chap. 9, this volume). These chapters raise some interesting issues, which we did not initially consider and that we take up further in the concluding commentary (Roberts, Stankov, Schulze, & Kyllonen, chap. 19, this volume).

Enhancement Over Time

Chapters in this section discuss time-related enhancement other than cognitive development. Both Horn's (chap.10, this volume) and Kliegl and Philipp's (chap.11, this volume) chapters concern the development of expertise, which is a particular kind of intellectual enhancement, with certain benefits (optimal performance), but some costs (e.g., intensive, time consuming, and little generalization) compared to other enhancement methods. Some are attempting to apply expertise-enhancement principles to various additional performance domains (Kliegl and Philipp, chap. 11, this volume; see also Kliegl, Philipp, Luckner, & Krampe, 2001). Another example of enhancement over time is the ubiquitous growth in scores on intelligence tests that has occurred in numerous settings, countries, and cultures over the past 50 years (Flynn, chap. 12, this volume; see also Flynn, 1999). A theme in this section of the volume is discussion of which factors are most important for enhancing intelligence over the long haul.

Enhancement via New Constructs

Beyond general cognitive ability, or intelligence, per se, there are factors, both cognitive and noncognitive, that might be said to support intelligent behavior. A theme of this section of the volume is that by enhancing these factors one can enhance intellectual or cognitive performance. For example, Sternberg (chap. 13, this volume; see also Sternberg, 1996) has suggested that creativity and practical intelligence are supplemental to analytic intelligence in producing intelligent behavior, and has suggested methods for enhancing those factors. One that has received particular attention with regard to enhancement is practical intelligence (Sternberg & Grigorenko, 2000). The concept of emotional intelligence extends the idea still further in suggesting that social and emotional factors can affect intelligent behavior (Mayer, Salovey, & Caruso, chap. 14, this volume; see also Mayer et al., 2000). A third new construct that we included here was critical thinking, addressed in the chapter by Halpern (chap. 15).

New Directions in Enhancement

Chapters in this section are concerned with methods for enhancing human intelligence other than instruction and development, methods normally not covered in scientific treatments of human cognitive abilities. We believe these may become increasingly popular as topics of future research and development efforts in the intelligence literature. Among these new intelligence enhancement methods are nutrition (Benton, chap. 16; see also Donohoe & Benton, 1999) and supplements (Benton, Griffiths, & Haller, 1997); external technological aids, such as "wearable intelligence" (Pentland, 1998) or "just in time information retrieval" (Rhodes, chap. 17; see also Rhodes, 2000); and the control of the sleep-wake cycle (Dinges & Rogers, chap. 18; see also Van Dongen & Dinges, 1999). Each of these enhancement methods may have transient effects that when multiplied over the course of a lifetime could have far-reaching consequences.

General Issues and Themes

Because of the diversity of perspectives we brought together for this volume, we thought it would be useful to have authors, the conference participants, and now the current reader reflect on a common list of questions related to evaluating enhancement effects and interventions.

These were not meant to be restrictive, but rather to stimulate thinking. These questions, which appear important to consider for any program of research aimed at enhancing cognitive ability, are as follows:

1. *What is the construct that is being enhanced?* There is a long list of candidate processes, including the general factor (*g*), fluid intelligence (Gf), crystallized intelligence (Gc), competence, talents, knowledge, and skills.

2. *What is the nature of the enhancement?* For example, is it via education, coaching and/or motivational techniques, a developmental phenomenon, a psychopharmacological one, or some combination of all of these factors?

3. *What evidence is there that the construct can be enhanced?* This question boils down to asking what are the tests, measures, or indicators suggestive of an enhancement effect; whether alternative hypotheses can be ruled out; and whether methods and design are adequate. A closely related question concerns determining from among a number of available methodologies (e.g., correlational, experimental) the technique that is most useful for studying enhancement effects.

4. *How generalizable are enhancement effects?* The possible answers to this question require ascertaining the range of other groups of (potential) participants, intervention procedures, measures, indicators, or criterion performances, settings, and time points where effects may be observed. A related question is the duration of enhancement: Do effects vanish after a short period or extend across the individual's life?

5. *How are cognitive enhancements made possible?* Again, there is a potentially long list of candidate processes, including practice, exposure to content, exposure to processes, and provision of specific exercises. Related issues include ascertaining whether interventions need to be tailored to the specific individual, whether such fine-tuning is unnecessary; and whether the intervention is expected to affect low- and high-ability groups to the same or varying degrees.

6. *What factors facilitate enhancement?* Candidate environmental factors include a good family, good teachers, and good mentors. Likely there is also a range of noncognitive or affective factors—including motivation, persistence, attitude, self-concept, self-confidence, values, and so forth—that play important roles.

7. *Does enhancement depend on biological makeup?* If there are neurological underpinnings associated with enhancements, what are these neurological substrates and how can they be measured and interpreted?

8. *What are the contextual limits to enhancement and what are the barriers to achieving those limits?* We might envisage the following as setting limits on what might actually be achieved in studies examining intellectual enhancement: theory, funding, ethical concerns, politics, and ideology. We asked the authors to keep these issues in mind as they wrote each chapter.

Anticipated Outcomes

Enhancement is a topic not typically covered in books or professional meetings on human intelligence. For example, an inspection of the programs for recent meetings of the International Society of the Study of Individual Differences (http://psyserver.uni-graz.at/issid2003/index.htm) and the International Society for Intelligence Research (http://www.isironline.org/abstracts/index.html) revealed no papers on enhancing intelligence. Nor was the topic covered in Sternberg's "Intelligence for the Next Millenium" conference (Sternberg, Lautrey, & Lubart, 2003).

In the 1990s the U.S. National Research Council and the Department of the Army conducted several meetings and assembled several volumes concerned with organizing what we know about intellectual enhancement (Druckman & Bjork, 1991, 1994; Druckman & Swets, 1988), but the perspective was different from the current effort. Their focus was on the learning and memory literature, whereas here we pay more attention to individual differences and the human intelligence perspective. This volume also includes a number of topics that were not reviewed in the earlier work, such as nutrition, psychopharmacology, circadian rhythms, rising test scores, emotional intelligence, and wearable intelligence. Some of these topics are treated in the nascent field of ergogenics (Angel, Brooks, Greenley, & Kumagi, 1999; Brabin-Smith, 2000).

In summary, we had several aspirations in assembling this volume. We believe that many research camps are addressing cognitive enhancement, but from different perspectives. We thought that putting them together might stimulate some new, productive interchanges. We also believe that enhancement is a worthy topic for the field of human intelligence, for a variety of reasons ranging from addressing the score gap to the aging of the population. Doubtless too, we concede that our assembled panel of stellar contributors is likely to uncover additional issues that we did not consider in either planning the conference or writing this introductory chapter. Nevertheless, it is our hope that this volume triggers an integration of perspectives that will move the field forward to address both scientifically valid and socially relevant concerns.

REFERENCES

Angel, H., Brooks, J., Greenley, M., & Kumagi, J. (1999). *Human factors integration requirements for armored fighting vehicles (AFVS): Part III—Literature review* (DCIEM No. CR-2000-075). Defence and Civil Institute of Environmental Medicine, Canadian Department of National Defence, Ontario, Canada. Retrieved March 25, 2005, from Defense Research Reports Database, Defense R&D Canada via http://pubs.drdc-rddc.gc.ca/pubdocs/pcow1_e.html

Barton, P. E. (2003). *Parsing the achievement gap: Baselines for tracking progress.* ETS' Policy Information Center. Retrieved March 24, 2005 from http://www.ets.org/research/pic

Benton, D., Griffiths, R., & Haller, J. (1997). Thiamine supplementation, mood, and cognitive functioning. *Psychopharmacology, 129,* 66–71.

Brabin-Smith, R (2000, March). Opening address. *International Conference on Physiological & Cognitive Performance in Extreme Environments.* Australian Defence Science & Technology Office, Canberra, Australia.

Brody, N. (1992). *Intelligence.* New York: Academic Press.

Collis, J. M., & Messick, S. (Eds.). (2001). *Intelligence and personality: Bridging the gap in theory and measurement.* Mahwah, NJ: Lawrence Erlbaum Associates.

Comer, J. P. (1998). *Waiting for a miracle: Why schools can't solve our problems—and how we can.* New York: Dutton.

Deary, I. J., Whalley, L. J., Lemmon, H., Crawford, J. R., & Starr, J. M. (2000). The stability of individual differences in mental ability from childhood to old age: Follow-up of the 1932 Scottish Mental Survey. *Intelligence, 28,* 49–55.

Dennis, I., & Tapsfield, P. (Eds.). (1996). *Human abilities: Their nature and measurement.* Mahwah, NJ: Lawrence Erlbaum Associates.

Donohoe, R. T., & Benton, D. (1999). Cognitive functioning is susceptible to the level of blood glucose. *Psychopharmacology, 145,* 378–385.

Druckman, D., & Swets, J. A. (Eds.). (1988). *Enhancing human performance: Issues, theories, and techniques.* Washington, DC: National Academy Press.

Druckman, D., & Bjork, R. A. (Eds.). (1991). *In the mind's eye: Enhancing human performance.* Washington, DC: National Academy Press.

Druckman, D., & Bjork, R. A. (Eds.). (1994). *Learning, remembering, and believing: Enhancing human performance*. Washington, DC: National Academy Press.

Flynn, J. R. (1999). Searching for justice: The discovery of IQ gains over time. *American Psychologist, 54*, 5–20.

Härnqvist, K., Gustafsson, J.-E., Muthén, B. O., & Nelson, G. (1994). Hierarchical models of ability at individual and class levels. *Intelligence, 18*, 165–187.

Herrnstein, R.-J., Nickerson, R. S., de Sanchez, M., & Swets, J. A. (1986). Teaching thinking skills. *American-Psychologist, 41*, 1279–1289.

Hunt, E. B. (2001). Themes in cognitive science and education. In S. M. Carver & D. Klahr (Eds.), *Cognition and instruction: Twenty-five years of progress* (pp. 427–437). Mahwah, NJ: Lawrence Erlbaum Associates.

Hunt, E. B., & Minstrell, J. (1994). A cognitive approach to the teaching of physics. In E. B. Hunt, J. Minstrell, & K. McGilly (Eds.), *Classroom lessons: Integrating cognitive theory and classroom practice* (pp. 51–74). Cambridge, MA: MIT Press.

Jencks, C., & Phillips, M. (Eds.). (1998). *The black–white test score gap*. Washington, DC: Brookings Institute Press.

Kliegl, R., Philipp, D., Luckner, M., & Krampe, R. T. (2001). Face memory skill acquisition. In N. Charness & D. C. Parks (Eds.), *Communication, technology and aging: Opportunities and challenges for the future* (pp. 169–186). New York: Springer.

Lubinski, D., & Benbow, C. P. (2000). States of excellence. *American Psychologist, 55*, 137–150.

Mayer, J. D., Salovey, P., & Caruso, D. R. (2000). Models of emotional intelligence. In R. J. Sternberg (Ed.), *Handbook of intelligence* (pp. 396–420). New York: Cambridge University Press.

McArdle, J. J., Prescott, C. A., Hamagami, F., & Horn, J. L. (1998). A contemporary method for developmental-genetic analyses of age changes in intellectual abilities. *Developmental Neuropsychology, 14*, 69–114.

Neisser, U. (Ed.). (1998). *The rising curve: Long-term gains in IQ and related measures*. Washington, DC: American Psychological Association.

Pentland, A. P. (1998). Wearable intelligence. *Scientific American Presents: Exploring Intelligence, 9(4)*, 90–95.

Powers, D. E., & Rock, D. A. (1999). Effects of coaching on SAT I: Reasoning test scores. *Journal of Educational Measurement, 36*, 93–118.

Ramey, C. T., Campbell, F. A., & Ramey, S. L. (1999). Early intervention: Successful pathways to improving intellectual development. *Developmental Neuropsychology, 16*, 385–392. (See also the project web site, http://www.fpg.unc.edu/~abc/)

Rhodes, B. J. (2000). *Just-in-time information retrieval*. Unpublished doctoral dissertation, MIT, Cambridge, MA. Retrieved on March 25, 2005, from http://www.bradleyrhodes.com/

Sternberg, R. J. (1996). *Successful intelligence*. New York: Simon & Schuster.

Sternberg, R. J., Forsythe, G. B., Hedlund, J., Horvath, J. A., Wagner, R. K., Williams W. M. et al. (2000). *Practical intelligence in everyday life*. New York: Cambridge University Press.

Sternberg, R. J., & Grigorenko, E. L. (2000). Practical intelligence and its development. In R. Bar-On & J. D. A. Parker (Eds.), *The handbook of emotional intelligence: Theory, development, assessment, and application at home, school, and in the workplace* (pp. 215–243). San Francisco: Jossey-Bass.

Sternberg, R. J., Lautrey, J., & Lubart, T. I. (Eds.). (2003). *Models of intelligence: International perspectives*. Washington, DC: American Psychological Association.

Sternberg, R. J., & Wagner, R. K. (1986). *Practical intelligence: Nature and origins of competence in the everyday world*. New York: Cambridge University Press.

Van Dongen, H. P. A., & Dinges, D. F. (1999). Circadian rhythms in fatigue, alertness, and performance. In M. H. Kryger, T. Roth, & W. C. Dement (Eds.), *Principles and practice of sleep medicine* (3rd ed., pp. 391–399). Orlando, FL: Saunders.

Zernike, K. (2000, August 13). Ideas and trends: A gap in test scores becomes a talking point. *New York Times*.

ENHANCEMENT VIA INSTRUCTION

2

▼▼▼▼▼▼▼

Improving Intelligence:
What's the Difference From Education?[1]

Earl Hunt
The University of Washington

This chapter discusses two things, the concept of crystallized intelligence (Gc) and ways to improve it. Some people may feel that the ideas presented here constitute educational methods rather than being part of a discussion of intelligence. If you take the attitude that intelligence is equivalent to biologically determined individual differences in mental competence, then that argument is right. One of the theses of this chapter, though, is that the argument is wrong. I believe that the study of intelligence should be the study of individual differences in human competence to perform cognitive tasks. That competence is determined by a biological capability to move information around in the head and by social conditions that facilitate the acquisition of information to be moved. Therefore reports of better ways to get information inside a person's brain ought to be of great interest to those who would study intelligence.

THE STATUS OF THEORIES OF INTELLIGENCE

Any proposal to improve something should be clear about what is to be improved. In the case of intelligence the subject matter is very sensitive to definitions. De facto, intelligence is often defined in terms of the results obtained using a particular technology, psychometric testing. Large numbers of people, said to be a sample more or less representative of the "general population" of school children, young adults, adults, or elderly adults, are asked to respond to a variety of questions. In order to facilitate objective scoring, and in order to get enough data to analyze, questions are chosen that have brief, well-defined answers. Appeals to assistance during testing, such as looking up material in a book or referring to one's notes, are regarded as cheating. The examinees are certainly not urged to consult each other. A typical test session lasts 2 to 8 hours, although occasional studies have reported tests over a period of days. The statistician Robert Mislevy has referred to this methodology as the "Drop in from the Sky" method of observing human performance.

---

[1]The research on which this chapter is based was supported by a grant from the National Science Foundation to the University of Washington (Earl Hunt, principal investigator) and several grants from the James S. McDonnell Foundation and the Hewlett-Packard Foundation.

Both my description and Mislevy's phrase are somewhat pejorative. Complete attacks are not warranted. Reliable, useful information can be obtained by this method of data collection. Test results can be used to predict extra-laboratory performance, both in academia and the workplace (Herrnstein & Murray, 1994; Hunt, 1995). Furthermore, and perhaps most importantly, no other method of evaluating cognitive performance does any better (Schmidt & Hunter, 1998). Those alternatives that predict as well as psychometric testing does, such as structured interviews and job samples, are far more expensive. By any cost–benefit criterion the conventional test is a bargain. Therefore it is worthwhile to conduct detailed analyses of the performance that the tests elicit. The study of intelligence is very much based on such analyses.

Psychometric studies of test performance have produced a coherent theory of intelligence. It is generally agreed that the most accurate model is a hierarchical one, in which three separate talents, Crystallized Intelligence (Gc), Fluid Intelligence (Gf), and Visual–Spatial Reasoning (Gv) stand out. A number of other dimensions of ability (e.g., short-and long-term memory retrieval, ability to deal with auditory stimuli) can also be identified, but I concentrate here on Gc and Gf.

As is well known, Gc and Gf are correlated, leading many investigators to argue that the separate abilities are actually special manifestations of a more general ability, "general intelligence," g (Gottfredson, 1997; Gustafsson, 1988; Jensen, 1998). However, the extent to which the different intelligences vary depends dramatically on the general level of ability. Detterman and Daniel (1989), and since them several others (e.g. Deary et al., 1996), have shown that there is a very large general factor in populations of low average ability, but that high-level talents are much more differentiated. This will be an important point in what follows.

Gf is defined as the ability to deal with new and unusual problems, whereas Gc is defined as the ability to apply previously learned problem-solving methods to the problem at hand. Because all old problems were new once, Raymond Cattell (1971), the initial developer of the Gc–Gf model, argued that Gc is largely the result of a person's having invested Gf into particular learning experiences. Viewed this way, Gf is a more basic ability than Gc. This is further backed up by the observation that performance in Gf-loaded rests is accompanied by activity in particular brain regions, notably the dorso-lateral prefrontal cortex (Duncan, Emslie, Williams, & Johnson, 1996) and by numerous studies showing that scores on Gf-loaded tests are sensitive to direct insults to the brain. Because this line of reasoning reinforces legitimate goals of reductionism in science, Gf has been said to be identical to g. A great deal of recent research has been devoted to finding the genetic and brain-based components of Gf or g.

However, Gf is not the whole story. Gc is both important and difficult to deal with in the standard psychometric framework. First I explain why we know that the two are different, then I look at the concept of Gc.

One of the classic experimental techniques for demonstrating that behaviors A and B are generated by different mechanisms is to show there is some experimental manipulation, C, that affects A and B in different ways. There is a "natural experiment" using this design that has shown, unequivocally, that Gf and Gc are different constructs, whatever their statistical association may be. It is well known that on a population basis, measures of Gf begin to fall in fairly early adulthood and continue to decline through the 50s and 60s, showing marked decline in the 70s and 80s. By contrast, Gc measures actually rise in early to middle adulthood and decline very slowly until great age is reached (Horn & Noll, 1994).

Although he did not use these terms, Flynn (1987) alluded to a second great experiment: the passage of generations. He documented rises in measures of Gf, and especially the Raven

Matrices, over the past seven decades. This supports earlier analyses by Schaie (1994), who, as early as the 1960s, documented cohort effects on intelligence tests in cross-longitudinal designs. Flynn also argued that measures of Gc, such as the Scholastic Assessment Test (SAT) may have actually fallen over the same time period. Raven (2000) reported data that could be used to support a similar conclusion. I am somewhat concerned that the data on generational effects are being oversimplified, a point that I expand on later. However, if one accepts the Flynn and Raven data at face value, one is forced to conclude that there is a strong case for distinguishing between Gc and Gf, as the logic of the cohort studies is analogous to the logic of the studies of aging.

Those authors who might be characterized as holding a strong *g* position are generally pessimistic about the chances to improve intelligence by overt interventions. See, for instance, Jensen's (1998) book. In this chapter I argue that it is indeed possible to improve intelligence, in the sense of improving Gc. Furthermore, I demonstrate how it can be done.

PSYCHOLOGICAL STATUS OF GC

Raymond Cattell (1971) stated "Crystallized intelligence (gc) expressions…operate in areas where the judgments have been taught systematically or experienced before" (p. 98).

This definition refers to how well someone can use information, and does not discriminate between different sources of that information. Horn (1985; Horn & Noll, 1994) make the de facto connection to testing clearer.

"(Gc is) …measured in tasks indicating breadth and depth of knowledge of the dominant culture" (Horn, p. 25).

This conceptual definition was extracted from the observation that tests of vocabulary, verbal comprehension, world knowledge, simple numerical operations, and general information load on the same factor.

The two definitions differ in an important way. Cattell made a psychological distinction; according to his definition, Gc reflects the use of previously acquired knowledge. Horn, reflecting empirical practices, added to the psychological definition the qualification that Gc refers to, or at least is measured by, the use of previously acquired knowledge that is associated with a particular (modern postindustrial) culture. According to the Horn definition, which has certainly been adopted by modern designers of tests, the only knowledge that is "fair" to test in evaluating Gc is that knowledge that is widespread in our current culture.

When it comes to the design of practical tests, and particularly for tests used either for academic selection or for general industrial personnel screening, Horn's cultural codicil makes sense. Tests used for these purposes are intended to predict performance in a certain cultural milieu that is part and parcel of Western society. Furthermore, it defies our concept of fairness to measure someone's possession of information when that person has not had the opportunity to acquire it. In practice, then, a Gc test is supposed to evaluate whether or not a person has picked up information that he or she had a "fair chance" to pick up. Many of the debates about the validity or invalidity of intelligence testing can be understood in this light. A debate about whether a vocabulary test based on upper-middle class White usage is "fair" to African American children often amounts to a debate about the extent to which it is reasonable to expect children to pick up usage both from their social context and from television!

This viewpoint suggests a straightforward way to "improve intelligence," by improving either the amount or efficiency of an individual's exposure to tested knowledge. This amounts to education, and there are at least assertions that education does not improve intelligence. Therefore, and in order to set the stage for some of my later argument, let us examine the evidence for one of the most highly publicized of such assertions.

In their widely publicized book *The Bell Curve*, Herrnstein and Murray (1994) asserted that educational level attained had no influence on "intelligence" (not further distinguished), on the basis that an analysis of covariance showed no statistical relationship between the educational level attained by young adults and their scores on the Armed Forces Qualification Test (AFQT), once statistical allowance was made for the predictive effects of a childhood intelligence test, taken prior to entering school. Winship and Korenman (1997) reanalyzed Herrnstein and Murray's data, using different techniques, and concluded that IQ (once again, not further distinguished) increased by two points per year of school attended. The details of the different analyses need not concern us. What does concern us is the way in which observations were generalized. Both sides in this debate stated their conclusions in terms of general intelligence, rather than in terms of AFQT scores.

This shows the danger of reifying concepts, without considering the nature of the data underlying the concept. It also shows the danger of concentrating on statistical analyses of relationships between test scores, without considering carefully the behavior required to take tests in the first place.

The AFQT is a weighted sum of several of the tests on the Armed Services Vocational Aptitude Battery (ASVAB). Not surprisingly, it is highly correlated with the first factor extracted from factor analyses of the ASVAB. This fact was the basis of Herrnstein and Murray's contention that the AFQT measured *g*; the first factor of a battery is often associated with general intelligence. Their generalization was incorrect. Roberts et al. (2000) conducted a factor-analytic study of the ASVAB combined with tests that previously had been shown to be markers for Gc or Gf. The results were clear-cut; the first general factor of the ASVAB is a marker for Gc. So the debate should be about Gc, not general intelligence. (And, I add, I think that a great deal of the argument in *The Bell Curve* could be rethought with Roberts et al.'s results in mind.)

Winship and Korenman's (1997) conclusion that "intelligence" was increased by schooling can similarly be criticized for dealing with abstractions rather than dealing with the behavior evaluated by the AFQT. In the version analyzed by Herrnstein and Murray (1994), the AFQT is a composite formed by nearly equal weighting of the ASVAB subtests of word knowledge, paragraph comprehension, arithmetic reasoning, and mathematics knowledge (p. 583). Every one of these topics is explicitly taught in American schools. If an additional year's schooling failed to produce improvement in these topics, school districts should be held accountable! (And, in fact, there is a considerable movement to do just that.)

The fact that conventional tests of Gc are essentially tests of school-taught subjects does invalidate the tests. E. D. Hirsch (1987) pointed out cultural knowledge is organized into *schema*, which are essentially preselected plans for solving certain types of problems. Hirsch used as an example the importance of understanding the Civil War in order to make sense of modern history. We also have a concept of a "fair trial," of the appropriate relationship between church and state, and, more prosaically, of how to behave in a restaurant, theater, or doctor's office. These schema tell us what to do, without having to have recourse to abstract first principles. People who can use these schema think more efficiently, and that is the definition of intelligence.

In addition to these schema, all of us have acquired specialized schema that are needed for our particular role in life. Questions about *linear regression model, residual legatee, balance-of-forces,* and *regulator gene* are not likely to appear on the typical test of Gc. They are more usually defined, and studied, as part of "expertise." However, the use of acquisition and use of these schema for reasoning is no different than the acquisition and use of general cultural schema. There is, therefore, a complete merging from the study of Gc to the study of expertise.

What is different, though, is the way that individual differences in the possession of schema have to be conceptualized. Quoting again from Horn, it is reasonable to believe that different people's "breadth and depth of knowledge of the dominant culture" (1985, p. 28) can be summarized in a unidimensional ordering. It is quite likely that a person who knows that the United States fought a war in Korea also knows that the United States fought a war in Vietnam. It is also likely that a person who knows who Colonel MacQuarie was also knows who Captain Cook was. In both cases the converse is not necessarily true.

Unidimensionality of knowledge breaks down rapidly when we begin to study deeper levels of knowledge acquisition and use. For instance, one would hesitate to say that physicians and lawyers have any generic differences in Gc, as expressed in Horn's definition. By and large, members of both groups are at the top of the intellectual heap. Beyond that, though, in terms of solving problems by acquired knowledge, that is, the Cattell definition, the two groups certainly use Gc in their everyday practice, but the knowledge bases from which they work are very different. This means that we have to find a new conceptualization, a metaphor if you will, to replace the geometric metaphor that has dominated intelligence testing (Sternberg, 1990). I now present two such conceptualizations.

One, which is easiest to think about, represents individual differences in mental competence as a "tree" that contains a variety of branches, each coming off at different points from a trunk representing general cultural schema. This is shown in Figure. 2.1. Note that the branches can come from different points along the trunk, thus representing the well-known fact that different levels of expertise are associated with different levels of knowledge about the culture in general. This representation can be thought of as a slight but significant generalization of the representations behind hierarchical models of intelligence.

An alternative representation is based on the concept of a knowledge space (Falmagne, Koope, Villaw & Doignant, 1990). The intuition behind a knowledge space is that virtually every problem we encounter requires the knowledge acquired in earlier problem-solving activities. For instance, solving calculus problems requires knowledge of algebra. This is simple enough. In other cases there may be several sufficient but no necessary conditions. There is an excellent example from industrial anthropology. Workers in a dairy delivery warehouse had to determine the optimal way to load milk-product deliveries onto a truck. This could be cast either as a task in arithmetic or as a task in visualization, where the worker imagined different-sized cases of dairy products being placed into a truck. If you observe someone successfully completing the loading task, all you know is that the loader must have mastered at least one of the two component skills.

Falmagne et al. (1990) suggested representing knowledge states of this sort by a directed graph, called a *knowledge space*. The graph for a knowledge space shows the direction of dependencies between skills. This is shown in Figure. 2.2. If knowledge is represented this way the purpose of assessment is to determine where a person is in the knowledge space, rather than to assign that person a number.

Jim Minstrell and I (Hunt & Minstrell, 1996; Minstrell, 2001; see also DiSessa, 1993) have proposed a similar idea, but with an important qualification. Falmagne et al.'s (1990) definition

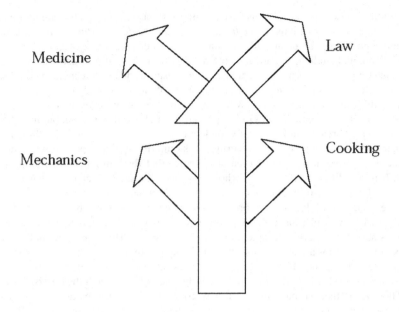

Medicine

Law

Mechanics

Cooking

General Cultural Knowledge

FIG. 2.1.   A depiction of the branching of cultural knowledge that is produced by specialization at various levels. In order to describe an individual completely it is necessary to say where that person falls on each of the arrows.

of a knowledge space implies that there are particular skills, and that having these skills is always good. Logically, and empirically, it is also possible to possess schema that allow you to behave a particular way, including solving some problems, but that will actively inhibit you in solving certain other problems. This is illustrated by an example from introductory physics, a topic that will occupy a good bit of the subsequent discussion.

Newton's laws of motion constitute our modern schema for reasoning about moving objects. The essence of these laws is that an object in motion continues in motion until some external force impinges on it. Aristotle's law of motion states that moving objects naturally come to rest, as the "force" of the motion dissipates. Aristotle's law provides an accurate schema for reasoning about the motion of objects here on Earth; things do not keep going unless somebody or something continues to push them. Aristotle's law fails in space, which is defined as a location where (a) gravitational forces can be disregarded, and (b) an object is surrounded by a perfect vacuum. Of course, this idealized situation is never actually reached. The fact that his law fails in space never bothered Aristotle, for he had no way of observing the failure.

Newton's laws provide a schema that can be applied both on Earth and in space, but a person who makes this application needs to use some supporting schema. It is necessary to understand the definition of space and to understand the concepts of friction and resistance to motion in a medium (air). Figure 2.3 shows the resulting knowledge space. An important

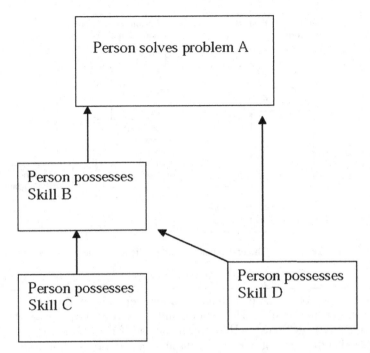

FIG. 2.2.   A knowledge–space representation. A Person who solves Problem A could do so using either skills B or D. However, in order to possess skill B it is necessary to possess skills C and D. The observation that a person solved problem A is evidence that the person possesses skill D, and that he or she may possess Skills B, and C.

point about this diagram is that some parts of the knowledge space cannot be observed directly. They have to be inferred by observations about what problems a person does or does not solve. Therefore one of the key steps in building an assessment of a person's crystallized knowledge about motion is to develop diagnostic problems that will assist in defining the person's knowledge space.

If we look at Gc in this way the whole point of education is to improve a person's crystallized intelligence, that is, to move a person toward a knowledge state that adequately covers the problems that that person will encounter. I now want to look at how this can be done, basing my argument on psychological principles. How should we instruct people in schematic reasoning?

EDUCATION: HOW TO IMPROVE CRYSTALLIZED INTELLIGENCE

The key point of my argument, and for that matter Hirsch's, is that the purpose of education is to develop schematic reasoning. And how do we do that? About 20 years ago Gick and Holyoak (1983) argued that schema are developed inductively, from a consideration of memorable examples that first served as analogies. To illustrate, Figure. 2.4 shows Duncker's X-Ray problem, which has frequently been used in studies of problem solving. This problem is rather hard.

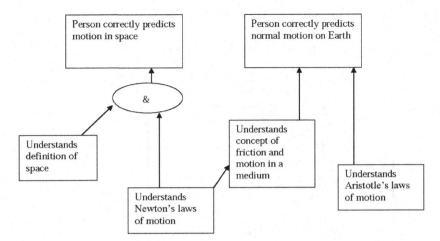

FIG. 2.3.   A knowledge space for the understanding and prediction of the motion of objects.

The X-Ray problem. A patient has a tumor deep in his body. An operation is not feasible. The tumor could be destroyed by X-rays of sufficiently high intensity. However, if such an X-ray beam were directed at the tumor it would pass through, and damage, vital tissue surrounding the tumor, and thus would kill the patient.

How can the tumor be treated ?

FIG. 2.4.   Duncker's X-Ray problem.

Fewer than 10% of college students solve it on their first attempt. It is also an unusual problem for most of us, so solving it fits the definition of a demonstration of Gf. However, if the students solve two or more problems analogous to the X-Ray problem, in different settings (Figure. 2.5), they induce a general "convergence of forces" schema (Figure. 2.6). The X-Ray problem then turns out to be quite easy. Finding a solution has changed from being a test of Gf to a test of Gc.

Glick and Holyoak (1983) demonstrated schema induction using artificial problems. Subsequently, Bassok and Holyoak (1989) made the same point, using data from high school students who were learning arithmetic progressions.

Minstrell (2001) came to the same conclusion, quite independently, on the basis of his extensive field experience as a high school mathematics and physical science teacher. Describing his method of instruction in the present terminology, he argued for

The General Story: A dictator has seized a vital fortress. A general leading the good guys wants to attack the fortress with a large force. However the dictator has set land mines along all the roads leading into the fortress, so if a large force goes over any of the roads it will set off the land mines.

The general decided to disperse his forces, sending lots of small forces by different routes. They joined together again at the fortress and seized it.

The Firefighter Story. A fire has broken out at an oil well. It can only be put out by directing lots of water on it. There are several pumps, but the fire chief only has low pressure hoses, so that none of them can pump enough water to put out the fire.

The fire chief decided to use all the hoses at low pressure. He told the firefighters to point each hose at the fire, but from a different position and direction. Enough water arrived at the point of the fire to extinguish the blaze.

FIG. 2.5.   Two analogs for the X-Ray problem.

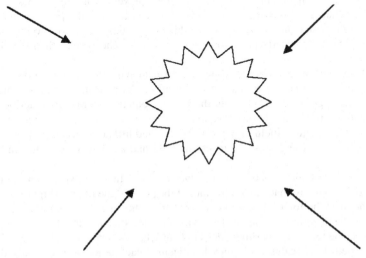

FIG. 2.6.   The Convergence Schema induced by seeing several examples similar to the X-Ray problem and its analogs.

FIG. 2.7.   A large football player crashes into a small cheerleader. What is the distribution of forces at the point of impact?

(a) carefully determining where students were in the knowledge space, and (b) constructing situations, which he refers to as "benchmark lessons," that serve as good analogies from which to build new schema that are a step closer to the desired knowledge state.

For the past dozen years, Minstrell and I have been working together to perfect this technique, which I refer to as *facet-based instruction*. (In Minstrell's terminology, a facet is equivalent to a unit in Falmagne's knowledge space.) I now offer a pair of examples, and then show some data (most of which has been published, but in the educational literature) to show how fruitful this approach can be.

The first example is an illustration of Newton's third law ("equal and opposite reactions"). Imagine a collegiate situation in which a large football player crashes into a small cheerleader (Figure. 2.7). What is the distribution of forces between them at the point of impact? Over half the high school students who were asked this question asserted, prior to instruction, that the large, mobile player exerts more force on the smaller cheerleader than the cheerleader exerts on the player.

Much of conventional instruction intended to deal with this sort of problem involves telling the students about Newton's laws of motion. As a result of this instruction it is indeed possible to get students to recite the slogan "equal and opposite reactions." But do they believe it? Probably not. In one case I particularly remember, a student answered every question on a physics quiz, including questions that had little or nothing to do with the third law, by reciting "equal and opposite reactions." He had a schema…say this and you pass physics!

A more convincing bit of instruction involves a simple thought experiment. Suppose that the cheerleader and the fullback held up scales at the point of the impact (Figure. 2.8). Clearly the scales measure the force of the person pushing on the balance. Wouldn't they be equal? In some cases the thought experiment alone will convince students that the scale readings will be the same. If the thought experiment does not suffice, an instructor can arrange that a large and small student hold scales while they lean against each other (less violently than in the illustration). The scale readings will indeed be the same. The students have been provided

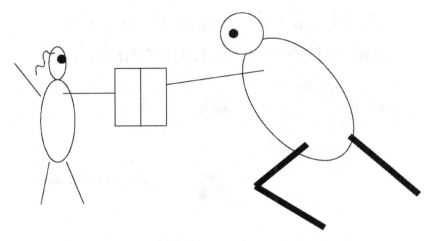

FIG. 2.8.   Suppose that at the point of impact the football player and the cheerleader push two scales together. What will be the relative readings on each of the scales? (It is possible to arrange a less violent demonstration in a schoolroom.)

with an analogy (in Minstrell's terms, a benchmark experience) around which they can build a schema.

My second example uses the same psychological principles in another area of physical mechanics. Figure 2.9 shows a situation in which the same block of material is weighed under three difference conditions: in an ordinary room, in a vacuum, and in a special chamber where the air pressure is twice the ordinary pressure. If the scale reading is 10 kg in the ordinary room, will it be the same, greater, or less than 10 kg in the vacuum? In the high pressure room?

I suggest that the reader write down his or her answer, and the reasons for it, before going further.

Two answers are frequently given. One is that the scale readings will be all the same, because a scale measures weight, weight is due to gravity, and gravity is the same in all three situations. The other is that the block will weigh more in the pressure chamber, due to the force of the high-pressure air pushing down on it.

At this point an instructor using the facet-based method would ask another question.

What would happen if the block were weighed in water? For that matter, suppose that you were to replace the block, and weigh yourself (Figure. 2.10)? People who are familiar with a feeling of floating, including anyone who ever took a bath, will agree that the scale reading drops when you are placed in water.

But water is denser than air! Water pressure certainly can be felt. So what is going on? A teacher (or a computer program) can use this example to conduct a guided discussion of a generalized buoyancy schema. And the students will have a good benchmark experience to guide their thinking.

Compared to conventional instruction, this method of instruction makes a marked improvement in students' thinking about introductory physics. Figure 2.11, taken from some of our early work (Hunt & Minstrell, 1994), shows the scores on a common examination that were achieved by students in two classes: a class taught using facet-based instruction and

A block of cement is weighed under three different conditions.

- What are the relative weights of the block in each condition?

 Air

 Vacuum chamber

 High-pressure chamber

FIG. 2.9. A diagnostic question intended to reveal a person's knowledge space with respect to the relation between weight, gravity, and the surrounding medium.

What if you weighed the block in water?

Isn't air an 'ocean,' just like water, but much less dense?

FIG 2.10. An example of a benchmark (analogical) presentation, made after observing answers to the diagnostic question of Figure 2.9.

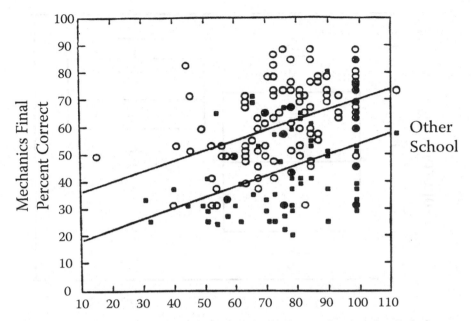

FIG. 2.11.   A comparison of scores obtained on a final examination as a function of method of instruction (facet-based instruction vs. standard instruction), and as a function of mathematics achievement scores, on a test taken prior to instruction (Hunt & Minstrell, 1994).

a class in a comparable school, taught by conventional methods. Scores are also shown as a function of the students' scores on a mathematics test, taken prior to entering the physics course. This is a reasonable covariate, for mathematical knowledge is a reasonably good predictor of how well a person will do in a physics course.

The comparison is marred by the fact that two different instructors were involved. Figure. 2.12, based on somewhat later work (Hunt & Minstrell, 1996) shows scores achieved by classes taught by the same (experienced) teacher, before and after adopting the facet-based instruction method. As you can see, substantial gains were achieved. Furthermore, the gains are achieved at all levels of student achievement in mathematics. We are dealing with a main effect, rather than a technique of instruction that differentially improves learning for the better prepared or poorly prepared students.

Similar gains can be achieved in other areas. Figure 2.13, based on a PhD dissertation by Andrew Schaffner (1997), is a comparison of examination scores obtained in two sections of a university statistics course, one taught using facet-based instruction and one taught by standard lecture methods. Substantial improvement occurred. This result is typical of other results that we have obtained. When an experienced instructor adopts facet-based instruction, student scores generally increase by about 15% in the first year and 4% in the second.

The data shown so far were obtained from courses in which an entire instructional method was utilized, including both new methods of quizzes and examination and marked changes in teacher behavior. My next example involves minimal use of the technique. To explain it I have to set the stage.

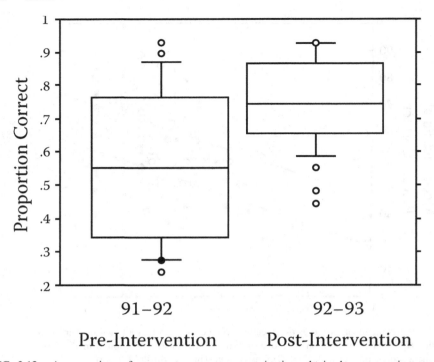

FIG. 2.12. A comparison of scores on a common examination, obtained on successive years in a course in high school physics taught by the same (experienced) instructor. During the second year the instructor switched from conventional to facet-based instruction (Hunt & Minstrell, 1996).

Group	
Traditional instruction	38.8
DIANA instruction alone	53.6
DIANA + Benchmark Lessons	60

FIG. 2.13. Data obtained in a university statistics course in which one group used a DIAGNOSER-style program for statistics instruction (DIANA), one group used DIANA plus in-class facet-based instruction, and one group received conventional instruction. Scores are presented as percentages of maximum score. Data from Schaffner (1997).

Early in our work we realized that a teacher could detect what facets seemed to predominate in thinking within a class, but simply would not have time to conduct inquiries with individual students. Socratic dialogues are hard to conduct with 30 students at a time. Therefore we constructed a computer program, the DIAGNOSER, that presented a branching series of questions and compared the responses to the responses that would be expected if a student

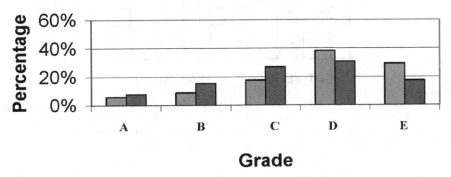

Percentage of class receiving indicated grade on review covered by DIAGNOSER (dark) or conventional review (light)

FIG. 2.14.   Results of a minimal application of facet-based instruction. Middle School students reviewed coursework in a course module on the water cycle, using DIAGNOSER or using a conventional paper and pencil review covering exactly the same material.

had a particular facet of thinking. The original DIAGNOSER ran on stand-alone, desktop Macintosh computers (Levidow, Hunt, & McKee, 1991). Today there is a World Wide Web version, which is described later.

What would happen if DIAGNOSER alone were to be injected briefly, as a review prior to an examination? We built a special DIAGNOSER for a middle school course on the water cycle, as part of a broader course on ecology. Students who had received instruction from the same teacher reviewed material either using DIAGNOSER, which permitted interaction, or by reviewing written material carefully designed to present exactly the same material. We regard this as a minimally effective dose of facet-based instruction. Nevertheless it had a reliable effect. Figure 2.14 shows the grades obtained by students using each type of material.

The relation between successful learning and conventional intelligence test measures is of interest. There are two interesting points here. Progressive matrices tests, which we have used in a variety of studies, clearly predict success in learning, with uncorrected coefficients of .3 to .4. This point is hardly surprising to people who deal with intelligence tests.

A second question one can ask deals with transfer. Does learning physics, one of our most demanding courses, have any effect on "intelligence" as measured by conventional tests? To answer this question, Levidow (1993) gave the even items on the Raven Progressive Matrices test to a class being taught by this method at the start of the academic year, and the odd items at the end of the year. There was no difference in test scores before or after the physics course, even though the physics course itself was clearly a success. The message is clear. If you study a specialized science you learn to perform well in that science, you do not learn "thinking in general." I strongly suspect that this is true of advanced instruction in virtually any field.

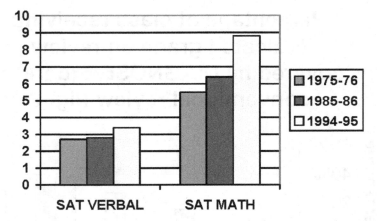

FIG. 2.15.   The number of test takers achieving Scholastic Assessment Test scores of 600 or higher, expressed as a percentage of the number of high school graduates in the relevant year. Note that not all test takers in a given year will be recent high school graduates, although the vast majority are. (Source: National Council of Education Statistics, Digest of Education)

As I indicated, the DIAGNOSER is now on the World Wide Web. In fact, the Web site goes well beyond the DIAGNOSER itself. The testing program integrates DIAGNOSER assessment with advice for teachers concerning the use of facet-based instruction and suggestions for in-class activities that a teacher might use as a benchmark lesson, either to elicit student ideas or to illustrate a scientific schema. In addition, and as a matter of more concern to educators than to scientists, the Web site makes a connection between the materials provided and the statewide assessment standards in middle school and high school science and mathematics.

A CLOSING REMARK

The work Minstrell and I have done is typical of numerous other efforts to reform American education over the past 30 years. This leaves us with something of a paradox. It is well known that "intelligence," as conventionally measured, has been increasing over the past 50 years. Two measures are usually cited for this conclusion: increases in various programs utilizing the Raven Matrices or similar tests of Gf, and changes in normalization for the Wechsler Adult Intelligence Scale (WAIS). It is also often stated, more as an assertion than as a statement based on evidence, that obviously the general social competence of individuals is not increasing. The evidence cited for the decline seems to be ephemeral, except for well-known declines in SAT scores. This seeming paradox has been resolved, if you will, by assertions that the tests really measure something special, a sort of test-taking skill, rather than real cognitive ability.

I believe that intelligence is increasing and that the paradox does not exist. If one examines the extent of improvement in progressive matrix scores by percentile it is immediately clear that the cohort effect is being driven by improvements in the lowest half of the distribution. See, for instance, the data on Raven Matrices standardizations recently published by Raven (2000). This is precisely in the area where the Gc–Gf distinction breaks down. Improving basic skills (especially literacy) that we associate with Gc, on the whole, probably does improve Gf-type reasoning at the lower half of the distribution.

My second reason for doubting the paradox is that, contrary to widespread belief, there is a small but real improvement in specialized, Gc-like, school-taught topics at the top end. In other words, the decline in "America's most talented," as documented by declines in SAT scores, simply does not exist. The reason that it appears to exist is that over the years progressively higher percentages of high school students have been taking the SAT. As a result, there has been a drop in the percentage of test takers that achieve exceptionally high scores on the SAT. However, if we allow for the change in the population, as is done in Figure. 2.15, we find that the percentage of U.S. high school students who achieve unusually high scores on the SAT has been steadily increasing!

Education does help improve intelligence, and better education would help even more. When I was in high school, in the late 1940s, one of my teachers had a very clearly stated theory of learning. He said, "You are here to learn. And what do I mean by learn? Memorize, retain, and be able to recite."

With the possible exception of a few utterly arbitrary pieces of information, such as the order of letters in the alphabet, this theory of education was utterly and completely wrong. Learning is an active process, and the purpose of learning, understanding, is only achieved by the development of schematic reasoning. Formative assessment, built into the classroom, industrial training session, or workplace can be used to improve learning. This, in turn, improves performance in cognitive tasks. Performance, not competence, is what drives a civilized society.

There is no reason to take an either–or position. Studies of those aspects of intelligence that are not driven by knowledge acquisition are certainly important. So are studies of knowledge-driven intelligence. The conceptualizations that are useful for one of these fields are not necessarily the same as the ones that are useful for the other.

ACKNOWLEDGMENT

This research was supported by a grant from the National Science Foundation to the University of Washington (Earl Hunt, principal investigator) and several grants from the James S. McDonnell Foundation and the Hewlett-Packard Foundation.

REFERENCES

Bassok, M., & Holyoak, K. J. (1989). Interdomain transfer between isomorphic topics in algebra and physics. *Journal of Experimental Psychology: Memory, Learning, and Cognition, 15*(1), 153–166.

Cattell, R. B. (1971). *Abilities: Their structure, growth, and action.* Boston: Houghton Mifflin.

Deary, I. J., Egan, V., Gibson, G. J., Austin, E. J., Brand, C. R., & Kellaghan, T. (1996). Intelligence and the Differentiation Hypothesis. *Intelligence, 23*(2), 105–132.

Detterman, D. K., & Daniel, M. H. (1989). Correlations of mental tests with each other and with cognitive variables are highest in low IQ groups. *Intelligence, 13,* 349–360.

DiSessa, A. A. (1993). Toward an epistemology of physics. *Cognition and Instruction, 10,* 105–225.

Duncan, J., Emslie, H., Williams, P., & Johnson, R. (1996). Intelligence and the frontal lobe. The organization of goal directed behavior. *Cognitive Psychology, 30*(3), 257–303.

Falmagne, J. C., Koope, M., Villano, M., Doignant, J. P. (1990). Introduction to knowledge spaces: How to build, test, and search them. *Psychological Review, 97*(2), 201–224.

Flynn, J. R. (1987). Massive IQ gains in 14 nations. What IQ tests really measure. *Psychological Bulletin, 101*(2), 171–191.

Gick, M. L., & Holyoak, K. J. (1983). Schema induction and analogical transfer. *Cognitive Psychology, 15*, 1–38.

Gottfredson, L. S. (1997). Why g matters: The complexity of everyday life. *Intelligence, 24*(1), 79–132.

Gustafsson, J-E. (1988). Hierarchical models of individual differences in cognitive abilities. In R. J. Sternberg (Ed.), *Advances in the psychology of human intelligence* (Vol. 4, pp. 35–71). Hillsdale, NJ: Lawrence Erlbaum Associates.

Herrnstein, R. J., & Murray, C. (1994). *The bell curve. Intelligence and class structure in American life.* New York: The Free Press.

Hirsch, E. D., Jr. (1987). *Cultural literacy: What every American needs to know.* Boston: Houghton Mifflin.

Horn, J. L. (1985). Remodeling old models of intelligence. In B. B. Wolman (Ed.), *Handbook of intelligence. Theories, measurements, and applications (*pp. 267–300). New York: Wiley.

Horn J. L., & Noll, J. (1994). A system for understanding cognitive capabilities: A theory and the evidence on which it is based. In D. Detterman (Ed.), *Current topics in human intelligence: Vol. 4. Theories of intelligence* (pp. 151–204). Norwood, NJ: Ablex.

Hunt, E. (1995). *Will we be smart enough? A cognitive analysis of the coming workforce.* New York: Russell Sage.

Hunt, E., & Minstrell, J. (1994). A collaborative classroom for teaching conceptual physics. In K. McGilly (Ed.), *Classroom lessons: Integrating cognitive theory & the classroom.* Cambridge, MA: MIT Press.

Hunt, E., & Minstrell, J. (1996). Effective instruction in science and mathematics: Psychological principles & social constraints. *Issues in Education: Contributions from Educational Psychology, 2(2),* 123–162.

Jensen, A. R. (1998) *The g factor: The science of mental ability.* Westport, CT: Praeger.

Levidow, B. (1993). *The effect of high school physics instruction on measures of general knowledge and reasoning ability.* Unpublished doctoral dissertation, University of Washington, *Seattle.*

Levidow, B., Hunt, E., & McKee, C. (1991). The DIAGNOSER: A Hypercard tool for building theoretically based tutorials. *Behavioral Research, Method, Instruments, and Computers, 23*(2), 249–252.

Minstrell, J. (2001). The role of the teacher in making sense of classroom experience and effecting better learning. In S. M. Carver & D. Klahr (Eds), *Cognition and instruction: Twenty-five years of progress* (pp. 121–150). Mahwah, NJ: Lawrence Erlbaum Associates.

Raven, J. (2000). The Raven's progressive matrices: Change and stability over culture and time. *Cognitive Psychology, 41*(1), 1–48.

Roberts, R. D., Goff, G. N., Anjoul, F., Kyllonen, P. C., Pallier, G., & Stankov, L. (2000). The Armed Services Vocational Aptitude Battery (ASVAB): Little more than acculturated learning (Gc)!? *Learning and Individual Differences, 12*(1), 81–103.

Schaffner, A. A. (1997). *Tools for the advancement of undergraduate statistics education.* Unpublished doctoral dissertation, University of Washington, Seattle.

Schaie, K. W. (1994). The course of intellectual development. *American Psychologist, 49*(4), 304–313.

Schmidt, F. L., & Hunter, J. E. (1998). The validity and utility of selection methods in personnel psychology: Practical and theoretical implications of 85 years of research findings. *Psychological Bulletin, 124*(2), 262–274.

Sternberg, R. J. (1990). *Metaphors of mind.* Cambridge, England: Cambridge University Press.

Winship, C., & Korenman, S. (1997). Does staying in school make you smarter? The effect of education on IQ in *The Bell Curve.* In B. Devlin, S. E. Fienberg, D. P. Resnick, & K. Roeder (Eds.), *Intelligence, genes, and success: Scientists respond to The Bell Curve* (pp. 215–234). New York: Springer-Verlag.

3

▼▼▼▼▼▼▼

Schooling and Intelligence: Effects of Track of Study on Level and Profile of Cognitive Abilities

Jan-Eric Gustafsson
Goteborg University

The field of research on intelligence is rich in paradoxes. There is, thus, ample evidence of stability of individual differences in intelligence over long periods of time, extending even from childhood to old age (e.g., Deary, Whalley, Lemmon, Crawford, & Starr 2000). Assumptions of stability are also made in many practical applications where it has proven useful to treat results obtained on tests of intelligence as representing fairly fixed characteristics of individuals that may be used for purposes of prediction, selection, and diagnosis. But there also is evidence that intelligence can change, and that these changes may be quite dramatic. The best example of this is the so-called secular change of intelligence, according to which there is a strong increase in the intelligence level of the population over time. This has been observed to take place since at least the 1930s, and since then the level of intelligence has risen by about one standard deviation (Flynn, 1999; Neisser, 1998). One of the many explanations that have been put forward is that the secular trend is due to the increased general level of education.

The possibility that education may affect intelligence is, however, an idea that has generated much controversy. The discussion following the publication of Jensen's (1969) paper on how much intelligence may be boosted through preschool participation is an example of this. Reviews of research by, among others, Ceci (1991), Herrnstein and Murray (1994), and Winship and Korenman (1997), also arrive at quite different conclusions about to which degree schooling affects intelligence. One of the reasons for the divergence in opinions among researchers is that the problem of determining effects of quality and quantity of schooling involves great methodological challenges.

Let me illustrate this by looking at the design and results of one of the classical studies in this field, namely the study by Härnqvist (1968a, 1968b). In this longitudinal study Härnqvist tested a representative 10% sample of the Swedish population of 13-year-olds with a test battery comprising a verbal, a spatial, and an inductive test. At the age of 18, the male subset of the sample took another test battery of a similar composition at the enlistment to military services. Härnqvist also had access to information about the educational careers of the subjects, which were differentiated into different tracks both in secondary school (Grades 7–9) and in upper secondary school (Grades 10–12). Some subjects left school for work after Grade 7, and quite a few did so after Grade 9. In the analysis of the data Härnqvist used the test results at age 13 to control for differences in entry characteristics to the different tracks of education, in order to determine treatment effects on intelligence of the differing kinds and amounts of schooling. A main finding was that students who had the most academically oriented education gained approximately .6 standard deviation units in intelligence as compared to those with the least amount of academic education. This is a fairly strong treatment effect, and estimated on a yearly basis the effect is approximately 0.12 sd units per year, or 1.8 IQ points.

This empirical result raises, however, a number of questions concerning validity and interpretation. The most fundamental question is, of course, the one about internal validity: Is the conclusion about a causal effect correct, or may this conclusion be challenged? Because this is a nonexperimental study in which subjects were not randomly assigned to treatments a selection effect is an alternative explanation of the findings. This alternative explanation was stressed by Brody (1992), who said:

> Individuals who chose or were assigned to an academic track might have gained in IQ even if they had been randomly assigned to a less rigorous academic education. Consider two individuals with the same IQ who elect to enter different educational tracks at the secondary school level. The student who chooses the academic track may like to read books more than the individual who chooses a less academic track. Differences in intellectual interests may be related to changes in IQ. (p. 187)

This objection certainly is valid in principle, as it raises all the fundamental problems that are related to making causal inferences from nonexperimental data. As was observed by Lord (1969), there is no dependable method for determining what is the appropriate adjustment of initial differences between groups. The only way out of this situation seems to be the recommendation made by Campbell (1963) to " ... vigorously attend to the specific plausible rival hypotheses appropriate to each situation" (p. 214).

If the Härnqvist finding, temporarily, is accepted to be internally valid, there is still the question of interpretation of what the finding means. Ceci (1999) argued, in essence, that there is a change of 1.8 IQ points for each additional year of academic schooling but he also emphasized that the change is a change in intelligence test scores and not in intelligence " ... while schooling seems to prop up IQ test performance, it does not seem as obvious that it increases intellectual development, particularly if we conceptualise the latter in terms of novel problem solving" (p. 171). This interpretation of may be a reasonable one, but Ceci does not supply any empirical support for it. The question of what the change in observed test performance signifies thus seems to be an open one.

The main purpose of the present chapter is to investigate effects of schooling on intelligence, with a particular focus on the two questions posed in relation to the Härnqvist example: (a) if it is possible to establish a causal effect of schooling on intelligence, and in that case how strong the effect is, and (b) what aspects of intelligence are being influenced?

REVIEWS OF STUDIES OF EFFECTS OF SCHOOLING ON INTELLIGENCE

The fact is that strong designs that involve randomization in this field of research has spurred researchers into being creative to find other ways to establish the effects of schooling on intelligence. Ceci (1991) identified some 200 studies with eight different types of designs in this area, and even though it is not possible to discuss all of them here, it may be worthwhile to bring up some of the main findings.

One class of evidence concerning the effect of schooling on intelligence is that during the summer vacation there is a small decrement in IQ, which effect seems to be stronger for children of low socioeconomic status (e.g., Jencks et al., 1972). Another similar type of study has investigated effects of intermittent school attendance on intelligence. Ceci (1991) referred to several early studies of children who were prevented from attending school regularly because of traveling, handicap, or living in areas without access to education. These studies have demonstrated a successive drop in IQ as a function of age for these groups of children.

Ceci (1991) also reviewed studies investigating length of academic schooling. One example of such a study is the Härnqvist study that has already been described. There are others studies, several of which are Scandinavian (Husén, 1951; Lorge, 1945; Lund & Thrane, 1983). These studies have arrived at estimates of increases of IQ similar to those obtained in the Härnqvist study.

Ceci (1991) argued that one of the strongest designs for investigating effects of schooling on intelligence is a cohort-sequential design in which children of the same age enter school at different times (i.e., they go in different grades), and stay there for similar lengths of time. One such study was reported by Cahan and Cohen (1989) who investigated the slope of within-grade regressions of intelligence test scores on chronological age, comparing the regressions across grades to determine the impact of years in school. They found that the effect of schooling was substantial, and, indeed, about twice as strong as the effect of chronological age.

Ceci (1991) observed that for each of the different categories of evidence reported, there is evidence that schooling affects intelligence. He also noted that it would be possible to challenge this as a causal conclusion in virtually every study, because they are all basically correlational. However:

> ... despite the many interpretive snarls one confronts with correlational data, when one considers the entire corpus of correlations that have been reported this century; the high correlations between IQ and schooling are difficult to account for on the basis of genetic selection or any other explanation (e.g., motivational differences or parental SES), because these mechanisms appear farfetched in many of the studies that were reviewed. The most parsimonious account of the correlations that have been reviewed is that of a direct causal link, namely, that the processes associated with schooling influence performance on IQ tests through a combination of direct instruction and indirect inculcation of modes of ... . (Ceci, 1991, p. 711)

On the basis of a review of the literature and an empirical study, Herrnstein and Murray (1994, chap. 17) arrived at quite a different conclusion, namely that there is little evidence that differences in the amount of schooling account for much of the intellectual variation. Herrnstein and Murray (1994, Appendix 3) also reported an empirical study of their own, which showed an increase of about one IQ point per year of additional schooling. This estimate is lower than what has been obtained in other similar studies. However, Winship and Korenman (1997) reanalyzed the Herrnstein and Murray data, using alternative model specifications and correcting some problems with the data. The reanalysis resulted in higher estimates of the effects of schooling on intelligence: According to the model preferrred by Winship and Korenman (p. 231) there was an estimated effect of 2.7 points of IQ per year of education.

Winship and Korenman (1997) also reviewed the research on effects of schooling on intelligence, with a special emphasis on studies using an analysis of covariance design. They tried to obtain a quantitative estimate of the magnitude of effects of schooling from each study. These estimates covered a quite large interval, the lowest being around one IQ point per year of schooling and the highest being around four IQ points per year of schooling.

Having concluded that the effect of schooling on intelligence is empirically established, Ceci (1991) pitted two possible explanations of the schooling effect against one another. According to one of these, schooling influences intelligence because the experience of being in school alters the individual's cognitive processes in a fundamental manner, such as through fostering more abstract and disembedded ways of thinking about the world. According to the other explanation, schooling only supplies the individuals with knowledge relevant for responding to IQ tests, and with efficient ways of responding to items in such tests. Evaluating the support for these hypotheses, Ceci favored the latter. He emphasized that schooling involves teaching answers to questions on IQ tests, and that it is in school that one is most likely to come across information relevant to IQ tests. Ceci also observed that schools teach modes of thinking that are rewarded on intelligence tests, such as using paradigmatic classifications. As a third explanation, Ceci emphasized that schools prepare students with values that support efficient testtaking.

However, intelligence is a multifaceted phenomenon and in the absence of more specific information about how schooling affects different aspects of intelligence, conclusions about the mechanisms involved are premature. It also seems necessary to focus more on effects of different types of education than has been done in previous research. Nowadays education covers a much greater part of life for most individuals, at the same time as the concept of education, particularly at upper secondary and tertiary levels, has been broadened to include much more of vocational education.

From the literature reviewed so far it thus seems that we may draw the general conclusion that schooling has an effect on intelligence. However, several concerns that need further attention have also been identified. There is, thus, a need for better control of omitted variables that are correlated both with the independent variable and the residuals of the dependent variable, and that therefore are threats to the validity of the inference that schooling causes improvements in intelligence. One example of such an omitted variable may be differences in intellectual interests, as was proposed by Brody (1992). Another factor that needs closer attention is type of education. Ceci (1991) suggested that only academically oriented types of programs cause effects on intelligence, and as proposed by Ackerman and Lohman (2003), it certainly is a worthwhile question to ask to what extent there are differences in the effects of different types of programs. A third aspect that needs refinement is the conceptualization and measurement of the construct of intelligence. The large majority of studies have relied on global and undifferentiated IQ measures, but considerably more information may be gained if instead a model of intelligence is adopted that allows for multidimensionality, such as a hierarchical model (Carroll, 1993; Gustafsson, 1984, 1988, 2001). Particularly when effects of different types of educational programs are studied, it would seem necessary to adopt a more multifaceted conception of intelligence.

A Swedish study by Balke-Aurell (1982) extended the Härnqvist study in such a direction. The main purpose of the Balke-Aurell study was to investigate changes in specific ability factors (primarily verbal/reasoning and spatial/technical abiliies). In order to study the influence of different types of educations and occupations on the pattern of abilities, Balke-Aurell classified the educations and occupations into verbal and spatial/technical domains, and used these classifications as independent variables. She concluded that specific ability factors develop in accordance with verbal and technical types of education, and, to a lesser extent, with type of occupation. These effects were mainly found, however, for spatial/technical ability, and to a lesser extent for verbal ability.

THE PRESENT STUDY

The Balke-Aurell (1982) study demonstrated that it is necessary to take into account the fact that education is not a homogeneous activity, but that the characteristics of different educational tracks are important for effects on intelligence. The study also showed that it is necessary to investigate differential effects of schooling on different aspects of intelligence. An empirical study is presented here that aims to extend the study of effects of different educational programs on different aspects of intelligence.

Sweden has 9 years of compulsory education, and 3 years of voluntary upper secondary education (or high school). However, even though upper secondary education is not compulsory, about 90% of the cohort participates in 12 years of education (OECD, 2001). This increase in participation rate compared to the cohorts studied by Härnqvist (1968a, 1968b) and Balke-Aurell (1982) is mainly due to an expansion of vocational education at the upper secondary level. This had started for the 1954 cohort, who went through upper secondary school in the early 1970s, but the great expansion occurred after that. Until the mid-1990s most vocational programs comprised 2 years of study, but after this time all upper secondary education programs in Sweden comprise 3 years of study, and have a higher level of ambition as to academic content.

The current study investigates the cohort born in 1976. Normally students born this year left compulsory school at the age of 16 (school started at age 7 for these students) in 1992 and started upper secondary school in the autumn the same year. At this time the old system of 2-year vocational programs was still in operation, but in some parts of the country the new 3-year programs had already been implemented. This makes it possible to make some comparisons between the vocational programs of different types.

This study also takes advantage of the fact that a new military enlistment battery was introduced in 1994. During the latter part of this year the old test battery consisting of four paper and pencil tests, which were designed to measure the general factor only, was replaced by a computer-administered test, consisting of 10 subtests designed to measure the factors Fluid intelligence (Gf), Crystallized intelligence (Gc) and General visualization (Gv) (Carlstedt, 2000; Mårdberg & Carlstedt, 1998). The three factors are estimated within a hierarchical modeling framework, according to which the Gf-factor is identical with the g-factor (Gustafsson, 1984, 1988, 2001).

This new test battery provides much more information about different aspects of intelligence than the batteries used in previous studies. What is of special interest to investigate in the current study is, of course, if schooling affects the g-factor, or if it affects the factors at lower levels of the hierarchical model, as was hypothesized by Ceci (1999). It is also of great interest to investigate if programs of education with special curricular emphasis affect special abilities, in a continuation of the investigation conducted by Balke-Aurell (1982).

The empirical study relies on information from official registers only, whereas the Härnqvist and Balke-Aurell studies used data collected through tests and questionnaires as well. Register information can easily be obtained for the entire population, so this method of data collection brings the advantage that a large set of data is available for analysis. The disadvantage is that certain types of information are not available, such as previous test performance and information about interests. However, there is information about school achievement and socioecenomic status, so a rather high degree of control of intial differences may be achieved.

Method

The design of the empirical study is fairly simple. Differences in results on the military enlistment test battery at age 18 for students who have followed different tracks in upper secondary school are analyzed, controlling for initial differences in grades and socioeconomic background. To the extent that the control for differences due to self-selection is successful, this design makes it possible to make causal inferences about effects of track of study on level and profile of intelligence.

Subjects. The data from the present study are taken from a large database consisting of everyone born between 1972 and 1979 living in Sweden in 1996. The database includes a large number of variables taken from different registers containing information about educational choice and educational achievement. Because every person in Sweden has a unique identification number that is used in almost all registers, it is possible to create longitudinal databases by combining the register data at individual level. Most of the registers are kept by Statistics Sweden, where the different registers have been combined, after which the data has been delivered to Göteborg University in anonymous form.

The data to be analyzed here are from the 1976 cohort. This is the only cohort for which information is available both about track of study at upper secondary school and results on the new version of the military enlistment test battery. This cohort also is interesting to study because it represents a large variety of upper secondary programs. As has already been mentioned a new version of the upper secondary school curriculum was successively implemented up until the mid-1990s. In the 1996 cohort some persons thus have followed the older version of the upper secondary school curriculum, in which vocational lines comprise 2 years of study, and some persons have followed the new curriculum, in which vocational programs comprise 3 years of study.

Because enlistment to military service in Sweden is compulsory for males only, the analyses reported here will be restricted to this gender. This not only limits the generalizability of the findings to males only, but it also entails a restriction on which programs of study can be investigated, because in many instances choice of program is highly correlated with gender. This is an unfortunate but inescapable consequence of relying on data collected for other purposes than research.

The database comprises 52,113 males born in 1976, although the analyses to be reported are based on a subset of 13,903 cases. The main reason why so many cases are lost is that only 17,588 cases have a score on the 10 subtests of the test battery analyzed here, which is because the new enlistment test was operational only from August 1994 (Mårdberg & Carlstedt, 1998). Only a few cases were not tested at all. Those who are not Swedish citizens are excluded from the military enlistment procedure, as are those who have been diagnosed to be mentally retarded. With these restrictions, there is little reason to believe that those taking the new enlistment test do not form a representative sample from the population.

Another reason why not all cases are analyzed is that some attend programs of study that are too small to be analyzed. Because of the successive implementation of the new curriculum for the upper secondary school, there were during the years 1992 to 1994, an unusually large variety of upper secondary school tracks. Not only did the old and new curricula coexist, but in some school districts an experimental precursor to the new curriculum, with 3-year vocational programs, also was in operation. These experimental programs are not so well defined as the others, so they have been left out of the analysis.

Information about the socioeconomic background of the students is available from the 1990 census. Parental occupation has been used to classify the background of the students according to the so called Socio-Economic Index, which here involves a categorization into one of eight groups (e.g., unskilled labor, positions requiring academic education). In the analyses, group belongingness has been represented as a vector of dummy variables.

Treatments. The old version of the upper secondary school curriculum consisted of five academic lines (Liberal Arts, Economics, Social Science, Natural Science, and Technology), which prepared for entry to university-level education. These programs all comprised 3 years of study. There also was a rather large number of vocational programs, which all comprised 2 years of study, and which did not allow entry to university level education without further education at the upper secondary level. The new system consists of 17 national programs of study along with a large number of local programs. These programs are all 3 years long, and they all provide formal access to university level education, even though the range of available educational programs varies highly. When the students born in 1976 entered upper secondary school the new system had been decided on, and in some parts of the country implementation started before the official starting date (i.e., the academic year 1994/1995). A smaller part of the cohort thus obtained their upper secondary education from one of the new programs. For most of the programs the number of students is, however, too small to allow analysis.

Table 3.1 presents the number of students born in 1976 who have graduated from different lines of the old upper secondary school curriculum, and for students who have graduated from some of the programs of the new upper secondary school curriculum. The table only includes lines and programs for which at least 100 students are available for analysis. This implies, regrettably, that the Liberal Arts program, for which only 90 cases are available, is excluded. For most programs the proportion of cases who have data on the variables to be analyzed is around 30%.

In the analyses to be reported here all the different lines and programs are analyzed as different treatments, and comparisons are made with the group of cases for which no information is available about their upper secondary education. To understand the nature of possible treatment effects it would be desirable to have a fairly detailed description of the amount of time allocated to different subject matters in the curricula. Given the large number of tracks this is not possible, but it may be useful to have a more detailed presentation of one example of each of the main categories of educations.

The Electro-Telecommunications line is the largest among the 2-year lines. This line had during the 2 years approximately 14% of the curriculum allocated to Swedish and an optional theoretical subject. The remaining time was allocated to electro-telecommunications subjects, divided between work technique and vocational theory, with a stronger emphasis on the former than on the latter. This curriculum thus had a weak emphasis on general academic subjects, and a strong emphasis on practical skills.

The new Electrical Engineering program to a certain extent consists of individually elective courses, which makes it impossible to identify a single common curriculum. However, according to the recommended time table approximately 33% of the time should be devoted to academic subjects and the remainder to vocational subjects. Thus, even though there is a stronger emphasis on academic subjects in this program than in the 2-year program, the main emphasis still is on vocational skills.

For the 3-year Natural Science line, to take yet another example, approximately half the time was allotted to mathematics, science subjects, and technology, approximately 25% of the

TABLE 3.1
Number of Male Students Born 1976 From Different Lines and Programs of Study

	Graduated	Included	Percent
Two-Year-Lines			
Building and Construction line	2,346	695	29.6
Consumer line	148		
Distribution and Clerical line	1,016	297	29.2
Electro-Telecommunications line	2,874	924	32.2
Food and Manufacturing line	721	239	33.1
Horticultural line	194		
Motor Engineering line	1,910	601	31.5
Music line	181		
Nursing line	135		
Operation and Maintenance line	690	232	33.6
Social line	1,609	503	31.3
Processing line	36		
Woodwork line	343	120	35.0
Workshop line	972	372	38.3
Three-Year Lines			
Economics line	3,861	1,136	29.4
Liberal Arts line	311		
Natural Sciences line	3,458	1,007	29.1
Social Sciences line	3,717	1,101	29.6
Technology line	5,356	1,551	29.0
Three-Year Programs			
The Construction Program	495	215	43.4
The Electrical Engineering Program	1,191	445	37.4
The Vehicle Engineering Program	834	271	32.5
The Business and Administration Program	961	309	32.2
The Industrial Program	822	324	39.4
The Use of Natural Resources Program	843	280	33.2
The Natural Science Program	1,425	488	34.2
The Social Science Program	1,913	634	33.1
No Information	8,404	2,087	24.8

time to Swedish and foreign languages, and the remaining time roughly evenly split between social subjects and other subjects. The main emphasis of this program thus is academic.

In the analysis each different track will be represented by a dummy variable of its own, using the No information group as the reference group.

Grades from Compulsory School.   As has already been pointed out there is a strong need to identify and control for possible self-selection of students into the different tracks. This is done through relying on the grades in 17 different subject matters given on the leaving certificate from compulsory school. The grades were assigned on a scale from 1 to 5 according to a norm-referenced grading system, in which national tests were used to achieve comparability of grades from different schools.

Andersson (1998) has fitted a 5-factor model to the grades data, which holds promise not only to capture differences in general level of school achievement for the different lines and programs of study, but also differences in the profile of performance over different areas. Andersson fitted her model to the population data for students born in 1972, and the standardized factor loadings for males are shown in Table 3.2, along with the results for the current sample.

The estimated factor loadings generally are very close to those previously obtained. The model fitted is an orthogonal model with so-called nested-factors (Gustafsson & Balke, 1993). There is a general factor (SchAch), which has positive and fairly strong relations to all the grades. The highest loadings are observed for social science subjects, which require heavy reading and much homework. Andersson (1998) interpreted this factor as involving a strong component of verbal ability, and also a strong motivational component.

There is also a rather broad factor that Andersson (1998) labeled NonVerb, and that is most highly related to technology, crafts, and physical education, but also to several other subjects involve figures or numbers. Andersson interpreted this to be a spatial–practical factor. The third factor relates to grades in mathematics and in science subjects, and was labeled MathSci by Andersson. The fourth factor has fairly strong relations to the grade in English and in Swedish, and weaker relations to grades in art education, mathematics, and music. This was interpreted as a language (Lang) factor by Andersson. The fifth factor, finally, has low relations to a fairly broad range of grades, and it was labelled the aesthetic–domestic factor (Ad) by Andersson.

These five factors will be used to control for possible selection and self-selection effects into the different lines and programs.

The Swedish Enlistment Battery.   Until 1994 the enlistment battery consisted of four tests (one inductive, one verbal, one spatial, and one technical; see Carlstedt, 2000), which where combined to measure a general factor. In August 1994 this batttery was replaced with a computer-administered test, consisting of 10 subtests designed to measure the factors g, Gc, and Gv within a hierarchical modeling framework (Carlstedt, 2000; Mårdberg & Carlstedt, 1998). This test is referred to as the Swedish Enlistment Battery (SEB). The following tests are included:

Synonyms 1 and *Synonyms 2*, with 25 and 20 items, respectively. These are multiple-choice tests with four or five options, from which the synonym of a given word is to be selected. There is also a test called *Opposites* (25 items) in which the task is to select the antonym of a given word. These three tests have been shown to measure Crystallized Intelligence (Gc).

Figure Series (20 items) presents sequences of four figures, and the task is to complete the series by selecting two figures out five given ones. In the *Groups* (20 items) test, five figures are presented, and the task is to identify the figure that does not fit thematically. These two tests have been shown to measure Fluid Intelligence (Gf).

In the items in *Dice 1* and *Dice 2* (20 items each) two cubes, on which three surfaces are visible, are presented. According to the instructions there is a unique symbol on each side of the cube, and on identical cubes, the symbols are placed in the same relation to each other. The task is to find out if the two cubes, if turned, are identical, or if they are different. In the *Metal Folding* test (16 items), a drawing of an unfolded piece of metal is presented and the task is to find the three-dimensional object out of four that corresponds to the two-dimensional drawing. The items in the *Block Rotation* test (20 items) present a three-dimensional target

TABLE 3.2

Standardized Factor Loadings in the Five-Factor Model for Grades

	SchAch		Non-Verb		MathSci		Lang		Ad	
	Males-72	Current	Males-72	Current	Males-72	Current	Males-72	Current	Males-72	Current
Child studies	0.78	0.79							0.23	0.30
Art education	0.49	0.50	0.25	0.25			0.12	0.12	0.14	0.12
English	0.73	0.73			0.10	0.12	0.42	0.41		
Domestic science	0.72	0.72	0.19	0.21					0.25	
Physical education	0.39	0.44	0.23	0.21						
Mathematics	0.75	0.75	0.14	0.16	0.29	0.28				
Music	0.63	0.62	0.10	0.12			0.12	0.14	0.13	0.12
Biology	0.85	0.84	0.08	0.11	0.24	0.27	0.19	0.19	0.11	0.11
Physics	0.83	0.82	0.15	0.17	0.34	0.36				
Chemistry	0.84	0.84	0.09	0.11	0.31	0.34			0.08	0.07
Technology	0.59	0.60	0.36	0.35	0.22	0.23				
Geography	0.88	0.89	0.03	0.02						
History	0.90	0.90							−0.09	−0.08
Religious studies	0.90	0.90							−0.02	−0.04
Civics	0.90	0.90								
Crafts	0.42	0.44	0.59	0.58					0.11	0.12
Swedish	0.83	0.84					0.25	0.24	0.04	0.07

TABLE 3.3
Standardized Loadings of the Tests in the SEB on the
Three Factors of the NF-Model

	g	Gv	Gc
Figure series	0.89		
Groups	0.80		
Dice 1	0.70	0.20	
Dice 2	0.68	0.29	
Metal folding	0.71	0.38	
Block rotation	0.69	0.34	
Technical comprehension	0.68	0.24	0.17
Synonyms 1	0.61		0.64
Synonyms 2	0.66		0.59
Antonyms	0.68		0.59

object, and the task is to select the identical three-dimensional rotated object out of five. In *Technical Comprehension* (16 items), the items all constitute illustrated technical and physical problems, and one out of three suggested solutions should be selected as the correct one. These five tests have been shown to measure General visualization (Gv). The Technical comprehension test has a loading on Gc as well, and there also is overlap between the specific components of Dice 1 and Dice 2 (Mårdberg & Carlstedt, 1998).

Factor models have been fitted to this test battery in several previous studies (e.g., Carlstedt, 2000; Carlstedt, Gustafsson, Ullstadius, 2000; Mårdberg & Carlstedt, 1998). These models have genereally been taken to be hierarchical models of the nested-factor kind (Gustafsson, 2001; Gustafsson & Balke, 1993) in which a general factor factor (g) is related to every test and Gc' and Gv' are introduced as residual factors to account for the remaining covariance between these two groups of tests. The model does not include a residual Gf-factor, because of the empirical equivalence between g and Gf (Gustafsson, 1984, 2001). Such a model has been fitted to these data as well, and the standardized factor loadings are shown in Table 3.3.

There are substantial loadings of all the tests on the g-factor, and particularly so for the two Gf-tests. The tests hypothesized to load on Gv' do so, but the loadings tend to be relatively low, which indicates that it is difficult to separate the g- and Gv'-factors in this battery of tests. For Gc', the three vocabulary tests have quite substantial loadings. Being restricted to vocabulary tests only, it may be noted that the Gc factor is a fairly narrow factor.

The model includes a covariance between the residuals of Dice 1 and Dice 2 as well, and when this covariance is introduced the model fit is quite acceptable, the RMSEA being 0.044, with a narrow confidence interval.

This hierarchical model is used to estimate the g-factor. However, this model is less useful for investigating effects of schooling on Gc and Gv, because g is partialed out from these dimensions, and g may be affected by treatment effects. For purposes of analysis of effects of schooling on the abilities at lower levels of the hierarchy an oblique measurement model will be used as well. This model specifes three correlated factor Gf, Gv, and Gc, with the pattern of standardized loadings shown in Table 3.4.

In this model there is no g-factor, and the Gf-factor is measured by Figure series and Groups alone. Otherwise the pattern of loadings matches that of the hierarchical model. In the oblique model there are, however, high correlations among the factors. Gf and Gv thus

TABLE 3.4
Standardized Loadings of the Tests in the SEB on the Three
Factors of the Oblique Model

	Gf	Gv	Gc
Figure series	0.90		
Groups	0.80		
Dice 1		0.74	
Dice 2		0.74	
Metal folding		0.79	
Block rotation		0.77	
Technical comprehension		0.56	0.23
Synonyms 1			0.87
Synonyms 2			0.89
Antonyms			0.91

correlate 0.90, Gc and Gv correlate 0.69, and Gf and Gc correlate 0.72. This model too fits well, with an RMSEA of 0.046.

Results

The analysis and reporting of results proceeds in three steps. First relations between the factors of the model for the grades and the SEB-factors are investigated. Next relations between tracks of study and the grades are studied, in order to investigate the extent of selection and self-selection to the tracks. In the third step relations between lines of study and the factors of the SEB-models are investigated with control for grades and socioeconomic status.

Relations Among Grades From Compulsory School and Test Performance at 18. To investigate the amount of relationship among the grade factors and the factors of intelligence at 18, the g-factor and and the factors of the oblique SEB-model have in two separate analyses been regressed on the five factors of the model for the grades. The standardized regression coefficients are presented in Table 3.5.

The pattern of results are highly similar for the g- and the Gf-factors, and no less than 64% of the variance in g is accounted for. The general SchAch factor contributes most, but MathSci and Lang also have substantial relations to g. For Gv there is a strong positive correlation with SchAch and Lang, which is because there is a very substantial amount of g-variance in this factor, but this factor also has rather strong relations with NonVerb and MathSci. For Gc there is a strong relation of .71 to SchAch, and there also are relations to Lang and MathSci.

Between 60% and 70% of the variance in abilities is accounted for by the grade factors. In spite of the fact that intelligence scores are not available, the amount of variance accounted for is at least as high as in previous studies. This is because a latent variable modeling approach is used that takes full advantage of the multidimensionality of grades and SEB tests, and that allows estimation of error-free latent variables. The problem of disattenuation of relations by unreliability in measures is thus not present here.

Tracks and Grades. Processes of self-selection may cause considerable differences in means of grades over the different tracks in upper secondary school. In order to investigate

TABLE 3.5
Standardized Relations Among the Latent Variables for the Grades and SEB Models

	SchAch	Non-Verb	MathSci	Lang	Ad	Expl var
g	0.64	0.19	0.31	0.30	−0.09	64%
Gf	0.63	0.19	0.33	0.28	−0.09	60%
Gv	0.52	0.36	0.36	0.24	−0.12	60%
Gc	0.71	−0.09	0.22	0.36	−0.05	70%

such differences the five factors of the model for the grades have been regressed onto the full set of dummy variables for the lines of study, and the partial regression coefficients have been estimated. This analysis expresses on a convenient scale, which is comparable across the different dimensions, track differences in the level of the five factors.

As may be seen in Table 3.6 choice of, and successful completion of, track accounts for no less than 55 % of the variance in SchAch. This is primarily due to the fact that the academically oriented 3-year lines have a much higher mean on the SchAch factor than have the vocationally oriented 2-year lines. Among the new programs the Natural Science Program and the Social Science program also have a higher mean on the SchAch factor, but not as high as the old lines. The 2-year Electro-Telecommunications line and the 3-year Electrical Engineering program have a higher level on SchAch than the other vocational programs.

In the MathSci factor 24% of the variance is accounted for, and this is almost entirely due to the fact that the Natural Sciences line, the Technology line, and the Natural Sciences program have a high mean on this factor. Here too the Electro-Telecommunications line and the Electrical Engineering program have intermediate means. The lines of study account for 8% of the variance in the NonVerb factor. The Technology line, the Electro-Telecommunications line, the Building and Construction line, the Motor Engineering line, and the Woodwork line all have correlations higher than .12. For the Lang factor 11.6% of the variance is accounted for. The academically oriented lines and programs have a higher level on this factor.

The results presented in Table 3.6 show that the different tracks have widely varying levels of entry performance, not only on the general school achievement factor, but also on the narrow achievement factors. It is quite interesting to see that these differences go along with the different contents and requirements of the lines. Thus, for the programs with an emphasis on mathematics and science the MathSci factor is high, and for programs in which spatial–practical skills are important the NonVerb factor is high. Unless these differences are controlled for, they will be confounded with treatment effects.

Effects of Track of Study on Test Performance at Age 18.   In the final step of the analysis a model has been constructed in which the intelligence factors at age 18 have been regressed onto the dummy variables representing track, and the latent variables representing individual differences in the compulsory school grades and the SES variables have been included as control variables. The model thus estimates the direct effects of line of study on test performance at age 18 controlling for entry differences.

The parameter estimates are presented in Table 3.7. Only significant (p < .01) parameter estimates are shown.

For the g and Gf factors positive effects of attending an academic program may be observed. The strongest effect is obtained for the Technology program, but a standardized

TABLE 3.6
Standardized Coefficients for the Differences in Grades Between Lines

	SchAch	Non-Verb	MathSci	Lang	Ad
Two-Year Lines					
Building and Construction line	0.05	0.15	−0.01	−0.01	0.04
Distribution and Clerical line	0.04	0.01	−0.01	0.03	0.04
Electro-Telecommunications line	0.15	0.19	0.12	0.03	0.08
Food and Manufacturing line	0.06	0.03	0.00	0.00	0.09
Motor Engineering line	−0.01	0.12	0.01	−0.02	0.03
Operation and Maintenance line	0.03	0.09	0.02	−0.01	0.00
Social line	0.10	0.02	−0.02	0.05	0.03
Woodwork line	0.00	0.12	−0.01	−0.01	0.02
Workshop line	−0.07	0.04	−0.01	−0.05	−0.02
Three-Year Lines					
Economics line	0.36	0.07	0.07	0.13	0.11
Natural Sciences line	0.53	0.06	0.32	0.25	0.07
Social Sciences line	0.43	0.02	0.02	0.16	0.05
Technology line	0.50	0.21	0.32	0.12	0.16
Three-Year Programs					
The Construction Program	0.01	0.06	−0.03	−0.05	0.03
The Electrical Engineering Program	0.10	0.10	0.10	0.01	0.07
The Vehicle Engineering Program	−0.02	0.08	0.03	−0.02	0.01
The Business and Administration Program	0.05	0.02	−0.03	0.04	0.03
The Industrial Program	−0.03	0.06	0.00	−0.05	−0.02
The Use of Natural Resources Program	0.04	0.07	0.00	−0.09	0.01
The Natural Science Program	0.31	0.09	0.24	0.09	0.07
The Social Science Program	0.25	0.02	0.05	0.07	0.05

regression coefficient around .10 or slightly lower is observed for all the academic programs, including the new programs. There also are weak positive effects on g/Gf of attending the Electro-Telecommunications line and the Electrical Engineering program.

For Gv there are effects of the Natural Sciences line (0.11), the Technology line (0.17), and of the Natural Sciences program (0.10). The latter program may be regarded as a combination of the Natural Sciences line and the Technology line. For Gc there are effects of the academic lines and programs, with correlations varying between .03 and .11. There also are very weak effects, both positive and negative ones, of some of the vocational lines, but these do not seem to form an easily described pattern.

In these analyses the effects of the different tracks of study have been expressed in terms of standardized partial regression coefficients, or as correlations with control for the other independent variables. As was observed by Lubinski and Humphreys (1996) correlations are often misinterpreted to indicate weaker relations and smaller effects than do other measures, such as effect size measures. However, they also pointed out that correlations can be translated into estimates of mean differences, so such misinterpretations can be avoided. Bobko, Roth, and Bobko (2001, p. 50) presented a formula for the transformation of a correlation

TABLE 3.7

Standardized Coefficients for the Differences the SEB Factors Between
Tracks, Controlling for Grades and Ses

	g	Gf	Gv	Gc
Two-Year Lines				
Building and Construction line	−0.03	−0.03	−0.03	−0.03
Distribution and Clerical line			−0.03	−0.03
Electro-Telecommunications line	0.04	0.04	0.04	0.03
Food and Manufacturing line				
Motor Engineering line				
Operation and Maintenance line	0.02	0.03		0.04
Social line				0.02
Woodwork line				
Workshop line				
Three-Year Lines				
Economics line	0.09	0.10		
Natural Sciences line	0.09	0.12	0.11	0.07
Social Sciences line	0.07	0.07		0.08
Technology line	0.14	0.17	0.17	0.10
Three-Year Programs				
The Construction Program				
The Electrical Engineering Program	0.02	0.02		
The Vehicle Engineering Program				
The Business and Administration Program				−0.03
The Industrial Program				
The Use of Natural Resources Program				0.05
The Natural Science Program	0.08	0.10	0.10	0.05
The Social Science Program	0.06	0.07	0.03	0.03

between a dichotomous variable indicating group membership and a continous variable into an effect size measure (i.e., a mean difference divided by the pooled standard deviation).

According to the Bobko et al. (2001) formula the standardized coefficient of .14 for the effect of the Technology program on g corresponds to an effect size of .45, which in turn corresponds to an increase of 6.8 IQ units. For Gf and Gv the estimated size of the effect of the Technology program is .55. For the Natural Science program the estimated effect on g is 0.35, on Gf it is 0.47, and on Gv it is 0.43. These estimates indicate considerable effect sizes for the increase in intelligence as a function of attending some of the uppersecondary school tracks.

DISCUSSION AND CONCLUSIONS

The results indicate that there are effects on the factors of intelligence of schooling at the upper secondary level. However, the effects seem to be restricted to the academic programs.

The estimates for the general factor are marginally stronger when the Gf-factor in the oblique model is taken to represent this factor, than when it is estimated as a truly general factor in the NF-model. There also is some variation between the programs, the lowest effect being observed for the Social Sciences program and the strongest for the Technology program. However, the mean standardized partial regression coefficient amounts to about .10, which for the groups under study here roughly translates into an effect size of 0.33. Assuming an IQ scale with a standard deviation of 15, this implies a change of 5.0 IQ units during the approximately two years that the treatment lasted, or 2.5 IQ units per year. This is somewhat higher than the estimated increase of 1.8 IQ units for each additional year of academic schooling reported by Ceci (1999), but it is at the midpoint of the interval of estimates of 1 to 4 IQ points arrived at by Winship and Korenman (1997).

There is no sign of any effect of the higher academic level of ambition of the new 3-year vocational programs. However, it must be emphasized that this increased level of ambition has caused the length of the programs to be extended from 2 to 3 years, although during each of the years the proportion of academic subject matter is still fairly small. The present data was collected during the autumn semester of the third and last year of upper secondary school, which implies that for most subjects there remained almost a full year of education in the track. These data thus were collected too early to tell about the full effect of this change.

For Gv there are fairly strong effects of the three academic programs that have an orientation toward technology and science. For the Electro-Telecommunications line there is also a weak effect, but otherwise there is no effect on this ability of the vocational tracks. Balke-Aurell (1982) found that both educations and occupations with a spatial/technical content caused a shift in the ability profile in the direction of the spatial/technical end of the bipolar v-s factor, but she also found that the effects were stronger at higher levels of education. The present results suggest that there is an effect on Gv only for the most academically oriented tracks.

For Gc there also are effects of the academic tracks, except for the Economics line, even though these effects tend to be somewhat weaker than for the other two factors of intelligence. There also are still weaker effects of some of the vocational tracks (Electro-Telecommunications line, Operation and Maintenance Line, Social line, Use of Natural Resources Program). Whereas for Gv there seems to be a fairly strong effect for certain specific programs, the effects of Gc are weaker and associated with a wider range of programs. It must be observed, however, that the fact that the tracks under study here are those that are popular among males implies a restriction of which tracks are actually included in the analyses. The Liberal Arts program is an example of a program that too few males had selected to allow inclusion in the study. Had it been possible to include this program, a strong effect on Gc might have been found of this track. Had females been included in the study as well, a wider range of vocational tracks would also have been included in the study, some of which may have had a strong influence on Gc.

When interpreting the Gc findings it must also be borne in mind that the Gc-dimension in the present study is quite narrowly defined as a vocabulary factor. It seems, however, that it would have been difficult in the present study to adopt such a broad definition of Gc as to also include achievement in subject matter areas (Carroll, 1993), because specific content taught in the different programs might then have been misinterpreted as general effects on intelligence.

These results thus indicate that participation in an academic track at upper secondary school has a positive effect on Gf and, to a lesser extent, on Gc. Furthermore, academic tracks with an orientation toward technology and science affect Gv positively. This shows that even after the length of education has been extended so that the natural variation in the number of years of education up to age 18 has been eliminated, there are effects on intelligence of the academic programs that are closely similar to those obtained when variation in years of schooling was investigated.

One of the main questions in the research on effects of schooling on intelligence is how the change should be interpreted. One hypothesis is that the change is a real and profound one, which fully reflects the meaning of the construct of intelligence. Another hypothesis is that the observed change only is a change in test performance without any concomitant change in the underlying ability. Ceci (1999) expressed the latter hypothesis as follows: " ... while schooling seems to prop up IQ test performance, it does not seem as obvious that it increases intellectual development, particularly if we conceptualise the latter in terms of novel problem solving" (p. 171). The results show quite clearly, however, that the strongest effect is observed for the Gf-factor, there being a marginally weaker effect on the g-factor, which is estimated from the full set of tests in the battery. The Gf-factor is measured by tests of inductive reasoning and it clearly involves novel problem solving, which provides support for the idea that the effects of schooling are not surface-level effects due, for example, to acquisition of specific pieces of information. One possible explanation for the positive effect on problem-solving abilities may be that the academic curricula put an emphasis on problem solving rather than on knowledge acquisition.

The weaker effects that have been obtained for Gc should, however, probably be accounted for in terms of the increased opportunities in education to acquire knowledge about the meaning of new words.

It could, of course, be asked if the design of the current study allows causal inferences to be made. Given that this is a correlational study, with a less than perfect statistical control of initial differences, the results could be rejected as being expressions of mechanisms of self-selection, rather than treatment effects. With Ceci (1991) it could, however, be argued that " ... in an inductive enterprise ... the usual inferential processes are relevant, namely that if studies using different methodologies, different mental measures, and different samples all converge on the same conclusion and if these studies possess uncorrelated weaknesses, then one can infer that their collective power is greater than that of their individual conclusions" (p. 718).

Compared to previous studies using the analysis of covariance design, the present study employs a weaker set of measures to control for entry differences in that only school achievement and no IQ measure is being used. However, this is partially compensated for by employing a multidimensional latent variable model that fully utilizes the information available, and that uses latent independent variables in which there is no attentuation of relationships due to errors of measurement. The amount of variance accounted for in the dependent latent variables therefore rather seems to be higher (60% to 70%) than in most previous studies.

One final caveat should be added, though. Even though a large amount of variance may be accounted for by the control variables, certain selection effects cannot be properly controlled for with the analysis of covariance design, because it is based on the assumptions of linearity and of additive effects of the independent variables on the dependent variable. Recently it has been established that abilities, interests, and personality variables tend to go together in clusters, referred to as "aptitude complexes" by Snow (1989; ses also Corno et al., 2002) and as "trait complexes" by Ackerman and Heggestad (1997). One of the basic notions of a trait complex is that the combined effect of the variables involved is greater than is the sum of the additive effects of the constituent variables.

Ackerman and Heggestad (1997) tentatively identified six trait complexes. An example is the Science/Math trait complex, which is associated with high spatial and reasoning abilities and with so-called realistic interests. Further studies (e.g., Ackerman, 2000; Ackerman & Rolfhus, 1999) have shown the Math/Science trait complex to be related, among other things, to math and science self-concept and to domain knowledge in physical sciences. According to Ackerman (2003), a trait complex is associated with choice of objects of study, and with the level of engagement invested in different areas of study. It is, therefore, predicted that the trait complex exerts influence on the person's development in schooling and over the life course.

The results of the present study indicate that there is a strong tendency toward self-selection into the different tracks of study, and the profile of differences in grades from comprehensive school shows that there is an overrepresentation of persons characterized by the Science/Math trait complex on the Natural Science and Technology tracks. Although the analysis of covariance technique may control for the additive effects of the intial differences, it may be that there are interactive effects that cannot be controlled for in this way. For example, persons with the the Math/Science trait complex may not develop their abilities within an upper secondary school track with a liberal arts orientation, and persons who are not characterized by the Math/Science trait complex may not develop at all well within the Technology and Science tracks. Such possible interactive effects between characteristics of the persons and characteristics of the tracks of study should be given serious attention in further research on the effects of schooling on intelligence.

REFERENCES

Ackerman, P. L. (2000). Domain-specific knowledge as the "dark matter" of adult intelligence: gf/gc, personality and interest correlates. *Journal of Gerontology: Psychological Sciences, 55B* (2), P69–P84.

Ackerman, P. L. (2003). Aptitude complexes and trait complexes. *Educational Psychologist, 38*(2), 85–93.

Ackerman, P. L., & Heggestad, E. D. (1997). Intelligence, personality, and interests: Evidence for overlapping traits. *Psychological Bulletin, 121*, 219–245.

Ackerman, P. L., & Lohman, D. F. (2003). Education and *g*. In H. Nyborg (Ed.), *The scientific study of general intelligence. Tribute to* (pp. 275–292) *Arthur R. Jensen,* New York: Elsevier.

Ackerman, P. L., & Rolfhus, E. L. (1999). The locus of adult intelligence: Knowledge, abilities, and non-ability traits. *Psychology and Aging, 14*, 314–330.

Andersson, A. (1998). The dimensionality of the leaving certificate in the Swedish compulsory school. *Scandinavian Journal of Educational Research, 42*(1), 25–40.

Balke-Aurell, G. (1982). *Changes in ability as related to educational and occupational experience.* Goteborg, Sweden: Goteborg Studies in Educational Sciences.

Bobko, P., Roth, P. L., & Bobko, C. (2001). Correcting the effect size of *d* for range restriction and unreliability. *Organizational Research Methods, 4*(1), 46–61.

Brody, N. (1992). *Intelligence (2nd ed).* New York: Academic Press.

Cahan, S., & Cohen, N. (1989). Age versus schooling effects on intelligence development. *Child Development, 60*, 1239–1249.

Campbell, D. T. (1963). From description to experimentation: Intepreting trends as quasi-experiments. In C. W. Harris (Ed.), *Problems in measuring change* (pp. 212–242). Madison, WI: Wisconsin University Press.

Carlstedt, B. (2000). *Cognitive abilities—Aspects of structure, process and measurement.* Goteborg, Sweden: Acta Universitatis Gothoburgensis.

Carlstedt, B., Gustafsson, J.-E., & Ullstadius, E. (2000). Item sequencing effects in the measurement of fluid intelligence. *Intelligence, 28*(2), 145–160.

Carroll, J. B. (1993). *Human cognitive abilities.* Cambridge, England: Cambridge University Press.

Ceci, S. J. (1991). How much does schooling influence general intelligence and its cognitive components?: A reassessment of the evidence. *Developmental Psychology, 27*, 703–722.

Ceci, S. J. (1999). Schooling and intelligence. In S. J. Ceci & W. M. Williams (Eds.) *The Nature-Nurture Debate. The Essential Readings.* (pp. 168–175). Oxford: Blackwell Publishers.

Corno, L., Cronbach, L. J., Kupermintz, H., Lohman, D. F., Mandinach, E. B., Porteus, A. W., & Talbert, J. E. (2002). *Remaking the concept of aptitude. Extending the legacy of Richard E. Snow.* Mahwah, NJ: Lawrence Erlbaum Associates.

Deary, I. J., Whalley, L. J., Lemmon, H., Crawford, J. R., & Starr, J. M. (2000). The stability of individual differences in mental ability from childhood to old age: Follow-up of the 1932 Scottish Mental Survey. *Intelligence, 28,* 49–55.

Flynn, J. R. (1999). Searching for justice: The discovery of IQ gains over time. *American Psychologist, 54,* 5–20.

Gustafsson, J.-E. (1984). A unifying model for the structure of intellectual abilities. *Intelligence, 8,* 179–203.

Gustafsson, J.-E. (1988). Hierarchical models of individual differences in cognitive abilities. In R. J. Sternberg, *Advances in the psychology of human intelligence* (Vol. 4, pp. 35–71). Hillsdale, NJ: Lawrence Erlbaum Associates.

Gustafsson, J.-E. (2001). On the hierarchical structure of ability and personality. In J. M. Collis & S. Messick (Eds.)., *Intelligence and personality. Bridging the gap in theory and measurement,* (pp. 25–42). Mahwah, NJ: Lawrence Erlbaum Associates.

Gustafsson, J.-E., & Balke, G. (1993). General and specific abilities as predictors of school achievement. *Multivariate Behavioral Research, 28*(4), 407–434.

Härnqvist, K. (1968a). Relative changes in intelligence from 13–18. I. Background and methodology. *Scandinavian Journal of Psychology, 9,* 65–82.

Härnqvist, K. (1968b). Relative changes in intelligence from 13–18. II. Results. *Scandinavian Journal of Psychology, 9,* 50–64.

Herrnstein, R. J., & Murray, C. (1994). *The bell curve. Intelligence and class structure in American life.* New York: The Free Press.

Husén, T. (1951). The influence of schooling upon IQ. *Theoria, 17,* 61–88.

Jencks, C., Smith, M., Acland, H., Bane, M. J., Cohen D., Gintis, H., Heyns, B., & Mitchelson, S. (1972). *Inequality: A reassessment of the effects of family and schooling in America.* New York: Basic Books.

Jensen, A. R. (1969). How much can we boost IQ and scholastic achievement? *Harvard Educational Review, 39,* 1–123.

Lord, F. (1969). Statistical adjustments when comparing pre-existing groups. *Psychological Bulletin, 70,* 162–179.

Lorge, L. L. (1945). Schooling makes a difference. *Teacher's College Record, 46,* 483–492.

Lubinski, D., & Humphreys, L. G. (1996). Seeing the forest from the trees: When predicting the behavior or status of groups, correlate means. *Psychology, Public Policy, and Law, 2*(2), 363–376.

Lund, T., & Thrane, V. C. (1983). Schooling and intelligence: A methodological and longitudinal study. *Scandinavian Journal of Psychology, 24,* 161–173.

Mårdberg, B., & Carlstedt, B. (1998). Swedish Enlistment Battery (SEB). Construct validity and latent variable estimation and profile prediction of cognitive abilities by the CAT-SEB. *International Journal of Selection and Assessment, 6*(2), 107–114.

Neisser, U., Boodoo, G., Bouchard, T. J. Jr., Boykin, A. W., Brody, N., Ceci, S. J., Halpern, D. F., Loehlin, J. C., Perloff, R., Sternberg, R., & Urbina, S. (1996). Intelligence: Known and unknowns. *American Psychologist, 51*(2), 77–101.

Neisser, U. (1998). (Ed.). *The rising curve. Long-term gains in IQ and related measures.* Washington, DC: American Psychological Association.

OECD. (2001). *Education at a glance. OECD indicators 2001 edition.* Paris: OECD.

Schmidt, F. L., & Hunter, J. E. (1998). The validity and utility of selection methods in personnel psychology: Practical and theoretical implications of 85 years of research findings. *Psychological Bulletin, 124,* 262–274.

Snow, R. E. (1989). Aptitude-treatment interaction as a framework for research on individual differences in learning. In P. L. Ackerman, R. J. Sternberg, & R. Glaser (Eds.), *Learning and individual differences. Advances in theory and research* (pp. 13–59). New York: W. H. Freeman.

Winship, C., & Korenman, S. (1997). Does staying in school make you smarter? The effect of education on IQ in *The Bell Curve.* In B. Devlin, S. E. Fienberg, D. P. Resnick, & K. Roeder (Eds.), *Intelligence, genes, & success. Scientists respond to the Bell Curve* (pp. 215–234). New York: Springer-Verlag.

4

▼▼▼▼▼▼▼

Early Childhood Interventions: The Abecedarian Project

Frances A. Campbell
Margaret R. Burchinal
University of North Carolina at Chapel Hill

Although psychologists and educators generally agree that early childhood educational intervention enhances the school progress of poor children (Lazar, Darlington, Murray, Royce, & Snipper, 1982; Schweinhart, Barnes, & Weikart, 1993; Campbell, Ramey, Pungello, Miller-Johnson, & Sparling, 2002; Reynolds, Temple, Robertson, & Mann, 2001), there is less consensus concerning whether early treatment has a lasting effect on intellectual development. Most who study the latter question have concluded that only fleeting gains of little practical importance have been demonstrated. As Arthur Jensen put it some time ago, "Compensatory education has been tried and it apparently has failed." (Jensen, 1969, p. 2). Eleven investigators who formed a Consortium for Longitudinal Studies to follow up their well-controlled early childhood programs concluded that "few program/control IQ differences [were found] when children were 10–17 years old, indicating that the effect of early education on [IQ] scores was probably not permanent" (Lazar et al., 1982, p. 56). More recently, Herrnstein and Murray (1994) once again considered the effects of early intervention on intellectual development and stated "The fact is that we and everyone else are far from knowing whether, let alone how, any of these projects have increased intelligence" (p. 409).

Why, in the face of so little encouragement, should we consider this question further? For one thing, almost no carefully controlled research on the long-term effects of early intervention on intellectual development actually exists, especially research in which intensive intervention began early in the life span and lasted for five or more years. For those studies that did begin intervention very early, such as the Syracuse University Family Development Project (Lally, Mangione, & Honig, 1988) or the Milwaukee study (Garber, 1988), either very long-term follow-up data are lacking, or participant numbers are very small, or both. Other studies, such as the Perry Preschool Program (Weikart, Bond, & McNeil, 1978), began treatment no earlier than age three. Thus, valid questions about intellectual malleability remain. The Abecedarian study, a prospective experimental study of early childhood educational intervention is pertinent to this issue because intellectual development among the participants was one of its major outcome measures and its intellectual test data extend from early childhood to young adulthood.

The Abecedarian Project was begun in 1972 in a university town in the Southeastern United States. Its primary purpose was to gain more knowledge about the malleability of intellectual development as a function of enriching the very early environment. Cross sectional research had shown a progressive decline in the cognitive development of children from poor families, to the point that they were disproportionately represented among the mildly retarded (IQs 50 to 70) by middle childhood (Heber, Dever, & Conry, 1968, cited in Jensen, 1969). Because no biologically based cause had yet been identified for most cases of mild retardation, many assumed that the environment in which the child developed was implicated in its etiology. Thus, the Mental Retardation and Developmental Disabilities Branch of the National Institutes of Child Health and Human Development (NICHD) was interested in funding a carefully controlled study of what might be accomplished through environmental enrichment.

The Abecedarian Project was launched amid the controversy created by disappointment over research indicating that any cognitive or academic gains shown by poor children who attended Head Start faded quickly (Westinghouse Learning Corporation, 1969). Many scientists were not prepared to accept that this apparent erosion of Head Start gains rendered early childhood intervention futile (e.g., Zigler & Muenchow, 1992). Perhaps Head Start and other programs for 3 or 4-year-olds began too late in the life span (e.g., Bloom, 1964). A rationale for starting intervention at a much earlier age was provided by the work of J. McVicker Hunt (1961) who argued that the right kinds of early experience were vitally important and had lasting effects on cognitive development. Concurrent reports from the Milwaukee study (Garber, 1988) encouraged optimism about very early intervention for high-risk infants. This quasi-experimental study, which enrolled infants born to poor women with low IQs, reported treatment/control differences as great as 25 IQ points during early childhood.

In this climate, the Abecedarian study was funded. The scarcity of infant day care made the program attractive to parents while at the same time affording researchers the opportunity to learn more about the extent to which cognitive and social competence could be enhanced through enriching the environment. The treatment was to begin in infancy, to be delivered in a full-time childcare setting, and to last for at least 3 years. Subsequently, funds were secured to expand the preschool program to five full years, and later still, to provide a school-age phase of treatment for the first three years in public school.

METHOD

Study Design

The setting for the Abecedarian study was a multidisciplinary research center with ties to psychology, education, social work, nursing, and medicine. The Principal Investigator, Craig Ramey, was a developmental psychologist interested in the enhancement of infant learning through a contingently responsive environment. He was joined by an educational psychologist and curriculum developer, Joseph Sparling. Three pediatricians studying the spread of infectious disease among young children in group care were also investigators on the original grant.

The design was a prospective longitudinal experiment in which infants were randomly assigned to treatment and control conditions. Treatment in this case consisted of full-time educational childcare starting in infancy. Screening for eligibility was based on a High Risk Index (HRI), shown in Table 4.1. The HRI included 13 sociodemographic factors such as parental education and other indications of risk for compromised cognitive development. A score of 11 or higher was required for consideration of the family.

TABLE 4.1
High Risk Index for Abecedarian Study

Factor	Weight
Mother's educational level (last grade completed)	
6	8
7	7
8	6
9	3
10	2
11	1
12	0
Father's Educational level (last grade completed)	
6	8
7	7
8	6
9	3
10	2
11	1
12	0
Family income (per year)	
$1,000	8
$1,001–2,000	7
$2,001–3,000	6
$3,001–4,000	5
$4,001–5,000	4
$5,001–6,000	0
Father absent for reasons other than health or death	3
Absence of maternal relatives in local area	3
Siblings of school age one or more grades behind age appropriate level with equivalently low scores on school-administered achievement tests	3
Payments received from welfare agencies within past 3 years	3
Record of father's work indicates unstable or unskilled and semiskilled labor	3
Records of mother's or father's IQ indicate scores of 90 or below	3
Records of siblings' IQ indicates scores of 90 or below	3
Relevant social agencies in the community indicate the family is in need of assistance	3
One or more members of the family has sought counseling or professional help in the past three years	1
Special circumstances not included in any of the above that are likely contributors to cultural or social disadvantage	1

To control for the possibility that any treatment related differences in cognitive development resulted from higher quality first-year nutrition for children who attended the treatment center, control group infants were supplied free iron-fortified formula for the first 15 months of life. Families in both groups had supportive social work services. Treated children received primary pediatric care at the child development Center, but low-cost medical care was available to control group families through local clinics.

Study Design

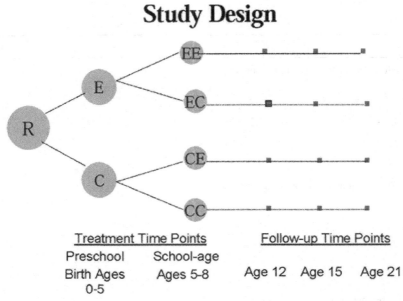

Treatment Time Points   Follow-up Time Points
Preschool   School-age
Birth Ages   Ages 5-8   Age 12   Age 15   Age 21
0-5

FIG. 4.1   Study Design. R = Random Alignment E = Treated C = Control

When children entered public kindergarten at age 5, the 48-month IQ score was used to match pairs of children as closely as possible within their respective preschool group, then one of each pair was randomly assigned to a school-age treatment or control group (see Figure 4.1). The resulting 4-group design thus permitted a test of the necessity of continuing treatment into public school in order to maintain preschool gains, and, alternatively, what could be accomplished through primary school intervention alone. Treatment varied in timing and duration from five years in preschool and three in primary school for a total of eight years (Experimental-Experimental or EE group), five years in preschool only (Experimental-Control or EC group), three years in primary school only (Control-Experimental or CE group), and no treatment at all (Control-Control or CC group).

Participants

One-hundred-eleven infants born to 109 families were originally enrolled. Although a range of circumstances existed among families in both groups, the trend in both was for children to be born to young, single women with less than a high school education. Table 4.2 gives entry-level demographic information by group. Ethnicity was not included as a risk factor, but given the characteristics of the local community, virtually all qualified families who enrolled in the study were African American. Approximately 3/4 of the sample lived apart from their fathers at birth.

Parents were recruited through contacts with social service agencies and prenatal clinics. Receptive families were visited at home to score the HRI. Those who appeared eligible were invited to visit the Center for further interviewing and an intellectual assessment of the mother. Information derived from all these sources was combined to arrive at a final determination of the family's suitability. In addition, study families had to live within commuting distance of the Child Development Center to allow treated children to attend, and the

TABLE 4.2
Entry Demographic Characteristics for Families in Abecedarian
Study by Preschool Group

Demographic Measure	Preschool Group		
	Treated[a]	Control[b]	Total[c]
Maternal age (years)			
M	19.6	20.3	19.9
SD	3.9	5.8	4.9
Maternal education (years)			
M	10.4	10.0	10.2
SD	1.8	1.9	1.8
Maternal Full Scale IQ (WAIS)			
M	85.5	84.2	84.8
SD	12.4	10.8	11.6
Percent two-parent family	23	26	24
Percent African American family	96	100	98
Percent male child	51	43	47

Note. WAIS = Wechsler audlt Intelligence Scale.
[a]– =55. [b]– = 54., [c]– = 1090

newborn infant had to appear free of biological conditions associated with developmental disabilities, such as Down Syndrome.

Once a pool of eligible participants was available, the families were divided into treatment and control groups using a table of random numbers (see the study model in Figure 4.1). The children were born over a 5-year period, from 1972 to 1977, and entered the study in four cohorts over that span. A cohort consisted of 28 infants, 14 treated and 14 not treated. Random assignments were typically made twice per cohort.

Attrition. Sixteen children were lost to attrition during the preschool years. Four children died, one proved to be ineligible because of a biological condition that was not apparent during the neonatal period, two were withdrawn from the study, and nine moved away. At school entry, 95 children had the 48-month IQ score used to equate pairs for school-age random assignments, and one preschool control child who had moved away as a toddler was placed in the CC group because it was considered justified to honor his first random assignment and continue it. This gave a total of 96 children assigned to a school-age group. However, three children in the CE group moved away at the point of kindergarten entry. Thus, 93 children comprised a "treated-as-assigned" sample upon which the research reported after school entry and during adolescent follow-up studies has generally been based (e.g., Ramey & Campbell, 1991; Campbell & Ramey, 1994; 1995; Ramey et al., 2000).

During adolescent follow-up studies, all eligible families (n = 105) were invited to take part. Six families were not eligible, either because of the death of the target child, the discovery of an excluding condition (see above) or because the family asked that the child be permanently withdrawn. The other two withdrawn children were invited to take part, as were all those who had moved out of the area. In all, 12 children earlier lost to attrition were seen as adolescents. At age 12, 102 children contributed data, 104 did so at 15. At neither age were the data from the attrition group entered into the "treated-as-assigned" analysis models, however.

For the young adult follow-up, all 105 living and eligible study participants were located and 104 agreed to take part. For those now living at a distance, travel costs to the study site were met. Fifty-four individuals from the preschool treated group and 51 from the control group were assessed as young adults.

For the present study, all cases ever admitted to the study were included if they met the following criteria: at least two intellectual test assessments were collected on the person and a score was available for each predictor included in the models. One-hundred five cases, 53 in the treatment group and 52 in the control group, met these requirements.

Treatment Program

Preschool. The mean age of the infants at treatment entry was 4.4 months (the range was 6 weeks to 6 months). The Center operated full days, five days per week, year round except for vacation and holiday closings. The children were provided a warm, secure and contingently stimulating environment in which each had an individualized program of learning activities. The activities were drawn from a curriculum designed especially for the program by Joseph Sparling and Isabelle Lewis (1979; 1984; updates, 2000; 2001). The game-like activities were interspersed in a seemingly spontaneous manner throughout the child's day. As the children grew past the toddler stage, the program more nearly resembled other quality preschools with a variety of learning activities provided.

Standardized assessments of cognitive development comprised the major outcome measure for the first five years of life. Examiners were persons not otherwise connected with the design or delivery of the preschool program. Although all testing took place at the childcare center, parents of children in treated and control groups were required to be present each time. Child care staff were not allowed to see the assessments to avoid any possibility that they might "teach" test items to the children. In addition to standardized tests, the evaluations included measures of parental attitudes and the early home environment. The family's demographic circumstances were continually updated throughout the study period. Other research included measures of language development, task-oriented behavior, and mother-child interaction. Growth data (height, weight, and head circumference) were also collected on children in both groups.

School-age program. Each family treated in the school-age phase was assigned a Home-School Resource Teacher (HSRT) who visited the home and classroom on alternate weeks. This individual (all were women) learned from the classroom teacher what basic skills in reading and math were being introduced at the time and also what, if any, skills the child needed extra help to acquire. The HSRT then devised an individualized packet of learning activities for parents to use at home. In addition, the HSRT served as a liaison between home and school to foster better communication between teacher and parent. She sought referrals for families to local agencies for housing, food supplements, or employment, as needed, in an effort to help families overcome barriers to full involvement in the child's learning.

Major outcome variables in this phase included standardized measures of intellectual development and academic achievement along with indices of adjustment to school as reflected in classroom observations and teacher ratings, parent ratings of socioemotional adjustment, and family demographic data.

Follow-up Studies

Adolescent follow-ups that included intellectual and academic tests were conducted for 12-year-olds in the summer after they completed seven years in school and again at age 15, after 10 years in school. The most recent, young adult follow-up study was conducted when the study sample reached age 21. In contrast to the two previous follow-ups that were linked to years of school attendance, the 21-year assessment was age-related. The target window for assessment was one month before or after the 21st birthday: 66% of the sample was seen within that window; 96% of the sample was seen within 3 months of turning 21. Young adult procedures included interviews where self-reported educational status, employment, and family circumstances were collected and also the administration of standardized tests of intellectual levels and academic achievement in reading and math.

Measures

Intellectual development. At every age, intellectual development was measured with widely used instruments that demonstrated high levels of validity and reliability and whose normative samples included African Americans. All normed scores reported are in comparison to the most up-to-date tables available when the oldest study child attained the target age. Tests included the Stanford Binet Intelligence Scale, Form L-M (SB; Terman & Merrill, 1972) at ages 2, 3 and 4 years; the Wechsler Preschool and Primary Scale of Intelligence (WPPSI; Wechsler, 1967) at age 5, the Wechsler Intelligence Scale for Children-Revised (WISC-R; Wechsler, 1974) at ages 6.5, 8, 12, and 15, and the Wechsler Adult Intelligence Scale – Revised (WAIS-R; Wechsler, 1981) at age 21. Maternal IQ was measured using the Wechsler Adult Intelligence Scale (Wechsler, 1955) unless the mother was younger than 16 years, in which case she was administered the Wechsler Intelligence Scale for Children (Wechsler, 1947). The score used in all present analyses is the derived IQ or Full Scale IQ. Preschool examiners were individuals not connected with the design of the study or the implementation of the curriculum. All examiners who tested participants aged 8 through 21 years were completely blind with respect to earlier treatment history.

Maternal attitudes. Maternal attitudes were assessed using Emmerich's (1969) modification of Schaefer and Bell's (1958) Parental Attitudes Research Inventory (PARI) which was administered to mothers when children were 6, 18, and 30 months of age and the Parental Modernity measure from the Parent as Educator Interview administered when children entered kindergarten (Schaefer & Edgerton, 1985). For the original PARI, reliability estimates obtained across a number of studies ranged from .40 to .77 for the scales used here (Schaefer & Bell, 1958). Split half-reliabilities of .90 and test-re-test reliabilities of .84 have been reported for the Modernity scale (Schaefer & Edgerton, 1985). The maternal attitudes data were converted to within-sample z scores and the cumulative sum entered for each child.

The home environment. Home visits occurred when children were 6, 18, 30, 42, and 54 months and 8 years of age. On each occasion the age-appropriate version of the Home Observation for Measurement of the Environment (HOME; Caldwell & Bradley, 1984) was scored. A score representing the proportion of items scored "yes" each time was created. The first five scores were summed to represent the quality of the home environment during the treatment phase, the age 8 score was added as representing the post-treatment phase, and the cumulative sum for both phases was entered into the model thereafter.

Mother's marital status. Annual updates of family demographic circumstances during the treatment phase and thereafter at follow-ups included questions about the mother's marital status or the presence of a male partner in the household. The data for each time point were entered cumulatively into the models, giving an overall measure of the extent to which there was an adult male in the child's home.

Task orientation.   Examiners completed the Infant Behavior Record (IBR) after each administration of the Bayley Scales of Infant Development (Bayley, 1969) to an infant or toddler. A factor analysis of the IBR scores within this sample yielded three factors: Activity Level, Sociability, and Task Orientation (MacPhee & Ramey, 1980). The Task Orientation factor reflected the extent to which the infant was responsive to the examiner and to objects in the environment. The scores at 6, 12, and 18 months were used in the present analysis. This characteristic was selected because previous work has indicated that it is a good infant predictor of later intellectual performance (DiLalla et al., 1990; Burchinal, Campbell, Bryant, Wasik, & Ramey, 1997). Inter-rater reliability for the IBR was established locally (r = .90) by determining the rate of agreement between the actual examiner and an observer who watched a subset of the sessions.

Verbal development.   Scaled scores for the Verbal Index of The McCarthy Scales of Children's Abilities (McCarthy, 1972), which is comprised of subtests measuring Pictorial Memory, Word Knowledge, Verbal Memory, Verbal Fluency, and Opposite Analogies, were available at 30, 42, and 54 months. These scores provided an estimate of verbal development that was independent of the Verbal IQ score derived from the Wechsler scales.

Data Analysis

Hierarchical Linear Models (HLM) were used to test the longitudinal hypotheses in this study, using the MIXED procedure in SAS (Singer, 1998). This analytic method estimates individual and group growth curves to describe patterns of change over time and factors associated with those patterns (see Bryk & Raudenbush, 1987; 1992; Laird & Ware, 1982). That is, investigators can examine both regression relationships among dependent and predictor variables and the ways in which these relationships vary over time. This approach accommodates randomly missing data points and inconsistent timing in data collection (i.e., unequal time intervals between data points) and allows for flexible specification of the within- and between-subject variance.

The full models included treatment group as a between-subject predictor and linear and quadratic change with age as within-subject factors. All main effects and two-way interactions among treatment group and the trends for age were included. Specifically, the aims were (1) to describe the nature of the growth curves of intellectual development as a function of time; (2) to learn if these trajectories differed as a function of assignment to the preschool treatment and control conditions; (3) to learn how characteristics of the child (gender) and family (maternal IQ, maternal attitudes, the early home environment and mother's marital status) might moderate treatment effects. Finally, two possible mediators of treatment effects were examined.

Because the HLM programs allow for missing data, it was possible to include in the current prediction models all individuals for whom age-21 data were collected (n = 104) since all could be classified according to a random preschool group assignment. Testing a two-group model for intellectual development is justified because there is no evidence from earlier 4-group analyses that the school-age treatment affected intellectual test performance. Moreover, including all individuals assigned to a preschool treatment or control group regardless of the amount of treatment received affords a more stringent test of the treatment hypothesis, and also increases the total number of cases available, which increases the power to detect treatment differences, if any exist.

TABLE 4.3
Longitudinal Means for Early Task Orientation and McCarthy Verbal Scores by
Preschool Treatment Group

	Group					
	Treated			Control		
Score	n	M	SD	n	M	SD
Task Orientation 3	52	11.1	4.0	52	11.4	3.6
Task Orientation 6	53	19.4	3.9	53	19.1	4.1
Task Orientation 9	51	21.5	3.1	53	20.6	3.7
Task Orientation 12	51	21.7	3.7	52	20.8	3.3
Task Orientation 18	51	23.4	3.5	49	20.8	4.2
McCarthy Verbal 30	50	51.3	8.0	48	44.6	8.2
McCarthy Verbal 42	50	52.8	6.7	47	47.7	7.4
McCarthy Verbal 54	47	54.7	7.4	46	48.1	9.5

A complex model was tested. Both individual and group IQ curves were estimated for two time periods – during treatment (infancy to age 5) and post-treatment. To learn if the rate of development was different while treatment was underway, one slope was estimated for the treatment period, using test scores collected each year from age 2 to 5. To control for the fact that two instruments were used during that period (i.e., the Stanford-Binet at ages 2, 3, and 4 years and the WPPSI at age 5) a term was entered in the preschool period to learn if some differences were attributable to the instruments themselves.

Intercepts and slopes for the post-treatment period (considering preschool alone as treatment) were estimated from scores collected at 5 time points: ages 6.5, 8, 12, 15, and 21 years. Because of the close similarity between the WISC-R and WAIS-R, no instrument term was entered in the post-treatment phase. Age changes were tested for linear and quadratic changes (age squared) in the slope during both the treatment and the post-treatment periods.

Mediation analyses. Baron and Kenny (1986) recommend that mediation hypotheses be tested as follows. First, the degree of association between the predictor and mediation variables is ascertained, then the relationship between the first predictor and the outcome of interest is established, and finally models are run to learn if that association is reduced when the mediator is added to the prediction equation. Two plausible mechanisms that might have mediated the effects of treatment on children's cognitive development were examined in this study. Enhanced engagement with persons and objects might be one way that the early childhood program contributed to better test performance later on; another explanation could be that treatment led to increased verbal skills. Table 4.3 gives longitudinal unadjusted scores for both measures in the treated and control groups.

RESULTS

Preschool findings

Infants in the treated and control groups were equivalent on the Bayley Mental Development Index (MDI; Bayley, 1969) at 3 months, but at each tested age thereafter those in the treated group began to earn higher scores, a difference that attained statistical significance at 18 months of age. All test scores after that significantly favored the treated children with the exception of the McCarthy Memory and Motor Scale Indices (McCarthy, 1972) at 42 months (Ramey & Campbell, 1984). The physical growth data showed no group differences in height, weight, and head circumference at 3 months or 60 months (Campbell, 2001, unpublished data).

School-age findings

The school-age phase of treatment had no apparent effect on children's intellectual test performance but dramatic effects on academic test scores. Analyses of Woodcock-Johnson reading and mathematics scores (Woodcock & Johnson, 1977) collected at the school-age treatment endpoint (after 3 years' attendance) showed that academic benefits were more strongly associated with the 5 years of preschool treatment than with the 3 years in primary school (Ramey & Campbell, 1991). There were linear trends in the data, however, indicating that academic scores increased as years of treatment increased, especially in reading.

Adolescent outcomes

At both adolescent follow-ups, longitudinal analyses using the 4 group models showed significant differences in intellectual and reading and mathematics test scores related to preschool treatment but no significant differences related to school-age treatment (Campbell & Ramey, 1994; 1995).

Long-term cognitive test findings

Table 4.4 gives the unadjusted means for intellectual test scores for the treated and control groups from age 2 to age 21, and Figure 4.2 contains smoothed IQ curves illustrating their developmental trajectories based on the HLM analysis for Model 1. Table 4.5 summarizes the regression weights obtained using the mixed-model procedure considering all included predictors of intellectual test performance in two separate developmental periods – treatment and post-treatment, as described above. The hierarchical longitudinal analyses considered only preschool treatment and participant age in the first model; model 2 added child gender, the home environment, maternal IQ, maternal attitudes, and the presence of a father-figure in the home; model 3 added the first mediator considered, child task orientation; and model 4 added the second, child verbal development.

As can be seen, the treated group earned higher scores during the entire period from age 2 to age 21 years ($F (1,659) = 7.56, p = .01$). A two-way treatment x age interaction indicated that the rates of change differed in the two groups (for treatment x age, $F (1,659) = 26.70, p = .0001$) and a treatment x period interaction indicated that the rates of change differed in the treatment and post-treatment periods (for treatment x period, $F (1,659) = 19.62, p = .0001$). The two-way interactions were in turn modified by a significant three-way treatment x age x period interaction ($F (1,659) = 5.49, p = .02$). This three-way interaction indicated that the slopes of the treated and control groups differed during the preschool period but the slopes were not significantly different in the post-treatment period. In the very early years, the treated group gained while the control group remained static, but an upward trend was seen in the control group after age 3. Although both groups showed declines after age 6, the treated group maintained its advantage in intellectual test performance such that the trajectories were generally parallel.

Model 2 showed a main effect for maternal IQ ($F (1,648) = 15.34, p = .0001$) that was modified by a maternal IQ $\times$ age^2 interaction ($F (1,648) = 5.30, p = .02$). Although child IQ

TABLE 4.4

Unadjusted Means for Abecedarian Treatment and Control Groups From Age Two
to Twenty-one Years

| | Treatment Group | | | Control Group | | |
Age and Test	n	M	SD	n	M	SD
2 years, Stanford-Binet	51	95.88	11.22	48	84.79	9.03
3 years, Stanford-Binet	50	100.70	13.97	48	84.27	13.45
4 years, Stanford-Binet	50	101.70	11.82	47	89.19	13.40
5 years, WPPSI	49	101.43	10.96	45	93.98	13.68
6.5 years, WISC–R	47	98.45	12.25	44	92.55	11.78
8 years, WISC–R	48	97.83	11.76	43	93.77	12.60
12 years, WISC–R	52	94.69	9.53	49	88.65	11.58
15 years, WISC–R	53	95.83	11.08	51	90.06	12.56
21 years, WAIS–R	53	89.66	10.09	51	85.24	8.61

Note.–WPPSI = Wechsler Preschool and Primary Scale of Intelligence; WISC–R = Wechsler Intelligence Scale for
Children–Revised; WAIS–R = Wechsler Adult Intelligence Scale–Revised.

was strongly influenced by maternal IQ across the entire time span, the slopes differed in the
two periods. The slopes were linear during the preschool period, but somewhat curvilinear
during the post-treatment phase. The effect of maternal IQ was stronger after the early years,
with offspring of brighter mothers doing relatively better during middle childhood and adolescence. The main effect for the quality of the home environment (F (1,648) = 4.57, p = .03)
was modified by a HOME × age interaction (F (1,648) = 3.85, p = .05). That is, the influence
of the early home environment declined over time. There was not a main effect for child gender, but gender × age interactions were found. For gender × age^2, F (1,648) = 4.64, p = .03.
This gender × age^2 interaction suggested that females outscored males in IQ test performance
in the early years, but thereafter, they declined at a slightly faster rate until middle adolescence. Males decline more sharply from middle adolescence to young adulthood. At age 21,
females scored slighter higher on intellectual tests than did males.

No instrument effect (Stanford-Binet vs. Wechsler) during the preschool period was found.
Nor did maternal attitudes or the presence of a father figure predict intellectual test performance in this sample.

Model 3 tested the first of two possible mediators, child task orientation. Preliminary
analyses showed that treated children earned higher scores on the measure of task orientation
derived from the Bayley IBR (F (1,92) = 4.18, p = .023), and they made significantly more
linear gains over time on this measure (F(1,92) = 7.40, p = .01). Model 4 added the second
mediator, child verbal development. Treated children also earned significantly higher scores
on the McCarthy Verbal Index (F (1,92) = 22.7, p = <.0001) but the treated and control groups
did not show differential patterns of change in verbal scores over time. Based on these results,
scores for these mediator variables were entered into the analytic models as follows. The Task
Orientation score at 18 months was selected as representing the last score obtained and the
one most representative of linear change (Model 3). Because there was no differential change
in the Verbal Index score, the mean of the three McCarthy Verbal Index scores was used as
best representing each child's overall performance (Model 4). Both infant Task Orientation
and early verbal development were significant predictors of IQ. For Task Orientation,
F(1,642) = 4.43, p = .04; for the McCarthy Verbal Index, F(1,639) = 110.59, p <.0001.

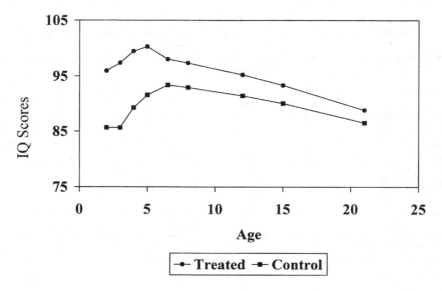

FIG. 4.2   Smoothed IQ trajectory – 2 to 21 years.

Models 3 and 4 indicated that the two factors examined as possible mediators of early treatment did fill this role, but to differing degrees. Infant task orientation only slightly changed the treatment effect on long-term IQ development. In contrast, the long-term effect of preschool treatment on intellectual test scores was well accounted for by early verbal development. The main effect for maternal IQ was also lost when early verbal development was entered into the model, but the maternal IQ $\times$ age^2 interaction remained significant. The main effect for HOME, however, remained significant with both mediators present, suggesting that its influence on intellectual test performance was mediated by neither. However, the HOME x age interaction is lost when mediators are added. Neither the presence of infant Task Orientation nor early verbal development as mediators altered the gender x age interaction seen in IQ test performance, but the gender x age interaction was not seen when Task Orientation was added. These interactions are reported for the sake of completeness, but, given the small size of the sample, they should not be overly interpreted.

Treatment effect sizes.   Although the MIXED procedure does not yield the r-squared statistic, treatment effect sizes (Cohen, 1977) can be calculated as described below. Table 4.6 summarizes treatment/control effect sizes on intellectual test scores at 44 ages, as a function of the four analytic models tested here. These were calculated by subtracting the difference between the adjusted means for the treated and control groups and dividing the result by the square root of the sum of the variance among the individual intercepts and the error variances. As can be seen, under Models 1 and 2, effect sizes during the preschool years were large. The addition of child and family characteristics slightly increases the treatment effect. Although under both Models 1 and 2 the effect sizes decrease by middle childhood, they remain medium (Cohen, 1977), and meaningful, up to seven years post treatment. By age 21, the treatment effect size is small. The addition of the first mediator, early task orientation, does reduce the effect sizes, but the change is minimal. The situation is very different, however,

TABLE 4.5

Summary of Hierarchical Mixed-Model Regression Analysis for Variables Predicting Longitudinal Intellectual Development

Source	Model 1 β	SE	Model 2 β	SE	Model 3 β	SE	Model 4 β	SE
			Preschool period 2–5 Years					
Intercept age = 2 years								
Treated	97.48	1.79	97.88	1.61	97.14	1.60	94.79	1.29
Control	83.19	1.75	84.04	1.66	84.65	1.66	86.98	1.31
Test (Stanford-Binet =1)	1.52	2.90						
Treatment × Age								
Treated	1.83***	.54	1.53**	.57	1.50*	.55	1.49***	.55
Control	3.22***	.55	2.97***	.57	2.94***	.57	2.99***	.56
Age^2	.33	.79	.36	.79	.35	.79	.40	.79
			Post-treatment period-6.5–21 years					
Intercept age = 6.5 years								
Treated	98.59	1.49	98.12	1.34	97.22	1.34	94.98	1.05
Control	92.41	1.53	92.71	1.37	93.05	1.39	95.78	1.10
Age								
Treated	−.31	.30	−.32	.30	−.39	.30	−.36	.31
Control	−.21	.30	−.20	.30	−.25	.31	−.19	.31
Age^2	−.01	.01	−.01	.01	−.01	.01	−.01	.01
			Moderators and Mediators					
Gender (male = 1)			−2.59	1.92	−1.57	1.92	−1.31	1.30
Gender × age			.62*	.26	.64*	.26	.65*	.26
Gender × age^2			−.03*	.01	−.03*	.01	−.03*	.01
HOME			.17*	.08	.21**	.08	.14	.07
HOME × age			.03*	.015	−.02	.02	−.03	.02
HOME × age^2			.001	.001	.001	.001	.001	.001
Maternal IQ			.36***	.09	.34**	.09	.10	.07
Maternal IQ × age			.02	.01	.02	.01	.022	.013
Maternal IQ × age^2			−.002*	.001	−.002*	.001	−.0015*	.0007
Parental attitudes			.50	1.04	.99	1.03	−.52	.79
Parental attitudes × age			−.19	.18	−.13	.18	−.14	.18
Parental attitudes × age^2			.003	.01	.001	.01	.002	.01
Married			3.48	1.92	2.97	1.86	1.46	.131
Married × age			−.14	.27	−.20	.27	−.11	.27
Married × age^2			.003	.01	.01	.01	.007	.01
Task 18					.45*	.21		
McCarthy Verbal							1.00***	.09

*p <.05; **p <.01; ***p <.0001

when early verbal development is entered under Model 4. In that case, after the preschool period, the treatment effect appears to be wholly accounted for by treatment's effect on early verbal development.

TABLE 4.6

Effect Sizes and Adjusted Mean Differences in Intellectual Test Scores for Abecedarian Preschool Treatment and Control Groups at Four Ages

Age at Testing	Model 1		Model 2		Model 3		Model 4	
	Effect Size	Difference	Effect Size	Difference	Effect Size	Difference	Effect Size	Difference
2 years	.96	11.70	1.10	11.99	1.07	11.34	.76	7.81
6.5 years	.38	4.6	.43	4.7	.40	4.3	.10	0.8
12 years	.31	3.8	.34	3.7	.31	3.3	-.21	-1.7
21 years	.19	2.3	.20	2.1	.17	1.8	-.38	-3.2

Note. Model 1 adjusts only for all parameters on the model. Model 2 adjusts for child and family characteristics. Model 3 adjusts for child and family characteristics and treatment effects on early task orientation. Model 4 adjusts for child and family characteristics and treatment effects on early task orientation and early verbal development.

DISCUSSION

The present longitudinal examination of intellectual development among the Abecedarian study participants was based on test performance from 2 to 21 years of age. The study provided a unique opportunity to learn how enriching the early environment through educational child care affected cognitive development, while at the same time considering the role of several relevant personal and family factors. The results showed that altering the educational stimulus value of the early caregiving environment modestly enhanced intellectual development in a lasting way. The findings generalize to African American children from low-income families.

This study highlights the role of early verbal development in intellectual test performance. Early verbal development was so powerful a mediator of treatment effects that it completely accounted for the long-term effect of treatment on intellectual test performance. In addition, the influence of verbal development grew stronger as child age increased and test performance became more and more dependent on the manipulation of verbal symbols. This finding affirms the importance placed on language development by the program planners, who specifically targeted this domain from infancy. The program emphasized the development of "communicative competence" including pragmatics, representational competence (ability to abstract), and linguistic competence throughout the preschool years (e.g., Ramey, McGinness, Cross, Collier, & Barrie-Blackley, 1982). Controlling for treatment effects on the other mediator we considered, early task orientation, reduced the treatment effect on IQ only slightly.

Within this sample, early childhood educational intervention and the characteristics of the family appeared to play complementary roles. Adding family characteristics to the prediction model slightly increased the size of the preschool treatment effect on IQ scores, probably by reducing random error associated with these factors. Maternal IQ, which might be construed as a surrogate for genetic factors, had a powerful effect on child intellectual development. So did the quality of the early home environment. Early treatment interacted with child gender in a complex way. As noted above, we would not overly interpret this outcome given the size of the sample, but the differential patterns of intellectual growth seen in males and females from low-income, African American families suggest that further research on the differential growth of intellect among poor children would be worthwhile.

The treatment/control difference in the unadjusted IQ scores of the Abecedarian young adults was modest, but the likelihood of testing within the mildly retarded range was reduced for treated children. Under the normal curve, 2% of the population would be expected to fall 2 standard deviations below the mean on an intelligence test. The Abecedarian investigators believed that their sample of children was at risk for exceeding the 2% rate. All the families admitted to the study qualified on the risk index (HRI) that screened for factors known to be associated with developmental delays. In addition, the maternal IQ obtained when the children were enrolled indicated that 12% of the mothers scored 70 or below on a Wechsler scale. Measures of age-21 IQ in the child generation showed that 4% of the control group scored 70 or lower on the WAIS-R, roughly double the expected population rate. In contrast, no one in the treated group did so. Expanding the range to include IQ scores of 80 or below, 29% of the preschool control group fell into this range compared with 13% of those in the treated group.

The cognitive gains shown by the Abecedarian program's treated group were associated with important benefits in later life. Significant gains in academic test scores (Woodcock & Johnson, 1989) and educational attainments were found at age 21 for those who had earlier been assigned to preschool treatment. Analyses reported elsewhere indicated that treatment effects on academic scores were mediated by child intellectual level (Campbell, Pungello, Miller-Johnson, Burchinal, & Ramey, 2001).

Meaningful differences between the treated and control groups were found in young adult adaptation and accomplishments. Those treated in preschool were more likely to be either in school or working at a skilled job as young adults. The treated group also reported more total years of education by age 21. The latter effect was largely confined to females. Treated females reported an average of 12.6 years compared to 11.3 years for control females. In contrast, males reported almost identical amounts of education irrespective of early childhood treatment: 12.0 years for treated males compared to 11.9 years for control males. More importantly, almost three times as many individuals in the treated group (35.9%) compared to the control group (13.7%) had attended, or were still attending, a 4-year college at age 21.

Fewer of the preschool treatment group members became teenaged parents. Among those (males and females) who did have children by age 21, the mean age at the birth of a first child was 19.1 years for the preschool treatment group compared with 17.7 years for preschool controls. However, the youngest parent in both groups was 15 years old when she or he reported having a first child. (The educational, vocational and child bearing results are reported in more detail in an earlier publication by Campbell, Ramey, Pungello, Sparling, & Miller-Johnson (2002).

Confidence in the findings is increased because the data are prospective. The intellectual test data used in the present models were collected across a 19-year span. Having prospective measures of family circumstances avoids errors inherent in retrospective family histories. The fact that this study was a randomized trial controls for possible bias associated with self-selection into the treatment program. The treated and control groups contained children from similar backgrounds. Although the initial equivalency of the two groups has been questioned (Herrnstein & Murray, 1994), there is no evidence to support this idea. By almost any standard – percent of teenagers among the original mothers, maternal marital status, family living circumstances, maternal educational levels – the treated and control groups were very similar. The percent of mothers earning IQ scores below 70 is almost identical in the two groups. All families lived in the same community when the children were enrolled. Almost all parents attended the same schools, and the same kinds of social services and prenatal care for mothers were available to both groups. Differences in the children's nutrition during the first year were at least partly ruled out by supplying high quality formula for control children during the first year. There is no evidence of differential growth patterns making it unlikely that differences in nutrition accounted for differences in cognitive growth in the two groups.

The estimated treatment effect is probably conservative. The study does not make comparisons between children reared at home with their mothers and those in high-quality educational childcare. About three-quarters of the control children were in out-of-home childcare at some time during their preschool years, some in state licensed full-day programs. Moreover, the study evaluators referred control group children who evinced early delays to appropriate agencies for follow-up assessments and treatment or intervention as indicated. The comparison is thus between high-risk children who had systematic educational intervention in the context of high-quality childcare versus those growing up in social circumstances typical of them all.

Why might the cognitive test score benefits have lasted so long in the Abecedarian study? Was it crucial to begin intervention in early infancy as was done here? The Perry preschool started with 3-year-olds and found its intellectual test score benefits faded by four years in school, although it must be noted that benefits in adult adaptation were found for its treated participants at age 27 (Schweinhart et al., 1993). Two differences between the Perry Preschool program and the Abecedarian study make comparison difficult. First, the Perry Preschool was a half-day program offered 10 months a year, whereas the Abecedarian program was provided for full days, year-round. Second, children in the Perry Preschool earned Stanford-Binet scores between 60 and 90 at age 3, although, like the infants in the Abecedarian study, they were free of biological conditions associated with developmental delays. Thus, we cannot really answer the question of whether the years 0-3 were crucial, nor can we rule out their importance.

Was it crucial to offer a full day program, year round, as was done here? The Milwaukee study started in infancy and offered a full day program year round plus a year of program-sponsored kindergarten. Although the Milwaukee sample was small and a number of criticisms have been raised about it (e.g., Flynn, 1984), it does compare in intensity to the Abecedarian program and its findings are worthy of consideration. The mean differences between the intellectual test performance of Milwaukee's treated and control groups appear to have lasted into adolescence and were larger than those obtained in the Abecedarian study. That study did not find comparable differences in academic achievement, however. The reason is unclear. The Milwaukee sample probably lived in more high-risk neighborhoods than the Abecedarian sample, and may have attended a public school system with a less advantaged majority than was true for the Abecedarian sample.

The characteristics of the Abecedarian program itself may have been one important factor in its long-term benefits. In contrast to the situation typical of many poor children in full-time care, where situations are often characterized by poor quality care during the preschool years (Peisner-Feinberg et al., 2001), the Abecedarian treatment program provided a stable and high quality early childhood environment for the children enrolled. Virtually every family who remained in the area used the facility throughout the child's preschool years. Barriers to attendance such as unreliable transportation were overcome because the center provided this service. Adult/child ratios exceeded state guidelines. Staff turnover was very low. State of the art medical care was available on site, and children attended sick or well (chicken pox excepted). All of these factors undoubtedly contributed to the success of the effort.

Caveats for this work include the fact that the study sample was relatively small and that the location of the study was atypical of many neighborhoods where poor minority individuals grow up in the United States, being a University community with a highly competitive school system and low unemployment rates. It would be unrealistic to expect that treatment benefits would be similarly maintained in very poor school systems or in much more high risk neighborhoods. That said, however, the children who participated in the Abecedarian early childhood program grew up in relatively disadvantaged circumstances. The school progress of the never treated control group illustrates how serious this disadvantage could be: half of them repeated a grade during the first 10 years of school (Campbell & Ramey, 1995). Slightly more than a third of them dropped out of high school. That more of those with preschool treatment enrolled in four-year colleges should make an important difference in the kinds of jobs for which they qualify. The implications of these findings for practitioners and policy makers are clear: early educational intervention in a childcare setting can make an important and lasting difference in the lives of poor children.

ACKNOWLEDGEMENTS

This research was supported by grants from the Child Health and Human Development Branch of the National Institutes of Health during the early years. The young adult work was supported by grants from the Maternal and Child Health Bureau, the Office of Educational

Research and Improvement, and the David and Lucile Packard Foundation. The authors wish to thank Dr. Elizabeth Pungello for helpful comments on the manuscript, and Dr. Lyle Jones for consultation on the presentation. They are also indebted to Dr. Craig Ramey for conceptualizing the original early childhood program, and to Dr. Joseph Sparling and Ms. Isabelle Lewis for developing and implementing the early childhood curriculum. Thanks are also due to Mrs. Carrie Bynum, the study's Family Coordinator for maintaining contact with the sample over many years and to Ms. Katherine Polk, Research Associate, for myriad contributions to the work. Finally, thanks are due most of all to the families enrolled in the study who have so generously shared their lives with us.

REFERENCES

Baron, R. M., & Kenny, D. A. (1986). The moderator-mediator variable distinction in social psychological research: Conceptual, strategic, and statistical considerations. *Journal of Personality and Social Psychology, 51,* 1173–1182.

Bayley, N. (1969). *Bayley Scales of Infant Development.* New York: The Psychological Corporation.

Bloom, B. S. (1964). *Stability and change in human characteristics.* New York: Wiley & Sons.

Burchinal, M. R., Campbell, F. A., Bryant, D. M., Wasik, B. H., & Ramey, C. T. (1997). Early intervention and mediating processes in cognitive performance of children of low-income African American families. *Child Development, 68,* 935–954.

Bryk, A. S., & Raudenbush, S. W. (1987). Application of hierarchical linear models to assessing change. *Psychological Bulletin, 101,* 147–158.

Bryk, A. S., & Raudenbush, S. W. (1992). *Hierarchical linear models.* Newbury Park, CA: Sage.

Caldwell, B., & Bradley, R. (1984). *Home Observation for Measurement of the Environment.* Little Rock, AR: University of Arkansas at Little Rock.

Campbell, F. A., Pungello, E. P., Miller-Johnson, S., Burchinal, M., & Ramey, C. T. (2001). The development of cognitive and academic abilities: growth curves from an early childhood educational experiment. *Developmental Psychology, 37,* 231–242.

Campbell, F., A., & Ramey, C. T. (1994). Effects of early intervention on intellectual and academic achievement: A follow-up study of children from low-income families. *Child Development, 65,* 684–698.

Campbell, F., A., & Ramey, C. T. (1995). Cognitive and school outcomes for high-risk African American students at middle adolescence: Positive effects of early intervention. *American Educational Research Journal, 32,* 743–772.

Campbell, F. A., Ramey, C. T., Pungello, E. P., Sparling, J.J. & Miller-Johnson, S. (2002). Early childhood education: Young adult outcomes from the Abecedarian Project. *Applied Developmental Science, 6,* 42–57.

Cohen, J. (1977). *Statistical power analysis for the behavioral sciences (Rev. ed.).* New York: Academic Press.

DiLalla, L. F., Thompson, L. A., Plomin, R., Phillips, K., Fagan, J. F., Haith, M. M., Cyphers, L. H., & Fulker, D. W. (1990). Infant predictors of preschool and adult IQ: A study of infant twins and their parents. *Developmental Psychology, 26,* 759–769.

Emmerich, W. (1969). The parental role: A functional cognitive approach. *Monographs of the Society for Research in Child Development, 34,* Whole Number 8.

Flynn, J. (1984). The mean IQ of Americans: Massive gains 1932 to 1978. *Psychological Bulletin, 95,* 29–51.

Garber, H. L. (1988). *The Milwaukee Project: Prevention of mental retardation in children at risk.* Washington, DC: American Association on Mental Retardation.

Herrnstein, R. A., & Murray, C. (1994) *The bell curve: Intelligence and class structure in American life.* New York: Free Press.

Hollingshead, A. B. (undated). *Four factor index of social status: Working paper.* Photocopied. New Haven, CT: Yale University, Department of Sociology.

Hunt, J. McV. (1961). *Intelligence and experience.* New York: Ronald Press Company.

Jensen, A. R. (1969). How much can we boost IQ and scholastic achievement? In *Environment, heredity, and intelligence, Harvard Educational Review. Reprint Series No. 2 (pp.1–123).* Cambridge, MA.

Laird, N. M., & Ware, J. H. (1982). Random-effects models for longitudinal data. *Biometrics, 38,* 963–974.

Lally, J. R., Mangione, P. L., & Honig, A. S. (1988). The Syracuse University Family Development Research Program: Long-range impact on an early intervention with low-income children and their families. In I. E. Sigel, (Series Ed.) and D. R. Powell (Vol. Ed.), *Annual advances in applied developmental psychology, Volume 3. Parent education as early childhood intervention: Emerging directions in theory, research, and practice.* (pp. 79–104). Norwood, NJ: Ablex Publishing Corporation.

Lazar, I., Darlington, R., Murray, H., Royce, J., & Snipper, A. (1982). Lasting effects of early education: A report from the Consortium for Longitudinal Studies. *Monographs of the Society for Research in Child Development, 47,* (2–3, Serial No. 195).

MacPhee, D. & Ramey, C. T. (1980, April). *Evidence for reliable and valid dimensions of infant temperament.* Paper presented at the Sixth Biennial Southeastern Conference on Human Development. Alexandria, VA.

McCarthy, D. (1972). *McCarthy Scales of Children's Abilities.* New York: The Psychological Corporation.

Peisner-Feinberg, E. S., Burchinal, M. R., Clifford, R. M., Culkin, M.L., Howes, C., Kagan, S. L., Yazejian, N. (2001). The relation of child-care quality to children's cognitive and social developmental trajectories through second grade. *Child Development, 72,* 1534–1553.

Ramey, C. T., & Campbell, F. A. (1984). Preventive education for high-risk children: Cognitive consequences of the Carolina Abecedarian project. *American Journal of Mental Deficiency, 88,* 515–523.

Ramey, C. T., & Campbell, F. A. (1991). Poverty, early childhood education and academic competence: The Abecedarian experiment. In A. Houston (Ed.), *Children in poverty: Child development and public policy* (pp. 190–221). New York: Cambridge University Press.

Ramey, C. T., Campbell, F. A., Burchinal, M., Skinner, M. L., Gardner, D. M. & Ramey, S. L. (2000). Persistent effects of early intervention on high-risk children and their mothers. *Applied Developmental Science, 4 (1),* 2–14.

Ramey, C. T., McGinness, G. D., Cross, L., Collier, A. M., & Barrie-Blackley, S. (1982). The Abecedarian approach to social competence: Cognitive and linguistic intervention for disadvantaged preschoolers. In K. Borman (Ed.). *The social life of children in a changing society* (pp. 145–174). Hillsdale, NJ: Erlbaum.

Reynolds, A. J., Temple, J. A., Robertson, D. L., & Mann, E. A. (2001). Long-term effects of an early childhood intervention in educational achievement and juvenile arrest: A 15–year follow-up of low-income children in public school. *Journal of the American Medical Association, 285(18),* 2339–2346.

Schaefer, E. S., & Bell, R. (1958). Development of a parental attitude research instrument. *Child Development, 29,* 339–361.

Schaefer, E. S., & Edgerton, M. D. (1985). Parent and child correlates of parental modernity. In I.E. Sigel (Ed.). *Parental belief systems* (pp. 83–105). Hillsdale, NJ. Erlbaum.

Schweinhart, L. J., Barnes, H. V., & Weikart, D. P. (1993). Significant benefits: The High/Scope Perry Preschool study through age 27. *Monographs of the High Scope Educational Research Foundation* (Number 10). Ypsilanti, MI: High/Scope Press.

Singer, J. D. (1998). Using SAS PROC MIXED to fit multilevel models, hierarchical models, and individual growth models. *Journal of Educational and Behavioral Statistics, 23,* 323–355.

Sparling, J. J., & Lewis, I. (1979). *Learningames for the first three years: A guide to parent-child play.* New York: Walker.

Sparling, J. J., & Lewis, I. (1984). *Learningames for threes and fours: A guide to adult and child play.* New York: Walker.

Sparling, J. J., & Lewis, I. (2000). *Learningames for Birth to 12 Months: The Abecedarian Curriculum.* Tallahassee, FL: Early Learning Press, Inc.

Sparling, J. J., & Lewis, I. (2001). *Learningames for 12–24 Months: The Abecedarian Curriculum.* Tallahassee, FL: Early Learning Press, Inc.

Terman, L. M., & Merrill, M. A. (1972). *Stanford-Binet Intelligence Scale, Third Revision: Form L-M.* Boston: Houghton-Mifflin.

Wechsler, D. (1947). *Wechsler Intelligence Scale for Children.* New York: The Psychological Corporation.

Wechsler, D. (1955). *Wechsler Adult Intelligence Scale.* New York: The Psychological Corporation.

Wechsler, D. (1967). *Wechsler Preschool and Primary Scale of Intelligence.* New York: The Psychological Corporation.

Wechsler, D. (1974). *Wechsler Intelligence Scale for Children-Revised.* New York: The Psychological Corporation.

Wechsler, D. (1981). *Wechsler Adult Intelligence Scale-Revised.* Allen, TX: The Psychological Corporation.

Weikart, D. P., Bond, J. T., & McNeil, J. T. (1978). The Ypsilanti Perry Preschool Project preschool years and longitudinal results through fourth grade. *Monographs of the High Scope Educational Research Foundation* (Number 3). Ypsilanti, MI: High Scope Press.

Westinghouse Learning Corporation (1969). *The impact of Head Start: An evaluation of the effects of Head Start on children's cognitive and affective development.* Athens, OH: Ohio State University.

Woodcock, R. W. & Johnson, M. B. (1977). *Woodcock-Johnson Psycho-Educational Battery: Part 2: Tests of Academic Achievement.* Boston, MA: Teaching Resources Corporation.

Woodcock, R. W., & Johnson, M. B. (1989). *Woodcock-Johnson Psycho-Educational Battery- Revised.* Allen, TX: DLM.

Zigler, E. & Muenchow, S. (1992). *Head Start: The inside story of America's most successful educational experiment.* New York: Basic Books.

Does Education Influence Intelligence?

Nathan Brody
Wesleyan University

EDUCATION AND INTELLIGENCE: THREE PROPOSITIONS

Consider three propositions dealing with the relationship between intelligence and education.

1. Individual differences in intelligence influence the acquisition of knowledge for individuals exposed to a common educational experience. This proposition has overwhelming empirical support and is not in dispute. None of the papers reviewed here address this issue and it will not be considered in this commentary.
2. What is learned (self-evidently) depends on what is taught. Individuals with the same intelligence may acquire different levels of expertise and knowledge if they are taught in different ways. Professor Hunt's paper deals with this issue. I agree with what I take to be the main thrust of Prof. Hunt's paper. The relationship between fluid ability and the mean level of knowledge acquired as a result of instruction is crucially dependent on what is taught and how it is taught. I have always been impressed with the results obtained by Stevenson and his colleagues (see Stevenson et al. 1990; Stevenson and Stigler, 1992) comparing the mathematical knowledge of American elementary school children and children in various Asian countries. Stevenson obtained aggregated indices of performance on tests of mathematical knowledge for children attending the same school. Comparisons of these indices for children attending schools in America with children attending schools in Asian countries indicate that virtually all indices for American schools are lower than all indices for Asian schools. The mean differences are large – typically on the order of 1.5 standard deviations. Differences in intelligence between children in Asian countries and children in American countries are either small or non-existent. Asian parents and children seem to value academic accomplishment more than American parents and children. More time is devoted to the study of math in Asian countries. The use of exceptionally well designed curriculum materials and whole class teaching methods suited for classrooms with large numbers of pupils may contribute to the superiority of achievement of Asian school children. Whatever the exact reasons for the differences, Stevenson's research demonstrates that children with roughly comparable levels of intelligence can obtain vastly different amounts of knowledge under different conditions of instruction.

3. Variations in education experiences influence intelligence. Professor Hunt's results do not provide support for this proposition. He found that variations in the educational experiences he studied had no influence on fluid intelligence. By contrast, Professors Campbell and Gustafsson obtained evidence indicating that variations in educational experiences influenced intelligence. I believe that the evidence in support of proposition 3 is opaque. No one doubts that extreme levels of educational deprivation will influence intelligence. Whether intelligence is substantially and enduringly influenced by variations in educational exposures that are commonly encountered among individuals in technologically advanced societies is unclear.

PROFESSOR GUSTAFSSON'S PAPER

Prof. Gustafsson's paper contains several methodological refinements. The use of a latent variable design provides better estimates of theoretical influences. Most importantly, the attempt to conceptualize education as a heterogeneous set of experiences that may have diverse impacts on several different components of intelligence represents an important mapping of the complexity of relationships that must be studied in order to understand the relationship between educational experiences and intelligence.

Prof. Gustafsson's study controls for entry characteristics related to academic achievement and social background. His research does not control for some entry characteristics that may be relevant to the choice of an educational track and to gains in intelligence. For example, individuals who select an academically rigorous academic track may have stronger intellectual interests than individuals with comparable social class backgrounds, intelligence, and prior academic achievements. Thus the controls used for entry characteristics in Prof. Gustaffson's study may be incomplete. And, some of the missing entry characteristics could account for some of the effects of education on intelligence.

Professor Gustaffson's study does not provide information about the enduring effects of the increments in intelligence associated with educational exposures. Do the increases decline or increase over time? There may be interactions between educational experiences and occupational experiences that determine the enduring effects of educational exposures on intelligence. It is often the case that experiences that change intelligence exhibit declining influences over time. Declining influences have been found for some of the influences discussed by Prof. Gustafsson in his review of the literature on educational effects on intelligence. Consider DeGroot's (1951) analysis of educational deprivations associated with World War II in the Netherlands. There were little or no effects on IQ for the oldest cohort in his study whose educational deprivation had occurred several years earlier. DeGroot's results may be understood as providing simultaneous evidence for the deleterious effects of educational deprivation on the development of IQ and for the resilience of IQ. The effects of severe educational deprivation were not permanent if individuals were provided with a normal educational exposure following the deprivation. It is also the case that variations in educational exposures associated with age of entry into formal education are of declining significance. Morrison, Smith and Dow-Ehrensberger (1995) studied reading skills as a function of educational exposures. They found that children who varied in age by one year at the start of their formal education differed in reading skills by .9 S.D. The difference in reading achievement for children of the same age who had one year of educational exposure versus those who had none was 2.63 S.D. The difference between children of the same age who had two years of exposure with those who had one year was .36 S.D. These results indicate that the effect of a year difference in educational exposure is proportional to total educational exposure. The impact of a year difference in exposure declines as individuals obtain increasing amounts of formal education.

I would like to compare Prof. Gustafsson's results with the results of analyses of the Spanish and Brazilian standardizations of the WAIS performed by Roberto Colom and his colleagues (Colom, in press; Escorial, Nascimento, Florez-Mendoza, Juan-Espinosa, & Colom, unpublished). For the analysis of the Spanish data, Colom divided his sample into four educational levels. He obtained five sets of difference scores for each of the sub-tests of the WAIS for groups differing in the number of years of formal education they had obtained. He also obtained g loadings for each of the WAIS sub-tests. He then correlated the vectors defining sub-test differences associated with levels of education with the vector defining g loadings. The mean of the five vector correlations was −.18. Groups with greater amounts of education tended to score higher than groups with less exposure to formal education on all of the sub-tests of the WAIS. The magnitude of the difference in favor of more highly educated groups was larger on sub-tests that had low g loadings.

For the Brazalian data, Escorial et al. performed a Schmid-Leiman analysis of the sub-tests and obtained vectors defining sub-test loadings on a g factor and on residual performance and verbal factors. The mean correlation between the g vector factor scores for groups with more education compared to groups with less education was −.29. Comparable correlations for vectors defining sub-test loadings and mean differences on sub-test scores for groups differing in amount of formal education for the performance and verbal factors were −.55 and .63, respectively. Thus, for these data, variations in educational exposure were positively associated with scores on sub-tests that had high loadings on a verbal ability factor and inversely associated with sub-tests that had high loadings on a g factor and high loadings on a performance factor.

These results appear to be at variance with those obtained by Prof. Gustafsson. His results indicate that individuals who were exposed to academically rigorous secondary school programs exhibited larger gains on g and gf than they did on gc (see his Table 7). By studying the effects of amount of education rather than variations in educational tracks, Colom and his colleagues are studying larger educational variations that might be assumed to have stronger influences on components of intelligence than the variations studied by Gustafsson. There are of course many differences in methodology, samples, and educational exposures between the studies reported by Colom et al. and Gustafsson. One difference that I think may be critical is the length of time between the educational exposure and the assessment of intelligence. Colom and his colleagues studied adult samples varying widely in age. Most of their subjects had completed their education years earlier. It is possible that gains in intelligence as a result of exposure to more formal education do not endure and are less manifest on measures of g than they may have been if intelligence was assessed shortly after the educational exposure had ended. Thus the enduring effects of educational experiences on g may be of declining significance.

PROFESSOR CAMPBELL'S PAPER

I believe that we should applaud Prof. Campbell's meticulous documentation of the enduring effects of early childhood interventions on intelligence and academic achievement. There are four issues that are germane to an analysis of these results.

- *Generalizability.* To what extent are these findings generalizable? Do the results obtained depend on the supervision of a university based research team?
- *Effect sizes and remediation.* The outcomes in this project, while certainly of great social significance, do not remediate the intellectual deficits of the target population. At age 12, subjects in the intervention group were compared to a representative group of children of the same age attending schools in the same community. The children in the experimental group had scores that were approximately one standard deviation lower than children in the community comparison group on various measures of academic achievement and intelligence. The children in the preschool intervention group had scores on these same tests that were approximately one third of a standard deviation higher than children in the control group. Thus these data indicate that the experimental intervention remediates approximately 25% of the intellectual deficit of subjects in the target population.
- The analysis of effect sizes of the intervention on intelligence reported in Table 6 indicates that the effects of the intervention decline with age. At age 21, the effect size of the intervention based on the model 1 analysis controlling for pre-school treatment group and age is .19. The data reported in Table 6 for Model 4 control for measures of verbal ability obtained at 30, 42 and 54 months. Professor Campbell notes that an aggregate verbal ability score based on these three assessments mediates the effects of the experimental treatment. The effects of the intervention become negative after controlling for pre-school verbal ability. Note that the negative effect size at age 21 for Model 4 in Table 6 (−.38) is actually twice the effect size for the experimental intervention reported for Model 1. These results may be explained by assuming that the gains in early intellectual development had two components − one is a gain in the hypothetical construct that is putatively assessed by tests of ability. The second component is a gain in test score for subjects in the intervention group that is relatively independent of the underlying disposition that is assessed by the test. Since the control groups scores are not artificially inflated by the latter component, the control groups scores are closer to the hypothetical "true" score of the underlying disposition. If the scores of the experimental group are artificially inflated they will be less predictive of performance over time and will predict higher adult scores on intelligence tests than the same score obtained from a subject in the control group. The declining effect sizes for the intervention observed for Model 1 over time are mirrored by the increasingly negative effect sizes reported for Model 4 that controls for early verbal ability. These results imply that the inflated test scores associated with changes in scores on tests of intelligence for the intervention group that are independent of changes in the hypothetical true score value of the intelligence disposition fade over time. A follow-up for the experimental sample at age 30 based on the Model 1 analysis might well indicate that the effect size for the intervention had declined to zero. These data indicate that the experimental intervention may very well have had a minimal enduring influence on intelligence construed as a latent disposition.

Intelligence is a relatively stable disposition. The best evidence for the stability of intelligence is contained in the results of the Scottish Mental Surveys based on the population of 11-year-olds who took an IQ test in 1932 and 1947 (see Deary, Whalley, Lemmon, Crawford, & Starr, 2000). Deary et al. a obtained a correlation of .63 (corrected to .73 for restrictions in range of talent) for a longitudinal study in which a subset of the original subjects was given the same Moray House test under identical conditions 66 years later. Deary and his colleagues also obtained evidence for the partial stability of the latent construct assessed by tests of intelligence.

Their subjects took the Ravens and Moray House tests in 1998 at age 77. The correlation between these tests was .57. The time-lagged correlation for the Moray House Test scores obtained at age 11 and the Ravens obtained at age 77 was .48. The correlation between these tests may be construed as an index of the commonality determined by the latent trait. The ratio of shared commonality for concurrent and time-lagged measures may be construed as an index of the stability of the underlying disposition of intelligence. The ratio of time lagged to concurrent correlations suggests that 70% of the variance in the underlying disposition of intelligence remains invariant from age 11 to 77. A claim to modify the hypothetical disposition of intelligence (as opposed to a score on an intelligence test) should be supported by evidence of enduring changes in the disposition rather than declining effects of interventions. It is not analytically or conceptually correct to argue that gains in intelligence attributable to an educational intervention should decline over time. True changes in intelligence might well change environmental encounters and exhibit increased effects over time. The Abecedarian Project does not provide evidence for enduring changes in the disposition of intelligence.

A completely effective intervention is one that remediates the risk of its target population. It may not be utterly Procrustean to expect individuals exposed to the Abercedarian intervention to perform at a level that is comparable to that of subjects attending schools in the same community who are not at risk for educational and intellectual deficits.

- *Target populations.* I believe that the Abecedarian sample does not constitute children at the highest risk for the development of low intelligence. The variables used to select children for the project de-emphasized parental IQ relative to various indices of poverty. Maternal IQ for project participants was quite variable (S.D. = 12.4) and included some mothers whose IQ exceeded 120. When maternal IQ was used as a covariate for the age 12 outcomes it accounted for approximately three to four times more variance than the experimental treatment. The predictive relationship between maternal IQ and the IQ of children in the Abecedarian Project exhibits an increase over time. The predictive relationship between maternal IQ and intellectual outcomes did not appear to be attenuated by the results of an educational exposure that to a significant degree provided children with a comparable early intellectual socialization exposure. The influence of maternal IQ is present for children living their lives in comparable conditions of poverty attending comparable schools.

I think that it is likely that a selection of a sample solely on the basis of maternal IQ would have larger educational and intellectual deficits than the sample included in the Abecedarian Project. Luster and McAdoo (1994) studied the variables associated with academic success for the African-American sample of the National Longitudinal of Youth study. They found that maternal IQ accounted for over twice as much variance in educational performance than various indices of social class background. The Abecedarian Project's sample is almost exclusively African-American. Approximately 15% of the African-American population have IQs of 70 or less. Thus it would not have been difficult to obtain a sample of individuals at highest risk for educational failure. It is interesting to compare the results obtained for the Abecedarian Project with those obtained for the Milwaukee Project that also studied the effects of intensive early intervention. The Milwaukee Project sample consisted solely of children whose mothers had low IQ. The Milwaukee Project obtained gains in intelligence test performance that were not accompanied by gains in educational achievement (Garber, 1988). Would the results obtained for the Abecedarian Project generalize to a sample of children whose mothers all had low IQ?

• *Is early socialization critical?* An emphasis on the importance of early socialization experiences in the development of intellectual competence may be misplaced. Behavioral genetic analyses indicate that early socialization experiences have declining influences on intelligence over time. Consider the results of the Colorado Adoption Project – a longitudinal study of the relationship between the IQs of biological and adoptive parents and their adopted children (Plomin, Fulker, Corley, & Defries, 1997). The correlation between adoptive parent IQ and child's IQ was near zero at age 16. The correlations between biological parent IQ and the IQs of their adoptive children with whom they had no post-natal encounters increased from early childhood to age 16. The changes in the magnitude of the correlations between parental and child IQ for biological parents were comparable for parents in a control group with comparable social backgrounds who were rearing their biological children and the biological parents whose children were adopted. Indeed, the correlation between biological parent IQ and adoptive child IQ at age 16 marginally exceeded the correlation between parent and child in the control group at age 16. These data (along with other longitudinal behavioral genetic analyses) indicate that early socialization experiences are of declining significance in the development of intellectual competence. If this is correct, it might be appropriate to attempt to intervene to change intelligence at later ages. The Abecedarian intervention after the start of formal schooling was not intense. Children were not provided with after school learning experiences or educational experiences during summer vacations. It is possible that a more intensive intervention after the children began their education would have been effective.

CONCLUSION

There is very little evidence indicating that attempts to increase intelligence lead to changes that are both large and long-lived. Assume that the upper bound of effect sizes derived from currently available educational interventions to increase intelligence is .5 (This estimate is compatible with the results obtained by Prof. Gustafsson for variations in educational tracks and with other data he cites in his review. Whether the estimate is appropriate for effects that endure over the adult life-span of individuals cannot be ascertained from the available data). Such an effect size is approximately equivalent to 6% of the variance of individual differences in intelligence. By contrast, variables operative prior to the first year of life account for far more variance in individual differences in intelligence. Parental IQ measurable prior to birth accounts for approximately 20 percent of the variance in adult intelligence. Genetic influences, present at the moment of conception, may account for anywhere between 50 to 80% of the variance in adult intelligence. Infant information processing measures obtainable prior to age 1 may account for as much as 50% of the variance in intelligence (this assumes that the obtained correlations are corrected for attenuation – a correction that may be problematic – see Colombo, 1993). These three influences are probably not independent of one another.

To a considerable degree influences that determine individual differences in intelligence prior to the start of education are far stronger than the influences associated with the variations in education that are likely to be encountered by a vast majority of children attending schools in technologically advanced countries. Individual differences in intelligence influence what is learned by individuals exposed to the same educational experience. If we wish to eradicate or substantially diminish this influence we shall have to develop radically new methods of instruction or finds ways of substantially increasing intelligence such that individual differences are radically reduced. The interventions considered by Profs. Campbell, Gustafsson, and Hunt do not accomplish either of these goals. Therefore, if we wish to increase intelligence or to diminish its long-lived influence on educational outcomes we shall have to consider interventions that are quite different from those considered in these papers. How this may be done is a topic for another paper.

REFERENCES

Colom, R. (in press). Education, Wechsler's full scale IQ, and g. *Intelligence.*

Colombo, J, (1993). *Infant cognition.* Newbury Park, CA: Sage.

Deary, I.J., Whalley, L.J., Lemmon, H., Crawford, J.R., & Starr, J.M. (2000). The stability of mental ability from childhood to old age: Follow-up of the 1932 Scottsih Mental Survey. *Intelligence, 28,* 49–55.

DeGroot, A.D. (1951). War and the intelligence of youth. *Journal of Abnormal and Social Psychology, 46,* 596–597.

Escorial, S., Nascimento, E., Florez-Mendoza, C., Juan-Espinosa, M., & Colom, R. (undated). Education, IQ, g, and cognitive abilities. Unpublished paper available from the authors at the Universidad Autonoma de Madrid.

Garber, H.L. (1988). *The Milwaukee Project: Preventing mental retardation in children at risk.* Washington, DC: American Association on Mental Retardation.

Luster, T., & McAdoo, H. (1994). Factors related to the achievement and adjustment of young African American children. *Child Development, 65,* 1080–1094.

Morrison, F.J., Smith, L., & Dow-Ehrensberger, M. (1995). Education and cognitive development: A natural experiment. *Developmental Psychology, 31,* 789–799.

Plomin, R., Fulker, D.W., Corley, R., & DeFries, J.L. (1997). Nature, nurture, and cognitive development from 1–16 years: A parent-offspring adoption study. *Psychological Science, 8,* 442–447.

Stevenson, H.W., Lee, S.Y., Chen, C., Lummis, M., Stigler, J., Fan, L., & Ge, F. (1990). Mathematics achievement of children in China and the United States. *Child Development, 61,* 1053–1066.

Stevenson, H.W., & Stigler, J.W. (1992). *The learning gap.* New York: Summitt Books.

III

ENHANCEMENT VIA DEVELOPMENT

ENHANCEMENT VA.
DEVELOPMENT

Child Development: The Underweighted Aspect of Intelligence

JAMES COMER
Yale University

Until very recently the general public and many researchers believed in what I call "the best brain notion." Many argue that success in school and in life is due largely to genetically determined intelligence and the willful expression of it. Those with the best brains who make the effort are expected to do well. And others are expected to do less well. The effects of child rearing, development, and the developmental context experience are underweighted. The notion is still held by many today.

Our Yale Child Study Center School Development Program work in elementary, middle, and high schools suggests that the determinants of school and life success go beyond intelligence and will. It was my own personal life experience that caused me to first challenge the "best brain notion." Thus, I begin my discussion with a brief review of my background.

My mother was born into extreme poverty in rural Mississippi in 1904; fourth in a family of seven. Her father was a sharecropper, the lowest rung of the socioeconomic ladder. And, they were an African American family in the poorest, most racist state in the nation. He was a good man and did the best he could to care for his family, but he was killed by lightning when my mother was about 6 years of age.

There were no family support programs and the children were too young to help their mother earn a living. As a result, a cruel stepfather came into their lives who was abusive in every way. They moved frequently from one shack to another. He physically abused her mother and the children. He would often go away and leave them for long periods of time. Neighbors, the storekeepers in town, and others provided them with just enough food to keep going. When home he would attempt to embarrass and demean them in every way possible. For example, he and his friends would eat all of the little food that they had in front of the hungry children. And he wouldn't let the children go to school.

When my mother was 8 years of age she decided that the way to a better life was through education. At the age of 16 she ran away to a sister in East Chicago, Indiana. She attended school for a few days but her sister didn't support her effort. She finally had to drop out and become a domestic worker. But when she dropped out she declared, "If I ever have children, I'm going to make certain that all of them get a good education."

Then she set out very, very, very carefully … find my father. (She didn't want to make the same mistake that her mother made.) She wanted to find someone with like goals and determination. She wasn't sure that my father was the right one in that he had been married once before and had a daughter by his first wife. She insisted that he obtain a letter of recommendation from his ex-mother-in-law before she would go out with him. The caution paid off. My mother, with no education, working as a domestic, and my father with a rural Alabama, approximately sixth-grade education, working as a steel mill laborer, sent the five of us to college for a total of 13 college degrees.

While this was happening in our family, something quite different was happening with my three best friends. The four of us went off to the same elementary school together. They were just as intelligent as anybody in my family and anybody in the predominantly White working, middle-to upper middle-class school that we attended. Yet all three of my friends went on a downhill course in life. One died early from alcoholism, one spent a good part of his life in jail, and the other was in and out of mental institutions all of his life until he died recently.

What was the cause of the difference between my outcome and that of my three friends? We attended the same school. Our families had the same kind of backgrounds and jobs. The cause was the quality of the developmental experience that I received before school age and that that they received.

One of my friends, said to be a bad boy and a poor student in school, often played on our porch. He was permitted to do so if he promised that he would not fight. My mother gave him instructions about what to do if he felt he was treated unfairly. He played without incident. The desire to belong and participate, and minimal structure, made this possible. He didn't receive the same experience at home.

Social and behavioral scientists often focus on poverty as the cause of social, behavioral, and academic performance problems. But the quality of the developmental experience, influenced by socioeconomic conditions, explains more. The interactions, exposure, opportunities to participate and belong, and the attitudes, values, skills, confidence, and competence that all of this generates are more important determinants of performance—intellectual and social.

I want to briefly describe my experience as a way of making the case for a greater focus on and a larger weighting of development.

Although we were a low-income family, my experience was not much different from that more often seen in middle- and upper income families. First, we were very much wanted by our parents. We were valued, and they had mainstream aspirations for us. We received a great deal of nurturance: trips to the Lake Front (Lake Michigan Park) where my parents would sit and talk while we played, or play and interact with us. We were served malted milk and popcorn on the porch on warm summer evenings. Every Sunday the four younger children would gather around my mother, two on her lap and two on the floor, as she read us the Sunday funnies. She could barely read and the funnies were not great literature. What was important was being close to her. Each of us would have her read our favorite comic strip over until she had read the paper two or three times, our way of sustaining the togetherness or nurturance.

All of this led to powerful attachment and bonding. It enabled us to imitate, identify with, and internalize the attitudes, values, and ways of our parents and the people in our family's primary social network of friend and kin.

There was also protection for the ideas and attitudes we were developing. My family doctor came to see me when I was about 4 years of age. When he left I said, "I'm going to be a doctor when I get to be a big man!" My parents responded to that by buying me a doctor's kit and playing doctor with me. A lady from the neighborhood observed this and asked my parents, "Why are you encouraging him to be a doctor? We are poor people. You know that he will never be a doctor!" My mother said, "Say that one more time and you're out of here."

On another occasion a new student to our school said to me, "I know your mother." I asked my mother about this. She explained that she had worked for her mother years before. I was about 10 or 11 years of age, and status and self-esteem issues were pressing. She could see that her explanation bothered me a bit. She said to me, "You are just as clean as she is, just as smart as she is, and you can do just as well in school as she can." And then she looked at me as only my mother could, and said, "And you had better!"

We gained mainstream attitudes, values, and skills through many of the activities that went on in our home. Around the dinner table every evening we gained the skills of conversation— talk about our experiences and ideas, not speak too long (or "hog" the conversation), listen to and not interrupt what others had to say; but not sit back or you'd lose your chance. Assertive, vibrant expression was welcome, even applauded.

Almost every evening those animated conversations would spill over into debates after dinner. Although not consciously planned (I don't think) the situation allowed for supervised thinking and expression. My mother usually rested in the bunk bed just off the kitchen where we were debating. On one occasion I expressed opposition to the public welfare program because it promoted dependency. This is a position my brother would ordinarily have taken, but catching me in it he accused me of being heartless. After a few charges and counter charges my mother said to me, "But Jim, what would become of poor people?" I indicated that the solution would be to have government provide jobs of *last* resort. She responded with, "Okay", and resumed her usual role as listener.

These were fierce discussions and emotions were high, but there was a rule that no matter how badly you were losing the debate, you could not fight. And losing was not a good thing in my house. So I found myself coming home from school fashioning my argument so that I would have a better chance that evening.

We were exposed to all things our parents felt to be educational and encouraged to participate in all wholesome mainstream activities. We visited the museums, the aquarium, the zoo, and many other places in Chicago. We often went to the Bud Billiken Parade, an African American community activity. And we went to the circus, ballgames, and other activities with parents of White friends. And a Black deacon from our church took us to Chicago Cubs baseball games.

In the 1940s many restaurants and other facilities were either racially segregated, or just beginning to open up. On one occasion after a visit to a marina in Chicago we stopped to have a meal at such a restaurant. And although there was no problem being served, some of the patrons stared at us. I observed my mother stare back until they dropped their heads or changed their gaze. The unspoken message I received: Don't let anybody intimidate you or stop you from going where you want to go because of your race. Indeed, what my mother said in behavior, my father said in words on many occasions.

On one occasion my mother was serving as a poll worker during the election. I passed by on my way back to school at noon and she called me over, which was probably against the rules. She took me inside the polling place, which was probably against the rules. I actually pulled the lever, which was against the rules. But this powerful, positive experience of participating has stuck with me across a lifetime. And when President Franklin Delano Roosevelt's entourage came through town my parents took us all down to see them come across the bridge. All of this encouraged participation in mainstream activities.

At the same time our family was deeply enmeshed in the African American church culture. It was a part of the primary social network of our family—a place where we felt belonging, a place where we made contributions. At one time my father was the Sunday School superintendent. At another period he was the president of the Baptist Young People's Training Union. And he was on the Deacon Board. My mother sat three or four rows back on the right hand side of the church, and we sat on the second row back on the left hand side, behind the Deacons. In that way she could keep her eyes on our necks and mouths if we turned and talked, which we were not supposed to do.

All of the activities and values of the church reinforced the activities and values of our home. Parents and church people, and other members of our primary social network, supported our growth and development along all the critical developmental pathways—physical, social interactive, psychoemotional, ethical, linguistic, intellectual cognitive. Indeed, on one occasion in church Mrs. Johnson caught me throwing a punch at another kid (a defensive blow, of course). She threatened to tell my father. And although my father never spanked me, I was greatly concerned that he might learn of my misbehavior. I didn't relax until he arrived for the evening service and I realized that she didn't tell him. But that was the power of a network of caretakers who knew, trusted, and interacted with each other and, in turn, together, supported the development of their children.

Interestingly, the same Mrs. Johnson had a vision about me, as people often did in the Baptist Church. She said that she saw me as a little minister traveling all over the country to spread the gospel. Every time I attend a meeting to discuss child development, I think of Mrs. Johnson. She was in the right church, wrong pew—child psychiatrist, not minister; child development, not religion.

All of this prepared us for school. We were able to sit and take in information when appropriate, able to be spontaneous and curious, and able to interact well with other children. These skills and dispositions made it possible for us to connect and elicit a positive response from school people. We could then imitate, identify with, and internalize their attitudes, values, and ways. We could identify with the program of the school. Now parents and school together could promote our growth along the developmental pathways. Already primed to be participants and learners, approval and support in school promoted enthusiastic academic learning.

I gained some support for my attachment and growth notion several years ago when I went back to visit my mother in the hospital. Ms. Walsh, my first-grade teacher, was a spry 80-plus-years-old volunteer. When she saw me she threw her arms around me and said, "Oh, my little James!" I was 55 years old. But of course you're always "little James" to your first-grade teacher.

After she hugged me she stepped back and said, "Oh, we just loved the Comer children! You came to school with those bright eyes, you were so eager to learn, you got along so well with other children," and she went on and on.

What was she describing? It was the outcome of the developmental experience that we received at home that made it possible for us to elicit a positive response from school people, and attach to the people and the program of the school. The outcome of the preschool experience of my three friends was problematic.

Their experience did not prepare them to attach and bond to school people and programs. A third-grade activity is illustrative.

A book-reading contest was organized to encourage us to use the public library. I read the most books over the assigned period of time, and my three friends did not read any. In frustration and anger my teacher said to them, "If you three little colored boys don't want to be like the rest of us, you should not come to our school!"

My teacher was not a die-hard racist. We walked the three blocks from her home to school hand-in-hand every morning. She did not understand that my three friends were the grandchildren and great-grandchildren of sharecroppers and tenant farmers whose families were intimidated by mainstream institutions. Their parents did not feel belonging and did not prepare their children to participate and belong. She, like most teachers, was not prepared to understand and to provide underdeveloped children with the kind of support they needed to be able to succeed in school. If she had understood, she would have taken them to the library and helped them get a card to be able to participate.

After I finished medical school I did my internship in my hometown as part of my plan to become a general practitioner there. My friends were already beginning to go on a downhill course. Others who had functioned well in school were not functioning well in life. And I was struck by the high level of depression among poor people in the city, and by the high level of poverty despite the fact that the steel industry and other parts of the economy were still strong. Also, a number of incidents of gratuitous racism caused me to reflect on the issues of poverty and race and to consider their contribution to the problems I observed. I decided to go into the U. S. Public Health Service to do my military service time, and to give myself time to think.

While in the service I worked as a volunteer in a "bootstrap" social service organization formed to help people who had been thrown off the public welfare rolls for minor violations. There I encountered a number of bright African American youngsters whose families were living under economic and social stress. The children weren't prepared for school. And the school wasn't prepared for the children. The economy had changed dramatically. The sense of community that I grew up in had broken down completely in these areas. High mobility and television had made life much more complex. It occurred to me that these children were going to go on the same downhill course that my friends were on without major interventions.

These concerns led me to the University of Michigan School of Public Health in order to develop a prevention perspective. In 1964 human ecology had not really emerged in social science but there were important parallels in environmental ecology that I believed could be used in preventive psychiatry. While training in psychiatry at Yale University I was introduced to milieu therapy, and the power of the group to influence individual behavior. This made me aware of the importance of a sense of belonging. The adult behavior problems I encountered suggested the importance of childhood rearing and development. This led me into child psychiatry.

It occurred to me that schools strategically located, organized, and focused to promote development, could reinforce desirable preschool development, and compensate for underdevelopment and damage. By drawing on my own background, I hypothesized that a positive environment would enable the adults in the school to promote development and learning.

In 1968, Dr. Albert Solnit, the director of the Yale Child Study Center, asked me to lead a school-intervention program in two of the lowest achieving inner city elementary schools in New Haven, Connecticut. The schools were 99% Black and poor. They were 32nd and 33rd in achievement out of 33 schools. They had the worst attendance and worst behavior in the city. Our strategy was to live in these schools and learn; and not to impose theories or beliefs on the system. With insight, and in collaboration with parents, teachers, administrators, and students, we were to develop a strategy for improving schools.

We found apathy, anger, acting up, and acting out on the part of all the participants—parents, school staff, students. These conditions led to a troubled school climate, low achievement, poor attendance, and many behavior problems. At the same time, everybody wanted to succeed. We concluded early in our work that they were all a victim of what we call "the best brain theory": Intelligence is genetically determined and fixed, influenced only by will. This led to a mechanical model of teaching and learning, with a focus on cognitive and linguistic development primarily, and with almost no focus on overall development.

We believed that the students were underdeveloped because they grew up in families that were living under economic and social stress. Parents could not provide their children with the kinds of interactions that would allow them to fully express their intelligence. This led to interactions in school that caused them to be perceived as "bad" and "dumb." The school's response was generally punishment and control. This led to a downward spiral in achievement and behavior among all in the school setting. In short, the problem was in the larger social system, and the school as a system, not with the kids. The challenge was to change the system we could influence, the school.

Our belief that the children were underdeveloped rather than "bad" and "dumb" stemmed from our public health interactive systems (ecological) and child and adolescent development perspectives. As a result, our staff and the administrators, teachers, and parents were often "miles apart" in thinking about child learning and behavior. We believed that children must be able to attach and bond with caring people in a supportive environment at home and at school; that this would permit the adults to help the children grow along the critical developmental pathways needed to make academic learning possible—physical, social interactive, psychoemotional, ethical-moral, linguistic, cognitive-intellectual. Without being fully aware of it, school people and parents believed that behavior and academic outcomes were a result of genetically determined intelligence and student will. They did not accept the notion that student will or motivation was influenced greatly by relationship conditions in the school. A change in understanding and relationships was needed.

We quickly learned that district and building leadership could not mandate change and achieve school improvement. Second, we learned that you can't just teach child development and expect the staff to be able to go in and successfully apply the principles in their classrooms, even when they are in agreement. What we had to do was to create a conceptual and operational framework that enabled the staff to create good relationship conditions among all the adults in school. We believed that this would allow the children to attach and bond to them; to imitate, identify with, and internalize attitudes, values, and ways that would lead to school success. The positive climate made the people and the program of the school meaningful to the children.

The framework literally evolved in self-defense. Conditions were so difficult in the first year that the parents threatened to throw us out of the school. We created a governance and management team that was representative of the parents, teachers, administrators, and non-professional staff, in short, all of the adult stakeholders. It was their job to work their way to success. This led to a nine-element change process that we now call the School Development Program. It contained three mechanisms, three operations, and three guidelines.

The governance and management team, the most important mechanism, was eventually called the School Planning and Management Team. This team carried out three operations: the development of a (a) Comprehensive School Plan, both social and academic; (b) staff and adult development geared to enabling them to meet their goals; and (c) assessment and modification on an ongoing basis. These operations permitted the school to identify and respond to student and staff needs. The Parent Team, a second mechanism, selected their representatives to serve on the School Planning and Management Team, and they carried out social and academic activities in support of the Comprehensive School Plan—Science Fair, Book Fair, and so on.

A group called the Student Staff Support Team, the third mechanism, was made up of all the helping professionals in the school: psychologist, social worker, special education teacher, nurse, and others. The work of this team was both preventive and problem solving. They helped all the adults make the school child friendly in a way that prevented behavior problems. They worked with individual children or small groups as indicated. They brought in service providers from outside the school as needed.

It would have been difficult to impossible to carry out these processes with the original control and punishment disposition of the staff and sense of exclusion experienced by the parents. These conditions led to both parent–staff and intra-staff conflict, and a difficult school climate. To respond to this situation we developed three relationship guidelines: no fault, consensus decision making, and collaboration.

The no-fault principle asked people to avoid blaming each other and to focus on problem solving. Action decisions were decided on through consensus rather than vote to avoid"winner–loser behavior." The losers often did not want to cooperate. With consensus decision-making based on what appeared to be in the best interest of the child, it was understood that we would go back and use the approach suggested by others, or we might discover a better approach that we had not discussed. We use whatever works to help children, and try to avoid "adult need" interferences. Finally, the collaboration principle was designed to avoid paralysis of the principal, and to ensure that the principal would not ignore the input of parents and staff. It encouraged all to work together to achieve school goals.

These nine elements coordinated all of the many potentially disorganizing activities in a school. They reduced overlap of efforts and program fragmentation. The processes gave all of the school participants a sense of ownership of the challenges and the successes, and a sense of belonging. All of this created a good culture in the school and a clear sense of direction.

The belief system of the school was that all children could learn; that the problem was under-development, not a lack of ability. The staff and parents believed that they could provide the children with what they needed to develop and function well in the school; that this would lead to improved learning. As we predicted, this culture made it possible for the students to make positive attachment and bond to the adults in the schools, imitate, identify with, and internalize their attitudes, values, and ways and, as a result, strive toward social and academic achievement.

The model was and is a response to the way that multiple social environments or contexts interact to interfere with the development of children. It recognizes that children develop and grow in three major social contexts—the primary social network of friend, kin, and institutions in which the family feels belonging; the secondary or service network, which includes the family workplace or source of income, and the school; and the tertiary or policy network that influences conditions in the primary and secondary networks. The influences on development are the greatest in the primary and secondary networks. The school is strategically located and can reinforce good development and compensate for poor development. But this requires structures and processes that create a culture that facilitates good development in school. Let me give some examples.

An 8-year-old child who grew up in a warm, tight-knit social network in rural North Carolina was brought to New Haven over a weekend and dropped off in school by an aunt the following Monday morning. She went on to work and the child was taken directly to the classroom without an orientation. His teacher had had three transfers the week before. She nodded her head in frustration and this was experienced as rejection by the child. This, and the abruptness of change and strangeness of the situation, caused him to panic. He kicked the teacher in the leg and ran out of the room. This is a situation where a child is often sent to the principal to be punished, and sent back to the classroom. If another child laughs at him, to protect his honor, he might pop his tormentor in the mouth. He would be sent back to the principal, and the process would go around and around until he was finally labeled disturbed, and sent off to someone like me to have his head fixed.

Our SSST discussed the matter with the staff, asking them to consider his stage of development at 8 years of age, and the stressfulness of this change. They began to realize that the child lacked the mental, social, psychological, and linguistic development necessary to manage this situation. Together they thought about ways to help the child be successful in the classroom: "Welcome Johnny" signs, assignment to a successful child to help him adjust, discussions about his previous home and the things he liked to do, and so on. And then the procedures of the school were changed. All new students received a supportive orientation, and the caretaker was expected to stay the first few hours until the adjustment had taken place.

Children treated in this way became the carriers of the attitudes and values established by the parents and school staff. A 9-year-old transferred into the school during the second semester, having transferred three times in the previous semester. Another child stepped on his foot during a classroom exercise and his dukes (fists) went up. He was ready to fight. In all the schools he had been in before you had to fight your way in. Another child looked at him and said, "Hey man, we don't do that in this school." He looked around and sure enough the expressions on the faces of the teachers and other children confirmed this. With relief he dropped his dukes and began to take on the culture of the school.

Another problem was the student assembly. It was always chaotic because several of the kindergarten children would become disruptive. They had to be disciplined or carried out. We used one well-known bit of child development knowledge to help the teachers develop a successful approach. We pointed out that 5-year-olds can't sit still very long. Using this knowledge about development they created a plan: Bring the kindergarteners in last, put them on the program first, have them sit and listen to a part of the program, and at the first intermission, and before they became disruptive, they left as a class in an orderly fashion. This reduced a great deal of student and staff stress.

A third grader did not look at her teacher directly for 8 months, but did just enough work to earn promotion. At the end of 8 months with a caring, predictable, responsible teacher she finally looked up and smiled. The teacher was devastated because she knew that in 2 more months she would have to pass her on and would not be able to build on the relationship.

We had an SSST–teacher discussion group about this situation in which we discussed the importance of attachment and bonding, continuity, and support for development, and its relationship to academic learning. We talked about how many children from low-income backgrounds experience multiple changes in adult authority figures in their lives, different and conflicting messages, different locations and the like. As a result, the school established a 2-year same teacher program, now commonly called looping. This greatly improved the performance of all children and some who made no academic gain during the first year made 2 academic years and more of gain during the second year with the same teacher. This also greatly reduced behavior problems.

A number of such building-based adjustments and student improvements helped the school staff and the parents begin to believe that the children could learn at a high level. We also reasoned that if we could provide the students with some of the same experiences that middle- and upper-income students from better-educated families receive by simply growing up with their parents that our students could do just as well in school. This led to the creation of a program called the "The Social Skills Curriculum for Inner City Children." We had discussions with parents about their expectations for their children, and what kind of skills the children would need to achieve them. Parents and staff together agreed that the students would need knowledge and skills in politics and government, business and economics, health and nutrition, spiritual–leisure time. During what would have been elective time we developed programs in these areas that integrated the teaching of basic academic skills, social skills, and an appreciation of arts and athletics.

The first unit implemented was in politics and government at the time of a local mayoralty election. The children wrote letters to the candidates inviting them to make presentations at the school, and then wrote thank you notes after the event. This made the linguistic and communication skills very meaningful. Parents contributed money from their activities for busses, and with the staff took the students on study tours around the city relevant to the role of government and politics. There were discussions on the bus and back in the school regarding this experience, and other related academic activities. The children were taught to be hosts for the candidates and their parents. They were taught how to raise tough and meaningful questions without being disrespectful. They rehearsed for and put on a dance drama program during the event and students served as the masters of ceremony, with the support of their teachers.

This was a powerful experience for all involved.

The interest of important adults from home, school, and the community, and the opportunity to engage them around adult life issues, raised the esteem of the students. They were motivated to perform well. Some students who had not previously demonstrated good academic skills turned out to have good personal presence and could express themselves well in interactions with the candidates. Some had artistic talents that teachers were unaware of. The interest and large turnout of the parents reminded everybody that low-income parents and children want to achieve at the highest levels possible. We believe that the changed perceptions of the staff led to changed expectations and treatment of the students, which in turn led to improved academic and social performance. They not only learned more about local politics and government but they demonstrated greater knowledge of regional and national politics and government. After this school experience some parents who had never voted before registered and voted for the first time.

In short, school conditions designed to promote learning and preparation for life led to improved outcomes. After the first year of this program there was a 7-month jump in academic improvement on nationally standardized tests, and then a 2-to 4-month per year gain for the next several years until the children who had been 32nd and 33rd in achievement out of 33 schools were eventually tie for third and fourth highest levels of academic achievement in the city. They went from having the worst attendance to the best. There were no serious behavior problems in these schools; and in one school, no teacher turnover for 15 years. Over the years, teachers from these schools have moved into top leadership positions in the school system.

The question raised by Professor Brody earlier was whether intervention programs could be transferred. We field tested our program in schools in Michigan, Arkansas, and Maryland. We had good outcomes where effective implementation took place. We could not use the "Social Skills Curriculum for Inner City Children" component because it can only be carried out effectively in reasonably well-functioning schools. Nonetheless, there was enough success using our basic nine-element model that in 1991 the Rockefeller Foundation provided us with the funds to begin a large-scale dissemination program.

By 1998 we were in almost 700 schools in 27 school districts across the country. But we discovered that it was difficult to sustain even successful implementations where the district was not supportive. One school serving low-income minority children moved from 24th to first in achievement. There was suspicion that they were cheating and so they were required to repeat the test under district supervision. The students scored slightly better the second time than they did the first. But then the principal was removed, and some key staff transferred, and a new principal and staff were brought in who were not trained in use of the model. The school immediately tumbled in achievement.

In a similar school in another district the students moved from 34th to first, and rivaled the middle-and upper-income schools in the suburbs in mathematics achievement by the eighth grade. Again the principal was removed. But the staff requested a principal who supported our developmental model. This school continued to achieve at this high level for 5 years, until staff turnover without adequate training reduced their achievement performance. With help, they are recovering. For these reasons we made a strategic decision to reduce the number of schools we are working in to about 400 and to work with districts that support systemic change guided by developmental principles. We will increase the number of schools we are working with within these committed districts.

How do we take this model to scale? We don't believe that it is possible to take this or any other model to scale. On the other hand, organic change at the building and district level that includes inherent accountability can promote continuous improvement in development and learning among parents, teachers, students, and policy makers. Our model is both a conceptual and operational framework that can be used to create building and district conditions that promote continuous development and learning. What is needed now is a deep and wide pool of educators and policy makers who are able to create and/or support the creation of development, teaching, and learning frameworks throughout our education enterprises. Schools of education can play a key role.

One of the projects we are now working on is an effort to create an Educational Extension Service inspired by the Agricultural Extension Service used at the beginning of the 20th century. Education at the beginning of the 21st century is what agriculture was to the economy at the beginning of the 20th century. Knowledge about better ways to farm were in research and development organizations in and outside of universities while the farmers practiced in traditional ways. The same is true of education today. Most important among the new knowledge is the effectiveness of applying child and adolescent development to all aspects of schooling.

We would like to infuse the child and adolescent development knowledge and practices into education policy and decision making throughout the education enterprise. In our design, schools of education would play a key role. A part of a school would serve as the education agency and would support school improvement in various districts using child and adolescent development knowledge and skills. They would also help policy makers and the public understand the usefulness and the way to create coordinated, coherent policy. The extension service would help infuse knowledge of practice needs into the general program of the school of education and the university, as well as utilize the knowledge and resources from both.

In summary, we rejected the notion that success in school and in life is due primarily to genetically determined intelligence. We demonstrated that the underlying problem was student underdevelopment and the fact that schools are not organized and managed, nor staff prepared, to support student development. With a focus on the building as a system, we created a conceptual and operational framework that created conditions that allowed the adults to support the development of students. This improved the school climate and permitted adequate academic and behavioral achievement among students. Our effort now is to infuse and inform all elements of the education enterprise about child and adolescent development and how to organize and manage in a way that creates coherent education policy and practice.

BIBLIOGRAPHY

Bransford, J. D., Brown, A. L., & Cockings, R. R. (Eds.). (2002). *How people learn: Brain, mind, experience, and school,* Washington, DC: National Academies Press.

Brown, F. E., & Murray, E. T. (2005). Essentials of literacy: From a pilot as Davis Street School to disctrict-wide intervention. *Journal of Education for Strudents Placed at Risk, 10: 2,* 185–197.

Comer, J. P. (1988). Educating poor minority children. *Scientific American, 259: 5,* 42–48.

Comer, J. P. (1998). *Waiting for a miracle: Why schools can't solve our problems and how we can.* New York: Plume.

Comer, J. P. (2004). *Leave no child behind: Preparing today's youth for tomorrow's world.* New Haven, CT: Yale University Press.

Comer, J. P. (2005). The rewards of parent participation. *Educational Leadership, 62:*6, 38–42.

Comer, J. P., Haynes, N. M., & Hamilton-Lee, M. (1987). School power: A model for improving black student achievement. *The Urban League Review, 11:1,* 187–200.

Comer, J. P., Joyner, E. T., & Ben-Avie, M. (Eds.). (2004). *The field guide to Comer Schools in action: When children develop well, they learn well.* Thousand Oaks, CA: Corwin Press.

Darling-Hammond, L. (1997). *The right to learn: A blueprint for creating schools that work.* San Francisco: Jossey-Bass.

Emmons, C. L., & Baskerville, R. (2005). Maintaining excellence while managing transtitions: Norman S. Weir revisited. *Journal of Education for Students Placed at Risk, 10: 2,* 199–206.

Haynes, N. M., Emmons, C. L., Gebreyesus, S., Ben-Avie, M. (1996). The School Development Program evaluation process. In J. P. Comer, N. M. Haynes, E. T. Joyner, & M. Ben-Avie (Eds.). *Rallying the whole village* (pp. 123–146). New York: Teachers College Press.

Healy, J. M. (2004). *Your child's growing mind: Brain development and learning from birth to adolescence.* New York: Broadway Books.

Henderson, A. T., & Mapp, K. L. (Eds.). (2002). *A new wave of evidence: The impact of family, school, and community connections on student achievement.* Austin, TX: Southwest Educational Development Laboratory.

Joyner, E. T. (1998). Large scale change: The School Development Program perspective. In A. Hargreaves, A. Lieberman, M. Fullan, & D. Hopkins (Eds.), *International handbook of school change part two.* Boston: Kluwer Academic.

Maholmes, V. (2002). What school is all about, *Education Week.*

Wood, C. (1997). *Yardsticks.* Greenfield, MA: Northeast Foundation for Children.

7

▼▼▼▼▼▼▼

Enhancing Development in Intellectually Talented Populations

David Lubinski
April Bleske-Rechek
Vanderbilt University

This volume is devoted to enhancing intellectual development. Our chapter contribution focuses on how this might be achieved in intellectually talented populations. Intellectually precocious individuals are endowed with dispositions that accelerate their intellectual growth, and they possess extraordinary promise for truly exceptional achievement and creativity. Their promise is often actualized if they are given access to *appropriate developmental placement*: educational settings that tailor the curriculum to progress at a pace commensurate with student learning. Our treatment of this population is particularly timely because, although well documented, the extent to which intellectually precocious youth thrive in developmentally appropriate learning environments remains underappreciated (Benbow & Stanley, 1996; Stanley, 2000).

For example, when seventh-grade students scoring in the top 3% on conventional achievement tests are given the opportunity to take college entrance exams, such as the SAT Reasoning Test, they routinely generate score distributions indistinguishable from college-bound high school seniors. Those scoring at or above the mean on such assessments are invited to major universities throughout the United States. (e.g., Duke, Johns Hopkins, Northwestern, University of Iowa, and Vanderbilt) to attend summer residential programs for intellectually talented youth. And each year, thousands of seventh- and eighth-graders attend these programs and assimilate a full high school course (e.g., a foreign language, chemistry, mathematics) in 3 weeks' time (Benbow & Stanley, 1996). That many educators and psychologists are unaware of this speaks to the benign neglect of this special population. In this chapter we review some modern findings that suggest how we can reach more youth, especially from lower socioeconomic status households, who would profit from such opportunities.

We begin this chapter by introducing a model of person–environment fit that can not only help forestall underachievement of intellectually precocious youth but also actually enhance their educational–vocational development. After introducing this model, we describe the sample on which our longitudinal studies are based, and we subsequently review findings supporting the model's verisimilitude. We then discuss recent findings on neglected intellectual and nonintellectual personal attributes associated with exceptional achievement and, hence, address the subtitle of this volume by "extending new constructs" to this special population. Our chapter culminates with a discussion of how theory and findings on talent development can shape educational policy to more fully develop the differential potentialities within this special population.

THEORETICAL UNDERPINNINGS: PERSON–ENVIRONMENT FIT AND THE THEORY OF WORK ADJUSTMENT

Our model of intellectual enhancement is premised on the idea that optimal learning environments are tailored to each individual's abilities and interests. The theory of work adjustment (TWA; Dawis & Lofquist, 1984; 1991), arguably the most comprehensive theory of person–environment fit to date, offers a formal presentation of this premise. Although it was developed initially to conceptualize work adjustment in adult populations, TWA has broader implications in areas ranging from educational to industrial psychology (Lubinski, 2000). Lubinski and Benbow (2000) have used it to conceptualize talent development and lifelong learning.

According to TWA, optimal learning and work environments are defined by the co-occurrence of two broad dimensions of correspondence. The first is *satisfactoriness,* a match between the ability of the person and the ability requirements of the environment. The second is *satisfaction,* a match between the preferences (e.g., needs, interests, and values) of the person and the rewards typical of the learning and work environments. To the extent that satisfactoriness and satisfaction co-occur, the person and environment are said to be in harmony. According to this model, ideal environments are those that match individuals' personal attributes; optimal development occurs when people's needs are met and their abilities are appropriately challenged. Figure 7.1 contains a graphical representation of TWA (on the right) and its related ability and interest components (on the left). The latter help guide assessment of the individual in terms of abilities and interests commensurate with the demands and rewards of contrasting educational-vocational environments. For further explication of this model and how it connects with other theoretical frameworks for understanding ability (cf. Carroll, 1993) and interest dimensions (cf. Holland, 1996), see Lubinski and Benbow (2000).

THE STUDY OF MATHEMATICALLY PRECOCIOUS YOUTH (SMPY)

Elements of many contemporary advances in the understanding of intellectual precocity may be traced to Julian C. Stanley. His longitudinal study of precocious youth significantly changed the landscape of gifted education. Because of his interest and experience in identifying and developing scientific talent, Stanley began in 1969 by studying mathematical reasoning ability (Keating & Stanley, 1972; Stanley, 1973; Stanley, Keating, & Fox, 1974). By 1980, however, he was devoting an equal amount of attention to verbal reasoning ability (Stanley, 1996). To study long-term outcomes and the development of talent across the lifespan, SMPY, now based at Vanderbilt University, is currently tracking more than 5000 intellectually precocious youth identified through talent searches by age 13 as being in the top 1% in verbal or mathematical reasoning ability (Lubinski & Benbow, 1994; Stanley, 1996). In this chapter we focus on research findings from SMPY, as this is one of the largest contemporary studies of intellectual talent.

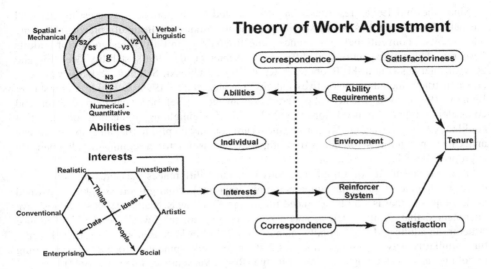

FIG. 7.1.   The Theory of Work Adjustment (right) combined with the radex scaling of cognitive abilities (upper left) and the RIASEC hexagon of interests (lower left) for conceptualizing personal attributes relevant to learning and work (Lubinski & Benbow, 2000). The letters within the cognitive ability arrangement denote different regions of concentration, whereas their accompanying numbers increase as a function of complexity. Contained within the RIASEC is a simplification of this hexagon. Following Prediger (1982), it amounts to a two-dimensional structure of independent dimensions: people/things and data/ideas, which underlie RIASEC. The dotted line running down the individual and environment sectors of TWA illustrates that TWA places equal emphasis on assessing the personal attributes (abilities and interests) and assessing the environment (ability requirements and reward structure).

Research Findings From SMPY

Above-Level Assessment.   Today, approximately 300,000 seventh- and eighth-graders from around the United States take the SAT or ACT each year. Identifying intellectually precocious youth through assessment tools initially designed for college-bound high school seniors is one of applied psychology's most impressive contributions to the conservation and development of human talent to date (Benbow, Lubinski, Shea, & Eftekhari-Sanjani, 2000; Benbow & Stanley, 1996; Lubinski, 1996, 2000; Lubinski, Webb, Morelock, & Benbow, 2001; Stanley, 1996). The assessment of gifted youth at ages 12 or 13 using above-level tests such as SAT-Math and SAT-Verbal uncovers an ability profile that is quite indicative of subsequent educational–vocational decisions. Over time, these differential areas of strength forecast the selection of contrasting educational and career paths (Achter, Lubinski, & Benbow, 1996; Achter, Lubinski, Benbow, & Eftekhari-Sanjani, 1999; Benbow & Lubinski, 1996; Benbow & Stanley, 1996; Lubinski & Benbow, 2000; Lubinski, Webb, et al., 2001). This information can meaningfully influence practice. Educators and counselors equipped with specific ability information can differentially plan educational programs for bright youth that are predicated on the concept of appropriate developmental placement (Lubinski & Benbow, 2000).

Since the mid-1990s, researches has documented the importance of assessing personal attributes beyond abilities in this special population. Among intellectually precocious young adolescents, conventional preference questionnaires initially designed for adults have revealed marked individual differences (Achter et al., 1996), stability over 15- and 20-year intervals (Lubinski, Benbow, & Ryan, 1995; Lubinski, Schmidt, & Benbow, 1996), and construct (including predictive) validity (Achter et al., 1999; Schmidt, Lubinski, & Benbow, 1998). The assessment of preferences in an above-level format can help educators and counselors refine recommendations to gifted youth by highlighting applications of talent that could maximize satisfaction. Such assessments are not only helpful for opening up educational and career possibilities for talented youth, they are useful for designing developmentally appropriate learning environments.

The practical utility of applying various individual differences measures initially developed on adults to bright youth supports the idea that intellectual giftedness is best construed as development that is simply advanced for its age (Benbow & Stanley, 1996). Studies have documented that ability, interest, and personality assessments reveal the same covariance structure in adults and intellectually talented youth (Lubinski & Benbow, 2000). Such structural similarity between groups indicates that similar developmental processes are operating in both groups, even though they differ in age (Rowe, Vazsonyi, & Flannery, 1994).

Teaming Abilities and Preferences.   Longitudinal research supports the TWA-based model for promoting talent development. Achter et al. (1999) administered the SAT and Study of Values (SOV; Allport, Vernon, & Lindzey, 1970) to 432 intellectually precocious young adolescents and surveyed them 10 years later, after they had secured college degrees. Achter et al. categorized college majors into three broad criterion groups: math–science, humanities, and other. They found that the SAT mathematical and verbal measures accounted for 10% of the variance between these groups by themselves, and the five SOV scales accounted for an additional 13% of the variance. Given the heterogeneity within these three broad degree-groupings, and considering that initial assessment occurred a decade earlier at age 13, accounting for 23% of the variance was truly impressive. By showing that age 13 assessments of preference dimensions provided incremental validity to age 13 assessments of mathematical and verbal abilities in predicting educational outcomes at age 23, Aditer et al. documented the distinctive advantage of assessing both abilities and preferences when working with talented youth.

Figure 7.2 depicts discriminant analysis classification accuracy into the three criterion groups, based on both ability and preference dimensions. Note that discriminant loadings (contained in the structure matrix) support interpretation of distinct math–science and humanities dimensions, with *math ability + theoretical values* loading most strongly on function 1 (coupled with negative loadings for social and religious values), and *verbal ability + aesthetic values* loading most strongly on function 2. The psychological difference between these two functions is profound. These functions provide powerful analytic tools for conceptualizing how individuals make educational and career choices, and how learning environments can be tailored to match the differential proclivities among students who differ markedly on them. Although it is beyond the scope of our treatment, these functions also afford insight into how members of different professions (manifesting significant group differences on these two functions) approach intellectual problems and create contrasting but dispositionally congruent organizational climates (Lubinski, 1996, 2000).

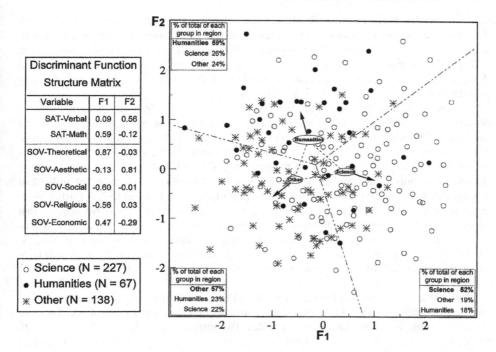

FIG. 7.2.   Group centroids and discriminant-structure matrix (Achter et al., 1999). The bivariate group centroids for the total sample were (Function 1, followed by Function 2): math–science (.43, −.05); humanities (−.29, .60); and other (−.57, −.21). To make the scatter plot less cluttered, each bivariate point represents an average of two participants' discriminant scores (most typically, the closest geometrically). Percentages were computed using all individual data points. SOV = Study of Values; SAT = Scholastic Aptitude Test; F1 = Function 1; F2 = Function 2.

We turn next to recent longitudinal findings that underscore the magnitude of psychological diversity found in intellectually precocious populations identified by modern talent searches. We focus on ability level and ability pattern.

Ability Level.   The range of individual differences in human abilities is huge, and the magnitude of these differences is sometimes underappreciated (Benbow, 1992). Consider, for example, general intelligence. In terms of IQ points, scores within the top 1% on general intellectual ability range from approximately 137 to substantially more than 200, reflecting a tremendous amount of quantitative variation among an already highly select group. The same is true for specific abilities. But the question often asked is whether these differences in ability level make real-world differences in people's lives.

To answer this question, Lubinski, Webb, et al. (2001) studied a sample of 320 profoundly gifted individuals identified for their exceptional (i.e., top 1 in 10,000) mathematical or verbal reasoning ability at age 13 (mean estimated IQ > 180). By age 23, 93% of this group had obtained bachelor's degrees, 31% had earned master's degrees, and 12% had completed doctoral degrees. Furthermore, fully 56% of this select group expressed intentions to pursue doctorates, a number more than 50 times the base rate expectation (viz, 1% in the general population, U.S. Department of Education, 1997). By comparison, studies of persons in the highly able, but less select, top 1 in 100 in cognitive ability have revealed pursuit of doctoral degrees at 25 times base rate expectations (Benbow et al., 2000)—still remarkable, but only half the rate observed among the top 1 in 10,000.

As informative as this is, it does not tell the whole story regarding the magnitude of achievement in the higher ability group. For example, among those pursuing doctorates in the top 1 in 10,000 study (Lubinski, Webb, et al., 2001), 42% were doing so at universities ranked within the top 10 in the United States, another indication of the extraordinary promise of this group. By comparison, "only" 21% of the top 1 in 100 (Benbow et al., 2000) were pursuing doctorates at universities ranked within the top 10. An abbreviated listing of individual achievements attained by the top 1 in 10,000 group by age 23 (see Table 7.1) further highlights the real-world significance of their extraordinary ability level. It certainly appears that higher ability level translates into higher achievement among those within the top 1%, just as it does in the general population even when opportunity is essentially held constant (Murray, 1998). It will be fascinating to observe the impact these highly talented individuals will have as SMPY tracks their lifespan development.

Ability Pattern.   Another critical factor for understanding and enhancing intellectual talent is ability pattern. Lubinski, Webb, et al. (2001) divided their top 1 in 10,000 sample into three groups based on individual ability profiles. Two groups were "tilted" (either High-Math or High-Verbal) and one was more intellectually uniform or "flat" (High-Flat). The High-Flat group had SAT-Math and SAT-Verbal scores that were within one standard deviation of the other. The other two groups had contrasting intellectual strengths: The High-Math group had SAT-M scores greater than one standard deviation above SAT-Verbal scores, whereas the High-Verbal group exhibited the inverse pattern. These three ability patterns, drawn from age 13 assessments, eventuated in distinct developmental trajectories.

Lubinski, Webb, et al. (2001) compiled the idiographic accomplishments and awards reported in open-ended questions and placed them in one of three clusters, like those found in Figure 7.2, "Humanities and Arts," "Science and Technology," and "Other" (Table 7.1). They then went back to ascertain whether these three clusters were differentially representative of their three ability groups. As shown in the bottom right panel of Table 7.1, three-fourths of the classifiable accomplishments of High-Math participants were in science and technology. By comparison, two thirds of the classifiable accomplishments of High-Verbal participants were in the humanities and arts. High-Flat participants reported similar numbers of accomplishments in the sciences and humanities clusters. It is evident that ability pattern relates to the types of activities to which these individuals devoted time and effort. Moreover, age 13 assessments of specific abilities anticipated differential course preferences among these three groups in high school and college (see Figure 7.3). The High-Math group consistently preferred math/science courses relative to the humanities, whereas the inverse was true for the High-Verbal group; results among the High-Flat group were, again, intermediate.

Other investigations of the longitudinal significance of ability pattern, using more comprehensive assessments, have generated even more refined predictions. For example, Shea, Lubinski, and Benbow (2001) tracked a group of more than 550 individuals representing the top 0.5% in general intellectual ability over 20 years. They demonstrated that verbal, mathematical, and spatial abilities, assessed in early adolescence, were related in distinct ways to subsequent educational–vocational group membership in engineering, physical sciences,

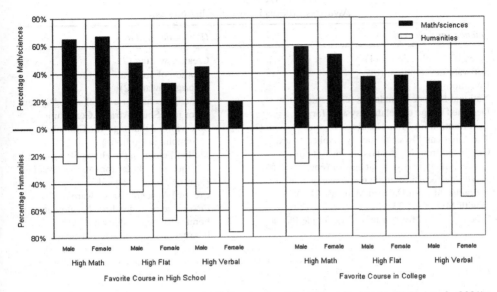

FIG. 7.3.   Participants' favorite course in high school and in college (Lubinski, Webb, et al., 2001). Percentages in a given column do not necessarily sum to 100% because only participants indicating either math/sciences or humanities courses are displayed. Significance tests for differences among groups for favorite course are as follows: high school math/science χ^2 (2, $N = 320$) = 20.7, $p < .0001$; college math/science χ^2 (2, $N = 320$) = 18.2, $p < .0001$; high school humanities χ^2 (2, $N = 320$) = 36.6, $p < .0001$; and college humanities χ^2 (2, $N = 320$) = 30.2, $p < .0001$.

biology, humanities, law, social sciences, and business. In five different educational–vocational outcomes over a 20-year span, each specific ability added incremental validity (Sechrest, 1963) to the prediction of group membership relative to the other two. Figure 7.4 highlights the configural arrangement.

Figure 7.4 tracks favorite and least favorite high school class (age 18), bachelor degree groups (age 23) and occupations (33) in three-dimensional space, organized by standardized units of mathematical (X-axis) and verbal (Y-axis) ability. For each grouping, the direction of the arrow represents whether spatial ability (Z-axis) were above (right) or below (left) the grand mean for spatial ability. (A and B are within gender, C and D are combined across gender). These arrows were scaled on the same units of measurement as the SAT scores (viz., z-scores), so one can envision how far apart these groups were in three-dimensional space as a function of these three abilities in standard deviation units. Across these time frames, exceptional verbal ability, relative to mathematical and spatial ability, was characteristic of group membership in the social sciences and humanities, whereas higher levels of math and spatial abilities, relative to verbal abilities, characterized group membership in engineering and math/computer science. Other educational–vocational groups, such as the natural and physical sciences, appeared to exhibit appreciable amounts of all three abilities. These findings illustrate that important individual differences factor into choices, whether or not they are assessed.

TABLE 7.1
Awards and Special Accomplishments

Sciences and technology	Humanities and arts
Scientific publications (11)	Creative writing (7)
Software development (8)	Creation of art or music (6)
Inventions (4)	Fulbright award (2)
National Science Foundation fellowship (2)	Wrote proposal for a novel voting system
Designed image correlation system for	for new South African Constitution
navigation for Mars Landing Program	Solo violin debut (age 13) Cincinnati
The American Physical Society's Apker Award	Symphony Orchestra
Graduated from Massachusetts Institute of	Mellon Fellow in the Humanities
Technology in 3 years at age 19 (entered at 16)	Presidential Scholar for Creative Writing
with perfect (5.0) grade point average and	Hopwood writing award
graduated from Harvard Medical School	Creative Anachronisms Award of Arms
with MD at age 23	First place in midreal-medieval poetry
Teaching award for "Order of Magnitude Physics"	Foreign language study fellowship
	International predissertation award

Other		Sciences & technology	Humanities & arts
Phi Beta Kappa (71)	High-math	16	5
Tau Beta Pi (30)			
Phi Kappa Phi (14)			
Entrepreneurial enterprises (2)	High-flat	6	6
Omicron Delta Kappa			
Olympiad Silver Medal	High-verbal	7	13
Finished bachelor's and master's in 4 years			
Received private pilot's license in 1 month at age 17			

Note. Numbers in parentheses represent the number of participants indicating each accomplishment. All other entries represent a single individual. Values in bottom right panel reflect accomplishments listed in top two panels.

Directions for Future Research

Spatial Ability.   Shea et al.'s (2001) study was among the first to document the unique developmental implications of spatial ability among gifted students identified by modern talent search procedures, further demonstrating the importance of comprehensive ability assessments. As we strive not to miss those students who might usefully contribute to our increasingly technological society, identifying spatially talented individuals is one of the current critical challenges in the field. Indeed, using normal curve theory, one can estimate that approximately half of the top 1% in spatial visualization is not identified by modern talent search procedures that focus only on mathematical and verbal talent. We are unaware of any greater loss of human capital than the neglect of this special population (cf. Gohm, Humphreys, & Yao, 1998; Humphreys, Lubinski, & Yao, 1993; Humphreys & Lubinski, 1996). These students will not necessarily find their own way if their exceptional spatial talents are not recognized and encouraged.

The need for recognition of spatial talent is especially important given that exceptional spatial ability is less associated with socioeconomic status than is exceptional math or verbal

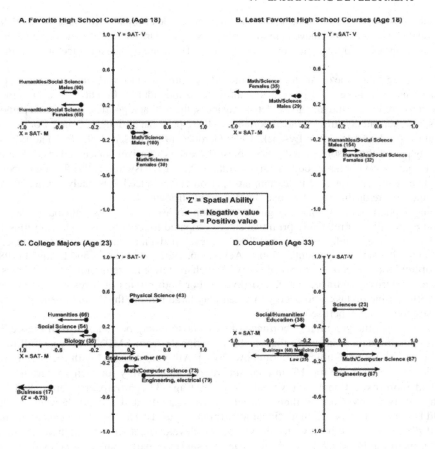

FIG. 7.4. Trivariate means for (A) favorite high school class and (B) least favorite class at age 18, (C) conferred bachelor's degree at age 23, and (D) occupation at age 33. SAT-V = Verbal subtest of the Scholastic Assesment Test; and Spatial Ability = A composite of two subtests of the Differential Aptitude Test (space relations and mechanical reasoning). Panels A and B are standardized within genders, panels C and D between genders (adapted from Shea et al., 2001). The large arrowhead in panel C indicates that this group's relative weakness in spatial ability is actually twice as great as that indicated by the displayed length.

ability (Humphreys et al., 1993). Thus, since a large number of spatially talented youth are found at lower socioeconomic levels, identification of spatial talent may not only facilitate the intellectual development of individuals who are at promise of excellence in technologically demanding fields, it may also help break down social class barriers.

Commitment to Work. Clearly, the landscape of intellectual precocity is not one-dimensional. Yet even with the multidimensionality reviewed up to this point, something is missing. Among individuals who exhibit comparable ability and preference profiles, and who have been given commensurate opportunities, huge individual differences in achievement are routinely observed. We do not know all the causal determinants relevant to modeling individual differences in achievement and creativity. One class of causal factors, however, is often underappreciated by counselors and educators. These are the conative factors (Lubinski, 2004).

Since at least the time of Aristotle, attributes like commitment to work, industriousness, persistence, and zeal have been posited to contribute to individual differences in achievement. Modern theoreticians studying art, athletics, business, the military, politics, and science, among others, have repeatedly stressed the importance of these personal attributes of energy or psychological tempo (Ericsson, 1996; Eysenck, 1995; Gardner, 1993; Jensen, 1996; Simonton, 1988). Probably part of the reason applied psychologists have not extensively discussed these determinants is that we do not have good measures of them. Yet, it is easy to surmise that they operate to explain significant variance in learning and performance. Indeed, it is likely that under- and overachievers are distinguished, in part, by this set of attributes.

Some modern theorists have begun to develop measures for these attributes, but the measures are still at a relatively primitive stage compared to tools for assessing abilities and preferences. For example, Ackerman (1996) has developed a measure for a construct he calls "typical intellectual engagement" (Goff & Ackerman, 1992). And Dawis and Lofquist (1984) have offered four aspects of "personality style" to characterize the temporal characteristics of behavior: celerity, endurance, pace, and rhythm. For both groups of investigators, concentrated effort, time on task, and energy invested play large roles in the development of knowledge structures and expertise.

A glimpse of the potential importance of these factors may be gleaned from Figure 7.5, which contains data from more than 1,700 participants from SMPY's 20-year follow-up (Benbow et al., 2000; Lubinski & Benbow, 2000). All were assessed with the SAT before age 13 and scored in the top 1% in quantitative reasoning ability for their age group (several had more exceptional SAT-Verbal scores). At age 33, participants were asked how much they typically work in their current job (top panel), and second, how much they would be willing to work in their "ideal job" (bottom panel). This figure reveals huge individual differences in time invested in vocational development. If these individual differences remain stable, which they will for at least a subset of participants, the amount of time invested in career development for some participants will be but a small fraction of what it is for others. Given the importance of time on task for predicting performance outcomes such as salary and position (e.g., Harrell & Alpert, 1989; Wood, Corcoran, & Courant, 1993), it is reasonable to suggest that these individual differences in work hours will eventuate in a vast array of achievement outcomes, ranging from considerably below typical to extraordinary.

Informing Educational Policy

Understanding individual differences in key psychological attributes is critical for designing policies that will facilitate development of all individuals (Lubinski, 1996). Policies that allocate opportunity according to individual differences have the potential to optimize the development of each individual (Dawis, 1992; Tyler, 1974; Williamson, 1965). These policies offer people opportunities to develop in areas where they have the most potential for growth, that is, according to the salient features of their individuality, defined by their unique constellation of abilities, drives, and interests (Lubinski & Benbow, 2000).

Individual assessment and appropriate developmental placement are as essential for the intellectually talented as they are for any other group of students (Tyler, 1974; Williamson,

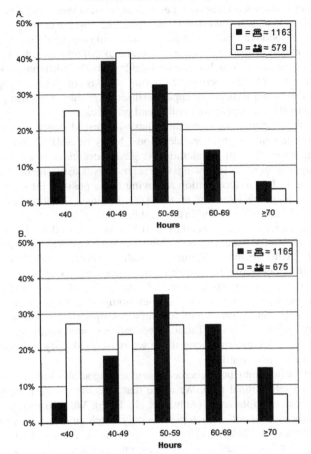

1972-1979 Talent Search Participants

FIG. 7.5.   Two questions about work taken from SMPY's 2-year follow-up questionnaire (adapted from Lubinski & Benbow, 2000). Participants were identified at age 13 as having quantitative reasoning abilities within the top 1% of their age group. At age 33, they were asked (top panel) how many hours per week they typically worked (excluding homemakers), and (bottom panel) how many hours per week they were willing to work, given their job of first choice.

1965). As we have documented, intellectually talented youth vary widely in their intellectual capabilities and nonintellectual proclivities. Furthermore, these personal attributes are longitudinally stable and predict long-term educational–vocational choices and subsequent performance. Such findings demonstrate the importance of tailoring the educational curriculum's level and pace to meet each individual's unique developmental needs. As Stanley (2000) aptly observed, effective educational systems allow intellectually talented students to "learn things that they don't already know."

Our emphases on multiattribute assessment and tailoring educational opportunities in accordance with student individuality are actually not new. Rather, they are reminiscent of past pleas by some of the most distinguished psychologists throughout the 20th century: Leta Hollingworth, Sidney Pressey, Carl Seashore, Lewis Terman, and Leona Tyler (Achter & Lubinski, 2003). They, among others, were invested in understanding positive development and stressed the importance of individually tailored educational–vocational planning. Given the robust empirical documentation of the importance of individual differences, why have mainstream educational practitioners not routinely embraced stable individual differences to shape educational policy and practice? In this section we examine various concerns and suppositions held by social scientists and practitioners that appear to discourage them from using individual differences attributes to inform educational policy and practice.

First, some social scientists and educators have expressed concern that students who accelerate will subsequently regret their decisions. Many of SMPY's participants did, in fact, report using some form of acceleration (e.g., honors classes, advanced placement courses, even skipping grades) following their above-level assessment. Yet, participants overwhelmingly viewed their acceleration as having had a positive influence on their educational and career planning (Benbow et al., 2000; Lubinski, Benbow, et al., 2001). For example, Figure 7.6, taken from Lubinski, Webb, et al. (2001), displays the relatively intense levels of acceleration experienced by SMPY's top 1 in 10,000 group, and their feelings about their accelerative experiences. If there are regrets among these participants, it is that they did not accelerate more. Similarly, another cohort of SMPY participants was asked how they felt about doing away with homogeneous grouping by ability, the vehicle by which acceleration often occurs (see Fig. 7.7). At age 33, after completing their formal education, SMPY participants seemed to favor grouping by ability for instruction. Eighty percent of participants were "somewhat" to "very" unsupportive of eliminating homogeneous grouping by ability in schools. Tailoring educational opportunities according to ability does not seem to be a concern among those whose individuality indicates a likelihood of profiting from such opportunities.

Second, some educators may be concerned that assessing adolescents will lead them to be pigeonholed in a set educational path. We agree that students should develop and achieve basic standards across multiple areas (Achter et al., 1996). We also recognize instabilities associated with early assessments, which provide only rough guideposts for facilitating educational and career planning. Indeed, periodic reassessment of individual differences over the course of one's development is advisable. Abilities, interests, and conative attributes can and do change for some individuals, and assessing the magnitude of such changes is helpful for making informed choices. Yet, intellectually precocious youth think seriously about their educational and vocational interests from an early age, and there is more than enough stability in these early assessments to warrant their routine use.

Third, many social scientists and educators appear to be more concerned with demographic group membership across advanced disciplines than with embracing each student's individuality. Many contemporary treatments of educational–vocational outcomes operate under the implicit assumption that parity in number across demographic groups is the decisive indicator of equity (Bleske-Rechek & Webb, 2002; Humphreys, 1991). Hence, psychologists and educational policymakers present parity in number across groups (e.g., gender, race) in educational and vocational outcomes as their primary goal (American Association of University Women Educational Foundation, 1998; Commission on the Advancement of Women and Minorities in Science, Engineering, and Technology Development, 2000; National Research Council, 2001). A recent NRC task force, for example, stated the following in reference to male and female representation in science and engineering:

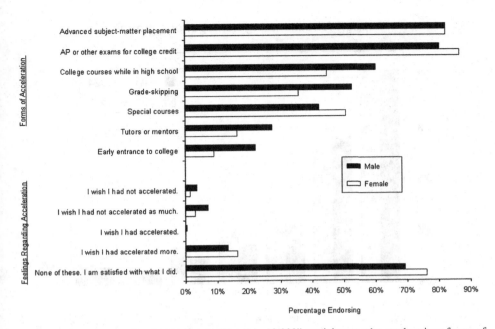

FIG. 7.6. Percentages of male and female "Top 1 in 10,000" participants who used various forms of educational acceleration (upper section), and their feelings regarding those accelerative experiences (lower section), AP = advanced placement (Lubinski, Webb, et al., 2001).

> Overall, since 1973 there have been impressive and promising changes in the entry into and participation of women in science and engineering ... But while women have clearly made enormous gains in their participation in science and engineering, it is also clear that these advances represent neither unconditional success in overcoming gender inequalities nor assurance of continuing progress in the future. (National Research Council, 2001, p. 10)

This emphasis on parity in number as an indicator of equity fails to take into account gender differences in specific abilities and nonintellectual personal attributes. The neglect of these individual differences attributes appears to lead to the sole, mistaken assumption that *differential representation* between groups as the result of *unequal treatment* between groups (e.g., Kite et al., 2001). We argue that differential representation between the sexes in the math/ science pipeline might be viewed more appropriately as the result of mean differences between the sexes on specific abilities, interests, and commitment to work. Next, we review these gender differences in key attributes necessary for the development of scientific expertise. Then, we show that these gender differences are virtually nonexistent in samples of men and women who have chosen environments that require the development of world-class scientific expertise. Finally, we review a set of findings that suggest that mathematically talented women who exit the math/science pipeline do not underachieve; to the contrary, they thrive in the disciplines they subsequently enter.

Abilities. Gender differences in quantitative reasoning ability, with males displaying a higher mean and greater variability, are robust across populations (Ackerman, Bowen, Beier, &

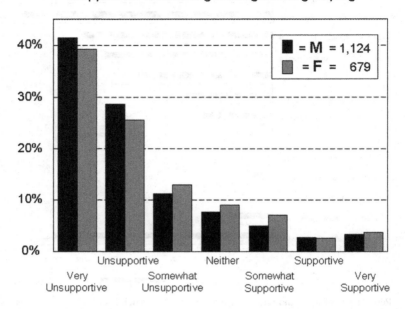

FIG. 7.7   Participants' attitudes toward eliminating homogenous grouping for instruction by gender (Benbow et al., 2000). At age 33, participants were asked the following question: "A number of educational policymakers have proposed the following: eliminating homogenous grouping for instruction (i.e., grouping students according to their abilities and skills, as in reading groups or honors classes) and instead, teaching students of all ability levels in the same group. How supportive are you of this proposal?

Kanfer, 2001; Hedges & Nowell, 1995; Lubinski & Humphreys, 1990). They also appear early: Gender differences in mathematical precocity have been documented before kindergarten (Robinson, Abbott, Berninger, & Busse, 1996), and young adolescent males who obtain a 700 or higher on the SAT-M outnumber adolescent females 13 to 1 (Benbow, 1988). A similar pattern is found with spatial ability. Because males are more variable than females on spatial ability and have a higher mean performance, males are substantially more represented at the upper ends. These gender differences in specific ability distributions are likely partly responsible for the greater representation of males in upper-level careers in the areas of math, engineering, and inorganic sciences (Hedges & Nowell, 1995, p. 45).

Interests.   As young as age 13, mathematically precocious boys and girls differ on average in their interests, with girls scoring higher on social values and boys scoring higher on theoretical values (Achter et al., 1996; Schmidt et al., 1998). This finding aligns with a large (effect size > 1) gender difference in the general population in preferences for working with people versus things (Lubinski, 2000, p. 421). On average, females more than males report interest in working with and helping people, and males more than females report interest in working with and manipulating objects (Feingold, 1994; Lippa, 1998; Maccoby & Jacklin, 1974). The importance of interests for understanding gender differences in career paths is underscored by recent research with undergraduates, which demonstrated that individual differences in interests accounted for the majority of the obtained gender difference in knowledge of the physical sciences and technology domains, after controlling for general intellectual ability and personality characteristics such as social potency (Ackerman et al., 2001).

Commitment to Work. Finally, males and females also differ in their commitment to work. Among equally precocious SMPY males and females, females consistently place more importance on having part-time career options. In contrast, males consistently place more importance on having a full-time career and earning a lot of money (Benbow et al., 2000; Lubinski, Webb, et al., 2001). Relative to women, men report working longer hours and a willingness to work longer hours (see Figure 7.5). These findings align with repeatedly documented gender differences, in other populations, in occupational aspirations and time devoted to work (Bhargava, 1986; Fuchs, 1988; Hoffman & Reed, 1982; Shye, 1991; Wood et al., 1993). That these findings are observed in a population of men and women who are similarly able, similarly aware of their abilities, and similarly satisfied with their current careers and life in general at age 33 (Benbow et al., 2000) is striking.

Collectively, these findings on quantitative reasoning and spatial abilities, interest in people versus things, and commitment to work combine to produce extreme male or female proportions on outcomes for which all of these attributes are relevant. This is what appears to be happening with the math/science pipeline, where men are more greatly represented relative to women.

The Math/Science Pipeline. Although men are more greatly represented than women in math/science domains, analyses of individual differences attributes among men and women who choose to pursue advanced training in math/science domains reveal that individual differences attributes are more important than group membership (i.e., gender) for understanding the pursuit of scientific excellence. In a recent study of 714 world-class math and science graduate students, Lubinski, Benbow, et al. (2001) found remarkably similar profiles across the sexes in abilities, preferences, and commitment to work. They found that both men and women at promise for scientific eminence display the pattern of abilities, interests, and commitment to work that have been linked in the past to exceptional scientific achievement (see Table 7.2). These graduate students, enrolled in elite math and science programs around the United States, displayed exceptional quantitative reasoning ability. Both genders displayed marked investigative and theoretical interests. A majority reported that their favorite high school class was in math or science. Both sexes also reported early participation in special programs and contests for the gifted such as math and science competitions, thus demonstrating their early commitment to math/science endeavors. Finally, both sexes devoted much of their time in graduate school to their educational vocational development, with a median of 50 hours per week spent on studying and research. This profile indicates that individuals' abilities, preferences, and commitment to work, regardless of gender, combine to promote the active pursuit of scientific excellence.

A second set of findings from a recent study by Webb, Lubinski, and Benbow (2002) is consistent with the idea that individual differences are more important than group membership for understanding educational–vocational outcomes. Webb et al. tracked over 1,100 adolescents who were identified as mathematically precocious (top 1%) at age 13 and reported plans to major in math/science at the onset of their undergraduate studies, and then compared those who eventually completed a degree in math/science to those who completed a degree outside of math/science. They found that more women than men eventually chose to pursue degrees in

TABLE 7.2
Similarities Between Male and Female Graduate Students in top Math,
Science, and Engineering Graduate Programs

Personal attribute	Men	Women
Specific abilities		
SAT-M	718 (67)	701 (64)
SAT-V	625 (82)	622 (94)
Preferences		
Investigative interests	59 (5.8)	58 (6.2)
Theoretical values	49 (6.9)	46 (6.7)
Educational experiences		
Favorite high school class was in math or science (%)	79	74
Math–science contest or special program before college (%)	58	54
Math–science contest or special program during college (%)	20	21
Commitment to work		
Median number of graduate school hours per week spent on:		
Studying	20	20
Research	30	30

Note. Values represent means unless otherwise indicated; standard deviations are in parentheses. Analyses are based on 368 men and 346 women. Maximum possible score on the SAT-V or SAT-M is 800. Investigative interest score is a *t*-score with a mean of 50 and a standard deviation of 10 in the general population. Theoretical values score is derived from an ipsative measure with a mean of 40 across scales and a standard deviation of approximately 10.

areas outside of math/science, a finding that appears negative from the view of contemporary literature on women in science, which focuses on demographic parity. But in-depth analyses of the participants' educational, vocational, and life outcomes revealed several positive findings and yielded new interpretations of the human capital that math/science domains attract.

First, Webb et al. (2002) found that individual differences in ability pattern and interests, not biological gender, surfaced as the central predictors of who actually completed a degree in math/science and who completed a degree outside of math/science. It thus appears that group status is a frail proxy variable for specific individual differences attributes (Lubinski & Humphreys, 1997), such as ability and preference patterns, that (more centrally) guide educational–vocational choices.

Second, Webb et al. found that those who completed degrees in math/science and those who completed degrees outside of math/science showed similar levels of success, career satisfaction, and life satisfaction. For example, participants who completed their undergraduate degrees outside of math/science, regardless of gender, earned comparable levels of graduate degrees to participants within math/science; they merely secured their graduate degrees in different areas. This finding mirrors other research from SMPY demonstrating that women and men with similar ability profiles achieve baccalaureate and post baccalaureate degrees at the same rate, yet women are more likely than men to pursue their credentials in organic fields such as the social sciences, law, biology, and medicine, and men are more likely than women to pursue their credentials in inorganic fields such as math, engineering, and the physical sciences (Achter et al., 1999; Benbow et al., 2000; Lubinski, Webb, et al., 2001).

Third, Webb et al. (2002) found that many individuals who completed their degrees in non-math/ science areas ultimately chose math/science occupations, and vice versa. On reflection, this fluidity is actually not surprising, particularly for mathematically precocious females. Within samples of males and females selected for mathematical ability, females display higher levels of verbal ability (Lubinski, Benbow, et al., 2001); thus, mathematically precocious females more often than mathematically talented males are endowed with talents that enable them to excel with distinction in domains that require highly developed verbal and linguistic skills. This fluidity also points to the multidimensional nature of modern work environments. Scientific and quantitative reasoning skills, for example, are valuable in chemistry as well as environmental law. Given the ever-changing nature of the modern world of work, it is not surprising that talented women are attracted to careers that capitalize on both quantitative and verbal reasoning skills, such as environmental law, medicine, or scientific journalism. Such career choices represent anything but a loss of scientific talent.

The findings from Webb et al.'s (2002) study support the idea that providing similar educational and vocational opportunities across individuals will not necessarily lead to similar outcomes (Cronbach & Snow, 1977; Lubinski & Humphreys, 1997). It thus seems somewhat ironic that the lesser representation of women in math/science domains has attracted so much attention and so many millions of precious educational dollars. When any two groups that manifest such marked differences are provided with opportunities to develop according to their differential strengths and proclivities, a difference between the two groups in representation, on outcomes for which their differences are relevant, is a predictable result.

SUMMARY

Our model for talent development stresses the importance of tailoring educational opportunities in accordance with each student's individuality. The study of individual differences has much to offer intellectually talented populations (and all populations). We must go beyond crude nominal scales or demographic groupings, which educators and policy makers appear to be focusing on, and use more fully the ordinal and interval scales that differential psychology has refined over the years. These methods uncover a wide range of talent among members of all groups and facilitate a more precise tailoring of educational curricula, allowing for a fuller utilization of both components of Cronbach's (1957) "two disciplines of scientific psychology"—aptitude and treatment. To the extent that educators choose not to respond to individual differences and tailor educational opportunities accordingly, academic underachievement is virtually guaranteed and, at extreme levels, the neglect of key individual differences attributes approaches educational malpractice.

Finally, we hope that current efforts to boost demographic representation in math, engineering, and the inorganic sciences (and other disciplines) do not interfere with individual development or, at the broader level, scientific progress. The implications for the former have been explicated above; the latter can happen as well because the breadth and depth of a curriculum changes as a function of the overall ability level of the class, even at distinguished universities (Davis, 1976, 1986, pp. 168–176). Likewise, the breadth and depth of a curriculum can be prompted to change as a function of the interests and average level of commitment displayed by the class (see Kardash & Wallace, 2001; Rosser, 1990; and Seymour & Hewitt, 1997, for examples of such prompting). Humphreys (1991) and Sackett, Schmitt, Ellingson, & Kabin (2001) have pointed out that, to the extent that two groups differ in key attributes relevant to performance in any domain, simultaneously maximizing performance and group parity is untenable. It is important to realize the implications of this fact: Lowering standards to accommodate students who are less capable or less committed simultaneously decreases the potential of learning environments to foster the development of world-class expertise—impeding, not enhancing, development.

REFERENCES

Achter, J. A., & Lubinski, D. (2003). Fostering exceptional development in intellectually talented populations. In W. B. Walsh (Ed.), *Counseling psychology and optimal human functioning* (pp. 25–54). Mahwah, NJ: Lawrence Erlbaum Associates.

Achter, J. A., Lubinski, D., & Benbow, C. P. (1996). Multipotentiality among the intellectually gifted: It was never there and already it's vanishing. *Journal of Counseling Psychology, 43,* 65–76.

Achter, J. A., Lubinski, D., Benbow, C. P., & Eftekhari-Sanjani, H. (1999). Assessing vocational preferences among gifted adolescents adds incremental validity to abilities. *Journal of Educational Psychology, 91,* 777–786.

Ackerman, P. L. (1996). A theory of adult intellectual development: Process, personality, interests, and knowledge. *Intelligence, 22,* 227–257.

Ackerman, P. L., Bowen, K. R., Beier, M. E., & Kanfer, R. (2001). Determinants of individual differences and gender differences in knowledge. *Journal of Educational Psychology, 93,* 797–825.

Allport, G. W., Vernon, P. E., & Lindzey, G. (1970). *Manual: Study of values.* Cambridge: Houghton Mifflin.

American Association of University Women Educational Foundation. (1998). *Gender gaps: Where schools still fail our children.* Washington, DC: Author.

Benbow, C. P. (1988). Sex differences in mathematical reasoning ability in intellectually talented preadolescents: Their nature, effects, and possible causes. *Behavioral and Brain Sciences, 11,* 169–183, 217–232.

Benbow, C. P. (1992). Academic achievement in mathematics and science between ages 13 and 23: Are there differences among students in the top one percent of mathematical ability? *Journal of Educational Psychology, 84,* 51–61.

Benbow, C. P., & Lubinski, D. (1996). (Eds.). *Intellectual talent.* Baltimore, MD: Johns Hopkins University Press.

Benbow, C. P., Lubinski, D., Shea, D. L., & Eftekhari-Sanjani, H. (2000). Sex differences in mathematical reasoning ability at age 13: Their status 20 years later. *Psychological Science, 11,* 474–480.

Benbow, C. P., & Stanley, J. C. (1996). Inequity in equity: How "equity" can lead to inequity for high-potential students. *Psychology, Public Policy, and Law, 2,* 249–292.

Bhargava, G. (1986). Professional identification: A study of female students at a medical college in India. *Social Science and Medicine, 20,* 1169–1175.

Bleske-Rechek, A., & Webb, R. M. (2002). Neglected aspects and unsupported claims. [Comment on Kite, M. E., Russo, N. F., Brehm, S. S., Fouad, N. A., Hall, C. C. I., & Hyde, J. S., et al. (2001). Women psychologists in academe: Mixed progress, unwarranted complacency. *American Psychologist, 56,* 108–109.]

Carroll, J. B. (1993). *Human cognitive abilities.* New York, NY: Cambridge University Press.

Commission on the Advancement of Women and Minorities in Science, Engineering, and Technology Development. (2000). *Land of plenty: Diversity as America's competitive edge in science, engineering and technology.* Reviewed from: http://www.nsf.gov/od/cawmset

Cronbach, L. J. (1957). The two disciplines of scientific psychology. *American Psychologist, 12,* 671–684.

Cronbach, L. J., & Snow, R. E. (1977). *Aptitudes and instructional methods: A handbook for research on interactions.* New York, NY: John Wiley & Sons.

Davis, B. D. (1976). Academic standards in medical schools. *The New England Journal of Medicine, 294,* 118–119.

Davis, B. D. (1986). *Storm over biology: Essays on science, sentiment, and public policy*. Buffalo, NY: Prometheus.

Dawis, R. V. (1992). The individual differences tradition in counseling psychology. *Journal of Counseling Psychology, 39*, 7–19.

Dawis, R. V., & Lofquist, L. H. (1984). *A psychological theory of work adjustment*. Minneapolis: University of Minnesota Press.

Ericsson, K. A. (1996). *The road to excellence*. Mahwah, NJ: Lawrence Erlbaum Associates.

Eysenck, H. J. (1995). *Genius: The natural history of creativity*. Cambridge, England: Cambridge University Press.

Feingold, A. (1994). Gender differences in personality: A meta-analysis. *Psychological Bulletin, 116*, 429–456.

Fuchs, V. R. (1988). *Women's quest for economic equality*. Cambridge, MA: Harvard University Press.

Gardner, H. (1993). *Multiple intelligences*. New York: Harper Collins.

Goff, M., & Ackerman, P. L. (1992). Personality–intelligence relations: Assessing typical intellectual engagement. *Journal of Educational Psychology, 84*, 537–552.

Gohm, C. L., Humphreys, L. G., & Yao, G. (1998). Underachievement among spatially gifted students. *American Educational Research Journal, 35*, 515–531.

Harrell, T. W., & Alpert, B. (1989). Attributes of successful MBAs: A 20-year longitudinal study. *Human Performance, 2*, 301–322.

Hedges, L. V, & Nowell, A. (1995). Sex differences in mental test scores, variability, and numbers of high-scoring individuals. *Science, 269*, 41–45.

Hoffman, C., & Reed, J. (1982). When is imbalance not discrimination? In W. Block & M. Walker (Eds.), *Discrimination, affirmative action, and equal opportunity* (pp. 187–216). Vancouver: Frasier Institute.

Holland, J. L. (1996). Exploring careers with a typology. *American Psychologist, 51*, 397–406.

Humphreys, L. G. (1991). Limited vision in the social sciences. *American Journal of Psychology, 104*, 333–353.

Humphreys, L. G., & Lubinski, D. (1996). Brief history and psychological significance of spatial-visualization abilities. In C. P. Benbow & D. Lubinski (Eds.), *Intellectual talent*. Baltimore, MD: Johns Hopkins University Press.

Humphreys, L. G., Lubinski, D., & Yao, G. (1993). Utility of predicting group membership and the role of spatial visualization in becoming an engineer, physical scientist, or artist. *Journal of Applied Psychology, 78*, 250–261.

Jensen, A. R. (1996). Giftedness and genius: Crucial differences. In C. P. Benbow & D. Lubinski (Eds.), *Intellectual talent* (pp. 393–411). Baltimore, MD: Johns Hopkins University Press.

Kardash, C. M., & Wallace, M. L. (2001). The perception of science classes survey: What undergraduate science reform efforts really need to address. *Journal of Educational Psychology, 93*, 199–210.

Keating, D. P., & Stanley, I. C. (1972). Extreme measures for the exceptionally gifted in mathematics and science. *Educational Researcher, 1*, 3–7.

Kite, M. E., Russo, N. F., Brehm, S. S., Fouad, N. A., Hall, C. C. I., & Hyde, J. S., et al. (2001). Women psychologists in academe: Mixed progress, unwarranted complacency. *American Psychologist, 56*, 1080–1098.

Lippa, R. (1998). Gender-related individual differences and the structure of vocational interests: The importance of the people–things dimension. *Journal of Personality and Social Psychology, 74*, 996–1009.

Lofquist, L. H., & Dawis, R. V. (1991). *Essentials of person–environment-correspondence counseling*. Minneapolis: University of Minnesota Press.

Lubinski, D. (1996). Applied individual difference research and its quantitative methods. *Psychology, Public Policy, and Law, 2*, 187–203.

Lubinski, D. (2000). Assessing individual differences in human behavior: "Sinking shafts at a few critical points." *Annual Review of Psychology, 51*, 405–444.

Lubinski, D. (2004). Introduction to the special section on cognitive abilities: 100 years after Spearman's (1904) "General intelligence," objectively determined and measured. *Journal of Personality and Social Psychology, 86*, 96–111.

Lubinski, D., & Benbow, C. P. (1994). The study of mathematically precocious youth: The first three decades of a planned 50-year study of intellectual talent. In R. F. Subotnik & K. D. Arnold (Eds.), *Beyond Terman: Contemporary longitudinal studies of giftedness and talent* (pp. 255–281). Norwood, NJ: Ablex.

Lubinski, D., & Benbow, C. P. (2000). States of excellence. *American Psychologist, 55,* 137–150.

Lubinski, D., Benbow, C. P., & Ryan, J. (1995). Stability of vocational interests among the intellectually gifted from adolescence to adulthood: A 15-year longitudinal study. *Journal of Applied Psychology, 80,* 196–200.

Lubinski, D., Benbow, C. P., Shea, D. L., Eftekhari-Sanjani, H., & Halvorson, M. B. J. (2001). Men and women at promise for scientific excellence: Similarity not dissimilarity. *Psychological Science, 12,* 309–317.

Lubinski, D., & Humphreys, L. G. (1990). Assessing spurious "moderator effects": Illustrated substantively with the hypothesized ("synergistic") relation between spatial and mathematical ability. *Psychological Bulletin, 107,* 385–393.

Lubinski, D., & Humphreys, L. G. (1997). Incorporating general intelligence into epidemiology and the social sciences. *Intelligence, 24,* 159–201.

Lubinski, D., Schmidt, D. B., & Benbow, C. P. (1996). A 20-year stability analysis of the Study of Values for intellectually gifted individuals from adolescence to adulthood. *Journal of Applied Psychology, 81,* 443–451.

Lubinski, D., Webb, R. M., Morelock, M. J., & Benbow, C. P. (2001). Top 1 in 10,000: A 10-year follow-up of the profoundly gifted. *Journal of Applied Psychology, 86,* 718–729.

Maccoby, E. E., & Jacklin, C. N. (1974). *The psychology of sex differences.* Stanford, CA: Stanford University Press.

Murray, C. (1998). *Income, inequality, and IQ.* Washington, DC: American Enterprise Institute.

National Research Council. (2001). *From scarcity to visibility: Gender differences in the careers of doctoral scientists and engineers.* Washington, DC: National Academy Press.

Prediger, D. J. (1982). Dimensions underlying Holland's hexagon: Missing link between interests and occupations? *Journal of Vocational Behavior, 21,* 259–287.

Robinson, N. M., Abbott, R. D., Berninger, V. W., & Busse, J. (1996). The structure of abilities in mathematically precocious young children: Gender similarities and differences. *Journal of Educational Psychology, 88,* 341–352.

Rosser, S. V. (1990). *Female-friendly science: Applying women's studies methods and theories to attract students.* Elmsford, NY: Pergamon.

Rowe, D. C., Vazsonyi, A. T., & Flannery, D. J. (1994). No more than skin deep: Ethnic and racial similarity in developmental process. *Psychological Review, 101,* 396–413.

Sackett, P. R., Schmitt, N., Ellingson, J. E., & Kabin, M. B. (2001). High-stakes testing in employment, credentialing, and higher education. *American Psychologist, 56,* 302–318.

Schmidt, D. B., Lubinski, D., & Benbow, C. P. (1998). Validity of assessing educational–vocational preference dimensions among intellectually talented 13-year olds. *Journal of Counseling Psychology, 45,* 436–453.

Seymour, E., & Hewitt, N. M. (1997). *Talking about leaving: Why undergraduates leave the sciences.* Boulder, CO: Westview.

Shea, D. L., Lubinski, D., & Benbow, C. P. (2001). Importance of assessing spatial ability in intellectually talented young adolescents: A 20-year longitudinal study. *Journal of Educational Psychology, 93,* 604–614.

Shye, D. (1991). Gender differences in Israeli physicians' career patterns, productivity, and family structure. *Social Science and Medicine, 32,* 1169–1181.

Simonton, D. K. (1988). *Scientific genius.* Cambridge: Cambridge University Press.

Stanley, J. C. (1973). Accelerating the educational progress of intellectually gifted youths. *Educational Psychologist, 10,* 133–146. Reprinted in W. Dennis & M. W. Dennis (Eds.), *The intellectually gifted: An overview* (pp. 179–196). New York: Grune and Stratton.

Stanley, J. C. (1996). SMPY in the beginning. In C. P. Benbow & D. Lubinski (Eds.), *Intellectual talent: Psychometric and social issues* (pp. 225–235). Baltimore: Johns Hopkins University Press.

Stanley, J. C. (2000). Helping students learn only what they don't already know. *Psychology, Public Policy, and Law, 6*, 216–222.

Stanley, J. C., Keating, D. P., & Fox, L. H. (Eds.). (1974). *Mathematical talent: Discovery, description, and development.* Baltimore: Johns Hopkins University Press.

Tyler, L. E. (1974). *Individual differences.* New York: Meredith.

U. S. Department of Education, National Center for Education Statistics. (1997). *Digest of Education Statistics, 1997* (NCES 98–015). Washington, DC: Author.

Webb, R. M., Lubinski, D., & Benbow, C. P. (2002). Mathematically facile adolescents with math/science aspirations: New perspectives on their educational and vocational development. *Journal of Educational Psychology, 94,* 785–794.

Williamson, E. G. (1965). *Vocational counseling: Some historical, philosophical, and theoretical perspectives.* New York: McGraw-Hill.

Wood, R. G., Corcoran, M. E., & Courant, P. N. (1993). Pay differences among the highly paid: The male–female earnings gap in lawyers' salaries. *Journal of Labor Economics, 11,* 417–441.

8
▼▼▼▼▼▼▼

Studies of the Impacts of Minimum Academic Standards (Prop 48) on the Academic Achievements of College Student-Athletes

John J. McArdle
University of Southern California

ACADEMICS AND ATHLETICS IN THE NCAA

The relationship between academic skills and athletic skills has unusual historical linkages within the American collegiate system (see Astin, 1971; Manski & Wise, 1983; Pascarella & Terenzini, 1991). In this educational system, it is possible for a small group of athletically talented high school students to matriculate in higher education by participating in athletic contests for a specific college or university. Although many nations and societies have a long history of athletic competition, often following the classical Olympic traditions, the need for terms such as *'student-athletes'* (SA) and *'scholarship-athlete'* are unique to the United States of America. Of course, this is not the only difference between the higher education system of the United States and other countries (e.g., cost, societal requirements, etc.). Nevertheless, the unique academic–athletic relationship within U.S. colleges seems to have created a great deal of tension among members of this community. This academic–athletic relationship is seen by some members in a positive light, especially when considering the life-long virtues of "team play" and "sportsmanship" (e.g., "Our future leaders are found on the playing fields of Eton"; see Falla, 1981). Other persons are concerned about academic–athletic "myths," and are concerned "how schools might best take advantage of the positive emotions that sports evoke without endangering the core of their educational missions" (Shulman & Bowen, 2001, p. xxvii).

The research discussed here is a direct offspring of the continuing tension surrounding academics and athletics in U.S. colleges. However, unlike most of the previous debates, this chapter is based on empirical research. The studies reported here are based on data collected by the *U.S. National Collegiate Athletic Association* (NCAA). These data include high school and college academic performances of groups of *student-athletes* (SA) in the highest level of athletic competition in U.S. colleges (Division I). The NCAA was created in 1906 by President Theodore Roosevelt to act as a national regulatory body for college sports and this competition extends to more than 30 different sports played at over 1,000 colleges by over 360,000 college students each year (for details, see Falla, 1981; cf., Fleisher, Goff & Tollison, 1992).

Since the early 1960s, the NCAA has attempted to deal with problems of "competitive equity" across different colleges and sports by legislating minimum academic requirements for participation in college sports. This report is based on studies of one of these national changes in educational policies, colloquially termed "Prop 48" (as detailed in the following section). Here, we examine how these policy changes may or may not be associated with subsequent changes in educational achievements of the college students. In terms of the central theme of this book, the "enhancements" discussed here are new academic rule changes in a collegiate system, and the "intelligences" discussed here are "academic attainments" of different cohorts of college students. In this view, the implications of any impacts could extend far beyond the collegiate playing fields studied here.

ACADEMIC REFORMS AND 'PROP 48"

At its national convention in early 1983, the NCAA membership passed minimum academic requirements for participation in the 1st year in college for NCAA sports. This legislation was the proposition numbered 48 at the national meeting, so it was termed 'Prop 48'. The revised academic standards required of all 1st-year college students included the presentation of: (a) a high school diploma, (b) at least a 2.0 overall grade point average (GPA), (c) a 2.0 grade point average in 11 "core" courses (e.g., English, math, science), *and* (d) a national achievement test score of either an SAT $\geq$ 700 or an ACT $\geq$ 17 (this was 15 at the time). This new rule was phased in during 1986 and 1987 and was fully in effect in 1988. These rules remained in effect until 1994 when additional restrictions were added. A graphic display of this eligibility rule is presented in Fig.8.1a, and the numerical details will be discussed in later sections. Under this rule, 1st year students who achieved above these minima are "eligible to practice and play" but those who do not achieve these minima are "ineligible to practice and play."

As with many other academic issues, there is a long and complex legislative history behind the creation of these rules. It is sufficient now to say that these specific rules were based as a mixture of political compromise and research evidence. The same eligibility rules were to be applied to all "prospective student-athletes," so they were considered "unbiased," created "competitive equity," and represented a "level playing field." The inclusion of a high school degree, core course curriculum, and the minimum GPA were not considered controversial. These requirements were basically consistent with the popular notions at the time (e.g., The "Nation At Risk" report) although the choice of the specific minima (11 courses and GPA of 2.0) were not clearly based on prior research. However, this new set of minimum standards generated a great deal of controversy due to the inclusion of the SAT and ACT test scores. The "Black–White gap" on the ACT–SAT tests raised issues of "test bias" and "adverse impact" and these were key concerns in all further NCAA discussions. The controversy was intensified after the implementation of this rule (1986–1988) when the impacts on minority groups became more evident. This controversy took on broader implications when the intended penalty of "no freshman play" seemed to be reinterpreted by colleges as a rule of "no athletic scholarship," and it became clear that under this new rule, some high school students might lose the opportunity to go to college.

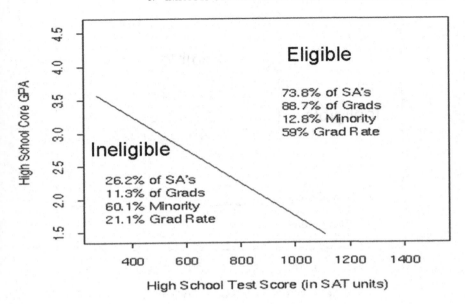

FIG. 8.1a. A summary of the NCAA "Prop 48" rules for high school GPA and ACT-SAT test scores and the projected impacts on the 1984–85 cohort of students athletes.

RESEARCH PERSPECTIVE

Much previous research has been done on these kinds of controversial topics. The previous literature on the use of the SAT and ACT are particularly useful here. In most prior research studies, high school academic indices have been used for prediction of college academic performances, and these results are widely known, discussed and criticized (Aitkin & Longford, 1986; Beatty, Greenwood, & Linn, 1999; Bock, 1989; Crouse & Trusheim, 1988; Pascarella & Terenzini, 1991; Sawyer, 1986; Willingham, Lewis, Morgan, & Ramist, 1990; Beatty,). In many studies of college grades the first predictor set is based on high school grades, and the second predictor set is based on some nationally standardized measurement, such as the ACT (American College Testing Program, 1995) or the SAT (see College Board, 1995). These two classical predictors are often correlated so a multiple linear regression model is used to separate the prediction of college grade point average into two independent components. The costs and benefits of including test scores in this predictive model equation, especially the consequences for selection of minority groups, have been studied in many ways by many researchers (e.g., Beatty et al., 1999; Bowen & Bok, 1998; Crouse & Trusheim, 1988; McArdle, 1998; Willingham et al., 1990; NCAA 1992).

These prior research issues were used in the development of our analysis of the impacts of Prop 48. As we highlight in the next section, there is no clear empirical methodology that can be used to disentangle all effects of restrictive regulations. This is partly due to the fact that the optimal approach, using randomized experiments, is not scientifically or ethically feasible for the current questions about academic attainments. In our own research, various impacts and the needed evidence for these impacts were first defined on a theoretical basis.

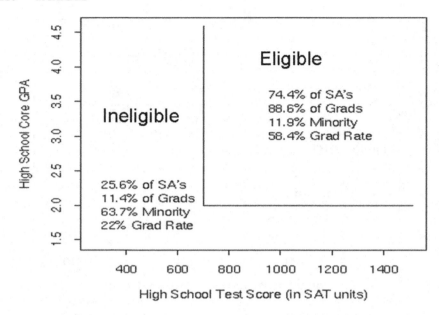

FIG. 8.1b.   A summary of the alternative "ARC 91–94" rules for high school GPA and ACT-SAT test scores and the projected impacts on the 1984–85 cohort of student athletes.

Our subsequent analyses used three different approaches. In a first set of analyses we examined the basic structure of each component of the Prop 48 rules, and we used the "Pre-Prop 48" data to make projections about the likely impacts on both colleges and students. One of our key results is depicted as the alternative eligibility rule presented in Fig. 8.1b. In a second set of analyses we examined the long-term longitudinal outcomes at the college level, including both matriculation and graduation. In a third set of analyses we compared students within the colleges "before and after" the implementation of Prop 48. The results from the three approaches are presented in the sections that follow.

The goal of this research is to provide an objective examination of the impacts of Prop 48 from a 15-year perspective, and some of the results presented here are new. This research uses NCAA data from relatively large and representative samplings of colleges ($N_c > 250$) and individual students ($N > 25,000$). This includes studies of the individual-level behaviors, including grades received, courses taken, SAT and ACT national test scores, and matriculation status. These studies also consider SAT and ACT test-taking changes due to additional policy changes, including age effects, time trends, and high school differences together with corrections for self-selection to test taking. From these projections we try to define the likely *benefits and costs* of specific regulations (see NCAA McArdle, 1991, 1998).

METHODS

NCAA Research Data

Year by year, changes in academic outcomes were monitored on NCAA Student–Athletes (SA) by the NCAA Research Team (see footnote). This research mainly focuses on data from three NCAA data collections:

1. *Academic Performance Study* (*APS*) focused on individual academic and demographic information from $N > 12,000$ SA entering college in 1984–1988.
2. *Graduation Rate Disclosure* (*GRD*) study was started in 1992 and is a collection of aggregate data on $N > 40,000$ SAs at $G > 600$ colleges in NCAA Divisions I and II.
3. *Academic Performance Census* (*APC*) is a follow-up of schools in the APS begun in 1994, and offers information on all $N > 12,700$ students in NCAA Division I who are on athletically related aid each year subsequent to 1994.

Three additional data sources were merged with the data just listed and used in several phases of this research:

4. *Initial Eligibility Clearinghouse* (*IEC*) data collections were started in 1994 and provide yearly data since 1994 on $N > 100,000$ prospective student-athletes.
5. *Basic Academic Skills Study* (*BASS*) was started in 1995 and was intended to be a more in-depth look at students at 24 colleges within the NCAA.
6. *College Board Survey of Colleges* provides yearly data on many characteristics of colleges and universities all across the United States.

Table 8. 1 is an outline of the selected student-level information used here. The first five sets of data listed here were collected between 1984 and 1992 using a representative stratification of colleges within a *cohort-sequential design* (e.g., Kish & Frankel, 1974; Nesselroade & Baltes, 1979). Each of $N_c = 252$ colleges was representatively stratified to 1 of 5 groups and asked to follow the individual student-athletes of one entering class for 5 consecutive years. The Division I data come from the 1984–1988 APS data on $N > 12,000$ student athletes (pre-1990). A set of reports have been based on the two cohorts with Pre-Prop 48 data (e.g., McArdle & Hamagami, 1994).

In this study all the available data on all five cohorts are considered. A 5-year record is available on the majority of participants ($N > 10,000$); some colleges (42/252) did not fully report the required individual-level information. The third dataset just listed (APC) was collected as part of a new survey requesting information on all freshman student–athletes in Division I schools selected for an athletically related scholarship. This study started with $N{\sim}38,000$ prospective student-athletes initially recruited by $Nc{\sim}280$ colleges. These data now include $N{\sim}12,700$ student-athletes including $N_c > 10,000$ with longitudinal information. Most importantly, some APC students are at the same colleges as the first 5 groups (from

TABLE 8.1
The Cohort Sequential design of the NCAA Academic Performance Study
($N_a = 252$ colleges randomly stratified to one 5 year cohort)

APS Cohort	Num. schools	Num. Student—athletes	5 Year Follow-up	5 Year Graduation Rate
1984 (pre48)	39	2,500	1,710	52.7%
1985 (pre48)	33	2,400	1,540	48.9%
1986 (part48)	46	2,870	2,440	58.2%
1987 (part48)	42	2,470	1,910	54.6%
1988 (post48)	34	2,470	1,990	61.1%
1994 (followups)	227	10,200	5,890	57.7%

APS). This means that some information is available for two generations of students at the same colleges.

Academic, Demographic, and Outcome Variables

In each data collection listed in Table 8.1, a similar data collection strategy was used. Requests for data were made to a specific college by the NCAA research staff. This was mainly in the form of a letter sent to the Office of the President and the Office of the Director of Athletics. Once a contact person was named a set of survey forms was mailed to the college, filled out by the contact person (i.e., not the student-athlete), and mailed back to the NCAA. After these surveys were completed and returned, additional variables were merged in from other NCAA data sources. Although we know these students attained a high level of athletic success at the high school level, we did not measure athletic performances at the college level. However, the combination of these resources allowed us to create individual and college level datasets with the following variables of interest:

1. *High school information:* number of core taken courses (i.e., English, math, science, etc.), grade point averages (GPA), national test scores (SAT or ACT).
2. *College academic information:* Year-by-year grade point averages, credit hours attempted and attained, major areas, academic probation, dropout or matriculation, and graduation status.
3. *College athletic information:* Year-by-year team, participation, injuries, and use of athletic advising systems.
4. *Demographic group information:* Gender, ethnicity, family income, sport played, etc.
5. *High school institutional information:* High school location and demographics, academic characteristics, specific SES levels, etc.
6. *College institutional information:* College location and demographics, college academic selectivity, college graduation rates, specific athletic advising systems, etc.

Hypothesized Policy Impacts

In theory, a set of broad alternative impacts are considered here. All of these are based on information about the *prospective student-athletes* (PSA) and those who entered the class of *matriculated student-athletes* (MSA). Some proposed impacts include:

1. *Rising Up*—The PSAs when faced with higher standards will "rise to meet those new challenges." This implies that the standards are within reasonable bounds, and the same group of MSAs will now be better prepared for college academic work.
2. *Replacement*—The PSAs who would have been admitted (based on athletic standing and potential talent) are replaced by others with higher academic standing and potential. This implies a somewhat different group of MSAs but these will be better prepared.
3. *Falling Down*—The PSAs when faced with higher standards will "fall at the sight of those new challenges" or "learn helplessness." This implies that the standards are unreasonable in some way, and some group of PSAs will do worse than expected as a result.
4. *Teaching-to-Test*—The PSAs when faced with higher standards will "meet the test criteria but not alter the construct." This implies the same group of students will matriculate, but the measurements used to indicate academic standing and potential will become less valid indicators of the construct (i.e., lack measurement invariance).

5. *Confounding Influences*—There are other influences that coincide with the rule changes that create the impacts, including a general awareness of the importance of the academic-athletics link, and the new effectiveness of the athletic-advising systems.
6. *Mixtures of Impacts*—Each of the impacts just noted is true to some degree. Obviously, this is the most complex result to identify but may be the most likely result.

Statistical Modeling Methods

The lack of clearly defined experimental and control groups limit both our measurement of alternative outcomes and the clarity of specific policy changes. In many problems like this, there is probably no empirical methodology that can be used to disentangle all effects of restrictive regulations. The methods we used to define and quantify the possible "academic enhancements" are presented in the form of a quasi-experimental analysis based on "regression–discontinuity" (after Campbell, 1988; Cook & Campbell, 1979; Reichardt, Trochim, & Cappelleri, 1995; Shadish, Cook, & Campbell, 2001; Thistlethwaite & Campbell, 1960). These statistical modeling analyses are attempts to separate the effects of students from colleges, maturation from training, and permit a clearer view of the impact of policy changes on changes in academic achievements.

The inclusion of the most recent 1994 data (entering freshman for the Class of 1998) permit some new longitudinal group comparisons *within the same colleges* (see Table 8.1). In this sense, each college is treated as a unit of analysis, and the students within the colleges are treated as the within-college replicates. This feature of the 15-year cohort longitudinal study is important because there are many differences among colleges that might overwhelm any within college policy effect. From this cohort-longitudinal perspective we can define three broad classes of different colleges:

1. *Pre-Post for Total Impacts*: $N_c = 50$ colleges were measured before Prop 48 went into effect (1984–1985) and these can be compared to current outcomes (1994) within the same schools.
2. *Pre-Post for Phase-In Impacts*: $N_c = 69$ colleges were measured immediately after Prop 48 went into effect (1986–1987) and these can be compared to current outcomes (1994) within the same schools.
3. *Pre-Post for Long-Term Impacts*: $N_c = 31$ colleges were measured after Prop 48 went into effect (1988) and these can be compared to current outcomes (1994) within the same schools.

Most statistical models used here are based on a standard logistic regression model presented in the path diagram of Fig. 8.2a. In this model the outcome is an individual binary outcome (e.g., graduation) and the predictors include categorical variables (i.e., group membership), continuous variables (i.e., z-scores based on GPA and a combined ACT/SAT index), and the possible interaction of both (e.g., GPA by group). To these models we add "multilevel" components based on college information (e.g., Aitken & Longford, 1986; Bock, 1989; Cronbach & Webb, 1975; McArdle & Hamagami, 1994). Technical details about this model are given in several previous reports and will not be repeated here (see McArdle, 1998; McArdle & Hamagami, 1994). These models are intended to yield reasonable (a) statistical estimates of differences in proportions or rates, (b) "specific contrasts" among cohorts of students at specific colleges, and (c) adequate power to test alternative models. Given the size of these samples, statistical accuracy (i.e., significance at the $\alpha = .01$ test level) is virtually assured. This allows our discussion to focus on the direction, size, and specific meaning of these impacts.

RESULTS

Phase I: Pre-Prop 48 Projections

To examine these issues, we first looked at what was already known about the specific components within the rule. For example, one important part of the Prop 48 rules was that the specific cut-off on the ACT–SAT score was a much more stringent requirement than the cut-off for core GPA (see NCAA 1991b). At the time, it was estimated that, in a national sample of college-bound students, this ACT–SAT score excludes 16.8% (700 = –1 Z-score) at the low end whereas the 2.0 GPA score only cut off 2.3% (2.00 = –2 Z-score) at the low end (see Fig. 8.1a Klitgaard, 1986; NCAA #1991b). This implies that the ACT–SAT was given substantially more "weight" in the eligibility outcomes of the Prop 48 rules (e.g., 16.8% vs. 2.3%).

In a series of studies we, examined the predictive validity of the variables involved (see NCAA, 1991a, McArdle & Hamagami, 1994, 1996; McArdle, Paskus, & Boker, 2004; NCAA 1991a). In a first study we examined $N{\sim}3,000$ students in $C{\sim}65$ colleges, and the observed graduation rate of students was predicted from both individual-level high school academic variables (e.g., total number of core courses taken, student core GPA, ACT, or SAT scores) as well as college-level characteristics (e.g., college graduation rate, overall student body ACT or SAT scores). The regression prediction models based on Fig. 8.2a initially focused on freshman grades and credit hours—these results showed both High School GPA ($R^2 > 10\% - 31\%$) and ACTSAT ($\Delta R^2 > 2\% - 5\%$) were useful predictors. The multilevel logistic prediction models were used on freshman dropout, survival and graduation, and these results showed the ACTSAT ($R^2 > 21\%$) was the best predictor but high school GPA ($\Delta R^2 > 3\%$) was also useful. Most importantly, these results also showed that a composite variable based on equal weights was the single best predictor. Although the Prop 48 rules were applied uniformly to all colleges, virtually any prediction model used here was improved substantially by the inclusion of the college graduation rate ($\Delta R^2 > 10\%$).

These statistical models were also used to evaluate the impacts of *prediction bias*. Although there were substantial differences in the distribution of most academic indicators among demographic and athletic groups, these regression analyses showed little or no evidence of prediction bias against the minority groups. A representation of this result is presented in Fig. 8.2b. Plotted on the X axis is an equally weighted composite of high school grades and test scores (the average Z-score) and this was found to be a positive predictor of the probability of graduation. However, the optimal logistic regression lines for the majority and minority groups have almost exactly the same shape and no prediction bias is evident. The African American minority SAs had poorer academic outcomes (i.e., GR = 29.8%) but this was predicted from their lower high school scores (i.e., GPA = 2.4, SAT = 667). In contrast, using the same models, the female SA's outcomes were much better than predicted (+5%) suggesting the possibility of gender prediction bias.

Finally, we used the same NCAA data to examine the potential *selection biases* apparent under different eligibility rules (McArdle, 1998; NCAA, 1991b). Using standard decision theory analyses (e.g., with cost-benefit utility weights) we found the rules proposed in 1983 would have created substantial selection bias against the minority group members of the 1984 and 1985 entering freshmen. When we applied the Prop 48 rules to the Pre-Prop 48 data, we

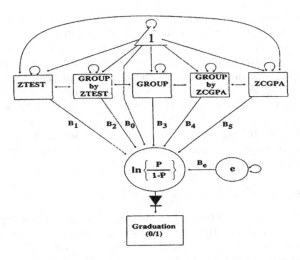

FIG. 8.2a   This is a path diagram of the logistic regression model describing individual level graduation.

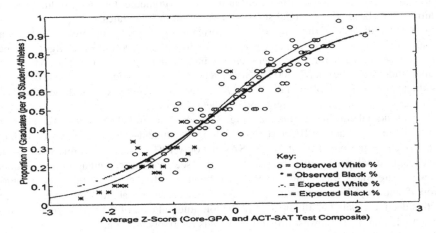

FIG. 8.2b   This is shows the results of the logistic regression where Y = probility of graduation and X = achievement composite Z score for white and black student athletes.

projected substantially higher graduation rates (GR) of students who were above these cut-offs (see Fig. 8.1) from the existing GR = 46% to a projected GR = 59%. However, using the same data, we also projected a substantial selection effect (SE) of students who were now in college, but did not meet the minimum standards ($n > 3,400$ or 27% of all student athletes). This selection effect also exhibited a large within-group difference between the majority ($n = 1,290$, 14%) and minority ($n = 2,090$, 66%) groups. Most importantly, we also estimated a substantial misidentification of the eventual graduates (False Negatives (FN) $n = 810$ or 6%) and a sizeable difference in the loss of graduates among the majority ($n = 370$, 4%) and minority ($n = 420$, 14%) groups.

These results led to the representation of a variety of alternative rules (see NCAA, 1991b). Perhaps the most important result was based on our projection that some of this bias could be overcome by using an "equally weighted sliding scale" based on the high school grades and the ACT–SAT test scores. This kind of an alternative eligibility rule is displayed in Figure 8.1b. Using this straight line selection variable, together with a cutoff placed near the graduation rate projected under Prop 48, we found diminished impacts on the overall group (GR = 56%, SE = 20%, FN = 3.8%), the majority group (GR = 59%, SE = 9%, FN = 3.8%), and the minority group (GR = 44%, SE = 52%, FN = 9%). This form of linear "compensatory" rule was projected to both increase the graduation rates and minimize adverse impacts. For these reasons, the alternative displayed in Figure 8.1b turned out to be a reasonable way to address some of the issues raised about Prop 48.

Phase II: Longitudinal Research on Graduation Rates

In our second phase of results, we focused on the striking differences among the graduation rates of different NCAA colleges. Here we examined data from the NCAA *Graduation Rate Disclosure* (GRD) study on $N > 25,000$ student athletes per year (NCAA, 1997). Initially mandated by the NCAA for all member colleges and universities in 1986 (predating U.S. federal guidelines; i.e., Bowen & Bok, 1998), the GRD data are used to monitor Minority and female enrollment and number of student-athletes who graduate. Our longitudinal research was aimed at isolating the potential sources of variation in these rates.

Fig. 8.3 is a display of the longitudinal information on enrollment rates (Fig. 8.3a) and graduation rates (Fig. 8.3b) over a recent 10-year period (1991–2000). In each figure, we have plotted the percentages for four operationally independent groups: (1) The White Non-Hispanic student–athletes in $N_c \sim 300$ Division I schools, (2) the African American (Black) student-athletes in these schools, (3) the White Non-Hispanic student body at these schools, (2) the African American (Black) student body at these schools.

The longitudinal enrollment statistics (Fig. 8.3a) show several clear trends. We can see the relatively large percentage of Black students among the student–athletes in Division I; that is, in 1983, Blacks represented about 27% of SAs, but only 10% of the comparable student-body. In this longitudinal perspective, however, we also see that the percentage of the student-athletes that are Black was reduced (−5%) in 1986 at exactly the year of the implementation of Prop 48 and stayed lower than the pre-Prop 48 percentage for about 4 more years. In contrast, this decline was not at all apparent in the longitudinal data of the Black student body at these schools; that is. the lowest line in Fig. 8.3a is relatively straight.

The longitudinal graduation statistics (Fig. 8.3b) also show several distinct trends. We can see the relatively low percentage of graduates among the Black student-athletes in Division I; that is, in 1983, the White student athletes graduated at about a 59% rate whereas the Black SAs graduated at a 35% rate. In this longitudinal perspective, however, we also see that the graduation rate of both White student athletes Black student athletes increased (+2% and +10%) after the implementation of Prop 48 (1986), and both rates remained higher for about 5 years. It is important to note that this upward trend was somewhat apparent in the longitudinal data of both the White and Black student–bodies at the same schools so, at best, only part of these graduation rate increases can be attributed to Prop 48. One other result is striking—within both White and Black groups, the student-athletes graduation rate is higher than the comparable rates for the student bodies at the same schools. The higher graduation

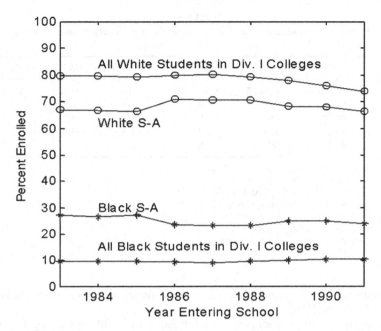

FIG. 8.3a College enrollment trends for two ethnic groups. (Date from NCAA Graduation Rate Disclosure reports.)

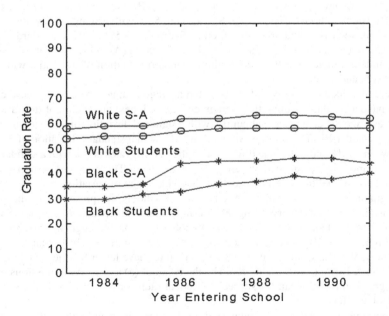

FIG. 8.3b College graduation trends for two ethnic groups. (Date from NCAA Graduation Rate Disclosure reports.)

TABLE 8.2
Summary statistics on variability in trends in graduation rates across
different NCAA colleges

Statistic	Ten Year GR Averages (Levels)			Ten Year GR Changes (Slopes)		
	SBGR10	SAGR10	Δ(SA–SB)	ΔSB10	ΔSA10	Δ(ΔSA–ΔSB)
Mean	53.1	57.1	4.0	0.3	0.7	0.4
(Stan Dev)	(19.2)	(15.1)	(9.0)	(1.3)	(3.2)	(3.5)
Minimum	10.2	21.0	23.4	–5.3	–13.9	–11.0
Maximum	96.1	90.8	–30.8	8.8	24.0	29.4

Notes: Nc = 310 colleges in Division I of the NCAA;
SBGR10 = Ten–year average of Student–Body GR;
SAGR10 = Ten–year average of Student–Athlete GR;
D(SA–SB) = Difference in ten-year average levels;
DSB10 = Annual change of Student–Body GR;
DSA10 = Annual change of Student–Athlete GR;
D (DSA–DSB) = Difference in ten-year average changes.

of student-athletes is a consistent result across many studies but does not seem to be widely known (see McArdle, 1998).

A more in-depth analysis of longitudinal information across different colleges is presented in Table 8.2. The variables described here for different schools include both (a) 10-year averages of graduation rates (GR10) and (b) 10-year slopes of graduation rates (10 year rates of change). These are presented for both the *student body* (SB) and the *student–athletes* (SA) in the same Division I schools. The average SB rates are 53% with a standard deviation of 19% and a range between 10% and 96%. The average SA rates are 57% with a standard deviation of 15% and a range between 21% and 91%. The differences (Δ) in the 10-year SA–SB rates show the student-athletes are 4% higher with a standard deviation of 9% and a wide range, between −31% and 23%.

Table 8.2 also includes the calculations of the average changes over time. These calculations also have a similar feature—the average changes (slopes) are small but the variation is large. The average SB changes are about 0% with a standard deviation of 1% but with a range between −5% and +9%. The average SA rates are 1% with a standard deviation of 3% and a range between −14% and 24%. The difference in the SA–SB rates is 0% with a standard deviation of 4% and a wide range between −11% and +30%. The aggregate comparisons of Fig.8.3 are less compelling when considering this wide range of variation.

These graduation rates for all NCAA Division I schools are presented in the plots of Fig. 8.4. Fig. 8.4a suggests a very strong relationship among the graduation rates of the student-athletes and the student body at the same schools ($r > .7$). Although most schools have SA rates higher than SB rates, some schools have lower SA rates. Further analysis of this problem shows that the schools with the highest SB rates have lower SA rates, and vice versa (cf, Schulman & Bowen, 2001). This could be the result of (a) a selective admissions process, (b) of a regression to the mean for subsets of student rates, or (c) some complex mixture of these and other effects.

Other possible explanations are suggested by the analysis of individual changes in rates over ten years. Figure 8.4b is a plot of the 10-year slopes for SA and SB at the same schools.

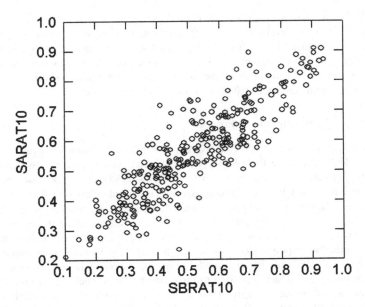

FIG. 8.4a A scatter plot of the relationship among the 10 year average of Xth Standard BodyGraduation rate and the Y = Student Athlete Graduation Rates. (for N_c = 310 NCAA Division Colleges, see Table 2)

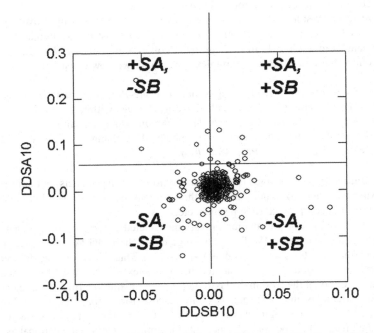

FIG. 8.4b A scatter plot of the relationship among the 10 year differences in X = Student Body Graduation Changes and the Y = Student Athlete Graduation changes (for N_c = 310 NCAA Division College see Table 2)

This plot shows most of the schools in the central part of the graph, but some schools appear in each of the four quadrants. In the upper left quadrant, a few schools exhibit increasing graduation rates for student-athletes but declining rates for the student body (+SA,−SB). In contrast, the lower right hand quadrant shows many schools with decreasing graduation rates for student-athletes but increasing rates for the student body (−SA,+SB). The other two quadrants show the schools with consistent patterns of SA-SB characteristics.

Phase III: Long-Term Impacts of Prop 48

In the early phases of this research (see NCAA, 1992) complete data were only available on samples from 1984–1986 (see Table 8.1) so we examined the changes across two groups of colleges: (a) $N_c = 71$ colleges measured pre-Prop 48 (1984–1985) and (b) $N_c = 46$ colleges measured Post Prop 48 (1986). Because the colleges were representatively stratified each year, these between-group comparisons could be considered indicative of general trends. These data allowed us to use regression–discontinuity analyses to directly estimate the initial impacts of Prop 48. In this model a regression is estimated over all occasions, but we include the possibility of a shift in the intercept and slope for occasions after Prop 48 was implemented.

Results based on the full logistic model (Fig. 8.2) showed large differences between groups on the intercepts, with the post-48 group estimated with much higher predicted scores, but there were no differences in regression slopes or interactions. We repeated these analyses using only SAs with scores meeting the Prop 48 minimum standards. The results of these above-average group comparisons no longer showed any differences in intercepts or slopes. The elimination of the time-related discontinuity implies the initial impacts were due to the initial selection at the implementation of Prop 48.

Our most recent results include the same groups of colleges measured over the last few years. Table 8.3 presents a current set of analyses using most of the longitudinal cohort-sequential data from Table 8.1. In this approach colleges are *compared to themselves* over time and cohort. For each of the 20 variables considered, we now consider:

1. *Pre-48* = scores for $N_c = 71$ colleges measured pre-Prop 48 (1984–85),
2. *ΔPre-Post #1* = the *total effects* calculated as changes within these schools,
3. *ΔPre-Post #2* = the *phase-in effects due to the initial impacts,* and
4. *ΔPre-Post #3* = the *long-term effects* calculated as changes within $N_c = 42$ colleges originally measured Post-Prop 48 (1988).

The consideration of both changes is a simple way to index the impacts, but simple changes are not always used here for a number of methodological reasons not detailed (e.g. noncomparable groups, noncomparable time periods, etc.).

In Table 8.3a we present information on variables related to the high school characteristics of the entering freshman class. We list the average high school *ΔGPA* = 2.81 and an increase over 10 years (the 1994 GPA = 3.16 so *ΔGPA#1* = +0.35). This relatively large difference in the students Pre-Post 48 needs to be considered in the context of the *ΔGPA#3* = +0.23, which implies that the GPAs of the freshman classes kept going up after the rule was already in place. The second variable is the ACT and SAT in *Z*-score form (for details, see McArdle & Hamagami, 1994). Here the high school ACTSAT = −0.21 (*Z* units), is just below the national average at the time, and the positive change, puts the group just above the national average (the 1994 ACTSAT = +.17, so *ΔACTSAT#1* = +0.36). This same difference is not found in the long

TABLE 8.3a:
Resulting estimates from comparisons of Entering Freshman

High School Variable	Pre 48 value	Pre Post #1	Pre Post #3
Core GPA	2.81	0.35	0.23
ACTSAT Z	−0.21	0.36	−0.11
Male SA %	63.3%	−10.6%	−6.6%
Black SA %	25.6%	−2.7%	2.3%
Eligible 48	69.8%	30.4%	0.9%

TABLE 8.3b
Resulting estimates from comparisons of College Outcomes

College Variable	Pre 48 value	Pre Post #1	Pre Post #3
1st Yr GPA	2.30	0.35	0.10
1st Yr Credit	26.5	0.9	−1.8
1stYr Persist	80.0%	8.9%	−2.3%
Final GPA	2.38	0.44	0.11
Graduation Rate	45.4%	12.4%	−0.1%

run (ΔACTSAT#3 = −0.11), meaning the average scores initially were higher but, over time, remained the same. The proportion of SA who were male (63%) was lower (−10.6) and this was true even after Prop 48 (-6.6%). Of course, this effect may be due to other factors (i.e., increasing numbers of females due to Title IX, increases in academic advising, etc.). The proportion of SA who were Black (25.6%) went down (−2.7%) but was higher afterwards (+2.3%). Within these schools, the proportion of SA who would have been eligible under Prop 48 (70%) clearly increased when the rule was put into effect (+30%) and has remained constant since (+1%).

In Table 8.3b we present information on variables related to the college academic characteristics of the comparable cohorts of students. Here we find a rise in 1st year GPAs (from 2.30 to 2.65), and this trend continues post-48 (+.10). The 1st year credits show small changes (+1, −2), but the 1st year persistence increased (from 80% to 89%) and then decreased a bit later (to 87%). Once again, this could be due to other contiguous factors (i.e., transfers, finances, etc.). The average GPA at the time of college graduation increased (2.38 to 2.82) and this increase continues (+.11). Within these colleges, the graduation rate of successive generations of student–athletes increased dramatically from 45.4% in 1984–1985 to 57.8% in 1994 (+12.4%) and this increase has remained since that time.

The pre-post cohort comparisons of Table 8.3 begin to isolate some impacts of Prop 48 on the collegiate system as a whole. However, this aggregation ignores the variation among colleges within each group (see Fig. 8.4). In Table 8.4 we present the same kinds of analyses, but here we relate the 10-year changes in the college graduation rate (ΔGR) for the student-athletes to other changes that occurred during the same time period within the college. The change from 1984-85 to 1994 in high school GPA for the class (ΔHSGPA) has a correlation (for 71 schools) of +0.39 with the change in subsequent graduation rate. These changes were

TABLE 8.4A
Resulting estimates from Group correlates of College ΔGR

College Changes	ΔPre Post #1	ΔPre Post #3	Part Δ #1: #3
HS GPA	0.39	0.29	0.26
ACTSAT	0.53	0.45	0.28
Male %	−0.18	−0.05	−0.17
Black %	−0.25	−0.31	0.18
Eligib 48	0.40	0.05	0.40

TABLE 8.4B
Resulting estimates from College Systemic correlates of College ΔGR

College Variable	Pre Post #1	Pre Post #3	Part #1 : D#3
Overall Size	0.17	0.38	−0.33
School ACTSAT	0.19	0.31	−0.25
Black %	−0.15	−0.33	−0.29
CEEB Supports	−0.24	−0.09	−0.22
NCAA Supports	−0.20	0.36	−0.29

also correlated +0.29 between 1988 and 1994 classes. Under a variety of simplifying statistical assumptions not detailed here (variance homogeneity and part correlations), we can calculate the part of the overall effect that could be considered unique to Prop 48 (i.e., added explained variance of .08). A stronger pattern of results is seen in the correlation of the changes for the entering ACTSAT and the subsequent graduation rates (+.53), and because this still occurs after Prop 48 (+.45) the part of the overall effect directly attributable to the ACTSAT cutoffs in Prop 48 is a bit less than that observed for GPA (+.28 or 8% added variance). The correlations of the changes among graduation rates and male percents of eligibility are notable only in the Prop 48 period and due to Prop 48. However, the changes in the graduation rates and the Black enrollment percentages are still apparent even after Prop 48 was in place.

In Table 8.4b we present the same kinds of analyses, but here we relate the 10-year changes in the college graduation rate (ΔGR) to other systemic features of the college. The changes are more notable in the larger schools, but become stronger after Prop 48 was put in place. The ACTSAT of the student body, a common indicator of college selectivity, and the percent of Blacks in the student body both show the same pattern of stronger recent history (Post-48) relationships with graduation rates. The number of "academic supports" in the college was recorded for both 1994 student body (labeled CEEB supports due to the source of information) and the student–athletes (labeled NCAA supports). Comparing colleges pre–post 48 there are negative relations among changes in academic supports and changes in graduation rate, and positive effects for increased NCAA supports in the post-48 era. These results are complex and may be confounded by a variety of other circumstances—that is, changes in support are often introduced after serious academic problems have already occurred.

DISCUSSION

Overview

This chapter overviews several interrelated studies of longitudinal changes in the academic performances of college students who also participate in high-level athletics. During the past two decades, the relationship between college academics and college sports has been questioned by many critics. In response, the U.S. National Collegiate Athletic Association (NCAA) has directed many efforts towards "academic reforms" for college "student-athletes" (SA), including a variety of academic eligibility policies and academic support systems. The studies presented here are an effort to isolate the impacts of the reforms on "academic enhancements" made during the last decade. In these studies we used data from relatively large and representative samplings of colleges ($N_c > 250$) and individual students ($N > 12,000$). We presented some of our initial methods and results used to estimate the impacts of a mandatory initial eligibility policy (termed Prop 48) on the academic outcomes of various colleges and groups of students who are participants in high-level college sports.

Impacts of Prop 48?

The overall impacts of Prop 48 remain hard to quantify from extant data, but both positive (desirable) and negative (undesirable) outcomes seem apparent. These analyses suggest a rise in several academic outcomes after the implementation of Prop 48, together with a corresponding decrease in male and Black enrollment. There are strong positive increases in academic performances of the eligible SA, together with increases in ineligible prospective student-athletes who later succeed. There remains somewhat lower eligibility for Black and lower income prospective student-athletes, and for different schools (e.g., public, historically Black colleges, etc.). Further multivariate analyses of these data are ongoing, and some critical multilevel comparisons have yet to be made.

The colleges vary a great deal, however, so it seems unwise to be overly confident about aggregate statements about academic impacts. There are important systematic differences among the colleges in the graduation rates for student-athletes and the student body. There are also important differences in the academic profiles of the Division I college student bodies and the recruited student athletes. For example, for some big colleges (e.g., Division I-A) the student-body average graduation rate changes are very small but the student-athlete rate changes are large (cf. Schulman & Bowen, 2001). Similar findings can be presented for public versus private schools, and other demographic features of the colleges. In general, these longitudinal analyses suggest that the colleges are changing over time in many different ways and the isolation of specific impacts is complex. This also means that an equitable rule from a "national" (aggregate) perspective is likely to have "inequitable outcomes" from a "local" perspective (e.g., on individual students or colleges).

These analyses provide broad evidence for choosing among alternative impacts:

1. *Replacement is likely*—A different group of SA seems to have matriculated, and these students are better prepared but represent far fewer minority SA.
2. *Rising up is unlikely*—The SA groups have changed, and there is little evidence that suggests these are the same people who simply achieved more in high school.
3. *Falling down is likely*—Some groups of prospective SA did do much worse than expected, and it is possible that they were not recruited or did not even apply to college.

4. *Teaching-to-test* is not yet seen—Within similar groups of tested abilities, the measurements do not seem to have lost validity. The one exception here may be the increasing percentage of SA who present almost exactly minimum scores and multiple tests.
5. *Confounding influences are clear*—Other influences are found, including increased female participation, high school and college advising, and the possibility of "an earlier wake-up call."
6. *Mixtures of impacts are likely*—There were many different local policies that may have a positive impact on academic performances, including academic advising and academic coaching—The degree to which all of these impacts are occurring was not yet possible to estimate, and this is a key concern for future research.

In sum, our current results show that there are both (1) intended gains and unintended losses in the academic outcomes, and (2) these gains and losses are not spread equally over different demographic groups and colleges. The largest overall gains are primarily due to the barriers placed on some academically poorer students, and only small gains are attributable to systematic changes in individual student achievements. These results also provide hints at some positive impacts of academic advising for all high school and college students, but these are hard to fully characterize using the current data. Further research on this question will need to recognize the differences among college support programs and the fact that many students within the same college do not receive all academic support benefits available. Nevertheless, in most respects, the student–athletes appear to be similar to other students at the same colleges (i.e., those who do not participate in high-level sports), so these results seem likely to generalize to academic enhancement programs for all students.

Impacts of Educational Policy Research

These analyses are limited by several uncontrolled features of the data collections and constantly evolving policy changes. For these and other reasons, it is often hard to judge whether empirical evaluation research of this kind makes any difference. After all, this research was initiated after the rule was approved, and there was little or no chance to change it immediately. The NCAA legislative history does not clearly show that these unbalanced cutoff scores had a specific empirical basis, and it is not even clear that this imbalance was intentional. In contrast, these cutoffs were later termed *arbitrary* by several NCAA committees (reports of NCAA Academic Requirements Committees) and criticized as "an inappropriate use of the test" by members of the testing companies (the College Board, ETS, ACT). The alternative form of "compensatory" rule (Fig. 8.3b) addressed many of the questions raised by previous critics, but the Prop 48 rules were not directly altered in response to these results by 2001 (see McArdle, 2004). However, recent changes in eligibility rules have more directly responded to some of the empirical findings of these studies.

On the other hand, although public policy research is often not completely scientific, the kind of experimental methodology advocated here may have improved the clarity of the debate concerning these topics (see Chelimsky, 1991). Many forms of "test bias" are now clearly defined in terms decision-makers do understand, and the most important questions are not simply considered in terms of "yes or no." It has become clear that the substantive problems surrounding academic reforms require much more clarification of "goals" and "subjective utilities" (see Zerbe, 1998). Because this research was carried out with the support of the NCAA research staff, reports have already been made to the constituent committees. Indeed, for the past decade many NCAA committees have discussed these rules, and many new rules are being considered only after an empirical base has been created.

Although the inferences made here were limited by the design and measurements available, the essential need for scientific objectivity cannot be understated. Our collaboration on this research with a national regulatory body might be seen to restrict the objectivity of this research in some intentional or unintentional way. Although the NCAA is well known for its role in the enforcement of academic regulations, it is less well known that all formal rules are created by the Presidents of the NCAA member colleges. Thus, it is neither necessary nor helpful for this kind of work to try to place the policies previously implemented by the NCAA in either a positive or negative light. Even for legal reasons it would be better for any monitoring committee to alter an inappropriate rule than to let it remain in place. It is also clear that a statistical model should not be chosen based on the results it yields—this is "advocacy" and not the "science" for finding facts. This research-based approach can only make a contribution if we attempt to, and are permitted to, accurately estimate the impacts of academic policies on the academic outcomes of various colleges and students (see McArdle & Hamagami, 1994; McArdle, 1998). Improvements in the ways objective information can be collected, analyzed, and communicated in policy debates may be the most important aspect of future research on this topic.

ACKNOWLEDGEMENTS

This chapter is dedicated to Dr. Ursula R. Walsh, the creator and first Director of the NCAA Research Staff. Dr. Walsh encouraged and contributed to the empirical analyses of all key issues studied here. These analyses were conducted in 2002 using data that were made available to the author at that time, and benefiting from the help of many others – Steve Boker, Aki Hamagami, Tom Paskus, and Todd Petr. Persons interested in updated information on these topics should contact the NCAA Research Staff.

REFERENCES

Aitken, M., & Longford, N. (1986). Statistical modelling issues in school effectiveness studies. *Journal of the Royal Statistical Society, 149*, 1–43.

American College Testing Program. (1995). *ACT assessment student information.* Iowa City, IA: Author.

Astin, A. (1971). *Predicting academic performance in college.* New York: Free Press.

Beatty, A., Greenwood, M.R.C., & Linn, R. L. (1999). *Myths and tradeoffs: The role of tests in undergraduate admissions.* Washington, DC: National Research Council Press.

Bock, R. D., (Ed.) (1989). *Multilevel analysis of educational data.* New York: Academic Press.

Bowen, W. G., & Bok, D. (1998). *The shape of the river: Long-term consequences of considering race in college and university admissions.* Princeton, NJ: Princeton University Press.

Campbell, D. T. (1969). Reforms as experiments. *American Psychologist, 24,* 409–429.

Campbell, D. T. (1988). *Methodology and epistemology for social sciences: Selected papers.* Chicago: University of Chicago Press.

Campbell, D. T. (1996). Regression artifacts in time-series and longitudinal data. *Evaluation and Program Planning, 19* (4), 377–389.

Campbell, D. T., & Stanley, J. C. (1966). *Experimental and quasi-experimental designs in research.* Stokie, IL: Rand McNally.

Chelimsky, E. (1991). On the social science contribution to governmental decision-making. *Science (254),* 226–230.

College Entrance Examination Board. (1995). *College bound seniors national report: 1995 Profile of SAT and achievement test takers.* New York, NY: College Entrance Examination Board.

Cook, T. & Campbell, D. (1979). *Quasi-experimentation: Design & analysis issues for field settings.* New York: Houghton Mifflin Company.

Cronbach, L. J., & Webb, N. (1975). Between class and within class effects in a reported aptitude x treatment interaction: A reanalysis of a study by G.L. Anderson. *Journal of Educational Psychology, 67*, 717–724.

Crouse, J. & Trusheim, D (1988). *The case against the SAT.* Chicago: University of Chicago Press.

Falla, J. (1981). *NCAA: The voice of college sports: A diamond anniversary history 1906–1981.* Mission, KS: The National Collegiate Athletic Association

Fleisher, A. A., Goff, B. L. & Tollison, R. D. (1992). *The National Collegiate Athletic Association: A study in cartel behavior.* Chicago: University of Chicago Press.

Kish, L., & Frankel, M.R. (1974). Inference from complex samples. *Journal of the Royal Statistical Society: Series B, 36,* 1–37.

Klitgaard, R. (1986). *Choosing elites.* New York: Basic Books.

Manski, C. F. & Wise, D. A. (1983). *College choice in America.* Cambridge, MA: Harvard University Press.

McArdle, J. J. (1998). Test bias. In J. J. McArdle & R. W. Woodcock, (Eds.), *Human cognitive abilities in theory and practice* (pp. 157–195). Mahwah, NJ: Erlbaum Associates.

McArdle, J. J. (2004). *Beyond the NCAA: Two decader of academic research on students atletes* (in progress).

McArdle, J. J. & Hamagami, F. (1994). Logit and multilevel logit modeling studies of college graduation for 1984-85 freshman student-athletes. *The Journal of the American Statistical Association, 89* (427), 1107–1123.

McArdle, J. J., & Hamagami, F. (1996). Multilevel models from a multiple group structural equation perspective. In G. Marcoulides & R. Schumacker (Eds.), *Advanced Structural Equation Modeling Techniques.* Hillsdale, N.J.: Erlbaum. 89–124.

McArdle, J. J., Paskus, T.S. & Boker, S. M. (2004). Multilevel predictions of college academic outcomes. *Multivariate Behavioral Research?* (under review).

National Collegiate Athletic Association. (1991a). *A statistical comparison of the college graduation of freshman student-athletes before proposition 48.* NCAA Research Report #91–02. Overland Park, KA.

National Collegiate Athletic Association. (1991b). *A decision theory analysis of proposition 48. and alternative rules* NCAA Research Report #91–05. Overland Park, KA.

National Collegiate Athletic Association (1992). *A statistical comparison of the college graduation of freshman student–athletes before and after proposition 48.* NCAA Research Report #92–02. Overland Park, KA.

National Collegiate Athletic Association. (1997). *A longitudinal analysis of NCAA Division I graduation rates–data.* NCAA Research Report #96–01. Overland Park, KA:

Nesselroade, J.R., & Baltes, P. R. (Eds.) (1979). *Longitudinal research in the study of behaviour and development.* New York: Academic Press.

Pascarella, E. T., & Terenzini, P. T. (1991). *How college affects students.* San Francisco, CA: Jossey-Bass.

Reichardt, C. S., Trochim, W. & Cappelleri, J. (1995). Reports of the death of the regression-discontinuity design are greatly exaggerated. *Evaluation Review, 19,* (1), 39–63.

Sawyer, R. (1986). Using demographic subgroup and dummy variable equations to predict college freshman grade point averages. *Journal of Educational Measurement, 23* (2), 131–145.

Shadish, W. R., Cook, T. D., & Campbell, D. T. (2001). *Experimental and quasi-experimental designs for generalized causal inference.* Boston: Houghton Mifflin.

Shulman, J. L. & Bowen, W. G. (2001). *The game of life: College sports and educational values.* Princeton, NJ: Princeton University Press.

Thistlethwaite, D. L. & Campbell, D. T. (1960). Regression-discontinuity analysis: An alternative to the ex post factor experiment. *Journal of Educational Psychology, 51,* 309–317.

Willingham, W.W., Lewis, C., Morgan, R, & Ramist, L. (1990*). Predicting college grades: An analysis of institutional trends over two decades.* New York: The College Board.

Zerbe, R. O. (1998). Is benefit cost analysis legal? Three rules, *Journal of Policy Analysis and Management- 17* (3), 419–456.

9

Is There a Standard for Standardized Testing? Four Sketches of the Applicability (or Lack Thereof) of Standardized Testing in Different Educational Systems

Elena L. Grigorenko[1,2,3]
Yale University
Moscow State University

Linda Jarvin[1]
Yale University

Weihua Niu[1]
Yale University

David Preiss[1,4]
Pontificia Univesidad Catolica de Chile

The issue of the applicability and usability of standardized achievement and aptitude testing approaches in different countries around the world is gaining importance in the context of world globalization. First, more and more people obtain their college and professional educations in places other than their country of birth and/or the country in which they practice their professions; thus, there appears to be a need for a unified metric of some kind that can com-

---

[1]All authors contributed to the chapter equally.

[2]The four authors of this chapter represent the educational systems they discuss and are, in essence, products of these educational systems. Thus, the authors present their "interval" views of their respective educational systems and engage in the discussion of the system's pluses and minuses.

[3]Unlike the case with achievement aptitude tests, there is no cultural tradition of standartized ability testing in China. The currently used IQ tests are mostly translations and identifications of foreign instruments, although there-are a few tests of abilities developed based on respective theories of Chinese psychologists (Shi, 2001). IQ tests are primarily used in clinical settings, personnel recruitment settings, and in educational settings with respect to identification of children with special needs.

TABLE 9.1

Brief Summaries of Matriculation and College Entry Examinations Administered in Chile, China, France, and Russia

Country	Chile	China	France	Russia
Relevant Tests	PAA (1967–2002) SIES (200?—to be introduced)	NCEE (1952–present, administration was discontinued during 1966–1976)	Baccalauréat (1808–present); not a standardized test	CSE (2001–present)
Main Contents Tested	Mathematics and Spanish; content tests in sciences and social sciences	Chinese, mathematics, English, and one of several comprehensive domain tests, depending on the chosen track	Contents vary depending on the type of Baccalauréat chosen	Mathematics, Russian language, and a number of optional subjects
Status	The aptitude test PAA is being replaced with more achievement-oriented SIES	An achievement-based NCEE is becoming more like an aptitude test	No standardized tests	Standardized tests are now in pilot stage
Preferred Format	Written multiple choice	Written essay, multiple choice, and fill-in-the-blank	Oral and written essay, open response	Written multiple choice, short answers, open response
Prototype Tests	SAT-I & II (USA)	SAT-I & II (USA)		SAT-II (USA)
High School Graduation Test	No	A set of separate graduation tests given 1 year to one semester prior to the NCEE	Yes	Yes
Connection with Secondary Instruction	PAA: limited; SIES: extensive	Both curriculum based (G1–G11) and aptitude driven	Curriculum based (G1–G12)	Curriculum based (G1–G11)
Relevance to University/College Admission	Directly relevant (selection and placement)	Directly relevant (selection)	Baccalauréat is a matriculation procedure; required for higher education enrollment but not a selection test	Relevant, but contributes only partially to admissions decisions

TABLE 9.1 (Continued)

Country	Chile	China	France	Russia
Relevance to Financial Support/Other Financial Issues	Indirectly relevant through placement (universities are rewarded for higher scores of their student body)	No	No	Directly relevant for issues of financial support
Public attitude	Endorsed (both by the government and the public), although the format is criticized	Endorsed (both by the government and the public), although the high-stakes nature is criticized	Criticized for subjectivity, but no alternative is being developed	Endorsed by the government, but criticized by the public
Relevant Social Issues	Direct connection to socioeconomic differentiation of the society (through placement)	Direct connection to socioeconomical differentiation of the society (through selection)	No connection	Uncertain
Future	The most important factor for selection to and placement in higher education institutions	Increasingly adopted as the major criterion for selection to higher education institutions	No introduction of standardized testing is foreseen	Uncertain

pare, at this advanced level, the academic aptitude and achievement of competing candidates. Presumably, standardized achievement tests eliminate educational borders between countries as they help to promote educational exchanges by increasing comparability. Moreover, such tests are assumed to help create a universal scale of measurement, which fosters a particular set of skills, deemed important in most developed economies.

Second, there is increasing unification in outcome expectations of graduates from different educational programs around the world, and the various standards employed by different nations reflect more similarities than differences across such standards. In other words, whether Indonesian, Canadian, or Israeli, students are expected to meet almost the same achievement criteria while mastering the body of school-taught knowledge. Given the similarities of school completion achievement requirements around the world, it only makes sense to devise assessments that can quantify and compare the success of different educational approaches in preparing the world's children for vocational activities or further studies (Martin et al., 2001; Mullis, Martin, Gonzalez, & Kennedy, 2003).

Third, the industrialized world tends to look for effective mainstream solutions that allow the dissemination of technological advancement and the homogenization of customers' needs—the most cost-effective answer is always the "one size fits all" solution. Standardized achievement and aptitude testing appears capable of providing such a solution, one that might work around the world.

Yet, although "standard," standardized testing is different in different cultural contexts. A comparison of different national systems that either employ or do not employ standardized testing might be of use for understanding how similar and how different these systems are, and how standardized testing develops and exists in different economic, social, and cultural contexts. Moreover, comparisons between countries can identify universal and specific aspects of standardized testing as well as aspects that foster or prohibit cultural communication.

In this chapter, we provide four sketches of standardized achievement and aptitude testing as the means of organizing matriculation from secondary school and entry into higher education institutions in four very different nations: China, France, Chile and Russia.[2] Specifically, we briefly investigate various economic, political, cultural, and psychological issues related to the distribution of the idea of standardized testing in these countries. The sketches are structured around three different themes: (a) a brief history of the standardized testing approaches in a given country; (b) the practices currently employed by each country for matriculation from secondary school and entry into higher-education institutions; and (c) each country's attitude toward standardized testing.

The main structural points of the four sketches are the description of the relevant tests and their history, their role in school matriculation and entry into the system of higher education, and their importance in the context of broader societal issues (see Table 9.1). We complete the chapter with a general discussion of three issues that arose in our investigations.

CHINA: THE OLDEST HIGH-STAKES ACHIEVEMENT TESTING SYSTEM IN THE WORLD

China has a long history of achievement testing. Over 10 centuries ago, guided by teachings of Confucius, Chinese educators started using the so-called Imperial Examination System (IES) to select government servants and leaders, based on how much and how deeply a candidate understood Confucian classics (Biggs, 1996; Feng, 1994; Miyazaki, 1976). This system, consistent with the imperial hierarchy and, thus, organized as a pyramid from a low-level county test to a high-level palace test, formed the backbone of Chinese education for more than 1,300 years. To reach the top of the hierarchy, applicants took the county test, provincial test, capital test, and finally, the palace test. Most students would be screened out level by level, leaving very few to take the final exam (Franke, 1960). Under the IES educational system, students spent almost their entire lives learning Confucian teachings. Even though the IES[3] was officially abolished in 1905, it still has a profound influence on modern Chinese education and its testing systems.

A distant relative of the IES, the National College Entrance Examination (NCEE), is the single most important test in Chinese society. The NCEE is required for university applications and is administered at the same time nationwide. Administration of the NCEE was established in 1952 under the Ministry of Education; it was discontinued during the Cultural Revolution (1966–1976) and resumed in 1977. The exam was based on a modification of the IES proposed by the Jiang Jie Shi government in 1939 (Feng, 1994) and was reflective of Chinese political centralism.

The initial purposes of the NCEE are to (a) select trustworthy, academically well prepared, and physically healthy youth for higher education, so they can be trained as "red experts" for the socialist construction and modernization of China; and (b) provide equal opportunities for education and employment to everyone nationwide. It is important to note that the graduation exam for high school is different and independent from the NCEE. Students normally take school graduation tests in their local schools 1 year before taking the NCEE (if they plan to take it). The administration of school graduation tests is less standardized than the NCEE both in terms of the procedure and the test formats (e.g., fewer multiple-choice items, less structured items, and local, rather than nationwide, scoring).

The original NCEE was knowledge-driven and very time-consuming. It was a 3-day examination based on multiple subtests in six or seven subject areas, the results of which were used to place students in specific professional domains to pursue in college. There were two tracks from which students could choose: (a) humanity, social sciences, and foreign languages, and (b) sciences and technology. Students who chose the first track were required to take six subtests in Chinese, mathematics, English, history, geography, and political sciences. Students who chose the second track were required to take seven subtests in Chinese, mathematics, English, physics, chemistry, biology, and political sciences (Luo & Wendel, 1999; Wang, 1995). After the 3-day exam, hundreds to thousands of high school teachers gathered together in each local area to grade the exams manually for several weeks. The final score was a total score on the NCEE subtests within a given track included in a given year. Central and provincial governments then set the cut-off scores for college enrollment. The scores varied from province to province, depending on the number of high school students taking the exam that year and the enrollment quota each province received from the central government. There was no item bank for the NCEE in the beginning, nor were there sufficient studies of the test's psychometric properties, such as its reliability and validity. In fact, one study showed that the correlation between test performance and students' achievement in college was much lower than the correlation between test performance and students' achievement in high school; thus, the original NCEE was targeted more to students' prior knowledge in high school than their aptitude for college studies (Zhang, 1988).

In short, the original version of the NCEE was extremely effortful for both examiners and examinees, and was not psychometrically sound. Consequently, in the early 1980s, Chinese psychologists called for the replacement of the knowledge-driven test with a more aptitude-oriented test, and for the standardization of test items. With the help of experts from other countries, such as the United States, Japan, and some European nations, the NCEE was evaluated. It was determined that the test needed significant revisions to become more adequately standardized and comparable with standardized tests administered in other countries.

Beginning in 1984, the Chinese Ministry of Education started to revise the format and content of the NCEE (Heyneman & Fagerlind, 1985). In 1985, the Office of the National Testing Group for Planning of Educational Research (ONTGPER) of the Chinese Ministry of Education called for a special group of testing experts to oversee and examine the processes and outcomes of standardizing the NCEE. To ensure the success of the process, two phases were identified in an effort to implement standardized testing for educational admission purposes at the national level in China. The pilot phase was instituted from 1985 to 1989. At the onset of this stage, the province of Guangdong was asked to generate and implement pilot standardized tests in mathematics and English for the college entrance exam in 1986. After the success of this pilot, three more provinces (Shandong, Guangxi, and Liaoning) joined the experiment in 1987. The subject areas were also extended so that the test now covered mathematics, English, physics, and chemistry. The 1987 pilot was recognized as a success, and more and more provinces began to use standardized tests in almost all tested subject areas of the NCEE. In 1988, the ONTGPER group received the Chinese National Science Advanced Award for its successful implementation of standardized testing in the first-round nationwide examination.

Two aspects were taken into consideration during the standardization of the NCEE. The first had to do with the standardization of the test format. In the beginning, some testing experts suggested applying the Educational Testing Service (ETS) model in every subject, which was to use exclusively multiple-choice items. However, this proposal was ruled out early on. A majority of Chinese testing experts believed that different types of test items served different purposes in different subjects. Correspondingly, they argued, test items should be designed to reflect the characteristics of each subject; thus, multiple choice, essay, and fill-in-the-blank items should be kept in the test. Hence, the modern version of the NCEE contains multiple types of items. The second aspect had to do with the standardization of the scoring system. Before establishing a standardized scoring procedure, scoring was undertaken manually each year by local high school teachers. Starting in 1986, with the help of international testing experts, particularly experts at ETS, Chinese testing experts started to produce scanning machines suitable for reading Chinese. Since 1992, machine-based scoring has been widely used in various standardized tests in China.

In 1989, the Chinese Ministry of Education distributed a document (Ed89-001) titled "The implementing plan to establish a standardized scoring system for the National College Entrance Exam" to the whole nation in which the administration of the new form of NCEE was made mandatory. The document introduced detailed instructions on procedures of standardizing item format, test administration, and scoring, and symbolized the official recognition of using standardized tests in the Chinese national examination system (Yang, 2000). China sees the reform of its educational testing system as a part of the national reform of modern science and technology and as a necessary action in shortening the educational gap between China and Western countries.

Since the 1990s, the NCEE has become increasingly aptitude driven, and the test format has become more similar to general ability tests such as the SAT. Multiple-choice items constitute more than 50% of test items in each subject. The rest of the items include essay and fill-in-the-blank items. Special testing organizations were formed in each local area under the administration of the National Ministry of Education to professionalize the testing procedure. At the national level, item banks were created for various kinds of standardized tests (the NCEE and other standardized tests such as a national accounting examination, a national bar examination, and a Chinese language proficiency test for non-Chinese speakers). A professional evaluation of test difficulty was conducted after each year's testing, and testing experts adopted modern testing theories to monitor test items for appropriateness. Moreover, scanning machines were widely used in scoring multiple-choice items.

Thus, during its existence, the NCEE has evolved and become more adequately standardized and comparable with standardized tests administered in other countries. The most recent large-scale modification, during the summer of 2002, is referred to as the *3 + X System*. The new NCEE includes only four subtests: Chinese, mathematics, English, and one of several comprehensive tests, depending on the track a student chooses (China Education and Research Network, 2001). Accordingly, the 2002 modification allows the examination time to be reduced from 3 days to 2.

Although the format and the content of the NCEE are changing, the purposes of the test and its role in students' lives have not changed. These few days generally have a tremendous impact on the lives of millions of students. For many teenagers, especially those living in rural areas, a high score on the NCEE is almost their only chance to change their life paths. For them, the amount of knowledge they have obtained, supposedly reflected in their scores, becomes less important than the scores per se. Both teachers and students are under intense pressure to invest long hours preparing for the exam with test-related materials, such as exams used in previous years (Seeberg, 2000). Given the limited capacity of the Chinese higher education system, only 25% of high school students can enroll in college (around 5% of all Chinese 18- to 21-year-olds). Given the importance of the NCEE in students' lives, it is referred to as the most competitive and, undoubtedly, the most important exam in China (Seeberg, 2000).

Recently, standardized tests have faced new criticisms from both psychologists and the public for their influential roles in people's lives and the limited validity of these tests in predicting future performance. More and more people are concerned about the overuse of standardized tests in people's everyday lives. However, despite this criticism, under government leadership, China is marching into a new era of using standardized tests as the major criteria in selecting the best of its vast human resources.

STANDARDIZED ACHIEVEMENT TESTING IN FRANCE: EVER OR NEVER?

French psychologist Alfred Binet (1857–1911) is often considered the father of standardized testing, and an updated edition of his test of intelligence, known in the United States as the Stanford-Binet–IV (Thorndike, Hagen, & Sattler, 2003), is still one of the most widely used intelligence tests in the world. Yet standardized tests[4] are not widely used in the French public educational system today, and there is no equivalent to the commercially produced standardized tests, such as the SAT, used in the U.S. (OECD, 1996).

For the broader student population, the key to graduation from high school and access to higher education is, and has been since 1808, the *Baccalauréat*. The percentage of students obtaining the *Baccalauréat* in a given age cohort has increased from 3% in 1945, to 25% in 1975, and 62% in 2000 (http://www.education.gouv.fr). Here, a detailed description of the *Baccalauréat* is presented, followed by a description of current entrance policies to higher education institutions. The sketch is completed by a discussion of the future of standardized testing in France.

---

[4]Standardized ability tests are used, but primarily in psychiatric evaluations and personnel assesment in the military.

Since 1808, graduation from high school has been sanctioned by the *Baccalauréat*, which once opened the doors to the job market, but is increasingly seen primarily as the required passport to higher education, which in turn gives access to the professional world. In June of 1808, 31 candidates took and passed the *Baccalauréat*, a series of oral exams in Greek & Latin literature, impersonal rhetoric, history, geography, and philosophy. In 1830, a written component was added and candidates were given the option of writing an essay or translating a classic author from Latin or Greek to French. Since 1968, both a technical and a general *Baccalauréat* have been administered, and in 1985 a professional *Baccalauréat* was created. There are currently eight different technological exams (clerical science and technologies, industrial science and technologies, laboratory sciences and technologies, medical/social sciences and techniques, food-processing sciences and technologies, agronomy and environmental sciences and technologies, music and dance, and hotel trade), and three different general series (economy and social studies, literary, and science). In 2000, 54% of students passed a general *Baccalauréat*, 28% passed the technical version, and 18% were enrolled in professional training.

In France, the first 9 years of schooling are general. To prepare for these different versions of the *Baccalauréat*, students are asked, at the end of grade 9, to select an exam to prepare for and are divided correspondingly into groups during grades 10 to 12. For example, a student interested and proficient in sciences might choose to prepare a scientific *Baccalauréat* and would study math and sciences predominantly during grades 10 to 12, whereas a student who decides to prepare a literary *Baccalauréat* would devote more time to studying literature and languages.

Thus, the *Baccalauréat* is a national curriculum-based oral and written exam that takes place in two stages: an examination in French language and literature at the end of grade 11 (*Baccalauréat de français*), and examinations in other subject matters at the end of grade 12, for a total of nine to 10 compulsory exams and up to two optional ones for each student. In addition, in the general literary and economy/social studies series, there is also a 1.5-hour written exam in "knowledge of science" at the end of grade 11, and a written exam in mathematics and computer science for students in the literary series.

The exams are administered in students' schools on the same day nationwide but time allocations and content requirements for both the general and technological examinations vary widely across the 30 educational districts licensed to supervise the administration of the exam. Successful completion of the *Baccalauréat* requires a certain number of points, and the respective weight of a given exam for the overall number of points varies. For example, all students have an exam in philosophy, but the weight is a coefficient of 2 for students in the scientific series and a coefficient of 7 in the literary series. In addition, even within one type of exam (e.g., the literary examination) the specific exam topics vary from one region of France to the next. In short, even though the generic term *Baccalauréat* is used to designate the required exam for high school graduation, the specific exam taken by any one student can be very different from that of another student.

For example, students preparing for a *Baccalauréat* in science have compulsory exams in mathematics, physics and chemistry, life science, ecology or engineering, history and geography, two foreign languages, philosophy, physical education, and an oral presentation of a year-long group project. In addition, students can choose one or two optional exams among the following: foreign language, regional language, Latin, ancient Greek, arts, physical education, and social and cultural practices. Similarly, students preparing for a literary *Baccalauréat* are expected to take written, oral, and practical exams, but in the content areas of the humanities (literature, philosophy, and languages).

As previously noted, to pass the *Baccalauréat*, a candidate must collect a fixed minimum points, and points beyond the minimum count toward honors (of which there are four levels: honors, high honors, very high honors, and *cum laude*). A candidate who is more than a few points from passing must repeat a year of schooling before taking the exam again; those who are close to the minimum requirement are given the oppurtunity to retake two exams.

Higher education in France is characterized by a great variety of institutions, with the majority of students attending either a public university or a public or private professional school. In the year 2000, 78.4% of students who passed the *Baccalauréat* in June enrolled in a course of higher education the following September. In the year 2000, approximately 15% of students who enrolled in a first-year university program dropped out. The probability that a student who completed the first year and enrolled to pursue a second year would obtain a diploma (DEUG) was 77.6%. However, the probability of obtaining this 2-year diploma in 2 years was only 45.7%, and the probability varies widely depending on the type of *Baccalauréat* obtained. Students with a technological *Baccalauréat* only had a 38.1% probability of obtaining a diploma, as compared to 92.3% for students with a scientific *Baccalauréat* (ftp://trf.education.gouv.fr/pub/edutel/dpd/rers02/chap8.pdf). France and other European countries are now moving toward a unified university system with three level of diplomas: bachelor's (3 years), master's (5 years) and doctorate.

Universities are professionally oriented and students are required to choose a specific course of study from the onset (e.g., law, economy, psychology, engineering). To enroll at a university, applicants must hold a *Baccalauréat* or the equivalent, or must have the national diploma providing access to university studies (*Diplôme d'Accès aux Études Universitaires*, DAEU). There is no *numerus clausus* rule, and a slot in a university is guaranteed to anyone meeting this requirement (there is no guarantee of a place in one's preferred area of study, however). The exceptions are the medical schools, which select a limited number of candidates based on an exam at the end of the first year of study at a university.

Students can also attend public and private institutions, which provide higher vocational education under the supervision of various ministries. Such education takes the form of short courses (technological, commercial, or paramedical training, and so on) or long courses of 3 or more years after the *Baccalauréat* (political science, engineering, commerce and management, veterinary science, legal skills, architecture, telecommunications, and art). The shorter courses are offered by general and technological *lycées* (schools) and so-called higher technical sections (STS); the latter can prepare students in two years for the *Brevet de Technicien Supérieur* (BTS). Longer courses are offered by the *Grandes Ecoles* (literally "big schools"), which can be private (as is the case for most business schools) or public (as is the case for teacher preparation and most engineering schools). To enter a *Grande Ecole*, students must, after obtaining the *Baccalauréat*, prepare for the entrance examination in a 1- to 2-year preparatory course. Admission to this preparatory course is itself subject to scrutiny of the applicant's school record by a committee of teachers. After the preparatory course, the entry examination is organized by the *Grandes Ecoles* themselves and admission to these institutions is very selective. Public *Grandes Ecoles* organize an entrance exam to ensure that all students have a threshold level of knowledge and skills, whereas private *Grandes Ecoles*, which operate on a *numerus clausus* basis, organize competitions to rank students and accept top candidates depending on the number of open slots. In addition to this exam, the selection criteria and methods vary from one school to another and are heavily based on a given school's approach to candidate selection.

The current system of the *Baccalauréat* is complex and time consuming, and each June the media have one or more scandal stories to report on the subjectivity of oral examinations or the dangers of essays graded by a single examiner. However, this system of graduation and selection has been in place for close to 200 years and there is virtually no debate regarding its necessity or a need for a fundamental reform. The graduation/entrance system is very unlikely to be substantially modified in favor of shorter, standardized testing practices. It is generally agreed that long written exams and shorter oral ones are necessary to fully assess students' knowledge and understanding of the use of that knowledge. Essays and oral exams are also the norm at the university level. Most students in France are likely to encounter only one multiple-choice test in their lives, and that is if they take a driver's license exam. Thus, it is likely that the system will maintain two forms of examination. There are few, if any, voices arguing for a movement toward a multiple-choice standardized format of examination.

The debate around entrance to higher education is livelier, and there is disagreement on the issue of restricting entrance to public universities to deal with the phenomenon of "massification" (the combination of higher enrollment and the inclusion of social groups not previously attending higher education; Phelps, Dietrich, Phillips, & McCormack, 2000). Currently the idea is to constrain the inflow of freshmen by imposing selection criteria such as grades obtained on the *Baccalauréat*. Once again, there is no discussion of introducing a national SAT-type standardized test for these purposes. The trend of "being more selective," as exemplified by the use of interviews in highly competitive university programs, is toward more qualitative decision criteria rather than a move from curriculum-based exams to shorter, minimum-competency examinations. Private institutions of higher education, such as business schools, are in some cases using standardized tests as a part of their admission battery and are likely to continue to do so.

CHILE: RELATIVELY YOUNG BUT VERY PROMINENT

Standardized testing has had a short but influential life in Chilean education. A national system of standardized testing was first implemented in the late 1960s, alongside the rapid expansion of enrollment in secondary and higher education. In 1967, the *Consejo de Rectores de las Universidades Chilenas*[5] (hereafter CRUCH) established a national test to select students for undergraduate higher education: the *Prueba de Aptitud Académica* ("Test of Academic Aptitude," hereafter PAA). The PAA was designed to replace the old *bachillerato* (Cox, 1993). Modeled after the French *Baccalauréat*, the *bachillerato* was intended for an educational system that admitted exclusively the elite of its students to higher education. Therefore, it was not conceived as a system suited to large-scale implementation and was not appropriate for a nationwide system of standardized testing. The new, revised PAA, on the other hand, is based on the SAT model and, therefore, is more appropriate to a growing university system of higher education. In addition, although there is no national test that certifies graduation from high school, the PAA has been used to gauge the relative success of secondary schools. Although the PAA is not used as a final graduation exam, it is still required for numerous jobs in the labor market.

The PAA came to serve a university system that was quite homogeneous and almost fully run by the state. Still, Chilean universities were quite protective of their academic autonomy.

---

[5]The CRUCH was established in 1954. Its mission is to provide, by way of its affiliated institutions, undergraduate and graduate education, scientific research, and cultural extension. More information can be found at www.cruch.cl.

When the PAA was introduced, higher education in Chile consisted of eight universities, two public and six private. The two oldest universities were, and still are, the country's most prestigious: the *Universidad de Chile* (hereafter UCH), established by the state in 1842, and the *Universidad Católica de Chile*[6] (hereafter PUC), established by the Catholic Church in 1888 as a counterpart to the secular, state-run UCH. Although the majority of the universities were private in name, the state was the main force behind the scenes, both politically and economically. Each university depended on state funding and was controlled by the same set of state regulations[7]. Since its introduction in Chile, the PAA has remained the most important test of admission for Chilean universities. The university system, however, has undergone huge changes since 1967. In the wake of these transformations, a new test is currently being developed to replace the PAA[8].

Although its history is brief, the PAA survived several intense periods of both societal and educational reforms. Its first years elapsed during a period of rapid expansion of the higher educational system in Chile, state-sponsored social reform, and great political turmoil. That period came to a close in 1973, with the coup d'état of Augusto Pinochet. Because the universities were a long-established hotbed of political activism and socialization, the military government put them under its charge and supervised them very closely. They decreased state funding for public institutions, transformed the UCH and UTE regional campuses into smaller regional public universities, and allowed and promoted the development of new private institutions (Brunner, 1994).

The PAA survived all these transformations and evolved from an admission test for eight universities, with the classic goals of liberal universities—teaching, research, and cultural extension—to an admission test serving 25 institutions diverse in size, capacity, political and ideological attitudes, and orientation. The PAA lived on for three reasons. First, it had a great deal of legitimacy and was considered a good predictor of academic achievement by the educational establishment. Moreover, taking the PAA was an established ritual for university applicants from the more prestigious traditional sector, so it was natural for the new institutions to require PAA scores as a part of their admission processes. Second, since 1981, the state linked some of its funding to the ability of the institutions to recruit students with high PAA scores. Stated simply, the higher the PAA scores of the recruited students in a given university, the higher that university's level of state funding. Finally, the PAA cost the new universities nothing, because it was administered by the public sector; students, however, paid a fee to take the exam.

Admission to traditional universities depended on students' PAA scores as well as their GPA. Although a minimum score on the PAA was required to apply to any of the traditional universities, the universities had some limited autonomy in determining the cut-off PAA scores for admission to their programs. Moreover, the institutions established the weight they gave to PAA scores as compared to GPA in making admission decisions. They could also determine which subject-tests to take into consideration and how they were weighted. As a result, the same students applying to the same academic major in different institutions could find that the same application information would be treated in different ways and gain or deny them an admission to a particular university.

---

[6]Subsequently named Pontoficia *Universidad Catolica de Chile*.

[7]In addition to the UCH, the state administered another large public university, the *Universidad Technical del Estado* (hereafter UTE).

[8]The PAA is administered in December because university entrance results are available in January and the universities start their academic year in March.

The PAA was designed to test academic aptitude and achievement, specifically in the domain of mathematical and linguistic knowledge. In Chile, the PAA was referred to as an academic *ability* test and scores on the PAA were considered to be good predictors of academic success at the university level. In addition to the aptitude tests, content-based tests measured knowledge in six subject areas: math, biology, physics, chemistry, social sciences, and Chilean history.

The democratic period following Pinochet's demise brought changes to the educational system (Brunner & Cox, 1993; Cox, 1993; Muga & Brunner, 2001) and the need to a adjust the PAA to new educational programs became evident. In 2001 the CRUCH reached an agreement to replace the old PAA with a new test of admission, the *Sistema de Ingreso a la Educación Superior* (hereafter SIES [CRUCH, 2002a, 2002b])[9]. A team of professionals based at the PUC and the UCH worked on the design of the new test, which would involve several drastic modifications of the PAA. First, the SIES would be not only a test of abilities but also a test of knowledge. Second, it would cover material taught during each year of secondary education, rather than the first only. Third, in addition to the traditional multiple-choice format, the SIES would use a multiple-choice format with graded responses (i.e., the format in which different options approximate the right answer to different degrees, and receive different scores accordingly). Whereas the traditional multiple-choice format would be used to test basic levels of knowledge, the multiple-choice format with graded responses would be used to test higher levels of knowledge (Rosas, Flotts, & Saragoni, 2002). Fourth, item construction would involve the use of item response theory (IRT), a methodology not used with the PAA. Fifth, it would include four compulsory tests: language and communication, math, sciences, history and social sciences, and advanced optional subtests in the sciences test.

The SIES was originally scheduled to debut in December 2003. However, its application was postponed, as it met with some criticism that spurred vigorous political debate. A large part of the criticism of the SIES focused on the impact it will inevitably have on secondary education. Specifically, critics claimed that the SIES would limit freedom of teaching, as it determines what content is relevant to such critical evaluation as the test of admission to universities. In addition, SIES critics argued that, because of the range of content covered by the test, the exam would prohibit students from specializing in a specific area or areas not covered by the SIES (e.g., the arts and religion). Moreover, critics suggested that it would generate greater inequalities, as public high schools lack the resources to cover all the content included in the SIES. Finally, it has been argued that the SIES would force teachers to focus solely on preparing students for the SIES and not on transmitting subject-relevant content (Dussaillant, 2002; Eyzaguirre & Foulon, 2002; Fontaine, 2002).

In response to these criticisms, the SIES development team argued that the implementation of the SIES would benefit secondary education. First, they said it would give more value to the content actually taught in high school and, consequently, to secondary teachers. Thus, it would bring students previously focused on the training of the PAA back to the classroom. Second, proponents of the SIES claimed that, as shown by some of the tests of knowledge employed by the Ministry of Education, testing knowledge instead of testing general aptitudes yields lower differences between students matriculating from public and private institutions. Conversely, it is claimed that preserving the PAA would ensure the maintenance of the gender and social inequality characteristic of the test. Regarding the problem of breadth, SIES proponents argued that both universities and students would benefit from recruiting applicants with a larger knowledge base (Bravo & Manzi, 2003; Rosas, personal communication, 2003).

---

[9]Official information on the SIES can be found online at www.sies.cl.

However, the SIES was never implemented as planned. In 2005, senior high school students were preparing to take the new *Prueba de Selección Universitaria* (hereafter, PSU), has a compulsory component that includes tests of Spanish language and mathematics, and was envisioned as a transitional test between the PSU and a new reformed test. The PSU voluntary component which includes tests of sciences and social sciences. Although still resisted by some critics, the PSU incorporates several of the proposals made by the SIES project. Among the most remarkable: It is thought of as a knowledge test and it covers material taught during the duration of high school. Notwithstanding these changes, most of the structure of the system of admission to universities maintains the framework used for the PAA; that is, although the test is administered by the UCH, most of the universities, both public and private, weight is different components independently.

Of great importance is that the PAA versus SIES debate has brought to the forefront the issue of the nature and content of the secondary school curriculum. As noted by several players involved in the debate, including the Minister of Education and the PUC Chancellor (Correa, 2003; Rosso, 2002), discussion of the SIES triggered a conversation on the structure and content of the curriculum introduced by the recent Chilean Educational Reform. All these topics go beyond the issue of standardized testing. However, without question, the final form of the new test of admission to Chilean universities will depend on the agreements reached by the institutions involved in discussing the new test on the larger relevant philosophical, educational, sociological, and pedagogical levels.

STANDARDIZED ACHIEVEMENT TESTING IN RUSSIA: TO BE OR NOT TO BE?

As is true for any social science, Russian psychology has had its glorious and its dark moments. One such dark moment is directly relevant to the discussion in this chapter and concerns the pressure standardized testing, in fact, all psychological testing, experienced in the early 1930s. Specifically, in 1936, educational psychologists' work came under fire. A decree by the Central Committee of All-Russia Communist Party (Bol'shevikov), known as the Decree of Pedology[10], criticized the social impact of their work, condemning those psychologists who had engaged in pedological and/or testological studies. Given that almost all work in educational psychology in the 1920s was called "pedology," one can imagine the consequences of this decree. All forms of intelligence testing were forbidden. Numerous trumped-up charges, including cosmopolitism (a tendency to analyze and refer to Western theories), idealism, and being an enemy of the Soviet people, severely complicated the lives of some psychologists and geneticists in high official positions[11]. Along with pedology, social psychology, psychotherapy, and behavioral genetic research were prohibited in the USSR for

---

[10]Pedology was the term used in the 1920s for research and testing in child and educational psychology.

[11]For example, Sergei L. Rubinstein, one of the most famous figures in Soviet psychology was awarded the State Premium of the USSR in 1941, but was fired in 1951 from his position as chair of the division of psychology in the philosophy department of Moscow State University. He was charged with cosmopolitism and forced to defend his research in front of various party and state committees (Zhdan, 1993).

The fate of Dr. Levit is an more unfortunate example. As director of the Medical Biological Institute in Moscow, he was severly criticized in 1936 in the first round of Vavilov–Lysenko discussions. (This meeting was an example of the idealogically driven struggle against "cosmopolitism," where genetics was announced to be a bourgeois science and prohibited.) Levit was subjected to repression in 1937, and imprisoned. He died there.

more than 40 years. Marxism was imposed on all research as the only possible philosophical underpinning for any science, including the study of thinking.

Needless to say, that testing was effectively eliminated from the list of officially approved professional tools and research topics did not aid the development of psychometrics and testology in Soviet Russia. Yet, testing never quite left Russian psychology. For example, testing was implicitly present in clinical psychology. Clinical psychologists in their diagnostic practice always used "experimental methods," which, in reality, were analogous to subtests of intellectual assessments (classification, analogies, vocabulary, and so on). The interpretation of these results, however, was done in the context of understanding generalization and categorization processes, and motivational and goal-oriented regulation of activity (Rubinstein, 1970; Zeigarnik, 1962).

In addition, the prohibition on testing did not mean that Soviet psychologists did not use diagnostic tasks of children's intellectual development. These tasks were designed, however, as criterion tasks or educational tasks, not as level-oriented tests (Gurevich & Gorbacheva, 1992; Podgoretskaya, 1980; Talyzina, 1981; Zaporozhets, 1986).

Testing "officially" reappeared in Soviet/Russian psychology in the 1960s and 1970s, with the first study using tests of intelligence performed at Sanct-Petersburg State University (Palei, 1974). In the late 1960s and 1970s, a number of Soviet/Russian psychologists used tests of intelligence in their research studies (e.g., Ananiev, Pansiuk, Iliasheva—as cited in Burlachuk & Morozov, 2000). Since then, Soviet/Russian psychologists have adapted and created many psychological tests and testing is widely used in experimental and clinical psychological research[12].

The absence of the tradition of testing in social sciences was only made clearer in the context of examinations administered for school diplomas and entrance to higher education institutions. In brief, the situation can be characterized by one sentence: There was NO *standardized* achievement testing at either school graduation or university entry. This is not to say that examinations were haphazard (they were carefully orchestrated and well structured), informal (they were very formal), or not stressful (they were very stressful!). Rather, they were not *standardized,* and every school and every higher education institution had its significant say in how educational rewards were distributed and admission decisions made.

This brief historical note sets the stage for the discussion to follow, which is one of both fascination and resistance caused by the recent introduction of the so-called *Единый Государственный Экзамен* (Common State Examination, CSE or ЕГЭ in Russian; www. ege.ru)—a federally administered, nationwide achievement-based exam that was conceived to serve as both a school graduation and a college entrance exam. The CSE typically consists of two mandatory components—math and Russian—and a number of optional subjects that can be included in the total scores at the students' request. The exam is administered in one day across participating districts, and students take the CSE, at this pilot stage, in their own classrooms. Participating school districts are given the months of June and July to administer the exam, but there is some flexibility in selecting a specific date. There are multiple versions of the CSE per 20 to 30 students, and the versions are mixed so that cheating is

---

[12]Although there are many translated tests of intelligence, there is only one test (WISC) that was properly adapted to and standardized for use with the Russian population. The standardization of the WISC in 1973 (Panasiuk, 1973) made available a reliable and valid instrument for diagnostic tasks. It is important to note that, although the test itself has been reprinted many times (by a company called IMATON), it has not been restandardized since the early 1970s.

difficult. The CSE is proctored, but at this pilot stage, the proctoring is organized by the local educational authorities. The CSE includes three types of items: multiple choice, short answers, and open response. Multiple choice and short answer responses are analyzed in the Federal Testing Center, but local experts analyze open response items. After administration, the exams are sent to a central location, where the data are processed and prepared for scoring. The results of the CSE can be appealed and each region in which the CSE is administered has an appeal board whose charge is to review complaints. All in all, the structure and procedures closely resemble that of ETS in the United States.

It is assumed that, for the purposes of school matriculation, the CSE score is transformed into a grade and this grade is then entered as a part of the school diploma. When treated as a component of the admission process into higher education institutions, the CSE score determines not only acceptance, but also eligibility for and level of financial support. Clearly, the stakes of the CSE are very high.

If a school district from which the appliant graduates does not participate in the pilot, or the applicant took time off between graduating from high school and applying to college, the applicant can take the CSE at the higher education institution s/he is applying to (if this instiuttion participates in the pilot).

The pilot administration of the CSE was launched in the spring of 2001, and by the fall of 2002, 400,000 Russian school graduates had taken it and 126 Russian higher education institutions had used the CSE scores in their admission processes. The pilot has been steadily expanding since then, and in 2004, 982,000 people took the CSE, and 946 higher education institutions accepted the CSE results as a part of their admission process. The Russian Ministry of Education and Science monitors the pilot; it reviews the results every year and makes an annual decision whether to continure the pilot or not. The decision to continue the pilot in 2005 was made on October 13, 2004, and, at the time of this writing (fall 2005), the final report on the results of the 2005 testing had not yet been released nor the decision with regard to the 2006 testing announced (http://ege.edu.ru/PortalWeb/index.jsp).

Let us start with the positive aspects of this innovation. What is good about the CSE? First, the CSE was introduced to the Russian public as a way to overcome the subjective machinery of both school graduation and higher education institution entrance examinations. The idea is to put everyone on the same scale, to obtain comparable measures of everyone's performance, to avoid the subjective nature of grading, and to combat corruption. However, the realization of these ideals is far from fulfilled. Specifically, even with the CSE in place, there is a lot of room for passing candidates for admission to certain institutions "behind the scene," as CSE scores contribute only partially to admission decisions.

Another reason for the introduction of the CSE was to reward high-achieving students from provincial towns and small villages across the vast territory of Russia for their scores on the CSE. The argument is that, were it not for the CSE, it would have been quite difficult for students from remote areas, especially economically disadvantaged students, to gain acceptance to the more prestigious higher education institutions in Russia, as the majority of these institutions require the presence of the student during entrance examinations held at the institution. Clearly, for parents in a country in which, according to World Bank estimates, approximately 58% of the population lives below the poverty line, the task of sending their daughter to Moscow or St. Petersburg for a month to take the entrance examinations presents a serious, if not impossible, financial challenge.

Third, for the first time the country received a mean to compare the quality of education as captured by the results of the CSE across Russia. Immediately after the preliminary announcements of the results of the CSE-2005, the newspaper *Izvestia* published an article titled "CSE in the regions of Russia: Where do they teach you best?" (Известия , 29 июня 2005). Of interest is that the scores of students from Moscow, especially of those from highly prestigious schools, are far from being the best. Similarly, the results were not impressive from students from St. Petersburg. Overall, the best results were shown by students from Chuvashia (Chuvas Autonomic Republic), Marii El (Marii El Autonomic Republic), and Mordovia (the Republic of Mordovia). The worst results were shown by students from Dagestan (the Republic of Dagestan), and the Rostov, Magadan, and Sakhalin regions.

There are many more points of criticism than support for the use of the CSE. Why is the CSE so criticized? First, the most serious criticism relates to its multiple-choice format. The Russian educational system, in the 300+ years of its "official" existence, has never dealt with this format on a large scale. Thus, the first reaction of the public was to label the format primitive and to refer to the CSE as a "stupidifying" exam.

Second, both teachers and parents criticize the substitution of an attitude of obtaining knowledge driven by curiosity and intellectual desire with a cynical view toward obtaining a good score. The mass media debates on this issue are endless.

Third, in response to the "threat" of the CSE, publishers have printed numerous applied texts aimed at preparing students for the CSE. There are thousands of such books, which take up most of the space in the school-relevant sections of bookstores. In all of these, the graduates who face the inevitability of the CSE are referred to as "our poor children."

Fourth, one of the features of the dissolution of the old Russian educational system, which was almost completely unified and standardized across the country, is a huge apparent differentiation of the quality of teaching and, correspondingly, levels of achievement of Russian school students in different regions of the country. Thus, the idea of having the same height pole for everyone, when the conditions of growing are so vastly different, is quite, problematic. For example, when considering the use of CSE scores in its admission procedures, the Moscow State Linguistic University (MSLU), the flagship of foreign language education in Russia, conducted a survey of foreign language achievement in different regions of Russia. The results were highly diverse, suggesting incredible variation in pedagogical qualification and strategies in the domain of foreign languages across Russia (Известия, June 14, 2002). Based on this survey, MSLU decided not to rely on CSE scores but to continue using their old-fashioned system of entrance examinations.

Fifth, there are a number of critical comments regarding the ability of the CSE to identify and promote real talent. The concern here is that the memory-oriented (rather than the analyses- or syntheses-oriented) content of the CSE will disadvantage creative students on the examination. Correspondingly, many leaders of prestigious higher education institutions actively oppose the installation of the CSE, arguing that their institutions are interested in developing professionals characterized by flexible and creative minds rather than "memory machines" (Известия, May 24, 2002).

Finally, it is of interest to consider the opinions of the "victims" of the CSE. A survey of school graduates conducted through the CSE Web site indicated that 26% of respondents found the idea of the CSE appalling; 21% thought the decision to take the CSE should be voluntary and not mandated by the federal educational system; 14% thought that the idea of the CSE might work, but it needs to be piloted more; 11.4% thought that the very idea of the CSE was stupid; 11.4% thought it was too early to make any conclusions and more piloting should be done; 10.8% stated that they did not have any information about the examination; 3.2% supported the CSE completely, and 2.2% preferred not to answer (as published in Известия, July 19, 2002).

Similarly, the opinion of the parents of the "victims" are also rather negative. As compared with the data from September 2003, by June 2005, the number of Russians with a positive attitute toward the CSE decreased from 23% to 11%. Conversely, the number of people with a clear negative attitude constantly increases. Of interest is that many who expressed a dislike for the CSE cited the presence of corruption at local sites of administration of the exam as a reason for their opinion (Известия, June 22, 2005). In other words, the very reason that was used as a major motivator for the introduction of the CSE to the Russian educational system appears to be a chief concern in the willingness of the Russian public to accept the innovation.

To summarize, the amount of turmoil produced by the introduction of a standardized achievement test in Russia, even at the pilot stage, can be explained by the interplay of multiple factors. The two most obvious ones: (a) There is no cultural tradition of standardized testing either in psychology or education in Russia and, therefore, such a large-scale innovation creates great tension among both the developers and users of the CSE, and (b) The Russian educational system is not quite sure how to use the CSE score. Thus, whether the CSE will survive the experiment and whether it will be a factor in the future of the Russian educational system has yet to be determined.

GENERAL DISCUSSION

In this chapter we briefly reviewed the applications of standardized testing of achievement and aptitude in four very different educational systems (see Table 9.1). Not surprisingly, there is no standard with regard to standardized testing in different countries. Although Chile and China have developed and promoted the implementation of national systems of standardized testing, France and Russia have been more reluctant to do so. The Chinese educational system is older and significantly more massive than the Chilean one; China is a communist society, Chile is a capitalistic one; and still both countries seem to be moving in a similar direction. France's reluctance to use standardized testing is quite paradoxical considering that it is in France where modern intelligence testing originated. Although those same tests blossomed in the United States, they found a restricted application in the French system. Although Russia has shown a similar cautious attitude toward standardized testing, this attitude originated in a different set of conditions, more related to political than cultural factors.

Differences notwithstanding, it quite surprising that the implementation of standardized testing seems to have some commonalities: As illustrated by Russia, Chile, and China, it seems that when applied, a combination of quantitative plus language-and content-based tests seems to fit the needs of different systems of education, which is reasonable, as the mastery of mathematical knowledge and literacy are the natural goals of modern education. Yet there are differences, as well: Whereas Chile intends to align standardized testing with the secondary curriculum, China is moving in the opposite direction. These differences are not only of policy but also of the underlying philosophies of testing and its practical applications.

Summarizing the material presented in this chapter, the first and most obvious comment that must be made is that the need for and, correspondingly, the use of standardized testing in the four countries is very different. In China, there is a need for a selection tool that will sort out the brightest of its huge population for a comparatively limited number of placements in higher education institutions. In Chile, the issue is matching—Who "deserves" to go to what school? In France, everyone can get higher education and, moreover, get it virtually for free. Correspondingly, there is no need to bother with the expense and headache of developing and administering the machinery of standardized testing. Of course, there is still a question of professional orientation and meeting the needs of the labor market, but these questions can be addressed in many other more humane and individualized ways than standardized testing. Finally, in Russia, the idea of introducing standardized testing, although masked by the discussion of "fairness" of admission, in fact surfaced in the context of the financial reform of Russian education. The Russian educational system is currently transitioning from being free and available to everyone at all levels to a system that needs a mechanism to fund it, because the state cannot afford the whole bill. Specifically, economical analyses of the current situation of higher education in Russia indicate that the system has available, considering all federal, local, and private sources of financial support, only ~30% of what it needs to support the standard-oriented level of education (*Известия*, July 5, 2002). So, the students (or rather their parents) need to be charged to keep the system going. But the question is how? How can the issues of tuition versus financial support be determined in a country in which half of the population lives below the poverty line? That is where standardized testing can be very helpful—charge the parents for the scores of their children! In short, in all of the discussed examples, standardized testing is either banned or promoted to solve other than straightforward educational or individual differences issues. In the three countries in which standardized testing is widely used, it is used as a tool to address specific societal problems.

There is no assessment, especially high-stake assessment, that is independent of instruction (Sternberg, 1998). In Russia, for example, the introduction of the CSE poses a threat to the established system of early gifted differentiation for talented children. For years now, there have been profile schools—schools that stressed education in a given domain (e.g., foreign languages, mathematics, literature) and produced very high-achieving graduates in these specialized domains. It did not mean that the children were underperforming in other subject matters—simply that more emphasis was placed on the domain that constituted the profile of a school (for a review, see Grigorenko, 2000). Given that the CSE score includes scores on all mandatory components of the examination, it will be quite difficult for schools for gifted children to maintain a traditional emphasis on specialization; the schools will need to spend a lot of time on areas other than their profile subjects, simply to make sure that their talented and gifted will be still competitive for high-prestige institutions (where teaching is very subject oriented).

In Chile, the development of the SIES seems to be resulting in stimulating talks about yet another educational reform. Many researchers (e.g., Sternberg, 1998) have argued that assessment cannot be changed without changing instruction and the other way around—consider the impact of accountability reform in the United States on the content of classroom pedagogical activities! Thus, any installation of a statewide, standardized examination inevitably results in relevant changes in pedagogy. Even in Russia, where the CSE has been around for only 3 years, teachers need to revise their methods of teaching to prepare their students for the test. Everything is done by the test and for the test.

Finally, there is certain hypocrisy inherent in the idea of standardized achievement testing when applied in diverse educational environments. The ideological basis of standardized achievement testing is to provide everyone with a chance to succeed: By definition, the content of the test, the testing procedure, its scoring and, therefore, its results, are objectified. The idea, then, is that whatever variation in scores is observed is all due to variation in students' performance and is directly reflective of their aptitudes. But what do we say about all other sources of variation in students' performance? In addition, what do we have to say about the idea of social justice, according to which everyone should be guaranteed a chance to obtain whatever education he or she desires? Can achievement be fairly assessed with standardized testing when the variation in teaching is great? It is not an easy question—and its answer captures the introduction of inequality even before the test, at the stage of test preparation! In other words, to prepare for the test, a child should attend a school in which he or she can get better prepared for the test. And thus the circle of inequalities starts.

In this chapter, we presented a series of sketches that exemplify the use of standardized achievement/aptitude tests in four different educational cultures. Although primarily through descriptive material, the chapter asserts that the use or lack of use of standardized tests is not a neutral event, at least in the four countries analyzed. This use is socially charged and can be understood and appreciated only in the context of a general analysis of an educational system that uses standardized tests. Although globalization of education seems to have made the educational systems of different countries more interconnected, the countries still develop specific, culturally grounded ways to select from and place their human resources. And, as we hope we have shown, there is no standard in doing this.

AUTHORS' NOTE

This research was supported by Grant R206R50001 from the Institute of Educational Sciences (formerly the Office of Educational Research and Improvement), U.S. Department of Education. Preparation of this report was supported by Grant R206R00001 from the same organization. Grantees undertaking such projects are encouraged to express freely their professional judgment. This article, therefore, does not necessarily represent the position or policies of the U. S. Department of Education, and no official endorsement should be inferred. We are thankful to Drs. Inna V. Ravich-Scherbo and Ricardo Rosas for their assistance with collecting relevant materials and Ms. Robyn Rissman for her helpful editorial comments. Correspondence should be sent to Elena L. Grigorenko, PACE Center, Yale University, Box 208358, New Haven, CT 06520-8358.

REFERENCES

Biggs, J. B. (1996). Western misperceptions of the Confucian-heritage learning culture. In D. A. Watkins & J. B. Biggs (Eds.), *The Chinese learner: Cultural, psychological and contextual influences* (pp. 45–68). Hong Kong and Melbourne: Comparative Education Centre and the Australian Council for Educational Research.

Bravo, D., & Manzi, J. (2003). *El SIES, la equidad y la elevación de los aprendizajes* [The SIES, equity and the improvement of learning]. Retrieved April 20, 2003, from www.sies.cl.

Brunner, J. (1966) Towards a theory of instruction. Cambridge, MA: Harvard University Press.

Brunner, J. J. (1994). *Educación superior: Chile en el contexto internacional comparado* [Higher education: Chile in the comparative international context]. [Work document No. 13/94]. Santiago, Chile: CPU.

Brunner, J. J., & Cox, C. (1993). *Dinámicas de transformación en el sistema educacional de Chile* [Dynamics of transformation in the educational system of Chile] [Education and Culture Series No. 38]. Santiago, Chile: FLACSO.

Burlachuk, L. F., & Morozov, S. N. (2000). *Slovar'-spravochnik po psikhodiagnostike* [*Psychometric dictionary*]. Sanct-Petersburg, Russia: Psychologia.

China Education and Research Network. (December, 2001). *Beijing to try new college entrance exam plan.* Beijing, China. http://www.edu.cn/20011212/3013800.shtml

Correa, R. (2003). *Entrevista a la Ministra de Educación Mariana Aylwin* [Interview with Secretary of Education Mariana Aylwin]. Retrieved April 20, 2003, from www.sies.cl.

Cox, C. (1993). *Chilean secondary education: Challenges and policies for the nineties.* (Education and Culture Series No. 39). Santiago, Chile: FLACSO.

CRUCH. (2002a). *Acuerdo del Consejo de Rectores de las Universidades Chilenas*, [Agreement of the Board of Chancellors of Chilean Universities]. Retrieved April 20, 2003, from www.sies.cl

CRUCH. (2002b). *Declaración pública del consejo de rectores* [Public Statement of the Board of Chancellors]. Retrieved April 20, 2003, from www.sies.cl.

Dussaillant, F. (2002). *El SIES: Su impacto en la calidad y libertad de la enseñanza*. [The SIES: Its impact on the quality and freedom of teaching] (Work document No. 333). Santiago, Chile: CEP.

Eyzaguirre, B., & Foulon, C. L. (2002). El SIES: Un proyecto prematuro [The SIES: A precipitate project]. *Estudios Publicos, 87*, 39–53.

Feng, Y. (1994 November). *From the Imperial Examination to the National College Entrance Examination: The dynamics of political centralism in china's educational enterprise*. Paper presented at the 19th Annual Meeting of the Association for the Study of Higher Education, Tucson, AZ.

Fontaine, A. (2002). *Peligro en el SIES* [Danger in the SIES]. (Work document No. 332). Santiago, Chile: CEP.

Franke, W. (1960). *The reform and abolition of the traditional Chinese examination system*. Cambridge, MA: Harvard University Press.

Grigorenko, E. L. (2000). Russian gifted education in math and science: Tradition and transformation. In K. A. Heller, F. J. Monks, R. J. Sternberg, & R. F. Subotnik (Eds.), *International handbook of research and development of giftedness and talent* (pp. 729–736) Amsterdam: Elsevier.

Gurevich, K. M., & Gorbacheva, E. I (1992). *Umstvennoe razvitie shkol'nikov: Kriterii i normy [School students' cognitive development: Criteria and norms]*. Moscow: Znanie.

Heyneman, S. P., & Fagerlind, I. (1985). *University examinations and standardized testing: Principles, experience, and policy options*. Paper presented at A Seminar on the Uses of Standardized Tests and Selection Examinations, Beijing, China.

Luo, J., & Wendel, F. C. (1999). Preparing for college: Senior high school education in China. *NASSP Bulletin, 83*, 57–68.

Martin, M. O., Mullis, I.V.S., Gonzalez, E. J., Gregory, K. D., Smith, T. A., Chrostowski, S. J., Garder, R. A., & O'Connor, K. M. (2001). TIMSS *1999 International Science Report*. Chestnut Hill, MA: TIMSS International Study Center.

Miyazaki, I. (1976). *China's examination hell: The Civil Service Examinations of Imperial China*. New York: Weatherhill.

Muga, A., & Brunner, J. J. (2001). Chile: Políticas de educación superior 1990–1995 [Chile: Policies of higher education 1990–1995]. In R. K. Serna (Ed.), *Experiencias de reforma en la educación superior en América Latina* [Experiences of reform in higher education in Latin America] (pp. 181–234). Mexico City, México: Plaza y Valdés.

Mullis, I. V. S., Martin, M. O., Gonzalez, E. J., & Kennedy, A. M. (2003). *PIRLS 2001 International Report: IEA's study of reading literacy achievement in primary schools*. Chestnut Hill, MA: Boston College.

Organization for Economic Co-Operation and Development (1996). *Education at a glance: OECD indicators 1996, country profiles*. ftp://trf.education.gouv.fr/pub/edutel/dpd/rers02/chap8.pdf

Palei, I. M. (1974). K differentsial' no-psikhologicheskomu issledovaniyu studentov v svyazi s zadachami izucheniya potentsialov razvitiya vzroslogo cheloveka [Toward differential-psychological studies of students in the context of adult development]. *Sovremennye psikhologo-pedagogicheskie problemy vyshei shkoly, 2*, 133–143.

Phelps, R. P., Dietrich, G. L., Phillips, G., & McCormack, K. A. (2000). *Higher education: An international perspective*. Available online at http:www.math.nyu.edu/mfdd/breams/k12mc

Podgoretskaya, N.A. (1980). *Izuchenie priemov logicheskogo myshleniya u vzroslych [Studying strategies of logical thinking in adults]*. Moscow: MGU.

Rosas, R., Flotts, M. P., & Saragoni, C. (2002). Modelo de representación del conocimiento para las nuevas pruebas de selección de ingreso a las universidades chilenas [Model of representation of knowledge for the new tests of selection to the Chilean universities]. *Psykhe, 11*(1), 3–14.

Rosso, P. P. (2002). *La Universidad Católica y el SIES* [The Catholic University and the SIES]. Retrieved April 20, 2003, from http://www.puc.cl/noticias/ficha/pub489.html.

Rubinstein, S. Y. (1970). *Eksperimental'nye metodiki patopsikhologii I opyt ikh primeneniya v klinike* [*Experimental methods in psychopathology and their applications in clinics*]. Moscow: Meditsyna.

Seeberg, V. (2000). *The rhetoric and reality of mass education in Mao's China*. Queenston, Canada: The Edwin Mellen Press.

Shi, J. (2004). Diligence makes people smart: Chinese perspectives of intelligence. In R. J. Sternberg (Ed.), *International handbook for psychology of intelligence* (pp. 362–390). New York: Cambridge University Press.

Sternberg, R. J. (1998). Ability testing, instruction and assessment of achievement: Breaking out of the vicious circle. *NASSP Bulletin, 82,* 4–10.

Talyzina, N.F. (1981). Printsipy sovetskoi psikhologii i problema psikhodiagnostiki poznavatel'noi deyatel'nosti [Principles of Soviet psychology and issues concerning the assessment of cognitive activity]. In I. I. Il'yasov & V. Ya. Lyaudis (Eds.), *Textbook on developmental and pedagogical psychology. Soviet psychologists' papers in 1918–1945* (pp. 38–43). Moscow: MGU.

Thorndike, R. L., Hagen, E., & Sattler, J. (2003). *Stanford–Binet Intelligence Scale* (4th ed.). Itasca, IL: Riverside.

Wang, J. (1995). *The college entrance examination and the development of higher education on the Chinese mainland* (in Chinese). Taipei, Taiwan: The Mainland Affairs Council.

Yang, X. (2000). *The two decades of National College Entrance Examination: Its relationship with the Chinese society and economics*. Wuxi Education (in Chinese). http://www.wxjy.com.cn/jywz/2000/cedu20/25.htm

Zaporozhets, A.V. (1986). *Izbrannye psikhologicheskie trudy (v dvykh tomakh)* [Selected psychological writings (Vols. 1–2)]. Moscow: Pedagogika.

Zeigarnik, B.V. (1962). *Patologiya myshleniya* [Thinking pathologies]. Moscow: MGU.

Zhang, H. (1988). Psychological measurement in China. *International Journal of Psychology, 23*(1), 101–117.

IV

ENHANCEMENT OVER TIME

SPEARMAN, g, EXPERTISE, AND THE NATURE OF HUMAN COGNITIVE CAPABILITY

John L. Horn
University of Southern California

SPEARMAN IN PERSPECTIVE

Spearman's contributors to scientific understanding of cognitive capabilities are well attested to in the chapters of this book. His g theory has been particularly influential. The extant evidence does not, however, support that theory. It is important to recognize this.

Spearman (and Binet) were principal pioneers in designing tests to describe the abilities of human intelligence. Tests developed in Spearman's laboratory (e.g., matrices, induction, classifications), and various off shoots of these tests, are still today among the major indicators of the abilities that are regarded as indicating intelligence. But Spearman's contributors went beyond identifying abilities of intelligence.

A Testable Theory

Spearman put forth the first scientifically testable theory of intelligence. He marshaled the then-extant evidence in support of this theory. Most important, he developed a rationale and method for testing principal hypotheses of the theory[1] (Spearman, 1904, 1914, 1923, 1927). This work founded the scientific study of human intelligence.

---

[1]This rationale and method was the first formulation of a structural equation model. Spearman thus may be said to be the originator of a structural equation modeling method. Lawley (1943–44), following the logic of Spearman's model, developed statistical tests of multi-factor models. Joreskog (1967) put together efficient algorithms in programs for calculating the parameters of the equations of these models, and these programs were referred to as structural equation modeling programs. Thus structural equation modeling was born. It has become a principal tool for research in the behavioral sciences. In a sense it all began with Spearman.

In the substance of his theory Spearman reasoned, in confluence with the influential neurologist Lashley (1929), that the brain functioned as a whole to produce a kind of neural energy that to some extent determined all the capabilities of human intelligence. All cognitive abilities would be products of this mass action. This would be manifested in a common g-factor. Other influences—neurological, physiological, environmental—would also operate to produce abilities, but these influences would be specific, not general. They would operate to produce abilities, but not all abilities. Spearman then showed that if these statements about the formation of abilities were correct and studies were carefully designed to measure abilities that are indeed indicative of human intelligence[2], but each measure is carefully selected to involve a different (one and only one) specific influence, then the intercorrelations among the different ability measures will have a particular, quite lawful, hierarchical form indicating the influence of g, and g alone. He showed how the g-factor could be extracted from a matrix of intercorrelations among abilities, how the matrix of residual correlations could be calculated, and why the distribution for these residuals would be symmetrical, normal, with an expected value of zero and a standard error for relationships occurring only by chance.

Spearman first put his theory to test in a study of the academic grades of 22 high school boys. He calculated the intercorrelations among rank-order measures of grades the boys received in classics, French, English, mathematics and music. He then demonstrated that, indeed, one common factor accounted for these correlations[3]. It has been said that in this work Spearman "discovered g" (Jensen, 1998). Unfortunately for those who like this story, the "discovery" did not hold up. Spearman's hypotheses have not been supported in other studies.

Insufficient Structural Evidence[4] and Attempts to Salvage the Theory

Using larger samples of subjects and more adequate measures of abilities than Spearman had employed, Burt (1909, 1911) found that one common factor simply did not fit the correlational data. He extracted a general factor in accordance with Spearman's stipulations, but then found that he had to calculate a second (numerical) factor to account for the residuals among one group of tests and then a third (verbal) factor to account for the residuals among another group of tests. In subsequent studies using broader samples of the tests that were then being developed to measure features of intelligence, Burt (1924) found that he had to calculate group factors of memory span, scholastic aptitude and manual skills—in addition to verbal and numerical factors—in order to account for the intercorrelations among the measures. To this list of group factors was added, even before the influence of Thurstone's (1931, 1935) studies began to be felt, a factor of spatial abilities, one involving mental speed, a visualization dimension, and several less clearly defined group factors (Carter, 1928; Cox, 1928; Kelley, 1928; Patterson & Elliot, 1930).

---

[2]Ideally the sample of abilities would be representative of all abilities that indicate human intelligence, but this ideal would not need to be realized in order to adduce evidence in support of the theory. Meredith (1964), citing Lawley (1943–1944) as the originator of the idea, showed that a common factor can be identified when neither the sample of indicator variables nor the sample subjects is representative of their respective populations.

[3]The symmetrical distribution of the residuals averaged .02 with a standard deviation of .00029.

[4]Evidence of the interrelationships among measures hypothesized to be indicative of a function is here referred to as structural evidence to distinguish it from other kinds of construct validation evidence such as that derived from studies of development or studies of neurological correlates.

The Overlapping Specific Attempt. Spearman argued that the findings of group factors indicated only failures in study design. The studies were not well designed to ensure that specific factors were not sampled in more than one test. He pointed out that specific factor overlap would produce group factors additional to the g factor. Recognizing the validity of this argument, a number of investigators (Alexander, 1935; Brown, 1933; Brown & Stephenson, 1933; El Koussy, 1935; Rimoldi, 1948) attempted to design studies in which the assembled tests would at once measure important features of intelligence and not introduce specific factor overlap. These efforts failed. In each case group factors were needed to account for intercorrelations among a good sampling of tests regarded as including important features of intelligence.

The Invariance of Indicator Attempt and Thomson's Bond Theory. Spearman came to grudgingly acknowledge that, as sampled and measured, abilities involved more than one common factor. In the face of this evidence he attempted to salvage g-theory with what was referred to as a theorem of indifference of the indicator. According to this argument, g was present in all ability tests among which multiple group factors were found, and was indicated by a finding (which by that time had become well established) of positive intercorrelations among all the tests. The fact that any one ability test correlated positively with all the other tests was said to support the theory of g. This argument for support has been widely accepted (e.g., Eysenck, 1982; Gottfredson, 1997; Jensen, 1998).

Unfortunately for the theory, what is called a theorem in this argument is not a theorem. It is not true that if each of a set of variables intercorrelate positively, then necessarily a general factor is indicated (at any level of analysis). Positive intercorrelations among all of a set of variables can be indicative of two or three or four or more common factors that are not indicative of a single higher order common factor.

Thomson (1919) demonstrated this early in the last century and put forth a theory of bonding of elementary cognitive processes to account for a positive manifold of ability test intercorrelations. If Test 1 involves elementary processes *a*, *b*, *c*, and *d*, for example, then if Test 2 involves processes *a*, *e*, *f*, and *g*, it can correlate with Test 1 in virtue of sharing process *a* (but not *b*, *c*, *d*, *e*, *f*, or *g*). Similarly, it Test 3 involves processes *b*, *e*, *h*, *j*, and *k*, it can correlate with Test 1 virtue of sharing processes *b*, and it can correlate with Test 2 in virtue of sharing processes *e*, (and not sharing any other processes with Test 1 or 2). Test 4 can share processes *c* with Test 1, processes *f* with Test 2, processes *h* with Test 3, and thus be positively correlated with all three tests without sharing any processes common to all four tests. Continuing in this way Thomson showed that all the tests of a battery of tests can be positively correlated and not involve a single common factor. He also pointed out that performance on any cognitive test can be seen to involve many processes of perception, apprehension, retention, association, reasoning, reflection, retrieval, and so forth, and that such processes can be configured—organized, called forth, applied, and expressed—in a great variety of different ways, and that these different configurations can overlap and be shared in an even larger number of ways in the performances on different tasks that can make up a battery of cognitive tests. The multiple factors found in analyses of tests designed to indicate important features of human intelligence are consistent with this conception of cognitive capabilities.

Thus, Thomson demonstrated that positive intercorrelations among cognitive tests is to be expected, but evidence of positive intercorrelations is not, in itself, indicative of a single common factor. The evidence accumulated thus far today is consistent with Thomson's theory. Humphreys (1971) alerted us to this over 30 years ago. The evidence is not consistent with g-theory.

The High Correlation Among Measures Attempt.   It has been pointed out that different tests designed to measure intelligence not only correlate positively, they correlate quite highly, near the limits of their reliabilities, and this, it is argued, indicates that g is operating throughout. But this finding, also, is consistent with bond theory, not with g theory.

Tests analyzed in these kinds of demonstrations—tests such as the Stanford-Binet (Thorndike, Hagen, & Sattler, 1986), those authored by Wechsler (e.g., 1955), the Hawaii Battery (DeFries et al., 1976), the Comprehensive Ability Battery (Hakstian & Cattell, 1974)—are conglomerates of measures of many abilities (that may be linked through a multitude of bonds).They correlate highly because they measure the same *things*, not because they measure the same *thing*.

This is well illustrated by correlations between conglomerate measures and rather homogenous measures regarded as indicating g. For example, if a rather homogenous test such as matrices (Raven, 1941, which is proclaimed to be a very good measure of g) is correlated with a conglomerate general intelligence test, the correlation is found to be somewhere in the range of about 0.40 to 0.80 (depending on the nature of the conglomerate test), well below the internal consistencies of the measures. This indicates that conglomerate tests measure factors in addition to the factor (or factors) measured by matrices. The different factors could all indicate a g, but, again, analyses of the tests of the conglomerates indicate that they do not. One g is not found.

Higher Order Common Factors Attempts and Multiple Factor Theories.   It is argued that if common factors at a primary level are factored to yield second-order factors, and these are factored to yield third-order factors, and factoring continues in this manner until only one factor is indicated at the kth-order, this one factor is evidence of g. A problem with this reasoning is that one factor calculated at the top of the higher order reflects the number and reliability of different kinds of abilities sampled in the test battery. If the test batteries differ, then factors calculated at the higher order will differ. If a battery contains reliable tests measuring spatial abilities, for example, the one factor calculated at the many highest order will have its highest correlations with spatial abilities. If the battery contains reliable measures requiring verbal comprehension, the one factor at the higher order will be a verbal comprehension factor. The factors are general factors, but they are not the same general factor.

Findings of this kind are well illustrated in Carroll's (1993) tour de force reanalysis of some 477 batteries of ability tests. A Table 15.4 in Carroll's monograph "...lists 153 factors, in 146 datasets, classified as measuring "general intelligence" or possibly Spearman's factor g" (p. 591). Inspection of these results indicates: (a) The general factors of different analyses often contain no abilities (tests) that are the same; the factors are thus "general" in respect to entirely different sets of variables; (b) Usually most of the tests (abilities) are different in pairs of factors that were classified as indicating the general factor, but some of the tests are the same.

The factors thus had a few variables in common. Factor invariance analyses (Meredith & Horn, 2001) might have indicated that the factors were the same for the few variables they had in common, but eliminating the other variables would mean that the factors could not be regarded as general. (c).The "general" factors are different even when they involve several of the same abilities: some were "general" visualization factors; other were "general" verbal comprehension factors; still others were primarily indicative of reasoning with novel materials or were mainly indicative of verbal fluency. Carroll's study illustrates that over the course of the last century studies designed to indicate the structure of human intellect often sampled notably different sets of tests and abilities.

A higher order factor analysis converging or one factor would provide evidence in support of Spearman's theory if (a) the factors at the kth-order satisfied the one-common-factor (rank-one) requirements of the Spearman model, and (b) the abilities that were sampled represented the full range of abilities accepted as indicating human intelligence[5]. An early study by Thurstone and Thurstone (1941) is also one of the best attempts to test Spearman's hypotheses in this way.

L. L. Thurstone (1938) had put forth a theory and a testable model that would account for the findings that Spearman's model did not account for. Rather than specifying a single common ability (Spearman) or overlapping bondings of many abilities (Thomson) Thurstone's theory specified a relatively small number of primary abilities, each of which could be identified as a common factor among several (three or four) different exemplar measures of the ability. In his landmark test of this theory, Thurstone (1938) identified primary abilities (nine in all) of verbal comprehension (V), word fluency (W), number facility (N), spatial thinking (S), associative memory (M), perceptual speed (P), general reasoning (R), inductive reasoning (I), and deductive reasoning (D).

In the Thurstone and Thurstone (1941) study it was reasoned that if these primary abilities are positively intercorrelated, that positive manifold could indicate a second-order factor that is equivalent to Spearman's g. They found, indeed, on rotating six on the nine primary abilities—V, W, N, S, M, and I—into oblique, positive manifold simple structure, the rank of the matrix of intercorrelations was close to unity, indicating support at this level for Spearman's claim of a general intellective factor.

Unfortunately, this finding was for a trimmed battery in which tests, and what Thurstone (1938) has identified as primary abilities, were left out. When, for example, tests marking the D primary ability were added to the battery, the rank-one condition no longer obtained. Generally, when other samples of what were found to be primary abilities were factored at the second order—or higher order—the g-factor hypothesis was not supported.

The results of several studies now indicate that one can select a subset of tests from a battery that well represents the abilities of human intelligence and demonstrate that a common factor for the selected tests satisfies the conditions of Spearman's one-and-only-one common factor model. Such a factor indicates a particular sampling of the ability tests from the larger domain of measures that are accepted as indicating human intelligence. The sample of tests of the Thurstone and Thurstone (1941) study, for example, represents a sampling to indicate primary abilities that define a second-order crystallized knowledge factor (Gc, also known as crystallized intelligence). When tests representing other primary abilities—the D factor, for example—are added to this battery, a single general factor no longer accounts for intercorrelations.

In a second kind of sampling from the domain of abilities of human intelligence, tests that well represent a second-order fluid reasoning factor (Gf, also known as fluid intelligence) are found to intercorrrelate in a manner that indicates a rank-one condition satisfying the conditions of Spearman's model (Horn, 1998). But this Gf factor correlates only about .50 with Gc, and tests that well represent both of two factors do not satisfy the rank-one condition.

This separation of Gf and Gc abilities was adumbrated in several studies in the 1920s and 1930s of ability correlates of brain damage and aging. Some abilities declined with brain damage and aging; others did not. Cattell (1941) and Hebb (1941), summarizing somewhat

---

[5] In accordance with the Lawley-Meredith theorem of footnote 2, the sample of abilities need not be representative of a population of abilities indicating human intelligence, but it must be broad enough to cover the abilities of the population.

different sets of the earlier findings, arrived separately at conclusions that two forms of intelligence were needed to account for the evidence. Cattell (1957) coined the terms "fluid intelligence" (Gf) to describe the declining abilities and "crystallized intelligence" (Gc) to describe the abilities that did not notably decline with brain damage and aging. In Cattell (1963, 1971) he presented structural and developmental evidence for a theory of two intelligences.

Gf appears to better represent Spearman's substantive theory of g than does Gc. The central processes of g, as specified by Spearman (1927), are apprehension of concepts, education of relations among concepts, and education of correlates of the relations. In Horn (1998), the following indicator variables of Gf were carefully chosen to not overlap in representing components of the Spearman processes (and a few other processes):

1. maintenance of concentration (required to attain awareness of the fundaments of a problem),
2. immediate (short-term) memory (required to retain the fundaments in awareness),
3. inductive reasoning (indicating education of relations among fundaments),
4. deductive reasoning (extending understanding of relations to new instances),
5. comparison speed (identifying many relations in a short unit of time, facilitating the process of educing relations), and
6. carefulness in avoiding incorrect inferences.

It was found that the matrix of intercorrelations among these measures very nearly met the rank-one conditions of the Spearman model. Thus, Gf-factor indicators chosen in accordance with Spearman's substantive theory well approximate the conditions of one, and only one, common factor.

The Gf factor is not g, however. It's not a general factor across all abilities indicative of human intelligence. If indicator variables for Gc are added to the battery of tests, the rank-one condition no longer obtains: Two factors are needed to describe the relationships, Similarly, if an indicator variable for a visualization second-order factor, or for an auditory second factor is brought into the system, the correlation matrix no longer meets the rank-one test of the Spearman model.

Results obtained by Gustafsson and Undheim (1996) point to the same conclusions. In a study that was well-designed to represent major second-order abilities indicating different forms of intelligence, Gustafsson and Undheim found that one factor (regarded as at the third order) could be rotated to perfect correlation with a second-order factor identified as Gf. This finding was interpreted as indicating that Spearman's g is best represented in Gf. The results thus indicate fundamentally that factors additional to Gf (g) are needed to account for the intercorrelations among ability measures that represent human intelligence, but that the intercorrelations among second-order factors can be associated with Gf[6]. Thus, there is no singular g, but Spearman's substantive theory is supported by findings indicating a Gf form of intelligence—one among several factors of human intelligence.

Insufficient Construct Validation Evidence

I have gone rather into detail in presenting structural evidence pertaining to Spearman's theory of g because claims of support for the theory have appealed primarily to that kind of evidence.

---

[6] Although the third order is underdetermined, so the correlations could just as well be associated with one of the other second-order factors—Gc, for example.

But the evidence that most convincingly indicates the inadequacy of the theory is of other forms: It has come from studies of development, neural function and brain damage, behavior genetics and environmental influences, and the prediction of criteria that are regarded as requiring human intelligence. Thurstone (1947) pointed out that a finding of a common factor is only a beginning in the work of building evidence that can establish that a unitary function is indicated by the factor. It is necessary to show that the elements of the factor work as a unit in relation to other variables that affect, and are affected by, the function the factor represents. The elements must relate lawfully across the span of development and in respect to genetic determiners and brain functions, for example.

Evidence form research on the development of abilities is particularly damning to theories of one general factor of intelligence. Studies of age changes and age differences show that the different abilities that characterize what we see as human intelligence have different trajectories over the course of development. The abilities develop at different rates. They are correlated in different ways with variables that represent biological and environmental determinants that operate in development. In adulthood, for example, some abilities that very much describe what is recognized as human intelligence (reasoning, working memory) decline over the same periods of development in which there is improvement in other abilities that indicate human intelligence (verbal comprehension, verbal fluency). No one process, mechanism, or principle has been found to account for these different developmental trajectories. Different processes and different mechanisms are needed. Different functions are indicated.

Behavior genetic research and studies of brain function and malfunction lead to the same kind of conclusion. There is very little direct information about relationships between neural functions and abilities, but what is known does not indicate a single neural function (neural speed or neural energy or neural mass action) that would correspond to a single factor common to all the behaviors that indicate human intelligence. The evidence suggests instead that there are several distinct neural organizations, centered in different locations in the brain, with pathways joining other functions in different ways, each founded in different sets of genetic and environmental determiners, and correlated with different kinds of abilities. The picture of the brain operating in association with behavior looks more like a set of interconnecting systems than like a single force running throughout everything.

With respect to learning, for example, which in itself indicates aspects of intelligence and that results in memories that become parts of expressions of intelligence, there appear to be at least three—or perhaps four—underlying neuronal systems that support different forms of learning and different aspects of what is seen as memory. One system is centered in the cerebellum; one is largely associated with the function of the hippocampus and nearby structures; one is related to function of the amygdala; and one is characterized by protein synthesis, perhaps mainly in the frontal lobes (Thompson, 1993).

For the function in the cerebellum, there is good direct-linkage evidence—laying out neural pathways and identifying what is lost when certain sections and pathways are lost— showing that elementary association learning requires the interpositus nucleus (Lavond & Kanzawa, 2000). Disabling the interpositus nucleus wipes out classical conditioning association learning. Any malfunction of this area, whether genetically based or environmentally produced, affects such learning and the retention that can be associated with it.

The hippocampus is in a quite different part of the brain than the interpositus nucleus, but it, too, is essential for learning and retention. The learning and retention are of a different form, however, than that associated with the interpositus nucleus. The hippocampus is essential for retaining the outcomes of instrumental learning in long-term memory; yet it is not the center for long-term memory storage. Several lines of evidence lead to these conclusions.

Most dramatic is evidence that has come from studies of H. M, a person whose hippocampus (on both sides of the brain) and some nearby tissue was surgically removed to cure life-threatening epilepsy. After he had recovered from the surgery H. M. seemed normal in conversation. He recalled things from the past. He could remember a telephone number long enough to dial it. Thus it seemed that his crystallized knowledge (Gc), his information retrieval from long-term memory (TSR), his immediate apprehension and short-term memory (of just a few seconds before) were all largely unaffected by hippocampus removal. But his intermediate memory (of a few minutes before) was lost. He was quite unable to remember experiences he had just a few minutes prior to a test for recall. Removal of the hippocampus removed the capacity for the consolidation part of learning and memory. His association learning of the kind that is mediated through the interpositus nucleus remained normal: He could learn a complex motor skill as well as most people. Also, his implicit learning—learning mediated through the amygdala—remained intact. Lost, however, was ability to remember experiences occurring a few minutes before.

The effects seen in H. M. have been observed in the other people who have had bilateral lesions in the hippocampus area. Analogous effects have been found in controlled experiments with monkeys (Thompson, 1998). Function of the hippocampus is central to one major ability to learn from experience, a very important part of intelligence.

A protein synthesis effect on long-term memory storage has not been as narrowly localized as effects associated with the functions of the hippocampus, amygdala and interpositus nucleus, but the evidence indicates that the effect is quite separate from those localized effects. If protein synthesis is inhibited, learning can occur, but there is loss of subsequent memory for what was learned (Thompson, 1998).

These various results are just a smattering of findings that indicate that different abilities of what we see as human intelligence stem from different parts and different functions of the brain. The absolute and relative size of these parts and functions of the brain are affected to different degrees by events that can occur at different points in development—events such as diminution of blood flow, anoxia, inebriation, and unfolding of genetic processes. Individual differences in these events produce aspects of individual differences in measured abilities.

Extended and heavy use of alcohol, for example, is associated with loss of function in the mammilary bodies and the nearby hippocampus, and this loss of function is associated with loss of memory and reasoning capacity. Similarly, although checks and balances work to ensure that all areas of the brain receive an adequate supply of blood, various conditions (illnesses, exhaustion, poisoning) bring about fluctuations in blood flow. Some areas of the brain—the hippocampus, for example—are particularly vulnerable to diminished blood flow (Hachinski, 1980). The arteries that supply blood to the hippocampus branch at right angles from the main trunks and terminate as end-arteries in the area, rather than as Y-branches from the main trunks. This means that any drop in blood flow can result in "drying-up" at the end-arteries, death of neurons, and associated loss of neural function. Indeed, infarcts have been found to occur more frequently in the hippocampus than in comparison structures (Corsellis, 1976). Such factors affect memory functions.

The conditions that bring on events such as fluctuations in blood flow can occur at almost any point in an individual human's development—before birth, at birth in infancy, childhood, adolescence, adulthood, old age. Also, such events can occur more and less frequently in the life of one person as compared to another. Abilities at the time such an event occurs, and development of abilities beyond that time, will be affected. Such factors occurring differently in different people result in the notable individual differences in measures of the various abilities that make up what we characterize as human intelligence.

There is little evidence of direct links between genetic factors and particular aspects of reasoning, learning, and retention, but such evidence as there is indicates that several separate sets of genes, transmitted independently, produce bases for the various different functions of the brain that support expression of the abilities we measure. Just as there are separate genetic factors affecting ear shape and nose length, so there are separate genetic factors affecting the size and shape and functions of the right and left hemispheres of the brain, particular parts of the cerebral cortex, the cerebellum, the limbic brain, neurotransmitters systems, and the pathways joining regions of the brain. Separate environmental influences also affect these regions and functions. Thus, genetic and environmental influences help produce the huge variety of patterns of abilities we see in people. It is unlikely that a single influence operates through the different systems to produce the learning, consolidation, retrieval, and so on—ultimately, the abilities—we measure and label as indicative of human intelligence. More likely there is a complex bonding among a melange of influences operating independently and the behavioral outcomes of these bondings are what we find in our measures of abilities and their interrelationships.

There is much more evidence of this kind. In sum it adds up to indicate that Spearman's beautifully simple idea of one general intellective factor is almost certainly incorrect. His ideas about measures, his substantive theory, the model he mounted to test this theory, his launching of testable theory, all are worthwhile contributions, still quite useful—standards in respect to which major research on human abilities can continue to be designed and evaluated. Spearman's work is valuable, but it should not be touted as demonstrating something it does not demonstrate. Spearman's work does not indicate that he discovered a psychometric basis for a general intellective factor that is now well established (Jensen, 1998). If g exists, the basis for it, psychometric and functional, has yet to be established.

Paths Not Followed

Spearman's influence on research on human intelligence has also had some negative effects. His (and Binet's) research focused and entrenched thinking about what constitutes a test to measure aspects of human intelligence. This work also focused and entrenched thinking that between-person—cum between-groups—research designs[7] are the designs to use to study human intelligence. These two entrenchments inhibited thinking about within-person measures and designs for research. But it is now becoming evident that these designs and measures are needed to explore the upper reaches of intellectual expertise (Charness, 1981a; de Groot, 1946; Ericsson, 1997; Ericsson & Kintsch, 1995; Krampe & Ericsson, 1996; Walsh & Hershey, 1993). It is becoming clear that can be identified in these upper reaches indicate capacities of human intelligence that are not seen in research of the kind that Spearman spawned.

The work of Spearman and Binet also led much research (under the aegis of studying general intelligence) down primrose paths of looking for the genetic basis for g, aiming to find it in the earliest displays of intelligence in infancy and early childhood, and seeking to demonstrate that it should show up in racial and ethnic differences.[8] These lines of research diverted attention away from studying outstanding displays of intelligence in different kinds of expertise, most of which reach their apex in adulthood. Tests of general intelligence were designed to

---

[7]Spearman probably is not mainly responsible for the dominance of mean-differences designs in the research of the last century, that honor probably should go to R. A. Fisher. But Spearman surely did lead the way in making the individual-differences covariance design very nearly dominant.

[8]This kind of research has done more to spark social dissension than to enhance understanding of the nature of human intelligence (Herrnstein & Murray, 1994; Horn, 2002).

measure abilities of childhood. Theory of general intelligence was derived primarily from study of these abilities. Even research on adulthood development of intelligence was based mainly on tests designed to measure abilities of children. Only belatedly in the latter part of the last century, when researchers began looking at expertise, did it begin to dawn on them that abilities seen in adulthood were culminations of the development of human intelligence. That thinking is still very fresh, but it should be a guide for future research on the nature of human intelligence.

BUILDING FROM SPEARMAN

So I wish to move our thinking about intelligence away from Spearman's contributions toward consideration of new kinds of research needed to raise our understanding to another level. The new research should focus on the development of intellectual expertise. We may look at the beginnings of this in childhood, but expect to find that the major abilities of intelligence emerge in adulthood.

Before going to that argument, it will be useful pass through a somewhat more specific review than was earlier provided of research that has led to our present multidimensional theory of human intelligence. This research provides an organizational system for classifying the myriad of abilities that have been put forth as indications of intelligence. Brief description of this system will set the stage for considering research on expertise.

Basic Constructs

What we presently know about the abilities of human intelligence is embodied to a considerable extent in extended Gf-Gc theory. This is a descriptive-interpretative account of evidence obtained primarily from two kinds of research: (a) structural research: studies of the covariation patterns among tests designed to indicate basic features of human intelligence, and (b) developmental research: studies designed to indicate the ways in which cognitive capabilities develop over age. To a lesser extent the theory incorporates findings from studies of neural organization, genetic influences, and the prediction of academic and occupational achievement.

Structural Evidence: Major Capabilities of Human Intelligence

The accumulated results from 100 years of research on covariations among tests, tasks, and paradigms designed to identify fundamental features of human intelligence indicate organization at what is referred to as primary mental abilities. At this level somewhat more than 60 kinds of abilities—dimensions indicated by common factors—are required to describe the individual differences variability that has been idenfied as indicating human intelligence (summaries by Carroll, 1993; Ekstrom, French, & Harman, 1979; Hakstian & Cattell, 1974).

The evidence of studies of structure also indicates that there is a broader, more general organization among the primary mental abilities and that this general organization can be represented largely (though not fully) by as few as nine major kinds of cognitive capacities. The common factors indicating these broad patterns of organization have been identified in samples that differ in respect to gender, level of education, ethnicity, nationality, language, and historical period. The nine kinds of abilities that represent this organization account for all or nearly all (depending on which particular test is considered) the reliable individual differences variability measured in conglomerate IQ tests and neuropsychological batteries. The abilities are positively correlated, but independent. The independence is indicated by structural evidence: A best-weighted linear combination of any set of eight of the factors does not account for the reliable covariance among the elements of the ninth factor. More fundamentally, independence is indicated by evidence of distinct construct validities: Measures representing the different factors have different relationships with a variety of other variables, including variables of neurology and age. The factors appear to represent distinct functions such as are realized through learning operating in conjunction with biological and genetic influences that directly determine brain structure and physiology. Although there are suggestions that some of the factors are somewhat more related to genetic determinants than others, the broad patterns do not define a clean distinction between genetic and environmental determinants. (Such distinctions appear to be better made at the level of primary mental abilities.) The nine classes of abilities are briefly described as follows.

Acculturation Knowledge (Gc), measured in tests indicating breadth and depth of knowledge of the language, concepts, and information of the dominant culture.

Fluency of retrieval from long-term storage (TSR), also labeled long-term memory (Glm). It is measured in tasks indicating consolidation for storage, tasks that require retrieval through association of information stored minutes, hours, weeks, and years before.

Fluid reasoning (Gf), measured in tasks requiring inductive reasoning (conjunctive and disjunctive). It indicates capacities for identifying relationships, comprehending implications, and drawing inferences within content that is either novel or equally familiar to all.

Short-term apprehension and retrieval (SAR), also referred to as short-term memory (Gsm) and working memory. it is measured in a variety of tasks that mainly require one to maintain awareness of elements in the immediate situation, that is, the span of a minute or so.

Processing speed (Gs), although involved in almost all intellectual tasks, this factor is measured most purely in rapid scanning and comparisons in intellectually simple tasks in which almost all people would get the right answer if the task were not highly speeded.

Visual processing (Gv), measured in tasks involving visual closure and constancy, and fluency in recognizing the way objects appear in space as they are rotated and flip-flopped in various ways.

Auditory processing (Ga), measured in tasks that involve perception of sound patterns under distraction or distortion, maintaining awareness of order and rhythm among sounds, and comprehending elements of groups of sounds.

Correct decision speed (CDS), measured in quickness in providing answers in tasks that are not of trivial difficulty.

Quantitative knowledge (Gq), measured in tasks requiring understanding and application of the concepts and skills of mathematics.

More detailed and scholarly accounts of the structural evidence are provided in Carroll (1993); Cattell (1971); Horn (e.g., 1968, 1994, 1998), Horn & Hofer (1992), Horn & Noll (1997), and McGrew, Werder, & Woodcock (1991).

Developmental Evidence

Most of the developmental research has been directed at describing age-related declines in cognitive capabilities—particularly the abilities of Gf, Gs, and SAR—but some of the prior work has adduced evidence of improvements and maintenance of abilities, in this case the abilities of Gc and TSR. The designs for the studies producing this evidence have been both cross sectional and longitudinal. These two kinds of designs have different strengths and weaknesses; they control for, and reveal, different kinds of influences (Horn & Donaldson, 1980). Yet in major respects as concerns age-related differences and changes, the findings from the two kinds of studies are largely congruent (Botwinick, 1978; Horn, 1994; Horn & Donaldson, 1980). The longitudinal findings suggest that the points in adulthood at which declines occur are later than is indicated by the cross-sectional findings, but the evidence of which abilities decline and which improve is essentially the same for cross-sectional and longitudinal studies (Horn & Donaldson, 1980; Schaie, 1996).

Research of the future should probably be most directed at understanding abilities that are maintained or that improve with age in adulthood, and our thought is that abilities of expertise, particularly, should be most carefully studies. To provide perspective for this view I first review evidence on abilities that do not decline, or decline little and late in adulthood, and then consider the more extensive evidence and theory pertaining to aging decline.

Capabilities for Which There Is Little or No Aging Decline. The results indicating improvement and maintenance of abilities has come largely from the same studies in which evidence of aging decline was found. The two most prominent kinds of abilities for which there is replicated evidence of improvement in adulthood are those of Gc, indicating breadth of knowledge of the dominant culture, and those of TSR, indicating fluency in retrieval of information from this store of knowledge.

Gc: Knowledge. The abilities of Gc are often referred to in efforts to specify what is more important about human intelligence. They are indicative of the intelligence of a culture, inculcated into individuals through systematic influences of acculturation. The range of such abilities is large. No particular battery of tests is known to sample over the entire range. The sum of the achievement tests of the Woodcock-Johnson Psycho-Educational Battery-Revised (Woodcock, 1996) probably provides the most nearly representative measure. The verbal subscale of the WAIS (Wechsler Adult Intelligence Scales) is a commonly used estimate. Indicators of the factor are measures of vocabulary, esoteric analogies, listening comprehension, and knowledge in the sciences, social studies, and humanities. Such measures correlate substantially with social class, amount and quality of education, and other indicators of acculturation.

On average, through most of adulthood, there is increase with age in Gc knowledge (e.g., Botwinick, 1978; Cattell, 1971; Harwood & Naylor, 1971; Horn, 1998; Horn & Cattell, 1967; Horn & Hofer, 1992; Kaufman, 1990; Rabbitt & Abson, 1991; Schaie, 1996; Stankov & Horn, 1980; Woodcock, 1995). Results from some studies suggest improvement into the 80s (e.g., Harwood & Naylor, 1971, for WAIS Information, Comprehension, and Vocabulary). Such declines as are indicated show up in the averages late in adulthood—age 70 and beyond—and are small (Schaie, 1996). If differences in years of formal education are statistically controlled, the increment of Gc with advancing age is increased (Horn, 1989; Kaufman, 1990).

TSR: Tertiary Storage and Retrieval. Two different kinds of measures indicate this class of abilities. Both of the two kinds of indicators involve encoding and consolidation of information in long-term storage and both involve fluency of retrieval from that storage. The parameters of association that characterize encoding and consolidation also characterize retrieval (Bower, 1972, 1975; Estes, 1974).

The first kind of test to identify TSR involves retrieval through association over periods of time that range from a few minutes to a few hours or longer. The time lapse must be sufficient to ensure that consolidation occurs, for this is what distinguishes these measures from indicators of SAR. For example, if a paired-associates test were to be used to measure the factor, recall would need to be obtained at least 5 minutes after presentation of the stimuli; if recall were obtained immediately after presentation, the test would measure SAR.

The second kind of test indicates associations among pieces of information that would have been consolidated and stored in a system of categories (as described by Broadbent, 1966) in the distant past, not just a few hours earlier. In a word associations test, for example, subjects provide words similar in meaning to a given word. The person accesses an association category of information and pulls information from that category into a response mode.

Tests to measure TSR may be given under time limits, but these limits must be generous, such that subjects have time to drain association categories. If given under highly speeded conditions, the tests will measure cognitive speed (Gs), not TSR.

The retrieval of TSR is from the knowledge store of Gc, but facility in retrieval is independent of measures of Gc—independent in the sense that the correlation between TSR and Gc is well below their respective internal consistencies and in the sense that they have different patterns of correlations with other variables.

For TSR abilities, as for Gc, the research results usually indicate improvement or no age differences throughout most of adulthood (Horn, 1968; Horn & Cattell, 1967; Horn & Noll, 1993; Schaie, 1996; Stankov & Horn, 1980; Woodcock, 1995).

Capabilities That Decline With Age

Principal aging declines have been found in Gf, SAR and Gs. These factors together are referred to as vulnerable abilities to contrast them with the maintained abilities of Gc and TSR.

Gf: Reasoning With Novel Materials. The research findings are consistent in indicating steady decline of Gf over most of the period of adulthood. The decline is seen with measures of syllogisms and concept formation (McGrew et al., 1991), in reasoning with metaphors and analogies (Salthouse, 1987; Salthouse, Kausler, & Saults, 1990), with measures of comprehending series, as in letter series, figural series, and number series (Horn, 1972, 1982, 1994; Noll & Horn, 1997; Salthouse, Babcock, Skouronik, Mitchel, & Palmon, 1990), and with measures of mental rotation, figural relations, matrices, and topology (Cattell, 1979). In each case the factor is most cleanly indicated—measures are most nearly unifactorial—if the fundaments of the test are novel or equally familiar to all—that is, give no advantage to those with greater knowledge of the culture. Although many of the tests that have indicated the aging decline of Gf have a speeded component, the decline is indicated very well by unspeeded tests that require resolution of high-level (difficult) complexities (Horn, 1994; Horn, Donaldson, & Engstrom, 1981; Noll & Horn, 1997). I return to a consideration of the relationship between Gf decline and cognitive speed in the section titled "Analysis of Interdependence Among Abilities."

SAR: Short-Term Apprehension and Retrieval. This organization of abilities involves the two major serial position memory functions—recency and primacy (Glanzer & Cunitz, 1966). Recency memory dissipates quickly; if there is delay of as much as 20 seconds, it is nearly absent in most people. Primacy memory can be retained somewhat longer (30 seconds). It has been regarded as an early indication of long-term memory (LTM) (Atkinson & Shiffrin, 1968; Waugh & Norman, 1965). Also defining the SAR factor are measures of the forward span memory—the "magical number seven plus or minus two" (Miller, 1956)—and indicators of working memory (Baddeley, 1993, 1994), including memory-span backward, although in factor-analytic studies this measure is more closely related to Gf than to SAR.

The findings of many studies indicate aging decline of all the memory abilities of SAR (Craik, 1977; Craik & Trehub, 1982; Horn et al., 1981; Salthouse, 1991; Schaie, 1996). The decline is small in tasks that involve very short periods of retention, such as recency measures. There are virtually no age differences for the Sperling (1960) kind of task, in which the retention is for only a few milliseconds. But for measures in which retrieval is required after short periods of roughly 10 to 60 seconds, age-related declines generally have been found. This is true of memory for information the subject could regard as meaningful, as well as for nonsense material, although age differences appear to be smaller for memory of the meaningful kind of information (Cavanaugh, 1997; Charness, 1991; Craik & Trehub, 1982; Ericsson & Delaney, 1996; Gathercole, 1994; Kaufman, 1990; Salthouse, 1991; Schaie, 1996). The more complex the memory task, and the more it requires that material be held in awareness while doing other things—as in definitions of working memory—the larger the negative relationship to age and, also, the more it relates to Gf.

Cognitive Speed and Aging.   Most tests of cognitive abilities involve speed in one form or another—speed of reacting, speed in behaving, speed of thinking. Studies of measures that mainly involve speed of reacting and/or speed of behaving—chronometric measures—and of their relationships with measures of cognitive capabilities that are not defined primarily in terms of speediness, indicate positive intercorrelations among all measures, the range of correlations being roughly .15 to .75 (Eysenck, 1987; Hertzog, 1989; Jensen, 1987; Nettelbeck, 1994; Salthouse, 1985; 1991). The more a speeded measure involves complexity, the higher this correlation becomes. Simple reaction time (SRT), in which one reacts as quickly as possible to a single stimulus, correlates at a low level ($r < .25$) with most measures regarded as indicating some aspect of human intelligence. For complex reaction time (CRT), in which one reacts as quickly as possible to one or another of several stimuli, the correlations increase systematically with increase in the number of different stimuli and patterns of stimuli one needs to take into account before reacting (Jensen, 1987).

Most speeded tests are negatively correlated with age in adulthood—that is, older adults behave more slowly than younger adults. Salthouse (1985, 1991) has provided comprehensive reviews of the evidence of how aging relates to speeded measures. He found slowing with age for all the chronometric measures that were considered: copying digits, crossing off letters, comparing numbers, picking up coins, zipping a garment, unwrapping Band-Aids, using a fork, dialing a telephone number, and sorting cards, digit-symbol substitution, movement time, trail making, SRT, CRT, and other indicators. There was a suggestion that the more a speeded measure involves complexity, the larger the absolute value of the negative correlation. For comparisons of standard score measures of SRT and CRT, for example, the age differences were larger for CRT. Moreover, in studies in which young and old subjects were provided opportunity to practice CRT tasks, practice did not eliminate the age differences and no noteworthy age-by-practice interactions were found (Madden & Nebes, 1980; Salthouse & Somberg, 1982).

These findings spawned theory that slowing with age in adulthood is a general feature of cognitive behavior (Birren, 1974; Kausler, 1990; Salthouse, 1985, 1991, 1992, 1993, 1994). Indeed, this theory has been regarded as a part of (supportive of) the theory of general intelligence. Spearmans (1927) had proposed that neural speed is the underlying function governing the central processes of g. Building on Spearman's hypothesis, Eysenck (1987), Jensen (1982, 1987, 1993), and Salthouse (1985, 1991) proposed that speed of information processing, reflecting speed of transmission in the neural system, is the essence of general intelligence.

Again, however, the existing evidence does not indicate either (a) a general cognitive speed factor, or (b) a general factor of slowing of cognitive processes with aging, or (c) a general intelligence factor the essence of which is cognitive speed.

A General Cognitive Speed Factor? There is evidence of several factors of speed— motoric, reactive, perceptual, in retrieval, in thinking. The factors are not intercorrelated in a manner that would indicate one common factor (much less one and only one common factor). The structural evidence reviewed in the previous section indicates three separate factors involving speeded tasks: (a) a broad Gs factor of speed of perception, defined primarily by simple tasks in which almost all people make no mistakes if the task is slowed, (b) a correct decision speed (CDS) factor defined by tasks in which incorrect answers are given even when the task is slowed, and (c) the fluency of retrieval (TSR) factor measured in tasks in which one retrieves information through association. Carroll (1993) found, in addition to these rather well-verified factors, a broad factor measured by various kinds of reaction time task, and a factor characterized by measures of psychomotor movement time. Carroll thus distinguished five separate speed factors.

The intercorrelations among measures of these five factors do not indicate a single common factor; indeed, the measures correlate in notably different ways with other variables (among them the variable of age to be considered next).

A General Factor of Slowing With Age? There is, first, evidence that the five speed factors identified by Carroll (1993) have notably different correlations with age and with other variables that correlate with age (Cunningham & Tomer, 1990; Hertzog, 1989; Horn et al., 1981; Hundal & Horn, 1977; Madden, 1985, Salthouse, 1991b; Walsh, 1982). The patterns of correlations are different even among measures all of which indicate slowing associated with aging. Walsh, for example, described two perceptual speed functions that correlated substantially (in the slowing direction) with age in adulthood, but correlated near the chance level (not significantly different from zero) with each other. Similarly, it has been found that the marker tests for the Gs factor correlates negatively with age and positively with Gf and SAR, which decline with age, where as the moderately speeded tests of the retrieval TSR factor correlate positively with age and with measures of Gc that do not decline with age (e.g., Horn et al., Horn & Noll, 1997).

A General Cognitive Factor Defined by Speediness? In respect to this hypothesis, there is, first, evidence reviewed in the previous section indicating that a g factor is unlikely. Secondly, there are serious defects in the studies interpreted as supporting the hypothesis; these defects render that interpretation dubious.

In the studies in question a chronometric measure was correlated with a conglomerate measure of intelligence, the correlation was corrected for attenuation due to unreliability, and the corrected high correlation was interpreted as indicating perfect correlation between the speeded measure and intelligence (Eysenck, 1987; Jensen, 1987). Intelligence thus was equivalent to cognitive speed. The following are major problems with these studies.

- The chronometric tests of these studies measured some of the same processes— attentiveness in dealing with complexities—that characterized the cognitive measures. Similarly, the cognitive measures were speeded. thus the correlations between the chronometric and cognitive measures were inflated by overlap in measuring the same processes. In studies in which the speed confound in cognitive tests was reduced by using power measures of Gf, only about one third of the reliable variance was accounted for by cognitive speed (Horn et al., 1981: Horn & Noll, 1997).

- In the sampling of subjects, there was heavy sampling at the extremes. For example, the samples contained subsamples of retarded people. Tests designed to distinguish between different cognitive capabilities do not do so in samples of retarded people because these people fail the most elementary requirements for dealing with the tasks—understanding what they are to do, getting started on time, sustaining attention to the task, remembering the test requirements—and these elementary requirements are much the same for quite different tests, including chronometric tests. This generates high correlations, high communality, and common factor covariance among tests that otherwise measure different factors. In a few homogeneous sample—people the same age and education level—Guilford (1964) found that highly speeded tests correlated negatively with lowly speeded tests that involved solving very complex problems, that is, tests regarded as indicating important features of human intelligence.

- The corrections for attenuation due to unreliability inflated the correlations. The reliability estimates were underestimates of the at-the-time internal consistencies in the samples in which the correlations between chronometric and cognitive measures were taken. The estimates were obtained from studies in which there was no sampling at the extremes. (Sampling at the extremes that would tend to increase the reliability estimates commensurate with the increase in the between chronometric and cognitive tests.) The inappropriately small reliability estimates enter in the denominator of the correction for attenuation, and thus inflate the estimate.

- There are several factors of chronometric measures, as well as several different general cognitive factors: A correlation between any one of either of these factors with any one of the other factors does not validly indicate that there is just one factor of each kind or that the obtained correlation represents the correlations among other chronometric factors and cognitive factors. The measures assumed to indicate g in the studies in question were mixtures of cognitive capabilities, different mixtures in different studies and no one of them indicative of a unitary g. Evidence that a particular cognitive speed factor accounts for variance in one such mixture measure is not evidence that it accounts for comparable variance in another mixture measure.

Together these conditions combine to produce substantial overestimates of the relationship between chronometric measures and estimates of different factors (incorrectly) regarded as indicating the same g factor. With appropriate corrections for unreliabilities in samples that are not loaded with extreme cases, the correlation between chronometric measures and mixture-measure of cognitive abilities are well below 1.0. For SRT the correlations are no larger than about .3; for CRT the correlations may run as high as .65. The relatively high correlations for CRT tests indicates that these tests measure complexity resolution, which overlaps with a principal process measured in cognitive ability tests regarded as indicating intelligence.

Although speeded functions do not fully account for the Gf, Gc, and the other cognitive capabilities indicating intelligence, they are intimately related to these capabilities. In particular, they are related to decline of the abilities of Gf, which, among several different intelligence factors, is the factor most similar to Spearman's concept of g. The relationships are seen in results from several studies of the interdependence among abilities. The results of these studies add to the evidence that speed is not the only process involved in the age differences of cognitive capabilities. Indeed, they suggest that cognitive speed is determined by a fundamental process of concentration.

Interdependence Among Abilities

The cognitive behavior displayed by a person is not, in itself, neatly partitioned into knowledge, reasoning, memory, speediness, and soon. It is a whole in which all such aspects of capability are interwoven. Gc, TSR, Gf, Gs, and SAR are constructs isolated by analyses with tests the requirements of which emphasize some aspects of capability relative to others. Such operational definitions never completely separate the different capabilities. This is seen in the positive intercorrelations among the factors. These intercorrelations indicate interdependence among capabilities. Gf, for example, is dependent on SAR: to reason effectively, as measured in Gf, one must apprehend the fundaments of a problem and hold them within the span of immediate awareness, processes emphasized in the measurements of SAR. Correlation between manifest indicators of Gf and SAR point to such latent interdependencies.

To describe the dependencies among different capabilities analytically, Horn (1982, 1989), Horn et al. (1981), Noll and Horn (1997), and Salthouse (1993) have used multiple-partialling procedures. These procedures have been directed mainly at describing aging decline of fluid reasoning in terms of elementary processes of memory, speed, concentration, attention, and incidental learning. Beginning with an observed age-related decline in Gf of approximately .25 standard deviation units (SDU) per 10 years of age (over a period from the early 20s through the mid-60s), Noll and Horn demonstrated that the decline of Gf is reduced by approximately .10 SDU per decade—to about .15 SDU—by controlling for process measures of SAR. Gs speediness also accounted for about .10 SDU of the age decline of Gf (as in previous studies). Part of this relationship reflected an interdependence of Gs and SAR. When this was taken into account in multiple parting, it was found that Gs, independently of SAR, accounted for about .055 of the Gf decline with age. This finding was replicated with different indicators of the basic constructs. More fundamentally, however, further analyses of interdependence suggested that the basic process involved in both the Gs and Gf decline with age is not speed at all, but a capacity for maintaining focused attention—a capacity that requires maintaining concentration.

The research leading to this conclusion is based on measurements of Gf that were designed to exclude speed of performance. Letter series and matrices tests have been constructed to provide measures of the average level of difficulty of problems solved, not count of the number of problems solved. One person may get a high score on these tests by solving few problems of high difficulty, whereas another person who solves many problems of low difficulty, but few of high difficulty, will get a low score. The measures obtained in this manner are referred to as power measures (Horn, 1997; see Noll & Horn, 1997, for fuller descriptions).

Power test operations tend to ensure that any variance Gf may share with Gs is not simply speed in producing answers. Such operations do not ensure that the Gf measurements are devoid of speed of thinking, however. In fact they are not. Gs measures of simple speed of scanning and comparing relate to power measures of Gf and account for significant portions of Gf aging decline (Horn, 1982, 1997; Horn et al., 1981; Horn & Noll, 1997; Noll & Horn, 1997). The simple measures appear to involve little memory or depth of processing or reasoning. The task may be simply one of quickly marking all the letter d's on a printed page, or determining whether sets of digits are the same or different.

What is involved may not be speed, per se, however. It may be capacity for concentration. The evidence for this idea comes from parting-out analyses with a very simple measure that relates to the aging decline of both Gf and Gs, but involves no speediness. The measure is obtained with a slow tracing test (first developed by Botwinick & Storandt, 1974). High score on the measure is obtained by tracing very slowly; the slower the tracing, the higher the score. To trace very, very slowly requires focused attention, that is, concentration. It has now been established in five studies (Horn et al., 1981; Noll & Horn, 1997) that this slowness/concentration measure accounts for most of the age-related variance that is associated with speediness, and most of the reliable age-related variance that the speediness has in common with measures of Gf. In other words, to think quickly requires concentration, and to solve reasoning problems requires concentration.

Age-related declines have been found for other sustained attention tasks. Measures of vigilance, for example (in which subjects must detect a stimulus change imbedded in an otherwise invariant sequence of the stimuli) decline with age (Kausler, 1990; McDowd & Birren, 1990). Age-related declines have been found for divided attention and selective attention tasks (Bors & Forrin, 1995; Horn et al., 1981; Horn & Noll, 1997; Madden, 1983; McDowd & Birren, 1990; McDowd & Craik, 1988; Plude & Hoyer, 1985; Rabbitt, 1965; Salthouse, 1991b; Wickens, Braune, & Stokes, 1987). When separate measures of concentration (slow tracing) and divided attention are partialled separately and together from measures of working memory, it is found that each independently accounts for some, but not all, the aging decline of working memory.

Older adults perform more poorly than their younger counterparts on the Stroop, a measure of resisting interference (Cohn, Dustman, & Bradford, 1984), and distracted visual search tasks (Madden, 1983; Plude & Hoyer, 1985; Rabbitt, 1965). Hasher and Zack (1988) suggest that aging decline in cognitive capability is due to distractibility and susceptibility to perceptual interference. These investigators found that manifest retrieval problems of older adults were attributable to inability to keep irrelevant information from obscuring relevant information. Horn et al. (1981) also found that measures of eschewing irrelevancies in concept formation related to measures of short-term memory, working memory, and Gf, and accounted for some of the age differences in these measures. All of these measures require concentration to maintain focused attention on a task. Hasher and Zack (1988) suggested that a basic process in working memory is one of maintaining attention. Baddeley (1993) suggested that working memory can be described as "working attention."

It is concluded from a number of these partialling studies that the Gf reasoning ability (that so resembles Spearman's g) involves processes of (a) gaining awareness of information (attention), and (b) holding different aspects of information in the span of awareness (working memory); these processes are dependent on a capacity for maintaining concentration.

Capacity for concentration may be dependent on neural recruitment—that is, synchronous firing of many neurons in patterns that correspond to the patterns of abilities involved in solving a complex problem. If neurons of a neural recruitment pattern are lost, the synchrony and hence the efficiency of the firing pattern is reduced. Grossly, this is seen in decline of Gf (SAR and Gs).

EMERGING THEORY OF HUMAN INTELLIGENCE: ABILITIES OF EXPERTISE

The results we have just reviewed provide some glimmerings of the nature of human intelligence. But only glimmerings; some things are missing in what we see in these ability test results. Aging decline is prominent. But decline doesn't characterize what we see with common sense assessments of adult intelligence. True, the results show some (Gc and TSR) enhancements of intelligence with age in adulthood, but these appear faint by comparison with the overwhelming picture of decline. The overall picture is one of increasing deficits of reasoning and memory in people (adults) who do most of the work of maintaining and advancing the culture, people who are the intellectual leaders in science, politics, business, and academics. The common-sense picture is one of maturing adults functioning at ever-higher intellectual levels, but the picture derived from research suggests the opposite of this. Common sense can be wrong, of course; nevertheless, it surely suggests that we should question the research results. Are the tests that are designed to measure intelligence really doing this?

Inadequacies of Current Theory

Indeed, there are some problems with the tests. Consider Gc, the factor that indicates enhancements of intelligence in adulthood. This factor should be a measure of the breadth and depth of knowledge of the culture that an individual has acquired. The abilities sampled in research to measure the factor are maintained with age, and in that sense are indicative of adult intelligence, but that sample is narrow and surface-like relative to the broad and diverse range of the knowledge of a culture. Tests used to measure the factor, for example vocabulary, information, and analogies, can provide only rough estimates.

A more fundamental problem is that the tests provide only a surface-like, introductory, dilettante measure of the knowledge of a culture. They don't measure the depth of knowledge, or the knowledge that is most difficult to acquire. Difficult reasoning is not measured in the factor. This can be seen in esoteric analogies, a test used to estimate a reasoning aspect of Gc. The items of this test sample relationships across several areas of knowledge, but the reasoning required in each area is simple. An item is of the form "Annual is to Perennial as Deciduous is to __?" If one has a cursory knowledge of botany or horticulture, completing the analogy is simple: It doesn't take much reasoning. The variance of the analogies test thus mainly indicates the extent to which one has introductory knowledge in several areas of scholarship. It does not represent ability in dealing with difficult abstractions in reasoning in any area. But difficult reasoning is what is called for in the work of a scientist or statesmen or engineer or plumber. Difficult reasoning is called for in measures of intelligence.

So, in-depth knowledge and in-depth reasoning are not measured in Gc. A dilettante, flitting over many areas of knowledge, will score higher on the measure than a person who has developed truly profound understanding in an area of knowledge. It is the latter, not the dilettante, who is most likely to make significant contributions to the culture and be judged to be most intelligent. Such a person is otherwise referred to as an expert. Such an expert best exemplifies the capabilities that indicate the nature and limits of human intelligence.

Defining Intelligence in Terms of Expertise

After childhood and adolescence and young adulthood people continue to think and solve problems, but usually—to an ever-larger extent as development proceeds—this thinking is directed to solving novel problems in fields of work. Adults develop abilities that help them to become expert. They come to understand a great deal about some things to the detriment of understanding other things. They neglect the work of maintaining and improving abilities previously developed that are not relevant for developing expertise. Thus, the intelligence of maturing adults becomes—more and more as development proceeds—manifested in abilities of expertise.

There are four principal implications of this analysis: (a) the measures currently used to estimate intelligence probably do not assess all the important abilities of human intelligence, (b) abilities that come to fruition in adulthood represent the quintessential expression of human intellectual capacity, (c) these abilities are abilities of expertise, and (d) the principal problems of design of research for describing these abilities are problems of identifying areas of expertise, designing measures of the abilities of expertise in these areas, and obtaining samples of people that can represent the variation that is needed to demonstrate the presence and range of expertise abilities.

Expertise Abilities of Intelligence.   The main premise of this argument is that expertise in some areas of human endeavor depends on effective application of a large amount of knowledge in reasoning to cope with novel problems. The abilities exemplified in these domains are indicative of human intelligence. The levels of complexities in reasoning resolved in expressions of expertise are comparable to the levels of complexities resolved in expressions of Gf abilities, and the problems solved often appear to be novel.[9]

In contrast to the reasoning that characterizes Gf, which is largely inductive, the reasoning involved in exercise of expertise is largely knowledge based and deductive. This is seen in descriptions of the thinking in several areas of expertise: in chess, financial planning, and medical diagnosis (Charness, 1981a, 1991; de Groot, 1978; Ericsson, 1996; Walsh & Hershey, 1993). For example, de Groot found that those at the highest level of expertise in chess chose the next move by evaluating the current situation in terms of principles derived from vast prior experience, rather than by calculating and evaluating the many move possibilities. Other work (Charness, 1981, 1991; Ericsson, 1996, 1997; Morrow, Leirer, Altieri, & Fitzsimmons, 1994; Walsh & Hershey, 1993) similarly has demonstrated that the expert characteristically uses deductive reasoning under conditions where the novice uses inductive reasoning. The expert is able to construct a framework within which to organize and effectively evaluate presented information, whereas novices, with no expertise basis for constructing a framework, search for patterns and do reasoning by trial-and-error evaluations. The expert apprehends large amounts of organized information, comprehends many relationships among elements of this information, infers possible continuations and extrapolations, and, as a result, is able to select the best from among many possibilities in deciding on the most likely outcome, consequence, or extension of relationships. The expert goes from the general (comprehension of relations, knowledge of principles) to the most likely specifics.

Expertise in problem solving also appears to involve a form of wide-span memory that is different from the forms of memory described (in current descriptions of intelligence) under the headings of short-term memory, short-term apprehension and retrieval (SAR), instantaneous memory (Sperling, 1960), and working memory (e.g., Baddeley, 1994). De Groot (1946, 1978) may have been first to recognize a distinction between expert memory and these other forms of memory. He described how, with increasing expertise, subjects became better able to rapidly access alternative chess moves of increasingly higher quality, and then base their play on these complex patterns rather than engage in extensive search. Ericsson and Kintsch, (1995) described this behavior as a form of memory. It's a capacity that emerges as expertise develops. It becomes a defining feature of advanced levels of expertise (Ericsson & Kintsch 1995; Ericsson & Delaney, 1996). It is a form of working memory, but it is functionally independent of what heretofore has been described as working memory. To distinguish it in language from this latter, which is referred to here as short-term working memory (STWM), expertise memory will be identified as wide-span working memory (WSWM). It is a capacity for holding relatively large amounts of information—large relative to STWM—in

---

[9] The difficulties of the problems solved in expert performance in chess, for example, appear to be as high as the difficulties of the items used to measure Gf. The complexities resolved in the game of GO appear to be even higher than those resolved in chess, and the problems are often clearly novel (Johnson, 1997; Mechner, 1998).

immediate awareness for periods of several minutes, and functions as an aid to solving problems and behaving expertly. WSWM is different from STWM in respect to two major features: apprehension-retention limits and access in a sequence.

The apprehension-retention limits of STWM are small and of short duration. For example, the apprehension limits for the recency effect in serial position memory, which is often taken as indicator of short-term memory, are only about three (plus or minus one), and this retention fades to zero in less than a few (sometimes estimated at 10) seconds (Glanzer & Cunitz, 1966; Roediger & Crowder, 1975). The apprehension limits for the primacy effect also are only about three (plus or minus one), with duration less than a few seconds. In a near-classic article, Miller (1956) characterized the apprehension limits for forward span memory as the "magical number seven plus or minus two"; and the duration for this memory (without rehearsal) is no more than 30 seconds. These kinds of limits have been demonstrated

For WSWM the apprehension limits are substantially eg longer than any of the limits accepted as indicating STWM—just how much larger and longer is not clear, but chess experts, for example, appear to be able to hold many more than seven elements of separate games within the span of immediate awareness for as long as several minutes (Ericsson & Kintsch, 1995; Gobet & Simon, 1996). In playing blindfold chess (Ericsson & Staszewski, 1989; Holding, 1985; Koltanowski, 1985) the expert is never able to literally see the board: All the outcomes of sequences of plays must be kept within a span of immediate apprehension. The number of elements the expert retains in such representations is much more than the seven and this retention is retained over several minutes.

It has been argued that successive chunking in STWM is sufficient to account for feats of memory displayed by experts and thus obviates any need for a concept of WSWM (Chase & Simon, 1973; Gobet & Simon, 1996). Chase and Simon reasoned that high-level chess memory was mediated by a large number (10,000 they estimated) of acquired patterns regarded as chunks, which could be hierarchically organized. The analyses of Richman, Gobet, Staszewski, and Simon (1996) suggested that the number of such chunks would have to be in excess of 100,000, rather than 10,000. In any case, the mechanism suggested by Chase and Simon was one of direct retrieval of relevant moves cued by perceived patterns of chess positions that are stored in a form of short-term working memory. They rejected a suggestion (Chase & Ericsson, 1982) that storage of generated patterns in long-term memory is possible within periods as brief as the 5-second presentations that were observed. Cooke, Atlas, Lane, and Berger (1993) and Gobet and Simon (1996), however, showed that this assumption is plausible. They found that highly skilled chess players could recall information from up to nine chess positions that had been presented one after the other as rapidly as one every 5 seconds without pauses. In the retrievals of blindfold chess, the number of chunks would appear to be larger than seven, and if chunks are maintained in a hierarchy or other such template, the representation would be changed with successive moves, and the number of sequences of such changes is larger than seven. Yet experts were able to use information of moves that were more than seven sequences removed from the point of decision.

Similarly, in studies of experts playing multiple games of chess presented on a computer screen, Saariluoma (1991) found that a chess master could simultaneously play six different games each involving more than seven relationships. The expert appeared to retain representations of many more than seven chess positions in a flexibly accessible form while moving from one game to another.

STWM is characterized by sequencing in retention, but such sequencing seems to be unimportant in WSWM. In STWM maximum span is attained only if items are retained and retrieved in the temporal order of apprehension. If a task requires retrieval in a different order, the amount recalled is substantially reduced: memory span backward, for example, is only about three-to-four, compared with the seven of forward span. In descriptions of chess experts displaying WSWM, on the other hand, information is almost as readily accessed from the middle or end of a sequence as from the front (Charness & Bosman, 1990).

The Ericsson and Kintsch (1995) analyses thus make the case that although chunking helps to explain short-term memory that is somewhat larger than seven plus two, it is not fully adequate to account for the very large apprehension, long retention, and flexibility of access that experts display. In particular, if the different sequences experts access are regarded as chunks that must be maintained if the retrieval of experts is to be adequately described, the number of such chunks must be considerably larger than seven plus two and they must be retained longer than a few seconds: thus, chunking cannot be the whole story (Ericsson & Kintsch, 1995; Gobet & Simon, 1996).

How might WSWM work? Prior theory has not spelled this out. Here the thought is that the development of expertise sensitizes the person to become more nearly aware of the large amount of information that is, for a very short period of time, available to all people (not just experts), but ordinarily is not accessed. Sperling's (1960) work indicates that for a split second the human is aware of substantially more information than is indicated by estimates of the limits of STWM. Similarly, the studies of Biederman (e.g., 1987) demonstrate recognition of complex visual stimuli involving many more than seven elements and retained for longer than 60 seconds.

Most of the information that comes into immediate awareness fades from awareness very quickly. It fades partly because new information enters awareness to take the place of previous information; it fades also because meaningful organizing systems are not immediately available to enable one to organize the incoming information. Biederman's findings demonstrate that information seen only briefly that is organized by the perceiver can be retained for long periods of time. Thus, if meaningful systems for organizing information are built up through expertise development (the systems of WSWM), and such systems are available in the immediate situation, then large amounts of briefly seen information might be organized in accordance with this system and retained for long periods of time for use in problem solving in an area of expertise. Such organized information (seen only briefly) would not be replaced by other incoming information.

The briefly-seen information would need to be that of a domain of expertise. That is, the development of expertise would not, in general, improve memory. It would do so only in a limited domain.

Further Notes on the Development of Expertise.   What we now know about expertise suggests that it is developed through intensive practice over extended periods of time and is maintained through continued efforts in regular, well-structured practice (Anderson, 1990; Ericsson, 1996; Ericsson & Charness, 1994; Ericsson, Krampe, Tesch-Romer, 1993; Ericsson & Lehmann, 1996; Walsh & Hershey, 1993). What is described as "well-structured practice" is essential for effective development of expertise. Such practice is not simply repetition and is not measured simply by number of practice trials. The practice must be designed to correct errors and move one to higher levels of performance. Practice must be well designed to identifying errors. There should be goals and appropriate feedback. Practice should be directed at advancing to ever more difficult levels of performance. It was found that in developing expertise in chess, self-directed practice using books and studying sequences of moves made by expert players, could be as effective as coach-directed practice (Charness, 1981a, 1981b, 1991; Ericsson, 1996).

Just how long it takes to reach the highest levels of expertise—one's own asymptote—is not known with precision for any domain. A "10-year rule" has been given as an approximation for domains characterized by complex problem solving, but this has been much debated (Anderson, 1990; Ericsson et al., 1993; Ericsson & Charness, 1994). The upshot of the debate is that the time it takes to become expert varies with domain, the amount and quality of practice and coaching, the developmental level at which dedication to becoming an expert begins, health, stamina, and a host of other variables. Ten years is a very rough estimation for some domains such as chess and medical diagnosis (Ericsson, 1996, p. 11).

Because it takes time (i.e., years) to reach high levels of expertise in complex problem solving, and because expertise in such domains is developed, at least partially, through the period of adulthood, it follows that expertise can improve in adulthood. Indeed, the research literature is consistent in showing that across different domains of expertise, people beginning at different ages in adulthood advance from low to asymptotic high levels of expertise (Ericsson et al., 1993). Advanced levels of expertise in chess, GO, and financial planning have been attained and maintained by older adults (Charness & Bosman, 1990; Charness, Krampe, & Mayr, 1996; Ericsson & Charness, 1994; Kasai, 1986; Walsh & Hershey, 1993). Rabbitt (1993) found that among novices, crossword-solving ability was positively correlated with test scores indicating Gf (r = .72) and negatively correlated with age (r = -.25), just as Gf is so correlated, but among experts crossword-solving ability was positively associated with age (r = +.24) and correlated near zero with Gf.

The results of Bahrick (1984), Bahrick and Hall (1991), Conway, Cohen, and Stanhope (1991), Walsh and Helshey (1993), and Krampe and Ericsson (1996) indicate that continued practice is required to maintain a high level of expert performance; if the abilities of expertise are not used, they decline. To the extent that practice is continued, expertise is maintained over periods of years and decades.

It appears, also, from the extant (albeit sparse) evidence that high levels of WSWM can be maintained into advanced age. Baltes (1997) found that in domains of specialization older adults could access information more rapidly than young adults. Charness (1981a, 1981b, 1991) found no age decrement in the depth of search for the next move and the quality of the resulting moves in chess.[10] Such findings suggest that there may be little or no decline with age for complex thinking abilities if these abilities are developed within a domain of expertise.

Also suggesting that expertise abilities indicative of intelligence can be developed and maintained in adulthood are results obtained by Krampe and Ericsson (1996) for speeded abilities. They obtained seven operationally independent measures of speed in a sample of classical pianists who ranged from amateurs to concert performers with international reputations, and who ranged in age from the mid-20s to the mid-60s. Independently of age, experts performed better than amateurs on all music-related speeded tasks. Age-related decline was found at the highest level of expertise, but reliably only for one of the seven measures and the decline was notably smaller than for persons at lower levels of expertise. The single best predictor of performance on all music-related tasks was the amount of practice participants had maintained during the previous 10 years,

In samples of practicing typists of different ages, Salthouse (1985) found that whereas abilities of finger-tapping speed, choice reaction time, and digit symbol substitution that would seem to be closely related to typing ability declined systematically with age, typing

---

[10]Depth of search is described as a point at which a player can no longer retain accurate information about the projected changes to a presented chess position (Charness & Bosman, 1990).

ability, as such, did not: Older typists attained the same typing speed as younger typists. The older typists had longer eye spans. This enabled them to anticipate larger chunks of the material to be typed. Salthouse interpreted this as a compensatory mechanism. It can also be viewed as indicating a more advanced level of expertise, for, seemingly, it would relate to improving the skill of a typist of any age.

In a study of spatial visualization in architects of different ages and levels of expertise, Salthouse, Babcock et al. (1990) found that high-level experts consistently scored above low-level experts at every age. In the abilities of expertise elderly high-level experts scored higher than youthful low-level experts. This suggests that with practice to increase and maintain expertise, cognitive abilities (of expertise) increase with advancing age.

CONCLUSIONS, IMPLICATIONS, AND EXTRAPOLATIONS

Thus it seems that some kinds of expertise require, and indicate, high levels of the abilities that indicate human intelligence. Attaining such expertise involves developing a deductive reasoning ability to solve very difficult problems. Also developed is a wide-span working memory that enables one to remain aware of, and work with, large amounts of information in the area of expertise. This facilitates expertise deductive reasoning. A cognitive speed ability also develops in the domain of expertise as high levels of expertise are attained. Very possibly there are other abilities that develop under the press to acquire expertise. Research should be directed at identifying such abilities. These expertise abilities are different from the somewhat comparable abilities of fluid reasoning (Gf), working memory (SAR), and cognitive speed (Gs) that also characterize human intelligence.

It takes a number of years to develop a high levels of expertise—10 years is a rough estimate time is needed to develop the highest levels. Much of this development must occur in adulthood. High levels of the abilities of expertise are displayed primarily in adults (not younger people). Expertise abilities of older high-level experts exceed the comparable abilities of younger persons at lower levels of expertise.

Thus, expertise abilities of intelligence are expected to increase (on average) in adulthood, that is, such abilities will increase at least in some people and in some parts of adulthood (perhaps mainly the early parts—the first 20 years, say). Burnout is common in activities that require an intense dedication and work. After working intensely for 10 years to develop expertise, one might burn out, and one would not continue to maintain and develop the abilities of expertise. Those abilities would then decline. On the other hand, people switch fields after burning out in a particular field, and such switching might be accompanied by launching a program to develop expertise in the new field. This could occur at fairly advanced ages in adulthood. Thus, generally, the average for the abilities of expertise could be expected to increase through much of adulthood.

Specifically, the implication is that deductive reasoning, wide-span memory, and expert speediness abilities associated with the development of expertise will increase concomitantly with the decreases that have been found for fluid reasoning, short-term working memory, and speediness defined outside a domain of expertise. It is possible that increase in expertise abilities necessarily results in decline in nonexpertise abilities, for the devotion of time, energy, and other resources to the development of expertise may of necessity take time, energy, and other resources away from maintenance of Gf, SAR, and Gs.

Such hypothesizing flows from sparse findings. The hypotheses may be correct, but for only some people, perhaps a small number. The extant results have often come from studies of a small number of people, sometimes only one person. The adults in these cases may be exceptional. There have been no longitudinal follow-up studies to determine the extent to which people become exceptional and maintain that status. If such development occurs only in a few cases, there are good questions to ask about how the development might be fostered in most people. There is need for further research.

GENERAL SUMMARY

The present science thus indicates that human intelligence is a melange of many abilities that are interrelated in many ways. The abilities and their interrelationships are determined by many endogenous (genetic, physiological, neurological) and exogenous influences (experiential, nutritional, hygienic). These influences operate over many minutes and months and years of life; they may be more and less potent in some developmental periods than in others. There is very little we know, much more we don't know, about the these interrelationships and determinants.

It is unlikely that there is one central deteminant running through the entire melange of abilities. If there is one such influence, it is weak, barely detectable among a chorus of other determinants: If g exists, it will be very difficult to ferret it out from all the other influences that operate to produce intellectual abilities. Small influences can be hugely important, of course, but we have no inkling that is true for g if, indeed, there is a g. Assertions that g has been discovered do nothing to help locate a possible g or indicate the importance of such an agent were it to be found.

It is known that almost any task that can be made up to measure a cognitive ability correlates positively with almost every such test. Very few exceptions to this generalization have been found, but there are a couple. The first is found in samples of very young children—under 2 years of age, particularly, perhaps under 3 years of age. In such samples, measures involving motor skill and speediness have been found to be not positively, and perhaps even slightly negatively, correlated with measures of awareness of concepts, that is, the beginnings of vocabulary. The second exception is found in very homogenous samples of young adults—all very nearly of the same age, same educational level, same ethnicity, same social class, and so on. Again measures in which there is much emphasis on speediness correlate near zero, perhaps negatively, with tests that require solving of difficult problems. But with these two exceptions, almost all cognitive ability tests are positively intercorrelated. This is referred to as a condition of positive manifold.

It is to the evidence of positive manifold that is referred to in assertions that g has been discovered. But a positive manifold is not sufficient evidence of a g. There are many ways for positive manifold to occur that do no involve one common factor.

Many variables that are not ability variables are positively correlated with ability variables (as well as among themselves). This does not indicate g. In our society variables scored in the "good" direction generally correlate positively with other things scored in the "good" direction: high ability correlates positively with ego strength, ambition, morale, family income, healthful habits, and so on, and variables scored in the "not good" direction generally correlate positively with other things scored in the "not good" direction: low ability correlates positively with neuroticism, other psychopathologies, inattentiveness, hyperactivity, boredom, lack of energy, delinquency, poverty, birth stress, and so on. Just as it is argued (e.g., by Jensen, 1998) that one can obtain a good measure of g by adding up scores on different ability tests that are positively intercorrelated, so one might argue that by adding over the presence of a long list of the aforementioned negative things and the absence of a long list of positive things one can obtain a good measure of c factor[11]— c standing for crud. The evidence for such c factor is of the same form as the evidence said to exist for a g factor. The problems with the science of the c factor are the same as the problems with the science of a g factor. In both cases many, many things can operate to produce the positive manifold of variable intercorrelations. In both cases it is not a scientific simplification to claim (or imply) that one thing produces this positive manifold. In both cases something like a bond theory of many causes is a more plausible model of the data than a one-common-factor model.

The extant evidence indicates that within the manifold of positive intercorrelations among cognitive abilities there are pockets of substantially higher intercorrelations among some abilities coupled with lower correlations of these abilities with other abilities. Such patterns of intercorrelations give rise to theories that somewhat separate sets of influences produce somewhat distinct common factors. Results from many studies now point to 60 or 70 such distinct common factors operating at primary level and some nine common factors operating at a second-order level.

One set of indicators a primary-level influences interrelate to indicate a second-order factor that rather well represents Spearman's hypotheses that human intelligence is characterized by keenness of apprehension, ability to discern extant relationships, and ability to extrapolate to generate new, implied relationships. It seems that a capacity for attaining and maintaining—concentrating—focused attention is an integral part of this clutch of abilities. This capacity for concentration appears to enable—or at least be an aspect of—speed in apprehending and scanning fundaments and possible relationships among fundaments in working toward solutions to complex problems. This set of cognitive functions is labeled fluid reasoning and symbolized Gf (the capital G in honor of Spearman and his g).

Gf does not represent a one-and-only-one common factor influence running through all abilities that indicate the nature of human intelligence. Another set of primary-level indicators interrelate to indicate a second-order factor of ready acquisition of information. It is manifested in acquisition of information that constitutes the culture of the dominant culture. The abilities of the factor are the abilities the society seeks to pass from one generation to the next through various process of acculturation, in particular those of formal education. This set of abilities is labeled crystallized knowledge and symbolized Gc.[12]

Gc and Gf together do not represent two-and-only-two common factor influences running through all abilities that indicate the nature of human intelligence. There are also common factor influences representing two forms of memory. One of these, labeled short-term working memory or short-term apprehension and retrieval (SAR), indicates span and capacity for holding information in awareness for very short periods of time—less than a minute—while, for example, working on a problem such as would be solved through the processes of Gf. The second form of memory indicates a facility for consolidating information in a manner that

---

[11]Indeed, Herrnstein & Murray (1994) obtained such a composite, scored in the opposite direction, and called it "The Middle Class Values Index." I owe the thought of calling it a crud factor to Paul Meehl, who referred to it in this manner in a conversation I had with him many years ago.

[12]The terms "crystallized" and "fluid" in the labels for Gc and Gf respectively were affixed by Cattell to represent his hypothesis that Gf was a necessary determinant of Gc—it "flowed" into production of a Gc that then became fixed rather in the way that polyps produce the calcareous skeletons that constitute a coral reef. The sparse evidence at hand suggests that something like this process may operate in the early years of development, but that as development proceeds, Gc may precede and do more to determine Gf than the reverse.

enables it to be stored and retrieved minutes, hours, and days later. This facility is labeled tertiary storage and retrieval (TSR).

Still other sets of primary-level abilities interrelate to indicate second-order factors representing cognitive functions associated with perceptual modalities. One indicates various visual functions that work together to facilitate visualization: This is labeled broad visualization, symbolized Gv. Another set of relationships is for abilities of listening and hearing and comprehending intricacies of sounds. It is referred to as auditory ability, symbolized Ga. There are very possibly somewhat comparable organizations of cognitive functions spinning off from the other sensory modalities, but there has been virtually no study of such possibilities.

Speed of reacting, speed deciding, speed of movement, speed of perceiving, various speeds in solving various different kinds of problems, speed in thinking, and other aspects of speed of responding and behaving are involved in very intricate ways in almost all the abilities that are regarded as indicating human intelligence. Five common factors involving different sets of indicators of speediness have been identified at what is approximately a second order among primary factors of speediness. The indicators of speediness do not indicate a general speed of thinking/behaving factor, nor do any of the speed factors represent a sine qua non of the other second-order systems. Indeed, as concerns Gf in particular, a capacity for behaving slowly, which seems to indicate focused concentration, largely accounts for any relationship between reasoning and speed of thinking: An ability to concentrate seems to determine any need to think quickly in solving the difficult, abstract problems that characterize Gf. It may be true that capacity for focusing concentration largely accounts for the speediness of the speed factors and their relationships to other broad cognitive factor, but these hypotheses have not been examined. Good research is needed in this area.

Systems involved in retaining information in immediate awareness, concentration, and reasoning with novel problems decline, on average, in adulthood. Yet an important referent for the concept of intelligence is high-level ability to deal successfully with complex problems in which the solutions require advanced, deep understanding of a knowledge domain. Cognitive capability systems involved in retrieving information from the store of knowledge (TSR) and the store of knowledge itself (Gc) increase over much of the period of adulthood development. These increases point to the development of expertise, but the Gc and TSR measures tap only surface-like indicators of expertise abilities. They do no indicate the depth of knowledge, ability to deal with many aspects of a problem, reasoning, and speed in considering possibilities that characterize high-level expertise performances. Gc and TSR do not measure the feats of reasoning and memory that characterize the most sublime expressions of adult intelligence. These capabilities have been described in studies of experts in chess, GO, medical diagnosis, and financial planning. Factor analytic studies have demonstrated that expert performances depend on abilities of deductive reasoning and wide-span working memory, and are associated with cognitive speed abilities, that are quite independent of the Gf reasoning, SAR short-term memory, and Gs speediness abilities of intelligence. Within a circumscribed domain of knowledge, wide-span working memory provides an expert with much more information in the immediate situation than is available in the system for short-term working memory. Wide-span working memory appears to sublimate to a form of deductive reasoning that utilizes a complex store of information to effectively anticipate, predict, evaluate, check, analyze, and monitor in problem solving within the knowledge domain. These abilities appear to characterize mature expressions of intelligence. Years of intensive, well-structured learning, and regular practice are needed to develop and maintain these abilities. To the extent that such practice occurs through the years of adulthood, these abilities will increase, to this extent important abilities of intelligence will not decline with advancing age.

JOHN LEONARD HORN 1928-2006

John Horn was born in St. Joseph, Missouri on September 7,1928, and he died in Los Angeles, California on August 18, 2006. His parents divorced when he was young and he moved with his mother to Denver, Colorado, where he grew up, first with his mother, then with an aunt and uncle, and finally with another family who took him in and treated him as their child. John dropped out of high school to join the Army during the Korean War. He saw action in the war, received a GED, attended the University of Denver on the GI Bill, and graduated Phi Beta Kappa with majors in Psychology and Chemistry. John went to the University of Melbourne to begin graduate studies in Psychology with Sam Hammond. In Australia he met Raymond B. Cattell from the University of Illinois, and he soon moved to Illinois for his Ph.D. study with Cattell where he also found time to be active in the local chapters of the NAACP and the ACLU. During his illustrious career, John received a Fulbright Fellowship (Australia), a Fulbright-Hays Award (Yugoslavia), he enjoyed visiting professorships at the University of California (Berkeley), University College (London), the University of Lund (Sweden), and a NIH Career Development Award (National Institutes of Aging). His early training in math and chemistry allowed him to take apart complex ideas and make them seem elemental and fundamental. In an era of specialization, John became an expert in Cognition and Aging, Personality and Motivation, Alcoholism, Child Abuse, and Multivariate Methodology all at once.

John Horn's dissertation work (1965) was the first empirical study of Cattell's (1941) "Theory of Fluid and Crystallized Intelligence." This theory suggested that Spearman's (1904) "Theory of General Intelligence" overlooked the key distinction between novel reasoning and thinking (Gf) and acquired knowledge (Gc), and these two broad factors had different trajectories over the life-span. John's other dissertation advisors were Lloyd Humphreys, Ledyard Tucker, and Henry Kaiser, all giants in the field of multivariate methodology. This dissertation was the first multivariate study designed with tests selected to allow a formal evaluation of these alternative theories. The empirical conclusion was quite provocative and suggested both prominent theories were flawed! The new "Horn & Cattell" theory (1966,1967, 1984) did start with broad roles for both Reasoning and Knowledge, but these were only clear in the context of several other broad cognitive factors, including Visualization, Speediness, Memory, and Auditory abilities. This result led to subsequent studies that merged concepts of individual differences with experimental studies of cognitive processes using novel methods for the separation of states, traits, and trait changes (see Horn, 1972). This early work has become the foundation of most current studies of adult cognitive aging, has been supported by large scale meta-analyses (e.g., Carroll, 1996), became the foundation of important test batteries (e.g, the Woodcock-Johnson), and it has even prompted changes in other classic test batteries (e.g., the WAIS-IU).

John returned to the University of Denver and joined the faculty of Psychology, where he worked for 25 years. During these years he published his most influential work on Psychometrics and Factor Analysis, Personality and Motivation, and the widely used Alcohol Use Inventory with Ken Wanberg (1986). One common theme in this work pointed out the problems with overly simplistic approaches to measurement and scale development and the problems with univariate analyses of multivariate phenomena. He also found time to write numerous popular articles on personality and intelligence, and on student activism and societal injustice. John published hundreds of articles and chapters, yet he only completed one book, this being a tribute to his academic mentor, Ray Cattell (1984). However, he wrote several other book length treatments on the General Linear Model approach to regression and ANOVA (1969) and factor analysis (1972), and these were widely circulated among numerous students and colleagues. In 1969 he was the first winner of the R.B. Cattell Award for early achievements in multivariate analysis, and in 1976 he was named President of the Society of Multivariate Experimental Psychology (SMEP). His scientific research at DU was sponsored by grants from the National Institutes of Health and the National Science Foundation, and he was a study section member for a decade. Two large research grants provided support for many pre-doctoral and post-doctoral students (including myself). In 1980 John was appropriately named "University of Denver Professor of the Year."

Throughout his academic career, John was involved in several well-known academic debates. A first debate, published in *Psychological Bulletin,* pitted a relatively young John Horn up against the famous USC psychometriciao, J. P. Guilford. The seeds of this debate can be found in John's classic works "A rationale and test for the number of factors in factor analysis" (1965) and "Subjectivity in Factor Analysis" (1967). But the debate became more focused when Horn & Knapp (1973, 1974) posed a complete refutation of the factorial basis of Guilford's popular "Structure of Intellect" (SOI) model of cognitive abilities. They criticized the evidence in favor of SOI theory and, supported by statistical simulations, showed how easy it was to use "Procrustean" target rotation to obtain virtually any factorial solution desired, especially one with as many dimensions as SOI theory (i.e., 120). The response by Guilford (1974) was heated, to say the least, but it is fair to say that over the next decade the popular SOI model lost its elevated status in psychometric practice. The second set of debates, published here in *American Psychologist,* started as a critique of the longitudinal work of the famous life-span researchers, Paul Baltes and Warner K. Schaie. The presentations of Horn & Donaldson (1976,1977) attempted to reinterpret the complex inferences of the age, time, and cohort conundrum in studies of adult development. Horn & Donaldson basically concluded that, no matter what data collection method was used, most human cognitive abilities decline relatively early in the adult life span (e.g., as early as age 65). The responses by Baltes & Schaie (1977) were compelling and this debate has since become enjoyable reading for many cohorts of life-span researchers. In his most recent debates, Professor Horn took on any and all researchers who tried to provide convincing evidence in support of Spearman's original g theory (e.g., Horn, 1988,1998). As with all other debates, John emphasized the importance of empirical evidence and multivariate methodology. John did a lot of this work himself, and concluded that Spearman's g did not meet the criteria Spearman himself defined (see Horn & McArdle, 2006).

John moved to the University of Southern California in August 1986 where he was Professor of Psychology and Head of the Adult Development and Aging program for the past 20 years. At USC, John was actively involved in graduate and undergraduate student education — including coordinating two large-scale training grants in aging research. In 1996 John won the Saul B. Sells Award for Lifetime Achievements in Multivariate Experimental Psychology from SMEP. For the past 15 years John was also an active member of the Data Analysis Research Network (DARN) of the National Collegiate Athletic Association (NCAA). In recent years he focused his research on "Adult Lifestyle and Intellectual Development," where he developed his "Extended Gf-Gc Theory" A new approach, it emphasized the intensive study of behavior at the individual level, and introduced new ideas about "expertise" and multiple pathways of knowledge acquisition.

John was quite sure that the concept of Fluid Intelligence was a good description of our basic brainpower, much as in Spearman's original conception of "g", but he was also convinced that the construct of Crystallized Intelligence needed to be measured in the context of the persons' own goals and experiences. His recent collaborations included an NICHD funded grant on "The Impact of Neglect on Adolescent Development," with the USC School of Social Work. John was certainly a larger-than-life professor and an active presence at USC. He taught his last class in the Spring 2006 semester where despite being ill, John, as always, was willing and eager to offer his time to others.

We can find the key source of John's atypical academic approach in his own writings. In his 1993 obituary for Henry Kaiser, John wrote the following:

> There were many admirable professors at Illinois at the time... but Kaiser was by far and away the least stuffy and stodgy, the least pompous and pretentious, the most unconventional, the most irreverent, the most individualistic, and the most refreshing... He enjoyed what he did, and what he seemed to like to do most was play - with ideas. It was also part of why he was regarded as eccentric - even outlandish... He scared the establishment, but not because he was a wild-eyed iconoclastic revolutionary; he wasn't that; he scared them with ingenious curiosity.... He also brought huge, comprehended knowledge to what he taught... Most of what I learned from Henry Kaiser I could not have learned from reading textbooks and articles — partly because it wasn't there yet, but mainly because it couldn't be found there in the thoroughly argued, hear-all-sides manner in which Henry presented it... I owe him for this... His joyous dedication to ideas was a great model. I think I speak for many when I say I have tried to emulate that model (J.L.Horn, 1993, *Multivariate Behavioral Research*).

We could not describe John Horn's unique academic style any better!

On a personal note, John had a wonderful sense of humor, and he laughed at everyone's jokes, all day long, even in the middle of classes. John was also an incredibly active person, and he loved competitive sports. He was a great boxer and gymnast in high school and college; became an exceptional softball player in his 50's; became a great racquetball player in his 60s; and worked hard at golf in his 70s. John is survived by his wonderful family - his wife, Penelope K. Trickett, Stein/Sachs Professor of Mental Health in the USC School of Social Work, his sister Ellen Demsky, his six children, and five grandchildren. John was extremely proud of the academic achievements of his children — John L. Horn Jr. with a B.S. from Stanford University (1982), James Brian Horn with an M.S. from Colorado State University (1985), Julia L. Banzi with an M.A. from UC Santa Barbara (2002), Kate Trickett with a BA from USC (2001), Jennifer Trickett with an MA from USC (2004), and Jennifer L. Zoltanski with a Ph.D. from Brandeis University (2006).

It was my pleasure to work with John Horn for the past 30 years, first as a post-doc at DU, and most recently as his colleague at USC. John Horn was a world-renowned scholar of immense intellect and he was highly respected in his time. So I think his major contributions to Psychology and influence on psychologists will continue to grow. His challenging factor analytic methods of the 1960s, the important methodological debates of the 1970s and 1980s, including his continuing resistance to faddish trends in psychological research, all represent fundamental contributions. Through his research and teaching he forced people to question popular assumptions, evaluate all the data available, and challenged us to think longer, harder, and better. His inspiration will continue to inspire important research in the fields of multivariate analysis and human cognitive abilities for many decades to come. For all of us who knew him well, John Horn will always remain a unique person and out friendly role model. John J. McArdle

REFERENCES

Alexander, W. P. (1935). Intelligence, concrete and abstract. *British Journal of Psychology: Monograph Supplement.*

Anderson, J. R. (1990). *Cognitive psychology and its implications (3rd ed.).* New York: W. H. Freeman.

Atkinson, R. C., & Shiffrin, R. M. (1968). Human memory: A proposed system and its control processes. In K. W. Spence & J. T. Spence (Eds.), *The psychology of learning and motivation: Advances in research and theory* Vol. 2, (pp. 89–195). New York: Academic.

Baddeley, A. (1993). Working memory or working attention? In A. Baddeley & Weiskrantz (Eds.), *Attention: Selection, awareness, and control. A tribute to Donald Broadbent* (pp. 152–170). Oxford, England: Oxford University Press.

Baddeley, A. (1994). Memory. In A. M. Colman (Ed.), *Companion encyclopedia of psychology* (Vol. 1, pp. 281–301). London: Routledge.

Bahrick, H. P. (1984). Semantic memory content in permaslore: 50 years of memory for Spanish learned in school. *Journal of Experimental Psychology: General, 113,* 1–29.

Bahrick, H. P., & Hall, L. K. (1991). Lifetime maintenance of high school mathematics content. *Journal of Experimental Psychology: General, 120,* 20–33.

Baltes, P. B. (1997). On the incomplete architecture of human ontogeny: Selection, optimization, and compensation as foundation of developmental theory. *American Psychologist, 52,* 366–380.

Biederman, I. (1987). Recognition-by-Components: a theory of human image understanding. *Psychological Review,* 94, 2, 115–147.

Birren, J. E. (1974). Translations in gerontology—From lab to life: Psychology and speed of response. *American Psychologist, 29,* 808–815.

Bors, D. A., & Forrin, B. (1995). Age, speed of information processing, recall, and fluid intelligence. *Intelligence, 20,* 229–248.

Botwinick, J. (1978). *Aging and behaviour: A comprehensive integration of research findings.* New York: Springer.

Botwinick, J. & Storandt, M. (1974). *Memory related functions and age.* Springfield, IL: Charles Thomas.

Bower, G. H. (1972). Mental imagery and associative learning. In L. W. Gregg (Ed.), *Cognition in learning and memory* (pp. 213–228). New York: Wiley.

Bower, G. H. (1975). Cognitive psychology: An introduction, In W. K. Estes (Ed.), *Handbook of learning and cognitive processes (Vol. 1, pp. 25–80)* Hillsdale, NJ: Lawrence Erlbaum Associates.

Broadbent, D. E. (1966). The well-ordered mind. *American Educational Research Journal, 3,* 281–295.

Brown, W. (1933). The mathematical and experimental evidence for the existence of a central intellective factor. *British Journal of Psychology, 23,* 171–179.

Brown, W. A., & Stephenson, W. (1933). A test of the theory of the two factors. *British Journal of Psychology, 23,* 352–370.

Burt, C. (1909). Experimental tests of general intelligence. *British Journal of Psychology, 3,* 94–177.

Burt, C. (1911). Experimental tests of higher mental processes and their relation to general intelligence. *Journal of Experimental Pedagogy and Training, 1,* 93–112.

Burt, C. (1924). *Report of consultative committee on psychological tests of educable capacity.* London: H. M. Stationery Office.

Carpenter, P. A., & Just, M. A. (1989). The role of working memory in language comprehension. In D. Clahr & K. Kotovski (Eds.), *Complex information processing: The impact of Herbert A. Simon* (pp. 31–68). Hillsdale, NJ: Lawrence Erlbaum Associates.

Carroll, J. B. (1993). *Human cognitive abilities: A survey of factory-analytic studies.* New York: Cambridge University Press.

Carter, H. D. (1928). The organization of mechanical intelligence, *Journal of Genetic Psychology, 35,* 270–285.

Cattell, R. B. (1941). Some theoretical issues in adult intelligence testing. *Psychological Bulletin, 38,* 592.

Cattell, R. B. (1957). *Personality and motivation structure and measurement*. New York: World Book.

Cattell, R. B. (1963). Theory of fluid and crystallized intelligence: A critical experiment. *Journal of Educational Psychology, 54*, 1–22.

Cattell, R. B. (1971). *Abilities: Their structure, growth and action*. Boston: Houghton- Mifflin.

Cattell, R. B. (1979). Are culture-fair intelligence tests possible and necessary? *Journal of Research and Development in Education, 12*, 1–13.

Cavanaugh, J. C. (1997). *Adult development and aging (3rd ed)*. New York: ITP.

Charness, N. (1981a). Search in chess: Age and skill differences. *Journal of Experimental Psychology: Human Perception and Performance, 7*(2), 467–476.

Charness, N. (1981b). Visual short-term memory and aging in chess players. *Journal of Gerontology, 36*(5), 615–619.

Charness, N. (1991). Expertise in chess: The balance between knowledge and search. In K. A. Ericsson & J. Smith (Eds.), *Toward a general theory of expertise* (pp. 39–63). New York: Cambridge University Press.

Charness, N., & Bosman, E. A. (1990). Expertise and aging: Life in the lab. In T. M. Hess (Ed.), *Aging and cognition: Knowledge organization and utilization* (pp. 343–386). New York: Elsevier.

Charness, N., Krampe, R., & Mayr, U. (1996). The role of practice and coaching in entrepreneurial skill domains: An international comparison of life-span chess skill acquisition. In K. A. Ericsson (Ed.), *The road to excellence* (pp. 51–80). Mahwah, NJ: Lawrence Erlbaum Associates.

Chase, W. G., & Ericsson, K. A. (1982). Skill and working memory. In G. H. Bower (Ed.), *The psychology of learning and motivation* (Vol. 16, pp. 1–58). New York: Academic Press.

Chase, W. G., & Simon, H. A. (1973). Perception in chess. *Cognitive Psychology, 4*, 55–81.

Conway, M. A., Cohen, G., & Stanhope, N. (1991). On the very long-term retention of knowledge acquired through formal education: Twelve years of cognitive psychology. *Journal of Experimental Psychology: General, 120*, 395–409.

Cooke, N. J., Atlas, R. S., Lane, D. M., & Berger, R. C. (1993). Role of high-level knowledge in memory for chess positions. *American Journal of Psychology, 106*, 321–351.

Corsellis, J. A. N. (1976). Aging and the dementias. In W. Blackwood & J. A. N. Corsellis (Eds.), *Greenfield's Neuropathology* (pp. 796–848) London: Arnold.

Cox, G. W. (1928). *Mechanical aptitude*. London: Methuen.

Craik, F. I. M. (1977). Age differences in human memory. In J. E. Birren & K. W. Schaie (Eds.) *Handbook of the Psychology of Aging*. New York: Van Nostrand-Reinhold.

Craik, F. I. M., & Trehub, S. (Eds.). (1982). *Aging and cognitive processes*. New York: Plenum.

Cunningham, W. R., & Tomer, A. (1990). Intellectual abilities and age: Concepts, theories, and analyses. In A.E. Lovelace (Ed.), *Aging and cognition: Mental processes, self awareness, and interventions* (pp. 279–406). Amsterdam: Elsevier.

DeFries, J. C., Vandenberg, S. G. & McClearn, G. E. The genetics of specific cognitive abilities. *Annual Review of Genetics*, 1976, 10, 170–207.

de Groot, A. D. (1978). *Thought and choice in chess*. The Hague, Netherlands: Mouton.

Ekstrom, R. B., French, J. W., & Harman, M. H. (1979). Cognitive factors: Their identification and replication. *Multivariate Behavioral Research Monographs, 79–82*.

El Koussy, A. A. H. (1935). The visual perception of space. *British Journal of Psychology, Monograph Supplement*, No. 20.

Ericsson, K. A. (1996). The acquisition of expert performance. In K. A. Ericsson (Ed.), *The road to excellence* (pp. 1–50). Mahwah, NJ: Lawrence Erlbaum Associates.

Ericsson, K. A. (1997). Deliberate practice and the acquisition of expert performance: An overview. In H. Jorgensen & A. C. Lehmann (Eds.), *Does practice make perfect?: Current theory and research on instrumental music practice* (pp. 9–51). NMH- publikasjoner.

Ericsson, K. A., & Charness, N. (1994). Expert performance. *American Psychologist, 49*, 725–747.

Ericsson, K. A., & Delaney, P. F. (1996). Working memory and expert performance. In R. H. Logie & K. J. Gilhooly (Eds.), *Working memory and thinking* (pp. 93–114). Hillsdale, NJ: Lawrence Erlbaum Associates.

Ericsson, K. A., & Kintsch, W. (1995). Long-term working memory. *Psychological Review, 105*, 211–245.

Ericsson, K. A., Krampe, R. T., & Tesch-Romer, C. (1993). The role of deliberate practice in the acquisition of expert performance. *Psychological Review, 100*(3), 363–406.

Ericsson, K. A., & Lehmann, A. C. (1996). Expert and exceptional performance: Evidence of maximal adaptation to task constraints. *Annual Review of Psychology, 47*, 273–305.

Ericsson, K. A. & Staszewski, J. (1989). Skilled memory and expertise: Mechanisms of exceptional performance. In D. Klahr & K. Kotovsky (Eds.), *Complex information processing* (pp. 235–268). Hillsdale, NJ: Lawrence Erlbaum Associates.

Estes, W. K. (1974). Learning theory and intelligence. *American Psychologist, 29*, 740–749.

Eysenck, H. J. (Ed.). (1982). *A model for intelligence.* Berlin, Germany: Springer-Verlag

Eysenck, H. J. (1987). Speed of information processing, reaction time, and the theory of intelligence. In P. A. Vernon (Ed.), *Speed of information processing and intelligence* (pp. 21–68). Norwood, NJ: Ablex.

Gathercole. S. E. (1994). The nature and uses of working memory. In P. Morris & M. Gruneberg (Eds.), *Theoretical aspects of memory* (pp. 50–78). London: Routledge.

Genshaft & Harrison (Eds), *Contemporary Intellectual Assessment* (pp. 53–91). New York: Guilford Press.

Glanzer, M., & Cunitz, A. R. (1966). Two storage mechanisms in free recall. *Journal of Verbal Learning and Verbal Behavior, 5*, 351–360.

Gobet, F., & Simon, H. A. (1996). Templates in chess memory: A mechanism for recalling several boards. *Cognitive Psychology, 31*, 1–40.

Gottfredson, L. S. (1997). Why g matters: The complexity of everyday life. *Intelligence, 24*, 79–132.

Guilford, J. P. (1964). Zero intercorrelations among tests of intellectual abilities. *Psychological Bulletin, 61*, 401–404.

Gustafsson, J. E., & Undheim, J. O. (1996). Individual differences in cognitive functions. In D. C. Berliner & R. C. Calfee (Eds.), *Handbook of educational psychology* (pp. 186–242). New York: Simon & Schuster Macmillan.

Hachinski, V.(1980) Relevance of cerebrovascular changes in mental function. *Mechanisms of Aging and Development*, 10, 1–11.

Haksitan, A. R., & Cattell, R. B. (1974). The checking of primary ability structure on a broader basis of performances. *British Journal of Educational Psychology, 44*, 140–154.

Harwood, E., & Naylor, G. F. K. (1971). Changes in the constitution of the WAIS intelligence pattern with advancing age. *Australian Journal of Psychology, 23*, 297–303.

Hasher, L., & Zack, R. T. (1988). Working memory, comprehension, and aging: A review and a new view. In G. H. Bower (Ed.), *The psychology of learning and motivation* (Vol. 22, pp. 193–225). San Diego, CA: Academic Press.

Hebb, D. O. (1941). The clinical evidence concerning the nature of normal adult test performance. *Psychological Bulletin, 38*, 593.

Herrnstein, R. & Murray, C. (1994). *The bell curve: Intelligence and class structure in American life.* New York: Free Press.

Hertzog, C. (1989). Influences of cognitive slowing on age differences. *Developmental Psychology, 25*, 636–651.

Holding, D. H. (1985). *The psychology of chess skill.* Hillsdale, NJ: Lawrence Erlbaum Associates.

Horn, J. L. (1968). Organization of abilities and the development of intelligence. *Psychological Review*, 75, 242–259.

Horn, J. L. (1972). The structure of intellect: Primary abilities. In R. M. Dreger (Ed.), *Multivariate personality research* (pp. 451–511). Baton Rouge, LA: Claitor's Publishing.

Horn, J. L. (1982). The aging of human abilities. In B. B. Wolman (Ed.), *Handbook of developmental psychology* (pp. 847–870). Englewood Cliffs, NJ: Prentice-Hall.

Horn, J. L. (1989) Models for intelligence. In R. Linn (Ed.), *Intelligence: Measurement, theory and public policy* (pp. 29–73). Urbana, IL: University of Illinois Press.

Horn, J. L. (1994). The theory of fluid and crystallized intelligence. In R. J. Sternberg (Ed.), *The encyclopedia of human intelligence* (pp. 443–456). New York: Cambridge University Press.

Horn, J. L. (1997). On the mathematical relationship between factor or component coefficients and differences between means. *Current Psychology of Cognition, 16*, 719–726.

Horn, J. L. (1998). A basis for research on a ge differences in cognitive capabilities. In J.J. McArdle, & R. Woodcook, (Eds.), *Human cognitive abilities in theory and practice* (pp. 57–92). Chicago: Riverside.

Horn, J. L. (2002). Selections of evidence, misleading assumptions, and over-simplifications: the political message of the Bell Curve. In J. Fish (Ed.). *Race and Intelligence: Separating Science from Myth* (pp. 297–325). Mahwah, NJ: Lawrence Erlbaum Associates.

Horn, J. L., & Cattell, R. B. (1967). Age differences in fluid and crystallized intelligence. *Acta Psychologica, 26*, 107–129.

Horn, J. L., & Donaldson, G. (1980). Cognitive development in adulthood. In O. G. Brim & J. Kagan (Eds.), *Constancy and change in human development* (pp. 445–529). Cambridge, MA: Harvard University Press.

Horn, J. L., Donaldson, G., & Engstrom, R. (1981). Apprehension, memory, and fluid intelligence decline in adulthood. *Research in Aging, 3*(1), 33–84.

Horn, J. L., & Hofer, S. M. (1992). Major abilities and development in the adult period. In R. J. Sternberg & C. Berg (Eds.), *Intellectual development* (pp. 44–99). New York: Cambridge University Press.

Horn, J. L., & Knapp, J. R. (1973). On the subjective character of the empirical base of Guilford's structure-of-intellect model. *Psychological Bulletin, 80*, 33–43.

Horn, J. L., & Knapp, J. R. (1974). Thirty wrongs don't make a right: A reply to Guilford. *Psychological Bulletin.*

Horn, J. L., & Noll, J. (1993). A system for understanding cognitive capabilities. In D. K. Detterman (Ed.), *Current topics in intelligence.* Norwood, NJ: Ablex.

Horn, J. L., & Noll, J. (1997). Human cognitive capabilities: Gf-Gc theory. In J. L. Flanagan, P.I.

Humphreys, L. G. (1971). Theory of intelligence. In R. Cancro (Ed.), *Intelligence: Genetic and environmental influences* (pp. 31–42). New York: Gune & Stratton.

Hundal, P. S., & Horn, J. L. (1977). On the relationships between short-term learning and fluid and crystallized intelligence. *Applied Psychological Measurement, 1*, 11–21.

Jensen, A. R. (1982). Reaction time and psychometric g. In H. J. Eysenck (Ed.), *A new model for intelligence* (pp. 93–132). New York: Springer-Verlag.

Jensen, A. R. (1987). Psychometric g as a focus of concerted research effort. *Intelligence, 11*, 193–198.

Jensen, A. R. (1993). Why is reaction time correlated with psychometric g? *Current Directions in Psychological Science, 2*(2) 53–56.

Jensen, A. R. (1998). *The g factor: The science of mental ability.* London: Praeger.

Johnson, G. (1997, July 2). To test a powerful computer, play an ancient game. *The New Times,* July 29 pp. B1, B13–14.

Joreskog, K. G. (1967). Some contributions to maximum likelihood factor analysis. *Psychometrika, 32*, 443–482.

Kasai, K. (1986). *Ido de atama ga yoku naru hon* [Becoming smart with GO]. Tokyo: Shikai.

Kaufman, A. S. (1990). *Assessing adolescent and adult intelligence.* Boston: Allyn & Bacon.

Kausler, D. H. (1990). *Experimental psychology, cognition, and human aging.* New York: Springer.

Kelley, T. L. (1928). *Crossroads in the mind of man.* Palo Alto, CA: Stanford University Press.

Koltanowski, G. (1985). *In the dark.* Coraopolis, PA: Chess Enterprises.

Krampe, R. T., & Ericsson, K. A. (1996). Maintaining excellence: Deliberate practice and elite performance in young and older pianists. *Journal of Experimental Psychology: General, 125*(4), 331–359.

Lashley, K. S. (1929). *Brain mechanisms and intelligence: A quantitative study of injuries to the brain.* Chicago: University of Chicago Press.

Lavond, D. G., & Kanzawa, S. A. (2000). Inside the black box. In J. E. Steinmetz, M. Gluck, & P. Solomon (Eds.), *Model systems and the neurobiology associative learning: A festschrift in honor of Richard F. Thompson* (pp. 245–269) Hillsdale, NJ: Lawrence Erlbaum Associates.

Lawley, D. N. (1943–1944). A note on Karl Person's selection formula. *Proceedings of the Royal Society of Edinburgh (Section A),* 28–30.

Madden, D. J. (1983). Aging and distraction by highly familiar stimuli during visual search. *Developmental Psychology, 19*, 499–507.

Madden, D. J. (1985). Adult age differences in memory-driven selective attention. *Developmental Psychology, 21*(4), 655–665.

Madden, D. J., & Nebes, R. D. (1980). Aging and the development of automaticity in visual search. *Developmental Psychology, 16*, 277–296.

McDowd, J. M., & Birren, J. E. (1990). Aging and attentional processes. In J. E. Birren & K. W. Schaie (Eds.), *Handbook of the Pychology of aging* (3rd ed., pp. 222–233). New York: Academic Press.

McDowd, J. M., & Craik, F. I. M. (1988). Effects of aging and task difficulty on divided attention performance. *Journal of Experimental Psychology: Human Perception and Performance, 14*(20), 267–280.

McGrew, K. S., Werder, J. K., & Woodcock, R. W. (1991). *Woodcock-Johnson technical manual.* Allen, TX: One DLM Park.

Mechner, D. A. (1998, January/February). All systems Go. *The Sciences,* 32–37.

Meredith, W. (1964). Notes on factorial invariance. *Psychometrika, 29*, 177–185.

Meredith, W., & Horn, J. L. (2001). The role of factorial invariance in modeling growth and change. In A. G. Sayer & L. M. Collins (Eds.), *New methods for the analysis of change* (pp.—). Washington, DC: American Psychological Association.

Miller, G. A. (1956). The magical number seven, plus or minus two: Some limits on our capacity for processing information. *Psychological Review, 63*, 81–97.

Morrow, D., Leirer, V., Altieri, P., & Fitzsimmons, C. (1994). When expertise reduces age differences in performance. *Psychology and Aging, 9*, 134–148.

Nettelbeck, T. (1994). Speediness. In R. Sternberg (Ed.), *Encyclopedia of intelligence* (pp. 1014–1019). New York: Macmillan.

Noll, J., & Horn, J. L. (1997). Age differences in processes of fluid and crystallized intelligence. In J. J. McArdle & W. Woodcock (Eds.), *Human cognitive abilities in theory and practice* (pp. 263–298). Chicago: Riverside.

Patterson, D. G., & Elliot, R. N. (1930). *Minnesota Mechanical Ability Tests.* Minneapolis, MN: University of Minnesota Press.

Plude, D. J., & Hoyer, W. J. (1985). Attention and performance: Identifying and localizing age deficits. In N. Charness (Ed.), *Aging and human performance* (pp. 47–99). New York: Wiley.

Rabbitt, P. (1965). An age-decrement in the ability to ignore irrelevant information. *Journal of Gerontology, 20*, 233–238.

Rabbitt, P. (1993). Crystal quest: A search for the basis of maintenance of practice skills into old age. In A. Baddeley & L. Weiskrantz (Eds.), *Attention: Selection, awareness, and control* (pp. 188–230). Oxford, England: Clarendon Press.

Rabbitt, P., & Abson, V. (1991). Do older people know how good they are? *British Journal of Psychology, 82*, 137–151.

Raven, J. C. (1941). Standardization of progressive matrices, 1938. *British Journal of Medical Psychology, 19*, 137–151.

Richman, H. B., Gobert, H., Staszewski, J. J., & Simon, H. A. (1996). Perceptual and memory processes in the acquisition of expert performance: The EPAM model. In K. A. Ericsson (Ed.), *The road to excellence* (pp. 167–188). Mahwah, NJ: Lawrence Erlbaum Associates.

Rimoldi, H. J. (1948). Study of some factors related to intelligence. *Psychometrika, 13*, 27–46.

Roediger, H. L., & Crowder, R. G. (1975). Spacing of lists in free recall. *Journal of Verbal Learning and Verbal Behavior, 14*, 590–602.

Salthouse, T. A. (1985). Speed of behavior and its implications for cognition. In J. E. Birren & K. W. Schaie (Eds.), *Handbook of the psychology of aging* (2nd ed., pp. 400–426). New York: Van Nostrand Reinhold.

Salthouse, T. A. (1987). The role of representations in age differences in analogical reasoning. *Psychology and Aging, 2*, 357–362.

Salthouse, T. A. (1991). *Theoretical perspectives on cognitive aging.* Hillsdale, NJ: Lawrence Erlbaum Associates.

Salthouse, T. A. (1992). *Mechanisms of age-cognition relations in adulthood*. Hillsdale, NJ: Lawrence Erlbaum Associates.

Salthouse, T. A. (1993). Speed medication of adult age differences in cognition. *Developmental Psychology, 29*, 727–738.

Salthouse, T. A. (1994). The nature of influence of speed on adult age differences in cognition. *Developmental Psychology, 30*, 240–259.

Salthouse, T. A., Babcock, R. L., Skouronik, E., Mitchel, D. R., & Palmon, R. (1990). Age and experience effects in spatial visualization. *Developmental Psychology, 25*, 128–136.

Salthouse, T. A., Kausler, D. H., & Saults, J. S. (1990). Age, self-assessed health status, and cognition. *Journal of Gerontology, 45*, 156–160.

Salthouse, T. A., & Somberg, B. L. (1982). Isolating the age deficit in speeded performance. *Journal of Gerontology, 37*, 59–63.

Schaie, K. W. (1996). *Intellectual development in adulthood: The Seattle longitudinal study*. Cambridge, England: Cambridge University Press.

Spearman, C. E. (1904). "General intelligence," objectively determined and measured. *American Journal of Psychology, 15*, 201–293.

Spearman, C. (1914) Theory of two factors. *Psychological Review, 21*, 101–115.

Spearman, C. (1923). *The nature of intelligence and the principles of cognition*. London: Macmillan.

Spearman, C. E. (1927). *The abilities of man: Their nature and measurement*. New York: Macmillan.

Sperling, G. (1960). The information available in brief visual presentations. *Psychological Monographs, 74*, 498.

Stankov, L. (1986). Age-related changes in auditory abilities and in a competing task. *Multivariate Behavioral Research, 21*, 65–71.

Stankov, L., & Horn, J. L. (1980). Human abilities revealed through auditory tests. *Journal of Educational Psychology, 72*, 21–44.

Thomson, G. A. (1919). On the cause of hierarchical order among correlation coefficients. *Proceedings of the Royal Society, A, 95*, 400–408.

Thompson, R. F. (1993). *The brain: A neuroscience primer*. New York: Freeman.

Thorondike, R. L., Hagen, E. P., & Sattler, J. M. (1986). *Stanford-Binet Intelligence Scale*, 4th ed. Chicago: Riverside.

Thurstone, L. L. (1931). Multiple factor analysis. *Psychological Review, 38*, 406–427.

Thurstone, L. L. (1935). *The vectors of mind*. Chicago: University of Chicago Press.

Thurstone, L. L. (1938). Primary mental abilities. *Psychometric Monographs, (1)*. Chicago: University of Chicago Press.

Thurstone, L. L. (1947). *Multiple factor analysis*. Chicago: University of Chicago Press.

Thurstone, L. L., & Thurstone, T. G. (1941). Factorial studies of intelligence. *Psychometric Monographs*.

Walsh, D. A. (1982). The development of visual information processes in adulthood and old age. In F. I. M. Craik & S. Trehub (Eds.), *Aging and cognitive processes* (pp. 99–125). New York: Plenum.

Walsh, D. A. (1990). *Brinley plots: A window to view psychological laws or a mirror for distorting psychological phenomena?* Psychology Department Papers. University of Southern California.

Walsh, D. A., & Hershey, D. A. (1993). Mental models and the maintenance of complex problem solving skills in old age. In J. Cerella, J. Rybash, W. Hoyer, & M. Commons (Eds.), *Adult information processing: Limits on loss* (pp. 553–584). San Diego: Academic Press.

Waugh, N. C., & Norman, D. A. (1965). Primary memory. *Psychological Review, 72*, 89–104.

Wechsler, D. (1955). *Manual for the Wechsler Adult Intelligence Scale*. New York: Psychological Corporation.

Wickens, C. D., Braune, R., & Stokes, A. (1987). Age differences in the speed and capacity of information processing: I. A dual-task approach. *Psychology and Aging, 2*, 70–78.

Woodcock, R. W. (1995). Theoretical foundations of the WJ-R measures of cognitive ability. *Journal of Psychoeducational Assessment, 8*, 231–258.

Woodcock, R. W. (1996). *The Woodcock-Johnson Psycho-Educational Battery—Revised*. Itaska, IL: Riverside Publishing.

11
▼▼▼▼▼▼▼

Become a Demosthenes! Compensating Age-Related Memory Deficits with Expert Strategies

Reinhold Kliegl
Doris Philipp
University of Potsdam

INTRODUCTION AND BACKGROUND

The primary association with the theme "extending intelligence" are training programs that improve abilities in the latent construct of intelligence. Two prominent problems with this approach relate to transfer of training. First, typically, training of intelligence tests show limited transfer even to other tests of the same latent construct. For example, training of induction with letter series does not show much benefit for induction with figural relations although both tests are standard markers of fluid intelligence (Baltes, Dittmann-Kohli, & Kliegl, 1986). Second, "extending intelligence" suggests a transfer of intelligent strategies to everyday behavior; we want persons to act more intelligently in life. The strong evidence for limits of transfer suggests that standard intelligence training programs are severely challenged with such a criterion. In this chapter we present an alternative approach to extending intelligent strategies to a specific real-life problem. The basic message is: Become a Demosthenes! Turn the behavior you want to improve into a topic of special competence, just as the famous Greek orator did with his speech impediment! We call this approach the expertise approach and we illustrate it for a problem that many of us find bothersome, namely our memory for persons, in particular their names. The approach worked for at least some old adults who as a group rank this problem very highly among what they consider negative cognitive changes associated with getting older.

The standard recommendation for age-related memory deficits is some form of mnemonic training (see Stigsdotter-Neely & Bäckman, 1993; Yesauage & Rose, 1984; Yesauage, Rose, & Brown, 1983). It is well known that healthy old adults can learn strategies to improve their memory for words or to increase their performance on intelligence tests (for reviews see

Camp, 1998, Verhaeghen, Marcoen, & Goossens, 1992). For example, old adults that were trained in generating mental images along with depositing them at mentally visited landmarks when learning a list of words recalled more words than untrained young adults (Baltes & Kliegl, 1992; Kliegl, Smith, & Baltes, 1989, 1990). At the same time such training studies also revealed that young adults profit more from training than old adults.

There are two problems with this research. First, such laboratory-acquired mnemonic skills do not transfer very well to everyday life. True: The method-of-loci mnemonic may generate amazement in an uninitiated audience at a party. However, somewhat surprisingly, even people proficient in its use rarely—if ever—use it for memorizing a list of groceries, the most cited prototypical application, or other purposes (Camp, 1998). Second, and unfortunately, such mnemonic strategies apparently do not work very well for one prominent memory problem—the problem of remembering names. Of course, bad memory for names is a very frequent complaint of both young and old adults but apparently it becomes much more severe with age than other deficits. For example, 61% of older adults mentioned learning and remembering of names among their top four choices of memory skills they wish to improve (Leirer, Morrow, Sheikh, & Pariante, 1990). Indeed, we carried out several studies that are in agreement with a somewhat pessimistic outlook on older adults' person memory. We review some of our experimental results obtained with this standard approach in the first section of this chapter. In the second section, we present an expertise approach that we think holds more promise in this respect. Note, however, that so far its principles are supported only by a few case studies. So whether this approach can be recommended as a general strategy needs to be seen; at present it is hardly more than a speculation. In the third section, we discuss the implications of this expertise approach for general approaches to extend intelligence.

THE STANDARD APPROACH

The standard approach consists of informing a group of persons of the powerful effects of mental images on memory. In the case of memory for faces, the mental images are to link features of facial physiognomy and name. This is a very well-known strategy and part of any book about how to improve one's memory (e.g., Higbee, 2001; Lorayne & Lucas, 1974). Basically, the idea is to look for an association between the name and a prominent feature of the person's face. For example, suppose you are introduced to "Mr. Seller," a man with noticeably larger than normal ears. One option is to imagine the person's ears in a very exaggerated form. Obviously, this is easier if the ears are already slightly "sail-shaped." Generating a mental image linking "sail ears" with "Seller" will increase the chances of remember the person's name at the next meeting. With some chance the ears will pop out in their caricature version, which in turn should trigger one's memory of the name "Seller." Similar strategies will work for other facial features: nose may look like hook, eyes like deep waters, mouths may have a heart shape.

Mnemonic Instruction for Artificial Faces (Experiments 1 and 2)

How do young and old adults respond to instruction in this mnemonic technique? In a first study we presented lists of face-place pairs in the format of the standard memory-span task (Kliegl, Krampe, Philipp, & Luckner, 2002). Faces were constructed from a limited set of facial features that made the faces unique but overall still very similar and, consequently, the task very difficult. We used places as names to make the task easier and to facilitate the transfer from the method-of-loci mnemonic in which these participants had been instructed for the recall of word lists. Face-place pairs were presented one at a time at a fixed rates of 2 s, 4 s, or 8 s per face-place pair. Each face was presented together with the complete list of places. Participants (8 young, $M = 24.5$ years, and 8 old adults, $M = 73.8$ years) indicated their response by clicking at the place label. The number of face-place pairs was increased by one in the next list after a perfect recall and decreased by one otherwise. The dependent variable was list length. Participants encoded and retrieved a total of 225 lists distributed across nine sessions.

The results are very clear: Young adults improved with practice; improvement was larger for longer encoding times. At the end of the experiment they maintained a list length of about 10 face-place pairs across trials with 8 s encoding time per pair. In contrast, there was zero change of performance for old adults. These results were very surprising because it was the first time in our laboratory that old adults did not profit from mnemonic instruction. The older adults represented a positively selected sample of our regular laboratory participants; for example, their average score was 51 on the WAIS digit-symbol substitution test; typical old adult scores in our and other laboratories are below 50 (in our lab: $M = 47$, $SD = 7$). We replicated this result of a zero training benefit with another, even more selected sample of five older adults ($M = 72$ years, WAIS digit symbol substitution = 58). Note that these scores are typical of those of young adults (18-30 years) in our studies.

Mnemonic Instruction for Recall of Person Information (Experiment 3)

The results of the last experiment could have been due to the highly artificial material and laboratory procedure. Therefore, we carried out a second study in which participants (20 young adults, $M = 22$ years, and 20 old adults, $M = 72$ years) were presented 12 distinct faces and at the same time they listened to an audio with the name of the person, her or his profession, and their special interest. At recall participants had to first identify the learned faces among new faces (face recognition). For recognized faces they were asked for the rest of the information as well. After pretest half of the young and half of the old participants received the standard mnemonic instruction for remembering faces. Then all participants attended four additional test sessions.

Young and old adults did very well in face recognition. Performance was better than 90% correct in both age groups. When asked about the names told with these persons, performance was very poor overall but clearly old adults did worse than young adults (old: 1.1, young: 2.5). Similar results were obtained for the memory for professions (old: 2.3, young: 5.1) and for special interests (old: 1.3, young: 4.0). Participants with standard mnemonic instruction recalled names somewhat better than those without such mnemonic instruction (2.0 vs. 1.2, averaged over four posttests) but the benefit of the training was very small compared to the age difference and statistically not different for young and old adults. Most likely such a small training benefit would be of little practical use in daily life.

To summarize, with more realistic experimental setups, cognitive training yielded benefits for young and healthy old adults but there are two problems. One problem is that training benefits related to memory for persons are very small even if the training and test material is realistic and accepted as representing a real-life encounter of a new person. The other problem is that, when trained in the laboratory, people usually do not use their new skill in everyday life (Camp, 1998). Of course, given the small returns from standard training this may not come as a big surprise.

THE EXPERTISE APPROACH: COGNITIVE ENGINEERING

So what can we recommend to older adults who would like to overcome a specific problem in their everyday life and who are in good health and active? We propose a general strategy and then illustrate this strategy for the case of memory for persons (see also Kliegl, Philipp, Luckner, & Krampe, 2001). We call the general strategy the "expertise approach" or "cognitive engineering," which basically involves turning your cognitive problem or deficit into something that you become an expert at. This may sound peculiar because expertise and cognitive deficit typically represent opposite ends of skilled behavior. How can I become an expert in an area in which I know that I have problems, an area in which I perform very poorly? The idea is to adopt behavioral components of experts to overcome a specific deficit. There is a very famous ancient Greek person who did exactly this: Demosthenes.

Demosthenes lived in Athens from 384 to 322 BC and became the greatest of the Greek orators despite a speech impediment. He lost his parents as a child. As a young man he pleaded his case in court against guardians who had misused his estate. Although he won some damages, he was not yet an outstanding speaker. To learn to speak distinctly, he took several measures. For example, it is said that he talked with pebbles in his mouth and recited verses while running. He also practiced speaking agaist the roar of the waves at the seashore to increase the volume of his voice. Demosthenes's deliberate practice paid off. At about 25 years of age he was a well-known and powerful public figure. He is best known for his orations against King Philip of Macedon (so-called "philippics") in which he tried to unite his countrymen.

Components of cognitive engineering

What do we learn from a person like Demosthenes? Despite a speech impediment he became one of the greatest orators and politically very influential persons in ancient Greece. He became an expert speaker. There are numerous other persons who turned a personal deficit into a superior skill. Why did Demosthenes succeed? In our conceptualization of changing a deficit into an expertise by means of cognitive engineering we distinguish between three major components: skill assembly, deliberate practice, and tailored learning (Kliegl et al., 2001).

Skill assembly.   To become an expert in a skill requires new knowledge and new procedures according to an expert model. There are proposals that expertise should be distinguished from high-level of skill. Krampe and Baltes (2003) distinguished an expertise-driven specific abilities versus expertise-driven broad abilities account. The trademark of expertise is that processing limitations characteristic of normal performance can be circumvented by experts. Expertise is based on a qualitatively different organization of behavior compared to normal behavior executed more efficiently. The observation that expertise is not a function of general intelligence is in agreement with this proposal. For example, level of chess expertise correlates only weakly with psychometric IQ-tests (Doll & Mayr, 1987). Strong evidence for such a dissociation of broad abilities (e.g., digit–symbol substitution) and expertise-specific abilities (e.g., finger sequencing of pianists) was provided by Krampe and Ericsson (1996). A large age difference was observed for broad abilities (irrespective of piano expertise) as well as a strong effect of expertise for specific abilities (almost irrespective of age). It is also compatible with limited transfer to tasks outside the specific expertise; that is, experts usually surpass normal persons only in a narrowly defined domain (Ericsson, 1996; Krampe & Baltes, in press 2003; Proctor & Dutta, 1995). If we want to engineer a skill or even an expertise in the laboratory, the behavioral organization of experts must be known and instructed.

Deliberate Practice. Of equal importance in the training program is deliberate practice. In this context Ericsson, Krampe, and Tesch-Römer (1993; see also Charness, Krampe, & Mayr, 1996; Krampe & Ericsson, 1996) distinguished between effort, intensity, and motivation. Effort, described with global measures such as amount of practice (e.g., hours), is not sufficient but must be coupled with intensity. "Exercising" a skill at a moderate level does not lead to the desired improvement. Rather, detailed feedback, ideally by a master coach in one-on-one instructional settings, must be available to uncover weaknesses in the performance and to develop appropriate strategies for their compensation. Krampe and Baltes (2003) linked the concept of deliberate practice to the concept of selective optimization with compensation (Baltes & Baltes, 1990), which has been developed into a framework of life-span development (Freund & Baltes, in press 2002). The Demosthenes example illustrates the willingness to select and optimize specific cognitive processes with the attempt to compensate a deficit. Indeed, in the Adlerian psychonanalytic tradition, he is often used as the prototype of overcompensation (Wyss, 1977). We consider the willingness to expend effort, intensity, and motivation over a long period of time as critical for achieving the transfer of a laboratory-based expertise into a real-life one.

Tailored Learning. The final component fine tunes the optimization process of deliberate practice. Tailored learning serves to keep a high level of motivation and reduces chances of *burnout*. Burnout can result from exaggerated training, setting unrealistic goals, or inadequate social comparisons. Long-term expertise acquisition requires control of demand and performance levels by the individual or a trainer. Acquisition of a real-life expertise is typically a process spanning many years of devoted practice and execution of the skill. Acquisition of an expertise in a laboratory setting can optimize practice in some ways. For example, we can provide training software that keeps task difficulty at an intermediate level to avoid boring as well as frustrating learning situations. We can also develop a large variety of training programs tailored to the individual needs.

The Demosthenes Case. Consider the example of Demosthenes once more. With respect to skill assembly, talking with pebbles in the mouth, speaking against roaring waves, and citing verses while running do not belong to the accepted therapy of speech impediments. Nevertheless we use these examples as an analogy of a selection of unconventional strategies that experts develop to circumvent processing limitations. With respect to deliberate practice, the comparison appears to hold very well. Demosthenes obviously was bothered very much by his speech impediment and was highly motivated to overcome this deficit. If one plans to overcome a specific deficit or improve on one, a high level of motivation to channel the required resources is a "must." One must be prepared to devote a major proportion of one's leisure time to the acquisition of expert strategies to overcome a specific problem by turning it into a specific domain of competence. If a problem is bothersome, but basically one that one can live with, then the expertise approach will probably not work. One must want to change one's behavior very much and make it a topic of special interest. One must be prepared to spend as much time on overcoming this problem as one would for acquiring a new skill such as learning a musical instrument or a new language or a new sport. In other words, the deficit must become something one wants to excel in—just as Demosthenes wanted to overcome his speech impediment and become a famous speaker.

Strategies for an Expertise in Person Memory

In this section we address the needs of mentally fit, healthy adults. We note at the outset that this is probably very different from the perspective one might take when facing the needs of other persons, in particular also those of children. A problem-centered approach, rather than an approach aiming for general solutions, may be uniquely suitable for adults. So how could the expertise approach be implemented? Given the central relevance of sufficient and sustainable levels of motivation, we do think that potential participants should have a clear ranking of the problems they wish to change. A simple strategy to find out about this is to have participants generate a list of cognitive or behavioral problems. Such problems may be misplacing glasses, insomnia, or problems with remembering the names of people, and so on. In the selective optimization with compensation framework, this is the selection stage. As some mental resources as well as available time appear to become scarcer with age, one should have clear priorities. At the outset it would be quite unreasonable to attempt to handle all problems with an expertise approach.

Now let us assume for the rest of this section that memory for persons is the top complaint and that we identified participants that are prepared to turn this deficit into an area of special interest, an area in which they want to become an expert. In this case there is a large repertoire of strategies one might want to work with. These strategies are in general agreement with the most basic principle of memory research: The more elaborate one thinks about a certain topic, the more likely one is to remember later. Applied to faces and names it means that the more one occupies oneself with a new face-name pair, the more likely one is to remember the name of a person when one meets her or him the next time. This principle is embodied in the following four illustrative activities.

Generation of Mental Images

First, generating mental images that link features of physiognomy and name as described earlier is useful. This strategy is most frequently taught in memory training programs. Note, however, that it did not consistently lead to better memory but that often participants by restricting their encoding to this aspect of facial processing actually perform worse after instruction (Sporer, 1991). If there are positive effects of such an instruction, they are typically very small and participants in training programs report that they use it very rarely in everyday life (Camp, 1998).

What are some of the problems with this strategy? First, when one is introduced to a new person, it is somewhat difficult to start thinking about caricature facial features. Typically, one is engaged in a conversation with the person and one simply does not find the time to think about funny associations between the name and facial features. A second problem is that most names (unlike Hook, Sailor, Water) do not lend themselves easily to mental images. What do you do with a name like Ballesteros, Kruse, or Kliegl?

The first problem one could solve by thinking of the image at your leisure, for example, in the evening. For the second problem, memory experts recommend to think of a similar imaginable noun. For example: Ballesteros = ball, Kruse = cruise, Kliegl = klieg light. As a matter of fact, some experts report that they keep dictionaries with conversions between low-imaginable names and imaginable nouns. As mentioned earlier, following up the null result for old adults participating in the second experiment reported we had asked a highly select subset of five older, participants to develop an expert-like knowledge for the facial features that were used to assemble the faces of the experimental material. This intervention by itself was not very effective either; indeed, as for the other older participants of Experiments 2 their was no gain at all.

However, as with any expert-like skill, participants did get better with deliberate practice (across test list to 121 to 260). After we introduced sessions in which participants could practice the same list until complete correct recall, we observed significant improvements in performances for each of our participants. These trends could be stabilized by furnishing their apartments with computers for daily practice starting with list 161. This type of deliberate practice was effective because it allowed our participants to identify the weak elements of the expert knowledge related to the conversion of facial features. They realized, for example, that they do not remember a specific recoding of lips as "helicopter." Thus, participants could selectively update their task-specific knowledge. Also, the more one practices, the more automatic will be the application of the strategy. In the end, some participants reported that the analysis of faces according to their special knowledge became a habit they engaged in quite spontaneously.

Use the Name

Mnemonic images by themselves are probably not sufficient. But in a problem-centered approach one does not need to rely solely on this strategy. The following three strategies seem to depart quite strongly from the standard mnemonic instructions. They were not systematically evaluated in our training program but we told our "expert" participants about these options. Moreover, some of the examples were actually reported to us by the participants. In terms of analytic research, this represents a problem because we do not know exactly to what degree the results about deliberate practice reported in the last section were actually due to the fact that at least some of our participants developed a "special interest" in face-place memory, a special interest that led them clearly beyond the instructional context. In terms of success of the training program, we would argue that the development of such strategies is essential for sustainable development. In other words, these strategies may actually carry more weight for the transfer of the laboratory skill to everyday life than the generation of mnemonics.

One of the oldest strategies for remembering something is to repeat it. Thus, if one wants to remember a new name, one should use it as frequently as possible in the initial conversation. From research about elaborate and maintenance rehearsal we know that the repetition of a name will be much more beneficial for memory if at the time one establishes links between the name and other information about this person. The more connections one builds between the new information and things one already knows, the better are the chances of recalling the name at a later occasion.

Using the name as often as possible in the conversation is one strategy. In addition one can make the name an initial topic of conversation. For example, one can pretend that one is uncertain about the name, that one may not have understood it correctly. This is a perfectly legitimate excuse in any conversation. From the perspective of memory research, one engineers a situation in which the new person uses his or her name a second time. That is twice as often than most of us normally encounter a new name.

Of course, there are other tricks to make the name the topic of a short conversation. For example, one can ask the person whether he is related to someone one knows. Again, whether one knows someone with this name may be true or not. Talking about the name, whether it is a frequent or infrequent name and about its etymological roots gives one the chance to use the name again. If one specializes in names, it becomes very likely that one can talk a lot about all sorts of names. So the expert knowledge lends itself to this end.

Collect Names, Plan to Meet New People

The problems of remembering names can also be greatly reduced if we make the persons whose names we are interested in remembering a topic of special interest. There are thousands of people who collect coins or stamps or pictures of locomotives, or cars. Many of them are true experts in the area in which they collect objects. They read about the history of stamps, when they were first sold, they know about misprints, they know the prices, and many other pieces of information.

Our proposal for persons who want to become a Demosthenes in remembering the names of persons is to become collectors of persons they care about. As a first step, one could make a list with all the persons whose names one would like to remember. This may seem daunting but probably the total number of persons on this list will not be much larger than 200 to 250. Also, we do not meet new people every day. So it should not be so difficult to add new persons. Ideally, one wants to have a picture and various pieces of information related to each person (such as birthday, profession, special interests, calling card). Maybe one also wants to list where one first met her or him and when and where one saw her or him the last time. Such albums can be used like a vocabulary booklet for testing one's memory of names. If one works through a album of names, or at least one's regular problem cases, it is highly unlikely that one will not remember the name of a person who is part of this collection.

One of the participants in our study came up with another idea. She noticed that she actually rarely meets new persons. However, she wanted to meet new persons because she wanted to practice her memory skill. So she decided to ask well-known people of her everyday life for their names. For example, she approached the man who sells her a newspaper every day in the following way: "We meet almost every day and I think it would be nice if we could address each other by our names. My name is Mertens. May I ask about your name?"

One reason why memory for names may be less efficient than in younger years is simply lack of practice. Ms. Mertens decided to counteract this tendency actively by "collecting" new names. This is not unlike a collector of stamps who will not wait until she or he hears about the release of a new stamp by chance. It is more likely that she or he will actively look for such information. Similarly, if "collecting new names" is your area of special interest, you may want to go about it in such an active way as well.

Inventing Excuses

As a final strategy, one may want to prepare in advance for the situation where one meets somebody whose name one is failing on. At one's leisure, one may think of excuses to master such embarrassing situations. Importantly, if the excuse is humorous, it may trigger a very distinct conversation that will allow one to remember the name of the person much better. Here are our personal three proposals. In third place:

"Your face/name simply did not inspire a creative thought." Obviously, one should be careful with this excuse. But the surprise reaction of the conversation partner might generate a very memorable response that will also include her or his name.

Somewhat better may be the second excuse: "You look very similar to a person I dearly love. Sorry, but all I can think of right now is this person's name." This excuse may still communicate ambiguity.

Our favorite excuse so far is the following: "I have basically given up remembering new names. But in your case I would like get a second chance."

DOES IT WORK?

We tried to sketch an ensemble of expert strategies that may improve memory for persons, especially their names. The core idea is to make "memory for persons" a topic of special interest. In our training studies there were two older adults who at an age of over 70 years were interested enough to try this approach. They were mentally very fit and very healthy. At the beginning their performance was not different from that of other older adults. At the end of training, however, they were much better, better even than young adults of Experiment 3 who had practiced for 7 hours

However, there was also one old adult who also tried and who did not achieve this level of performance. At this point we do not know who will succeed and who will not. Our opinion is that as long as persons are healthy and mentally fit otherwise, success of the expertise approach is primarily determined by the level of enthusiam for this task: Am I prepared to invest the time to turn my poor person memory into an expertise? And it will be critical whether the kind of activities or strategies described in this section are deployed to increase the chances for a sustainable development of this expertise.

GENERAL CONCLUSIONS AND DISCLAIMERS

There are some general pieces of advice we like to offer. First, whether one remembers a name or not will depend on how much one does with the name. The more one thinks about the name and the person, the more one uses the name of the person, the more likely one is to recall the name at the next encounter. This proposal is a simple extension of the beneficial effects of elaborative memory.

The second piece of advice serves to put expertise studies like the ones presented in this chapter in perspective. Nobody with a bad memory for persons should feel obliged to engage in such a program. The proposals presented here were meant to illustrate the options for those persons who consider this a serious subjective problem or for persons who just want to find out themselves whether they can overcome this problem.

At this point there is only evidence from a few older adults that suggests that the strategies we proposed will work. There was also one old adult for whom it did not work. More research is clearly needed. Indeed, perhaps there are participants in programs of this kind who will implement such strategies for themselves.

Person memory is but one very frequent age-related deficit. In principle, the general idea of turning a deficit into an area of expertise—remember Demosthenes—can be applied to any other deficit as well. For example, one could easily conceive of an expertise about insomnia (e.g., Morgan & Gledhill, 1991). There are strategies, some of them quite counterintuitive, that will effectively deal with this problem but, as in the case of mnemonics, the success is not guaranteed and it is not clear which factors determine success and failure. The acquisition of these expert strategies takes time and deliberate practice—just as it will take time and deliberate practice to acquire the strategies for a good person memory.

There is the question of the returns on the investment of time and energy. Asking persons to rearrange their lives in order to attain a better person memory seems like asking a lot. There are basically two reasons why some persons may be prepared to engage in a "cognitive engineering" program. First, they may suffer from the embarassment of not remembering someone's name more than most of us who do not feel particularly happy in these situations but can live with it. Most of us would be happy to get rid of this deficit if there were a quick fix to it but making our memory for persons a domain of special interest would be asking too much. Obviously, the decision whether the cognitive engineering approach is a practical option cannot be decided abstractly and independently of an assessment of individual needs and the perceived seriousness of the problem. Moreover, person memory is but one example of a problem we may want to deal with in such a manner. For other examples, such as insomnia, it is easier to imagine that suffering can be sufficiently large that persons would be ready to convert the problem in a special interest even if it requires a rearrangement of life habits. Although the example is drastic, we see the large potential and willingness to change in response to serious medical conditions such as required in the treatment of cancer.

The second reason why people may not be bothered by the imbalance of a large investment of time and effort for the potentially small returns of being spared a few embarassing situations a month is that they simply enjoy the new domain of special interest. After all, why should collecting faces be less stimulating, exciting, or rewarding than collecting coins or stamps? How often do we need the muscles built up in an exercise room in daily life? Maybe we simply have not thought about an expertise in person memory or any other problem area as a potential domain of special interest.

How does the expertise approach relate to questions about "extending intelligence"? There are basically two perspectives on this issue. The traditional perspective is to look at the theoretical construct of intelligence as a general-purpose skill. Then, the goal is to determine the conditions leading to its optimal development. The assumption is that more intelligent people will handle just about any task better than less intelligent people. And there is good evidence on this from correlation research. The alternative approach presented in this chapter is a problem-oriented perspective. We look at the specific behavioral deficit, analyze what activities might lead to expert-like performance, and implement an instructional program based on deliberate practice and tailored learning that might achieve this goal. The selection of activities and strategies is eclectic, it also ignores traditional taxonomies of cognition. It aims at changing the life context such that the behavioral deficit figures as an area of special interest that motivates a substantial investment of time. The focus is on achieving a level of performance that is clearly above average. The goal is to engineer a performance that qualifies the learner as an "outlier" in standard correlation research. At the current stage of research the goal would be to demonstrate that the approach could work in principle for a large variety of special skills. Subsequently one could carry out research to determine which of the components of the program are critical for performance and tune the training accordingly.

Obviously the theoretical foundation of this approach is very general. In most cases it probably suffices to start with well-established principles related to the content of the skill, such as "degree of elaboration" in the case of memory-related skill, and some general principles derived from theories of skill acquisition, such as power-law of practice or the benefits of distributed versus massed practice. Consequently, we suspect that the initial return for these theories would be very small. The benefit would rest primarily with the participant.

A final comment concerns potential target populations. In general, interest in extending intelligence is part of psychological and educational research on child or adolescent development. For these populations an approach staying as general as possible may be well advised because it might be difficult to justify the commitment of time in the amount required for the acquisition of a specific skill. In contrast, our research emanates from work with older adults. It seems that for this population, as well as for adults in general, the reverse holds: Adults know precisely (or should know) which deficits they want to overcome and if they are willing to invest the required amount of time given the returns to be expected from such an intervention. What could be new is that psychology could offer much larger potential returns if it recognizes that, in principle, expert performance might be in reach for persons with a deficit in this domain. Sustainable development of an expertise may depend on participants going beyond conventional instructional techniques.

ACKNOWLEDGMENTS

We thank Petra Grüttner and Nadine Liebs for research assistance. Address: Reinhold Kliegl, Department of Psychology, P.O. Box 601553, University of Potsdam, 14453 Potsdam, Germany. e-mail: Kliegl@rz.uni-potsdam.de

REFERENCES

Baltes, P. B., & Baltes, M. M. (1990). Psychological perspectives on successful aging: The model of selective optimization with compensation. In P. B. Baltes & M. M. Baltes (Eds.), *Successful aging: Perspectives from the behavioral sciences* (pp. 1–34). Cambridge, England: Cambridge University Press.

Baltes, P. B., Dittmann-Kohli, F., & Kliegl, R. (1986). Reserve capacity of the elderly in aging-sensitive tests of fluid intelligence: Replication and extension. *Psychology and Aging, 1,* 172–177.

Baltes, P. B., & Kliegl, R. (1992). Further testing of limits of cognitive plasticity: Negative age differences in a mnemonic skill are robust. *Developmental Psychology, 28,* 121–125.

Camp, C. J. (1998). Memory interventions for normal and pathological older adults. *Annual Review of Gerontology and Geriatrics, 18,* 155–189.

Charness, N., Krampe, R. T., & Mayr, U. (1996). The role of practice and coaching in entrepreneurial skill domains: An international comparison of life-span chess skill acquisition. In K. A. Ericsson (Ed.), *The road to excellence: The acquisition of expert performance in the arts, sciences, sports, and games* (pp. 51–80). Mahwah, NJ: Lawrence Erlbaum Associates.

Doll, J., & Mayr, U. (1987). Intelligenz und Schachleistung—eine Untersuchung an Schachexperten [Intelligence and achievement in chess—A study of chess masters]. *Psychologische Beiträge, 29,* 270–289.

Ericsson, K. A. (1996). *The road to excellence: The acquisition of expert performance in the arts, sciences, sports, and games.* Mahwah, NJ: Lawrence Erlbaum Associates.

Ericsson, K. A., Krampe, R. Th., & Tesch-Römer, C. (1993). The role of deliberate practice in the acquisition of expert performance. *Psychological Review, 100,* 363–406.

Freund, A., & Baltes, P. B. (2002). Life-management strategies of selection, optimization, and compensation: Measurement by self-report, and construct validity. *Journal of Personality and Social Psychology, 82,* 642–662.

Higbee, K. (2001). *Your memory: How it works and how to improve it* (3rd ed.). New York: Marlowe & Company.

Kliegl, R., Krampe, R. T., Philipp, D., & Luckner, M., (2002). *Face memory skill acquisition.* Manuscript submitted for publication.

Kliegl, R., Philipp, D., Luckner, M., & Krampe, R. T. (2001). Face memory skill acquisition. In N. Charness, D. C. Park, & B. A. Sabel (Eds.), *Communication, technology, and aging: Opportunities and challenges for the future* (pp. 169–186). New York: Springer.

Kliegl, R., Smith, J., & Baltes, P. B. (1989). Testing-the-limits and the study of adult age differences in cognitive plasticity of a mnemonic skill. *Developmental Psychology, 25,* 247–256.

Kliegl, R., Smith, J., & Baltes, P. B. (1990). On the locus and process of magnification of adult age differences during mnemonic training. *Developmental Psychology, 26,* 894–904.

Krampe, R. T., & Ericsson, K. A. (1996). Maintaining excellence: Deliberate practice and elite performance in young and old pianists. *Journal of Experimental Psychology: General, 125,* 331–359.

Krampe, R. T., & Baltes, P. B. (2003). Intelligence as adaptive resource development and resource allocation: A new look through the lenses of SOC and expertise. In R. J. Sternberg & E. L. Grigorenko (Eds.), *Perspectives on the psychology of abilities, competencies, and expertise* (pp. 31–69). Cambridge, England: Cambridge University Press.

Leirer, V. O., Morrow, D. G., Sheikh, J. I., & Pariante, G. M. (1990). Memory skills elders want to improve. *Experimental Aging Research, 16,* 155–158.

Lorayne, H., & Lucas, J. (1974). *The memory book.* New York: Stein & Day.

Morgan, K., & Gledhill, K. (1991). *Managing sleep insomnia in the older person.* Bicester, England: Winslow Press.

Proctor, R. W., & Dutta, A. (1995). *Skill acquisition and human performance.* Thousand Oaks, CA: Sage.

Sporer, S. (1991). Deep—deeper—deepest? Encoding strategies and the recognition of human faces. *Jorunal of Experimental Psychology: Learning, Memory, & Cognition, 17,* 323–333.

Stigsdotter-Neely, A., & Bäckman, L. (1993). Long-term maintenance of gains from memory training in older adults: Two 3 1/2-year follow-up studies. *Journals of Gerontology: Psychological Sciences, 48,* P233–P237.

Verhaeghen, P., Marcoen, A., & Goossens, L. (1992). Improving memory performance in aged through mnemonic training: A meta-analytic study. *Psychology and Aging, 7,* 242–251.

Wyss, D. (1977). *Die tiefenpsychologischen Schulen von den Anfängen bis zur Gegenwart—Entwicklung, Probleme, Krisen* (5th ed.). [The psychoanalytical schools from the beginning to the present: Development, problems, crises]. Göttingen: Vandenhoeck & Ruprecht.

Yesavage, J. A., & Rose, T. L. (1984). The effects of a face-name mnemonic in young, middle-aged, and elderly adults. *Experimental Aging Research, 10,* 55–57.

Yesavage, J. A., Rose, T. L., & Bower, G. H. (1983). Interactive imagery and affective judgements improve face-name learning in the elderly. *Journal of Gerontology, 38,* 197–203.

12
▼▼▼▼▼▼▼

The History of the American Mind in the 20th Century: A Scenario to Explain IQ Gains Over Time and a Case for the Irrelevance of *g*

James R. Flynn
University of Otago

The history of how American minds have adapted to social demands in the 20th century can be written only if the evaluation of IQ gains is distanced from g. The relationship between IQ gains and g can be clarified only if a causal scenario about the former is stated. Until now, I have been reluctant to endorse or state a causal scenario. However, the mathematical model of William T. Dickens (Dickens & Flynn, 2001) has made plausibility possible because it does two things: suggests how environmental change could be potent enough to cover the magnitude of IQ gains, and identifies a bridge between IQ gains and g that illuminates the significance of whether the two correlate or not. I should add that Dickens is not to be held responsible for the detail of the scenario I offer or the implications drawn herein. The scenario has two dominant themes: the industrial revolution as the creator of exogenous causes, and the reciprocal causality of IQ and environment as the multiplier of effects. The latter requires some explanation.

IQ AND ENVIRONMENT

The huge size of IQ gains over time, exemplified by the Dutch gain of 20 points (1.33 SDs) between 1952 and 1982 on a derivative of Raven's Progressive Matrices, and the fact that the causes had to be overwhelmingly environmental always stood out in stark contrast to evidence that environmental influences on IQ were feeble. Scholars in general tended to be intimidated by the evidence of kinship or heritability studies. As discussed later, I suffered from a personal inhibition: using a wrong-headed method (weighting the data) to measure the impact of environmental factors like rising affluence or socioeconomic status (SES).

The kinship studies, such as measuring the IQs of identical twins raised apart, show genes becoming overwhelmingly potent as people age. They produce h^2 or heritability estimates that show shared environmental factors accounting for only about 25% of IQ variance in children and fading away to almost nil by late adolescence. The Dickens/Flynn model hypothesizes that this is because genes have a dual effect. They have a direct effect on brain physiology but their influence is much magnified by "reciprocal causality." Someone born with a small genetic advantage for learning school-taught subjects is very like someone born with better genes for height and reflexes. The latter kind of person is very likely to become matched with increasingly enriched environments for basketball skills. At the start, they may take satisfaction in doing a bit better than their playmates; then they practice more, find others more willing to play with them, make teams, get professional coaching. The former kind of person is very likely to become matched with increasingly enriched environments for cognitive skills. They do better in the lower grades, are pleased to be praised, study harder, visit the library more often, are selected for advanced classes, win scholarships to good universities, practice cognitively demanding professions. In both cases, the feedback between genetically influenced skill and environment serves as a multiplier. Each increase in skill gets matched to a better environment, the better environment raises the skill further, they bat the ball back and forth until a small genetic advantage becomes a large skill advantage.

Now let us turn to identical twins. If the reciprocal-causation process entails that genetic differences will be magnified into much larger ultimate cognitive skill differences, it by definition also entails that a complete absence of genetic differences will mean comparatively small cognitive differences. It is this outcome that the kinship studies register, that is, the comparative similarity of the IQs of identical twins. But they say nothing about why genes appear so dominant. The full story of how genes, within a given generation, come to drive the powerful feedback process is told in the model (genetic differences have the advantage of persistence—they are with us throughout our entire lives). Here, I can only assert that the kinship studies show that genes do indeed dominate. And stress what those studies omit: that much of the potency of genes is derived from co-opting the potency of environment—from driving the dynamic reciprocal causation between better (or worse) skill level, better environment, even better skill level, even better environment, and so forth.

However, there is nothing intrinsic that makes the powerful multiplying effects of skill/environment intercausation into the slave of genes. Between generations, as distinct from within generations, they are captured by persistent environmental trends and these trends thereby multiply their effects and cause huge IQ gains over time. The processes have the same enormous potential no matter whom they serve. The scenario offered for the causes of massive IQ gains over time will make the mechanics of the capture of reciprocal causation by environment explicit.

Before embarking on that scenario, I wish to enter a plea to specialist readers. The process just described simply refers to reciprocal causation between a skill and the environment relevant to enhancing (or inhibiting) that skill. It has nothing to do with "gene x environment interaction" as used by biologists to refer to the conditioning of gene expression by environment. It has nothing to do with the technical terminology of the analysis of variance. Keep your eye on the basketball analogy and much confusion will be avoided.

1900 TO 1948: IQ GAINS AND SCHOOLING

The mighty engine of the industrial revolution has propelled the major social trends of the last century, particularly the trends toward enhanced affluence and leisure. It may have begun to lift IQ at its very inception, even before IQ could actually be measured (Flynn, 1998). In America, certainly no later than 1900, the industrial revolution created a new middle class and this trend was accelerated by the advent of the assembly line and mass production. More and more people filled professional, managerial, or technical jobs and these people became fully aware of the possibilities of upward social mobility and saw education as the way forward for their children. The emancipation of women, and the first hints of the instability of marriage, placed a higher premium on the education of females.

In 1900, it was not at all uncommon for children to enter the labor force anywhere from the ages of 11 to 14, after no more than 6 years of schooling. Herrnstein and Murray (1994, p. 144) use the graduation ratio, that is, the number of high school graduates divided by the relevant age cohort, to trace the trend toward more schooling during the 20th century. It rose from a mere 6% in 1900, to 55% in 1950, attaining a peak of about 75% by the early 1960s, which has remained relatively stable ever since. I believe that the growth in years of schooling was the primary proximate cause of IQ gains in America from 1900 to 1950. It would not have been the sole cause, of course. There were significant advances in nutrition and child health: Well-fed and healthy children learn better at school.

At this point, I wish to underline my skepticism about the persistence of some of these causes into the post-1950 era. Elsewhere, I have argued the case against nutrition (Flynn, 1998). Rutter (2000, p. 223) argued persuasively that post-1950 improvements in obstetric and neonatal care may have had no net effect: For every child who has escaped mental impairment, another has been saved who would have died without modern techniques. Hybrid vigor, or outbreeding due to greater mobility, looks promising until one does the relevant calculations. In the United States at least, the growth of mobility over the last century or so has been modest: In 1870, 23% of Americans were living in a state other than the one of their birth; in 1970, the figure was 32% (Mosler & Catley, 1998). Taking that trend as a rough measure of increased outbreeding gives 2.7% of the population per generation (32 minus 23 = 9; 9 divided by 3.33 = 2.7). As for the effects of outbreeding, 3 IQ points is the advantage of not breeding with one's cousins (Jensen, 1983; Bouchard, 1998). This gives 0.08 as the IQ-point gain per generation explained by increased outbreeding (.027 times 3 = .081). Someone will have to find reason to increase that estimate by 12 times to explain even one IQ point.

Tuddenham (1948) provides the best data on American IQ gains in the first half of the 20th century. His comparison of the 1917/18 draft with a representative sample of the 1943 draft on the Army Alpha, a test of verbal intelligence similar to the Otis, shows a gain of .80 SDs or 12 IQ points. Flynn (1984, p. 33; 1993; 1998a, pp. 35-37) checked this result against Stanford-Binet and Wechsler data and found that gains between 1918 and 1948 amounted to at least 12 points. Storfer (1990, pp. 89–94) analyzed Stanford-Binet data and longitudinal studies and concluded that substantial gains began in America in the early 1890s.

Tuddenham (1948) provided evidence that enhanced quantity and quality of schooling were a major component of inter-war IQ gains. He noted that the mean number of years of schooling had risen from 8 to 10 years and that weighting the 1917/1918 sample to match the 1943 sample eliminated half of the score difference. There is reason to believe that the weighting method underestimates the influence of changes in education over time. Tuddenham was aware of this although he did not use the language of social multipliers. Just to hint at these, when society lifts the population mean for school-relevant cognitive skills, each student is surrounded by fellow students who are more competent, better students make better teachers for the next generation of students, parents become more serious about schooling and homework, the lengths of the school day and school year tend to increase. Only a fragment of this is captured by adding on to the 1917/1918 sample the benefit of an extra 2 years of schooling of the kind that existed in their day. Or conversely, reducing the 1943 sample to match the

TABLE 12.1
American Gains on WISC[a] From 1947-49 to 1989 Expressed in IQ Points (SD = 15)[b];
American Rate of Gain per 30 Years (one generation) Compared to Other Nations[c]

	America (1948 to 1989)	America (30 years)	Scotland (30 years)	Germany & Austria (30 years)
Information	0.65	0.47	4.75	3.68
Arithmetic	3.30	2.39	−6.00	−3.23
Vocabulary	3.90	2.82	0.00	11.78
Comprehension	6.30	4.55	21.80	7.13
Picture Completion	8.20	5.93	4.15	16.05
Block Design	10.90	7.88	—	21.50
Object Assembly	12.70	9.18	—	11.23
Picture Arrangement	14.15	10.23	—	17.43
Coding	14.50	10.48	—	12.78
Similarities	20.35	14.71	25.15	22.60
Verbal IQ	8.96	6.48	13.25	9.03
Performance IQ	15.77	11.40	—	22.12
Full=Scale IQ	13.21	9.55	—	17.32

[a]WISC used generically to refer to subtests common to the WISC, WISC-R, and WISC-III.
[b]Subtest gains in terms of scaled scores (SD = 3) were multiplied times 5 to approximate IQ points (SD = 15).
[c]The comparative data came from the following samples: America: WISC (1947–1948) to WISC-R (1972) to WISC-III (1989); Scotland: WISC (1961–1962) to WISC-R (1983–1984); West Germany: WISC (1954) to WISC-R (1981); Austria: samples whose midpoint of testing was 1970–1971 were scored against the 1954 German WISC norms. A rate of gain in terms of IQ points per year was calculated for each nation and multiplied times 30 to get estimates of gains over a common period of 30 years. The West German and Austrian estimates were averaged to get an estimate for "German-speaking nations".
Source: James R. Flynn, IQ gains, WISC subtests, and fluid *g*; *g* theory and the relevance of Spearman's hypothesis to race. In G. R Bock & J. A. Goode (Eds.), *The nature of intelligence* (Novartis Foundation Symposium 233), pp. 202–227, Table 1. New York: Wiley (2000). Adapted with permission from publisher.

8 years of schooling of the earlier sample would not mean that both samples are benefiting from 8 years of the same kind of school experience.

INTERLUDE: THE TWO GREAT ATTITUDE SHIFTS

Unfortunately, the pre-1948 data do not include trends on WISC (Wechsler Intelligence Scale for Children) subtests. Therefore, I can only lend probability to something I suspect to be true: that there were sizable gains *both* on IQ tests close to classroom-subject skills (e.g., Arithmetic) *and* those removed from such skills (Similarities or Block Design). The case for the former is strong: The Army Alpha measures skills with very heavy classroom-subject loading. The case for the latter is inferential: Formal schooling normally encourages the kind of abstract thinking useful on Similarities and Block Design; and the magnitude of gains on Wechsler-Binet tests, which include many items well removed from classroom subjects, are so great that gains on such items must have been significant. As this account of pre-1948 trends is the most likely, I assume it in what follows.

Table 12.1 shows the IQ gains of American schoolchildren (ages 6–16) from the standardization of the WISC (1947–1948) through the WISC-R (1972) to the WISC III (1989). Now we can trace differential trends and we see something surprising: The four WISC subtests closest to classroom subjects show by far the lowest gains. From 1947/1948 to 1989, Information shows almost no gain, Arithmetic and Vocabulary show a gain of 3 or 4 points, and Comprehension shows just over 6 points (SD = 15).

The case for linking these subtests to classroom subjects is reinforced by comparison with trends on the National Association of Educational Progress (NAEP) tests given to representative samples of 9-, 13-, and 17-year-old students (U.S. Department of Education, 2000 The similarity of the trends suggests that classroom subjects are causally linked to certain IQ-subtest scores in the post-1948 era. In saying this, I am not trying to decide the vexed question of whether achievement gains raise "intelligence" or whether "intelligence gains" raise achievement (Williams & Ceci, 1997, p. 1229). I am merely noting that trends on corresponding NAEP and WISC that if mastery of classroom subjects is held responsible for one, it makes sense to hold it responsible for the other.

However, after 1948, classroom-subject gains became too modest to do much to drive America's global IQ gains. As Table 12.1 shows, the sum of the gains on the four "classroom-subject" subtests is only 15% of the sum for all subtests. The non-American data serve as a reminder that IQ gains are not uniform across national boundaries. It is quite clear that the Scots have made much more robust gains on verbal comprehension than Americans have. That they seem so deficient on Arithmetic is probably an artifact of the data: Scottish gains were measured on items unaltered from the WISC to the WISC-R and these were fewest on the Arithmetic subtest (Flynn, 1990, p. 47). It is clear that the German-speaking nations made more robust vocabulary gains than the English-speaking nations did. The diminished role of classroom subjects in IQ gains after 1948 may be more pronounced in America than elsewhere. Note in passing the fact that huge gains on the Similarities subtest are universal; and that they match the huge gains usually associated with Raven's Progressive Matrices. Also note the illuminating study of Case, Demetriou, Platsidou, and Kasi (2001, pp. 322–327). When 23 test or subtests including both traditional psychometric items (Matrices, seven WISC subtests, etc.) and Piagetian tasks (tilted boxes task, weights task, class inclusion, etc.) were analyzed, Matrices and Similarities were virtually identical. They had by far the highest g loadings (.643 and .641) and by far the highest loadings on a logic/analysis factor described as Cattell's fluid g (.756 and .753).

Let us focus on the "psychology" involved in taking the classroom-subject subtests. Having an adequate fund of general information, being able to do arithmetic, having a large vocabulary, and comprehending everyday life situations have an immediate practical payoff. They help children meet the demands that formal schooling places on them, get good marks, bring home a good report card. They involve applying what has been learned more than they involve on-the-spot problem solving: You apply the arithmetical techniques you know, you have the vocabulary and information needed to understand a piece of prose or you do not, you either know that Rome is the capitol of Italy or you know only of Rome, Georgia.

The psychology of the other subtests is different. Similarities requires an investment of "mental energy" with no obvious pragmatic payoff. When asked "how dawn and dusk are alike", children have to imagine alternatives and select the one that best catches an intrinsic similarity. Something like: "You get up in the morning and go to bed at night but that makes no sense because I often sleep past dawn and go to bed after dark. They are alike in that the sky is half-lit and often very pretty but of course that is not always true. What they really have in common is that they are the beginning and end of both the day and the night. The right answer must be that they separate day and night." The other non-classroom-subject subtests also have no obvious practical payoff and require taking problem solving for its own sake seriously. They require arranging blocks so that the view from above duplicates a presented pattern, building an object out of its disassembled parts, arranging pictures to tell a story.

I believe that post-1948 IQ gains signal a development so odd as to tax the imagination. Table 12.1 shows that during the period of 1947/1948 to 1989, the gains on the six non-classroom-subject subtests were all very large: They range from 8.20 points or 0.55 SDs (Picture Completion) to 20.35 points or 1.36 SDs (Similarities). These gains signal a profound attitude shift toward taking nonpractical mental problems seriously; and being willing to invest enough mental energy to develop the "habits of mind" needed to solve them. This attitude shift has nothing to do with test sophistication, that is, feeling comfortable with the format of IQ tests or test strategy; and it has nothing to do with trying in the test room. There is no reason to believe that these were absent or weak before 1948. It is what went on outside the test room that changed. To illustrate this, I appeal to those who in middle age have taken up crossword puzzles. As soon as I got interested in them, I tried hard. But it took awhile to develop the "habits of mind" needed to do well. The normal thing with words is to choose the one meaning that best conveys your intent. It takes awhile to adjust to looking for puns, always being careful to note that the clue word could be either a verb or a noun or an adjective, running through unusual meanings that you never actually use the word to convey. Unless you can take all of that seriously, despite its lack of a practical payoff, you can try as hard as you like and still not do well.

There is still a piece of the puzzle missing: that is why I have referred to *two* great attitude shifts. After all, just because nonpractical problem solving took off after 1948, that did not dictate that enhancement of classroom-subject skills would fall off. The best I can do to account for the low rate of gain on classroom-subject subtests since 1948 is to introduce the concept of a saturation point. Perhaps at a certain point, subjects like reading and arithmetic became about as cognitively demanding and time demanding (homework) as children and parents and even teachers were willing to put up with. This attitudinal reaction may have been a matter of physiology (their brains were approaching overload) or sociology (affluence at a certain point fosters the pursuit of pleasure rather than hard work)—take your choice. I realize that this is the very lowest level of causal explanation—positing psychological causes created to fit the data of psychological effects. I should also add that the psychology of different ethnic groups may dictate different saturation points. Between 1971 and 1996, the gains of White children on NAEP mathematics and reading were no more impressive than the gains of the total population (U.S. Department of Education, 2000, pp. 54, 63, 104, 113). Elsewhere, I have argued that Chinese and Japanese Americans show greater tolerance to the cognitive demands of classroom subjects than White Americans (Flynn, 1991).

Just to avoid a misconception, I recognize that school for children is not just classroom subjects, rather it constitutes a large portion of their social milieu. For children, teachers compete with parents and relatives and media personalities to provide role models, schools compete with neighbors and siblings to supply peers, and classmates substitute for work-mates. Boozer and Cacciola (2001) have shown that when smaller classes raise mean performance, peer interaction multiplies that rise to the extent that long-term performance gains are "almost entirely due" to feedback. If our second attitude shift had neutralized the school environment as a socializer and as a multiplier of effects, I would be at a loss to offer a plausible explanation of why schoolchildren have made massive IQ gains over time. It is not the school portion of the social environment that is failing to promote IQ gains. It is classroom subjects that have lost most of their capacity to promote IQ gains. Better teaching of and more exposure to that material may have been the dominant cause of IQ gains before 1948 (we will never know for sure) but their role has ebbed since.

1948 TO 2000: IQ GAINS AND THE SOCIAL MULTIPLIER

The mighty engine of the industrial revolution and the attendant growth of affluence continue unabated. Increasing affluence has engendered a number of social trends that would trigger something like the first great attitude shift. For example, the continuing post-World War II economic boom has done much to weaken the "depression psychology" of the 1930s and earlier. Preoccupation with practical concerns like earning a living may have diminished, so that nonpractical problem solving has moved from being perceived as a trivial distraction to something that appeals and attracts investment of mental energy. The growth in leisure, the fact that leisure is no longer exhausted by recuperation from the demands of work, may be a factor that has pushed leisure activities toward games and hobbies and conversation that exercise the mind. The number of jobs emphasizing manipulation of symbols or abstractions and on-the-spot problem solving has increased.

A factor worthy of mention in its own right: Middle-class mores and aspirations have reduced family size. This means that only children and first-born children have become an increasing percentage of cohorts over time. A study by Leong, Hartung, Goh, and Gaylor (2001) suggests that such children tend to have more cognitive and analytic interests, whereas later-borns are more artistic and oriented to the outdoors. They hypothesize that parents discourage only children from activities thought to be dangerous. I would add that even the later-borns may have a greater proclivity to cognitive problem solving than in the past. The fact that families have become smaller means that parents have more energy and time and inclination to take all of their children's "hypothetical" questions seriously. They may be more prone to answer rather than dismiss the eternal string of "whys" to which children are prone.

We want, of course, not only to hypothesize causes for the peculiar kind of IQ rises America has enjoyed since 1948 but also to assess their real-world effects. I beleive that cause and effect are functionally interrelated thanks to the social multipler.

First, a scenario from sport intended as an explanatory device rather than as history. After World War II, the fact that the small TV screen suited basketball better than baseball enhanced interest in the former. Soon young people were investing their physical energy in basketball to an unprecedented degree. A basketball culture emerged, plenty of people to play with, ever-more skilled opponents spurring one another on, better tactics taught by better coaches. As for the concept of a "social multiplier," when a persistent environmental trend raises the population mean for a skill, the *rising mean* tends to become a causal factor *in its own right*— a causal factor of enormous potency. The greater investment of numbers and energy in basketball means that people play and practice more and the average player becomes a better passer and shooter. Individual after individual finds, all players find, that if they are to be competitive with their peers they must upgrade their skills. To be better than average you have to be able to pass with either hand, then the average becomes passing with either hand, so you have to be able to shoot with either hand, then the average becomes shooting with either hand, and so forth. The skill level bounces back from higher group mean to individual to still higher group mean, resulting in an explosion of competence over a relatively brief time.

Now take chess, the sort of leisure pursuit that one would think would both benefit from the first great attitude shift (effect) and habituate people to be better at nonpractical problem solving (cause). Quite independently of Dickens and Flynn, Howard (2001) has posited the existence of the social multiplier in the sense of "cascading feed-back loops": More people want to play chess, the average skill rises, chess clubs form, coaching and chess books improve with rising demand, so you have even better average performance, and so on. He evidenced the trend toward enhanced skills by documenting the decline in the age of chess grandmasters. He made the same case, although the evidence is less compelling, for feedback loops in other leisure activities that are cognitively demanding, such as bridge and Go. Patricia Greenfield (1998) has argued that video games, popular electronic games, and computer applications have meant a shift toward problem solving in visual and symbolic contexts. Feedback loops would operate here as well. A new game develops skills; when the game is mastered, it becomes boring and, therefore, a more complex game is marketed.

Feedback loops are not, of course, confined to formalized leisure activities. The rising mean of cognitive skills dictates that every person everywhere is surrounded by people who demand a higher level of performance: A sharpens his wits on B, then places higher demands on B, she places higher demands on him, and so forth. The assumption is that in a more sophisticated and urbanizing society, a variety of social multipliers fill the whole day, whether we interact with schoolmates or workmates, spouses or peers or family (Schooler, 1998). Rosenau and have Fagan (1997) argued that today, even political discourse is expected to offer more complex accounts of events and issues.

Setting aside separating cause and effect, what real-world trends are most likely to accompany post-1948 IQ gains? A change in the cognitive tenor of human interactions. An escalation of skills in games like chess. Probably a larger pool of people who have an interest and therefore an inclination to pursue theoretical disciplines like mathematics, science, even philosophy. Sadly, the realization of this potential is often thwarted by unwillingness to fund university training and careers for the fields named. Willingness to take hypothetical problems seriously enhances performance in at least some jobs. As for the "job" most schoolchildren are asked to perform, current trends are surprisingly compartmentalized. Clearly there has not been much of a feedback loop operating between hypothetical problem solving and learning core subjects like arithmetic and reading. Finally, there is the vexed question of whether IQ gains have enhanced "intelligence" in a way that affects mental retardation. If so, either the mentally retarded should have virtually disappeared or, looking to the past, a huge proportion of previous generations must really have been mentally retarded but escaped detection.

As to eliminating most of the mentally retarded, I do not think this has occurred. The minds of people respond to social demands. The social demands on the individual to be capable of cognitive independence in everyday life, going to the corner shop, chatting about distant relatives, keeping score at a baseball game, have been so powerful for so long that all who could meet them have done so in every generation—and consequently, their numbers have not been much diminished over time. As Howard (2001) pointed out, verifying this is complicated by the fact that, aside from the severely handicapped, mental retardation and associated classifications like "learning disabled" are social rather than fixed categories. However, as Spitz (1986) has shown, even the most dramatic environmental interventions have not done much to thin out the ranks of the mentally retarded and I suspect the environmental triggers of IQ gains have been equally helpless. The lower 2% of the population have had a physiologically imposed "saturation" point and until perhaps now, the medical and biological sciences did not know how to affect it. As to whether say 40% of Americans were "really" mentally retarded in 1918, they were not. Their IQ scores according to today's norms were below 75 but only because their lives predated the factors that lifted IQ scores, first by more years of education, then by attitudes and habits of thought congenial to nonpractical problem solving—see Flynn (2006).

Emphasis on the feedback loops of the social multiplier should not get in the way of facts. Just as tolerance or capacity may have sets limits on the cognitive demands of classroom material, certainly people cannot be willing to invest endless time and mental energy into nonpractical problem solving. This is to say that we may soon reach a saturation point that puts an end to the kind of IQ gains that have been so prominent since 1948. This may have already happened in Scandinavia (Emanuelsson, Reuterberg, & Svensson, 1993; Teasdale & Owen, 2000). On the other hand, huge gains on Ravens at all levels appear unabated in Spain and Argentina (Colom, Andrés-Pueyo, & Juan-Espinosa, 1998; Flynn & Casé, 2005). In addition, the fact that we have lived in a time of IQ gains must not blind us to a less salutary possibility: History shows periods of progress followed by retrogression. Affluence sometimes turns into decadence. Up to now, it may have encouraged more competition at school, smaller families with better parent–child interaction, more cognitively demanding work roles, and more mental energy invested in leisure pursuits. But the next chapter may be one of "spoiled" children resisting instruction, the collapse of the family, and mindless hedonism.

A confession: Until recently, I have had a personal inhibition that made me resistant to some of the points made by Howard, and Greenfield, and Schooler. It was Bill Dickens introducing me to the mathmatics of the social multiplier that proved liberating. I realized that I had been inhibited by using a wrong-headed method to assess the potency of environmental causes: the method of weighting factors from two static contexts so as to measure the effects of dynamic processes over time. This method made putative causes of IQ gains look too feeble to be taken seriously.

A hypothetical example: Over 30 years, a nation enjoys an IQ gain of 20 points and an SES gain such that the top 75% in 1980 match the top 50% of 1950. To calculate the impact of rising affluence on IQ gains, I would do something like:

1. 1950: The top 50% of an IQ curve has a mean of 112. Assuming a correlation between SES and IQ of 0.50, the top 50% in SES would have a mean IQ of 106. The bottom 50% would have a mean of 94.
2. 1980: Weighting for the fact that the top 75% matches the SES of the top 50% of 1950: $106 \times 75 = 7{,}950$. Weighting for the fact that the bottom 25% matches the SES of the bottom 50%, 1950: $94 \times 25 = 2{,}350$.
3. Result: $7{,}950 + 2{,}350 = 10{,}300$; and that divided by 100 equals 103. So SES seems to explain only 3 points of the 20-point IQ gain.

The seductive appeal of this method must have been that it offered nice neat calculations. Because I had always known (and often said) that the significance of SES within a generation is completely different from its significance between generations. Within generations, competition for wealth and status is the major factor that correlates IQ and SES. Why should IQ differentials that are a product of a status competition be in any way indicative of IQ differentials between generations? Imagine that by 1980, the total income curve duplicated the top half of the 1950 curve. Would we assume that the mean IQ of 1980 was identical with the mean IQ of the top half of 1950? The top half of 1950 would have out-competed the bottom half of 1950. The totality of people in 1980 could hardly have out-competed anyone. If the intensity of the competition is the same within each of the two generations, then the correlation between SES and IQ should remain the same: but this tells us zero as to what has happened to mean IQ over time.

To assess what effect growing affluence over time might really have, we must put on a completely different pair of spectacles. It is possible that if competition became more intense over time, people would try harder to get the educational credentials needed for high-status jobs; and the enhanced education that resulted would raise mean IQ. But growing affluence might make competition less intense because fewer now fear poverty. And at any rate, this rise or fall in the intensity of competition for high SES from one generation to another would be a very minor factor compared to factors that affect mean IQ over time. The dynamic role of enhanced affluence over time rests on the impact it has on a host of factors such as easier access to necessities, family size, the quality of leisure, the nature of work, culminating in the first great attitude shift, and most of all, on the fact that once you have a rising average skill level, it participates in a reciprocal causality between skill and environment that multiplies gains with great potency. None of this is captured by the weighting method.

The same point could be made about other trends, for example, urbanization. Drawing on data from Flieller, Saintigny, and Schaeffer (1986), I did the usual weighting calculations for a shift from rural to urban and found almost nil effect. But the urban–rural IQ differential at any given time also reflects a kind of competition: a competition for desirable space, that is, going to the city for better jobs or fleeing the inner city because of crime. These shifts lead to either positive or negative urban/rural IQ differentials but these differentials are irrelevant to what urbanization is really doing over time. They miss the greater sophistication urbanization brings not only to cities but also to rural areas now less isolated thanks to travel and the media. I have already commented on how Tuddenham's weighting method undoubtedly underestimated the impact of schooling between the two world wars.

It is as if we tired to measure the tremendous explosion in basketball skills triggered by the advent of TV by using some weighting method. The hypothesis is that the small screen of TV was more suited to basketball than baseball and caused a shift of interest and investment of physical energy toward the former and away from the latter. Ghetto kids, and not just ghetto kids, found heroes and role models in an activity that could be played in a confined space with inexpensive equipment. As more and more kids played basketball more and more often, the mean skill level began to rise and the interaction process between mean skill and environment brought the powerful social multiplier into play. Imagine trying to measure all of this by weighting—a weighting based on correlations between "watching basketball on TV" and "basketball skill" drawn from two static contexts, say 1950 and today. The correlations might be pretty modest, even negative, and when weighted by a rise in the proportion of the population watching basketball, the result might be a very modest estimate. But whatever the result, the method is absurd.

Just as weighting cannot calculate the effects of social trends on IQ, it is equally unable to calculate the effects of IQ trends on soceity. In *The Bell Curve*, Herrnstein and Murray (1994, pp. 363–368) used it to estimate the effect of an IQ shift of 3 points on social problems. The results, of course, tell us nothing whatsoever about what would really happen. It would all depend on the causal interaction between social processes and IQ. If middle-class children became intellectually lazy, thanks to corruption by affluence, the average IQ might drop even if the lower classes were solving their social problems. Herreinstein and Murray did add that the exercise assumes that everything else but IQ remains constant and that in the real world, things would be more complicated. But since poweral social processes are never constant over time, this amounts to saying that if we ignore all of the truly significant factors, then the factor (IQ) artificially isolated takes on an exaggerated significance.

To be fair, Herrnstein and Murray did assume a certain dynamic was at work: dysgenic trends. They posit that people with less education are having more children than those with more education and that, over a few generation, this will lower brain quality. No one thinks that desirable. However, there is no reason to believe that a small decline in brain quality will make us unable to solve social problems. We know today that in 1900, we were far from exhausting our brain capacity. No one knows that at present, we are near our limits – or whether we will be in 2100.

THE LIMITATIONS OF g

The positive correlations between g and outcomes for individuals in competition with one another, plus evidence that g has a physiological substratum, make g an attractive choice to assess the significance of IQ gains over time. Jensen (1998) used his method of correlated vectors for this purpose. However, Dickens and Flynn (2001) called its relevance into question.

The method consists of this: ranking various IQ tests, usually the subtests of the WISC, in a hierarchy from the subtest on which IQ gains have been least to the subtest on which they have been greatest; ranking the same subtests into a hierarchy in terms of the size of the their g-loadings (the extent to which they correlate with g); calculating whether there is a positive or negative correlation between the two hierarchies. Clearly, whether this is meaningful depends on why IQ gains and g might or might not correlate. I am going to treat this question as essentially the same as why there might be a correlation between an IQ-gain hierarchy and an h^2 hierarchy, that is, one in which subtests are ranked according to the extent to which their score variance is explained by genetic variance. The heritability of IQ and the heritability of g are very close. This is hardly surprising in that g is the first principal component derived by factor analysis of a matrix of IQ scores.

Think back to the introductory section on the relationship between IQ and environment and note what gives genes their huge share of IQ variance. At a particular time, a person's slight genetic advantage gives a slight ability advantage through its direct effect on brain physiology; but then that ability advantage is greatly multiplied by its seeking out an enriched environment that engenders a series of feedback loops. Assume that the direct effect of genes on various WISC subtests is roughly equal. We do not know this to be true but the direct-effect differentials are likely to be less than the differentials engendered by reciprocal causation given the sheer power of the latter. The more potent the factor, the more likely it causes heritability variation between subtests. So the ranking of WISC subtests for h^2 is probably a function of their ranking for the potency of their reciprocal-causation processes. Now recall what made environmental factors so potent in causing IQ gains. Over time, they seize control of the reciprocal-causation processes; and these processes determine the potency of the social multipliers relevant to each subtest. So the ranking of WISC subtests for IQ gains is *also* a function of the potency of their reciprocal-causation processes. The gene-created h^2 hierarchy and the environment-created IQ-gain hierarchy will tend to correlate because they share the very same processes as their instruments.

In passing, if this analysis is correct, the method of correlated vectors has no relevance to the race and IQ debate. If the Black–White IQ-gap hierarchy on various subtests is due to environmental factors driving reciprocal-causation processes, it too will tend to correlate with gene-driven subtest hierarchies, such as h^2 and g-loading and inbreeding depression. Positive correlations will tell us nothing about whether the Black–White IQ gap is caused by environment or genes.

Reverting to the correlation between score gains and h^2, the analysis may seem to imply that it ought to be perfect: at least, if we set aside measurement error and the fact that the direct effect of genes on brain physiology may not be equal over all subtests. However, an analysis of Vocabulary and Similarities shows why discrepancies would occur. We have hypothesized that Similarities shows huge gains after 1948 because of the first great attitude shift: People began to take nonpractical problem solving more seriously. This may have had some effect on vocabulary, the need for more abstract terms, but it has not added much to the mainstream vocabulary we use for social intercourse. So score gains have been far greater for Similarities than for Vocabulary. However, Vocabulary is more influenced by genetic differences between individuals and has higher g-loadings (Flynn, 2000, Table 2; Rushton, 1995, Table 9.1). This suggests that it is relatively easy for individuals with better genes for Vocabulary to get a match with quality of environment for Vocabulary: They will tend to read more, take advanced literature courses, gravitate naturally toward people with larger than average vocabularies. Individuals with better genes for Similarities will also tend toward a match with quality of environment for Similarities, but perhaps not as unerringly: They will certainly find no courses in Similarities and may find compatibility for an interest in nonpractical problem solving less of a social glue than compatibility for vocabulary. So the heritability and g-loading of Similarities will be less than for Vocabulary.

In other words, Vocabulary has an advantage for the potential potency of its reciprocal-causality process, and within a generation genes have no trouble seizing control of that process; but as far as score gains over time are concerned, the environmental triggers during any given time may be too weak to capitalize on that potential. A great advantage between two subtests in trigger potency will overwhelm a handicap in reciprocal-causation potency. This alone would be sufficient to "force" the method of correlated vectors to give a less than perfect correlation (between score gains and h^2 or score gains and g). If there was a substantial negative correlation between trigger potency and process potency over the full range of subtests, the method would give a negative correlation.

If that is what determines the results of the method of correlated vectors, its results do nothing whatsoever to assess the significance of score gains over time. Americans really have made small gains in vocabulary, reading, and arithmetic; and they really have gotten a lot better at nonpractical problem solving. Negative correlations between this pattern of gains and h^2 or g are simply beside the point. Those who believe that IQ gains can be dismissed as an artifact should make a direct case to that effect—by trying to show that they are the result of enhanced test sophistication over time or better test-taking strategies over time. The only one to attempt this is Brand and his case has been overwhelmingly falsified (Flynn, 1998, pp. 42–43).

It may be said that because g is the common factor that underpins performance on various IQ tests, gains that do not correlate with g simply cannot be very significant. Such a view must not be a dogma but must be subject to the test of the historical record. Thanks to shifting social demands, Americans have made differential cognitive gains of great social significance, and their social significance stands no matter what correlations with g have to say. Take a final sporting analogy. If you have the speed and upper body strength to run a great 100 meters, you will tend to do well on all 10 events of the decathlon, particularly the 400 meters and the hurdles, but also weight events like the shot put, discuss and javelin. So when you engage in competition at a given time with others g factor will emerge. However, American soceity over 30 years may radically re-prioritize events in terms of glamor. Spectators may begin to find the shot put dull, the pole vault breathe-taking, the 100 meters exciting, the 1500 meters tedious. The pattern of performance gains over time may not yield a g factor. But the new records in the 100 meter and pole vault, and the absence of such in other events, will be not less real for that.

Our reasoning about correlations with g should be just the reverse: If highly significant skill gains can occur without g gains, so much the worse for g. Wicherts et al. (2004) have gone beyond jensen to show that IQ gains may not be factor invariant: they may not represent gain on any of the factors yielded by factor analysis, whether g or a quantitive fctor, or a verbal factor, and so forth. Flynn (2006) responds and concludes, so much the worse for factor analysis. Also, so much the better for me: it is good that society can make differential cognitive demands without facing some kind of psychometric veto. It is good that basketball skills could explode without waiting for baseball skills to tag along. Social multipliers are contemptuous of factor analysis.

This is not to say that g is unimportant. I am assuming that it has a physiological substratum even though Deary and Crawford (1998) have produced a worrying piece of evidence to the contrary. They found negative correlations between the g-loadings of WAIS-R (Wechsler Adult Intelligence Scale – Revised) subtests and both inspection time and word identification, two measures of "mental speed". However, their results conflict with those of most studies and perhaps some explanation will be forthcoming. If the physiological substratum of g is real, it will have relevance for periods, no matter how brief, during which serious nutritional deficiencies are alleviated thus upgrading brain physiology. During a longer period, I would say a much longer period, when dysgenic reproduction dominates, it will be relevant. It is certainly relevant to predicting social outcomes when genes drive reciprocal-causation processes, which is to say relevant for all of us in that all of us compete with one another for limited social goods.

THE COMPARTMENTALIZATION OF 'INTELLIGENCE"

Having sidelined g in our account of enhanced cognitive skills, we must consider whether it is profitable to ask whether or not IQ gains are intelligence gains. I will take the pragmatic approach of looking at the expectations the word 'intelligence' is likely to raise, and determining which are likely to bring disappointment and which are not. If it is expected that teachers of long experience will say that the intellectual quality of their students has dramatically escalated over time, I anticipate disappointment. Howard (2001) offered the first empirical evidence that this is so. If it is expected that the mentally retarded should virtually disappear, then the disappointment will be even more acute. Before identifying more realistic expectations, let us review what we have learned thus far.

People use their minds to adapt to the demands of their social environment. During the 20th century, an American society in rapid flux because of the industrial revolution altered its demands over time. Long before the beginning of that century, people felt a strong need to be cognitively self-sufficient in everyday life and by 1900, virtually everyone who could meet the demands of everyday life had done so, and the small percentage that could not has not varied much over the last 100 years. Since 1900, American society has been demanding that the mass of people come to terms with the cognitive demands of secondary education. They did so but this had little effect on the ability of the bottom 2% to be self-sufficient at the corner shop, keeping score at baseball, and so forth. The willingness or the capacity to respond to enhanced demands from core classroom subjects began to reach a limit about 1950. Growing affluence engendered a new set of demands: competence in nonpractical problem solving, nonpractical in the narrow sense of not seeming directly relevant to school marks or dealing with the concrete realities of everyday life. Thanks to the social multiplier, those new demands have been met to a surprising degree but that has had little effect in terms of escalating classroom-subject performance. It is likely that the tolerance of Americans to ever-increasing cognitive demands on their leisure and work time also has its limits; there is no reason to think that the post-1950 IQ gains will go on forever.

All of this implies a large degree of compartmentalization of skill enhancement over time. However highly correlated at a given time, dynamic processes over time show that skill at solving nonpractical problems, mastering core subjects, and coping with the simpler tasks of everyday life do not necessarily cross-fertilize. Neisser (1999) carried the compartmentalization of "intelligence" further still: He divided post-1950 cognitive gains into increased skills of visual analysis, use of abstract concepts, and complexity of verbal argument, all largely independent of one another.

There is nothing odd about cognitive enhancement taking place without either radical cross-fertilization or an escalation of what is often called "intelligence". All the social multiplier needs to work its magic are persistent environmental trends that raise the mean of a real-world cognitive competence. Even though there is probably a strong correlation between basketball and baseball skills at a given time, the relevant social multiplier can raise basketball skills dramatically without affecting baseball skills. I suspect that it has enormously enhanced basketball skills without much increasing the speed with which people master sporting skills in general, and without affecting the number of people who find themselves physically incapable of dealing with everyday life.

There is a romance in the history of the American mind in the 20th century. Many of the privileged did not believe that the masses could meet the demands of secondary education and they were proved wrong. The mastery of classroom-subject skills had profound real-world effects: an educated work force that could meet the needs of progressive industrialization, a mass clientele for books, plays, and the arts, contributions from those whose talents had hitherto gone undeveloped. The expanded population of secondary school graduates was a prerequisite for the chief educational advance of the post-1950 era, that is, the huge increase in the number of university graduates, but I have nothing interesting to add to what social historians say about that phenomenon.

As for the post-1950 IQ gains, I believe that they have had a significant but less dramatic real-world impact. No doubt, the first great attitude shift has enhanced the capacity of Americans to perform some work roles. People who take nonpractical problem solving more seriously are likely to be more innovative and independent. However, the fact that people have no better basic vocabularies or quantitative skills may set limits on whether they are better lawyers, technicians, managers, white collar, and blue collar workers. However, even the amount of real-word change that seems most certain has significance. A greater pool of those suited by temperament and therefore inclination to be mathematicians or theoretical scientists or even philosophers, more contact with people who enjoy playing with ideas for its own sake, the enhancement of leisure, these things are not to be despised. And all of this has come about without an upgrading of the human brain through eugenic reproduction or (since 1950 at least) the help of environmental factors that have a direct impact on brain physiology.

What of the future? Thus far, the cognitive skills enhanced have been caught in the net of current IQ tests. It will be sad if cognitive skills begin to escalate, perhaps insight into the social behavior or world views of other people, of a kind that go unnoticed because they are unmeasured. Or the next step may be the escalation of something noncognitive, such as moral maturity. Or, as has been foreshadowed, affluence may show its darker side and throw us into a retrogression both intellectual and moral.

REFERENCES

Boozer, M., & Cacciola, S. E. (2001). *Inside the black box of Project STAR: Estimation of peer effects using experimental data*. Center Discussion Paper No. 832. New Haven, CT: Yale University Economic Growth Center.

Bouchard, T. J. (1998). Genetic and environmental influences on adult intelligence and special mental abilities. *Human Biology, 70*, 257–289.

Case, R., Demetriou, A., Platsidou, M., & Kasi, S. (2001). Integrating concepts and tests of intelligence from the differential and developmental tradtions. *Intelligence, 29*, 307–336.

Colom, R., Andrés-Pueyo, A., & Juan-Espinosa, M. (1998). Generational IQ gains: Spanish data. *Personality and Individual Differences, 25*, 927–935.

Deary, I. J., & Crawford, J. R. (1998). A triarchic theory of Jensenism: Persistent, conservative, reductionism. *Intelligence, 26*, 273–282.

Dickens, W. T., & Flynn, J. R. (2001). Heritability estimates vs. large environmental effects: The IQ paradox resolved. *Psychological Review, 108*, 346–369.

Emanuelsson, I., Reuterberg, S.-E., & Svensson, A. (1993). Changing differences in intelligence? Comparisons between groups of thirteen-year-olds tested from 1960 to 1990. *Scandinavian Journal of Educational Research, 37*, 259–277.

Flieller, A., Saintigny, N., & Schaeffer, R. (1986). L'evolution du niveau intellectuel des enfants de 8 ans sur une periode de 40 ans, 1944–1984 [The evolution of the intellectual level of 8-year-old children over a period of 40 years, 1944–1984]. *L'orientation scolaire et professionelle, 15*, 61–83.

Flynn J. R., & Casé, L. R. (2005). *Standardization of Raven's in Argentina 1964 and 1996–2000: IQ gains huge, gender differences nil*. Manuscript submitted for publication.

Flynn, J. R. (1984). The mean IQ of Americans: Massive gains 1932 to 1978. *Psychological Bulletin, 95*, 29–51.

Flynn, J. R. (1990). Massive IQ gains on the Scottish WISC: Evidence against Brand et al.'s hypothesis. *Irish Journal of Psychology, 11*, 41–51.

Flynn, J. R. (1991). *Asian Americans: Achievement beyond IQ*. Hillsdale, NJ: Lawrence Erlbaum Associates.

Flynn, J. R. (1993). Skodak and Steels: The Inflated Mother-Child IQ cap. *Intelligence, 17*, 557–561.

Flynn, J. R. (1998). IQ gains over time: Toward finding the causes. In U. Neisser (Ed.), *The rising curve: Long-term gains in IQ and related measures* (pp. 25–66). Washington, DC: American Psychological Association.

Flynn, J. R. (2000). IQ gains, WISC subtests, and fluid g: g theory and the relevance of Spearman's hypothesis to race (followed by discussion). In G. R. Bock & J. Goode (Eds.), *The nature of intelligence* (pp. 202–227). Novartis Foundation Symposium 233. New York: Wiley.

Flynn, J. R. (2006). The Flynn Effect: Rethinking intelligence and what affects it, In C. Flores-Mendoza & R. Colom (Eds.), *Introducao A psicologia Das differencas individuals* [Introduction in the psychology of individual differences]. Porto Alegre: ArtMed. English translation available from author.

Greenfield, P. (1998). The cultural evolution of IQ. In U. Neisser (Ed.), *The rising curve: Long-term gains in IQ and related measures* (pp. 81–123). Washington. DC: American Psychological Association.

Herrnstein, R. J., & Murray, C (1994). *The ell curve: Intelligence and class in American life*. New York: The Free Press.

Howard, R. W. (2001). Searching the real world for signs that population intelligence is rising. *Personality and Individual Differences, 30*, 1039–1058.

Jensen, A. R. (1983). Effects of inbreeding on mental-ability factors. *Personality and Individual Differences, 4*, 71–87.

Jensen, A. R. (1998). *The g factor: The science of mental ability*. Westport, CT: Praeger.

Leong, F. T. L., Hartung, P. J., Goh, D., & Gaylor, M. (2001). Appraising birth order in career assessment: Linkages to Holland's and Super's models. *Journal of Career Assessment, 9*, 25–39.

Mosler, D., & Catley, B. (1998). *America and Americans in Australia.* Westport, CT: Praeger.

Neisser, U. (1999 July). *The secular rise in intelligence: Many gains, many causes.* Paper presented at a joint session of the Behavior Genetics Association and the International Society for the Study of Individual Differences, Vancouver.

Rosenau, J. N., & Fagan, W. M. (1997). A new dynamism in world politics: Increasingly skilled individuals? *International Studies Quarterly, 41,* 655–686.

Rushton, J. P. (1995). *Race, evolution, and behavior.* New Brunswick, NJ: Transaction Publishers.

Rutter, J. M. (2000). Comments in discussion on James R. Flynn. In G. R. Bock & J. Goode (Eds.), *The nature of intelligence* (pp. 222–223). Novartis Foundation Symposium 233. New York: Wiley.

Schooler, C. (1998). Environmental complexity and the Flynn effect. In U. Neisser (Ed.), *The rising curve: Long-term gains in IQ and related measures* (pp. 67–79). Washington, DC: American Psychological Association.

Spitz, H. (1986). *The raising of intelligence: A selected history of attempts to raise retarded intelligence.* Hillsdale, NJ: Lawrence Erlbaum Associates.

Storfer, M. D. (1990). *Intelligence and giftedness: The contributions of heredity and early environment.* San Francisco: Jossey-Bass.

Teasdale, T. W., & Owen, D. R.. (2000). Forty-year secular trends in cognitive abilities. *Intelligence, 28,* 115–120.

Tuddenham, R. D. (1948). Soldier intelligence in World Wars I and II. *American Psychologist, 3,* 54–56.

U.S. Department of Education, Office of Educational Research and Improvement. National Center for Educational Statistics (2000). *NAEP 1996 trends in academic progress, NCES 97–985r.* Washington, DC: Author.

Wicherts, J. M., Dolan, C. V., Hessen, D. J., Oosterveld, P., Van Ball, G. C. M., Boomsma, D. Z., & Span, M. M. (2004). Are intelligence tests measurement invariant over time? Investigating the Flynn effect *Intelligence, 32,* 509–537.

Williams, W. M., & Ceci, S. J. (1997). Are Americans becoming more or less alike? *American Psychologist, 52,* 1226–1235.

V
▼▼▼▼▼▼▼

ENHANCEMENT VIA NEW CONSTRUCTS

V

ENHANCEMENT IN NEW
CONSTRUCTION

13
▼▼▼▼▼▼▼

g, g's, or Jeez:
Which Is the Best Model for
Developing Abilities,
Competencies, and Expertise?

Robert J. Sternberg
Tufts University

There are three kinds of views of intelligence that compete for attention in today's world of intelligence. I refer to these three kinds of theories as *g, g's,* and *jeez.*

The first kind of view, dating back to Spearman (1904), is the theory of *g,* or general ability (Jensen, 1998; Spearman, 1927), according to which, for whatever other abilities there may be, general ability—an ability that is believed to pervade performance on any intellectual task (hence, its name)—is critical for success of various kinds.

A second kind of view, with antecedents dating back to Thurstone (1938), argues that general ability is not, in fact, central to an understanding of human intelligence. Thurstone believed that there are multiple (correlated) primary mental abilities. General ability is, at best, a secondary phenomenon. Gardner (1983, 1999) has argued for distinct multiple intelligences, each of which is relatively distinct from the others. Sternberg (1997, 1999b; Sternberg et al., 2000) has argued that there are three aspects of intelligence—analytical, creative, and practical—that are relatively distinct. Analytical and practical abilities tend each to yield a general factor, but the two general factors are relatively distinct from one another psychometrically. Creative abilities appear to be more domain specific (Sternberg & Lubart, 1995).

The third kind of view is based on no theory at all. It involves empirical work with no anchored theoretical basis. Much of the intelligence testing that has been done in the United States and elsewhere has been of this kind—unanchored in psychological theory. A great deal of research also is atheoretical, producing empirical findings in the absence of any theory that would help one interpret what the results mean. Work of this kind is perhaps more prevalent in the study of intelligence than in the study of almost any other psychological phenomenon.

My goal in this chapter is to argue that one of these kinds of views—*g's*—is particularly useful for the development of instructional programs to develop intellectual, academic, and other skills. It may be that the other views could also yield useful programs. But I believe the data supporting one theory of *g's*, the triarchic theory of successful intelligence (Sternberg, 1997, 1999b), are at least worthy of serious consideration.

Although our data are consistent with the theory of *g's*, they are not inconsistent with a certain version of the theory of *g*, as originally proposed by Spearman (1904), the theory of *g*. We believe that so-called general ability is applicable to a very wide range of tasks and situations. But its applicability is not equally strong in all situations. Its applicability is greater in academic tasks, for example, than in some kinds of practical tasks. In practical tasks, there also appears to be a *g* factor, but one distinct from psychometric *g*. Thus, the question becomes one of whether one takes a stronger or a weaker version of *g* as viable. I believe the weaker version is upheld, according to which *g* is quite general although perhaps not entirely general, and according to which its relevance varies across tasks and task domains. I do not believe a stronger version is upheld, according to which *g* pervades *all* tasks, and perhaps, pervades them equally strongly.

THE THEORY

According to the proposed theory of human intelligence and its development (Sternberg, 1980b, 1984, 1985, 1990, 1997, 1999b), a common set of processes underlies all aspects of intelligence. These processes are hypothesized to be universal. For example, although the solutions to problems that are considered intelligent in one culture may be different from the solutions considered to be intelligent in another culture, the need to define problems and translate strategies to solve these problems exists in any culture.

Metacomponents, or executive processes, plan what to do, monitor things as they are being done, and evaluate things after they are done. Examples of metacomponents are recognizing the existence of a problem, defining the nature of the problem, deciding on a strategy for solving the problem, monitoring the solution of the problem, and evaluating the solution after the problem is solved.

Performance components execute the instructions of the metacomponents. For example, inference is used to decide how two stimuli are related and application is used to apply what one has inferred (Sternberg, 1977). Other examples of performance components are comparison of stimuli, justification of a given response as adequate although not ideal, and actually making the response.

Knowledge-acquisition components are used to learn how to solve problems or simply to acquire declarative knowledge in the first place (Sternberg, 1985). Selective encoding is used to decide what information is relevant in the context of one's learning. Selective comparison is used to bring old information to bear on new problems. And selective combination is used to put together the selectively encoded and compared information into a single and sometimes insightful solution to a problem.

Although the same processes are used for all three aspects of intelligence universally, these processes are applied to different kinds of tasks and situations depending on whether a given problem requires analytical thinking, creative thinking, practical thinking, or a combination of these kinds of thinking. In particular, analytical thinking is invoked when components are applied to fairly familiar kinds of problems abstracted from everyday life. Creative thinking is invoked when the components are applied to relatively novel kinds of tasks or situations. Practical thinking is invoked when the components are applied to experience to adapt to, to shape, and to select environments.

More details regarding the theory can be found in Sternberg (1985, 1997). Because the theory of successful intelligence comprises three subtheories—a componential subtheory dealing with the components of intelligence, an experiential subtheory dealing with the importance of coping with relative novelty and of automatization of information processing, and a contextual subtheory dealing with processes of adaptation, shaping, and selection—the theory has been referred to from time to time as *triarchic*.

Consider instructional studies that have been done on the basis of the triarchic theory. The review of these studies will be divided into four parts: studies aimed at (a) analytical skills, (b) creative skills, and (c) practical skills, and studies aimed at (d) all three kinds of skills.

INSTRUCTIONAL STUDIES

This section of the chapter—the main section—is organized as follows.

First I describe studies aimed at improving *intellectual skills*. The initial studies were motivated by the componential subtheory of the triarchic theory. I describe, successively, studies aimed at instruction directed at analytical intelligence using metacomponents, performance components, and knowledge components. Then I describe a study motivated by the experiential subtheory, focusing on an important aspect of creative intelligence, namely, insight. Next I describe a study motivated by the contextual subtheory, one focusing on teaching practical intelligence.

Second I describe three instructional studies aimed at improving *academic skills and knowledge*. These studies compare teaching of subject matter triarchically to teaching of subject matter in alternative ways. The first study, focusing on science (psychology) instruction at the upper secondary level, was aimed at exploring aptitude-treatment interactions between students' ability patterns and the ways subject matter is taught. The second study, focusing on teaching of social studies at the elementary level and science (psychology) at the middle-school level, was aimed at exploring main effects in terms of efficacy of alternative instructional treatments. The third study, focusing on teaching of reading skills across the high school curriculum, also was aimed at exploring main effects in terms of efficacy of alternative instructional treatments.

DEVELOPING ANALYTICAL ABILITIES

Metacomponents

The goal of this study was to evaluate dynamic assessment as a means for understanding, developing, and assessing intellectual skills. The study involved metacomponential interventions.

PARTICIPANTS

A total of 358 experimental-group children, 161 boys and 197 girls, participated in the study. The children were spread throughout four grades (2–5) in 10 schools, even though their age was limited to 11 through 13 years of age. In terms of grade levels, 4.5% were in second grade, 37.7% were in third grade, 31.8% were in fourth grade, and 26.0% were in fifth grade. The reason for this spread in grades relative to ages was primarily that children first enrolled in formal schooling at different ages.

To verify whether the expected changes in performance were due to the impact of test-specific intervention rather than an outcome of repeated test administration (i.e., a practice effect), we recruited a sample of children to whom the intervention was not administered.

The sample included 100 children—40 boys and 60 girls—spread out through grades 2 to 5 (11 through 13 years of age). In terms of grade levels, 5.0% were in second grade, 30.0% were in third grade, 35.0% were in fourth grade, and 30% were in fifth grade. The children were recruited from five of the 10 schools from which the experimental sample's participants were drawn. No control sample's participants were included in the experimental sample (and, in fact, the control sample data were collected after the completion of the experimental study).

Tasks

Three tasks were administered dynamically: Syllogisms, Sorting, and Twenty Questions. Each task measured analytical skills of various kinds. Examiners were always instructed to ensure that the children understood what they were being asked to do. At the very start, if a child did not understand a task, the task was further clarified until he or she did understand it. After each pretest, the examiner would indicate to the child that he or she did very well, but that he or she had made some mistakes. The examiner explained that the examiner would now show the child how to solve the problems to help the child solve them correctly.

Syllogisms.   Thirty-four linear syllogisms were used—17 three-term series problems and 17 four-term series problems. Six of each appeared in the pretest, five of each in the intervention, and five of each in the posttest. An example of a three-term series problem would be "Alan is taller than Ken. Dan is taller than Alan. Who is the tallest, Alan, Ken, or Dan?" An example of a four-term series problem would be "Bill is smaller than Joe. Joe is smaller than Peter. Peter is smaller than Tom. Who is the smallest, Joe, Peter, or Tom?" Items could be about names of people, or about other things, such as lengths of roads, sizes of balls, sounds of school bells, and so forth. The posttest was similar to the pretest. The statements were read aloud to the children. In the intervention, the tester worked with drawings prepared in advance. The child was shown how visual representations of items in a vertical or horizontal line (spatial mental representations) could facilitate problem solution. Children were shown how the same representations that were drawn on a sheet of paper could be visualized mentally.

Scoring of items was for number correct at pretest, intervention, and posttest.

Sorting.   The pretest for the Sorting task used the Wisconsin Card Sorting Test (Heaton, Chelune, Talley, Kay, & Curtiss, 1993). Each card contained from one to four identical figures of a single color printed on white cardstock. There were four kinds of figures: stars, crosses, triangles, and circles. There were also four colors in which the figures could appear: red, yellow, blue, and green. Each card, then, could be categorized in terms of number of figures, form, and color.

Children were shown four target stimulus cards. The target cards contained one red triangle, two green stars, three yellow crosses, or four blue circles. The four stimulus cards were placed in front of the child in a row. The children also were given a single pack of 64 cards varying in the attributes described. The task was to sort the cards in the pack into the four piles. Children were not told any rules for sorting nor were they informed in advance that the rule for sorting would change over the course of sorting the 64 cards.

Whether a given card was sorted correctly depended on a rule that was not disclosed to the child. The rule could be that correct sorting was by form, number, or color. If a child placed a card from the pack under a target stimulus card that matched in the "correct" attribute, the child was told that he or she was correct. Otherwise, the child was told that he or she was incorrect. The child then sorted the next card. After a child did six correct sortings, the rule was changed.

The intervention for the sorting task involved foam figures of four colors (yellow, green, black, and blue) and four sizes (large, medium, small, and very small), four shapes (octagon, square, triangle, and rectangle), and four possible numbers of figures (1, 2, 3, and 4). Children were explicitly asked questions about attributes and about finding attributes in common between sets of figures. They were shown how to compare relative attributes and how to sort on the basis of the various attributes.

The posttest for the sorting task involved sorting of threaded beads rather than cards. The beads were of four shapes, four colors, and four combinations (number of beads per thread). The procedure with the beads was comparable to that with the cards.

Scoring of the pretest and posttest was for number of perseverative errors and the number of categories produced. Scoring of the intervention was for number of hints required for the child to reach criterion performance.

Twenty Questions. In the pretest for the Twenty Questions task, the participant was told that the examiner was thinking of an object. The child was then given up to 20 questions to figure out what the object might be. All questions asked by the child had to be answerable either by "yes" or "no." Objects were geometric designs from six rows of figures that varied in shape, size, and color. The shape could be a rectangle, square, or circle. The size could be large, medium, small, or very small. The color could be black or white. There were a total of 24 ($3 \times 4 \times 2$) different objects to choose from.

The intervention consisted of showing the children how to ask those questions that maximally narrowed the search space. For example, they learned that asking whether the figure is "black" would enable them to eliminate all black or white objects, depending on the examiner's response. Or they learned that asking whether the figure was a rectangle could create an included and an excluded set of eight and 16 objects, with the identities of the included or excluded objects depending on the examiner's answers.

The posttest for the Twenty Questions task was comparable to the pretest except that it used different attributes. There were crosses, circles, triangles, and rectangles that could be black or white and that could be large or small, for a total of 24 items in all.

Scoring for the pretest, intervention, and posttest was for ratio of constraint-seeking questions to the total number of questions asked.

Reference Ability and Achievement Tests. Results were also available from a number of other tests of abilities and achievement that serve as reference measures for our own new tests. The reference-abilities tests were digit span forward and backward (averaged), Corsi block, Stroop task, word fluency, and Spanish vocabulary, all of which are used to measure working memory and related cognitive skills. The digit-span forward test involved children's repeating back digits they had heard orally in forward serial order. The Corsi block test involves having children view an examiner tap a number of blocks; the children then have to repeat in forward serial order the pattern of block taps they have seen. The Stroop task was modified for the children so that they either had to say "tick" when they saw a tick and say "cross" when they saw a cross, or else say "cross" when they saw a tick and "tick" when they saw a cross. Word fluency required children to recall, separately, as many foods and animals as quickly as they could. Spanish vocabulary involved the children's learning Spanish vocabulary words (all of which are unfamiliar to them) paired with pictures of objects and then their having to show their recall of the meanings of the words via paired-associates recall. The reference achievement tests were of school achievement in three subject-matter areas: reading, spelling, and arithmetic adapted from the Wide Range Achievement Test (*WRAT*; Jastak & Jasktak, 1978).

The main dependent variables were pretest scores, intervention scores, and posttest scores for our new measures, and reference abilities (digit span, Corsi block, Spanish, Fluency, Stroop errors, Stroop time) and achievement (reading and mathematics). The main independent variables were gender, socioeconomic status, and grade in school.

Dynamic tests were administered in a fixed order: Syllogisms, then Sorting, and then Twenty Questions. All testing was done individually in Kiswahili in an empty classroom that served as a special testing room. Testing occurred in the morning for all participants. It consisted of the three pretests, instruction, and posttests occurring in a single session. Total testing time (actual time spent on tasks), including intervention and instructions for testing, ranged from 42 to 101 minutes. The mean testing time was 71 minutes. Total pure testing time without the intervention or instructions ranged from 14 to 46 minutes with a mean of 25 minutes. Intervention time ranged from 11 to 28 minutes with a mean of 17 minutes. None of these times include time spent in establishing rapport, distributing and collecting materials, changing materials, and so forth.

Static ability tests and educational tests were administered at another earlier time as part of another study.

What We Found

Reliabilities of Measures.   Test–retest reliabilities at a 2-week interval (for the pretest) were calculated on two distinct weighted (by *N*) samples of 50 and 19 individuals obtained by two testers. The weighted averages were .54 for syllogisms, .58 for perseverative errors on the sorting task and .64 for the number of categories on the sorting task, and .66 for the Twenty Questions task.

Dynamic testing makes a difference in terms of test performance on posttest versus pretest. To register this difference, we employed general linear modeling analysis (the mixed procedure). Given that pre- and posttest indicators were not independent, we introduced individuals (participants) as a random effect. There was a significant pre- to posttest performance difference for all three tasks.

This set of analyses was followed by profile analyses, whereby the pattern of performance on the three tasks was compared at pretest and posttest. The analysis revealed a significant effect of task, suggesting the importance of task-specific variation; a significant task × time interaction effect, suggesting that the pre- to posttest changes varied across tasks; and a significant task × individual interaction, suggesting that individuals responded differently to different tasks. As for between-subject effects, there was an effect of individual. All within-subject effects were significant.

Scores on all measures showed significant gains from pretest to posttest. Specifically, performance on the Syllogisms task improved by 117%, performance on the Sorting Task improved by 111%, and performance on the Twenty Questions Task improved by 220%. However, it is not possible to infer how much of the gain is due to the intervention and how much to practice effects from pretest to the posttest.

To address the question of experimental versus control-group differences, we analyzed the data from both experimental and control groups utilizing repeated measures analysis of variance with the four variables (number of syllogisms solved correctly, number of perseverative errors, number of categories detected, and the proportion of constraint-seeking questions) specified as within-subject effects measured in two groups (experimental and control; this variable was specified as a between-subject factor) across two time points (pretest and posttest). The effect of special interest was the Time X Group interaction effect: If this effect is significant, then two groups show different patterns of responses across time (e.g., greater gain from pretest to posttest for the experimental than for the control group).

What did this analysis reveal? First, the results showed the effect of time ($p < .01$), indicating that there were significant differences in the participants' pre- and posttest performance. Second and most importantly, there was a significant Time X Group interaction effect ($p < .01$), indicating that the two groups changed differently across the two time points. This result could not have been due to ceiling effects, because scores were well below the ceilings of the tests. Third, the results showed an effect of task ($p < .01$), which, of course, was expected due to the nature of the three variables (i.e., all variables were measured on different scales). Fourth, there was also a Task X Group interaction, indicating differences in the levels of performance for the four tasks in the two groups ($p < .001$). Fifth, the results showed the presence of the Time X Task interaction, showing that the profiles of changes differed for the four tasks ($p < .001$). The critical second result shows that, in fact, the training had an effect over and above that of a mere practice effect obtained by retesting.

Associations with Demographic Variables. The results of multivariate analysis of variance showed the presence of a multivariate main effect of grade. The effect of children's grade was significant for all indicators of performance on the Syllogisms task. The effects of SES and attendance were borderline. The effect of SES was significant for both pre- and posttest indicators of numbers of categories in the Sorting task and for performance on the pretest of the Twenty Questions task. The effect of school attendance was significant for all three indicators of intervention performance. There were no multivariate effects of gender or gender grade interaction. Of the 11 univariate models tested, follow-up analyses revealed four significant for all posttests.

Pretest-Intervention-Posttest Correlations for Dynamic Tests. Of much interest was the analysis of the correlations between scores for pretest, posttest, and intervention both within and between dynamic tests (corrected for attenuation). Two conclusions were drawn from these data.

First, pretest–posttest correlations ranged from trivial to moderate. They were .05 (NS) for the Syllogisms task, .14 ($p < .01$) for perseverative errors, .42 ($p < .001$) for number of categories on the Sorting task, and −.02 (NS) for the Twenty Questions task. These generally low correlations suggest that even a very brief and minimal intervention can have substantial effects on ability-test scores. Certainly, conclusions drawn on the basis of the pretest would have to be considered suspect, given the instability of the scores after the brief intervention. It appears as though it would be unwise to draw strong conclusions about a person's abilities based only on pretest scores. Second, the various dynamic tests were not very highly correlated with each other either. The correlations (corrected for attenuation) ranged from trivial (around 0) to moderate (.43).

It is interesting to compare these pretest–posttest correlations for the experimental group with the corresponding correlations of pretest and posttest for the control group. The control-group correlations, corrected for attenuation, were .84, .50, .71, and 1.00, respectively, all of which are statistically significant. Clearly, the brief intervention substantially lowered the magnitudes of the correlations: .79, .36, .29, and 1.02 correlation points respectively. The

z values of the group differences for the original correlations are all statistically significant at the 5% level, and the first and last are statistically significant at the 1% level (one-tailed tests of whether the correlation for the control group is higher than that for the experimental group). The most dramatic effect, obviously, is for the Twenty Questions task ($-.02$ vs. 1.00). The reason for this effect is probably a feature of the Twenty Questions task that does not apply to the other tasks: The participant "gets it" or does not. If one knows the strategy of cutting the solution space by 50% with each question, then one usually converges on the correct answer. If one does not know this strategy, one rarely converges on the correct answer and often simply makes chance guesses.

Correlations of Dynamic Tests With Reference Ability and Achievement Tests.   The correlations with both pretest and posttest scores were in the expected directions and many of them are statistically significant although small in magnitude. On the whole, the tests appeared to be measuring related constructs although probably not the same ones. Note that correlations of the posttests with the reference ability measures tended to be higher than the correlations of the pretests with the reference-ability measures. Comparing pretest and posttest correlations with reference-ability tests where at least one correlation in each pair was statistically significant, the pretest correlation with the reference-ability measures was higher in absolute value in two instances and the posttest correlation was higher in absolute value in 20 instances, with only two instances where correlations with both pre- and posttest indicators were nonsignificant. (Absolute values were used because for some measures, higher scores indicated higher levels of abilities, whereas for other measures, lower scores indicated higher levels of abilities.) Looked at in another way, the median of the absolute values of the correlations of the pretests with the reference ability measures was .10 and for the posttests was .21. Looked at in still another way, in every case where the disattenuated correlation of the pretest with the reference-ability measures differed significantly from the correlation of the posttest (11 pairs out of 24), the difference in correlation was significant in favor of the posttest. These results suggest that the posttests are better predictors of the reference ability measures than are the pretests.

Correlations With Achievement Tests.   The correlations with the school achievement tests ranged from trivial to moderate. The correlations were variable. In all cases, the correlation of the posttest was higher than the correlation of the pretest. The median correlation of the pretest with the school achievement measures was .08; the median correlation of the posttest with the school achievement measures was .34. Where there were significant differences of the disattenuated correlations between the pre- versus the posttests and the school achievement measures, all seven favored the posttest. Thus, once again, the posttests tended to correlate more highly with the reference measures, in this case of school achievement, than did the pretests.

Performance Components

One of our early instructional studies was aimed at improving the solution of linear-syllogism problems, that is, problems such as "Mary is taller than Jean. Jean is taller than Barb. Who is tallest?" or "John is not as good as Pete. Eric is not as good as John. Who is the worst?" Our research had shown that most participants use a mixture strategy that involves both spatial-visualization and verbal strategies for solving such items (Sternberg, 1980a), although it was likely that some participants used primarily a spatial strategy and other participants largely a verbal strategy.

We have sought to teach students to solve linear syllogisms by teaching them strategies based on a sequence of performance components (Sternberg & Weil, 1980). Forty-eight college students were given standard instructions for solving linear syllogisms. Of these participants, 30 yielded latency data best fit by the mixture theory, but 18 yielded data best fit by other theories: seven by a linguistic theory, five by a spatial theory, and six by an algorithmic theory (which is based on a participant strategy that uses a shortcut for solving linear syllogisms that bypasses transitive inference altogether). Group fits again indicated the superiority of the mixture theory, but clearly this superiority indicated that the mixture strategy was the most widely used strategy, not that it was the only one used.

The main experimental manipulation in this experiment was one of instructions for solving the linear syllogisms. The group noted previously, of 48 individuals, received standard instructions and was a control group. A second group of 48 individuals received instructions in how to use a strategy involving spatial visualization; and a third group of 48 individuals received instructions in how to use a strategy involving a shortcut algorithm that practically bypassed altogether the need for deductive reasoning of any kind. It was originally expected that the groups would yield different regression patterns when solution latencies were correlated with scores on verbal and spatial ability tests. In particular, it was expected that the uninstructed group would show significant correlation with both kinds of psychometric tests (because the mixture strategy that they would presumably use involves both verbal and spatial elements), that the spatially instructed group would show significant correlations only with the spatial tests, and that the algorithmically instructed group would show only minimal or trivial correlations with the two kinds of tests, in that standard verbal and spatial patterns of reasoning would be bypassed by these participants. The results that emerged, however, were a "mishmash." There was no clear pattern at all.

Analyses of individual participant data revealed the reason for the lack of clearly differentiable correlational patterns: Not everyone followed the strategy they were told to follow. For example, in the algorithmically instructed group, the number of participants using the instructed strategy was more than three times as great as the number in the untrained group (21 as opposed to six), but there were still substantial numbers of people using other strategies. In particular, about as many people (22) used the standard mixture strategy (which most subjects use spontaneously) as used the instructed algorithm strategy. Participants were therefore re-sorted into new groups on the basis of the strategy the mathematical modeling showed they actually used, as opposed to the strategy that we, the experimenters, had hoped they would use on the basis of the instructions. The number of participants in each group thus differed, reflecting the number of participants using the particular strategy characterizing the performance of that group. When participants were re-sorted, the correlations showed the kind of aptitude-strategy interactional pattern we had hoped for. Correlations in the mixture-strategy group were significant with both verbal (−.45) and spatial (−.27) tests. Correlations in the linguistic-strategy group were significant only with the verbal (−.76) but not spatial (−.28) tests. Correlations in the spatial-strategy group were significant only with the spatial (−.61) but not the verbal (−.08) tests. And correlations in the algorithmic-strategy group were significant, but reduced, with verbal (−.32), and marginal with spatial (−.28) tests.

Thus, it is important to consider individual differences in strategy, even in the face of instructional manipulations designed to eliminate such differences. When we teach students ways of solving problems that fail to correspond to their pattern of abilities or stylistic preference, the students may simply disregard our instruction and solve the problems in their preferred way. Or worse, they may become confused, trying not always successfully to integrate their preferred strategy with the one they are being taught. For this reason, it is helpful to know students' ability patterns in advance, and teach them, at least part of the time, in a way that fits these patterns.

KNOWLEDGE-ACQUISITION COMPONENTS

The goal of this study was to teach individuals more effectively to use knowledge-acquisition components. In this experiment (Sternberg, 1987), 150 New Haven area adults (nonstudents) of roughly average intelligence were divided into one of five conditions. There were three training conditions and two control conditions. Participants in all three training conditions and one of the control conditions received exactly the same practice words and passages, but differed in the instruction they received (if any) regarding the passages.

Participants

The 30 participants in each condition were given a 25-item pretest and a 25-item posttest measuring skill in figuring out word meanings, as well as other tests. The pretest and posttest were transfer tests, in that they measured skill in figuring out word meanings: They did not merely test recall of words in the practice materials. Our goal was not to train specific vocabulary, but rather, to train vocabulary-building skills. All words in the experiment were extremely rare English-language words. The same pretest and posttest words were used in each condition, and training words were the same across conditions. Items were scored on a 0 to 2 point scale, for a maximum score of 50 points per test. Each training session lasted 45 minutes, exclusive of various kinds of testing, which brought session length to 2 ½ hours. The conditions, which were between-subjects, were as follows.

Materials

In a *process-training condition,* participants were taught and given practice using three mental processes—selective encoding, selective combination, and selective comparison (Sternberg, 1987; Sternberg & Powell, 1983) alleged by the theory to be involved in figuring out meanings of new words from context.

For example, selective encoding was described as the process of sifting out relevant from irrelevant information. Students were presented with several lines of text that contained a rare word, and were given a detailed explanation of how selective encoding could be used to discover the relevant information about the word's meaning in the text. For example, one of the texts read:

He first saw a *macropodida* during a trip to Australia. He had just arrived from a business trip to India, and he was exhausted.

Processing of these sentences was described as follows:

There is much information to weed out. For example, we need not know that the man in the passage was on a business trip. We do not need to know that he had been to India or that his first exposure to *macropodida* occurred in Australia. That he saw a *macropodida* in Australia is relevant, but we could care less whether he had seen one a hundred times before in every zoo imaginable. In the first sentence there are two important cues: (a) the man saw a *macropodida,* so *macropodida* must be visible, and (b) *macropodida* can be seen in Australia. The second sentence does not contain any relevant information; the facts of this sentence relate to the man, not to the unknown word.

Practice exercises were then presented in which participants were asked to underline portions of the text that seemed relevant to the meaning of the unknown word.

In a *contextual-cue training condition,* participants were taught and given practice using the contextual cues on which the mental processes operate (e.g., class membership, stative-descriptive).

For example, for Cues I (temporal, spatial, stative-descriptive, and equivalence), setting cues were described as temporal, spatial, and situational information about contexts in which an unknown word may be found. Examples of each type of cue were given. Participants were told to judge cues by sorting out information specifically relevant to the unknown word. For example, one of the texts began:

Two ill-dressed people, the one a haggard woman of middle years and the other a lean young man, sat around a fire where the common meal was almost ready. The mother, Tanith, peered at her son through the *oam* of the bubbling stew.

Cues in the text were explained as follows:

There are three setting cues in the first sentence, and the phrase, "around a fire where the common meal was almost ready," contains them all. "Around a fire" is a spatial cue because it tells where the action takes place. The words, "common meal," provide a situational cue, and "almost ready" is an important temporal cue.

Participants were then given practice in identifying setting cues.

In a *moderating-variable training condition,* participants were taught and given practice using the moderating variables that affect how well the processes can be applied to the cues (e.g., the location of a cue in the passage relative to the unknown word).

For example, for number of occurrences of an unknown word, participants were told that multiple occurrences signal a word's importance to a text and provide additional information about its meaning, but they also require integration of information from the cues surrounding each appearance.

One of the passages used as an example follows:

The *flitwite* was only one of the judicial remedies available to the justices of the Court of the King's Bench in the 11th century, but it was perhaps the most important. Its frequent use added enormously to the treasury's coffers, and new royal expenditures were often financed by the issuance of an increased number of *flitwites.* However, even the most impartial of justices must have handed them down in multitudes, for the *flitwite* was as much a part of 11th century society as the civil tort is of our own. Medieval men and women related in direct and personal ways; therefore, conflict was likely to take the form of actual fighting. In our litigious culture, the law must often deal with more subtle forms of conflict.

The word's definition is given at the end of the passage: "a fine for fighting." The information from each occurrence of the word was explained as follows:

We learn from the first sentence that the *flitwite* was an important remedy in the 11th century. The context of the second occurrence tells us that the *flitwite* was important because it "added enormously to the treasury's coffers." The context of the third use of the term informs us that *flitwites* were an important part of 11th century culture. As we read on, we learn that the flitwite appears to be a penalty for fighting.

Participants were then given practice passages and asked to define the target words.

In a *vocabulary-memorization control condition,* participants were asked to memorize definitions of 75 extremely rare words (that otherwise did not appear in the experiment), and were tested on their memory for these words.

In a *context-practice control condition,* participants were given exactly the same practice that was given to the participants in the three training conditions, except that the practice occurred in the absence of training.

What We Found

The mean pretest–posttest gain scores (out of 50 points possible on each test) were 7.2 for the process condition, 5.2 for the contextual-cue condition, 7.6 for the moderating-variable condition, 1.1 for the word-memorization control condition, and 2.6 for the context-practice control condition. The results are clear: The training groups showed significantly greater gains than did the control groups. Two additional features of the means are worthy of note: First, as would be expected, the controls receiving relevant practice showed greater gain than did the controls receiving irrelevant memorization. The practice control condition is actually similar to many contextual training programs, which consist of little more than practice. Second, to the extent that other programs involve any training at all, it is in contextual cues, which provide the least facilitation of all three training conditions.

In summary, theoretically motivated instruction in learning words from context can make a significant and substantial difference in people's ability to learn word meanings from context. In just 45 minutes of training, substantial gains in decontextualization ability were obtained. Of course, the durability of this training was not shown.

DEVELOPING CREATIVE ABILITIES

A second kind of skill that should be susceptible to instruction is that of creative thinking. One aspect of creative thinking is insight.

We instituted a training program for fourth, fifth, and sixth graders based on the tenets of the experiential subtheory (Davidson & Sternberg, 1984). The training was spread out over a period of 7 weeks, and lasted for a total of 14 hours, including a pretest and posttest.

The program involved both verbal and quantitative training, but I restrict this report to quantitative problems, which seem at this point to provide the better measures of insight. Students participating in the program were either previously identified as "gifted" (via a combination of group and individual IQ tests, the Torrance Creativity Test, and teacher and parent input) or as "nongifted" by the school system.

Participants

A total of 40 gifted and 40 nongifted groups in grades 4, 5, and 6 were taught separately. In addition, 10 gifted and 13 nongifted students served as "controls" involved in testing but not the training procedures.

Materials

All experimental and control students received a pretest before the training and a posttest after training. There were two forms of the testing instrument. Half the students received one form as a pretest; the other form as posttest; the other half received the opposite pairing. Because scores did not differ significantly on the two instruments, it was possible to combine their results.

Relevant portions of each pretest and posttest consisted of 15 mathematical insight problems (such as those described earlier, but always without cueing), 10 mystery problems, and 15 deductive reasoning problems. The mathematical problems were included as a direct measure of the results of the training program, as problems of these kinds had constituted a primary basis for the training. The mystery problems were included as a transfer measure, presenting a brief mystery story, requiring students to indicate via free response how the detective assigned to the case had figured out who was the guilty party. These problems were appropriate as a transfer measure because they seemed to measure the insights of the kinds taught by our program, but also because the problem had contained no instruction on mystery problems. The deductive reasoning problems were included as a discriminant measure to show that what we had trained was insightful problem solving rather than problem solving in general. Although we hoped to obtain significant improvements in the experimental groups on the mathematical and mystery problems, we had hoped that significant improvements would not be obtained on the deductive reasoning problems, which measure problem-solving skills that were essentially irrelevant to anything we had taught in our training program.

The training program itself consisted of four types of activities: direct instruction, group problem solving, individual problem solving, and games. Direct instruction consisted of training by the experimenter in the nature and application of the three processes of insight specified by our theory. Group problem solving consisted of class discussion of how the processes applied to various kinds of insight problems, and especially mathematical ones. Individual problem solving consisted of each student solving insight problems on his or her own, with feedback from the experimenter only after the problem solving was completed. Games consisted of class activities (such as variants of "Twenty Questions") that were included as motivators and breaks from the regular instruction. However, all of the games did involve application of the insight skills taught by the program, thus serving to reinforce these skills in an informal way.

What We Found

The results of the training program suggest that insight skills are at least somewhat trainable.

On the mathematical insight problems, both gifted and nongifted experimentalgroup students showed significant improvements from pretest to posttest: 8.45 to 10.65 for the gifted students, 5/12 to 8.02 for the nongifted students. In the control group, no significant gains were shown from pretest to posttest: 8.75 and 8.75 for the gifted students, and 5/25 and 4/12 for the nongifted students. Gains in the experimental groups were significantly greater than in the control groups.

On the mystery (transfer) problems, again both gifted and nongifted experimental-group students showed significant improvements from pretest to posttest: 6.06 to 7.80 for the gifted students, 3.40 to 5/48 for the nongifted students. In the control groups, no significant gains were shown from pretest to posttest: 5/40 and 5/50 for gifted students, 4/50 to 4.77 for nongifted students. Gains in the experimental groups were significantly greater than gains in the control groups.

No significant gains were shown by any groups on the deductive reasoning test. In the experimental groups, results for the pretest and posttest were: 4.15 and 3.60 for the gifted students, 1.59 and 1.71 for the control students. In the control groups, results for the pretest and posttest were: 4.10 and 4/40 for the pretest, and 2.00 and 2.83 for the control students.

In conclusion, then, there is at least preliminary evidence for the trainability of certain aspects of insight performance. Improvements were obtained for both gifted and nongifted students, suggesting the feasibility of a training program for students who are at least average in intellectual abilities.

DEVELOPING PRACTICAL ABILITIES

We developed a program called Practical Intelligence for Schools (Williams et al., 2002) that was designed to teach practical thinking skills. The description here is based on Williams et al. (in press).

The intervention program is a curriculum intervention designed to enhance the practical-thinking skills of early adolescents, especially those in the fifth and sixth grades. We focused on fifth- and sixth-grade students because we believed that the point at which a child leaves primary school and enters intermediate school (usually around sixth grade) is a time when the child is ripe for instruction in practical thinking skills. The child at this juncture is old enough to assimilate and use the skills (many of which require a degree of metacognitive awareness not usually evident in younger children), but young enough to be open to learning them. Around the time of entry into middle school, the child's practical thinking skills become more essential as he or she must change classes several times a day and deal with the demands of different teachers, and, for the first time, a limited number of elective courses.

Participants

There were sites in both Connecticut and Massachusetts. I present here only the description of the Connecticut methods and results. Similar methods and results were applicable in Massachusetts.

In Year 1, 87 students from northwestern Connecticut served as subjects (43 girls and 44 boys). Their ages ranged from 10 to 13 years with a mean of 11.33 (sd = .62). Subjects were fifth- (n = 29) and sixth-grade (n = 58) students. Forty-four subjects (in three classes) received the PIFS program and 43 subjects (in three classes) served as controls. The PIFS and control groups were equivalent with respect to age, sex, and achievement level. This information is determined by the school principals and administrators at the end of each school year and is used to group students for the upcoming school year into heterogeneous classes (two classes per grade) with equivalent numbers of gifted, average, and learning disabled students.

In Year 2, 106 students from the same region participated (51 girls and 55 boys). Their ages ranged from 9 to 12 years with a mean of 10.68 (sd = .64). Subjects were fifth- (n = 42) and sixth-grade (n = 64) students. Fifty-four subjects (in three classes) received the PIFS program and 52 subjects (in three classes) served as controls. The PIFS and control groups were equivalent with respect to age, sex, and achievement level (as a result of the class-grouping procedure described previously).

Materials

Themes of the Practical Intelligence for School (PIFS) Curriculum. Based on extensive classroom observation, teacher and student interviews, and a review of the literature on metacognitive awareness (Metcalfe & Shimamura, 1996), our research team identified five major questions or themes that helped us understand the focus and mechanics of practical thinking skills. These themes became the basis of our curricular intervention, which we called the Practical Intelligence for School (PIFS) program. These five themes were further refined through discussions with teachers during the implementation and during subsequent revisions of the curriculum. Each theme focuses on an aspect of metacognitive awareness that pertains to a particular academic domain.

The first theme is *Knowing Why*. We believed that students would benefit from understanding the purposes behind the tasks they are asked to do in school. (What is the point of homework? Why is it important to read?)

The second theme is *Knowing Self*. Assessing one's own work and one's personal strengths and weaknesses is an integral component of practical competence, both in school and in life.

The third theme is *Knowing Differences*. A working style that is very successful in handling math assignments may be ineffective in writing an essay. The differences among subject matters, and, therefore, the need to learn varied approaches to work, become more pronounced as students move through middle school and into high school.

The fourth theme is *Knowing Process*. How should a student tackle an assignment or a problem? The classroom is a world of its own, and success in it requires an awareness of the academic process. The curriculum describes processes involved in completing work within four focal areas (discussed later): reading, writing, homework, and testing. Students learn to recognize and define problems for themselves. Lessons help students plan their work, develop effective strategies for problem solving, and draw on a wide variety of resources in overcoming difficulties.

The fifth and final theme is *Revisiting*. Each booklet in the PIFS curriculum focuses on a particular kind of reflection that is especially useful to its focal area: re-reading texts, revising writing, reworking homework, and reviewing tests. Children learn that going the extra mile to review and revise is the hallmark of the successful student.

Contents of the Practical Intelligence for School (PIFS) Curriculum. We focused the curriculum on four major areas in which students require practical intelligence to succeed in school. This is not to say that these are the only salient areas or that our curriculum addresses *all* the practical thinking skills children need. Rather, we focused on these four areas because our observations and interviews suggested that practical intelligence in each of these areas is important to school success. The four PIFS focal areas are reading, writing, homework, and testing.

The *Introduction* to the PIFS curriculum contains a series of lessons that asks students to think about the nature of school and why they attend it. Students also reflect on their own personal strengths and interests, developing a profile of themselves that they can use to help them draw their interests into future school assignments. The *Thoughtful Reading* booklet invites students to consider the role that reading plays in adult life. They develop their own reading profiles and identify their best strategies for overcoming difficulties in reading. They also compare and contrast different kinds of reading. *Expository Writing* lessons cover the practical side of planning, writing, and revising clear, coherent pieces that convey students' ideas, incorporate their particular interests, and capitalize on their strengths.

The *Homework Planning and Execution* booklet covers issues such as understanding the purposes of homework, identifying personal strengths and weaknesses in homework habits, developing organizational skills, and making use of a variety of resources to overcome homework problems. Finally, *Preparing for and Using Feedback from Tests* includes lessons in which students discuss the importance of and uses for tests; develop important classroom and study skills like listening carefully, taking notes, and memorizing; practice various study strategies in preparing for tests; anticipate and plan for problems they might encounter while testing; and, finally, consider how best to make use of feedback from tests.

Procedure

In both implementation years, experimental-group teachers approached the teaching of PIFS lessons as though these lessons were a normal part of the curriculum. Students were not told the material was "extra work" or "enrichment," they were simply taught from the PIFS perspective rather than from the more traditional purely academic perspective. The assessments used to evaluate PIFS, which were administered to all students (experimental and control), were also used by teachers to evaluate their students' proficiency in reading, writing, homework, and test taking. The use to which the researchers put these assessments was unknown to the students, who viewed the assessments as simply a part of normal classroom procedure.

Assessments

Description. In Year 1, we developed pretests and posttests designed to assess the quality of students' practical knowledge in each of the four focal areas (reading, writing, homework, and testing). All of the tests were based on the kinds of tasks students are typically asked to do in school to make them fair to students not exposed to the curriculum.

Scoring. Yale and Harvard researchers collaboratively developed a 5-point rating scheme for each test, in which a 1 was defined as "No Ability—very poor or essentially blank," a 2 as "Low Ability—poor but shows effort," a 3 as "Some Ability—generally good answer," a 4 as "Good Ability—very solid effort and performance," and a 5 as "High Ability—excellent in every respect." Each score was further defined with specific examples of student work that corresponded to that score. Separate scoring keys and sets of student work were developed for each academic and practical measure, reflecting the different emphases of academic and practical thinking skills. The same levels of relative and absolute performance were associated with the scores from 1 to 5 for both academic and practical measures, in both Years 1 and 2, at both the Connecticut and Massachusetts sites. Once the scorers had studied the anchors for the scale, they referred back during scoring to a key that contained the student examples corresponding to each score. Assessments were scored by three independent raters blind to student group membership (students' names, classes, teachers, and schools were masked, and pretests and posttests were intermixed).

What We Found

Practical and academic performance ratings showed good interrater reliability for both Year 1 and Year 2. The median reliability for Year 1 was .85 (range: .66 to .91). The median reliability for Year 2 was .86 (range: .82 to .92)

Analyses of covariance were conducted on all academic- and practicalintelligence variables, using the pretest score for each measure as the covariate, and comparing the fall-to-spring score changes for the PIFS and control group students.

Academic Measures. In general, for Year 1 academic measures, there were pretest-to-posttest increases for both the PIFS and control groups. However, the PIFS group was not significantly different from the control group. For Year 2, the PIFS and control groups were approximately equal at pretest on the academic measures. Both the PIFS and control groups increased at posttest. The PIFS group gains were significantly greater than the control group gains, showing beneficial effects of the PIFS curriculum on each type of academic work. For the academic summary score (based on reading and writing ability), the covariate-adjusted posttest improvement was .47 points greater for the PIFS group compared to the control group, which is a 17% larger gain (above the sample's pretest mean) for the PIFS subjects. For the academic testing score, the covariate-adjusted posttest improvement was 6.55 points greater for the PIFS group compared to the control group, which is an 18% larger gain for the PIFS subjects.

Practical Measures. For Year 1 practical measures, there were pretest-to-posttest increases for PIFS and control groups. The PIFS group gains were significantly greater than the control group gains on reading, homework, testing, and the practical-4 summary score (representing the mean of reading, writing, homework, and testing). On these variables, the PIFS subjects began lower than the controls at pretest but PIFS subjects overcame this initial difference and matched the posttest gains by controls. For the practical-4 summary score, the covariate-adjusted posttest improvement was .34 points greater for the PIFS group compared to the control group, which is an 11% larger gain over the sample's pretest mean for the PIFS subjects.

For Year 2, the PIFS and control subjects started equal at pretest and showed pretest-to-posttest increases. The PIFS group gains were significantly greater than the control group gains for all parts of the curriculum. For the practical-4 summary score, the covariate-adjusted posttest improvement was .56 points greater for the PIFS group compared to the control group, which is a 21% larger gain above the sample's pretest mean for the PIFS subjects.

The student evaluation form was used only at the Connecticut sites. It was designed to be completed by teachers, and it described how well each child performed both generally and specifically with regard to PIFS skills. The form asked the teachers to rate each student on a 1-to-9 scale in terms of her or his grades, general behavior, and attendance. It then asked teachers to evaluate the extent to which each student recognized and incorporated personal strengths into schoolwork, compensated for weaknesses, questioned the purpose of school, made connections between subjects and ideas, used different approaches and a variety of resources, persevered with work, organized time, and sought feedback.

The student evaluation form results showed that PIFS teachers observed significantly more improvement in their students overall than did control teachers from October to June. PIFS students' mean rating moved from 6.24 (fall) to 7.16 (spring), an increase of .92 on a 1-to-9 scale. Control students' mean rating moved from 5.55 (fall) to 5.82 (spring), an increase of .27 units. The relatively higher PIFS gain was significant.

PIFS teachers observed significantly greater improvements than control teachers in the following areas: recognizing and making use of personal strengths and interests, noticing differences across subject matters, using different approaches in different subjects, using a variety of resources, persevering in the face of difficulties, organizing time and materials, and seeking and using feedback. There was no significant change in grades or general behavior in class. PIFS students showed less improvement than control students in attendance and the tendency to speculate about the purposes of studying particular topics or doing particular tasks. In general, however, the trend was positive for the PIFS students as compared to the control students.

Overall Summary. In general, the PIFS program successfully enhanced practical and academic skills. Positive results were observed in both years of the program in Studies 1 and 2 at Connecticut (and Massachusetts) sites. The first year results varied depending on the curriculum component, with PIFS advantages occurring for practical variables in particular. Consistently significant benefits of the PIFS curriculum were found for practical and academic variables in Year 2 at the Connecticut (and Massachusetts) sites. The PIFS effect occurred across a variety of initial conditions in which the PIFS group at pretest scored lower than, equal to, or higher than the control group. In general, there was no interaction between PIFS treatment and gender (with a few exceptions for the Massachusetts site's Year 1 data), and there was consistency of the pretest–posttest gains across the PIFS teachers (classes).

COMBINED THINKING SKILLS TO IMPROVE ACADEMIC COMPETENCIES AND EXPERTISE INTERACTION STUDY: TEACHING SCIENCE

In this study (Sternberg, Ferrari, Clinkenbeard, & Grigorenko, 1996; Sternberg, Grigorenko, Ferrari, & Clinkenbeard, 1999), we sought to teach students primarily analytically, creatively, practically, or for memory, in order to determine whether there was an aptitude-treatment interaction between students' ability patterns and the methods by which they were taught.

Participants

The participants in the present study were high school students, ranging in age from 14 to 18, who attended the 1993 Yale Summer Psychology Program (YSPP). The program was advertised through brochures and newsletters distributed to schools in the United States and abroad. Schools were asked to submit nominations of gifted and talented students, by whatever criteria they used, to the Program Committee of the YSPP. A selection procedure was based on the students' performance on the *Sternberg Triarchic Abilities Test (STAT)*, Level H, designed for advanced high school and college students (Sternberg, 1993). The *STAT* was sent to schools that placed nominations, where the test was administered to the nominated students.

A total of 199 students (146 females and 53 males), from among 326 who were tested, were selected for participation in the summer program of 1993, on the basis of their patterns of ability-test scores (as described later). Of these students, 3 (1.5%) were entering grade 9, 25 (12.6%) were entering grade 10, 77 (38.7%) were entering grade 11, and 94 (47.2%) were entering grade 12. The program participants were fairly widely distributed ethnically (based on students' own reports): 60% European American, 11% African American, 6% Hispanic American, and 17% American from another ethnic minority. Furthermore, 4% of the students were from South Africa, and 2% "other."

The STAT subtest scores for the students were standardized, so they could be compared across different subtests. Based on their STAT performance, all students enrolled in the program were classified into five different groups. Students were identified as "high" in an aspect of ability based on their strongest test score and their score in respect to group average. For students to be classified as "high" in analytical, creative, or practical ability, their total score for a given ability was required to be at least a half-standard deviation above the group average and at least a half-standard deviation above their own scores for the other two abilities measured by the STAT (e.g., analytical higher than creative and practical). Thus, the first three groups included: (a) a group in which students were high in analytical ability ($N = 39$, 19.6%); (b) a group in which students were high in creative ability ($N = 38$, 19.1%); and (c) a group in which students were high in practical ability ($N = 35$, 17.6%). In addition, a "high balanced" group was also defined ($N = 40$, 20.1%). For students to be classified as high balanced, they had to score above the group average for all three abilities. Finally, the fifth group comprised students who scored at or below the group average for all three abilities ($N = 47$, 23.6%). This was a "low balanced" group.

Materials

Description of Abilities Test.   Participants for this study were selected on the basis of scores on the Sternberg Triarchic Abilities Test (STAT) (Sternberg, 1991a, 1991b, 1991c, 1993), a research instrument constituting one theory-based alternative to traditional intelligence tests. The test is based on the triarchic theory of intelligence (Sternberg, 1985), which views intelligence as comprising three aspects: an analytical aspect, a creative aspect, and a practical aspect.

In a nutshell, the analytical aspect of intelligence involves analyzing, evaluating, and critiquing given knowledge; the creative aspect involves discovering, creating, and inventing new knowledge; and the practical aspect involves using, implementing, and applying knowledge in everyday contexts.

The test has nine 4-option multiple-choice subtests, each comprising four items. The test takes roughly 1½ hours to administer, which was the maximum time that participating schools wished to allow for testing. In addition, the test includes three performance or essay subtests—one emphasizing analytical, the second creative, and the third practical thinking.

The nine multiple-choice subtests represent a crossing of three kinds of process domains specified by the triarchic theory—analytic, creative, and practical—with three major content domains—verbal, quantitative, and figural. The idea behind this design is to measure the three aspects of processing in content domains that involve different basic abilities. Because the test is unpublished and is not widely known, it is briefly described here.

The nine multiple-choice subtests plus the three performance tests are

1. *Analytical-Verbal* (neologisms [artificial words]). Students see a novel word embedded in a paragraph, and have to infer its meaning from the context.
2. *Analytical-Quantitative* (number series). Students have to say what number should come next in a series of numbers.
3. *Analytical-Figural* (matrices). Students see a figural matrix with the lower right entry missing, and have to say which of the options fits into the missing space.
4. *Practical-Verbal* (everyday reasoning). Students have to solve a set of everyday problems in the life of an adolescent (e.g., what to do about a friend who seems to have a substance abuse problem).
5. *Practical-Quantitative* (everyday math). Students have to solve math problems based on scenarios requiring the use of math in everyday life (e.g., buying tickets for a ballgame or making chocolate chip cookies).
6. *Practical-Figural* (route planning). Students are presented with a map of an area (e.g., an entertainment park), and have to answer questions about navigating effectively through the area depicted by the map.
7. *Creative-Verbal* (novel analogies). Students are presented with verbal analogies preceded by counterfactual premises (e.g., money falls off trees), and must solve the analogies as though the counterfactual premises were true.
8. *Creative-Quantitative* (novel number operations). Students are presented with rules for novel number operations (e.g., *flix*, for which numerical manipulations differ depending on whether the first of two operands is greater than, equal to, or less than the second). Students have to use the novel number operations to solve presented math problems.
9. *Creative-Figural* (novel series completion). Students are first presented with a figural series that involves one or more transformations; they then must apply the rule of the original series to a new figure with a different appearance, to complete a new series.

There are also three essay items, one each stressing analytical, creative, and practical thinking. In the current version, the analytical problem requires students to analyze the advantages and disadvantages of having police or security guards in a school building. The creative problem requires students to describe how they would reform their school system to produce an ideal one. The practical problem requires students to specify a problem in their life, and to state three practical solutions for solving it. Essays are scored for analytical, creative, and practical qualities, respectively, by trained raters.

Psychometric Properties of Test. Because the test we used is unfamiliar, we briefly describe here its main psychometric properties as elicited from our sample.

Basic statistics for the STAT took into account both multiple-choice and essay items. Scores for essays represent an average of two independent raters. Maximum score for each essay (analytical, creative, and practical) was 4. Mean scores ($N = 267$) were 2.78 (SD = 0.73) for analytical; 2.54 (SD = 0.71) for creative; and 2.85 (SD = 0.81) for practical essays. Maximum score for each of the analytical, creative, and practical multiple-choice sections was 12. Multiple-choice subtest means for all students initially screened ($N = 326$) were 7.90 (SD = 2.52) for the analytical section, 8.75 (SD = 2.09) for the creative section, and 8.09 (SD = 2.11) for the practical section. These statistics show what appear to be acceptable levels of mean performance and dispersions around these means.

Total ability (analytical, creative, and practical) scores are all calculated as sums of standardized scores on the multiple-choice and essay sections of the test. Overall correlations across subtests, all statistically significant at the $p < .01$ level, were .47 between analytical and creative, .41 between analytical and practical, and .37 between creative and practical. In general, multiple-choice items tended to intercorrelate with each other moderately (median $r = .52$) and the essay items to intercorrelate weakly (median $r = .21$), although all intercorrelations were statistically significant. The median intercorrelation of multiple choice with essay items was also weak (median $r = .14$) but statistically significant.

Because we used two different forms of test items (multiple choice and essay) and hypothesized three latent abilities (analytical, creative, and practical), the multitrait–multimethod approach via structural-equation modeling (Bollen, 1989) was utilized in order to assess what the correlations across the abilities would be if method variance were accounted for. In this model, we allowed the abilities (analytical, creative, and practical) to correlate, but the abilities and methods were uncorrelated. The errors were fixed. The overall fit of the model was satisfactory. The analysis enabled us to take out elements of the intersubtest correlations that are due solely to shared forms of testing (which are especially relevant to the multiple-choice subtests). Using such analysis, we found the correlations between latent abilities (as measured by multiple-choice subtests and essays) to be −.07 for analytical and creative, .00 for analytical and practical, and .06 for creative and practical. The correlation between the methods was 0.25.

The KR-20 internal-consistency reliabilities of the multiple-choice items, averaging across contents, were .63 for the analytical items, .62 for the creative items, and .48 for the practical items. These reliabilities are relatively weak, but perhaps reflect the facts that item content was diverse (verbal, quantitative, figural) and the number of items was small (12 for each of the analytical, creative, and practical sections). Interrater reliabilities (Spearman-Brown corrected correlation coefficients) of the essays were .69 for the analytical, .58 for the creative, and .68 for the practical essays.

In a pilot use of the STAT with a similar population (Sternberg & Clinkenbeard, 1995), a variety of tests of abilities was administered to 64 participants. The other tests used were the Terman Concept Mastery Test (primarily a test of crystalized abilities), the Watson-Glaser Critical Thinking Appraisal (a verbal test of critical thinking), the Cattell Culture Fair Test of *g* (primarily a test of fluid abilities), and a homemade test of insight problems (adapted from Sternberg, 1986). Respective correlations of the STAT with these tests were, for the analytical, .49, .50, .50, and .47 (all significant); for the creative, .43, .53, .55, and .59 (all significant); and for the practical, .21, .32, .36, and .21 (the second and third significant).

Instructional Material. The text for the course was a prepublication version of In Search of the Human Mind (Sternberg, 1995), an introductory psychology text comprising 20 chapters. The text covers at a college level the topics typical of introductory psychology courses. It includes analytical, creative, and practical questions embedded within each chapter and at the end of each chapter. Thus, all students, regardless of instructional placement, received at least some triarchic instruction through their reading.

Assessment of Achievement. Students in the program were evaluated in three ways: They were given two assignments, a final project, and two examinations (midterm and final). Each of the assessments involved analytical, creative, and practical thinking, as well as use of memory.

With regard to homework, one assignment required students to (a) compare and contrast two theories of depression (analytical); (b) propose their own, improved theory, which could be based in part on past theories (creative); and (c) show how they could apply their theory of depression to help a depressed friend (practical). The other homework required similar thought processes applied to the Festinger-Carlsmith (1959) forced-compliance paradigm.

With regard to the examinations, the midterm consisted of a multiple-choice portion measuring primarily recall but also simple inference, and three essays: one analytical, one creative, and one practical. The final exam again consisted of multiple-choice and essay sections, differing from the midterm only in the length of the multiple-choice section (it was longer) and the number of essays (three per type rather than one).

The independent project required students to come up with their own investigation and to pursue it analytically, creatively, and practically.

Four raters scored all performance assessments (i.e., assignments, exam essays, final project). Each (analytical, creative, practical) part of each assessment was rated for analytical, creative, and practical quality. To reduce redundancy, and to arrive at a purer assessment of each of these abilities, analyses are reported in this article only for ratings matched to assessments (e.g., analytical ratings for the analytical performances, creativity ratings for the creative performances, and practical ratings for the practical performances). Results were similar when all three ratings were used for all three types of performance.

All ratings were on a scale of 1 (low) to 9 (high). Raters met frequently in order to ensure common standards and use of the rating scales. Averaged Pearson interrater reliabilities for quality ratings by the four judges of the achievement measures were .59 for the assignments, .45 for the final project, and .71 for the examinations, and were comparable for analytical, creative, and practical ratings. If one applied the Spearman–Brown formula to take into account the use of the four judges whose ratings were ultimately averaged, the reliabilities rose to .85, .78, and .90 respectively. The ratings were subjected to principal-component analyses. First principal component standardized scores were utilized in the subsequent analyses as the measures of course performance.

Design. Students were selected on the basis of their ability test score profiles to be either (a) high-analytical, (b) high-creative, (c) high-practical, (d) high-balanced, or (e) low-balanced. They were then placed at random in sections of the introductory psychology course that emphasized (a) analytical instruction, (b) creative instruction, (c) practical instruction, or

(d) memory instruction (control). Thus, some students were better matched, and others more poorly matched, with respect to ability patterns and instructional treatment. All students were assessed for (a) analytical, (b) creative, (c) practical, and (d) memory achievement. Thus, participant ability and method of instruction were between-subjects variables, and method of assessment was a within-subjects variable.

Procedure.   Ability tests were sent out to schools from which students were nominated. The tests were administered in the schools, and then returned to us for scoring and data analysis. Students were then selected for participation in the study on the basis of their ability pattern. They came to the 4-week summer program at Yale, where instruction lasted all day. The students were housed in a common dormitory. Students used a common text and attended common lectures in the morning, given by a psychology professor who had won a university teaching award.

In the afternoons, students were assigned to sections, which constituted the experimental treatment. There were eight sections in all, two for each of the four instructional conditions. Half the sections were taught by high school advanced placement psychology teachers, the other half by trained graduate assistants. The two types of teachers were equally distributed across instructional conditions. Although students and their parents signed informed consent forms and thus knew they were part of a study, they did not know exactly what the study was about, nor that it involved ability patterns. Of course, they did not know their test scores nor how the sections were intended to differ. All examinations were administered in class. At the end of the course, participants were debriefed.

What We Found

Predictive Validity of STAT for Course Performance.   Before testing for ATI, we wanted to ascertain whether the STAT even had empirical validity for predicting course performance.

Subtests for all three processing domains measured by the *STAT* reliably predicted each of the analytical, creative, and practical aspects of course performance. Of course, because the subtests are themselves correlated, there may be redundancy in these predictions. Hence, we need to use multiple regression in order to assess levels of prediction for all three ability subtests.

The results of multiple regressions show that in every case at least two variables, and in one case, all three variables, significantly contributed to prediction: the analytical and either or both of the creative and practical scores.

Analysis of Variance.   To investigate the effects of the demographic factors, three sets of multivariate analyses of variance were conducted. These analyses separately employed multiple measures of performance on analytical, creative, and practical tasks as dependent measures and gender, ethnicity, and grade as independent measures. With the exception of one test (the main effect of ethnicity for performance on practical tasks), none of the multivariate tests of the main effects or interactions was significant. The follow-up univariate analyses revealed that there were significant differences for three out of the five measures of performance on practical tasks: the second homework assignment, the final exam, and the independent project. Closer analyses of the means showed that these differences were consistently due to the lower performance of Black students on these tasks. However, when conservative Bonferroni procedures correcting for the level of significance were applied, these findings were no longer significant.

The overall conclusion from the analyses of possible differences in task performance due to demographic factors showed that the students' performance did not vary significantly depending on such characteristics as their gender, ethnicity, and grade. Consequently, in the further investigation, these demographic factors were excluded from the tested models.

To investigate the effect of the interaction between the students' abilities and the method of teaching, a set of repeated-measures analyses of variance was conducted. Students were considered as matched if they scored high on the ability test (analytical, creative, practical) corresponding to the instructional condition (analytical, creative, practical), and mismatched otherwise. Thus, high balanced were always matched, low balanced always mismatched.

The repeated-measures analyses of variance employed five different assessment procedures as different assessment points spaced in time. The within-subject effect was specified as the assessment factor and the match/mismatch was specified as the between-subject effect.

For the measures of performance on the analytical tasks, there were no significant assessment or assessment-by-match effects. However, the between-subject effect of match was significant. The follow-up profile analysis, which allowed a comparison between performance of matched and mismatched groups across all five measures, showed the significant differences in level of performance of matched and mismatched students. The tests of parallelism and flatness were nonsignificant: The profiles appeared to be parallel and the various forms of assessment elicited the same average responses from both matched and mismatched students.

For creative tasks, there were no significant assessment or assessment-by-match effects. However, the between-subject effect of match was significant. The follow-up profile analysis, which allowed a comparison between performance of matched and mismatched groups across all five measures, showed significant differences in levels of performance of matched and mismatched students. The tests of parallelism and flatness were nonsignificant: The profiles appeared to be parallel and the various forms of assessment elicited the same average responses from both matched and mismatched students.

Finally, for practical tasks, there also were no significant assessment or assessment-by-match effects. However, the between-subject effect of match was significant. The follow-up profile analysis, which allowed a comparison between performance of matched and mismatched groups across all five measures, showed significant differences in levels of performance of matched and mismatched students. The tests of parallelism and flatness were nonsignificant: The profiles appeared to be parallel and the various forms of assessment elicited the same average responses from both matched and mismatched students.

The total sample of 326 children was recruited through the children's schools, which nominated them for participation in the program as gifted and talented. Thus, even the total sample was comprised of fairly selected children. The selection of 199 children for participation in the ATI analyses gave us groups with balanced as well as unbalanced patterns of triarchic abilities. Yet, one could argue that the observed difference between the matched and mismatched groups might have resulted from the fact that the "high" balanced group was included in the matched group and the "low" balanced group was included in the mismatched group, thus confounding the ATI-based effect with the effect of the g-factor (i.e., general intelligence). To test this hypothesis, we repeated the analyses previously described on a subsample of children that included only those high on specific abilities (analytical, creative, or practical). The balanced groups were not included in this analysis.

This procedure, however, significantly decreased the size of the sample, especially the size of the matched group ($N = 71$ to $N = 31$). In such a small sample, random fluctuations of scores (which might have been due to the impact of nonacademic factors of the YSPP, such as staying up late in the dormitory, etc.) are especially noticeable. In order to control for the impact of random variance, the data were screened for deviant scores and those extreme scores were deleted from the analyses.

In the framework of repeated-measures analyses of variance, the between-subject effect of match was significant for the measures of performance on the analytical and creative tasks. There was no overall effect of match on the performance of the five practical tasks, but the effect held for three of the five individual tasks (first homework assignment, final exam, and independent project).

COMBINED THINKING SKILLS TO IMPROVE ACADEMIC COMPETENCIES AND EXPERTISE MAIN-EFFECTS STUDY: TEACHING SCIENCE AND SOCIAL STUDIES

In a further study, we investigated main effects rather than interactions in triarchic teaching (Sternberg, Torff, & Grigorenko, 1998). The idea was to determine whether triarchic teaching would improve students' academic performance, regardless of their ability patterns.

We did two studies, Study 1 with primary school students, and Study 2 with secondary school students.

Study 1

Participants. In the primary-school project, the participants included 213 third-grade students (106 boys and 107 girls) in two elementary schools in Raleigh, NC. Both schools serve a diverse population of primarily lower SES students, including large groups of African American, Hispanic, and Asian students. Both schools are designated by the school district as "gifted and talented magnet" schools, but they serve both gifted and nongifted populations. A total of nine classes of 20 to 25 students participated in the research. These classes were taught by nine experienced teachers who were certified to teach third grade in North Carolina.

Ability Testing. Participating students took a standardized test of cognitive abilities, the Otis-Lennon Intelligence Scales, as part of a district-wide testing program for identification of giftedness. In the results section that follow we use the Otis-Lennon scores as a covariate with the effects of different instructional treatments.

Instructional Treatments. Prior to the intervention, participating teachers were divided into three groups, one for each form of instructional treatment. The teachers then received extensive training programs focusing on techniques for implementation of the appropriate instructional strategies. Each of the training programs comprised a series of workshops that included (a) descriptions and models of appropriate teaching strategies, and (b) opportunities for teachers to create lesson plans and classroom activities and to receive feedback on their work. Each workshop included techniques for infusing the appropriate strategy into all aspects of instruction, including lecture, discussion, collaborative-learning groups, and individual assignments.

There were three training programs in all, one for each instructional treatment. In the triarchic group, the teachers participated in workshops devoted to techniques for using and strengthening analytical, creative, and practical skills in the classroom. The critical-thinking group focused exclusively on analytical abilities. The traditional-instruction group participated in workshops focusing on an irrelevant topic—procedures for portfolio assessment. None of the teachers collected portfolios during the intervention.

Because primary school teachers have only one class at a time, each teacher was trained only for the instructional treatment to which he or she was assigned. The five teachers at School A, where the triarchic and critical-thinking groups were located, were divided between the triarchic and critical-thinking groups. All teachers at School B, which functioned only as a control school in this study, were assigned to the traditional-instruction group. The separation of the traditional control group by school was intended to minimize the cross-contamination that can result within a school when experimental-group teachers interact with control-group teachers.

During the intervention, the students received an instructional unit on the topic of "communities"—a social studies unit required for third-grade students in North Carolina. The unit centered on four curriculum objectives published in the Curriculum Guide given to teachers by the North Carolina Department of Education. Curriculum objectives for the unit included: (a) citizenship; (b) similarities and differences between individuals, families, and communities; (c) concepts of authority, responsibility, and justice; and (d) relationships between people and their governments. No text was used for the unit; materials for the courses were developed individually by the teachers. The intervention took place for 10 weeks, 4 days per week, 45 minutes per day, for a total of 30 hours of instruction.

A total of nine sections of the unit were taught at the two schools. Of the five sections at School A, three were given triarchic instruction ($n = 74$) and two received critical-thinking instruction ($n = 45$). At School B, all four sections received traditional instruction ($n = 92$).

To illustrate the three different instructional treatments, consider three ways in which a third-grade unit on public services (e.g., fire, police) can be taught. The approach taken in traditional instruction is to have children memorize the names and functions of the various public services. In critical-thinking instruction, an additional analytical effort is undertaken, perhaps one assigning students to compare and contrast the different services and evaluate which ones to keep in case of a budget crisis. In the triarchic group, creative and practical skills are used as well as analytical ones; students might be assigned to come up with their own public service, to describe its means and ends, and to compare this new public service with conventional ones.

During the intervention, the students received instruction that reflected the differences among these three instructional treatments. A typical activity in the traditional-instruction group emphasized memory abilities:

A police officer came to visit the class. He answered questions from the students and talked about what police officers do. He also talked about the equipment police offers use and how a person goes about becoming a police officer. After he left, each student wrote a letter thanking him and describing what he or she learned during the officer's visit.

In the critical-thinking group, the teachers designed and implemented activities that encouraged students to engage in analytical reasoning:

Class discussion concerning authority figures: Each student records information on a sheet with three columns. At the top of each column is a symbol for the following: USA/President, NC/Governor, and Raleigh/Mayor. The students take notes in each column as a range of issues are discussed (e.g., comparative powers, privileges, responsibilities).

Analytical activities as such were also used in the triarchic-instruction group, which focused as well on activities drawing on creative and practical skills:

The students invented their own government agency. They had to decide what service to provide, give it a name, tell why it's important, and why the government should pay for it.

Then students were asked to make an advertisement for the invented government agency. The class shared about the agencies for the rest of the class time. (Creative)

The students were given a problem situation of littering in the community. They brainstormed consequences that could be used in that situation. The teacher listed them on the board. Students then decided which consequences were appropriate (fair vs. unfair). Then we tied our "make believe" littering-in-the-community problem to our real-life problem of litter on the school grounds. In groups, the students brainstormed possible solutions to the problem. They regrouped to pick the best solution and discuss consequences for future "offenders." They came up with a schoolwide litter pick-up day for each grade level. (Practical)

Knowledge-Based Assessment.   Following the intervention, students completed a battery of assessment instruments designed to capture how much they learned and how they were able to use that knowledge. Three types of assessments were employed: (a) a total of 16 multiple-choice items; (b) essay items designed to capture analytical, creative, and practical abilities; and (c) performance assessments (assignments relying less heavily on students' writing skills, such as drawing a map) also implemented to measure analytical, creative, and practical abilities.

The battery of assessments included three essay items—an analytical one, a creative one, and a practical one—that required students to compose paragraph-long responses to the following prompts:

Students were asked to respond to three self-assessment questions: (a) How much did you like the course? (b) How much do you think you learned (in the course)? (c) How well do you think you did (in the course)? Responses were made on a 5-point Likert scale.

Data Analysis.   Following the intervention, the performance assessments were scored by three raters—undergraduate students majoring in psychology who had no knowledge of the research design or hypothesis. The raters used a 5-point Likert-type scale to rate the overall quality of each of the responses. The raters met frequently for several weeks to tune the rating process and to increase rater reliability. For the 15 items that required subjective ratings (one item, Performance Item #3, could be scored directly), interrater correlations for pairs of raters ranged from .77 to .88. The overall interrater correlation of .83 was deemed sufficiently high to provide a reliable assessment of students' responses to the essay items and performance assessments.

What We Found

As described previously, there were 10 main outcome measures of this study: a multiple-choice test score, six performance measures (analytical, creative, and practical assessed by the means of a project and an essay), and three students' self-evaluation scores. The corresponding ability measures correlated significantly (project-essay correlations for analytical, creative, and practical abilities were .25, .56, and .21 [all $p < .000$], respectively), suggesting that derivation of summary scores across the two types of evaluation would be appropriate. This conclusion was supported by the principal-component analyses, where for all three abilities (analytical, creative, and practical) there was only one component, accounting for 60% (for practical) to 78% (for creative) of the variance in the data. The correlations between the summary ability measures and ability scores as assessed by the project and the essay ranged between .78 and .88, demonstrating that both project and essay assessments contributed highly to the summary scores. Consequently, in the following analyses seven outcome measures were utilized: (a) ability measures (analytical, creative, and practical) and the multiple-choice measure, and (b) three self-evaluation measures.

Prior to conducting a series of analyses directed toward testing the hypotheses of the study, we investigated the association between the outcome performance variables (analytical, creative, practical, and multiple choice) and potential covariates, such as gender and scores on the Otis-Lennon ability test. The results revealed no significant differences between performance of boys and girls on any of the dependent measures. Moreover, there was no difference in the pattern of correlations between boys and girls.

In contrast, students' performance was significantly associated with the Otis-Lennon score. The significant correlation coefficients varied between .17 (p < .02), for performance-based scores obtained on the project, and .66 (p < .0001), for the multiple-choice test. Consequently, even though there were no differences in Otis-Lennon scores between the treatment groups the patterns of correlation between the outcome measures and the ability measures differed across treatment groups. Thus, although all outcome measures correlated significantly with the Otis-Lennon scores in the triarchic and critical thinking groups, only the multiple-choice performance score correlated with the Otis-Lennon score in the control group. In order to control the variance in the response to the treatment that might have had differential impact on children with different levels of abilities, the Otis-Lennon score was utilized as a covariate in all subsequent analyses of the four performance measures.

Students' self-assessments neither differentially correlated with the Otis-Lennon ability score nor showed mean differences between the treatment groups. Similarly, we did not find any gender-related differences. Therefore, in these analyses, the ability measure was not included as a covariate in the equation.

Multivariate analysis of variance, profile analysis, and pairwise least-square mean comparisons were implemented to evaluate the effect of teaching on students' performance. Two sets of analyses, one for the ability measures and the multiple-choice score and the other for self-evaluation scores, were conducted.

Three different tests were performed comparing the profiles of scores in the three treatment groups. The first test, the so-called flatness test of the group profiles, investigated whether, with groups combined, the differences between various assessments differed from zero (i.e., whether the group profiles were nonhorizontal). For this test, the obtained profiles were not horizontal. The second test, the parallelism test, asked if the difference between, for example, analytical and creative assessments, was the same for students receiving instructions based on the triarchic theory, the critical-thinking approach, and traditional teaching. For this test, the data led to rejection of the hypothesis of parallelism. Finally, the levels test examined differences between the means of the three treatment groups combined over the four evaluations. This analysis demonstrated that, overall, there was a significant difference between treatment groups in average performance on different types of assessments. The subsequent contrast analysis conducted on the transformed performance variables showed that the triarchic group performed consistently better than either the critical thinking group (the contrast estimate was .75 ± .30) or the traditional group (the contrast estimate was 2.38 ± .25).

A series of subsequent univariate analyses revealed significant F-values for the equations, modeling the sources of variation in the four dependent variables.

Specifically, the performance on analytical tasks model was statistically significant and accounted for 37% of the variance. Similarly, the F-statistic for the performance on the practical tasks model was significant. The R^2 for this model was equal to .21. The model for the performance on creative tasks accounted for 56% of the variance. Finally, the multiple-choice model explained 46% of the variance in the children's performance.

These results were followed up by a series of pairwise comparisons of least-square means. For performance on analytical tasks, the triarchic group performed significantly better than did both the critical-thinking and the conventional groups. Moreover, the critical-thinking group performed better than did the conventional group. For performance on practical tasks, there was no significant difference between the triarchic and critical-thinking groups, but both groups performed better than did the conventional teaching group. On the creative tasks, students from the triarchic group performed significantly better than did students either in the critical-thinking or the conventional-teaching groups. Students in the critical thinking group were also better in their creative performance than were those in the conventional teaching group. Finally, the triarchic group students performed better on the multiple-choice test. This difference was statistically significant when compared with the performance of the students whose teaching was based on the critical-thinking approach and borderline significant when compared with the performance of the conventional teaching group.

The profiles of least-squares means for the three self-assessment questions were also assessed. The profiles were horizontal, so the hypothesis of flatness could not be rejected. The profiles, however, were not parallel and the levels test was significant. The contrast analyses pointed to the differences between the averaged transformed variables: The students' self-evaluations in the triarchic group were consistently higher than those of the students in both the critical-thinking (the contrast estimate was equal to $.93 \pm .20$) and the traditional teaching (the contrast estimate was $1.44 \pm .17$) groups. A series of subsequent univariate analyses revealed significant F-values for all three dependent measures.

A series of pairwise comparisons of least-square means decomposed the observed multivariate effects. For the first question (*How much the students liked the course*), the triarchic group students scored the highest. Their ratings were significantly higher than both the critical-thinking group students and the conventional-group students. Critical-thinking group students were more satisfied with the course than were the conventional-group students. For the second question (*How much the students thought they learned*), there was no difference between the triarchic and critical thinking groups, but both groups showed ratings significantly higher than those of the conventional-teaching group. Finally, for the third question (*How well the students thought they did*), the triarchic group students gave higher ratings than did the students in either the critical-thinking group or the conventional group, but the two nontriarchic groups did not differ from each other.

Study 2

Participants.   The middle-school project was conducted in collaboration with the Center for Academic Advancement (CAA), a program in gifted education at the Johns Hopkins University. In summer of 1996, researchers at Yale designed and implemented a summer-school course in introductory psychology for CAA students. The participants included 141 rising eighth-grade students (68 boys and 73 girls). Drawn from around the nation, the predominantly Caucasian student population hailed largely from middle-class and upper-middle-class backgrounds. The course was taught by six experienced teachers of secondary-level psychology, all of whom were active in Teaching of Psychology in Secondary Schools (TOPSS), a special-interest group of the American Psychological Association.

Ability Testing.   A central goal of CAA is to identify gifted students and to provide them with academically challenging courses. CAA employs scores on the verbal battery of the SAT examination as the basis for identification of the gifted. Students were admitted to the psychology course based on an SAT-verbal score of 420 or higher. Admitted students had a mean SAT-verbal score of 471.13 with a standard deviation of 40.85.

Instructional Treatment.   As in the primary-school project, participating secondary-school teachers received an extensive training program prior to the intervention. The training program focused on techniques for infusing the appropriate instructional strategy into all aspects of the course—lecture, discussion, collaborative-learning groups, and individual assignments. In the triarchic-instruction group, teachers participated in workshops emphasizing the application of analytic, creative, and practical skills to the teaching of psychology. For example, having students frame their own research questions and design their own experiments were considered as tactics for bringing creative abilities to bear in the classroom. The critical-thinking training program was devoted to explication of the use of analytical reasoning in psychology; for example, tactics suggested for encouraging critical thinking in the classroom included having students analyze the flaws in a research project. The traditional-instruction group received a training program on an irrelevant topic: portfolio assessment in the middle-school classroom. None of the teachers collected portfolios during the intervention.

The 10-section course took place in two intensive 3-week sessions. Classes met 5 days per week with 7 hours of class time per day. An introductory psychology text by Myers (1996) was used in all sections. Topics included neuroscience, development, perception, consciousness, learning, memory, language, intelligence, motivation, affect, personality, psychological disorders, therapy, and social psychology.

Research activities were conducted at two sites. At Goucher College in Baltimore, MD, eight sections of the course were taught to 120 students. Of these eight sections, four received triarchic instruction ($n = 60$), two received critical-thinking instruction ($n = 30$), and two received traditional instruction ($n = 30$). At the California State University at Fresno (in Fresno, CA), two sections of the course were taught to 21 students. Students at Fresno received critical-thinking instruction, bringing to 51 the total number of students in the critical-thinking group. Six teachers were involved in the project, five located at Goucher and one at Fresno. Two teachers were assigned to each of the three instructional treatments.

To illustrate the three different teaching strategies as they apply to introductory psychology, it is useful to compare three ways to teach about a common psychological disorder—depression. In traditional instruction, a typical approach is to have students memorize theoretical constructs and research findings (e.g., summarize a biological perspective on depression). In critical-thinking instruction, students are typically asked to compare, contrast, and evaluate different theories of depression (e.g., compare and contrast the biological and sociocognitive perspectives). In triarchic instruction, students are encouraged to bring a combination of analytical, creative, and practical abilities to the fore; for example, students might be asked to generate their own theories of depression (creative), design therapeutic regimes that draw on the new theories (practical), and contrast these ideas with the work of biological and sociocognitive theorists (analytical).

During the intervention, students received instruction that reflected the differences between the three strategies. In the traditional-instruction group, the students participated in activities (e.g., discussions, writing tasks) that emphasized memory abilities:

Obedience to authority is a topic of interest to social psychologists. Who are some of the psychologists that conducted important research on obedience? What motivated this research? What sorts of research methods did they use? What did the researchers find?

In the critical-thinking group, the activities typically required students to employ analytical-reasoning abilities:

Sigmund Freud and Gordon Allport put forth different theories of human personality. What did each theorist seek to explain? On what assumptions does each theory rely? How are the theories similar? How are they different? Which of the two do you agree with more, and why?

In the triarchic-instruction group, creative and practical abilities were emphasized as well as analytical and memory-based abilities:

Why do you think that people sometimes fail to transfer skills or information when they need to? Think of a time when you did transfer when you should not have. Then think of a time when you did not transfer but should have. Why did these things happen? From your own life, come up with an explanation for why transfer does and does not occur when it is appropriate. (Creative)

Measurement error is a problem for many kinds of tests. This error is due to extraneous influences that can make people's scores unreliable. Imagine that you have a new job at the Educational Testing Service (ETS) to reduce measurement error on the Scholastic Assessment Test (SAT). What kinds of measurement errors do you want to reduce, and how will you do it? Feel free to suggest strategies that ETS might not like but which you think will reduce measurement error. (Practical)

Knowledge-Based Assessment.   To evaluate student achievement during the course, two types of assessment instruments were employed. First, multiple-choice questions from the Myers (1996) test bank were used to capture students' understanding of course content. The midterm examination and the final examination each included 21 multiple-choice questions, yielding a total of 42 multiple-choice items. Second, performance assessments were employed to capture students' abilities on analytical, creative, and practical tasks. The midterm and final exams included analytical, creative, and practical performance assessments in the form of short-answer essay items. There also were three assignments in the form of extended essays (one each was analytical, creative, and practical). The three short-answer items on the final exam give the flavor of the performance assessments used in the study:

June is so preoccupied with keeping her house absolutely spotless that she has no time to do anything but clean. After each meal she not only washes the dishes, but also the table, chairs, floor, and cupboards. Although these cleaning rituals irritate her family, June is unable to discontinue them without experiencing intense feelings of discomfort. Use the *psychoanalytic* and *learning* perspectives to explain June's behavior. How do these perspectives compare and contrast? What are the strengths and weaknesses of each approach? (Analytical)

Psychologists have shown that people sometimes cling to their beliefs in the face of contrary evidence. This is called belief perseverance. Give an example of belief perseverance. Then come up with your own theory that explains why people act this way. Be specific about how the theory explains your example of belief perseverance. (Creative)

You are in charge of the fund-raising committee for a club at school. You want to make sure that candy bar sales are strong. How would you go about training your club members to be effective salespersons? Design and describe your sales program, basing it on principles of social psychology. (Practical)

Data Analysis.   As in the primary-school project, the performance assessments were scored by three raters who had no knowledge of the research design or hypothesis. The raters used a 5-point Likert-type scale to rate the overall quality of each of the responses and met frequently for several weeks to tune the rating process. Correlations among the ratings given by pairs of raters for the nine performance items ranged from .76 to .80. The overall correlation of .83 is sufficiently high for us to conclude that the ratings provide a reliable assessment of learners' responses to the performance assessments.

What We Found

To reduce the number of dependent variables, we investigated whether summary measures of the students' performance on the two exams and the homework assignment would be adequate representations of the initial nine outcome measures. The principal-component analyses resulted in a one-component solution for the analytical performance measure, and in two-component solutions for both practical and creative performance measures. In both cases, the first component accounted for about 40% of shared variance in exams and assignment measures, whereas the second component (about 35% for both) was introduced by the variance in the assessment method (the examination scores and the assignment score loaded with opposite signs). Based on these results, in the subsequent analyses six different outcome measures were utilized: analytical, creative, and practical measures for the homework assignment and the two exams (summary measure). Thus, there were seven main outcome variables in the analyses: measures of assignment and examination performance on analytical, creative, and practical tasks, and the multiple-choice measures.

Two variables—gender and the SAT ability score—were considered to be of potential importance in the treatment-effect analyses. Multivariate analysis of variance did not reveal the presence of gender effects on any of the outcome variables. Similarly, the SAT scores did not appear to be significantly related to the performance measures. When the correlations between the SAT scores and the initial performance measures (two examinations and the assignment) were examined, only one correlation, the correlation with the analytical subtest of the final exam, was significant ($r = .189$, $p < .05$). Moreover, there were no SAT-related group differences or differentiative correlation patterns across the treatment groups. Therefore the subsequent analyses of variance did not include any covariates.

Multivariate analysis of variance, profile analysis, and pairwise least-squares mean comparisons were implemented to evaluate the effect of teaching on students' performance.

Three different tests were performed comparing the profiles of scores in the three treatment groups. The least-squares means groups profiles suggested that the investigated group profiles were nonhorizontal. The parallelism test demonstrated that the compared profiles were different for the three groups. Finally, the levels test examined differences between the means of the three treatment groups combined over the seven assessments. This analysis demonstrated that, overall, there was a significant difference between treatment groups in average performance on different types of assessments. Specifically, the contrast analyses across averaged transformed variables resulted in the following estimates: $2.08 \pm .30$ (the triarchic group vs. the critical thinking group) and $3.35 \pm .36$ (the trarchic group vs. the conventional group). There were no differences between the critical-thinking and the conventional group. These results suggest that the triarchic group, on average, performed significantly better than either the critical-thinking group or the traditional-teaching group.

A series of subsequent univariate analyses revealed significant F-values for six out of the seven investigated equations.

These results were followed up by a series of pairwise comparisons of least-square means. For performance on analytical tasks assessed through homework, both the triarchic group and the critical-thinking group performed better than did the traditional group but did not differ from each other. Similarly, for homework assignment performance on creative tasks, there was no significant difference between the triarchic and critical-thinking groups, but both groups performed better than did the traditional group. The pattern was also replicated for the practical homework assignment. Students from both the triarchic and the critical thinking group performed significantly better than did students from the conventional teaching group. The two groups, however, did not differ from each other.

For the examinations, the pattern of the least-square means was very different. The three groups did not differ in their average performance on the analytical tasks of the examination. The groups differed significantly, however, on both creative and practical tasks. For the creative tasks, the triarchic group did better than did either the critical-thinking group or the traditional group. The difference between the critical-thinking and the traditional group was borderline significant, with the traditional group performing slightly better than did the critical-thinking group. Similarly, on the practical tasks, the triarchic group performance was the highest and significantly different from the performance of both the critical-thinking group and the traditional group. Students in the critical-thinking group and the conventional teaching group did not differ.

Finally, the triarchic group students performed better on the multiple-choice test. This difference was statistically significant both when compared with the performance of the students whose teaching was based on the critical-thinking approach and when compared with the performance of those who received traditional teaching. Moreover, the critical-thinking group did better than did the conventional teaching group.

COMBINED THINKING SKILLS TO IMPROVE ACADEMIC COMPETENCIES AND EXPERTISE MAIN-EFFECTS STUDY: TEACHING READING ACROSS THE CURRICULUM

The main objective of this set of studies (Grigorenko, Jarvin, & Sternberg, 2002) was to develop, implement, and evaluate a triarchic enrichment of an existing reading curriculum. Only the first study is described here. We sought to modify the current reading program of the New Haven Public School District so that its content would be preserved but the methods of teaching could be enriched. The main question was whether we could improve students' reading skills by enrichment of teaching methods within the context of an extant basal-based reading program. In this program, experimental-group teachers taught the subject matter they would have taught anyway, but they taught it triarchically. Control-group teachers taught in their normal manner with enhanced emphasis on the use of mnemonics and other strategies for enhancement of memory for material that has been learned. Thus, enhancement in the experimental groups was in terms of triarchic thinking and in the control groups was in terms of memory.

The program was implemented for 2 consecutive years, serving, altogether, 809 students. In each year, the program was administered in three phases. In Phase 1, *Conventional Instruction and Evaluation,* all students received identical, conventional reading instruction with the materials they normally used and were evaluated for their reading performance. In Phase 2, *Transition,* the control group continued with conventional reading instruction with their normal materials taught with enhanced emphasis on mnemonics and other memory aids, whereas the experimental group transitioned to triarchic instruction. The purpose of this (unevaluated) phase was to give experimental-group students an opportunity to adjust to triarchic instruction and to continue conventional but memory-enhanced reading instruction with control-group students. In Phase 3, *Differentiated Instruction and Evaluation,* the control group continued with conventional but memory-enhanced instruction and the triarchic group continued with triarchic instruction. Both groups were again evaluated for their reading performance. Thus, the overall goal of the program was to verify whether triarchically enhanced instruction based on commercial textbooks will improve students' performance as compared with traditional instruction based on same commercial textbooks.

Thus, in terms of specific differences between this study and our other studies, this research (a) attempted to improve children's reading skills by building vocabulary and enhancing comprehension skills, (b) relied exclusively on the standard program material, (c) implied a test of the robustness of the program by administering the program in 2 consecutive years, (d) included a population of low-SES, inner-city, ethnically diverse fifth graders, (e) implemented elements of action research to change teachers' behavior in the classroom and to supplement these changes with instructional material, and (f) implied a test of the generalizability of the triarchic instruction by upscaling the research to larger groups of participants and making the program a component of a school's routine.

Participants

The participants in the present study were middle-school students. For the first-year study, the participating schools were nominated by the New Haven Public School District.

Year 1. A total of 323 fifth-grade students—149 girls (46.1%), 151 boys (46.7%), and 23 children whose gender was not specified (7.1%)—participated in the study. Of these students, 40.9% were African American, 20.1% Hispanic American, 9.3% European American, 5.9% from other ethnic minorities, and 23.8% for whom ethnicity was not registered. These 323 students attended four middle schools, two of which were randomly assigned to the triarchic teaching condition and two to the control condition.

Assignment to conditions was by school in order to minimize the cross-contamination that can occur when teachers talk to one another about what they are teaching and how they are teaching it. All but one of the fifth-grade teachers in the four schools participated in the study. The teacher who did not participate was a new teacher just starting her career, and her decision not to participate was supported by her school's principal. This teacher, however, did take part in the study in Year 2. Altogether, there were 13 teachers. The triarchic sample included 147 students (45.5%), and the control sample, 176 students (54.5%). There were no significant differences in gender or ethnic composition between the two samples.

Year 2. As in Year 1, school recruitment was done by officials of the New Haven Public School District. A sample of 486 fifth-grade students—238 girls (49%), 230 boys (47.3%), and 18 children whose gender was not specified (3.7%)—participated in the study. The ethnic breakdown of the sample was 39.5% African American, 19.3% Hispanic American, 13.0% European American, 9.1% of other ethnic backgrounds, and 19.1% for whom ethnicity was not registered. These 486 students attended seven middle schools, four of which (two triarchic and two control schools from Year 1) were in the Year 2 triarchic teaching group, and three of which were newly enrolled schools from the New Haven School District. In Year 2, 20 teachers participated in the study. Seven of the experimental-group teachers had previously served in the control group, but none of the control-group teachers previously had served in the experimental group. The triarchic sample included 350 students (72%) and the control sample included 136 students (28%). There were no significant differences in gender composition between the two samples. There were, however, ethnic differences: Hispanic American and children of other ethnic backgrounds were underrepresented, whereas European American children were overrepresented in the control sample.

To explore the possibility of combining the samples from Year 1 and Year 2 for the analyses, we investigated the group differences in the samples' performance by year. Half of the year-based comparisons were significant; however, the directions of higher performance were variable. Specifically, in some cases, Year 1 students outperformed Year 2 students, whereas in others, Year 2 students outperformed Year 1 students. Therefore, the decision was made to combine the two samples, controlling for the year of program administration (e.g., specifying the variable *Year* as a covariate).

Combined Sample.   Thus, altogether, 809 fifth-grade students participated in the study. However, only 708 students were present in school at the time when all of the eight assessments (four for pretest and four for posttest) were administered. (There were no demographic differences between those students who completed all assessments and those students who missed some assessments). Here we present the data only from those 708 students. Of them, 298 were boys (42.1%) and 313 were girls (44.2%) girls; the district files did not provide information on the gender of 97 children (13.7%). The ethnic composition of the sample was as follows: 309 (43.6%) of the children were African American, 155 (21.9%) Hispanic American, 53% (7.5%) European American, 83 (11.7%) were from other ethnic minorities, and 108 (15.3%) either did not register any ethnicity or had multiple entries in the district files. There were 450 students in the triarchic group and 258 students in the memory control group.

Materials

Instructional and Assessment Materials.   Six stories from the fifth-grade basal reader, *Light Up the Sky* (Farr & Strickland, 1993), were used in the program. Two stories ("The Speech" and "Teacher for the Day") served as Phase 1 units, two other stories ("New Home in Ohio," "The Great Caravan on the National Road") served as Phase 2 units, and two further stories ("Like Jake and Me" and "Many Moons") served as Phase 3 units. For all units for all students, the following assessment materials were developed: (a) homework assignments (from which students were given a choice of one assignment from a list, including memory–analytical, creative, and practical assignments); (b) vocabulary assessment (18 items: six memory–analytical, six creative, and six practical); and (c) comprehension assessment (18 items: six memory–analytical, six creative, and six practical). The assessments for different stories were designed to approximate each other in degree of difficulty. Homework assignments were graded by teachers but because the homework was viewed as an instructional activity the grades were not analyzed as part of the study. Teacher' guides were developed for the Phase 2 and Phase 3 stories based on the triarchic paradigm. These guides showed teachers how to teach traditional language arts skills (vocabulary, spelling, reading comprehension, and writing) so as to call into play and develop students' analytical, creative, and practical abilities and achievement. In addition, the instructional materials were designed to help students develop the triarchic-theory-based skills so that they could apply these skills directly to the improvement of their proficiency in reading subject matter. Teachers in the control group were shown how to apply mnemonic strategies to material to be taught.

Consider some examples of each kind of material, as manifested in in-class and homework assignments. The materials were designed for the actual textbook the children were using, *Light Up the Sky* (Farr & Strickland, 1993). Although activities are classified loosely as *analytical*, *creative*, and *practical*, these classifications represent emphases rather than fully discrete categories. Ultimately, we wanted children to learn to combine these skills rather than merely to use them separately.

In-Class Instructional Material.   These materials are used in class to develop analytical, creative, and practical thinking skills applicable to reading.

Affective Evaluations.   To evaluate affective outcomes of the reading program, affective evaluation forms were offered to students and to teachers. Teachers were asked whether they found the program to be professionally interesting and motivating. In addition, they were asked to evaluate the educational and motivational relevance of the program to their students and to estimate the power/suitability of the program for working with diverse groups of students attending urban schools. Students were asked whether/how much they liked the program and what their favorite components of the program were.

Design

The design was identical for Year 1 and Year 2. The critical independent variable in the study was teaching condition. There was one experimental condition and one control condition. The two conditions covered the same units from the basal reader used in the New Haven Public School District. The duration of the program was the same in each condition (4.5–5 months). Where the conditions differed was in the methods used in Phases 2 and 3 for teaching these skills: *triarchic instruction* (experimental) and *conventional (primarily memory-based) nstruction* (control). The impact of the triarchic intervention was measured through (*a*) assessments of students' performance, and (*b*) affective evaluations by teachers and students. The performance assessments were administered both before (Phase 1) and after (Phase 3) the in-service program for the teachers. Thus, it was possible to compare pretest and posttest scores in the experimental versus the control groups. The four pretest assessments were the vocabulary and comprehension assessments for the two stories from Phase 1 ("The Speech" and "Teacher for the Day"). The four posttest assessments were the vocabulary and comprehension assessments for the stories from Phase 3 ("Like Jake and Me" and "Many Moons").

Procedure

Teacher Training.   Teachers in the experimental group were invited to participate in a two-part workshop, of which the first part was dedicated to triarchic instruction and assessment and the second part to general issues of teaching reading in middle school. The training involved teaching teachers how to teach analytically, creatively, and practically. For example, teachers learned how to use prompts for analytical teaching (such as *analyze, evaluate, critique, judge*), creative teaching (such as *create, invent, discover, explore*), and practical teaching (such as *use, apply, implement, put into practice*). Instruction was based on material in Sternberg and Grigorenko (2000). Teachers in the control group were offered a workshop on memory mnemonics and related techniques relevant to the teaching of reading. These mnemonics included techniques such as use of interactive imagery, pegwords, keywords, acronyms, acrostics, the method of loci, categorical clustering, and hierarchical mental representations to recall material one has read (see Pressley, 1991; Pressley, Levin, & Delaney, 1982). Instruction was based on material in Sternberg and Grigorenko (in press). Each year of the study closed with a round table discussion in which teachers from both groups, triarchic and control, participated. The first-year discussion resulted in adding new units to the instruction materials. Because second-year control-group teachers were all new (and hence did not participate in the round table discussion), their teaching could not have been affected by this discussion.

Thus, both the control and experimental groups received special interventions, but of different kinds. The control group received an intervention based on enhancement of memory for material that is read based largely on mnemonic techniques, an intervention not made available to the experimental group. The experimental group received an intervention based on enhancement of analytical, creative, and practical thinking, an intervention not made available to the control group.

What We Found

Students' skills were assessed separately by vocabulary and comprehension assessments at pre- and posttest in two different samples, Year 1 sample and Year 2 sample. For clarity and ease of interpretation, in this article, the student-performance results and the affective-evaluation results are presented in a combined fashion for vocabulary and comprehension, together for Year 1 and Year 2.

Achievement Indicators. At the baseline, the groups were compared on (a) scores on a State of Connecticut standardized achievement test (the *Connecticut Mastery Test, CMT*), and (b) level of performance at the baseline (i.e., performance on pretest assessments). The CMT was administered to children approximately a year and a half before they entered the study (in the fall of fourth grade); thus, although the CMT scores might have not been good indicators of the concurrent validity of our program, they served as the covariates of interest. For the baseline *CMT* scores, the performance of students in the triarchic and control groups were compared on *Degrees of Reading Power* (DRP, a standardized reading test) and *Holistic Writing* (a standardized writing test) indicators. Both subtests assess skills that are called for in the performance assessments included in the study (open-ended items required writing). A multivariate test of the main effect of group (triarchic vs. control) was significant; there was no effect of year of the study. Follow-up univariate analyses revealed two significant effects: (a) the *DRP* reading scores of the children in the triarchic group were significantly lower than those of the children in the control group; and (b) the *Holistic Writing* scores of the children in the triarchic group were significantly lower than those of the children in the control group. Therefore, the *DRP* and *Holistic Writing* indicators were included as covariates in subsequent analyses.

Baseline Differences in Performance. At the pretest, there was no significant multivariate difference on performance indicators among the groups. This result is of particular interest in conjunction with the presence of significant differences between groups on indicators provided by standardized achievement tests (see previous sections). Although the control group might have performed better before, at the time of entry to the study, both groups performed approximately at the same level.

Demographic Characteristics. The demographics of the triarchic and control groups were similar in gender composition: Specifically, there was no significant difference in numbers of boys and girls in the study groups. However, the groups differed in ethnic background composition: Hispanic American children and children of other ethnic backgrounds were underrepresented in the control and overrepresented in the triarchic group, whereas European American children were overrepresented in the control and underrepresented in the triarchic group.

Both demographic variables (*Gender* and *Ethnic Background*) were examined via multivariate analysis in association with the baseline dependent measures. There was an effect of *Ethnic Background.* There was no multivariate effect of *Gender* or *Gender* x *Ethnic Background* on the performance indicators, but the interaction effects were significant for two variables (memory–analytical and creative). Therefore, we decided to keep both variables in the models for pretest–posttest comparisons.

Pretest-Posttest Comparisons.   Following the recommendation of Campbell and Kenny (1999), repeated-measures analysis of variance was employed to quantify the differences between pretest and posttest performance of students in the two groups. This data-analytic approach allows for better control for the artifact of the regression to the mean than the more traditional approach of utilizing pretest scores as covariates in all contrasts of posttest group differences. The model specified two repeated factors: (a) *Time* (pre- vs. posttest), and (b) *Type* (three types of assessments—memory–analytical, creative, and practical). In addition, based on the information obtained through the analysis of the baseline differences, the linear models included the between-subject factor of *Group* (triarchic vs. control) and a number of covariates (*Degrees of Reading Power [DRP], Holistic Writing [HW], Gender, Ethnic Background,* and *Year of Study*). Thus, the main effect of interest was that of the interaction between *Time* and *Group* (i.e., whether the difference between performance on pre- and posttest assessments varied across the triarchic and control groups). Additional within-subjects effects of interest were the effects of *Type* and all interactive effects between the repeated factors and covariates. In addition, the between-subjects effects of all covariates were evaluated.

The analysis produced a number of significant results. We start with the report of within-subject effects.

First, and most interestingly, the results showed a significant *Time* x *Group* effect, indicating a statistically significant difference in the profiles of performance scores' changes over time in the two study groups (triarchic and control). Students in the triarchic condition excelled on the tasks of all three types—memory–analytical, practical, and creative. For comparison, the time profiles of the performance in the control group look very different—the students remained approximately at the same level of performance on memory–analytical tasks, improved on the practical tasks, and slightly declined on creative tasks. This decline should be interpreted with caution—it is possible that it is only a random fluctuation, but it is also possible that it indicates that traditional classrooms inadvertently tend to suppress creativity rather than encourage it. Yet another indicator of the change in reading performance introduced by the triarchic teaching is the difference in the patterns of correlations between pre- and posttest scores in the study groups. Specifically, in the control group, the pretest scores predicted the posttest scores more effectively than in the triarchic group—that is, all control group correlations were statistically higher than the respective triarchic group correlations for memory–analytical, practical, and creative in the control and triarchic groups, respectively.

Second, the performance on different types of tasks differed in terms of their absolute values, with the highest scores observed for practical tasks, the second highest, for memory–analytical tasks, and the lowest, for creative tasks. In addition, the three types of tasks showed different patterns over time so that the highest gains over time were obtained for practical tasks and the lowest, for creative, with the memory–analytical tasks in between.

Third, the *CMT* standardized scores on the reading test (*DRP*) appeared to differentiate the impact of the program over time, for different tasks, and for the *Time* x *Type* interaction effect.

To investigate the role of *DRPs* in the time changes in the performance scores of various types (memory–analytical, practical, and creative), we calculated the posttest-to-pretest difference scores and, based on these scores, divided the sample into three groups (separate for scores on memory–analytical, practical, and creative tasks): gainers (those students, whose difference score was above the 75th percentile), decliners (those students, whose difference score was below the 25th percentile), and steady-staters (those students, whose scores were within the 25th–75th percentile range). Then we compared performance scores in these three groups. For memory–analytical tasks, there was a statistically significant difference in *DRP* scores among gainers, steady-staters, and decliners. Specifically, the highest *DRP* scores were characteristic of steady-staters (39.09), with gainers and decliners far behind, but in close proximity to each other (35.8 and 36.6, respectively). For practical tasks, higher *DRPs* were characteristic of both decliners (39.2) and steady-staters (38.8), and gainers, once again, demonstrated significantly lower scores (34.4) *DRPs*. Finally, for creative tasks, gainers showed the lowest *DRPs* (34.5), with both steady-staters and decliners showing *DRP* scores that were significantly higher than those of gainers, but statistically not different from each other (37.9 and 40.0, respectively). Thus, students who benefited from the program the most tended to have somewhat lower *DRPs*. The highest *DRPs* were characteristic of decliners on practical and creative tasks, and of steady-staters on memory–analytical tasks.

Finally, the last group of within-subject interactive effects included the variable of *Year of Study*. First, the time dynamics varied for students who participated in the study in Year 1 and for those who participated in the study in Year 2. Specifically, in Year 1, there were more than expected steady-staters and fewer than expected gainers for practical tasks, and more than expected decliners and fewer than expected gainers for creative tasks. Second, there were differences in performance on different types of tasks. In addition, there was a significant *Time x Type x Year of Study* interaction, demonstrating that the time trajectories for different types of tasks differed for Years 1 and 2.

The analyses also revealed a set of between-subject effects. First, there was an effect of *Gender*, indicating that girls' performance was slightly different from that of boys. Second, there was an effect of *Ethnic Background*, demonstrating that different ethnic groups performed differently. Third, there was an effect of *Group*, indicating different levels of performance in triarchic and control groups. Fourth, there was an effect of *DRP*. Fifth, there was an effect of *HR:* Students with higher levels of writing proficiency demonstrated higher levels of performance. Finally, there was an effect of *Year of Study*. Specifically, the Year 1 sample performed better on the pretest creative task, whereas the Year 2 sample performed better on the posttest memory–analytical and on the posttest practical.

To summarize, the analyses showed that training has a significant impact on performance scores over time whereby students taught triarchically profit more over time from instruction than do students not taught triarchically. In addition, all variables in the equation were found to impact the performance scores. Of most importance was the impact of the standardized reading achievement indicator (*DRP*). This variable predicted both (*a*) the levels of performance on the task (so that children with higher *DRP* scores demonstrated better performance), and (*b*) the susceptibility to the triarchic intervention (children who gained from the program the most tended to demonstrate lower *DRP* scores). Moreover, even though there were some nonsystematic differences in performance in children from Years 1 and 2 of the study (e.g., for practical and creative tasks, there were more gainers in Year 2 than in Year 1), children in the triarchic group in both years advanced more than their peers in the control group. Finally, the variables of *Gender, Ethnic Background,* and *Holistic Writing* all accounted for significant portions of variance in the performance scores, but did not show differential links with either the time factor (i.e., boys and girls of all ethnic backgrounds at all levels of writing abilities benefited equally from the project) or the type of the task (i.e., neither boys nor girls of any specific ethnic background showed differential improvement for a particular type of tasks—memory–analytical, creative, or practical).

Affective Indicators.   To evaluate the affective aspect of the program, we asked teachers and students from the triarchic group to provide an affective view of the program.

On a 7-point scale where 1 was low and 7 was high, teachers rated the interestingness of the program to them at 6.3 and the interestingness of the program to the students at 5.6. They rated the level at which it motivated them at 6.1 and the level at which it motivated their students at 5.7. In addition, the teachers thought that the triarchic teaching strategies addressed the needs of students with various levels of skills (6.0) and that the program was inclusive of a wide range of children (5.9).

Students were also asked how they liked the program. We found that 36.4% of the children indicated they liked the program very much; 44.4% liked it; 12.1% did not feel one way or another; and only 7.1% disliked it.

CONCLUSIONS

Instructional programs that attempt to teach "critical thinking" are largely based on the model of g. These programs may be useful, but arguably, they are incomplete. For example, a program such as that of Feuerstein (1980) teaches many analytical skills—including metacomponential, performance-componential, and knowledge-acquisition-componential—but perhaps fewer creative and practical ones. It does not explicitly teach creative and practical thinking.

Programs based on the Jeez model, such as the numerous Head Start offerings as well as many other such programs, are based on no theory at all. As a result, it is difficult to know what they are supposed to achieve (at a theoretical level) and it is difficult to measure their success against a theory-based set of criteria.

Other programs are based on the $g's$ model. Some of these, such as those of Gardner (1993), have yet to be quantitatively evaluated. Our own programs, though, show at least some promise for increasing intellectual and academic skills. We thus believe that programs based on this kind of model show particular promise, if evaluated, for increasing intellectual skills and academic achievement.

We view our work as building on Spearman's (1904), not as contradicting it. It would be a rare science in which someone proposes a theory in 1904 that, almost 100 years later, still proves to be totally viable as originally proposed. Rather, theories are scientifically useful to the extent to which they have heuristic value for building more comprehensive and hopefully valid theories. In these terms, perhaps no theory in psychology has been more valuable than Spearman's (1904, 1927) two-factor theory.

ACKNOWLEDGEMENTS

Preparation of this chapter was supported by grant REC-9979843 from the U. S. National Science Foundation, and by a grant supported under the Javits Act Program (Grant No. R206R000001) as administered by the Office of Educational Research and Improvement, U.S. Department of Education, and by grant REC-9979843 from the U. S. National Science

Foundation. Grantees undertaking such projects are encouraged to express freely their professional judgment. This chapter, therefore, does not necessarily represent the position or policies of the National Science Foundation, the Office of Educational Research and Improvement, or the U. S. Department of Education, and no official endorsement should be inferred.

Requests for reprints should be sent to Robert J. Sternberg, Yale University, The Yale Center for the Psychology of Abilities, Competencies, and Expertise, P.O. Box 208358, New Haven, CT 06520-8358.

REFERENCES

Bollen, K. (1989). *Structural equations with latent variables.* New York: Wiley.

Campbell, D. T., & Kenny, D. A. (1999). *A primer on regression artifacts.* New York, Guilford Press.

Caruso, D. R., Mayer, J. D, & Salovey, P. (2002). Relation of an ability measure of emotional intelligence to personality. *Journal pf Personality Assesment, 79,* 306–320. [Ed: potentially relevant to all tables]

Ciarrochi, J., Dean, F. P., Anderson, S. (2002). Emotional intelligence moderates the relationship between stress and mental health. *Personality and Individual Differences 32,* 197–209 [Ed: potentially relevant to all tables]

Davidson, J. E., & Sternberg, R. J. *(1984).* The role of insight in intellectual giftedness. *Gifted Child Quarterly, 28, 58–64.*

Farr, R. C., & Strickland, D. S. (1993). *Light up the sky.* Orlando, FL: Harcourt Brace Jovanovich. Inc

Festinger, L., & Carlsmith, J. M. (1959). Cognitive consequences of forced compliance. *Journal of Abnormal and Social Psychology, 58,* 203–210.

Feuerstein, R. (1980). *Instrumental enrichment: An intervention program for cognitive modifiability.* Baltimore: University Park Press.

Gardner, H. (1983). *Frames of mind: The theory of multiple intelligences.* New York: Basic. Books.

Gardner, H. (1993). *Multiple intelligences: The theory in practice.* New York: Basic Books.

Gardner, H. (1999). *Intelligence reframed: Multiple intelligences for the 21st century.* New York: Basic Books.

Grigorenko, E. L., Jarvin, L., & Sternberg, R. J. (2002). School-based tests of the triarchic theory of intelligence: Three settings, three samples, three syllabi. *Contemporary Educational Psychology, 27,* 167–208.

Heaton, R. K., Chelune, G. J., Talley, J. L., Kay, G. G., & Curtiss, G. (1993). *Wisconsin Card Sorting Test Manual (Revised and expanded).* Odessa, FL: Psychological Assessment Resources.

Ivcevic, Z., Brackett, M. A., & Mayer, J. D. (2006) *Emotional intelligence and emotional creativity. Manuscript under review.*

Jastak, J. F., & Jastak, S. R. (1978). *The Wide Range Achievement Test (Rev. ed.).* Washington, DC: Jastak Associates.

Jensen, A. R. (1998). *The g factor.* Westport, CT: Greenwood/Praeger.

Mayer, J. D., Salovey, P., & Caruso, D (2002). *Mayer-Salovey-Caruso Emotional Intelligence Test (MSCEIT) Users Manual.* Toronto, Ontario: Multi-Health Systems.

Mayer, J. D., Salovey, P., & Caruso, D (2004). Emotional intelligence: Theory, findings, and implications. *Psychological Inquiry, 15,* 197–215.

Mayer, J. D., Panter, A. T., Salovey, P., Caruso, D.R., & Sitarenios. G. (2005). A discrepancy in analysis of the MSCEIT-Resolving the mystery and understanding its implications: A reply to Gignac (2005). Emotion, 5, 236–237.

Mayer, J. D. (2006). A new field guide to emotional intelligence. In Ciarrochi, J., Forgas, J. P., & Mayer, J. D. (Eds). Emotional intelligence in everyday life (2nd edition). New York and Hove: Psychology Press.

Metcalfe, J., & Shimamura, A. (1996). *Metacognition*. Cambridge: MIT Press.

Myers, D. (1996). *Exploring psychology* (3rd ed.). New York: Worth.

Pressley, M. (1991). Comparing Hall (1988) with related research on elaborative mnemonics. *Journal of Educational Psychology, 83*, 165–170.

Pressley, M., Levin, J., & Delaney, H. D. (1982). The mnemonic keyword method. *Review of Research in Education, 52*, 61–91.

Salovey, P., Mayer, J.D., Caruso, D., & Lopes, P. N. (2003). Measuring emotional intelligence as a set of abilities with the MSCEIT. In S. J. Lopez and C. R. Snyder (Eds.), *Handbook of positive psychology assesment* (pp. 251–265) Washington, DC: American Psychological Association. [Ed: potentially relevant to all tables]

Salovey, P., Kokkonen, M., Lopes, P. N. (2004). Emotional Intelligence: What do We Know? In A. S. R. Manstead, N. Frijda, & A. Fischer (Eds). *Feelings and emotions: The Amsterdam symposium* (pp. 321–340). New York, NY, US: Cambridge University Press.

Spearman, C. (1904). "General intelligence," objectively determined and measured. *American Journal of Psychology, 15*(2), 201–293.

Spearman, C. (1927). *The abilities of man*. London: Macmillan.

Sternberg, R. J. (1977). *Intelligence, information processing, and analogical reasoning: The componential analysis of human abilities*. Hillsdale, NJ: Lawrence Erlbaum Associates.

Sternberg, R. J. (1980a). Representation and process in linear syllogistic reasoning. *Journal of Experimental Psychology: General, 109*, 119–159.

Sternberg, R. J. (1980b). Sketch of a componential subtheory of human intelligence. *Behavioral and Brain Sciences, 3*, 573–584.

Sternberg, R. J. (Ed.). (1984). *Mechanisms of cognitive development*. San Francisco: Freeman.

Sternberg, R. J. (1985). *Beyond IQ: A triarchic theory of human intelligence*. New York: Cambridge University Press.

Sternberg, R. J. (1986). *Intelligence applied*. Orlando, FL: Harcourt Brace College Publishers.

Sternberg, R. J. (1987). The psychology of verbal comprehension. In R. Glaser (Ed.), *Advances in instructional psychology* (Vol. 3, pp. 97–151). Hillsdale, NJ: Lawrence Erlbaum Associates.

Sternberg, R. J. (1990). *Metaphors of mind: Conceptions of the nature of intelligence*. New York: Cambridge University Press.

Sternberg, R. J. (1991a). Giftedness according to the triarchic theory of human intelligence. In N. Colangelo & G. A. Davis (Eds.), *Handbook of gifted education* (2nd ed., pp. 45–54). Needham Heights, MA: Allyn & Bacon.

Sternberg, R. J. (1991b). Theory-based testing of intellectual abilities: Rationale for the Triarchic Abilities Test. In H. Rowe (Ed.), *Intelligence: Reconceptualization and measurement* (pp. 183–202). Hillsdale, NJ: Lawrence Erlbaum Associates.

Sternberg, R. J. (1991c). Triarchic abilities test. In D. Dickinson (Ed.), *Creating the future: Perspectives on educational change* (pp. 76–81). Aston Clinton, England: Accelerated Learning Systems.

Sternberg, R. J. (1993). *Sternberg Triarchic Abilities Test (STAT)*. Unpublished test.

Sternberg, R. J. (1995). *In search of the human mind*. Orlando, FL: Harcourt Brace College Publishers.

Sternberg, R. J. (1997). *Successful intelligence*. New York: Plume.

Sternberg, R. J. (1999a). Intelligence as developing expertise. *Contemporary Educational Psychology, 24*, 259–375.

Sternberg, R. J. (1999b). The theory of successful intelligence. *Review of General Psychology, 3*, 292–316.

Sternberg, R. J., Clinkenbeard, P. R. (1995). A triarchic model of identifying, teaching, and assessing gifted children. *Roeper Review, 17*, 255–260.

Sternberg, R. J., Ferrari, M., Clinkenbeard, P. R., & Grigorenko, E. L. (1996). Identification, instruction, and assessment of gifted children: A construct validation of a triarchic model. *Gifted Child Quarterly, 40*(3) 129–137.

Sternberg, R. J., Forsythe, G. B., Hedlund, J., Horvath, J., Snook, S., Williams, W. M., Wagner, R. K., & Grigorenko, E. L. (2000). *Practical intelligence in everyday life*. New York: Cambridge University Press.

Sternberg, R. J., & Grigorenko, E. L. (2000). *Teaching for successful intelligence.* Arlington Heights, IL: Skylight Training and Publishing.

Sternberg, R. J., Grigorenko, E. L., Ferrari, M., & Clinkenbeard, P. (1999). A triarchic analysis of an aptitude-treatment interaction. *European Journal of Psychological Assessment, 15*(1), 1–11.

Sternberg, R. J., Grigorenko, E. L., Ngrosho, D., Tantufuye, E., Mbise, A., Nokes, C., Jukes, M., & Bundy, D. A. (2002). Assessing intellectual potential in rural Tanzanian school children. *Intelligence, 30,* 141–162.

Sternberg, R. J., & Lubart, T. I. (1995). *Defying the crowd: Cultivating creativity in a culture of conformity.* New York: Free Press.

Sternberg, R. J., & Powell, J. S. (1983). Comprehending verbal comprehension. *American Psychologist, 38,* 878–893.

Sternberg, R. J., Torff, B., & Grigorenko, E. L. (1998). Teaching triarchically improves school achievement. *Journal of Educational Psychology, 90,* 374–384.

Sternberg, R. J., & Weil, E. M. (1980). An aptitude-strategy interaction in linear syllogistic reasoning. *Journal of Educational Psychology, 72,* 226–234.

Thurstone, L. L. (1938). *Primary mental abilities.* Chicago: University of Chicago Press.

Trinidad, D. R., & Johnson, C. A. (2002). The association between emotional intelligence and early adolescent tobacco and alchohol use. *Personality and Individual Differences, 32,* 95–105

Tucker, J. S., & Riggio, R. E. (1988). The role of social skills in encoding posed and spontaneous facial expressions. *Journal of Nonverbal Behavior, 12,* 87–97.

Williams, W. M., Blythe, T., White, N., Li, J., Sternberg, R. J. & Gardner, H. I. (1996). *Practical intelligence for school: A handbook for teachers of grades 5–8.* New York: HarperCollins.

Williams, W. M., Blythe, T., White, N., Li, J., Gardner, H., & Sternberg, R. J. (2002). Practical intelligence for school: Developing metacognitive sources of achievement in adolescence. *Developmental Review, 22,* 162–210.

14

▼▼▼▼▼▼▼

What Is Emotional Intelligence and What Does it Predict?

John D. Mayer
University of New Hampshire

Peter Salovey
Yale University

David R. Caruso
Work-Life Strategies

At the Third Annual Spearman Conference from which this chapter comes, emotional intelligence was then assigned, appropriately, to the session on "New Constructs," a designation indicating its still uncertain, albeit promising, status. The concept of emotional intelligence—the idea that one can reason with emotion or, conversely, that emotion can enhance thought—joins two areas of psychological function that are more commonly thought of as separate. Indeed, areas of research into emotion and intelligence are separate, and their practitioners don't often have reason to enter into dialogue.

That conference was convened in New South Wales, Australia, in Sydney. New South Wales itself conjures up joining of seemingly contradictory ideas aside from emotion and intelligence, this one in the field of biology. It was from New South Wales, in 1799, that the first platypus was shipped to England. The English naturalist George Shaw, on examining the specimen, noted that the platypus seemed "most extra-ordinary," when compared with other mammals, and exhibited "the perfect resemblance of the beak of a Duck engrafted on the head of a quadruped." Only after the most minute examination of the specimen could he bring himself to believe it was not a deception (cited in Hall, 1999, p. 211–212). After decades of controversy, the existence of the platypus was accepted, along with its designation as a mammal. At the Sydney Aquarium, a very much alive, cheerful platypus was swimming around at conference time.

In this chapter we make the case that emotional intelligence really exists, and is a standard intelligence, and predicts matters of importance in an individual's life. The platypus, it is true, stretched the idea of a mammal a bit. Unlike other mammals, for example, its young are hatched from eggs. Emotional intelligence, too, stretches the idea of an intelligence. For example, emotional problems are often problems in "fuzzy logic," having more than one answer, and indeed, there may be more than one reasonable criterion for correctness. It is those qualities that make it such a fascinating example of an intelligence. The next sections of this chapter (a) briefly describe the origin of the emotional intelligence concept, (b) review our theory of emotional intelligence and an approach to measuring it, (c) examine what emotional intelligence predicts, and (d) takes a look at where EI research might extend in the future.

ORIGIN OF THE EMOTIONAL INTELLIGENCE CONCEPT

The term "emotional intelligence" was used on an occasional basis at least from the 1960s forward. An incidental use of the term can be found in some literary criticism describing the characters of Jane Austen. A few additional mentions arose in the psychological literature. The term was employed, however, as a rhetorical device—a mere suggestion that such an intelligence might exist—moreso than in any serious, formally defined, sense.

In hindsight, the central issue in establishing emotional intelligence involved understanding that emotions conveyed reliable information and that intelligence might reason about those emotions. During the 1970s and 1980s the scientific groundwork that could potentially decipher the meanings of emotional communication gradually accrued (Mayer, 2000). First, emotions researchers rediscovered the possibility that emotions were not primarily idiosyncratic and chaotic, but, in fact, were universally experienced and evolved—an idea specifically developed by Darwin (1872/1965) in his book *The Expression of Emotion in Man and Animals.* As a consequence of that work, emotions were viewed as a signal system conveying information. Experimental psychologists examined the possible positive adaptations emotions might bring with them to thought. Other such researchers examined the role nonverbal communication played in interpersonal understanding, with a partial focus on emotional facial and postural expressions. Clinical psychologists and psychiatrists examined people who suffered deficits in interpersonal relations (e.g., Taylor, Ryan, & Bagby, 1985), and suggested that there existed a subgroup they called alexithymics (for: a = without, lexi = words, thymic = emotions). Such individuals experienced a specific inability to use emotional words and a more general deficit in emotional understanding. Neuroscientists became interested in the crosstalk between emotion and cognition in the brain. Finally, cognitive scientists working in artificial intelligence began to teach computers the rules of emotions so that computers could better understand human interaction (e.g., Dyer, 1983).

In 1990, two of us reviewed the foregoing literatures, and suggested that there might exist an emotional intelligence. In one article, we developed a theory of what emotional intelligence might be and might describe (Salovey & Mayer, 1990). In a second article, we presented an initial measure of emotional intelligence, and a test of whether a common ability might underlie emotional perception across faces, colors, and abstract designs (Mayer, DiPaolo, & Salovey, 1990). The present chapter examines what we have learned about EI in the decade since those first articles.

There exist a number of other theories of emotional intelligence than our own, but few other theories that treat it both seriously and scientifically as an intelligence. Rather, the term emotional intelligence was popularized in a best-selling book in the mid-1990s (Golemar, 1995). Due to a very general and shifting definition of the term in that source, emotional intelligence has often been treated since as synonymous with well being, optimism, delay-of-gratification, social competencies, and other desirable and/or adaptive personality characteristics. Elsewhere, we have reviewed the influence of the popularization and its sequellae (Mayer, 2001), as well as compared the intelligence model with the other models (Mayer, Salovey, & Caruso, 2000b). Here we provide evidence that measures of EI stemming from our own theory, and those from others' theories using such alternative conceptions as well being, are essentially independent in what they assess. This brief overview of the origin of the concept is admittedly incomplete in a number of details.

THE THEORY OF EMOTIONAL INTELLIGENCE AND ITS MEASUREMENT

Emotional Intelligence As an Intelligence

The central characteristic of an intelligence is the capacity to reason abstractly about a problem to a correct solution with a given set of symbols. Nowadays, we speak of many different kinds of intelligences (Gardner, 1983; Guilford, 1959; Stemberg, 1997). In each case, intelligence refers to the capacity to perceive, understand, and use symbols. For example, one can talk of verbal, spatial, and social intelligences, as well as other interrelated intelligences. The modifier—verbal, spatial, or social—specifies the content domain or symbol set on which the intelligence operates. So, verbal intelligence denotes the capacity to reason, understand, and use words. Spatial intelligence denotes the capacity to reason, understand, and use objects in spaces. Within psychology, emotional intelligence belongs to this same group of interrelated intelligences, and denotes the capacity to reason, understand, and manage emotions. In addition, emotional intelligence plausibly reflects the emotion system's capacity to use emotion to enhance thought.

Foundational Ideas

To move from the general idea of "reasoning with emotion" and "emotion enhancing reasoning" to establishing a true intelligence, requires some additional work. First, emotions must be shown to convey reliable information about relationships; second, emotional information must be understood in relation to other types of information, and third, it must be possible to create test questions in the area that have correct answers and that can be used to measure the intelligence.

Emotions Convey Information About Relationships. Emotions appear to have evolved so as to signal and respond to changes in relationships between the individual and the environment (including one's imagined place within it). Early philosophical treatments of emotion concerned themselves with the meanings of emotions. Philosophers recognized that much emotional information was consistent across people, although the reason for that consistency was unknown. Operating on that idea, Spinoza and others attempted to explain, more and more precisely, what the meanings of feelings were.

In the mid-19th century, Charles Darwin argued that emotional expression had evolved across species (Darwin, 1872/1998). Compelling cross-cultural research by Ekman (1973) and others on facial expressions supported Darwin's hypothesis, strongly implying that emotional information—and the capacity to read it—would show some universals across human beings and even closely related mammalian species. Any apparent differences in human emotional expression from culture to culture could be attributed to the fact that different societies taught different display rules about when it was appropriate to express one or another feeling. Additional evidence for the regularity of emotional information can be found in the area of artificial intelligence, where cognitive scientists created expert systems that could understand emotions in rudimentary stories (Dyer, 1983). Today, artificial intelligence researchers have gone far further, adding recognizable emotion to computer interfaces and robots (Picard, 1997). The international success of their emotional mechanisms provides additional, albeit more informal, confirmation of the universality of emotional recognition.

Psychological researchers added an empirical component to the philosophical investigations into the meanings of emotion. Those psychologists surveyed groups of people as to the meaning of emotion terms (e.g., Ortony, Clore, & Collins, 1988; Plutchik, 1984). In so doing, the researchers created a substantial body of knowledge about what emotions mean. For example, anger arises in response to threat or injustice; fear arises in response to danger. Emotions follow no rigid time course but instead respond to external changes in relationships (or internal perceptions of them). Moreover, each emotion organizes several basic behavioral responses to the relationship; for example, fear organizes fighting or fleeing (Lazarus, 1991). Emotions are therefore more flexible than motivations, though not quite so flexible as cognition.

Emotions Can Be Understood and Studied as Are Other Information Sources.   The foregoing indicates that emotions are a source of information, and yet emotional information, like verbal, spatial, and other areas of information, has its unique properties. First and foremost, emotional information is biosocial: It applies primarily to the world of the human (and, perhaps, some animal) society. In other words, emotional information pertains primarily to the relations of people (and animals) to one another, and their relation to cultural institutions, ideas, artifacts, and socioemotional contracts, including rules of behavior (Mayer, 1998a; Mayer & Salovey, 1995). This can be contrasted with information on tests such as the WAIS that focus on cognitive information. The highly cognitive world of mathematics, for example, has been elaborated far beyond its application to human beings alone, to equations and scientific laws that describe gravity, acceleration, and the like, and applies to rocks, stars, and galaxies.

The fact that emotional information pertains to the human sphere means that the reference point for correct and incorrect emotional meanings will be human (and, perhaps, primate and mammalian) societies. So, the expert becomes an expert to some extent by studying the group consensus, and becoming, as it were, more accurate about the group consensus than other individuals or small groups. For example, some emotions experts can reliably distinguish sincere or real, from false, tense smiles (cf., Ekman, 1985). It is likely, however, that the general consensus of all people can do this as well in many instances. The decisive contribution of expertise is probably to identify and distinguish between facial expressions of emotions more cleanly, and better elucidate the rules going on, than can the average person. Thus, our theory of emotional intelligence is based on an approximate convergence between groups of unselected people, and experts, as to what a correct answer might be.

Compare that state of affairs to the cognitive domain. There, expert and general consensus as to a correct answer are not necessarily the same. The general consensus (e.g., among young children today) is that heavier objects fall faster than lighter ones. As experts know from empirical demonstration, this is a false notion: Objects of different weight fall equally fast.

It is interesting to speculate about whether, in principle, some divergence between the expert and group consensus will occur as emotional information is further systematized and institutionalized. For example, even now, curricula for the study of emotion are under development (e.g.,

Cohen, 1997, 2001; Elias et al., 1997) and textbooks about emotions may be written in the future. As this develops, opportunities for further divergence in the knowledge of experts and the general consensus might arise. In the meantime, strong convergence is to be expected (Mayer, Salovey, Caruso, & Sitaraneos, 2001). People converge on the consensus to different degrees, of course. It is, in fact, the inability of some individuals to converge, and accurate and reliable convergence of others to correct emotional answers, that makes EI so interesting to measure as an individual differences variable.

Emotional Intelligence As a Convergent Intelligence. The foregoing discussion raises the issue of whether tests of EI would encourage emotional conventionality rather than creativity, by rewarding those who converge to the group (e.g., Roberts, Zeidner, & Mathews, 2001). Emotional intelligence is what Guilford (1959) referred to as a "convergent" intelligence; that is, as with most other cognitive intelligences, people are expected to converge to the correct answer. This is not much different from, say, a reading comprehension test, where the correct answer involves "getting the same point" as everybody else has (or as the established, conventional experts have).

A person who can converge to the correct answers has the potential to be far more creative than others (although there is no necessity they are emotionally creative at all). That is because creativity often begins with an expert sense of the conventional meaning of elements, and then proceeds to the capacity to put those elements together in novel ways. Musical creativity seldom involves creating new notes (although in rare instances it has), but more typically involves arranging the standard notes in new orders, new combinations, and with different overtones produced by different instruments.

To make the case more clearly with emotion, consider Averill and Thompson-Knowles' (1997) "triad" task of emotional creativity. In that task, participants are asked to create a story in which a character experiences three emotions together. In response to "serene, bewildered, and impulsive," one participant described the following scene:

> The clouds are few, the sky is clear. I'm at the top of the cliff. It's real peaceful up here. Suddenly, I want to jump. I don't know why, I just want to. Calmly, I look down at what would be my unquestioned doom. It looks peaceful; warm and friendly. But why, why do I want to dive into the hands of the grim reaper? What does this mean? I hesitate, then motion to jump, something strange pulls me back. It is the peacefulness of the cliff. I can't destroy the peacefulness. The wind feels like velvet against my skin as I slowly shake my head. Why? (Averill & Thompson-Knowles, p. 280)

The passage was rated high in novelty, authenticity, and creativity. And yet what makes it work is that its anonymous author did understand the meanings of emotion in a "conventional" sense. What was novel was the creation of a new situation to elicit the feelings.

Is it Possible to Create Tasks with Right Answers that Measure Emotional Intelligence?

If what we have argued is correct, then correct answers to emotional intelligence questions can be obtained either by using a general group consensus, or the consensus of emotion experts. It is worth noting at the outset that cognitive IQ tests have at least a few items that are "objectively scored." For example, in "digits forward" on the WAIS-III, participants hear a series of digits (3...5...2) and simply must repeat them. The extent to which they match the sequence determines their score.

Most WAIS subtests, however, employ a consensus among experts. Such items include the Similarities subtest items, of the type, "How are a chair and a table similar?," and other items on other scales. For these sorts of items, the WAIS-III manual states that various answers were first placed with a group of similar responses. Once that was done, "…the team evaluated the quality of the responses and assigned a score value (0, 1, or 2) to each code on the basis of the accuracy of the response" (The Psychological Corporation, 1997, p. 37) This can be referred to as an "Expert Consensus" method: Various experts combine their judgments together to select a correct answer.

The Convergence of General and Expert Consensus.   Let us say we have an EI test item asking a person to identify an emotion in a face (e.g., How Happy is it?). To score the right answer across that and other questions, we could use a general consensus criterion, or expert consensus criterion. In the group consensus, if .56 of the sample says that there is a moderate amount of happiness in a face, and a participant agrees, his or her score is incremented by .56. If on the next face, a mere .02 of the sample said a moderate amount of happiness was in the face, and the participant endorses that alternative, his or her score would be incremented only by .02. A parallel procedure could be used to score the participant against the consensus of experts. Our first, full-length test of emotional intelligence, the Multifactor Emotional Intelligence Test (MEIS), was scored both ways. When the expert group is small (our first expert group included only two test authors), the converge between general and expert consensus scoring methods is substantial, but imperfect. Small numbers of experts (such as the two), are typically unreliable; experts must aggregated to obtain reliability (Legree, 1995).

In our newest test of emotional intelligence, the Mayer-Salovey-Caruso Emotional Intelligence Test (MSCEIT), we asked 21 members of the International Society of Research in Emotion (ISRE) to answer the MSCEIT questions. We then scored the MSCEIT according to an expert-consensus criterion, based on the proportion of experts from ISRE who answered each item in a particular way. When over 2,000 participants' scores on the MSCEIT were calculated by general- and by expert-consensus scoring, the intercorrelation between the two sets of scores was over $r = .90$ (Mayer et al., 2001). This supports our previous theoretical arguments concerning the evolved, general, nature of emotional consensus.

THE FOUR-BRANCH MODEL AND ITS MEASURE

With those foundational ideas covered, let us now turn to our further specification and description of emotional intelligence. Our theory of EI was developed along with specific attempts to measure it. For that reason, we co-present our theory and measure here. Separate, more detailed overviews are available of both the theory (Mayer & Salovey, 1997; Mayer, Salovey, & Caruso, 2000a) and the measures (Mayer, Caruso, & Salovey, 2000).

We have described EI as a general capacity concerning two parts: (a) the ability to reason with and about emotion, and (b) the capacity for emotion to improve thinking. From the start we have also divided these two areas into subsidiary abilities (Salovey & Mayer, 1990). The "map" of emotional intelligence we presently use was described in 1997 (Mayer & Salovey, 1997). It divided EI into four areas, called branches, after the tree-like diagram that introduced them. The four areas are: (a) perceiving emotion, (b) using emotion to enhance thought, (c) understanding emotion, and (d) managing emotion.

The Perception of Emotion

All intelligences require the accurate input and identification of information in the course of information processing. Verbal intelligence requires inputting and recognizing words, spatial intelligence requires inputting and recognizing shapes, and emotional intelligence involves inputting and recognizing feelings. Branch 1 skills concern the accurate perception and identification of emotion in the self and others. As a measurement approach, the MSCEIT (and earlier MEIS) uses several tasks. The first, *faces*, asks people to identify the emotions present in a facial expression. The second, *pictures*, asks people to identify emotions in a picture of a landscape or abstract design. People who can match the expert or general consensus (which mostly are the same), are scored as able to perform this task. Although no direct measure is taken of identifying emotion from the inside (i.e., in oneself)—and indeed, it would be difficult to know how to go about doing so—experimental research indicates that people able to identify emotions in others are better able to detect the physiological manifestations of emotions in their own bodies (Zuckerman, Hall, DeFrank, & Rosenthal, 1976; Zuckerman, Lipets, Koivumaki, & Rosenthal, 1975). Additional prior research indicates that emotionally expressive behavior is well correlated with the ability to perceive emotion (Riggio, 1992; Tucker 1988).

Using Emotion to Facilitate Thought

An important part of emotional intelligence is the idea that emotions themselves can facilitate reasoning. This is not unique to EI. In verbal intelligence, a person's possession of a large vocabulary is likely to support an individual's capacity to reason with words. For example, it should assist with the capacity to understand words' interconnected meanings. In addition, some words convey rhythmic sounds or meanings, and thereby may facilitate certain verbal productions such as poetry. In the case of emotion, the frequent experience and consideration of emotions can enhance reasoning about them, because the individual has frequent occasion to sense the feelings and compare them to other sensations. In addition, emotions and moods change a person's thoughts, and those who are most familiar with such changes may use them to their advantage (e.g., Mayer, McCormick, & Strong, 1995; Palfai & Salovey, 1993–1994; Schwarz, 1990).

Based on those ideas, the MSCEIT test uses two quite different tasks to assess emotions' positive influence on cognition. In one, people are asked to extract sensory experiences similar to emotions, such as whether anger is hot or cold (or sometimes one, sometimes the other), and whether jealousy is green or red. In the second task, people are asked to identify the moods that are most facilitated by certain activities. For example, a test taker might be asked what mood: happy, angry, or calm, would be best to feel when brainstorming.

Understanding Emotions

The core of any intelligence is the abstract reasoning it represents: the identification of similarities and differences, of valid versus invalid thought sequences, of analysis and synthesis. In the case of emotional intelligence, this is no different. Once an emotion is perceived, it must be understood. This may be as simple as being able to translate emotions into their meanings about relationships, or, at a more demanding level, understanding how a person who experiences a sequence of events would, as a consequence, feel various changes in emotions, including blends and complex composites.

For example, most people understand that happiness indicates a harmonious relationship with other people and the world. Sadness typically emerges in response to loss; anger in response to frustration or obstacles to pleasure; fear in response to threat. Beyond that, more complex emotions serve as blends of simpler ones. For example, contempt might be viewed as a combination of anger and disgust.

Based on those ideas, the MSCEIT uses two subtests to measure emotional understanding. The first task, Blends, asks several related sorts of questions including requiring people to (a) identify definitions of emotions, (b) identify which emotions emerge from combinations of simpler emotions, and (c) analyze complex emotions into the simpler feelings that make them up. A sample Blends item might be, "What emotion reflects displeasure about an event that has made someone else happy? (a) Guilt, (b) Anger, (c) Envy, (d) Jealousy, (e) Sadness." The second task, Changes, asks people how emotions change over time. For example, it asks, "If you are angry at someone, and later ashamed, what is likely to have happened in between? (a) You found out they did something worse than you first thought, (b) You expressed your anger in an over-the-top way, (c) You had a thoughtful conversation with the person in which you expressed your displeasure in a way they responded to well, or (d) You talked to them and found out they didn't care about your feelings."

Managing Emotions

The final branch of the emotional intelligence model concerns knowledge of how to manage emotions effectively in oneself and others. In oneself, this involves being open to one's own feelings enough to perceive, use, and understand emotions. Thereafter, however, it can involve attempts to maintain positive emotions in oneself in the face of difficult personal or social circumstances.

The MSCEIT test uses two tasks: Emotion Regulation and Socioemotional Management to assess the capacity to manage emotions in oneself and others. Items on these tasks are the same except that emotional regulation items pertain to the self and socioemotional items pertain to other people. An example of an Emotion Regulation item is the following: "You're having a great time with friends when one of them starts talking about people he really values and doesn't mention you which hurts your feelings. What would be the best way to make yourself feel better? (a) Reminisce aloud about people who were important in your own life and not mention him, (b) Tell him that his family was full of ungrateful people, so you aren't surprised that he is ungrateful too, (c) Break your diet, cut yourself a second piece of chocolate cake and change the subject, or (d) Remind yourself about the times he's told you how important you are and remain positive in your conversation."

SUMMARY

The four-branch model, then, is a way of organizing various emotional intelligence abilities and test items to measure those abilities. It describes four areas of capacities: (a) accuracy at emotional perception and expression, (b) the capacity to use emotions to facilitate thought, (c) the ability to understand emotion, and (d) the ability to manage emotion. The MSCEIT test, and its precursor, the MEIS, have been designed around this four-branch model. Next, we turn to findings with the MSCEIT test and its precursors.

WHAT DO ABILITY TESTS OF EMOTIONAL INTELLIGENCE MEASURE?

We present our discussion of tests of EI according to four broad questions: (a) Is the test acceptable to test takers? That is, are its administrative procedures, length, and face validity adequate? (b) Do the tests adequately reflect the factor structure of emotional intelligence, and do they measure that factor structure with consistency? This concerns the tests' reliability and factor validity. (c) Do the tests measure something unique and different from what has been measured before? This concerns technical issues of discriminant validity. And, (d) What do the tests measure and predict? This concerns questions of content and predictive validity.

The MSCEIT V2.0 is a new ability test of EI (Mayer, Salovey, & Caruso, in press). For that reason, some of the data to be cited is from (as yet) unpublished studies. Moreover, it makes sense to supplement this coverage of the MSCEIT V2.0 with an examination of the very similar performance of its precursor tests, the MEIS and MSCEIT RV1.0. There was considerable consistency in the development processes of the MEIS, the MSCEIT RV1.0, and the MSCEIT V2.0. The three tests sample items from the same four-domain model of EI (Mayer & Salovey, 1997). All three tests use multiple tasks to measure each branch of the four-branch model. We know that, in the same sample, the correlation between the MSCEIT RV1.1 and its shortened version, the MSCEIT V2.0, is $r = 96$ for the full scale score. Although the MEIS and MSCEITs are only now being intercorrelated, our experience suggests that, given the similarity in construction, content-domain sampling, format, and scoring, they will likely correlate at a high enough level to be useful proxies for one another at the Full Scale EI level.

Is the Test Acceptable to Test Takers?

People object to taking tests that are too long, too difficult, or that seem irrelevant. More technically, these issues concern test length, readability, and "face validity"—the idea that people perceive the test to measure what it is supposed to measure. The MSCEIT V2.0, our briefest measure, takes about 35 minutes to administer. Relative to the MSCEIT RV1.1, which was roughly twice as long, and MEIS, which was roughly three times as long, the MSCEIT V2.0 is a convenient test to take. With an approximate eighth-grade reading level, it is most appropriate for adults. Adolescents may be better assessed with the Adolescent Multifactor Emotional Intelligence Scale (A-MEIS; Mayer, Caruso, & Salovey, 1999).

Pusey analyzed the face validity of the similar MSCEIT RV1.1 in a work setting. Participants took the MSCEIT RV1.1, and afterward, all participant-reported thoughts and reactions to the MSCEIT were recorded and then coded by two independent raters. Participant reports indicated that the MSCEIT had good face validity. The MSCEIT V2.0 is a relatively brief test that is readily acceptable to adults as a measure of EI.

Do the Tests Measure With Consistency and Are its Scales and Subscales Warranted? (Reliability and Structural/Factorial Validity)

Reliability   Table 14.1 shows the reliability of the MSCEIT V2.0 and its precursor measures. As can be seen, split-half and alpha full-scale reliabilities are excellent, ranging from $r = .90$ to .96. Area scores of the MSCEIT V2.0 are excellent also, falling between $r = .90$ and .88. The branch score reliabilities of both the MEIS and MSCEIT are somewhat lower but still

TABLE 14.1
Reliability of the MSCEIT and Precursor Measures

TEST	Total EIQ	Area EIQ's		Branch EIQ's				N	Comments	Reference
		Exp	Strat.	Perc.	Using	Under.	Manage			
MEIS	.96	N/A	N/A	.96	.86	.89	.81	503	Reliabilities for the four-factor solution	Mayer et al., 1999, p. 286
MEIS	.90	.88	.70	N/A	N/A	N/A	N/A	114	Note, this two-factor solution was labeled as area scores post-hoc	Clarrochi et al., 2000)
MEIS	.95	N/A	N/A	.94	.84	.74	.76	183	Time 1	(Caruso, Mayer, & Salovey, 2002)
MEIS	.96	N/A	N/A	.96	.85	.80	.78	150	Time 2	"
MEIS	.75	N/A	N/A	.68	.60	.62	.61	150	Test-Retest	"
MSCEITV V. 2.0	.93	.90	.88	.91	.79	.80	.83	2015	Consensus -scoring	(J.D. Mayer et al., 2001

in the very good to excellent range (e.g., $r = .78$ to $.96$), over a series of studies. In one study, test–retest reliability of the MEIS was $r = .75$, with somewhat lower reliabilities for individual branches than would be desirable ($r = .61$ to 68). A recent test–retest reliability of the MSCEIT is $r = .78$. All told, the MEIS and MSCEIT are reliable tests at the total, area, and branch levels.

The tests are not designed to be highly reliable at the individual task level. At that level, task reliabilities are somewhat lower ($r = .64$ to $.88$; see Mayer, 2001; Roberts et al., 2001). Even the individual tasks, however, are not much different in reliability than those task reliabilities reported for the Wechsler Adult Intelligence Scale—Revised, used through 1988 (e.g. Matarazzo, 1972). Thus, overall, the MSCEIT and its precursors measure reliably, and particularly so at the branch, area, and full scale levels.

Factorial Validity. The factor, or covariance, structure of a test refers to how many distinct things it measures. For a test to be structurally (or factor-) valid, it must measure as many distinct things as it has scales. In the case of the MSCEIT V2.0, the primary EIQs are reported at the full-scale level, two area levels, and four branch levels. In fact, the MSCEIT V2.0s fit to one-factor (i.e., Total EIQ), two factor (i.e., Area Scores), and four-factor (i.e., Branch Scores) mathematical model is excellent (Mayer et al., 2003). Indeed, from the MEIS forward, evidence for all three solutions has been consistent.

For example, the MEIS was analyzed by testing a variety of factor solutions with it early on. Mayer et al. (1999) found that one three and four-factor solutions of the test were all supported (a two-factor solution was not tested). Ciarrochi, Chan, and Caputi (2000) found a one-factor solution and reported a fairly robust two-factor solution of the MEIS as well. Roberts et al. (2001) argued for a four-factor solution. Thus, one two and four-factor solutions were all found across at least two data sets of the MEIS. This pattern of solutions was repeated with the MSCEIT V1.1, where exploratory factor analyses clearly supported one, two, and four factor solutions aligned with the full-scale EIQ, Area EIQs, and Branch EIQ's. Confirmatory analyses with the MSCEIT V2.0 further indicates an acceptable fit of the one-factor model, and excellent fits for the two-and four-factor models to the data. Thus, the scales and subscales of the MSCEIT V2.0 are both reliable, and justified in regard to their structural validity.

Does the Test Measure Something New and Different? (Discriminant Validity)

If we are correct in arguing that EI is a new, previously unmeasured concept, then issues of distinctiveness arise. That is, the MSCEIT V2.0 ought to measure things different from other tests. The MSCEIT V2.0 (and its precursors) should be mostly independent of tests of cognitive intelligence, of emotion, and other self-report scales focusing on well being, positive affect, optimism, and other qualities sometimes informally included in the popular label "emotional intelligence" (e.g., Bar-On, 2000; Goleman, 1995).

Test-to-test correlations can range fully from zero to near 1.0. Generally speaking, among tests, correlations between $r = .00$ to .25 indicate the tests are unrelated; $r = .25$ to .50 indicate minimal to moderate overlap, $r = .50$ to .75, moderate to high overlap, and $r = .75$ and 1.00 indicate high overlap or, perhaps, equivalence between tests. This interpretive scale pertains solely to test-to-test correlations. Predicting from tests to life outcomes must be evaluated according to an entirely different yardstick. When predicting from tests to life outcomes, even extremely low correlations, such as $r = .10$ or lower, can be of pragmatic importance, especially when they are not inflated by correlated measurement error.

Distinctiveness refers to the issue of whether a test is different from those that have come before. As there has been a proliferation of psychological tests, the importance of distinctiveness has increased. As Ciarrochi, Chan, Caputi, and Roberts (2001) put it:

> Generally, we should not make up a test and call it EI when really it is a measure of some other, well-established personality trait. If we did this repeatedly, we would end up inventing thousands of new (but redundant) tests each year. Even worse, two scientists might be studying exactly the same thing and not realize it, because they have given different names to the same test. (p. 28)

EIQ and Social Desirability. With the foregoing in mind, the MSCEIT V2.0's distinctiveness can be evaluated vis-à-vis other tests. Wherever possible, we restrict our reports to studies conducted with at least about 100 participants, so as to avoid misleading data from small samples. In addition, the following findings focus on total EIQ and branch-level EIQ scores, because area EIQ's are a relatively late addition to scoring.

EIQ Is Distinct From Social Desirability, Traditional IQ, and Measures of Emotion. A number of test-to-test correlational studies have been conducted. For example, the MSCEIT V2.0s (and predecessors) are unrelated to socially desirable responding measured by the 16PF or Marlowe-Crowne scales (see Table 14.2). EIQ is also somewhere between unrelated and minimally related to scales of general intelligence, including a nonsignificant $r = .05$ (for Raven's Progressive Matrices), to a high of $r = .36$ (p < .01), for the Army Alpha Vocabulary Scale (see Table 14.3).

EI also is different from emotional experience itself. The MSCEIT EIQ and mood state correlate $r = .08$, n.s., using a scale "based on the circumplex model of emotion" in a sample

TABLE 14.2

Representative Relationships Between the MEIS, MSCEIT, and
Measures of Social Desirability

IQ TEST	Total EIQ	Branch EIQs				N	Comments	Reference
		Perc.	Using	Under.	Manage			
16PF: Impression Management (Cattell, Cattell,& Cattell, 1993	.00	.11	−.04	−.08	−.04	183	MEIS	(Caruso et al., 2002)
Marlowe-Crowne Social Desirability (Crowne & Marlowe, 1960)	.12	.09	.01	.08	.15	97	MSCEIT V2	(Salovey et al., 2003)

of 97 participants. Likewise the MEIS scale had no relationship to reports of depression, or hopelessness: r's: −.03, .08, .06, .12. (Ciarrochi, Deane, & Anderson, 2002, Table 2) Pelletteri (1999) found that higher EI, as measured on the MEIS, correlated with more adaptive defense styles among 107 ethnically diverse college students. These are reported in Table 14.4

Correlations With Other Scales of Emotional Intelligence and Related Constructs. Because the MSCEIT V2.0 was designed as an ability measure of the four-branch theory of EI (Mayer & Salovey, 1997), it should be unique among other measures of EI that are typically based on the popularized interpretations of the term, and that mix in measures of well being and personality. The MSCEIT EIQ correlates moderately with self-report scales of empathy (e.g., $r = .33$ to $.43$, $p < .01$), and lower with other EI scales such as the Bar-On EQi and Schutte's Self-Report Emotional Intelligence Scale (e.g., $r = .18$ to $.01$; p's n.s. to $< .01$). The MSCEIT is also independent of Levels of Emotional Awareness Scale (LEAS, Lane, Quinlan, Schwartz, Walker, & Zeihin, 1990). This is somewhat surprising as the LEAS is closest of all the scales to an ability scale in design (Table 14.5).

Predictions to General Personality Dimensions. The MSCEIT V2.0 and its precursors are also largely independent of general personality dimensions. In relation to the Big 5 personality traits, the MSCEIT V2.0 EIQ shows its most consistent patterns with the Big 5 dimensions of extroversion, agreeableness, and conscientiousness; those relations, however, are mostly below $r = .30$ (Table 14.6). It also correlates in the same range with self-esteem and life satisfaction.

Summary of Test-to-Test Relations. In summary, large-sample results from the MEIS precursor scale, and newer results from the MSCEIT V2.0, are consistent in indicating that the MSCEIT V2.0 is reliable, factor valid, and largely independent of a variety of self-report scales of socially desirable responding, intelligence, positive affect, and other scales measuring emotional intelligence and related constructs, including traditional personality traits such as the Big Five.

TABLE 14.3
Representative Relationships Between the MSCEIT and Precursor EI Measures
and Measures of Traditional IQ

IQ TEST	Total EIQ	Branch EIQs				N	Comments	Reference
		Perc.	Using	Under.	Manage			
Army Alpha Vocabulary Scale (Yerkes, 1921)	.36**	.16**	N/A	.40**	.20**	503	MEIS; Adults	Mayer et al., 1999, (p. 287)
Army Alpha Vocabulary Scale (Yerkes, 1921)	.38	N/A	N/A	N/A	N/A	239	A-MEIS; Adolescents	Mayer et al., 1999)
Raven's Progressive Matrices	.05	.10	N/A	−.03	N/A	114	MEIS; Note, this was a two-factor-based solution of the MEIS; Perception and Understanding/Management might best be considered area scores	(Ciarrochi et al., 2000)
16PF: Reasoning (cattell et al., (1993)	.21**	.01	.20**	.29**	.20**	183	MEIS	(Caruso et al., 2002)
ASVAB: Services Vocational Aptitude Battery: AFQT cited in Roberts et al., 2001	.32**	.09*	.22**	.40**	.16**	667 to 669	MEIS, Consensus scoring	(Roberts et al., 2001)
Verbal SAT's	.30**	N/A	N/A	N/A	N/A	207	MSCEIT V2	(Brackett & Mayer, October 5–7, 2001)
WAIS-III Vocabulary (Wechsler, 1997)	.15	.07	−.03	.38*	.03	97	MSCEIT V2	(Salovey et al., 2003)

*p < .05; **p < .01

TABLE 14.4

Representative Relationships Between the MSCEIT, Precursor EI Measures, and Measures of Emotions, Emotional Styles, and Affectivity

IQ TEST	Total EIQ	Branch EIQs				N	Comments	Reference
		Perc.	Using	Under.	Manage			
Mood-Adjectives based on Mood Circumplex	.08	.03	.01	.07	.13	97	MSCEIT V2	(Salovey et al., 2003)
Beck Depression Inventory-II (Beck, Steer, & Brown, 1996)	.06	N/A	N/A	N/A	N/A	302	Note: "Full scale" EIQ in this case is based on the MEIS "Stories" task, which measures Emotional Perception and Understanding	(Clarrochi et al., 2002)
Beck Hopelessness Scale (Beck, Steer, Kovacs, & Garrison, 1985)	.12	N/A	N/A	N/A	N/A	302	Note: "Full scale" EIQ in this case is based on the MEIS "Stories" task, which measures Emotional Perception and Understanding	(Clarrochi et al., 2002)

*p < .05; **p < .01

To the extent moderate relationships are detectable, the high EI person is somewhat more agreeable and emotionally sensitive and empathic than others, and perceives herself or himself as undergoing personal growth. The individual is a bit more conscientious and extroverted than others, and a bit higher in general intelligence as well. Given the minimal-to-modest size of these relations with prior-tests, however, one cannot escape the conclusion that the most important application of EI will be in the realm of life predictions. It is to that area of prediction we turn next.

Predictions to Life Criteria

Introductory Considerations. When evaluating test to real-life predictions, even very modest correlations of $r = .02$ or $.03$ can be of considerable importance. For example, the impact of chemotherapy on breast-cancer survival is $r = .03$, yet, given the life and death circumstances, it is almost always strongly recommended because it will save 1.5 lives per 100. In selection, hiring, and counseling contexts, the outcome does not regularly involve life and death circumstances, but it can involve important calculations of personal happiness,

TABLE 14.5

Representative Relationships Between the MSCEIT, Precursor EI Measures, and Measures of Constructs Related to Emotional Intelligence

Comparison Measure	Total EIQ	Branch EIQ's				N	Comments	Reference
		Perc.	Using	Under.	Man			
Overall Empathy (Mayer et al., 1999)	.33**	.20**	N/A	.25**	.34**	503	MEIS	(Mayer et al., 1999)
Overall Empathy (Mehrabian & Epstein, 1972	.43**	.24*	N/A	.37**	N/A		MEIS; The factor scores may best represent two "Area Scores" for the test.	
Bar-On Emotional Quotient Inventory (Bar-On, 1997)	.18**	–	–	–	–	207	MSCEIT V2.0	(Brackett & Mayer, October 5–7 2001)
Bar-On Emotional Quotient Inventory (Bar-On, 1997)	.15*	.16*	n.s.	.17*	.19*	130	MSCEIT V2.0	(Pelletieri, 2001, 2002)
Self-Report Emotional Intelligence (Schutte et al., 1998)	.19**	–	–	–	–	207	MSCEIT V2.0	(Brackett & Mayer, October 5–7, 2001)
Trait Meta-Mood Scale: Attention (Salovey, Mayer, Goldman, Turvey, & Palfai, 1995)	.01	.05	–.10	.04	.04	97	MSCEIT V2.0	(Salovey et al., 2002, Table 4)
Trait Meta-Mood Scale: Clarity (Salovey et al., 1995)	.05	.08	–.13	.11	.07	97	MSCEIT V2.0	(Salovey et al., 2002 Table 4)
Trait Meta-Mood Scale: Clarity (Salovey et al., 1995)	.29	N/A	N/A	N/A	N/A	318	MSCEIT V2.0	(Gohm & Clore, 2003)
Levels of Emotional Scale Awareness (Lane et al., 1990)	n.s. to .21*	N/A	N/A	N/A	N/A	107	Four subtests of MEIS used; two not sign; two were.	(Ciarrochi, et al.,)

TABLE 14.6

Representative Relationships Between the MSCEIT, Precursor EI Measures, and General Measures of Personality

Comparison Measure	Total EIQ	Branch EIQs				N	Comments	Reference
		Perc.	Using	Under	Manage			
Neuroticism (Costa Jr. & McCrae, 1985)	.04	−.03	N/A	.09	N/A	114	MEIS; Note; understanding was combined scoring for understanding and management	(Ciarrochi et al., 2000)
Anxiety (Neuroticism) (Cattell et al., 1993)	−.06	−.16*	−.01	.04	.01	183	MEIS	(Caruso et al., 2002)
Neuroticism (Christal, 1994)	−.18*	−.13*	−.13*	−.15*	−.11*	656 to 671	MEIS; Consensus	(Roberts et al., 2001)
Neuroticism. (Costa Jr. & McCrae, 1985)	−.13*	−.07	−.03	−.10	−.17	97	MSCEIT	(Salovey et al., 2003)
Extroversion (Costa Jr. & McCrae, 1985)	.26**	.19*	N/A	.19*	N/A	114	MEIS; See note for Ciarrochi, above	(Ciarrochi et al., 2000)
Extroversion (Cattell et al., 1993)	.16*	.08	.19*	.07	.18*	183	MEIS	(Caruso et al., 2002)
Extroversion. (Christal, 1994)	13*	.10*	.09*	.05	.14*	656 to 671	MEIS	(Roberts et al., 2001)
Extroversion (Costa Jr. & McCrae, 1985)	−.04	−.04	−.01	.11	.08	97	MSCEIT	(Salovey et al., 2003)
Toughmindedness (Agreeableness, reversed) (Cattell et al., 1993)	−.21*	−.13	−.19*	−.13	−.19*	183	MEIS	(Caruso et al., 2002)
Agreeableness (Christal, 1994)	.24*	.17*	.17*	.10*	.29*	656 to 671	MEIS	(Roberts et al., 2001)
Agreeableness (Costa Jr. & McCrae, 1985)	33*	.17	.23*	.18	.37*	97	MSCEIT	(Salovey et al., 2003)

TABLE 14.6 (*Continued*)

Comparison Measure	Total EIQ	Branch EIQ's				N	Comments	Reference
		Perc.	Using	Under	Manage			
Openness (Christal, 1994)	.13*	.01	.07	.18*	.12*	656 to 671	MEIS; Consensus	(Roberts et al., 2001)
Openness (Costa Jr. & McCrae, 1985)	−.23*	−.12	−.28*	−.03	−.24*	97	MSCEIT	(Salovey et al., 2003)
Conscientiousness (Christal, 1994)	.16*	.08*	.09*	.11*	.22*	656 to 671	MEIS	(Roberts et al., 2001)
Conscientiousness (Costa Jr. & McCrae, 1985)	.25*	.09	.10	.25*	.29*	97	MSCEIT	(Salovey et al., 2003)
Private Self-Consciousness	−.13	.01	−.11	−.17	−.14	97	MSCEIT	(Salovey et al., 2003)
Public Self-Consciousness	.06	.02	.08	.03	.04	97	MSCEIT	(Salovey et al., 2003)
Self-esteem (Rosenberg, 1965)	.31**	.25**	N/A	.19*	N/A	114	MEIS; Note that the factors employed "perception" and "understanding/ management" may represent what are now referred to as area scores.	(Clarrochi et al., 2000)
Self-Esteem (Rosenberg, 1965)	−.04	.00	−.07	−.04	.10	97	MSCEIT	(Salovey et al., 2003)
Life Satisfaction (Mayer et al., 1999)	.11*	.01	N/A	.11*	.13*	503	MEIS	(Mayer et al., 1999)
Life Satisfaction (Mayer et al., 1999)	.28**	.20*	N/A	.20*	N/A	114	MEIS	(Ciarrochi et al., 2000)
Secure Attachment (Bartholomew & Horowitz, 1991)	.28**	.08	.26	.28	.31	197	MSCEIT RV1.1	(Kafetsios & Mitchell, May, 2001)

success at school or a job (and hence, happiness at home), and the avoidance of associated costs in disruption brought about by poor placements. Current interpretations suggest that correlations as low as $r = .02$ or $.03$, are meaningful, with many psychological (and medical test) assessments and real life criteria falling in the $r = .10$ to $.30$ level, and a few rising beyond that level (Abelson, 1985; Meyer et al., 2001; Rosenthal & Rubin, 1982). Correlations between the MSCEIT V2.0, its precursor tests, and real life criteria follow that same pattern of low to modest relationships.

Qualitative Considerations of the High EI Person: Evidence from Case Studies.   The forgoing review of psychological tests suggests that the high EI individual is primarily defined by his or her ability at solving emotional problems. Beyond that, however, the individual is somewhat more likely to be extraverted, conscientious, intelligent, and to have more secure attachments than others. Case studies of people high in EI seem to bear this out and expand on the picture somewhat. In qualitative studies of both nursing leaders (Vitello-Cicciu, 2001) and adolescents (Mayer, Perkins, Caruso, & Salovey, 2001), those high in EI seem to be socially connected, sensitive to the feelings of others, and often, actively working to enhance socioemotional relations in and around themselves. For example, one high EI nurse leader (EIQ = 155) wrote that she was very proud of how she was able to find a compromise between opposing sides of a patient care problem, on a very stressful day during which much was going on. As she put it, ". . . we were able to come up with a solution that both the physician, the nurse, and the patient seemed to be satisfied with, but it took five to ten minutes talking, exploring different options and she [the nurse] felt good about it. I felt good. The physician was more than happy" (Vitello-Cicciu, 2001, p. 14–23). A case study of a high EI adolescent yielded a similar picture. When one young woman saw her friends preparing to paint someone in his sleep as a practical joke, she stepped in and discussed with them how their actions would be likely to hurt his feelings and demean his dignity; she ended up putting a stop to the incident (Mayer et al., 2001). By contrast, low EI nurse leaders and low EI teenagers appear relatively confused about their socioemotional relationships, and are often inappropriately assertive or aggressive in response to frustrations that they face.

Measures of Scholastic and Occupational Performance.   Emotional intelligence has sometimes been found to predict higher scholastic grades and occupational performance ratings. For example, Barchard (2001) found that measures of emotional and social intelligence incremented predictions of college GPA, although their predictive variance overlapped. Pusey (2000) administered the MSCEIT RV1.1 to 42 United Kingdom employees and found that Total EI scores (and, individually, the facilitation branch) correlated with job performance: $r = .28$, $p < .05$. These and subsequent effects are summarized in Table 14.7.

Rice (1999) studied the EI of customer service teams (11 leaders, 26 teams; 164 individuals) in an insurance industry setting. She found that the average EI of a team significantly predicted higher customer service in claims adjustments, $r = .46$, $p < .01$, although it was unrelated to either productivity or commitment to improvement. Team leader EI was also related to supervisors' rankings of the team leaders' effectiveness, $r = 51$, $p < .01$, although it was assessed on an N of 11. Conversely, when team leaders had high EIQ, team members had lower assessments of their accuracy and productivity: $r = -.35$, $p < .05$, for the 26 teams.

Relationships.   Several studies indicate stronger social relationships in context, for those higher in emotional intelligence. Kafetsios and Mitchell (May, 2001, Study 2) examined

TABLE 14.7
Representative Relationships Between the MSCEIT, and Precursor EI Measures, and
Measures and Life-Space Criteria

Comparison Measure	Total EIQ	Branch EIQs				N	Comments	Reference
		Perc.	Using	Under	Man.			
GPA	e.g., increase in R² of .42 for women	N/A	N/A	N/A	N/A	303 college students	Emotional and social intelligence both predicted individually	(Barchard, 2002)
High school rank	.23**	—	—	—	—	207	MSCEIT	(Brackett & Mayer, October 5, 2001)
Customer satisfaction in claims adjustments	.46*	N/A	N/A	N/A	N/A	164 individuals divided into 24 teams	Some contrary findings as well	(Rice, 1999)
Independent job performance ratings	.28*	N/A	N/A	N/A	N/A	42 UK employees	MSCEIT RV1.1	(Pusey, 2000)
Secure attachment among married couples	.37* wives; .24 husbands	N/A	N/A	N/A	N/A	41 long-term married couples	MSCEIT V2.0; rho coefficient reported	(Kafetsions & Mitchell, May, 2001)
Ratings of support network	.15* to .28*	N/A	N/A	N/A	N/A	176 ethnically diverse under-graduates	MSCEIT RV1.1	(Fullam, Siegel, in preparation)
Relatedness (pictures of friends, family, scrapbooks, sentimental items)	.30**	.21**	N/A	.26**	.22**	208 under-graduate students	MEIS; the two most salient life-space dimensions are reported here; others reached significance as well	(Formica, 1998)

TABLE 14.7 *(Continued)*

Comparison Measure	Total EIQ	Branch EIQs				N	Comments	Reference
		Perc.	Using	Under	Man.			
Destructive Behavior (drug use, high school detentions, criminal mischief, etc.)	−.33**	−.17*	N/A	−.27**	−.29**	208 under-graduate students	See note above	(Formica, 1998)
Overall peer-rated aggression	−.48**	N/A	N/A	N/A	N/A	49	Grade school children in an inner-city school	(Rubin, 1999)
Drug use	−.01	—	—	—	—	207	Used MSCEIT Life-space data	(Brackett & Mayer, October 5, 2001)
Alcohol use	−.04	—	—	—	—	207	MSCEIT	(Brackett & Mayer, October 5, 2001)
Smoking	.−.00	—	—	—	—	207	MSCEIT	(Brackett & Mayer, October 5, 2001)
Social Deviance	−.20**	—	—	—	—	207	MSCEIT: Social deviance = gun ownership, fights, arguments	(Brackett & Mayer October 5, 2001)

attachment relations in 41 couples in the Cambridgeshire area, all of whom had been married for a number of years (average age 51). The emotional management subscale was positively correlated with secure attachment in wives (rho = .37) and negatively associated with fearful and dismissing attachment (rho = −.34, −.32). Emotional perception was positively related to secure attachment in husbands (rho = .24), and negatively but nonsignificantly related to fearful and preoccupied attachment (rho = −.21, −.23).

In one study, Fullam and Siegel (in preparation) examined 176 ethnically diverse Rutgers University undergraduates with the MSCEIT V1.1. Most of the MSCEIT tasks individually showed significant correlations with perceptions that one's social network provided social support, that one was close to others, reassured about one's own worth, and provided nurturance to others (e.g., r's = .15 to .28, individually significant between p < .05 and < .0001). They also found a number of negative predictions to symptom reports (at about the same effect level). On the other hand, Salovey, Mayer, Caruso, and Lopes (2002), in a sample of 97 Yale University participants, found no significant intercorrelations between the MSCEIT V2.0 and Furman's Network of Relationship Inventory, which also measures social support. (Perhaps Yale Undergraduates require good social networks as a prerequisite to attending the school.)

Using life space inventories with (see Mayer, 1998b; Mayer, Carlsmith, & Chabot, 1998) with 208 students (79 men, 129 women), Formica (1998) found that high EI individuals expressed a great deal more relatedness in their environment, including being more likely to own and display pictures of others and family members, to keep scrapbooks and other sentimental objects, and to work as a caretaker or nanny r = .30, p < .01. Brackett (2001) found similar relationships in his sample of 322 for a slightly different set of scales.

Problem Behaviors and Violence.   Perhaps the earliest pattern to emerge with the MSCEIT series of tests was that they predict lowered problem behavior. For example, Trinidad and Johnson found that those higher in EI reported lower rates of drinking and smoking (r's = −.12 to −.20 on some questions only, p's from n.s. to < .01). In another study, children in an inner-city school with higher EI engaged in substantially lower levels of peer-rated violence, r = −.45, p < .05. (Rubin, 1999) In an early study of EI employing life space survey data (see Mayer et al., 1998), Formica (1998), found a correlation of r = −.33 p < .01, between MEIS EI and lower levels of problem behaviors including cigarette and other drug use, fighting, and handgun ownership, in a sample of 208 participants. Brackett (2001) performed a larger-scale study with 332 college students (243 women, 89 men) using life space data, using the MSCEIT V2.0. He obtained the following scales of (or related to) problem behavior: (a) physical fights and vandalism, (b) substantial alcohol use, (c) illegal drug use, (d) fighting with friends, and (e) knife and gun ownership. Higher EI scores meant lower (i.e., reduced, better) levels in all these problem areas for men, with r's between −.18 and −.38, p < .05. In four out of five cases the relationship held for men only. Finally, in an aforementioned qualitative analysis of 11 adolescents, the highest scorers in EIQ (based on several MEIS subscales) appeared to possess better social understanding, empathy, and to proactively refrain from, and even to discourage, teasing and interpersonally destructive behavior in the people around them (Mayer, Perkins et al., 2001).

SUMMARY AND CONCLUSIONS

The theory of emotional intelligence described earlier in this chapter gave rise, beginning in 1990, to a set of ability scales that are now relatively brief, efficient, and comprehensive instruments for the study of emotional intelligence. The scales indicate that EI exists in the form described by the theory, it can be objectively measured, and it predicts important life outcomes, independent of many other existing measures. Emotional intelligence is, in many respects, a standard intelligence, although it admittedly stretches some of our preconceived notions about intelligence.

There can be no "last word" regarding either modern IQ tests or theories of intelligence theories. Thus, we hope that the field of emotional intelligence continues to stimulate scientific inquiry and vigorous debate. For example, discussion of EI at the 3rd Spearman conference in Sydney raised several further questions particularly relevant to EI as an intelligence, and its measure. First, some wondered whether there existed an emotional memory that is sufficiently distinct from cognitive memory to warrant its independent assessment. Second, Dyke, Ferguson, and Shochet (2001) noted that, although cognitive IQ and emotional IQ are relatively unrelated in adults, in their sample of disordered and normal children at least, the correlation was far higher (e.g., $r = .35$ to $.90$). Whether this is due to their use of extreme groups, a relatively small sample, or some more general developmental process is an interesting issue. Third, one of the first cross-cultural studies of an EI ability test (using the MEIS) indicated that much of the scoring generalized across cultures, although some Branch 2 items generalized least of all. More generally, the further validation of the tests above should lead to a further understanding of the nature of people high and low in EI. We hope the contents of this chapter will encourage others interested in the area to further explore EI and its correlates.

REFERENCES

Abelson, R. (1985). A variance explanation paradox: When a little is a lot. *Psychological Bulletin, 97*, 129-133.

ACER. (1989). *Standard progressive matrices: Australian Manual.* Hawthorne, Victoria: Australian Council for Educational Research, Ltd.

Averill, J. R., & Thompson-Knowles. (1991). Emotional creativity. In K. T. Strongman (Ed.), *International review of studies on emotion* (Vol. 1, pp. 269-299). London: Wiley.

Barchard, K. A. (2002). *The relation of emotional intelligence to academic success.* University of British Columbia, Vancouver, BC.

Bar-On, R. (1997). *BarOn Emotional Quotient Inventory: Technical manual.* Toronto, Canada: Multi-Health Systems.

Bar-On, R. (2000). Emotional and social intelligence: Insights from the Emotional Quotient Inventory. In R. Bar-On & J. D. A. Parker (Eds.), *The handbook of emotional intelligence: Theory, development, assessment, and application at home, school, and in the workplace* (pp. 363-388). San Francisco: Jossey-Bass.

Bartholomew, K., & Horowitz, L. M. (1991). Attachment styles among young adults: A test of a four-category model. *Journal of Personality & Social Psychology, 61*, 226-244.

Beck, A. T., Steer, R. A., & Brown, G. K. (1966). *BDI-II Manual.* San Antonio, TX: Psychological Corporation.

Beck, A. T., Steer, R. A., Kovacs, M., & Garrison, B. (1985). Hopelessness and eventual suicide: A 10-year prospective study of patients hospitalized with suicidal ideation. *American Journal of Psychiatry, 142*, 559-563.

Brackett, M. (2001). *Describing the life space and its relation to emotional intelligence.* Unpublished master's thesis, University of New Hampshire, Durham, NH.

Brackett, M., & Mayer, J. D. (2001, October). *Comparing measures of emotional intelligence.* Paper presented at the Third Positive Psychology Summit, Washington, DC.

Brackett, M. A., & Mayer, J. D. (2001, October). *Comparing measures of emotional intelligence.* Washington, DC: Third Positive Psychology Summit.

Caruso, D. R., Mayer, J. D., & Salovey, P. (in press). Relation of an ability measure of emotional intelligence to personality. *Journal of Personality Assessment.*

Cattell, R. B., Cattell, A. K., & Cattell, H. E. P. (1993). *16 PF (5th ed.).* Champaign, IL: Institute for Personality and Ability Testing.

Christal, R. E. (1994). *Non-cognitive research involving systems of testing and learning (Contract # F33615-91-D-0010).* Brooks AFB, TX: USAF.

Ciarrochi, J. (in preparation). *A critical evaluation of the Levels of Awareness Scale.*

Ciarrochi, J., Chan, A., Caputi, P., & Roberts, R. D. (2001). Measuring emotional intelligence. In J. Ciarrochi, J. P. Forgas, & J. D. Mayer (Eds.), *Emotional intelligence in everyday life* (pp. 25-45). Philadelphia, PA: Psychological Press.

Ciarrochi, J., Deane, F. P., & Anderson, S. (in press). Emotional intelligence moderates the relationship between stress and mental health. *Personality & Individual Differences.*

Ciarrochi, J. V., Chan, A. Y., & Caputi, P. (2000). A critical evaluation of the emotional intelligence concept. *Personality and Individual Differences, 28,* 539-561.

Cohen, J. (Ed.). (1997). *Educating minds and hearts: Social emotional learning and the passage into adolescence.* New York: Teachers College Press.

Cohen, J. (Ed.). (2001). *Caring classrooms/intelligent schools: The social emotional education of young children.* New York: Teachers College Press.

Costa Jr., P. T., & McCrae, R. R. (1985). *The NEO Personality Inventory. Manual.* Odessa, TX: Psychological Assessment Resources.

Crowne, D. P., & Marlowe, D. (1960). A new scale of social desirability independent of psychopathology. *Journal of Consulting Psychology, 24.*

Darwin, C. (1872/1965). *Expression of the emotions in man and animals.* New York: Philosophical Library.

Darwin, C. (1872/1998). *The expression of the emotions in man and animals; with an introduction, afterword, and commentaries by Paul Ekman* (3rd ed.). New York: Oxford University Press.

Dyer, M. G. (1983). The role of affect in narratives. *Cognitive Science, 7,* 211-242.

Dyke, M. J., Ferguson, K., & Shochet, I. M. (2001). Do autism spectrum disorders differ from each other and from non-spectrum disorders on emotion recognition tests? *European Child and Adolescent Psychiatry, 10,* 105-116.

Ekman, P. (1973). *Darwin and facial expression: A century of research in review.* New York: Academic Press.

Ekman, P. (1985). *Telling lies.* New York: Norton.

Elias, M. J., Zins, J. E., Weissberg, R. P., Frey, K. S., Greenberg, M. T., & Haynes, et al. (1997). *Promoting social and emotional learning: Guidelines for educators.* Alexandria, VA: Association for Supervision and Curriculum Development.

Formica, S. (1998). *Description of the socio-emotional life space: Life qualities and activities related to emotional intelligence.* Unpublished senior honors thesis, University of New Hampshire, Durham, NH.

Fullam, A., & Siegel, H. I. (in preparation). *Adult attachment, emotional intelligence, health and immunological responsiveness to stress.*

Gardner, H. (1983). *Frames of mind: The theory of multiple intelligences.* New York: Basic Books.

Gohm, C. L., & Clore, G. L. (in preparation). Affect as information: An individual differences approach. In L. Feldman Barrett & P. Salovey (Eds.), *The wisdom of feelings: Psychological processes in emotional intelligence.* Guilford Press.

Goleman, D. (1995). *Emotional intelligence.* New York: Bantam Books.

Guilford, J. P. (1959). *Personality.* New York: McGraw-Hill.

Hall, B. K. (1999). The paradoxical platypus. *BioScience, 49,* 211-218.

Kafetsios, K., & Mitchell, V. (2001, May). *Adult attachment and emotional intelligence.* Paper presented at the 8th Conference of Psychological Research, University of Thrace, Alexandroupolis, Greece.

Lane, R. D., Quinlan, D. M., Schwartz, G. E., Walker, P. A., & Zeitlin, S. B. (1990). The Levels of Emotional Awareness Scale: A cognitive—developmental measure of emotion. *Journal of Personality Assessment, 55,* 124-134.

Lazarus, R. (1991). *Emotions and adaptation.* New York: Oxford University Press.

Legree, P. I. (1995). Evidence for an oblique social intelligence factor established with a Likert-based testing procedure. *Intelligence, 21,* 247-266.

Matarazzo, J. D. (1972). *Wechsler's measurement and appraisal of adult intelligence* (5th ed.). New York: Oxford University Press.

Mayer, J. D. (1998a). Socialization, society's "emotional contract," and emotional intelligence. *Psychological Inquiry, 9*, 300-303.

Mayer, J. D. (1998b). A systems framework for the field of personality psychology. *Psychological Inquiry, 9*, 118-144.

Mayer, J. D. (2000). Emotion, intelligence, emotional intelligence. In J. P. Forgas (Ed.), *The handbook of affect and social cognition* (pp. 410-431). Mahwah, NJ: Lawrence Erlbaum & Associates.

Mayer, J. D. (2001). A field guide to emotional intelligence. In J. Ciarrochi, J. P. Forgas, & J. D. Mayer (Eds.), *Emotional intelligence and everyday life.* (pp. 3-24). New York: Psychology Press.

Mayer, J. D., Carlsmith, K. M., & Chabot, H. F. (1998). Describing the person's external environment: Conceptualizing and measuring the life space. *Journal of Research in Personality, 32*, 253-296.

Mayer, J. D., Caruso, D. R., & Salovey, P. (1999). Emotional intelligence meets traditional standards for an intelligence. *Intelligence, 27*, 267-298.

Mayer, J. D., Caruso, D. R., & Salovey, P. (2000). Selecting a measure of emotional intelligence: The case for ability scales. In R. Bar-On & J. D. A. Parker (Eds.), *The handbook of emotional intelligence: Theory, development, assessment, and application at home, school, and in the workplace* (pp. 320-342). San Francisco, CA: Jossey-Bass.

Mayer, J. D., DiPaolo, M. T., & Salovey, P. (1990). Perceiving affective content in ambiguous visual stimuli: A component of emotional intelligence. *Journal of Personality Assessment, 54*, 772-781.

Mayer, J. D., McCormick, L. J., & Strong, S. E. (1995). Mood-congruent recall and natural mood: New evidence. *Personality and Social Psychology Bulletin, 21*, 736-746.

Mayer, J. D., Perkins, D., Caruso, D. R., & Salovey, P. (2001). Emotional intelligence and giftedness. *Roeper Review, 23*, 131-137.

Mayer, J. D., & Salovey, P. (1995). Emotional intelligence and the construction and regulation of feelings. *Applied and Preventive Psychology, 4*, 197-208.

Mayer, J. D., & Salovey, P. (1997). What is emotional intelligence? In P. Salovey & D. Sluyter (Eds.), *Emotional development and emotional intelligence: Educational implications* (pp. 3-31). New York: Basic Books.

Mayer, J. D., Salovey, P., & Caruso, D. R. (2000a). Emotional intelligence as zeitgeist, as personality, and as a standard intelligence. In R. Bar-On & J. D. A. Parker (Eds.), *Handbook of emotional intelligence* (pp. 92-117). New York: Jossey-Bass.

Mayer, J. D., Salovey, P., & Caruso, D. R. (2000b). Models of emotional intelligence. In R. J. Sternberg (Ed.), *Handbook of intelligence* (pp. 396-420). Cambridge, England: Cambridge University Press.

Mayer, J. D., Salovey, P., & Caruso, D. R. (in press). *Manual for the MSCEIT* (Mayer-Salovey-Caruso Emotional Intelligence Test). Toronto, Canada: MHS Publishers.

Mayer, J. D., Salovey, P., Caruso, D. R., & Sitaraneos, G. (2001). Emotional intelligence as a standard intelligence. *Emotion, 1*, 232-242.

Mehrabian, A., & Epstein, N. (1972). A measure of emotional empathy. *Journal of Personality, 40*, 525-543.

Meyer, G. J., Finn, S. E., Eyde, L. D., Kay, G. G., Moreland, L. K., & Dies, R. R., et al. (2001). Psychological testing and psychological assessment: A review of evidence and issues. *American Psychologist, 56*, 128-165.

Ortony, A., Clore, G. L., & Collins, A. M. (1988). *The cognitive structure of emotions.* Cambridge: Cambridge University Press.

Palfai, T. P., & Salovey, P. (1993-1994). The influence of depressed and elated mood on deductive and inductive reasoning. *Imagination, Cognition & Personality, 13*, 57-71.

Pelletteri, J. (1999). *The relationship between emotional intelligence, cognitive reasoning, and defense mechanisms.* Dissertation Abstracts International: Section B: The Sciences & Engineering, 60, 403 [AAM9917182].

Pelletteri, J. (2001, in preparation). *A comparison of two measures of emotional intelligence: The MSCEIT and EQi.*

Picard, R. (1997). *Affective computing.* Cambridge, MA: MIT Press.

Plutchik, R. (1984). Emotions: A general psychoevolutionary theory. In K. R. Scherer & P. Ekman (Eds.), *Approaches to emotion* (pp. 197-219). Hillsdale, N J: Lawrence Erlbaum.

Pusey, F. (2000). *Emotional intelligence and success in the workplace: Relationship to job performance.* Unpublished masters thesis, Guildhall University, London.

Rice, C. L. (1999). *A quantitative study of emotional intelligence and its impact on team performance.* Unpublished master's thesis, Pepperdine University, Malibu, CA.

Riggio, R. E. (1992). Social interaction skills and nonverbal behavior. In R. S. Feldman (Ed.), *Applications of nonverbal behavioral theories and research* (pp. 3-30). Hillsdale: NJ: Lawrence Erlbaum.

Roberts, R. D., Zeidner, M., & Matthews, G. (2001). Does emotional intelligence meet traditional standards for an intelligence? Some new data and conclusions. *Emotion, 1*, 196-231.

Rosenberg, M. (1965). *Society and the adolescent self-image.* Princeton, NJ: Princeton University Press.

Rosenthal, R., & Rubin, D. B. (1982). A simple, general purpose display of magnitude of experimental effect. *Journal of Educational Psychology, 74*, 166-169.

Rubin, M. M. (1999). *Emotional intelligence and its role in mitigating aggression: A correlational study of the relationship between emotional intelligence and aggression in urban adolescents.* Unpublished dissertation, Immaculata College, Immaculata, PA.

Salovey, P., & Mayer, J. D. (1990). Emotional intelligence. *Imagination, Cognition, and Personality, 9*, 185-211.

Salovey, P., Mayer, J. D., Caruso, D. R., & Lopes, P. N. (in press). Measuring emotional intelligence as a set of abilities with the MSCEIT. In S. J. Lopez & C. R. Snyder (Eds.), *Handbook of positive psychology assessment.* Washington, DC: American Psychological Association.

Salovey, P., Mayer, J. D., Goldman, S., Turvey, C., & Palfai, T. P. (1995). Emotional attention, clarity, and repair: Exploring emotional intelligence using the Trait Meta-Mood Scale. In J. W. Pennebaker (Ed.), *Emotion, disclosure, and health* (pp. 125-154). Washington, DC: American Psychological Association.

Schutte, N. S., Malouff, J. M., Hall, L. E., Haggerty, D. J., Cooper, J. T., & Golden, C. J., (1998). Development and validation of a measure of emotional intelligence. *Personality & Individual Differences, 25*, 167-177.

Schwarz, N. (1990). Feelings as information: Informational and motivational functions of affective states. In E. T. Higgins & E. M. Sorrentino (Eds.), *Handbook of motivation and cognition* (Vol. 2, pp. 527-561). New York: Guilford Press.

Spinoza, B. (1675). *Ethics* (Part III: On the origin and nature of emotions).

Sternberg, R. J. (1997). The concept of intelligence and its role in lifelong learning and success. *American Psychologist, 52*, 1030-1045.

Taylor, G. J., Ryan, D. P., & Bagby, R. M. (1985). Toward the development of a new self-report alexithymia scale. *Psychotherapy and Psychosomatics, 44*, 191-199.

The Psychological Corporation. (1997). *WAIS-III, WMS-III Technical Manual.* San Antonio, TX: Author.

Trinidad, D. R., & Johnson, C. A. (in press). The association between emotional intelligence and early adolescent tobacco and alcohol use. *Personality and Individual Differences.*

Tucker, J. S. R. (1988). The role of social skills in encoding posed and spontaneous facial expressions. *Journal of Nonverbal Behavior, 12*, 87-97.

Vitello-Cicciu, J. M. (2001). *Leadership practices and emotional intelligence of nurse leaders.* Unpublished doctoral dissertation, The Fielding Institute.

Wechsler, D. (1997). *WAIS III: Wechsler Adult Intelligence Scale (3rd ed.).* San Antonio, TX: The Psychological Corporation.

Yerkes, R. M. (1921). Psychological examining in the United States. *Memoirs of the National Academy of Sciences, 15,* 890.

Zuckerman, M., Hall, J. A., DeFrank, R. S., & Rosenthal, R. (1976). Encoding and decoding of spontaneous and posed facial expressions. *Journal of Personality & Social Psychology, 34,* 966-977.

Zuckerman, M., Lipets, M. S., Koivumaki, J. H., & Rosenthal, R. (1975). Encoding and decoding nonverbal cues of emotion. *Journal of Personality & Social Psychology, 32,* 1068-1076.

15

▼▼▼▼▼▼▼

Is Intelligence Critical Thinking?
Why We Need a New Definition
of Intelligence

Diane F. Halpern
Claremont McKenna College

Suppose that it is your job to hire someone who will serve in an important decision-making capacity at your office. You find that you are having difficulty writing a good job description or even suggesting appropriate qualifications because your office is about to undergo a major reorganization and the nature and title of this position will surely change. You ponder several choices. Unfortunately neither Superman nor Superwoman is available, Mighty Mouse is busy saving rodents in distress, and besides even if they were job hunting, they probably wouldn't apply for this position. Whoever is hired will have to manage a tidal wave of change, be able to make sound decisions with incomplete information, know how to work cooperatively with a diverse group of people, think creatively because new solutions will be needed for both old and new problems, identify a problem before it explodes, and learn very quickly. This is a description for many of the jobs of the future, jobs that may not even exist today; yet we are educating our students and making long-term personnel decisions now to fill them. Some of our students will be in the workforce in the year 2050 and beyond. In a jargon that you are undoubtedly familiar with, the KSAs (knowledge, skills, and abilities) are unknown. You need to identify intelligent people. How can you make the best choices?

Suppose that you had to select from among the following five applicants. Which of the following would you select?

1. The applicant with the highest IQ score
2. The applicant with the highest GPA from a prestigious graduate school
3. The applicant who is a grand chess master
4. The applicant who is an award-winning poet
5. The applicant who is a single parent and raised 3 sets of twins while attending graduate school on welfare

The way you decide among these five hypothetical and paper-thin applicants is an indication of the skills that you think are needed by the prospective employee and which of these profiles is indicative of a person who can learn quickly and adapt well to change. But, it is not just at the highest levels of administration where the necessary job skills are changing.

Here is a riddle for you:

What do you call a secretary who has not learned new job skills in the last 10 years?

The answer is unemployed—the same answer you would give if it were a riddle about almost any other occupation you can name. Call it "intelligence" or "job smarts" or the "ability to learn"—we need more of it than ever before. Today's workforce requires more complex skills and abilities at every level. The number of jobs available in manufacturing is shrinking; those workers with low levels of education can expect more competition for fewer jobs that pay poorly, while at the same time, there is increased demand for a new type of worker—this new job category has been dubbed the "knowledge worker" or the "symbol analyst" (a term that is used by the U.S. secretary of labor), to describe someone who can carry out multistep operations, manipulate abstract and complex symbols and ideas, acquire new information efficiently, and remain flexible enough to recognize the need for continuing change and for new paradigms for lifelong learning. Whatever term is used to describe these KSAs, it sounds like intelligence to me. How can we select, educate, and retrain individuals who can survive and thrive in the changing workplace—a place that has been described as "constant white water," a reference to the dangerous rapids that river rafters must negotiate in changing and sometimes dangerous and unknown conditions.

Workers in almost every job category can expect to face novel problems because the nature of the workplace is changing repeatedly at an increasingly rapid rate. Familiar responses no longer work. Certainly the military knows this and the rest of the world has been forced to ponder the new realities of war. Like every other type of work, the work of war has changed dramatically. War is no longer two armies facing off against each other on a battlefield or two strong men engaged in arm-to-arm combat. Modern warfare means wars of intelligence—both in the sense of acquiring and recognizing information and in the intelligent use of information.

Indicators of Intelligence

Let's consider indicators of intelligence—tests or other measures that we can use to identify prospective leaders in a world where intelligence is more important than ever before. What sort of questions would you want on your intelligence test?

Here are some choices:

1. The classic: a right triangle with sides 3" and 4". What is the hypotenuse? (In fact, what is a hypotenuse?)

This is a trivial question for many eighth graders, a more time-consuming question for most of us in this room, and an impossible question for most of the adult working-world.

2. What about the number of digits you can repeat backward? Try it, repeat these digits in reverse order: 5 9 8 6 9 4 1 8 5 7.

3. Or the time in milliseconds that it takes to mentally rotate an irregular 3-dimensional meaningless form? Try it with these figures. How quickly can you decide if the figure on the right be made congruent with the one on the left by rotating it in the depth or picture plane?

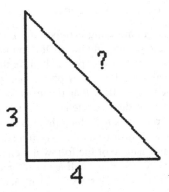

FIG. 15.1 A classic example of the type of test item used to infer intelligence: Given a right angle triangle with sides 3" and 4", what is the hypotenase?

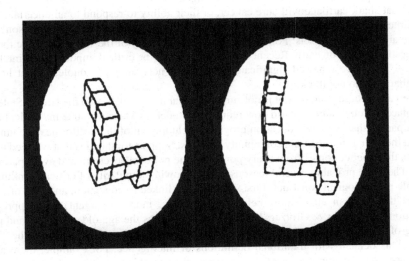

FIG. 15.2 This is mental rotation task where the dependent measures are the time in milliseconds for a correct response to determine if the two figures can be rotated in space to be identical and the percentage of correct responses.

4. What about vocabulary questions. What is the meaning of the word "travesty?" Now, I don't know why that word came to mind in this example.

I do not mean that these measures don't have a place in a cognitive assessment (in fact, I often use these measures in my own research on cognition), but are they meaningful indicators of intelligence? Will any of these measures allow us to identify future workers who can learn efficiently and think critically so that our various countries can remain competitive and cooperative in the 21st century? We need a new way of thinking about intelligence, one that is compatible with the heavy cognitive demands of contemporary life.

Why We Need a New Definition of Intelligence

I want to persuade you that what I am saying is important. Perhaps it will help if I scare you first—just to be sure that you are paying attention. Did you know that a large percentage of people start everyday by reading their horoscope and believe that it is so often correct that it's as though it was written especially for them; they phone their personal psychic, at a cost that many cannot afford, for advice on matters that range from how to invest their money to whether or not a loved one should be disconnected from life support systems; they spend huge sums of money on a variety of remedies for which there is no evidence that they work or are even safe to take—sometimes with disastrous results. In a survey of college students, more than 99% expressed belief in at least one of the following: channeling, clairvoyance, precognition, telepathy, psychic surgery, psychic healing, healing crystals, psychokinesis, astral travel, levitation, the Bermuda triangle mystery, unidentified flying objects (UFOs), plant consciousness, auras, and ghosts (Messer & Griggs, 1989). Would an intelligent person believe in phenomena for which there is no credible evidence to support the belief? Will someone's knowledge about the hypotenuse of a triangle or their ability to repeat digits in a reverse order predict their response to an advertisement for snake oil, or their willingness to believe that shark cartilage will cure cancer, or their ability to respond to an uncertain financial market, or any of the other responses we would expect from an intelligent person?

Here are more scary facts: For the first time in the history of the world, we have the ability to destroy all life on earth. Recent events have shown the critical importance of intelligent thinking. They give renewed significance to Hitler's now infamous quote, "What luck for rulers that men do not think."

Given all of these examples, it is not surprising that many colleges in the United States and other places throughout the world now require all students to take a course in "critical thinking" as part of their general education program, including all of the California state universities and the over 106 California community colleges. Support for the idea that we need to help students think better comes from every portion of the political spectrum and every part of the world. There are probably several reasons for the growing popularity of critical thinking as a desirable psychological construct. First, it is directly linked to education, and thus offers the promise that we can all become better thinkers (i.e., more intelligent) with appropriate instruction (cf. Perkins & Grotzer, 1997). Thus, it obviates the age-old, tiresome, and pointless tug-of-war between nature and nurture. Critical thinking does not come with the "heavy baggage" associated with traditional definitions of intelligence. For example, there are no arguments over the importance of "g" in the critical thinking literature. Finally, there are direct links between the construct definition and what looks like intelligent behavior. It is a more meaningful way to conceptualize intelligence for a generation of knowledge workers.

There is virtually no disagreement over the need to help American students improve how they think. Both George Bush, senior, and Bill Clinton, when he was governor, supported the national education goal for higher education that declared that it was a national priority to enhance critical thinking in college students, although I might add that this national priority was never funded (National Educational Goals Panel, 1991). It was a great idea that both Democrats and Republicans agreed on, until it was time to pay for it, causing some to cynically wonder if politicians really want a thinking public.

In his award-winning book, Earl Hunt (1995) examined the skills that will be needed by our workforce in the early decades of this century and asked, "Will we be smart enough?" The way we answer this question will determine the quality of life that we and our children can expect to live as well as the future of our countries and our planet.

CRITICAL THINKING: A CONSTRUCT DEFINITION

Although it sometimes seems that there is very little that academics can agree on, there is considerable agreement among experts in the field of critical thinking about its definition. Several recent reviews of this topic have found common themes. For example, in a recent review of the literature on critical thinking, Fischer and Spiker (2000) found that most definitions include judgment, reasoning, metacognition, and reflective thinking. Jones et al. (1995) also conducted an extensive review of the critical thinking literature and came up with a long list of skills that can be categorized in various ways, but contain the same components as listed in the Fischer and Spiker review. The Cornell Critical Thinking Test (Midwest Publications) contains sections on induction, credibility, prediction, experimental planning, fallacies, deduction, and definitions; and the Ennis-Weir Critical Thinking Test (Ennis & Weir, 1985) includes getting the point, reasons and assumptions, seeing other possibilities, and responding to and avoiding fallacies. Different authors use different terms and vary in the breadth of their definition, but overall there are no major disagreements about the sorts of skills that are included under a critical thinking rubric.

The definition of "critical thinking" that I have used is in accord with many of the tests of critical thinking and curricular materials designed for critical thinking. I have found this to be a useful working definition (not a brief definition; Halpern, 2003):

The term critical thinking is the use of those cognitive skills or strategies that increase the probability of a desirable outcome. It is purposeful, reasoned, and goal directed. It is the kind of thinking involved in solving problems, formulating inferences, calculating likelihoods, and making decisions. Critical thinkers use these skills appropriately, without prompting, and usually with conscious intent, in a variety of settings. That is, they are predisposed to think critically. When we think critically, we are evaluating the outcomes of our thought processes—how good a decision is or how well a problem is solved. Critical thinking also involves evaluating the thinking process—the reasoning that went into the conclusion we've arrived at or the kinds of factors considered in making a decision. In the term "critical thinking," the word "critical" is not meant to imply "finding fault," as it might be used in a pejorative way to describe someone who is always making negative comments. It is used instead in the sense of "critical" that involves evaluation or judgment, ideally with the goal of providing useful and accurate feedback that serves to improve the thinking process. Some people are uncomfortable with the word "critical" and prefer to substitute terms like "clear and effective" in the term "critical thinking."

Here are the five category headings for organizing college-level critical thinking skills (Halpern, 1994; 1998):

1. Verbal Reasoning Skills
   The skills listed under this rubric include those skills that are needed to comprehend and defend against the persuasive techniques that are embedded in everyday language (also known as natural language). Thinking and language are closely tied constructs, and the skills included in this category recognize the reciprocal relationship between language and thought in which an individual's thoughts determine the language used to express them, and the language that is used shapes the thoughts.

2. Argument Analysis Skills
   An argument is a set of statements with at least one conclusion and one reason that supports the conclusion. In real-life settings, arguments are complex with reasons that run counter to the conclusion, stated and unstated assumptions, irrelevant information,

and intermediate steps between the conclusions and the evidence that supports them. Arguments are found in commercials, political speeches, textbooks, and anywhere else where reasons are presented in an attempt to get the reader or listener to believe that the conclusion is true. The skills of identifying conclusions, rating the quality of reasons, and determining the overall strength of an argument should be sharpened in college course work.

3. Skills in Thinking as Hypothesis Testing
    The rationale for this category is that much of our day-to-day thinking is like the scientific method of hypothesis testing. In many of our everyday interactions, people function like intuitive scientists in order to explain, predict, and control the events in their lives. The skills used in thinking as hypothesis testing are the same ones that are used in scientific reasoning—the accumulation of observations, formulation of beliefs or hypotheses, and the use of the information collected to decide if it confirms or disconfirms the hypotheses.

4. Using Likelihood and Uncertainty
    Because very few events in life can be known with certainty, the correct use of probability and likelihood plays a critical role in almost every decision. The critical thinking skills that are subsumed under this heading are an important dimension of a college-level critical thinking taxonomy.

5. Decision Making and Problem-Solving Skills
    In some sense, all of the critical thinking skills are used to make decisions and solve problems, but the ones that are included here involve the use of multiple problem statements to define the problem and identify possible goals, the generation and selection of alternatives, and judging among the alternatives. Many of these skills are especially useful in quantitative reasoning problems.

Taken together, these five categories define an organizational rubric for a skills approach to critical thinking. They have face validity and can be easily communicated to the general public, and they offer one possible answer to the question of what college students need to know and be able to do when they graduate from college, thus are commonly used on measures designed to assess educational outcomes (e.g., American Psychological Association's Outcomes Assessment Taskforce, 2006). A skills approach to critical thinking has the benefit of focusing on skills that are teachable, testable, and generalizable. These are skills that are needed for success in the workplace and in handling the other complexities of modern life. These are not, of course, independent skills, and many real-world tasks require the use of several of these skills and often, selection of the best thinking skill for the task. It is useful to consider these categories as test specifications, just as one would include some multiplication, division, addition, and subtraction problems in a test of computational mathematics. They are not separable dimensions.

Can People Learn to Think Critically?

Critical thinking instruction is predicated on two assumptions: (a) that there are clearly identifiable and definable thinking skills that students can be taught to recognize and apply appropriately, and (b) if recognized and applied, the students will be more effective thinkers.

I can probably guess what you are thinking. This is a great list of critical thinking skills and you could easily add more, but is there good evidence that adults will improve in these skill areas in ways that transfer to novel situations and endure beyond the term of instruction when they are specifically taught these skills. First, there is no reason to believe that they wouldn't. Most students improve in their ability to write after taking coursework in writing; similarly, most students will become better at oral communication after appropriate instruction, and so on for math and other cognitive skill areas. We now have a sufficiently large body of research that shows that it is possible to teach in ways that help students become better thinkers and that these skills transfer to novel situations when we teach specifically for transfer.

One of the largest and most ambitious studies of the benefits of instruction designed to improved thinking was conducted in the 1980s in Venezuela. Unlike most other studies, this one used a "strong" experimental design, including the random assignment of participants to different learning conditions and "blind" evaluations of the outcomes (Herrnstein, Nickerson, de Sanchez, & Swets, 1986). Students who received the critical thinking instruction were better thinkers than students in the control groups that received standard instruction. Unfortunately, because of a change in the political leadership in Venezuela, there has been no long-term follow-up to determine if these gains were sustained over time. There are many studies where the dependent measures are student self-reports and self-assessments of how well they can think (e.g., Block, 1985). These studies provide only weak data because the belief that one can think well is not always correlated with actual performance, but it is reassuring to know that students believe that their thinking has improved as a result of instruction designed to improve thinking.

A strong case for critical thinking instruction comes from several different studies by Nisbett and his colleagues (Nisbett, 1993). For example, in one study, Nisbett and his coauthors phoned students at their homes after the coursework was completed, under the guise of conducting a survey. They found that students spontaneously applied the thinking skills that they had been taught in school when they encountered novel problems, even when the school-related context cues were absent (Fong, Krantz, & Nisbett, 1986). In a different study, college students learned inductive reasoning tasks using realistic scenarios from many different domains. The authors concluded that critical thinking is "a skill" and that "it is transferable" (Jepson, Krantz, & Nisbett, 1993, p. 82).

Kosonen and Winne (1995) studied the transfer of critical thinking skills to a novel domain in college students, secondary school students, and middle-school students. Like Nisbett, they found that when students learned general rules about reasoning and practiced these skills with everyday "ill-structured" problems, the thinking skills transferred to new contexts and different domains. More recently, Lovett and Greenhouse (2000) (building on the work of Paas, 1992) reported similar results. When students learned to solve multiple problems using "varied" problem sets during learning, the initial learning took significantly longer, but the students who learned with a variety of examples performed better on transfer problem sets than students who practiced only on similar problems. Thus, it seems that critical thinking skills are learned best and are most likely to transfer to novel situations when they are taught using a variety of contexts. Principles derived from empirical studies like these (and others) that show the successful transfer of critical thinking skills can serve as a model for instructional design for instructors who want to teach for critical thinking.

Critical thinking instruction can also be used to help students resist the appeal of paranormal claims, offering the promise of fewer sales of copper bracelets to cure arthritis and miracle weight-loss vitamins. Wesp and Montgomery (1998) found that college students were better able to recognize the flawed thinking found in claims for these sorts of products after completing coursework designed to enhance critical thinking.

Dispositions for Effortful Thinking and Learning

It is important to separate the disposition or willingness to think critically from the ability to think critically. Some people may have excellent critical thinking skills and may recognize when they are needed, but they may also decide not to engage in the effortful process of using them. This distinction calls attention to what people *can do* and what they *actually do* in real-world contexts. Good instructional programs help learners decide when to make the necessary mental investment in critical thinking and when a problem or argument is not worth it.

Dispositions for effortful thinking and learning include

- the willingness to engage in and persist at a complex task
- the conscious use of plans and suppression of impulsive activity
- flexibility or open-mindedness
- the willingness to abandon nonproductive strategies in attempts to self-correct
- the awareness of social realities that need to be overcome so that thought can become actions.

Thus, critical thinking has both and skills and dispositional components.

Tests Available to Assess Critical Thinking

There are a number of so-called critical thinking tests currently available. I have commented on them in several different publications and settings, so I summarize some of my concerns here. One test is the Watson-Glaser Critical Thinking Test in which short passages are read and test takers respond using a multiple-choice format (Watson & Glaser, 1980). This is essentially a reading test that correlates extremely high with other reading tests, such as the well-known Nelson-Denny. The passages are short; the response format does not allow for original or unprompted thinking or for assessing the propensity to think critically in real-life situations (Loo & Thorpe, 1999). The National League of Nursing, the accrediting body for nursing programs, requires that all nursing programs teach their students the skills of critical thinking. Nursing programs that have used this off-the-shelf measure have been very disappointed with the results. I believe the disappointment is caused by the lack of fit between the skills that the program administrators want their students to know and those that are tapped on this test.

There are other commercially available tests that rely on single sentence prompts with multiple-choice answers. One reviewer of the California Critical Thinking Skills Test (also a multiple-choice test) described it as having "Low internal consistency and poor construct validity" (Jacobs, 1999). There is even a so-called critical thinking test that relies on self-report of one's own belief about the quality or her or his thinking. The problems with self-report measures are well known—studies of metacognition have shown that people are often very poor judges of how much they know or understand about a subject. Most of these tests have dubious or unknown psychometric properties. The issue of validity is almost never mentioned in the same sentence as these tests. In a study with 1,300 college sophomores and over 100 faculty, researchers at Western Washington University concluded that three so-called tests of critical thinking (Academic Profile, College Outcomes Measurement Program, and Collegiate Assessment of Academic Proficiency) were basically tests of verbal and quantitative knowledge, not critical thinking (Western Washington University, www.ac.wwu.edu/~assess/).

A Better Measure

The need for providing information about the status of critical thinking skills is relatively non-controversial. There is currently little or no information to inform the decision makers in the workplace, higher education, the military, or in any other setting that is concerned with adult-level thinking skills. The controversies arise over questions of whether the information can be provided in a way that is meaningful, valid, useful, used, fair, and cost effective. A high-quality assessment can provide many benefits, but, if the assessment is not well done, the results will be costly and, possibly, harmful. Public confidence and trust are the sine qua non for an undertaking of this significance.

The type of measure of critical thinking that I am advocating is based on clearly defined skills that are assessed in realistic scenarios that could apply to a wide range of racial, ethnic, and socioeconomic groups. The United States is one of the most culturally diverse countries in the world, and as the globe shrinks in response to advances in technology, diversity of experiences and backgrounds need to be considered in test design for all countries. In order to provide a fair estimate of the ability of people from all cultures, the skills selected must be those that are used and needed in most cultural settings. Consider for example, a frequently cited example of a question that is not culturally fair, taken from the Wechsler Intelligence Scale for Children (WISC). The question concerns what children should do if someone younger and smaller hits them. This question has been criticized by African American psychologists who believe that "hitting back" (the wrong answer) is more acceptable in the African American community than in other cultures because of the emphasis on caring for younger children. If the test developers had probed the thinking that went into the responses that children selected, they would have found this potential bias. The inclusion of questions like this one casts doubt on the validity of the WISC because prospective users become wary of other possible biases. This problem could have been avoided if greater concern for cultural fairness had been demonstrated at the time the test was written and at every stage of test development. A culture-free test is not possible (or even desirable), but fairness for various groups can be improved with careful preparation (cf. Greenfield, 1997).

TESTING FOR TRANSFER

The goal of all formal education, and most explicitly, instruction that is designed to help students become better thinkers, is transfer to real-world, out-of-the-classroom situations. With this goal in mind, the ideal assessment would occur naturally in the course of one's life, in multiple settings, and provide comparable measures before, during, and long after the instruction. It would tell us what an individual thinks and does when reading a political advertisement, selecting a career objective, or voting on a bond issue, at times when the individual is not aware of being assessed. Unfortunately, this sort of intrusive and surreptitious assessment is not feasible, and probably not even legal. As a near approximation of a "truly authentic" test, we can create realistic scenarios from a variety of common contexts.

The Sequential Question

My own preference for test format, when the goal is to assess critical thinking, is to use believable examples with an open-ended response, followed by specific questions that probe for the reasoning behind an answer. If, for example, the thinking skill of understanding and recognizing the distinction between correlation and cause were being assessed, it would be tested with examples taken from medical research (e.g., coffee drinkers reported more headaches), social policy analysis (e.g., welfare mothers who received job training were more likely to be employed after 1 year than welfare mothers who did not receive job training), and numerous other believable scenarios. Such materials are ecologically valid in that they are representative of the many examples that could be found in newspapers and everyday discussions. The open-ended portion of the question allows test takers to demonstrate whether or not they spontaneously use the skill. Do the test takers recognize the fact that these are correlational designs that do not permit causal statements when there are no obvious hints to consider the issue of design?

Specific probes would follow the open-ended responses. These probes allow test takers to demonstrate their understanding of the concepts, such as whether they are able to recognize the problem of determining cause when they are provided with hints (e.g., In understanding these results, is it important to know if the participants were assigned randomly to the different conditions?). Such additional probes would show if students are able to use the skill when they are told that it is needed in a specific situation, even if the student did not spontaneously recognize that it was needed.

A good critical thinking question with several sequential parts would allow for different types of information about the test taker with a minimal number of questions. The open-ended constructed portion of the question could be graded simply as "recognized the need for the particular thinking skill" or "did not recognize the need for a particular thinking skill." The open-ended or constructed response portion is a test of the type of remembering that cognitive psychologists call "free recall" because there are few restraints on the type of response that the test taker can generate. (It is a type of recall that is free from restraints.) The multiple-choice or multiple-rating portion would show if the respondent were able to recognize the appropriate skill when it was presented in a list of alternatives. This sort of response is a measure of "recognition memory." Cognitive psychologists distinguish between recall and recognition paradigms in the assessment of memory. It is believed that these two types of recall utilize different cognitive processes and that students prepare differently for tests that require free recall (e.g., essay tests) than those that require recognition (e.g., multiple choice tests). In general, lower scores are expected on free recall tests than recognition tests because free recall requires a search through memory plus some sort of verification that the answer retrieved is correct; recognition requires only the verification stage and provides a less stringent measure of memory.

There is good evidence that multiple choice questions and open-ended essays are measuring somewhat separable constructs (Bridgeman & Moran, 1996). In a study of the Advanced Placements tests, which are taken by college-bound, high school seniors, a significantly greater proportion of females than males obtained scores that were high on the essay questions and low on the multiple-choice questions. Males showed an opposite pattern of results, with a significantly greater proportion obtaining high scores on the multiple-choice questions and low scores on the essay questions than the females. Thus, a mix of the two types of questions would also help to ensure equity for females and males in these tests.

The multipart nature of the questions makes it possible to assess both the dispositional aspect of critical thinking and the ability to use a skill when a prompt is provided. The constructed response can be either written or oral. I suggest that constructed responses be limited in length to a maximum of two to four sentences so that scoring costs can be contained, and good answers can be readily identified. If the questions and responses were presented on a computer, so that presentation times and scoring could be controlled and automated, the time needed for administering and scoring could be greatly reduced. A computer-administered assessment can also provide reaction time data, a major dependent measure in cognitive psychological studies. Reaction times are sometimes used as measures of intelligence, and although it is not an appropriate use in this assessment, reaction times can help psychologists understand a great deal about the microcomponents of the underlying cognitive processes. They permit a much more fine-grained analysis of mental events than other commonly used dependent measures such as percentage of questions answered correctly. Reaction time data could be made available to cognitive psychologists for secondary analyses. They would not be provided to respondents or reported to the public because it is difficult to convince the general public that a difference of a few hundred milliseconds relates to any practical notion of intelligence. No one can answer the philosophical question of whether differences of a few hundred milliseconds add up over the course of a day, so that "fast thinkers" have an extra hour or so every day that "slow thinkers" lose or whether these fractions of a second "get lost" in the ebb and flow of everyday events.

Although open-ended free response questions show how test takers approach a question and communicate knowledge, they can only be used to sample a few skills because they require a longer administration time than multiple-choice questions. They are also much more expensive to grade and lack the high level of reliability that can be obtained with carefully written multiple-choice items. Multiple choice responses can be machine graded at a relatively low cost. The multiple choice portion of the assessment can also include multiple-ratings items in which there is more than one correct response or a judgment made about the quality of each alternative.

It is also suggested that two or three of the questions be presented in a video format because so much information is currently obtained with this medium. There are many video possibilities. For example, a hypothetical analysis of employment data presented in a news show context, a group of mid-level executives discussing ways to improve profits for a hypothetical company, or a physician explaining the risks and benefits associated with the use of a particular drug. Response format for the test taker who views video segments can be the same as that used with written questions.

The nature of the proposed questions differ from those used on earlier assessment instruments in several ways. The questions are relatively complex in that they contain several types of information. Like real world thinking tasks, some of the information available may not be relevant, and part of the question involves deciding which information is important to the problem. What is important in an assessment of critical thinking skills is what test takers are required to *do* with the information. The tasks for the test taker should require thoughtful analysis and synthesis. Here are some suggestions for defining the task for the test taker:

After context-rich information is provided, the test taker is asked a question or told to perform a task. For example,

- Draw a diagram or other graphic display that organizes the information provided in the question.
- What additional information would you want before answering the question?
- Explain why you selected a particular multiple-choice alternative. Which alternative is second best? Why?
- State the problem.
- Which information is most important? Which information is least important? Why? Categorize the findings in a meaningful way.

- List two solutions for the problem.
- What is wrong with an assertion that was made in the question?
- Present two reasons that support the conclusion and two reasons that do not support the conclusion.
- Identify the type of persuasive technique that is used in the question. Is it valid or is it designed to mislead the reader? Explain your answer.
- What two actions would you take to improve the design of the study that was described?

I have been working on the Halper–Critical Thinking Assessment using everyday situations based on these principles for more than 20 years. I briefly report here the results of two early studies. This attempt to devise a psychometrically sound critical thinking assessment is a "work in progress."

STUDY 1:	1. 80 high school students—juniors and seniors from three high schools in California.They were all students who were present on the day of testing in one Advanced Placement English class and two regular English classes. (34 male, 46 female)
	2. 80 college students—juniors and seniors from California State University, San Bernardino (31 male, 49 female) Prizes were awarded to the 5 highest scoring individuals in each group as an incentive. (The prizes were lottery tickets and books.)
Format:	The test was administered in paper and pencil format.
Other Asessments:	All participants also took the Arlin Test of Formal Reasoning (a Piagetian level test). The content of Arlin includes volume estimates, proportional reasoning, combination, equilibrium, and correlation items.
Results:	College students scored higher than high school students on both tests (all *p's* < .001) Correlations between the Halpern Critical Thinking assessment using everyday situations and Arlin Test were .32 for both groups. There were no significant differences among college students for major, but the number in each major was small in this study (18 social science, 16 natural science, 17 humanities, 20 business). There were no gender differences for either group.
STUDY 2:	1. 145 undergraduate students (juniors and seniors) from California State University, San Bernardino (55 males and 90 females). Undergraduate participants received class credit for their participation.
	2. 32 second year master's level students from California State University, San Bernardino (11 males and 21 females) from English and psychology programs. Prior to data collection, it was decided that any participant who finished the assessments in less than 50 minutes or more than 100 minutes would not be included in data analyses (assuming that they did not take the task seriously or did not work consistently). Six additional participants were eliminated using these criteria and are not included in these analyses.

Format: The test was administered on IBM-compatible PCs (Dell computers). The use of computers to present items greatly reduced the reading load for the test because participants first read a short scenario and then typed a response in a response box. When they were finished writing their response, the same scenario remained on the monitor and the response box changed to a multiple-choice format (radio buttons) or multiple-rating format. The scenario did not have to be reread to answer the multiple-choice questions because the scenarios remained unchanged when the response-type changed. WebCT test software was used to present the assessment tests.

Other Assessments and Measures: In their informed consent (which was also presented on the computer), participants granted permission to access data from their student academic files. We collected information about age, major, grade point average, SATs, and GREs, when these data were available. Additionally, we collected data on ACTs and college freshman tests in English and mathematics (Educational Testing Service tests—English Placement Test [EPT] and Entry-Level Mathematics Test—[ELM]). There were not enough participants with these data, so they were not used in any of the analyses.

In an attempt to assess the dispositional aspects of critical thinking, two self-report questionnaires were administered when the participants completed the Critical Thinking Assessments. The 20-item "Conscientiousness Scale" (Costa & McCrae, 1992) is one of the assessments used with the "Big 5" Factor Theory of Personality. Participants rate items using a 7-point scale to indicate the extent to which the item is an accurate description of themselves. For example,

_____   I do things according to a plan.
_____   I waste my time.
_____   I am always prepared.
_____   I neglect my duties.

The Need for Cognition Scale, an 18-item self-rating scale, was also administered to all participants upon completing the Critical Thinking Assessment (Cacioppo, Petty, & Kao, 1984). It is designed to assess an individual's tendency to "engage in and enjoy effortful cognitive endeavors" (Cacioppo, Petty, Feinstein, & Jarvis, 1996, p. 17). Like the Conscientiousness Scale, participants rate items using a 7-point scale to indicate the extent to which the item is an accurate description of themselves. Sample items are:

_____   I like the responsibility of handling a situation that requires a lot of thinking.
         The notion of thinking abstractly is appealing to me.
_____   It's enough for me that something gets the job done; I don't care how or why it works.
_____   I like tasks that require little work once I've learned them.

Results:

• Scoring rubrics were created for each of the Halpern Critical Thinking assessment using everyday situations items. A small team of students, with graduate student leaders, were

TABLE 15.1
Mean Test or Measure Scores for Undergraduate and Graduate Studentsa

Test or Measure	Undergraduate	Graduate
Constructed Response CTA	28.89 (.69)	35.38 (1.50)
Multiple Choice CTA	57.42 (9.47)	63.97 (8.76)
Grade Point Average	2.89 (.56)	3.59 (.34)
Need for Cognition	75.35 (15.2)	88.63 (12.3)
Conscientiousness Scale	102.17 (17.12)	109.46 (15.32)
SAT or GRE	SATV 419.18	GREV522 GREQ554
	SATM 441.22	GREA 492

Note Standard deviations are in parentheses.

trained in grading the items. Every item was scored by at least 2 raters. In those cases where raters disagreed, they met with a third rater to discuss the item. All discrepancies were resolved with discussion, and after the training, disagreements were rare.

- Mean testing time for the Halpern Critical Thinking Assessment using everyday situations was 81.1 minutes (standard deviation = 19.4 minutes). The Conscientiousness Scale and Need for Cognition Test took 5 to 10 minutes (combined time) to complete.
- A Chronbach alpha reliability coefficient was computed using 10 scale scores as the items (constructed response and multiple-choice for argument analysis, hypothesis testing, probability and likelihood, verbal reasoning, and creative thinking), alpha = .81.
- Mean scores for the Constructed Response and Multiple-Choice portions of the Critical Thinking Assessment and other tests and measures are presented separately for undergraduate and graduate students in Table 15.1.

Correlations with total scores on the Halpern Critical Thinking Assessment using everyday situations were computed for Need for Cognition Scale, Conscientiousness Scale, Grade Point Average, SAT-Verbal, SAT-Mathematics, GRE-Analytic, GRE-Verbal, and GRE-Quantitative. These are shown in Figure 15.3.

It is interesting to note the there is virtually no relationship between scores on the Halpern Critical Thinking Assessment using everyday situations and the Conscientiousness Scale and the GRE-Verbal Test. The Critical Thinking Assessment does, however, show moderate correlations with the Need for Cognition Scale, the SAT-Verbal, but not the GRE Verbal Scale, the SAT Math Scale, but not the GRE Quantitative Scale, with highest correlations with the GRE Analytic Scale. It is premature to speculate about these relationships until these results are replicated with different samples.

To test for possible differences among undergraduates who selected different disciplinary fields for their academic major, total scores on the critical thinking assessment were analyzed as a function of grade point average for students grouped into three different disciplinary fields—humanities, social sciences, and natural sciences. These data were tested with an analysis of variance with five levels of GPA (2.0, 2.5, 3.0, 3.5, 4.0) and three levels of disciplinary field. Total score on the Halpern Critical Thinking Assessment using everyday situations differed significantly for disciplinary field, $F(2, 122) = 4.05$, $p < .02$. These data are shown in Fig. 15.4. It is interesting to note that the differences in grade point average by disciplinary field were not significant for disciplinary field when SATV, SATM, or their total

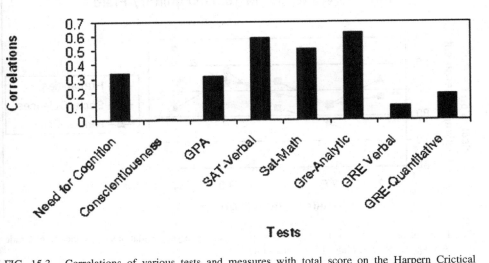

FIG. 15.3. Correlations of various tests and measures with total score on the Harpern Crictical Thinking Assesment Using Everyday Situations.

was used as the dependent measure. Thus, the Halpern Critical Thinking Assessment using everyday situations scores varied by disciplinary field, whereas the SAT measures did not.

SUMMARY OF FINDINGS AND RECOMMENDATIONS

As expected, the Halpern Critical Thinking Assessment using everyday situations with constructed response and multiple-choice item pairs that are based on real-life scenarios shares variance with some, but not all, of the tests on the SAT and GRE. It also seems to be related to the Need for Cognition, but not the Conscientiousness Scale. The Halpern Critical Thinking Assessment using everyday situations also differentiated among different disciplinary majors, as hoped. It seems reasonable to expect that students select a major area of study based on a personal assessment of their own talents and interests. There is a general, but uneven, trend for higher critical thinking scores to be associated with higher grade point averages, but again, the relationship is imperfect. Many critics of education have complained that schools neither teach nor reward critical thinking in students, thus a modest relationship could be interpreted as somewhat supportive of these critic's concerns.

Next Steps

Findings reported here have now been replicated using different high school and university samples with the Halpern Critical Thinking Assessment using everyday situations, but more importantly, there is a need to obtain data from working adults who have high-quality job performance records. There are few indicators that can accurately predict job-related performance, including advancement and job ratings. I obtained permission to administer the

Scores on Critical Assessment as a Function of Grade Point Average and Major Disciplinary Field

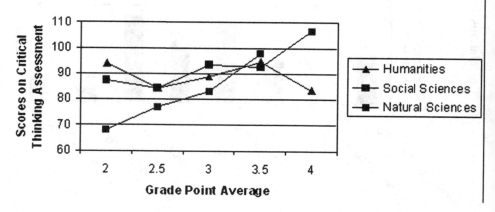

FIG. 15.4.   Scores on Critical Thinking Assessment Using Everyday Situations as a Function of Grade Point Average (GPA) and Major Disciplinary Field.

Halpern Critical Thinking Assessment using everyday situations to a wide range of employees in a large county in California and was promised access to the employee's personnel files to validate the scores. Unfortunately, I found that virtually all county employees received satisfactory ratings of job performance unless a supervisor was establishing the legendary "paper trail" as a prelude to disciplinary action. In fact, the problem with this area of work is finding a good measure to use for validation. I have resisted the most common suggestion, which is to validate scores for working adults using their salary as the criterion. The idea that the most intelligent people are paid the highest salaries is repugnant to me, especially as a (relatively) low-paid college professor. I would expect some relationship between these variables, but I also hope that the data would be so noisy that I could not detect the signal without a huge sample. Other traditional measures are possible for validation, such as reaction time measures or even standardized intelligence tests, but theoretically I would expect only a modest relationship, which is why a test of critical thinking is proposed as a better measure so it is difficult to see what would be gained with these sorts of studies. The problem of validation is inherent in any study of intelligence, so it is not surprising that it rears its ugly head in thinking about new constructs for assessing intelligence.

In closing, I ask you to ponder this question, "Why should you go to all of the effort to assess critical thinking skills and dispositions in prospective high-level employees?" Here is a sad, but true story that may provide the answer: "In 1994, Orange County, California filed for bankruptcy after its treasurer had lost $1.7 billion in highly speculative bond investments. The treasurer's top aid testified to a grand jury investigating the matter that the treasurer had consulted a psychic and relied on interest-free forecasts from a mail-order astrologer while making the ill-fated investments." (Quackwatch, http://www.quackwatch.com/01quackeryrelated topics/psychic.html). Aren't you glad you aren't the one who hired him?

Bertrand Russell said it well: "Most people would sooner die than think, in fact, they do." Traditional measures and conceptions of intelligence would not have revealed this treasurer's belief in financial psychics, whereas the Halpern Critical Thinking Assessment using everyday situations may have. The assessment of critical thinking is not an easy or casual undertaking, but I believe that it is important. As we adjust to a world with an ever-increasing pace of change, it is time for our understanding of what it means to be intelligent to also change.

AUTHOR NOTES

I sincerely thank Amy Latta, Luci Heymig, and the students in Psychology 437 in Spring 2001 at California State University, San Bernardino for their assistance with data collection and scoring.

REFERENCES

American Psychological Association's Outcomes Assessment Taskforce. (2006). *Standards for undergraduate psychology majors.* Unpublished manuscript available from American Psychological Association, Washington, DC.

Block, R. A. (1985). Education and thinking skills reconsidered. *American Psychologist, 40,* 574–575

Bridgeman, B., & Moran, R. (1996). Success in college for students with discrepancies between performance on *multiple*-choice and essay tests. *Journal of Educational Psychology, 88,* 333–340.

Cacioppo, J. T., Petty, R. E., Feinstein, J. A., & Jarvis, W. B. G. (1996). Dispositional differences in cognitive motivation: The life and times of individuals varying in Need for Cognition. *Psychological Bulletin, 119,* 197–253.

Cacioppo, J. T., Petty, R. E., & Kao, C. F. (1984). The efficient assessment of Need for Cognition. *Journal of Personality Assessment, 48,* 306–307.

Costa, P. T., & McCrae, R. R. (1992). *Revised NEO personality inventory (NEO-PI-R) and NEO five-factor inventory (NEO-FFI) professional manual.* Odessa, FL: Psychological Assessment Resources.

Ennis, R., & Weir, I. (1985). *Critical thinking essay test.* Pacific Grove, CA: Midwest Publications.

Fischer, S. C., & Spiker, V. A. (2000). *A framework for critical thinking research and training.* (Report Prepared for the U. S. Army Research Institute, Alexandria, VA)

Fong, G. T., Krantz, D. H., & Nisbett, R. E. (1986). The effects of statistical training on thinking about everyday problems. *Cognitive Psychology, 18,* 253–292.

Greenfield, P. M. (1997). You can't take it with you: Why ability assessments don't cross cultures. *American Psychologist, 52,* 1115–1124.

Halpern, D. F. (1994). A national assessment of critical thinking skills in adults: Taking steps toward the goal. In A. Greenwood (Ed.), *The national assessment of college student learning: Identification of the skills to be taught, learned, and assessed* (pp. 24–64). Washington, DC: U.S. Department of Education, National Center for Education Statistics.

Halpern, D. F. (1998). Teaching critical thinking for transfer across domains: Dispositions, skills, structure training, and metacognitive monitoring. *American Psychologist, 53,* 449–455.

Halpern, D. F. (2003). *Thought and knowledge: An introduction to critical thinking (4th ed.).* Mahwah, NJ: Lawrence Erlbaum Associates.

Herrnstein, R. J., Nickerson, R. S., de Sanchez, M., & Swets, J. A. (1986). Teaching thinking skills. *American Psychologist, 41,* 1279–1289.

Hunt, E. B. (1995). *Will we be smart enough?* New York: Russell Sage.

Jacobs, S. (1999). The equivalence of Forms A and B of the California Critical Thinking Skills Test. *Measurement & Evaluation in Counseling & Development, 31,* 211–222.

Jepson, C., Krantz, D. H., & Nisbett, R. E. (1993). Inductive reasoning: Competence or skill? In R. E. Nisbett, (Ed.). *Rules for reasoning* (pp. 70–89). Hillsdale, NJ: Lawrence Erlbaum Associates.

Jones, E. A., Hoffman, S., Moore, L. M., Ratcliff, G., Tibbetts, S., & Click, B. A. (1995). *National assessment of college student learning: Identifying college graduates' essential skills in writing, speech and listening, and critical thinking. (NCES 95-001)*. Washington, DC: U.S. Government Printing Office.

Kosonen, P., & Winne, P. H. (1995). Effects of teaching statistical laws on reasoning about everyday problems. *Journal of Educational Psychology, 87*, 33–46.

Loo, R., & Thorpe, K. (1999). A psychometric investigation of scores on the Watson-Glaser Critical Thinking Appraisal new forms. *Educational & Psychological Measurement, 59*, 995–1004.

Lovett, M. C., & Greenhouse, J. B. (2000). Applying cognitive theory to statistics instruction. *The American Statistician, 54*, 196–209.

Messer, W. S., & Griggs, R. A. (1989). Student belief and involvement in the paranormal and performance in introductory psychology. *Teaching of Psychology, 16*, 187–191.

National Education Goals Panel. (1991). *The national education goals report: Building a nation of learners*. Washington, DC: U.S. Printing Office.

Nisbett, R. E. (1993). *Rules for reasoning*. Hillsdale, NJ: Lawrence Erlbaum Associates.

Paas, F. G. W. C. (1992). Training strategies for attaining transfer of problem-solving skill in statistics: A cognitive-load approach. *Journal of Educational Psychology, 84*, 429–434.

Perkins, D. N., & Grotzer, T. A. (1997). Teaching intelligence. *American Psychologist, 52*, 1125–1133.

U.S. Department of Education, National Center for Education Statistics. (2000). *The NCES sourcebook on assessment. Vol. 1: Definitions and assessment methods for critical thinking, problem solving, and writing*. (NCES 2000-172). Prepared by T. Dary Erwin for the Council of the National Postsecondary Education Cooperative Student Outcomes Pilot Working Group: Cognitive and intellectual development. Washington, DC: U.S. Government Printing Office.

Watson, G., & Glaser, E. M. (1980). *Critical thinking appraisal*. New York: Psychological Corporation.

Wesp, R., & Montgomery, K. (1998). Developing critical thinking through the study of paranormal phenomena. *Teaching of Psychology, 25*, 275–278.

Western Washington University. Validity study of three national tests: A general report. Retrieved November 2, 2001 from http://www.ac.wwu.edu/~assess/

VI

NEW DIRECTIONS IN ENHANCEMENT

16

▼▼▼▼▼▼▼

Nutrition and Intellectual Development

David Benton
University Of Wales Swansea

"Can intelligence be increased?" Although psychologists will naturally consider psychological means of enhancing human intelligence, an alternative approach, the improvement of diet, has arguably as much potential.

Pollitt (1990) commented that: "Educational policy-makers and planners have, for the most part, overlooked nutrition and health as determinants of school entry and attainment....rarely is there recognition that a major improvement of school efficiency could come about by improving learning potential through the child's health and nutritional status" (p. 13). Potentially diet can influence many measures of psychological functioning, including mood, memory, the ability to sustain attention and intellectual functioning. In the present chapter only some of the many possible roles played by diet in infants, children, and the aging adult, are considered.

To a considerable extent the ability to use improved diet to enhance intelligence will reflect the adequacy of the existing diet. Although most attention is directed to those with the luxury of a Western diet, it is appropriate initially to acknowledge that hundreds of millions of children, in many parts of the world, are malnourished if not starving. Solving the problem of world poverty would stimulate intellectual functioning on a grand scale. Apart from protein-calorie malnutrition, clinical deficiencies of particular nutrients, including iron, iodine, vitamin A, and zinc, occur commonly.

NUTRITION IN THE DEVELOPING WORLD

Protein-Energy Malnutrition

In the developing world protein-energy malnutrition is the most common nutritional problem. Measures such as weight for age, height for age, and weight for height, are used as indications of past nutrition. As a generalization those who are currently well fed, and have a history of better nutrition, produce better scores on cognitive tests and perform better in school. Such observations, however, fail to distinguish the impact of diet from the many correlates of poverty: a history of disease; infestation; poor if any schooling; low birth weight; parents who are apathetic due to their own malnutrition.

The study of the influence of malnutrition on development produces many problems. It is difficult to distinguish the relative importance of various nutrients and whether there are critical periods when their absence has a lasting influence.

Based on animal studies it has been suggested that when malnutrition occurs during the period of myelination the development of the brain is most retarded (Davison & Dobbings, 1966). Kaplan (1972) reviewed studies where postmortems were carried out on malnourished children. In a study of 16 poor Jamaican children who had died before the age of 2 all had a low number of brain cells. Even in the United States the brains of babies who died in the first 48 hours of life were found to be 15% smaller if they had been born to poor rather than richer parents (Naeye, Diener, & Dellinger, 1969). It appears that all areas of the brain are similarly adversely affected by malnutrition.

One possibility taken when considering the impact of malnutrition is to take a retrospective approach. For example, Nigerian children aged 9 to 10 years were traced, if hospital records reported that they had suffered with Kwashiorkor (low protein and moderately low calorie intake) in the first 3 years of life. Their performance on an intelligence test was poorer than their brothers and sisters, and poorer than children from similar backgrounds who had not been severely malnourished (Nwuga, 1977). These types of study have many problems as they are nonexperimental and it is very difficult to establish the nature of the diet and the length of time when it was severely deficient. Allowing for the problems, the review of Barrett and Frank (1987) concluded that such studies "strongly suggest that early malnutrition has long-term and adverse consequences."

A much better experimental design is to randomly allocate children to groups that receive different types of dietary supplement. When they reviewed this type of approach, Barrett and Frank (1987) concluded that all of the studies they considered "demonstrated significant effects of protein-energy supplementation on behavioral developments."

Iron

Iron-deficiency anemia is the world's most common single nutrient deficiency. In developing countries an association has been reported repeatedly between iron deficiency, poorer school performance, and tests of intellectual ability: "iron deficiency affects selective learning aptitudes required in the classroom such as concentration and the appropriate selection of information (Pollitt, 1990 p 43). Iron deficiency is, however, also the most common nutritional problem in industrialized countries. In the United States, among poor African American and Hispanic babies, the rate of anemia is as high as 20% to 24% (Pollitt, 1994). In the United Kingdom, iron supplementation increased the growth rate of iron-deficient infants (Aukett, Parks, Scott, & Wharton 1986).

Although an association between iron deficiency and poorer performance on intelligence tests has been reported, the actual mechanism may not be straightforward. Infants with iron-deficient anemia have been found to differ on a number of measures from those with good iron status (Lozoff et al., 1998). They were less playful, tended to stay with their caregiver, showed less pleasure in their surroundings, and displayed a poorer ability to sustain attention. It is an obvious suggestion that such a pattern of behavior would result in less intellectual stimulation.

The adverse effects of iron deficiency that are not severe enough to result in anemia, has been little studied. There are large amounts of iron found in the brain but it is possible that in times of shortage the use of iron for the manufacture of hemoglobin takes priority. A study in Ireland reported that children with low levels of ferritin, the iron storage protein, who were not anemic, performed worse on a test of nonverbal intelligence (Lynn & Harland, 1998).

In this area ideally we need two groups that are similar in all respects other than iron status, a characteristic that is impossible to achieve as one risk factor is often correlated with another. Those researching in the developing world have a growing body of evidence suggestive of an association between poor iron status and intellectual functioning (Pollitt, 1990), although the many correlates make interpretation difficult.

Iodine

Iodine deficiency disorders are among the world's most common nutritional problems as it has been estimated that they afflict over one billion people (Delange, 1994). The only confirmed function of the trace element iodine is the role played in the synthesis of thyroid hormones that play a critical role in the metabolism of all cells and in the early growth of most organs, in particular the brain. Brain development in humans is particularly rapid in the fetus and in the first 18 months of life. A deficit of iodine and/or thyroid hormone during this critical period will result in irreversible damage to the brain.

A lack of iodine during a critical period in brain development, the end of the first trimester, and the early part of the second trimester of gestation, is associated with cretinism. However, cretinism will be apparent in only about 5% of a population, even when there is a serious lack of iodine in the diet. In those who appear normal there is some evidence that psychological functioning will be compromised. In China it has been calculated that in areas with severe iodine deficiency there is a loss of 10 to 15 IQ points in those who are apparently normal (Tai, 1997). In Papua New Guinea, performance on tests of visual perception and motor control was better in children, aged 10 to 11 years, if their mothers had higher levels of thyroid hormones in their blood during pregnancy (Pharoah, Connoly, Ekins, & Harding, 1984). Similarly there are general problems of psycho motor coordination (Azizi et al., 1993; Bleichrodt, Drenth, & Querido, 1980) and hearing (Wang & Yang, 1985) that respond to iodine supplementation during childhood.

It is clear that in areas of low iodine, there are serious implications for intellectual development, schooling, and economic development.

Vitamin A

Vitamin A deficiency is the leading cause of childhood blindness in developing countries. It has been estimated that between 190 and 240 million children have either subclinical or clinical problems (Sommer & West, 1996). Vitamin A has a role in vision and is particularly important during periods of rapid growth, both during pregnancy and in early childhood. A metaanalysis of eight vitamin A intervention trials reported a decrease of 23% in mortality (Beaton, Martorell, & L'Abbe, 1992).

There is clear evidence that severe vitamin A deficiency can impair the visual system (Sommer, 1982). With more severe and prolonged deficiency the eye becomes dry; small foamy spots form over the conjintival surface, so called Bitot's spots; ulcers may develop. Total blindness may result with the need for special schooling. There is no study that has considered the impact of night-blindness on the social and psychological development of children.

Zinc

Zinc plays a central role in the growth of cells and is involved with the activity of over 200 enzymes, in particular those necessary for the synthesis of RNA and DNA. It is found in high levels in the brain where it plays both structural and functional roles (Black, 1998). In animals, severe zinc deficiency during the period of brain growth has a similar impact to protein-energy malnutrition; animals display increased emotionality, decreased appetite, reduced activity, and disrupted memory and attention (Golub, Keen, Gershwin, & Hendricks 1995).

In human studies there is a need to distinguish the age when zinc supplements were given. There is evidence that zinc may have an impact when given to the mother, or when it is added to the milk and fed to the newborn. In Canada low birthweight babies were randomly allocated to a baby formula with or without a zinc supplement. Their development was assessed at 3, 6, 9, and 12 months. Those with the additional zinc grew more quickly and displayed better motor development. (Friel et al., 1993). Similarly, low zinc status has been associated with decreased activity in Indian children (Sazawal et al., 1996) and poorer attention in Egyptian infants (Kirksey, Wachs, & Yunis, 1993). It seems possible that any influence of zinc may prove to be mediated via changes in activity or emotionality.

In contrast in older children there is less evidence that zinc supplementation is beneficial. Zinc supplementation of 5 to 7 year old boys, for 12 months, did not influence attention span or taste acuity, although a subgroup pf boys with low hair zinc levels responded with increased growth. A study of Chinese children, aged 6 to 9 years, for the first time reported that a zinc supplement improved neuropsychological functioning (Penland et al., 1997). This study also found that zinc when combined with a range of micronutrients had the largest influence on the growth rate.

NUTRITION IN INDUSTRIALIZED COUNTRIES

Perinatal Diet

As early as 1929 Hoefer and Hardy reported that breast-fed rather than the formula-fed infants displayed more rapid cognitive development, a report that has been replicated on many occasions. Although in itself a robust observation, its interpretation is controversial. As infants are not allocated randomly to their method of feeding the possibility arises that it is not the nature of the diet that is important but rather some correlate. Mothers who choose to breast-feed are on average more intelligent, better educated, more affluent, less likely to smoke, and come from smaller families (Statement, 1994). Perhaps the decision to breast-feed reflects a systematic attitude and preoccupation with childrearing that will result in a multitude of differences in childrearing style. The act of breast-feeding itself may favor cognitive development. Breast-feeding involves more physical contact and mothers speak more to their child when breast rather than bottle-feeding. Lactating women have higher levels of prolactin and oxytocin, hormones known to trigger feelings of calmness and reduce maternal stress. Thus the act of breast-feeding, rather than the milk itself, could potentially facilitate mother–child bonding.

Clearly the possible influence of breast-milk needs to be distinguished from this range of correlates, all of which potentially influence the rate of development.

TABLE 16.1

The Cognitive Development at Different Ages of Children Either Breast- or Formula-Fed

AGE	BREAST-FED Sample size	FORMULA-FED Sample size	SUPERIORITY OF BREAST-FEEDING
6–23 months	2283	1169	+3.11
2–5 years	3674	5166	+2.53
6–9 years	1575	1461	+3.01
10-15 years	1116	4120	+3.19

Note. The data are from the meta-analysis of Anderson et al. (1999).

One approach is to try to statistically control for important covariates. Whereas some studies found that the nature of diet was unimportant when account was made for appropriate variables (Pollock, 1989; Jacobson & Jacobson, 1992), others reported that breast-feeding was still beneficial after this type of control (Morley, Cole, Powell, & Lucas, 1988; Rogan & Gladen, 1993; Florey et al., 1995). This inconsistency of finding encouraged Anderson, Johnstone, and Remley (1999) to perform a metaanalysis of 11 studies that met their inclusion criteria. They distinguished 15 characteristics that were correlated with the likelihood of breast-feeding and included a study in the metaanalysis if at least five of these were included as covariates. Initially those who had been breast-fed had an advantage of 5.32 points, a figure that declined to 3.98 points when taking account of the covariates. The conclusion of the metaanalysis was that "after adjustment for appropriate key cofactors, breast-feeding was associated with significantly higher scores for cognitive development than was formula feeding" (p. 531).

Table 16.1 summarizes the data depending on the stage at which cognitive functioning was assessed. A benefit of breast-feeding was apparent as early as 6 to 23 months of age and a benefit of similar magnitude was still apparent after 10 to 15 years. The impression gained from such data is that the augmentation gained from breast-feeding is established at an early stage and persists at least until the mid-teenage years. Although long-term data are rare, a study in the United kingdom measured the IQ of 994 elderly subjects, born between 1920 and 1930, whose feeding as infants was known. After appropriate controls were taken into account no association between feeding method and IQ was found (Gale & Martyn, 1996).

Table 16.2 presents similar data depending on the duration of breast-feeding. Breast-feeding for less than 8 weeks was without effect, although after this time as the duration of breast-feeding increased so did the relative benefit in terms of cognitive performance. The meta-analysis also concluded that the benefit from breast-feeding was greater in babies with a low birthweight. Compared with formula-fed infants those with a low birthweight had an average benefit of 5.18 points when breast-fed whereas those of normal weight benefited to the extent of only 2.66 points.

Another review suggested that we should not see breast-feeding as a dichotomous variable but consider the length of time it occurred and the daily dose of milk. As many studies have included in the same category infants exclusively and partially breast-fed, it is possible that the suggested impact of breast-feeding has been diluted. Drane and Logemann (2000) found that studies that distinguished exclusively breast-fed babies reported greater IQ advantages than those that did not. The advantage in term-infants was in the order of two to five IQ points, whereas it was eight points for those of low-birth weight.

TABLE 16.2
The duration of breast-feeding and its effect on cognitive development

DURATION OF BREAST FEEDING	BREAST-FED Sample size	FORMULA-FED Sample size	SUPERIORITY OF BREAST-FEEDING
4–7 weeks	2609	8413	−0.71
8–11 weeks	3070	10198	5.84
12–19 weeks	2458	9569	5.72
20–27 weeks	1232	2767	6.50
>28 weeks	2910	1840	4.82

Note. The data are from the meta-analysis of Anderson et al. (1999).

Even with the benefits of metaanalysis this remains a topic that is difficult to interpret. There is always the possibility that covariates that are poorly assessed, or are even as yet unrecognized, play an important role. However, the finding that the benefits are greater in those with lower birth weights, and those who consumed breast-milk for a longer period, suggests that the structure of the brain is influenced.

The major problem with the data summarized by Anderson et al. (1999) in their metanalysis is that the validity of observational studies, no matter how well controlled, is restricted by the potential (unknown) if not actual biases associated with the choice of the method of infant feeding. Although a rare design, considerable benefits result when children are randomly allocated to the consumption of either breast-milk or cows' milk-based formula. In such studies there is no concern about the correlates of the decision to breast-feed. Lucas, Morley, Cole, and Gore (1994) assessed Bayley psychomotor and mental development indices at 18 months in premature infants who were randomly assigned to consume expressed breast-milk or an enriched preterm formula. Although the donor milk was of lower nutritional content the development of the children was similar to those consuming the preterm formula. In contrast those randomly offered a standard term formula, less nutritious than the preterm formula, performed more poorly than those either consuming the enriched preterm formula, or breast-milk, consumed on average for 1 month. These data very strongly suggested that the nature of diet, at least in preterm infants, influences the rate of development. As the diet was allocated randomly, and was delivered by nasogastric tube in all cases, the possible confounding factors associated with either choosing to breast-feed, or the act of breast-feeding, are removed. Verbal and total intelligence, measured using the Wechsler Intelligence Scale for Children, was poorer at 7 1/2 to 8 years in boys, but not girls, who had received at birth the standard rather than enriched cow-milk based formula (Lucas, Morley, & Cole, 1998). Thus early diet can have long-term consequences although it is unclear why the male brain is more susceptible to inadequate nutrition. It is equally unclear whether the data of Lucas et al. (1994, 1998) can be generalized from the preterm babies used in these studies to full-term infants. We must await relevant data from full-term children before drawing conclusions about the majority of the population.

The view that cognitive functioning benefits from breast-feeding is not universally accepted as it is a topic where unequivocal data are difficult to collect. However, although researchers may agree that a conclusive statement awaits the results of future studies, the parent with a newborn child requires immediate guidance and the best available advice, even if with the passing of time this may change. Assuming that the mother is capable, the decision to breast-feed will do no harm and even if it does not help intellectual development it will bring other benefits. Arguably the burden of proof should be for those who advocate bottle-feeding to demonstrate that it is at least equivalent to breast-feeding.

If you suspect that breast-feeding is associated with developmental advantages the question of possible mechanisms arises. The presence of long chain polyunsaturated fatty acids (LC-PUFA) in human milk, but not cow's-milk based formula, has attracted attention given the possible developmental advantages of breast-feeding.

Fatty Acids and the Nervous System.   Lipids account for about 50% to 60% of the dry weight of the brain, of which a large proportion comprises of PUFAs. Arachidonic acid (AA) is the major omega-6 fatty acid, and docsohexaenonic aicd (DHA) the major omega-3 fatty acid in the brain. When compared with the rest of the body, the grey matter of the cortex, and the retina, contains a high level of DHA, in fact it is about a third of the total fatty acids in the brain. The ratio between omega-3 and omega-6 fatty acids in the brain is characteristic of the brain and similar in a wide range of species. In fact DHA is scarce in non-neural tissue. PUFAs are found primarily in phospholipid membranes rather than in storage lipids. Many cells in the brain have a large surface area; that is there is a large area of cell membrane. Cell membranes are highly selective barriers that contain specific pumps and gates that allow the passage of molecules and ions. The nature of the cell membrane plays a central role in bodily communication; the nature of the fatty acids determines its "fluidity" and thus the ease with which substances pass into the cell.

As the levels of PUFAs increase rapidly during the intrauterine and early postnatal period, the question arises as to whether their availability influences the structural development of the infant brain. Is there a critical period of rapid development during which the provision of PUFAs influences the structure of the brain?

Unlike plants, animals are unable to insert double bonds at the n-3 and n-6 position, and, for example, are unable to synthesize DHA. A so-called essential fatty acid is essential in the sense that it must be part of the diet as it cannot be manufactured in the body. Oily fish, for example, have high levels of DHA and can efficiently reverse a deficiency. The possibility that omega-3 fatty acids are necessary for the optimal development of the infant nervous system had led to concern that the cow's-milk-based formulas may be deficient in fatty acids. It had been found that formula-fed infants have lower levels of plasma and tissue DHA than those consuming breast-milk (Carlson, Rhodes, & Ferguson, 1986; Heird, 2001). In formula rather than breast-fed infants, postmortem brain tissue from infants who died in the first year of life was lower in DHA (Farquharson, Cockburn, Patrick, Jamieson & Logan, 1992 Mekride, Neumann, Byard, Simmer & Gibson, 1994). The significance of this observation is unclear as the levels of DHA associated with normal functioning have not been established.

However, the fact that breast-milk and formula differ in many ways other than LC-PUFAs (e.g., hormones) meant that without other data you could not conclude that fatty acids account for the benefits of breast-feeding. The way forward was to compare cow's-milk-based formulas with or without added LC-PUFA supplements. If LC-PUFAs were critical, infants fed with such a supplement should have better visual, motor, and cognitive development. Early studies on preterm infants fed formula supplemented with fish oil, that provided DHA but not arachidonic acid, as now recommended, suppressed growth; for example head circumference was reduced (Carlson, Cooke, Werkman, & Tooley, 1992; Carlson, Ford, Werkman, Peeples, & Koo, 1996; Montalto, Mimouni, & Sentipal-Woletius, 1996).

The high levels of DHA in the retina are selectively retained within the retinal photoreceptors suggesting that its intake may influence visual acuity. Whereas some studies have reported that the DHA supplementation of infants improved visual acuity (Birch, Hoffman, Uauy, Birch, & Prestidge, 1998; Carlson et al., 1996), others have reported no differences (Auestad et al., 1997; Innis, Nelson, Ford, Lwanga, Rioux, & Waslen, 1996). These differences have been explained as either a reflection of the measure of visual acuity that was used, or, alternatively, the nature and amount of the LC-PUFA used as a supplement. Heird (2001) noted that most, but not all, studies that reported no significant effect on visual acuity used a control formula with a high level of alpha-linolenic acid. Metaanalysis found that both human milk and DHA-supplementation was advantageous compared with unsupplemented formula (San Giovanni, Berkey, Dwyer, & Colditz, 2000). They concluded that in full-term infants dietary omega-3 intake was associated with better visual acuity as judged behaviorally at 2 months and at 4 months of age using electrophysiological measures. There is an impression that the benefits decrease with age and whether these effects offer any lasting advantage is being questioned. However, those with omega-3 deficiency due to metabolic problems have visual deficits that respond to omega-3 fatty acid supplementation (Martinez, 1996).

Thus some have assumed that omega-3 fatty acids act by influencing the rate of development of the visual system and that after a catch-up period any differences disappear. Although a plausible explanation, Neuringer (2000) cautioned against assuming that this was the only possibility as there is much evidence that early visual experience can critically influence functioning in later life. She argued that as the organization of the visual cortex is determined by inputs received during the early postnatal period the possibility should be considered that there maybe consequences in later life.

When turning to the influence of DHA-supplementation on cognitive development the comments of Heird (2001) should be kept in mind. Few studies of term infants have data beyond the first year of life. Even if significant, early estimates of cognitive development poorly predict later scores. In most studies the sample sizes have been so small that Power Statistics would predict negative findings given any likely degree of improvement.

When children who have and have not consumed LC-PUFA supplemented formulas have been compared the data are inconsistent. Some show lower and others higher cognitive scores with supplementation (Makrides, Neuman, Simmer, Pater & Gibson, 1995; Carlson, Werkman, Peeples, & Wilson 1994; Carlson, Ford, Werkman, Peeples, Koo, 1996; 1996). To date there is only one published study of term infants that used a sample of an appropriate size (Lucas et al., 1999). For the first 6 months of life, randomly term infants were offered an unsupplemented formula or one to which DHA and AA (0. 32% and 0.3% of total fatty acids) had been added as purified egg phospholipid. At 18 months neither the Bayley mental nor psychomotor developmental indices differed significantly. The possibility that there may be some longer term benefit needs to be considered in due course.

A review of the existing studies concluded that there is little evidence from randomised trials that LC-PUFA supplementation confers any benefit on visual or cognitive development. In addition There are no data from randomised trials that to indicate that LC-PUFA supplements influence the growth of term infants (Simmer, 2001).

LC-PUFA Supplementation of Lactating Women.   The supplementation of breast-feeding mother with LC-PUFAs increased the DHA content of human milk (Makrides, Neuman, & Gibson 1996) that in turn correlated with the plasma phospholipid levels in the infant (Jensen, Maude, Anderson, & Heird, 2000). When breast-feeding women received doses of DHA that varied from 0 to 1.3 g/day, the level of DHA in the milk and plasma increased in a dose-dependent manner. The levels in infant blood peaked when the DHA in breast milk was about 0.8% of total fatty acids (Makrides et al., 1996). However, enriching the mother's milk by this means did not influence visual functioning (Gibson, Neuman, & Makrides, 1997). The level of erythrocyte DHA predicted the Bayley mental development index at 1 but not 2 years of age (Gibson et al., 1997), raising the question as to whether there is a long-term benefit. In a second study breast-feeding mothers randomly received DHA supplements for 4 months although no differences in either visual acuity or behavior was found in their offspring at either 4 or 8 months of age (Jensen, Llorente & Voigt, 1999).

In summary, there is good evidence that DHA supplements prevent the decrease of DHA levels in the milk, and the plasma of the infant, that may be associated with prolonged breast-feeding. Although the data are limited these low levels of DHA have not been associated with adverse consequences.

Conclusions Concerning Breast-Feeding

In summary, many studies have found higher cognitive scores and visual acuity in breast-fed babies, although as the majority of studies have not randomly allocated the type of feeding, at least in part demographic factors may account for the differences. The evidence in preterm babies that breast milk promotes neurodevelopment is more compelling (Lucas et al., 1994). However, it is unclear to what extent LC-PUFAs are responsible for any benefits associated with breast-feeding. DHA supplementation appears to have a short-term effect on visual acuity but the long-term influence, if any, is unknown. The small scale of the trials of the impact of DHA on cognitive development to a large extent precludes a conclusion. A large study produced negative findings, although it was concluded that such a finding did not preclude differences at an older age (Lucas et al., 1999).

Although there is biochemical evidence that more DHA is incorporated into the brains of breast-fed babies (Farquharson et al.,1992; Makrides et al., 1994) its clinical significance is uncertain. There is no consensus concerning the DHA intake needed to saturate tissue membranes. In fact, there is no clear indicator of sufficiency or deficiency. Although the level of DHA supplied by mother's milk has been suggested to represent an optimal intake (FAO/WHO, 1994) and has been the basis on which recommended levels have been established, the levels vary geographically and with ethnic background. There is need to explore the level, duration, and timing of the supply of DHA and to consider its influence over a number of years. Although the evidence of an advantage from breast-feeding in term babies is less than for its advantage in preterm or small-for-age babies, in future the use of a wider range of neuropsychological tests may distinguish more subtle effects.

MICRONUTRIENT SUPPLEMENTATION AND INTELLIGENCE

Benton (2001) reviewed the effects, in double-blind placebo-controlled studies, of vitamin/mineral supplementation on the intelligence of children in industrialized countries. For example, Benton and Roberts (1988) reported that the giving of a mineral/vitamin supplement, to 12-year-old children for 8 months, increased scores on a nonverbal but not a verbal intelligence test. Although this finding has been replicated (Benton & Buts, 1990; Benton & Cook, 1991; Schoenthaler, Amos, Doraz, Kelly, & Wakefield, 1991, Schoenthaler, Bier, Young, Nichols, & Jansenns, 2000) there are also negative reports (Crombie et al., 1990;

Nelson, Naismith, Burley, Gatenby, & Geddes, 1990). In 10 out of 13 studies a positive response has been reported, always with nonverbal measures, in at least a subsection of the experimental sample. A selective response to nonverbal tests was predicted as they reflect basic biological functioning that could be expected to be influenced by diet. A possible explanation of the inconsistencies in the area is that not all children respond to supplementation, rather there is a minority who benefit, whose diet offers low amounts of micronutrients. Such observations are consistent with dietary surveys that typically report a subset of children with a low intake.

A Belgian study gave school-children either a multivitamin/mineral supplement, or a placebo, for 5 months (Benton & Buts, 1990). Although not all children responded, boys who ate diets supplying fewer vitamins and minerals scored significantly better on a nonverbal intelligence test following supplementation. The majority of those who responded to supplementation came from schools for the less academically able, in less economically privileged areas. Clearly the choice of subjects was critical. The data from the largest study of the topic were inconsistent; those taking micronutrients at 100% of the recommended daily amount responded to supplementation, but those taking either 50% or 200% did not (Schoenthaler, Amos, Eysenck, Peritz, & Yudkin, 1991). The answer became apparent after several years, when frozen blood samples were analyzed (Eysenck & Schoenthaler, 1997). The children who had responded to supplementation with changes in nonverbal intelligence were found to have had significantly greater increases in micronutrient status. The reason that the children responded to 100% of the RDA was that, by chance, they were more poorly nourished. Those who were well nourished did not respond.

The data relating nutrient status to the response to supplementation are limited, however, they suggest an approach with the potential to account for the inconsistencies in this area. The suggestion is not that micronutrient supplementations improves intelligence but rather that a poor diet can have an adverse effect.

Benton (2001) concluded that the topic was at a very early stage and needed the clarification gained from a series of large-scale studies that consider children of a wide range of ages, dietary styles, and social backgrounds. The nutrients and dosage required should be established. What is it that is missing from the diet, a little bit of everything or are particular nutrients important? Are other aspects of psychological functioning disrupted as well as nonverbal intelligence? Is the phenomenon more likely to occur at some stages of development rather than others? What proportion of children have an inadequate diet? These are questions that we have not begun to consider, never mind answer.

Thiamine

There is some evidence for the importance of specific nutrients, for example, thiamine.

In the United States, Harrell (1946) examined 120 children who lived together on a farm that was used as an orphanage in the United States. They ate the same diet that was estimated to supply 1 mg of thiamine a day. The WHO recommended daily allowance for children aged 10 to 12 is 1 mg a day for boys, and 0.9 mg for girls, so the diet was believed to supply an adequate amount of thiamine. Under a doubleblind procedure the children took either a placebo, or 2 mg thiamine, each day for a year. There were remarkable improvements. Those taking the thiamine rather than the placebo were significantly taller, had better eyesight, quicker reaction times, and scored better on tests of memory and intelligence. The status of such an isolated study, carried out half a century ago, is uncertain, although it raises the interesting possibility that at least some children would benefit today in a similar manner. There are data suggesting that the thiamine status of some British adults adversely influences mood (Benton, Griffiths, & Haller, 1997; Benton, Haller, & Fordy, 1995).

NUTRITION IN THE ELDERLY AND COGNITIVE DECLINE

Although early development has attracted attention, there is no reason to believe that diet may not have an influence throughout the life span. Antioxidants protect cells against oxidative damage by destroying single oxygen molecules (also called free radicals). Antioxidants are essential to good health and are found naturally in a wide variety of foods including many fruits and vegetables. Antioxidants commonly consumed as supplements include beta carotene, vitamin C, vitamin E, and selenium. Although supplements of these micronutrients have been used for their antioxidant properties, it is not clear whether they provide the same benefits as when they occur naturally in foods.

As the brain consumes a large amount of oxygen it is a good substrate for oxidation, in particular polyunsaturated fatty acids are highly susceptible. In fact it has been frequently proposed that neurodegeneration, for example Alzheimer's disease (Smith, Rottkamp, Nunomura, Raina, & Perry, 2000), results from oxidative stress. In addition there are low concentrations of antioxidants in the brain and a number of areas are rich in the pro-oxidant iron (Launer & Kalmijn,1998). Age-related changes in diet, and the decreased ability to absorb and metabolize antioxidant micronutrients, can lead to the elderly being at particular risk of oxidative damage. In brief, it has been suggested that free radicals in the body are associated with aging and antioxidants in the diet may slow its progress.

A review of the topic concluded that vitamin E may play an important role in maintaining neuronal integrity and preventing cell loss (Cantuti-Castelvetri, Shukitt-Hale, & Joseph, 2000). As vitamin E is the only lipid-soluble, chain- breaking antioxidant found in biological membranes, it was logical to consider whether it plays a role in neurological disorders where oxidative stress has been implicated. In those with Alzheimer's disease vitamin E supplementation for 2 years delayed entry into an institution, death was delayed by an average of 230 days (Sano et al., 1997). In epidemiological studies supplementation has been associated with a slower cognitive decline when vitamin E (median 29.3 mg/day) (La Rue et al., 1997), or both vitamin C and vitamin E, were taken as supplements (Masaki et al., 1994, 2000). However, in this type of study it is unclear to what extent the decision to take supplements is a marker for other health-related behaviors. Oral supplementation of vitamin E (1000 mg/day + 300 mg/day vitamin C) for 12 months improved memory, motor performance, and mood (Sram et al., 1993). Perrig, Perrig, and Stahelin (1997) reported a positive association between the levels of plasma beta-carotene, vitamin C, and memory. In a French study of Alzheimer's patients, although the intake of vitamin C reached accepted levels, plasma levels were low (Riviere, Birlouex-Aragon, Nourhashemi, & Vellas, 1998).

Thus there are several reports that the intake and status of antioxidant vitamins are associated with cognition in the elderly. These limited findings do not constitute a body of evidence that allows the drawing of a firm conclusion. The evidence does, however, encourage future research, the results of which will be examined with interest.

Vitamins other than those with antioxidant actions have been associated with aspects of cognition. An American study found that low levels of vitamin B_{12}, folate, riboflavin, and vitamin C were associated with poor cognitive functioning (Goodwin, Goodwin, & Garry, 1983; La Rue et al., 1997). Alzheimer's patients have often been found to have low serum levels of vitamin B_{12} (Selhub, Bagley, Miller, & Rosenberg, et al., 2000). Although the underlying mechanism is not fully understood, a deficiency of vitamin B_{12}, folate, or both, restricts the synthesis of methionine and S-adenosylmethionine, thus reducing the availability of methyl groups essential for the production of myelin, membrane phospholipids, and some neurotransmitters. A deficiency of folate, vitamin B_{12} or vitamin B_6 is associated with increased levels of plasma homocysteine. Given that homocysteine may damage the walls of blood vessels, cognitive impairment may be mediated through homocysteine-related cerebrovascular lesions (La Rue et al., 1997).

In summary, although there are suggestions that the intake of antioxidant micronutrients maybe associated with a slower rate of cognitive decline, the topic remains to be fully addressed. Questions that need to be considered include the importance of the age at which supplementation is started and the active dose. Aging is a lifelong process and it may well be easier to slow a decline than to reverse it. A 5 year trial maybe too short when considering changes in cognition. Safety is of paramount consideration and the effect of consuming large amounts of vitamins for many years is largely unconsidered. A recommendation, that must be considered to be preliminary until data are available, is that a diet rich in fruits and vegetables, and thus antioxidants, may contribute to the maintenance of cognition and memory. This is a suggestion that reflects the theory that oxidative stress is associated with neural degeneration rather than empirical evidence that such a diet is beneficial. When the dietary intake of antioxidants was estimated in the Rotterdam study a relationship was found between low beta-carotene intake, but not vitamin E and vitamin C intake, and cognitive impairment (Jama et al., 1996). However, the similar Zutphen Elderly Study failed to find an association between antioxidant intake and cognitive functioning (Kalmijn, Feskens, Launer, & Kromhout, 1997), although the measures used were extremely crude and more sensitive measures may have demonstrated more subtle relationships. In conclusion there are preliminary indicators that a diet rich in vegetables and antioxidants may in the future be proved to contribute to rate of cognition decline in the elderly.

DISCUSSION

A frequently discussed question is whether there are critical or sensitive periods in development when we need a certain standard of nutrition. The term critical period implies that when that stage has passed any damage is permanent and cannot be made up by subsequent good nutrition. The idea of a sensitive period implies that there is an optimal period when nutrition has a particular impact; however, at later stages good nutrition still has an influence, although the influence is not as great as during the sensitive stage. A more recent approach is to use a transactional model where both nutrition and environmental stimulation are said to be important. In animals environmental stimulation is able to increase the ability to learn and changes the structure of the brain (Rosenzweig & Bennett, 1972). It is assumed that a stimulating environment may decrease the influence of poor nutrition.

The young of all mammals, particularly humans, have large heads compared to the rest of their body, a reflection of the rapid rate at which the brain develops. The rate of the growth of the human brain is greatest in the last third of pregnancy and the first year of life. At birth a baby is 5% of the adult body weight yet the brain is already 25% of the final weight. At the end of the first year of life 90 to 95% of the adult number of brain cells are present (Ortega Torres, 1988). Clearly such a rapidly growing organ requires a good source of nutrition, and it is reasonable to ask if malnutrition at this time may have long-term, irreversible consequences.

Barrett and Frank (1987) considered the possibility that protein-energy malnutrition might have a more profound influence during the stage of rapid brain development. Human studies preclude an experimental approach. Children are not malnourished for precise periods that are preceded and followed by adequate nutrition. The existing studies produce inconsistent findings. It is unclear whether pre- or postnatal malnutrition plays a greater role, or even whether malnutrition during these stages of brain development has a greater impact than in the older animal.

With some micronutrients, such as iodine and iron, there is support for the view that a deficiency has an impact during a limited critical stage of development, and that a subsequent supply of the nutrient has a limited influence. However, even with the examples of iron or iodine, a deficiency has an impact later in life. In such cases the diet needs to be placed in an environmental context, with stimulation having an important modulating influence. The impact of other nutrients such as thiamine (Harrell, 1946) has been shown to take place long after the critical stage of brain development. Whether thiamine and other micronutrients have a critical role during the stage of brain development has not been considered. It is reasonable to assume that early malnutrition places a child at greater risk, although it is often unclear whether the prenatal or the immediately postnatal period is the more critical.

Firm conclusions are limited but some broad generalizations can be made. Children are susceptible to nutritional stress although different environments may provide protection. It is interesting to consider children who were malnourished because of illness, but never lived in poverty. Such children typically display no lasting intellectual problems (Lloyd-Still, 1976). Rutter (1998) monitored children from Romania who were adopted in Britain. The children were severely deprived; about a half of the sample were below the third percentile for height, weight, and head circumference. At 4 years of age, those who arrived before 6 months of age were of a similar size to British children. The developmental catch-up of those coming after 6 months of age was also impressive, although not as marked as with the younger children.

An impression repeatedly gained is that measures of emotional responsiveness and social interaction are most influenced by dietary problems. A syndrome associated with poor nutrition includes problems of sustaining attention, apathy, decreased persistence, emotionality, decreased activity, curiosity, and initiative. It is easy to see how such a response will help to conserve energy when food is in short supply. It is also easy to see how such a behavioral profile will decrease intellectual stimulation. With such a picture you would expect that slower intellectual development would only be apparent when considered over a long time scale; a time scale longer than that taken with many studies.

Harrell's (1946) study of thiamine supplements illustrates that there is much to learn about the impact of diet on child development. In this study of children who already consumed the level of thiamine recommended by nutritionists, supplementation improved cognitive functioning. It should be remembered that the RDA that is used to assess the adequacy of diet, is intended to avoid a deficiency disease rather than achieve optimal functioning. Although nutritionists have not traditionally used psychological measures to monitor nutritional status, it may be argued that they are a particularly appropriate way of examining the possibility that a subclinical deficiency exists (Benton, 1992). Cognitive tasks involve the summated activity of billions of neurons and countless biochemical pathways and their associated enzymes. It may be that relatively small dietary deficiencies have a measurable and potentially important cumulative influence on the brain, given its complexity. Thus it may be argued that if subclinical deficiencies exist then psychological changes may be one of the first indications. The use of existing RDAs to assess the adequacy of diet may ignore potential benefits from an optimal diet. This comment is speculative and awaits further investigation. When compared with the clinical deficiencies that exist in parts of the developing world such concerns are likely to seem relatively unimportant.

The present review has presented evidence that a poor diet will limit the intellectual development of the child. If clinical deficiencies exist, for example of iron, iodine, or zinc, intellectual functioning will be adversely effected. The suggestion that subclinical deficiencies may exist in industrialized societies, and that psychological functioning is disrupted, is a more controversial suggestion (Harrell, 1946; Benton, 2001). Because of the rapid growth of the brain, infant nutrition has attracted particular attention. There is growing evidence that breast-feeding is beneficial although the mechanism is uncertain. There is more evidence that nutrition has a long-term impact in preterm (Lucas et al., 1994) rather than term infants. The possibility that diet continues to have an impact throughout adulthood into old age is theoretically plausible although difficult to demonstrate over extended periods.

This chapter has done little more than argue that it is reasonable to consider that the nature of diet may potentially either inhibit or enhance intellectual functioning. The clearest examples are those of clinical deficiency, for example of iron or iodine. In those living in industrialized societies, consuming a diet that would be the envy of much of the rest of the world, the effects of minor differences in generally good diets are inevitably at the most subtle. It is an area with obvious methodological problems. For example, the available diet, or the decision to choose particular food items from those available, has many correlates that are in themselves influential. We have more questions than answers but the available data suggests that the questions deserve more attention.

REFERENCES

Anderson, J. W., Johnstone, B. M., & Remley, D. T. (1999). Breast-feeding and cognitive development: A meta-analysis. *American Journal of Clinical Nutrition, 70*, 525–535.

Auestad, N., Montalto, M. B., Hall, R. T., Fitzgerald, K. M., Wheeler, R. E., Connor, W. E., Neuringer, M., Connor, S. L., Taylor, J. A., & Hartmann, E. E. (1997). Visual acuity, erthyrocyte fatty acid composition and growth in term infants fed formulas with long chain polyunsaturated fatty acids for one year. *Pediatric Research, 41*, 1–10.

Aukett, M. A., Parks, Y .A., Scott, P. H., & Wharton, B. A. (1986). Treatment with iron increases weight gain and psychomotor development. *Archives of Disease in Childhood, 61*, 849–57.

Azizi, F., Saarshar, A., Nafarabadi, M., Kimiagar, M., Noohi, S., Rahbar, N., Bahrami, A., & Kalantari, S. (1993). Impairment of neuromotor and cognitive development in iodine-deficient schoolchildren with normal physical growth. *Acta Endocrinologia, 129*, 501–504.

Barrett, D. E., & Frank, D. A. (1987). *The effects of undernutrition on children's behavior.* New York: Gordon & Breach.

Beaton, G. H., Martorell, R., & L'Abbe, K. A. (1992). *Effectiveness of vitamin A supplementation in the control of young child morbidity in developing countries.* Final report to CIDA, Internation Nutrition Program, University of Toronto, Canada.

Benton D. (1992). Vitamin-mineral supplements and intelligence. *Proceedings of the Nutrition Society, 151*, 295–302.

Benton, D. (2001). Micro-nutrient supplementation and the intelligence of children. *NeuroScience and Biobehavioral Reviews, 25*, 297–309.

Benton, D., & Cook, R. (1991). Vitamin and mineral supplements improve the intelligence scores and concentration of six year old children. *Personaity and Individual Differences, 12*, 1151–1991.

Benton D., & Buts, J-P. (1990). Vitamin/mineral supplementation and intelligence. *Lancet, 335*, 1158–60.

Benton, D., Griffiths, R., & Haller, J. (1997). Thiamine supplementation mood and cognitive functioning. *Psychopharmacology, 129*, 66–71.

Benton, D., Haller, J., & Fordy, J. (1995). Vitamin supplementation for one year improves mood. *Neuropsychobiology 32*, 98–105.

Benton, D., & Roberts, G. (1988). Effect of vitamin and mineral supplementation on intelligence of a sample of schoolchildren. *Lancet, 1*, 140–143.

Birch, E. E., Hoffman, D. R., Uauy, R., Birch, D. G., & Prestidge, C. (1998). Visual acuity and the essentiality of docosahexaenoic acid and arachidonic acid in the diet of term infants. *Pediatic Research., 44*, 201–209.

Black, M. M. (1998). Zinc deficiency and child development. *American Journal of Clinical Nutrition, 68* (Suppl.), 464S–469S.

Bleichrodt, N., Drenth, P. J., & Querido, A. (1980). Effects of iodine deficiency on mental and psychomotor abilities. *American Journal of Physical Anthropology, 53*, 55–67.

Cantuti-Castelvetri, I., Shukitt-Hale, B., & Joseph, J. A. (2000). Neurobehavioral aspects of antioxidants in aging. *International Journal of Developmental. Neuroscience, 18*, 367–381.

Carlson, S. E., Cooke, R. J., Werkman, S. H., & Tooley, E. A. (1992). First year growth of preterm infants fed standard compared to marine oil (fish oil) n-3 supplemented formula. *Lipids, 27*, 901.

Carlson, S. E., Rhodes, P. G., & Ferguson, M. G. (1986). Docosahexaenoic acid status of preterm infants at birth and following feeding with human milk or formula. *American Journal of Clinical Nutrition, 44*, 798–804.

Carlson, S. E., Ford, A. J., Werkman, S.H., Peeples, J.M., & Koo, W. W. (1996). Visual acuity and fatty acid status of term infants fed human milk and formulas with and without docosahexaenoate and arachidonate from egg yolk lecithin. *Paediatric Research, 39*, 882–888.

Carlson, S. E., Werkman, S. H., Peeples, J. M., & Wilson, W. M. (1994). Long chain fatty acids and early visual and cognitive development of preterm infants. *European Journal of Clinical Nutrition, 48*, S27–S30.

Carlson, S. E., Werkman, S. H., & Tolley, E. A. (1996). Effect of long chain n-3 fatty acid supplementation on visual acuity and growth of preterm infants with and without bronopulmonary dysplasia. *American Journal of Clinical Nutrition, 63*, 687–697.

Crombie, I. K., Todman, J., McNeill, G., Florey, C. Du V., Menzies, I., & Kennedy, R. A. (1990). Effect of vitamin and mineral supplementation on verbal and non-verbal reasoning of schoolchildren. *Lancet, 335*, 744–747.

Davison, A. N., & Dobbings, J. (1966). Myelination as a vulnerable period in brain development. *British Medical Bulletin, 22*, 40–44.

Delange, F. (1994). The disorders induced by iodine deficiency. *Thyroid, 4*, 107–128.

Drane, D. L., & Logemann, J. A. (2000). A critical evaluation of the evidence on the association between type of infant feeding and cognitive development. *Paediatric and Perinatal Epidemiology, 14*, 349–356.

Eysenck, H. J., & Schoenthaler, S. J. (1997). Raising IQ level by vitamin and mineral supplementation. In: Grigorenko R. J. & Sternberg E. L. (Eds.), *Intelligence heredity and environment* (pp. 363 –392). Cambridge, England: Cambridge University Press.

FAO/WHO (1994). *Food and nutrition paper*. Expert committee on fats and oils in human nutrition. Rome: FAO.

Farquharson, J., Cockburn, F., Patrick, W. A., Jamieson, E. C., & Logan, R. W. (1992). Infant cerebral cortex phospholipid fatty-acid composition and diet. *Lancet, 340*, 810–813.

Florey, C.D., Leech, A. M., & Blackhall, A. (1995). Infant feeding and mental and motor development at eighteen months of age in first born singletens, *International Journal of Epedemiology, 24*, 521–526.

Friel, J. K., Andrews, W. L., Matthew, J. D., Long, D. R., Cornel, A. M., Cox, A. M., McKim, E., & Zerbe, G. O. (1993). Zinc supplementation in very low birth weight infants. *Journal of Pediatric Gastroenterology and Nutrition, 17*, 97–104.

Gale, C. R., & Martyn, C. N. (1996). Breastfeeding, dummy use and adult intelligence. *Lancet, 347*, 1072–1075.

Gibson, R. A., Neumann, M. A., & Makrides, M. (1997). Effect of increasing breast milk docosa-hexaenoic acid on plasma and erythrocyte phospholipid fatty acids and neural indices of exclusively breast fed infants. *European Journal of Clinical Nutrition, 51*, 578–584.

Golub, M. S., Keen, C. L., Gershwin, M. E., & Hendricks, A. G. (1995). Developmental zinc deficiency and behavior. *Journal of. Nutrition. 125*, 2263S–2271S.

Goodwin, J. S., Goodwin, J. M., & Garry, P. J. (1983). Association between nutritional status and cognitive functioning in a healthy elderly population. *Journal of the Medical Association, 249*, 2917–2921.

Harrell, R. F. (1946). Mental responses to added thiamine. *Journal of Nutrition, 31*, 283–298.

Heird, W. C. (2001). The role of polyunsaturated fatty acids in term and preterm infants and breastfeed-ing mothers. *Pediatric Clinics of North America, 48*, 173–188.

Hoefer, C., & Hardy, M. C. (1929). Later development of breast fed and artificially fed infants. *Journal of the American Medical Association, 92*, 615–620.

Innis, S. M., Nelson, C. M., Lwanga, D., Rioux, F. M., & Waslen, P. (1996). Feeding formula without arachidonic acid and docosahexaenoic acid has no effect on prefential looking actuity or recognition memory in healthy full-term infants at 9 months of age. *American Journal of Clinical Nutrition, 64*, 40–46.

Jacobson, S. W. & Jacobson, J. L. (1992). Breast feeding and intelligence. *Lancet, 339*, 926.

Jama, J. W., Launer, L. J., Witteman, J. C., den Breeijen, J. H., Breteler, M. M., Grobbee, D. E., & Hofman, A. (1996). Dietary antioxidants and cognitive function in a population-based sample of older persons. The Rotterdam Study. *American Journal of Epidemiology, 144*, 275–280.

Jensen, C. L., Llorente, A. M., & Voigt, R. G (1999). Effect of maternal docosahexaenoic acid (DHA) supplementation on visual and neurodevelopmental function of breast-fed infants and indices of maternal depression and cognitive interference. *Pediatric Research, 45*, 284.

Jensen, C. L., Maude, M., Anderson, R. E., & Heird, W. C. (2000). Effect of docosahexaenoic acid sup-plementation of lactating women on the fatty acid composition of breast milk lipids and maternal and infant plasma phospholipids. *American Journal Clinical Nutrition, 71* (Suppl.), 292–299.

Kalmijn, S., Feskens, E. J. M., Launer, L. J., & Kromhout, D. (1997). Polysaturated fatty acids, antiox-idants and cognitive function in very old men. *American Journal Epidemiology, 145*, 33–41.

Kaplan, B. J. (1972). Malnutrition and mental deficiency. *Psychological Bulletin, 78*, 321–334.

Kirksey, A., Wachs, T.D., & Yunis, F. (1993). Relation of maternal zinc nutriture to pregnancy outcome and infant development in an Egyptian villiage. *American Journal of Clinical Nutrition, 60*, 782–792.

La Rue, A., Koehler, K. M., Wayne, S. J., Chiulli, S. J., Haaland, K. Y., & Garry, P. J. (1997). Nutritional status and cognitive functioning in a normally aging sample: A 6-year reassessment. *American Journal of Clinical Nutrition, 65*, 20–29.

Launer, L. J., & Kalmijn, S. (1998). Anti-oxidants and cognitive function: A review of clinical and epidemiologic studies. *Journal of Neural Transmission, 53* (Suppl), 1–8.

Lloyd-Still, J. D. (1976). Clinical studies on the effects of malnutrition during infancy on subsequent physical and intellectual development. In J. D. Lloyd-Still, (Ed.), *Malnutrition and mental develop-ment* (pp 103–161). Littleton. MA: Publishing Sciences Group.

Lozoff, B., Klein, N. K., Nelson, E. C., McClish, D. K., Manuel, M., & Chacon, M. E. (1998). Behavior of infants with iron-deficiency anemia. *Child Development, 69*: 24–36.

Lucas, A., Morley, R., & Cole, T. J. (1998). Randomised trial of early diet in preterm babies and later intelligence quotient. *British Medical Journal, 317*, 1481–1487.

Lucas, A., Morley, R., Cole, T. J., & Gore, S. M. (1994). A randomised multicentre study of human milk versus formula and later development in preterm infants. *Archieves of Disease in Childhood, 70*, F141–F146,

Lucas, A., Stafford, M., Morley, R., Abbott, R., Stephenson, T., MacFadyen, U., Elias-Jones, A., & Clements, H. (1999). Efficacy and safety of long-chain polyunsaturated fatty acid supplementation of infant-formula milk: A randomised trial. *Lancet, 354*, 1948–1954.

Lynn, R. & Harland, E. P. (1998). A positive effect of iron supplementation on the IQs of iron deficient children. *Personality and Individual Differences, 24*, 883–885.

Makrides, M., Neumann, M. A., Byard, R. W., Simmer, K., & Gibson, R. A. (1994). Fatty acid composition of brain retina and erythrocytes in breast- and formula-fed infants. *American Journal of Clinical Nutrition, 60,* 189–194.

Makrides, M., Neumann, M. A., & Gibson, R. A. (1996). Effect of maternal docosahexaenoic acid (DHA) supplementation on breast milk composition. *European Journal of Clinical Nutrition, 50,* 352–357.

Makrides, M., Neumann, M. A., Simmer, K., Pater, J., & Gibson, R. (1995). Are long-chain polyunsaturated fatty acids essential nutrients in infancy? *Lancet, 345,* 1463–1468.

Martinez, M. (1996). Docosahexanoic acid therapy in docosahexanoic acid deficient patients with disorders of peroxisomal biogenesis. *Lipids, 31,* S145–152.

Masaki, K. H., Losonczy, K. G., Izmirlian, G., Foley, D. J., Ross, G. W., Petrovitch, H., Havlik, R., & White, L. R. (2000). Association of vitamin E and C supplement use with cognitive function and dementia in elderly men. *Neurology, 28,* 1265–1272.

Masaki, K. H., White, L. R., Petrovitch, H., Ross, G. W., Curb, J. D., Ardo, E., & Grove, J. (1994). The influence of prior and concurrent use of aspirin and vitamins on cognitive function scores in elderly Japanese-American men. *Neurobiology of Aging, (Suppl. 1),* S74.

Montalto, M. B., Mimouni, F. B., & Sentipal-Walerius, J. (1996). Reduced growth in hospital discharged low birth-weight infants fed formulas with added marine oil (fish oil). *Pediatric Research, 39,* 316A.

Morley, R., Cole, T. J., Powell, R., & Lucas, A. (1988). Mother's choice to provide breast milk and developmental outcome. *Archieves of Disorders of Childhood, 63,* 1382–1385.

Naeye, R., Diener, M. M., & Dellinger, W. S. (1969). Urban poverty: Effects on prenatal nutrition. *Science, 166,* 1206.

Nelson, M., Naismith, D. J., Burley, V., Gatenby, S., & Geddes, N. (1990). Nutrient intake vitamin/mineral supplementation and intelligence in British schoolchildren. *British Journal of Nutrition, 64,* 13–22.

Neuringer, M. (2000). Infant vision and retinal function in studies of dietary long-chain polyunsaturated fatty acids: Methods, results and implications. *American Journal of Clinical Nutrition, 71,* 256–267.

Nwuga, V. C. B. (1977). Effect of severe kwashiorkor on intellectual development among Nigerian children. *American Journal of Clinical Nutrition, 30,* 1423–1430.

Ortega Torres, J. (1988). Effect of malnutrition in pregnancy and childhood on early brain development: Methodological, pathophysiological, anthropological and psychological considerations. *Journal Clinical of Nutrition and Gastroenterology, 3,* 69–80.

Penland, J. G., Sandstead, H. H., Alcok, N. W., Dayal, H. H., Chen, X. C., Li, J. S., Zhao, F., & Yang, J. J. (1997). A preliminary report: Effects of zinc and micro-nutrient repletion on growth and neuropsychological function of urban Chinese children. *Journal of the American College of Nutrition, 16,* 268–272.

Perrig, W. J., Perrig, P., & Stahelin, H. B. (1997). The relation between antioxidants and memory performance in the old and very old. *Journal of the American Geriatrics Society, 45,* 718–724.

Pharoah, P. O. D., Connolly, K. J., Ekins, R. P., & Harding, A. G. (1984). Maternal thyroid hormone levels in pregnancy and subsequent cognitive and motor performance of the children. *Clinical Endocrinology, 21,* 265–70.

Pollitt, E. (1990). *Malnutrition and infection in the classroom.* Paris: UNESCO.

Pollitt, E. (1994). Poverty and child development: Relevance of research in developing countries to the United States. *Child Development, 65,* 283–95.

Pollock, J. I. (1989). Mother's choice to provide breast milk and development outcome. *Archieves of Disease in Childhood 64,* 763–764.

Riviere, S., Birlouex-Aragon, I., Nourhashemi, F., & Vellas, B. (1998). Low plasma vitamin C in Alzheimer's patients despite an adequate diet. *International Journal of Geriatric Psychiatry, 13,* 749–754.

Rogan, W. J., Gladen, B. C. (1993). Breast-feeding and cognitive development. *Early-human Development, 31,* 181–193.

Rosenzweig M. R., & Bennett, E. L. (1972). Cerebral changes in rats exposed individually to an enriched environment. *Journal of Comparative Physiological Psychology, 80,* 304–313.

Rutter, M. (1998). Developmental catch-up and deficit following adoption after severe global early privation. *Journal of Child Psychology and Psychiatry, 39*, 465–476.

San Giovanni, J. P., Berkey, C. S., Dwyer, J. T., & Colditz, G. A. (2000). Dietary essential fatty acids long-chain polyunsaturated fatty acids, and visual resolution acuity in healthy fullterm infants: A systematic review. *Early Human Development, 57*, 165–188.

Sano, M., Ernesto, C., Thomas, R. G., Klauber, M. R., Schafer, K., Grundman, M., Woodbury, P., Growdon, J., Cotman, C. W., Pfeiffer, E., Schneider, L. S., & Thal, L. J. (1997). A controlled trial of selegiline, alpha-tocopherol, or both, as treatment for Alzheimer's disease. The Alzheimer's Disease Cooperative Study. *New England Journal of Medicine, 24*, 1216–1222.

Sazawal. S., Bentley M., Black, R. E., Dhingra, P., George, S., & Bhan, M. K. (1996). Effect of Zinc supplementation or., observed activity in low socioeconomic Indian preschool children. *Pediatrics, 98*, 1132–1137.

Schoenthaler, S. J., Amos, S. P., Doraz, W. E., Kelly, M. A., & Wakefield, J. (1991). Controlled trial of vitamin-mineral supplementation on intelligence and brain function. *Personality and Individual Differences, 12*, 343–350.

Schoenthaler, S. J., Amos, S. P., Eysenck, H. J., Peritz, E., & Yudkin, J. (1991). Controlled trial of vitamin-mineral supplementation: Effects on intelligence and performance. *Personality and Individual Differences, 12*, 351–362.

Schoenthaler, S. J., Bier, I., Young, K., Nichols, D., & Jansenns, S. (2000). The effect of vitamin-mineral supplementation on the intelligence of American schoolchildren: A randomized double-blind placebo-controlled trial. *Journal of Alternative and Complementary Medicine, 6*, 19–29.

Selhub, J., Bagley, L. C., Miller, J., & Rosenberg, I. H. (2000). B vitamins, homocysteine and neurocognitive function in the elderly. *American Journal of Clinical Nutrition, 71* (Suppl), 614S–620S.

Simmer, K. (2001). *Longchain polyunsaturated fatty acid supplementation in infants born at term.* The Cochrane Database Systematic Reviews. Issue 4, Article number CD000376.

Smith, M. A., Rottkamp, C. A., Nunomura, A., Raina, A. K., & Perry, G. (2000). Oxidative stress in Alzheimer's disease. *Biochimica et Biophysica Acta, 1502*, 139–144.

Sommer, A. (1982). *Nutritional blindness, xerophthalmia and keratomalacia.* New York. Oxford University Press.

Sommer, A., & West, K. P. (1996). *Vitamin A deficiency, health, survival and vision.* New York. Oxford University Press.

Sram, R. J., Binkova, B., Topinka, J., Kotesoved, F., Fojtikova, I., Hanel, I., Klaschka, J., Kocisova, J., Prosek, M., & Machalek, J. (1993). Effect of anti-oxidant supplementation in an elderly population. *Basic Life Science, 61*, 459–477.

Statement of the Standing Committee on Nutrition of the British Paediatric Association. (1994). Is breast feeding beneficial in the UK? *Archives of Disease of Childhood, 71*, 376–380.

Tai, M. (1997). The devastating consequences of iodine deficiency. *South East Asian Journal Tropical Medicine and Public Health, 28* (Suppl. 2), 75–77.

Wang, Y. Y., & Yang, S. H. (1985). Improvement in hearing among otherwise normal schoolchildren in iodine-deficient areas of Guizhou, China, following use of iodized salt. *Lancet, ii*, 518–520.

17

▼▼▼▼▼▼▼

Challenges and Opportunities for Intelligence Augmentation

Dr. Bradley Rhodes
Ricoh Innovations

Intelligence Enhancement

Intelligence Enhancement is for the mind what an athletic coach is for the body. A coach takes an athlete through exercises and warm-ups to prepare the muscles. In the mental realm, the analogous mind-strengthening exercises include making sure a person gets good nutrition, good sleep, and does his or her thanking in a quiet and stress-free environment. Education in facts and pattern that can be applied to a particular task can also be thought of as ways to strengthen the mental muscle. Beyond strength training, a coach will teach an athlete how to use his or her muscles most effectively. In the physical realm these techniques include breathing techniques, and when to hold back, and when to exert energy. The analogous mental training is in brainstorming, problem solving, and memory techniques.

Intelligence Augmentation

Intelligence Augmentation (IA) is not about improving the mind itself, but rather giving a person tools that help the thinking process. In our analogy, IA is not the athlete's training but rather the athletic shoe that supports and guides the mental muscle. Like athletic shoes, tools for intelligence augmentation are often specific to a given task, environment, and individual.

Douglas Engelbart

The term "intelligence augmentation" was coined over 40 years ago by Dr. Douglas Engelbart, a computer visionary also known for the invention of the mouse, e-mail, teleconferencing, integrated help systems, and interactive hypermedia. Engelbart was interested in tools and techniques that could increase "the capability of a man to approach a complex problem situation, to gain comprehension to suit his particular needs, and to derive solutions to problems" (Engelbart, 1962' p.1). In his general framework he described three kinds of "repertoire" that people use to break down and solve complex problems. The first is what he calls explicit-human process capabilities, which are executed completely within the human mind. The second are explicit-artifact process capabilities, which are capabilities possessed entirely by tools or things and executed without human intervention. The third are composite process capabilities, which are processes that emerge from an interaction between people and artifacts. We are most familar with explicit-human process capabilities; these are the problem-solving skills we use every day. On the other end of the spectrum are the explicit-artifact process capabilities that are task-solving abilities that can be fully and autonomously carried out by artifacts such as computers. The most recent developments in such autonomous systems has been in the field known as "software agents."

Software Agents: Your Faithful Butler.   The motivating metaphor is that a software agent is like a butler. An agent understands your task, knows your likes and dislikes, and will act on your behalf with only minimal instruction (Maes, 1994,) More specifically, software agents are programs that can autonomously act to accomplish tasks for a user within a narrowly defined domain. They tend to be long-lived, running in the background even when not actively interacting with a user. They also tend to be personalized, often learning a profile for a user over time. In order to accomplish these tasks, agents usually have the ability to sense a person's environment (either computational or physical), as well as the ability to sense the actions of the user and of other agents. Software agents, and autonomous processes in general, are especially useful when the tasks requires too much information or attention for a human to process. For example, an agent might watch all the complex sensors in a car and alert the driver when maintenance is required. An agent might also watch the stock market day and night and alert a trader when a stock goes below a preset value. However, agent technology tends to do less well on tasks that require either an intimate knowledge of the user's current mental state, or that require an understanding of the broad context surrounding a task. For example, the Microsoft Office Assistant (otherwise known as "that infernal paper clip") is intended to help MS-Office users when they need it and not interfere otherwise. The agent needs to understand the context of the user's current task to know what information would be useful. It also needs to know the user's goals and motivations to know whether the user actually wants help, and whether the distraction would be worth information given. In spite of the sophisticated pattern recognition techniques used, the MS Office Assistant still makes a wrong prediction all too often. In these cases the agent is no longer the quiet yet effective butler. It instead is the annoying new employee who asks questions every 5 minutes and needs constant supervision. It's no wonder one of the most frequently asked questions of the paper clip is "How do I turn you off?!?" (In all fairness to software agents in geneal, the MS office Assistant suffered from several interface design problems beyond those described in this chapter.)

Intelligence Augmentation: A Prosthesis for the Mind.   Halfway between the entirely human and entirely automated capabilities lies Intelligence Augmentation, where the computer acts as a kind of prosthesis for the mind. The software agent design metaphor works best with zero communications between human and agent, punctuated by the occasional high-bandwidth communication to clarify a goal or to report an end state. The intelligence augmentation on metaphor, on the other hand, is most appropriate when there is a constant low-load communication between human and augmentation. Through this communication the human can provide appropriate context for the actions of the prosthesis, and the prosthesis can provide speed, extra sensors, and extra computational ability that the human may lack. The main challenge in these systems (as is discussed later) is how to minimize the amount of human attention required to maintain this constant communication.

EXAMPLES

Remembrance Agent (Desktop)

The Remembrance Agent (RA) is a system that automatically suggests notes, documents, or e-mails that might be relevant to what a person is currently writing or reading within the Emacs[1] text editor (Rhodes & Maes, 2000a). For example, as this paragraph is being written the RA is showing previously written papers and e-mails that describe the Remembrance Agent (including reviewer comments regarding those papers). These suggestions are continuously displayed and updated, one to a line, in a section at the bottom of the editor window. Given other databases, the RA could show notes, newspaper articles, abstracts from published papers, or any other corpus of text documents. The RA's list of suggestions updates every 5 seconds with suggestions for the documents most relevant at that moment. Long-term studies have shown there are many ways the Remembrance Agent can be valuable. The most significant effect is when a suggestion from the RA changes how the current task is performed. For example, one user of the RA was using it while writing a proposal for a new project. The RA suggested an e-mail describing another project that was very similar to the one he was proposing, and he was saved a great deal of embarrassment by incorporating the other project into his proposal. The RA can also provide supporting material, thus helping a person make stronger arguments. For example, in a controlled study where people were asked to write an essay about housing in the Cambridge, Massachusetts area, several people using the RA remarked that they would write down generalities such as "rent has risen a lot in the past year" and the RA would automatically produce newspaper articles giving the exact percentage of rent increases. Users have also found that information produced by the RA helps contextualize the current task. For example, one student writing a paper for a class found the RA displaying e-mail archives from a previous year's versions of the same class. Although he did not actively use the information in those e-mails, he commented that it was nice to see other people use technical terms the same way he did (Rhodes, 2000b). There are two main technical challenges with the Remembrance Agent. The first is how to determine what information might be valuable, given the text a person is currently reading or writing. The second is how to display that information without driving the reader nuts with constant interruptions and distractions. Both these issues are discussed in the section on challenges facing intelligence augmentation.

Jimminy (Wearable RA). The Remembrance Agent was designed for helping with desktop applications such as e-mail and word processing, but the basic idea of "just-in-time information" can also be applied to the physical world. That is the idea of Jimminy, also known as the "Wearable Remembrance Agent" (Rhodes, 1997). Jimminy ran on a wearable computer: a portable computer with a small 720 x 280 monochrome head-mounted display and one-handed keyboard. The wearable can also be equipped with sensors to determine where the wearer is and to whom he or she is speaking, with the help of radio-frequency beacons placed in rooms and an infrared-transmitting badge system. When beacons or badges were not available, locations and names of people in the area could still be entered by hand using the one-handed keyboard, which allowed between 35 and 60 words-per-minute typing speeds. These wearables were used as a part of a several-year "living experiment" at the MIT Media Lab, where researchers wore the computers and used them in their daily lives. Using the sensor

---

[1]Emacs, a popular Unix text editor, tends to be used for a wide variety of tasks including word processing, e-mail, Usenet, and sometimes even web browsing.

information, any notes taken using the one-handed keyboard would be automatically marked with the time, date, location, and people who were around when the note was taken. Because these computers were research prototypes there was a significant cost to wearing them in terms of size, weight, and certainly fashion sense. However, these costs were up-front; once the system was already being worn it was trivial to take a new note or jot down a new idea. This ease-of-use encouraged frequent notetaking. During the 4 years the author used the system at MIT, over 1,000 notes were taken, ranging in topic from technical conversations to class notes to notes on new dance steps. Jimminy would also show suggestions in the same way as the Remembrance Agent. However, instead of suggesting documents based on text being written or read, Jimminy would also suggest notes that had been previously written in the same room, or around the same people, or during the same time of day or day of week. So, for example, on entering a lecture hall on a Thursday at 3 pm, Jimminy would start suggesting other notes taken in that lecture hall on Thursdays at 3 pm. These would invariably be other notes from the same class. One downside to Jimminy was the way in which suggestions were displayed, which was essentially the same as the display for the RA only on a head-mounted display (this was primarily due to hardware limitations). This output interface was fine when quietly taking notes in a lecture or classroom setting, but took too much attention to retrieve information in more demanding situations such as when in a conversation. In these high-load situations, an output interface that integrates more smoothly with the environment is necessary.

Augmented Reality

Augmented Reality (AR) is the overlay of computer-generated graphics on top of a person's vision of the real world. For example, Columbia's KARMA system (Feiner, Mac Intyre, & Seligman, 1993) used a head-up display to overlay graphical instructions and diagrams on top of real-world devices to aid in tasks such as copy-machine repair. More recently, the group has created a wearable "historical campus tour" system that overlays 3D graphics of what the Columbia campus used to look like on top of the real world (Feiner Macintyre, Hollerer, & Webster, 1997). Jun Rekimoto at Sony CSL (Rekimoto Ayatsuka, & Hayashi, 1998) described a similar systems where a person wears a see-through head-up display, which displays graphical "Post-it notes" that appear to float on top of real objects. By tracking a person's head position via a CCD camera mounted on the display, the computer system can move the graphical overlay as if it were a part of the physical world. The term augmented reality often refers to the visual domain, but the technique can also be extended to audio annotations on physical locations and objects. For example, Audio Aura (Mynatt, Back, Want, Baer, & Ellis 1998) is an audio-based wearable system that uses ambient sound to automatically indicate e-mail, group activity, and information delivered based on the wearer's location. The goal of Audio Aura is to present serendipitous information via background audio cues. The information provided is often tied to the user's physical actions in the workplace, for example, when the user passes by an office he or she hears the name of the person who works there.

Nomadic Radio

Nomadic Radio (Sawhney & Schmandt, 2000) is a wearable system that delivers news, voice mail, and e-mail via audio. Information is played into two shoulder-worn speakers, starting with low ambient sounds and then scaling through levels of intrusiveness from a subtle auditory cue to full foreground presentation of the message. This system, which Sawhney called Dynamic Scaling, follows a predetermined sequence of increasing intrusiveness from silence (no intrusion) through ambient sounds to full speech being played. The level of intrusiveness for a given message can be overridden through voice commands. To keep the interface from being distracting, Nomadic Radio uses the user's history, local context, and the importance of the message being played to decide how intrusive a message should be. If the user has not recently used the system, if he or she is in the middle of a conversation (as detected via the microphone), or if a message is unimportant, then the system will follow a relatively nonintrusive ramp for outputting information. For example, the system might play a quiet sound of water running that slowly increases in volume (thus getting the user's attention), followed by an auditory cue and a short summary. The full body of the message would only be played if the user requests it. On the other hand, if the system expects that the user is not busy or if a message is judged to be important then a faster ambient sound and perhaps a full preview will be played. The system also maintains a model of how interruptible the user is at the moment and uses machine learning techniques to change that model based on how often the user overrides the default level of dynamic scaling with which a message is played.

CHALLENGES FOR INTELLIGENCE AUGMENTATION

There are many challenges facing designers of intelligence augmentation systems. The biggest problem is the human/machine interface bottleneck: how to communicate enough information between the computer and human such that they cover each other's weaknesses without becoming burdensome. Techniques to handle this problem stem mainly from the field of Human–Computer Interaction and Cognitive Science. The second problem is how a computer can sense and in some way "understand" the context of a task. Solutions to the context problem come primarily from Artificial Intelligence and Pattern Recognition. Finally, there is the problem of understanding a task domain in sufficient detail to design a device that is very tightly coupled to that task and its user. Methods for understanding the task domain come largely from the field of Ethnography, and to some extent decision psychology.

Human/Machine Interface Bottleneck

So that human intelligence and computer intelligence can each cover for the other's shortcomings, intelligence augmentation systems usually rely on continuous communication between the computer and the augmented human. One of the biggest challenges is how to design these systems without the communications being a bigger distraction and burden than the problem the system intends to solve. This is the problem of the human/machine interface bottleneck. Science fiction novels often describe the process of "jacking in" to a computer system, where skills such as flying a plane can be gained instantly when the mind and computer chips seamlessly merge to form one entity

> The microsoft Conroy had sent filled his head with its own universe of constantly shifting factors: airspeed, altitude, attitude, angle of attack, g-forces, headings. The plane's weapon delivery information was a constant subliminal litany of target designators, bomb fall lines, search circles, range and release cues, weapons counts. Conroy had tagged the microsoft with a simple message outlining the plane's time of arrival and confirming the arrangement for space for a single passenger. (Gibson, p. 88)

Unfortunately, until such miracle devices are developed the only way to get information into our brains is through our five senses, and the only way to get information from our brain into a computer is through our hands, voice, or other parts of our body. As this is an interface question and a question of human attention, most of the techniques to solve the bottleneck come from the fields of Human Computer Interaction and Cognitive Science. Two techniques employed to circumvent the interface bottleneck problem are progressive disclosure of information and the use of context.

Progressive Disclosure. Sometimes it is not clear how much information needs to be conveyed. For example, the Remembrance Agent can't know for sure whether a document it wants to suggest is already known by the user of the system. Similarly, Nomadic Radio can't know whether the user would like to hear the contents of a message, or whether just knowing that the message has been received is enough for the moment. In these cases it is the human who needs to be able to judge whether the information is useful. Progressive disclosure is the process where pieces of information are displayed in stages, where at each stage the user knows a little more about the nature of the information and can decide whether any more is necessary. The Remembrance Agent uses one form of progressive disclosure called a "ramping interface," where at each stage the user must take some small action in order to see more information. In the first stage, a suggestion sits in the user's peripheral vision. The user knows it is there, but can choose to ignore it. When the user becomes interested in whether a good suggestion is available, he or she can glance down and read one or more columns of information containing author, subject, date, and other information about the suggestion. This quick read, taking no more than a second, is usually enough to tell what a suggestion is about and whether it might be useful. If the user decides the information is useful, he or she can left-click on the suggestion to see the full document, or right-click on the suggestion to see keywords associated with it if he or she is still not sure. Through this design the user is distracted the minimal amount while still receiving enough information to deceide whether more information is valuable. Nomadic Radio's dynamic scaling system is similar, but it follows a predetermined sequence of increasing intrusiveness, and requires action on the part of the user to stray from the chosen presentation. This difference stems from the fact that Nomadic Radio is audio-based whereas the RA's output is visual. It is easy to avert one's gaze away from a suggestion and thus not see more. It is much more difficult to "avert one's ears" and not hear another stage.

The Use Of Context. Context is the part of the environment that is not directly a part of the human-computer interface but can still be useful in interpreting that interface. Human-to-human communication uses context all the time to compress complex meanings into a small number of words. For example, if I'm trying to open a door while carrying numerous packages and ask "Could you help me with this?" you know from context that "this" is the act of opening the door, that my trouble is in not having my hands free, and that opening the door for me is the obvious way to help. If came to you holding a math problem and asked the same question the meaning would be very different. In human–computer interaction, context can be similarly used to reduce the amount of direct, conscious communication between human and computer. In short, the environment that is already being noticed and thought about is used as a part of the interface.

In communication from the computer to the human, augmented reality is one technique that uses context. AR can be thought of as what might be called *"deictic interface"*: an interface that uses the real world to contextualize information being provided by linking the interface to parts of the real world. For example, in Rekimoto's system a virtual Post-it note might be attached to a VCR and read "It is broken." The interface itself is using the real-world object that is physically collocated with the post-it note to let the user know the object to which "it" refers. Audio Aura uses a similar technique when a name is spoken next to person's office. The location in which the name is spoken (a feature of the physical world) is associated with the virtual information being provided (the name). Similar to these more traditional AR systems is the Microsoft Spelling and Grammar Checker, which automatically underlines misspelled words and grammatically incorrect sentences within MS Word. The underline interface conveys its information in a very nondistracting way by using the location of the underline to indicate the incorrect part of the document. Imagine if the task were instead handled by the Microsoft Paper clip and upon typing a misspelled word it popped up a dialogue box saying "the third word in the second sentence of the fifth paragraph is incorrect."

In the opposite direction, any context that the computer can sense without direct human input can potentially reduce the amount of communication necessary. For example, the Remembrance Agent and Jimminy both use the environment as a sort of query into a database of potentially useful information, much like a search engine would use a human-supplied query. Although the automatically generated query will not be as precise as a human-created one, the fact that no information needs to be entered more than makes up for it. Similarly, Nomadic Radio uses the fact that the wearer is in a conversation (as detected by the microphone) to automatically increase the priority a message must be before intruding.

Understanding Context

Computers not only need to understand the context of a task to help the interface, they also need to understand context to know what actions and processes to perform to all. For example, the Remembrance Agent needs to know the context of what is being written in order to guess what documents should be suggested. Jimminy and Audio Aura rely on physical context in the same way. Some contexts are easier for a computer to detect and understand than others. If all a system needs to know is "he is using a word processor" or "a word has just been typed," then the context is easy to detect. This is all the context the MS Spelling Checker needs, for example. It's much harder to detect "he's in a conversation," as Nomadic Radio requires to determine whether the user is interruptible. Nomadic Radio uses something called "scene analysis," which uses machine-learning and pattern-recognition techniques to classify audio from the microphone (Clarkson, Sawhney, & Pentland, 1998). With enough training, such systems can distinguish between being in a conversation and being in a room where others are talking, and even between being outdoors, in a grocery store, in a car, or in the office. Hardest is understanding context that requires complex social understanding, such as "he's in a conversation with someone he wants to impress."

Proxies for Context. In spite of some successes such as scene analysis, most machine understanding of context is still quite limited. The most common technique is to use parts of the contexts that can be sensed, such as location, as proxies for more complex contexts. For example, if a person is at home the computer might assume that he or she is not working and therefore doesn't care about work-related information. Of course, the user may actually be working from home that day, so using such proxies is not perfect. Even Nomadic Radio uses whether the user is in a conversation as a proxy for a more complex piece of contextual information: whether the user minds being distracted at the moment. The state of the art still often resembles the joke about the man looking for his keys under a street lamp, and when asked where he lost them replies, "Well, I lost them over there, but the light is better over here."

Understanding the Task Details

At its most effective an intelligence augmentation system is so integrated with the task that it becomes invisible, or rather transforms the task so that the system becomes a part of it. The philosopher Daniel Dennett described a simple example of such transformation: using the letter Scrabble tray. The task of ordering seven letters in one's head to form words is quite difficult, but when given those seven letters as Scrabble tiles and a tray in which to arrange them the task becomes much easier. The tray and tiles in essence transform the task from an entirely cognitive one into a manipulation and perceptual-recognition task. Real-world tasks tend to be more complex than arranging letters to form words, but intelligence augmentation systems must still be tightly coupled to their tasks. Designing these systems therefore requires a sophisticated understanding of how the task is actually performed in real life, and how the introduction of a new tool might change the task. For example, Carnegie-Mellon University's Navigator-2 wearable computer was designed to aid Air-Force avionics specialists to inspect aircraft. In evaluating the system, researchers found that inspectors actually took longer during inspections because the specialists would go through each step in the checklist, rather than skip steps as they would using the paper-based system (Seigel, & Bayer 1997). In other experiments researchers found online instruction did not provide one of the most important features of paper-based manuals: penciled-in comments and corrections from previous maintenance workers.

CONCLUSION

Engelbart's vision was that by making computers interactive they could do more than automate certain tasks, they could make us smarter. The advent of the personal computer and all the tools that come with it is a testament to that vision. Now computer technology is on the verge of another revolution in size and power equal to the shift from mainframe to personal computer: from the desktop to computers on our person, in our everyday objects, and in our very clothing. This shift gives us the opportunity to integrate artificial computation and human intelligence even further than we have in the last 40 years. The challenges this entails will require skills from fields as diverse as Human–Computer Interaction, Cognitive Science, Artificial Intelligence, and Ethnography. It is only through this diverse range of methodologies and techniques that we can move from vision to living the next stage of augmented life.

REFERENCES

Clarkson, B.,Sawhney, N. & Pentland, A. (1998). *Auditory context awareness via wearable computing. Proceedings of the Perceptual User Interfaces Workshop*, San Francisco, CA.

Engelbart, D. (1962). *Augmenting human intellect: A conceptual framework*, Summary Report, Contract AF 49(638)–1024, Stanford Research Institute, Palo Alto, CA.

Feiner, S., MacIntyre, B., & Seligmann, D. (1993). Knowledge-based augmented reality. *Communications of the ACM, 36*(7) 52–62,

Feiner, S., MacIntyre, B., Höllerer, T., & Webster A. (1997). *A Touring Machine: Prototyping 3D Mobile Augmented Reality Systems for Exploring the Urban Environment*. Paper presented at the First International Symposium on Wearable Computers, Cambridge, MA.

Gibson, W. (1986). *Count Zero*. New York: Ace Books.

Horvitz, Eric, J. Breese, D. Heckerman, D. Hovel, and K. Rommelse (1998). "The Lumiere Project: Bayesian User Modeling for Inferring the Goals and Needs of Software Users," in *Proceedings of the Fourteenth Conference on Uncertainty in Artificial Intelligence,* Madison, WI, July 1998, Morgan Kaufmann: San Francisco, pp. 256-265.

Licklider, JCR (1960) "Man-Computer Symbiosis," IRE Transactions on Human Factors in Electronics, volume HFE-1, March 1960, pp. 4-11.

Maes, P. (1994). Agents that reduce work and information overload. *Communications of the ACM, 37,* 7, 31–40, 146.

Mynatt, E., Back, M., Want, R., Baer, M., & Ellis, J. (1998). "Designing Audio Aura." *Conference Proceedings on Human Factors in Computing Systems* 566–573.

Rekimoto, J., Ayatsuka, Y., & Hayashi, K. (1998). *Augment-able Reality: Situated communications through physical and digital spaces.'* paper presented at the Second International Symposium on Wearable Computers Pittsburgh, PA.

Rhodes, B. & Maes, P. (2000). Just-in-time information retrieval agents. *IBM Systems Journal (*Special Issue on the MIT Media Laboratory*), 39,* 3 & 4, 685–704.

Rhodes, B. (2000). *Just-in-time information retrieval.* Doctoral dissertation, MIT, Cambridge, MA.

Rhodes, B. (1997). The Wearable Remembrance Agent: A system for augmented memory. *Personal Technologies* 1, 218–224.

Sawhney, N. & Schmandt, C. (2000). Nomadic Radio: speech and audio interaction for contextual messaging in nomadic emviroments. ACM Transactions on Computer-Human Interaction, 7 (3), 353–383.

Siegel, J., & Bauer, M. (1997). *A field usability evaluation of a wearable system,* paper presented at the First International Symposium on Wearable Computers, Cambridge, MA.

Starner, Thad, Steve Mann, Bradley Rhodes, Jeffrey Levine, Jennifer Healey, Dana Kirsch, Rosalind W. Picard, and Alex Pentland (1997) "Augmented Reality Through Wearable Computing." Presence, Special Issue on Augmented Reality, vol 6(4), Fall 1997.

18

The Future of Human Intelligence:
Enhancing Cognitive Capability
in a 24/7 World

David F. Dinges, PhD
Naomi L. Rogers, PhD
University of Pennsylvania

Whether theorized to be a general factor or a collection of factors, or the atheoretical product of a given sets of cognitive tests, measures of human intelligence are typically taken without regard to biological timing. Human cognition capability, however, is temporally dynamic reflecting endogenous biological forces genetically programmed into all brains. These forces derive from an increasingly well-described neurobiology, and they appear to reflect evolutionary pressures via Earth's fundamental orbital mechanics (i.e., daily rotation on its axis and around the sun), which have provided perhaps the most pervasive and planetary-wide evolutionary pressure for appropriately timed behavior in complex animals. However, the development of the cortex, and especially of the prefrontal cortex, has resulted in higher order cognitive abilities (intelligence), which in turn has led to the expansive use of tools by humans and ultimately to modern industrialized societies. The technologies and systems created by higher brain development have allowed our species to attempt to step beyond the influence of daily light–dark and seasonal environmental behavioral controls. The continued development of societal systems that operate 24 hours a day, 7 days a week (i.e., 24/7) appears to be fed by the desire to control time. In this sense, human intelligence has created a lifestyle for millions that is, paradoxically, cognitively incapacitating, because biological forces that require us to sleep also appear to be critical to waking cognitive capability. The response to this dilemma has been the invention of preventative and operational, socially acceptable "countermeasures" to overcome the neurobehavioral deficits from a 24/7 world. These enhancements to cognitive capability include pharmacological, behavioral, and technological strategies that are rapidly and almost invisibly integrated into industrialized societies. The more effective these enhancements become in promoting or sustaining cognitive capabilities in all persons, regardless of individual differences in cognitive abilities, the more they challenge our concept of intelligence as a predetermined and predetermining force. Research is reviewed that illustrates the biologically programmed, temporally dynamic nature of human cognitive capabilities, their deficits during sleep deprivation, and emerging efforts to use pharmacological, behavioral, and technological strategies to maintain optimal cognitive functions and behavioral capability by society as a whole, and specifically in 24/7 human endeavors. One consequence of this growing use of strategies to promote human cognitive performance capability (or at least avoid catastrophe when cognitive skills are endogenously reduced) is that it is focused on pragmatic goals (e.g., operate the truck safely at night or ensure the blood gases of the patient on the operating table remain steady). It is largely undertaken without theoretical or operational distinctions among analytic, creative, or practical expressions of intelligence. Achievement of broader behavioral goals is typically the ultimate criterion for effectiveness of these countermeasures in a 24/7 world.

The cognitive capabilities that have been at the heart of various theories and tests of human intelligence are typically measured during wakefulness, which has historically been presumed to be a temporally static platform for cognitive functions. This has led intentionally or unintentionally to some practices that appear benign but which may contribute to test error variance. For example, it is not uncommon for high school students in the United States to complete the Scholastic Aptitude Test (SAT), which is a key factor in access to colleges and universities, early on a Saturday morning, after a week of classes with an accompanying sleep debt. Although assumptions that time-of-day matters little in testing intelligence, or that all waking moments are the same in terms of cognitive performance, may seem socially accepted, there is growing scientific evidence that they are neither warranted nor prudent. What is becoming clear is that cognitive performance depends on a stable waking state, but wakefulness itself is temporally dynamic by virtue of its dependence on two interactive neurobiological processes—a sleep drive and a temporal control process (i.e., the biological clock) that produces circadian rhythms (Czeisler & Khalsa, 2000).

Endogenous Circadian Timing and Sleep Need

Circadian rhythms are endogenously produced biological rhythms, characterized by repetitive oscillations with a frequency of one cycle approximately every 24 hours that are sustained in constant environmental conditions (Czeisler & Wright, J., 1999). In humans the endogenous biological clock (or circadian pacemaker) is located in the suprachiasmatic nuclei (SCN) of the anterior hypothalamus (Moore, 1983; Miller, Morin et al., 1996). The circadian system modulates the functional timing of a range of physiological and behavioral processes, including the endocrine, thermoregulatory, immune, cardiovascular, respiratory, gastrointestinal, renal, and the sleep–wake systems (see Fig. 1). Following lesions of the SCN, a loss of the circadian organization of sleep and waking (e.g., shorter bouts of waking), and increased total sleep time occurs, suggesting a role for the SCN in actively facilitating initiation and maintenance of wakefulness, and opposing the homeostatic sleep drive at certain circadian times (Edgar, Dement et al., 1993).

The circadian pacemaker is entrained to the 24-hour day via information received from the ambient environment. These environmental time cues are termed zeitgebers. In most animals, including humans, the most salient zeitgeber is the environmental light–dark cycle (Czeisler & Khalsa, 2000). In addition to entraining, zeitgeber are able to alter the timing of the circadian system, and consequently the circadian rhythms of the physiological and behavioral systems under its control.

A considerable number of neurobehavioral and cognitive functions have been reported to demonstrate circadian rhythmicity, including alertness, short-term memory, psychomotor vigilance, and cognitive throughput (Dijk, Duffy et al., 1992; Folkard, Marks et al., 1985; Monk,

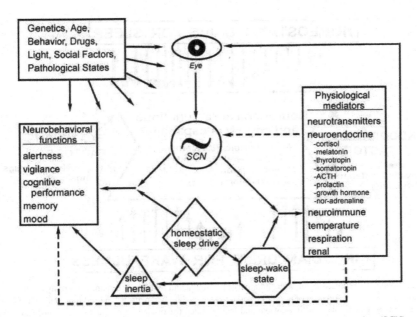

FIG. 18.1   Schematic representation of the interaction of the endogenous circadian pacemaker (SCN) and sleep homeostatic drive on a variety of neurobehavioral and physiological variables. A variety of experimental paradigms, especially forced desynchrony experiments, have established that under normal conditions the pacemaker and sleep–wake state each influence these variables. Their relative contributions and interactions depend on the variable (e.g., cortisol and melatonin are heavily influenced by the circadian system). Light is the most potent stimulus for entrainment of the circadian pacemaker, whereas the cognitive desire to be awake for school, work, leisure, and so on is the primary influence on the sleep–wake state among humans. The influence (feedback) of physiological variables on the circadian clock and on neurobehavioral functions is indicated by dashed arrows, whereas the influence of neurobehavioral demands on sleep-wake state is indicated by a solid arrow. The influence of environment, behavior, age, psychosocial factors, genetics, and drugs on virtually all elements contributing to sleep–wake regulation is also shown in the upper left hand area of the schematic. (Adapted from and reprinted with permission from C. A. Czeisler, & S. B. S. Khalsa (2000). The human circadian timing system and sleep wake regulation. In M. H., Kryger, T., Roth, & W. C. Dement (Eds.), *Principles and practice of sleep medicine* (3rd ed pp. 353–375), Philadelphia: W. B. Saunders.

Buysse et al., 1997; Wyatt, Cecco et al., 1999) The importance of the circadian system and sleep need to cognitive functions is easily demonstrated by the effects of jet lag—few European or American invited speakers to a Spearman Conference in Sydney, Australia would agree to speak within a few hours of arriving.

Interacting with the circadian timing system is the homeostatic drive for sleep (see Fig. 18.1). Sleep is among the most basic biological imperatives that occur in all humans. By 70 years of age, the average person will have spent a cumulative total of between 20 and 25 years asleep (approximately one third of their life). Although species-specific differences in the timing parameters of sleep exist, human sleep is remarkably similar to the sleep of most other mammals with regard to brain physiology, body posture, reduced environmental responsivity, and rebound following deprivation.

Deprivation of sleep in humans and other species does not prevent the circadian rhythm in core body temperature and many other biological functions, but it quickly leads to an elevated

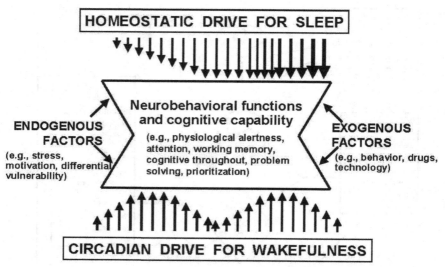

FIG. 18.2   Schematic representation of the putative oppositional and temporally dynamic interplay of circadian and homeostatic drives in the regulation of alertness, performance, and related neurobehavioral functions. The homeostatic drive for sleep, which involves time awake and loss of sleep (or disruption of the recovery function of sleep), decreases neurobehavioral functions and cognitive performance (and increases fatigue and subjective sleepiness) as it accumulates over time. Unlike the circadian component, which is limited by its amplitude, the homeostatic drive for sleep can accumulate far beyond the levels typically encountered in a 24hr day (illustrated by the increasing density of downward arrows). The neurobiology of the cumulative homeostatic pressure is unknown. In opposition to this downward influence on performance and alertness is the endogenous circadian rhythmicity of the biological clock, which through its promotion of wakefulness modulates the enhancement of performance and alertness. Although the neurobiology of the biological clock is increasingly elucidated, the precise way in which it controls the drive for wakefulness and enhances alertness and cognition is still unknown. The improvement in waking neurobehavioral functions by the circadian drive is an oscillatory output with some phases involving robust opposition to the homeostatic drive, although the phase of the lowest circadian opposition may involve a complete absence of circadian drive for wakefulness. Critical modulators of neurobehavioral functions other than the sleep and circadian drives are subsumed in the schematic under the broad categories of endogenous and exogenous stimulation. Like sleep need and circadian rhythmicity, these modulating factors are ubiquitous, yet are rarely considered in tests of intelligence. The neurobiological underpinnings of these exogenous and endogenous processes are undoubtedly diverse, and few of their interactions with the circadian and homeostatic systems have been studied systematically. (Adapted from and reprinted with permission from H. P. A. Van Dongen, & D. F. Dinges. (2000). Gircadian rhythms in fatigue, alertness, and performance. In M. H. Kryger, T. Roth, & W. C. Dement (Eds.), *Principles and practice of sleep medicine* (3rd ed. pp. 391–399), Philadelphia: W. P. Saunders.

pressure for sleep that appears to override the endogenous, wake-promoting, circadian opposition to sleep (Carskadon & Dement 1987; Dinges & Kribbs 1991). However, neither sleep homeostasis nor the circadian pacemaker has independent control of cognitive functions. Rather, these temporally bound regulatory processes interact neurobiologically to dynamically and endogenously control neurobehavioral functions and cognitive capabilities (Dijk, Duffy et al., 1992) (see Fig. 18.1). Although other endogenous factors (e.g., stress, motivation, differential vulnerability to the effects of sleep loss) and exogenous factors (e.g., behavior, drugs, technology) may further modulate the interaction, the need to sleep and the need to do so at an appropriate circadian phase are among the most powerful controls of neurobehavioural functions in human biology (see Fig. 18.2).

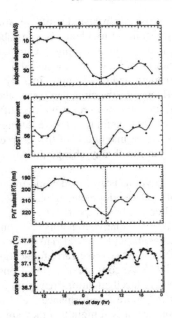

FIG. 18.3   The apparent circadian variation in neurobehavioral and cognitive functions across the day and night is in fact the product of an interaction between the circadian system and the sleep homeostatic drive. The figure shows covariation of changes in subjective sleepiness; cognitive throughput as assessed by the digit symbol substitution task (DSST); fastest reaction times; and body temperature assessed by rectal thermistor. Data are mean values from five subjects who remained awake in dim light, in bed, in a constant routine protocol, for 36 hours (a distance-weighted least-squares function was fitted to each variable). Note that functions are not stable (flat lines) even across the first 16 hr of waking, which would be typical of a normal day. The circadian trough is evident in each variable (marked by vertical broken lines). A phase difference is also apparent, such that all three neurobehavioral variables had their average minimum between 3 hr and 4.5 hr after the body temperature minimum. Although body temperature predominantly the endogenous circadian clock, neurobehavioral and cognitive performance functions also are clearly affected by the homeostatic pressure for sleep, which escalates with time awake or lack of adequate sleep. For reasons not entirely understood, cognitive performance following a night of wakefulness was worse between 6 a.m. and 10 a.m., which appears to be a zone of maximum vulnerability to loss of alertness and cognitive performance deficits. Interestingly, endogenous alertness and cognitive performance are often improved if the subject continues to remain awake until the evening. In fact, there is now extensive scientific evidence that for most healthy adolescents and adults, the circadian peak in alertness and performance is at a counterintuitive time—namely, in the evening, a few hours prior to habitual nocturnal bed time (note the curves around 8 p.m. [2000 hr] during the first day of waking). Adapted from and reprinted with permission from HPA. Van Donghen, & D F. Dinges, (2000). Circadian rhythms in fatigue, alertness and performance. In M. H., Kryger, T., Roth, W. C. Dement, (Eds.), Principles and Practice of sleep medicine (3rd ed., pp. 391–399), Philadelphia: W. B. Saunders.

Cognitive Performance as a Function of Circadian Phase and Sleep Need

Experimentally it has been demonstrated that under normal conditions, there is significant variation across the 24-hour day in cognitive and psychomotor performance. As shown in Fig. 18.3, following a full night of sleep, cognitive functioning and alertness levels are high across the day, increasing from about 8:00 a.m to 9:00 a.m. onward. Depending on sleep drive and time of morning awakening, there can be a decrease in cognitive performance in the early afternoon, known as the postprandial dip or siesta zone. Alertness and cognitive performance levels remain relatively high across the remainder of the afternoon, peaking—somewhat counter intuitively—in the early evening, 1 to 3 hours before habitual bedtime (circa 8:00 p.m. to 10:00 p.m.). If wakefulness is maintained overnight, alertness and cognitive performance begin to decline, reaching a minimum between 3 hr and 4.5 hr after the body temperature minimum (also termed the circadian nadir), or approximately between 6 a.m. and 10 a.m. Demonstrating the dynamic influence of the circadian pacemaker on wake state stability and cognitive functions, if the subject continues to remain awake after a night without sleep cognitive performance and alertness again begin to improve during the day, although the degree of functional recovery depends on the magnitude of the sleep drive as well. Factors such as night shift work and transmeridian travel may change the timing of these rhythms, but usually not the magnitude.

A shift in the timing of these rhythms is also evident during the adolescent years, and may occur as a consequence of pubertal development. A phase delay in the timing of daytime sleepiness in mid-pubertal children has been reported (Carskadon, 1990). In addition, adolescents typically report later sleep times relative to adults and younger children, due to school, work, social, and family commitments, and likely also to the delay in the timing of their daily sleepiness rhythm. They are then forced to wake early for school, thus shortening their sleep duration on a chronic basis (Link & Ancoli-Israel, 1995). Consequently, increased daytime sleepiness, reduced alertness, and reduced attention are reported in this population. Typically the highest levels of sleepiness and poorest performance are observed in the morning, during the first classes of the day. In contrast, it is at night that they are at their most alert, with sleep propensity at its lowest. When allowed to sleep without time constraints, for example on weekends, adolescents choose to go to bed and rise later than on weekdays, and sleep for longer—"catch-up" sleep (Link & Ancoli-Israel, 1995; Reid, Zeldow et al., 2002).

As the duration of sleep loss progresses, performance and alertness decrements occur in response to both increasing homeostatic sleep drive and circadian variation, resulting in an acceleration of the performance decrements superimposed on increased circadian modulation over time (see Fig. 18.4). Such performance deficits commonly occur during operations requiring optimal performance under high (or variable) workload conditions that often continue for extended periods of time, such as 3 to 5 days, during which time sleep opportunities are typically limited (e.g., fighting a forest fire; sustained military operations). Fig. 18.4 illustrates the temporally dynamic interaction of the circadian system and sleep homeostatic drive on cognitive performance across an 88-hour period without sleep.

Throughout the past century, the neurobehavioural and cognitive effects of both acute total sleep deprivation and chronic partial sleep deprivation (Carskadon & Dement, 1981; Dinges, Pack et al., 1997; Van Dongen, Maislin et al., 1999) have been evaluated in laboratory studies using many types of cognitive performance measures (Bohnen & Gaillard, 1994; Bonnet & Arand, 1994; Dinges, 1995; Harrison & Horne, 1998; Horne, 1988; Johnson & Naitoh, 1974; Kjellberg, 1977a, 1977b, 1977c; Kleitman, 1963; Linde & Bergstrom, 1992; Wilkinson, 1969; Williams, Lubin et al., 1959). The effects consistently found across studies are summarized in Table 18.1. Wake "state instability" appears to underlie the majority of these effects (Doran, Van Dongen et al., 2001), with deficits in attention, cognitive throughout, and working memory being most dramatically affected by sleep loss. There is reason to believe that virtually all the cognitive deficits due to sleep loss involve a decline in these core capabilities.

These core neurocognitive functions are putatively subserved by the prefrontal cortex (PFC), with brain imaging studies demonstrating activation of these cortical areas during performance tasks (Dagher, Owen et al., 1999; Diwadkar, Carpenter et al., 2000; Kroger, Sabb et al., 2002; Mottaghy, Gangitano et al., 2002; Zysset, Huber et al., 2002). A small number of

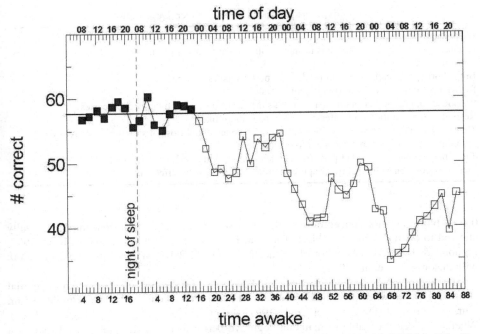

FIG. 18.4   Cognitive throughput performance on a 90-second digit symbol substitution task (DSST) in 12 healthy adults (mean age 29 yr) at baseline (filled squares) and while remaining awake for 88 hours (open squares). Interactions of the circadian system and the homeostatic drive for sleep are evident in the daily downward oscillation of performance. The horizontal line reflects average baseline performance (i.e., performance following 8-hr time in bed for sleep). The vertical line shows the final night of sleep before the period of continuous waking.

studies has investigated cortical activation and neurobehavioral performance during sleep deprivation. A decrease in performance on arithmetic tasks during sleep deprivation was associated with a decrease in prefrontal activation (Drummond, Brown et al. 1999; Thomas, Sing et al., 2000). In addition, PET studies have demonstrated reduced uptake of glucose during 72 hours of sustained wakefulness, with the greatest reductions observed in the frontal cortex (Thomas, Sing et al., 1993).

More recently, however, there are suggestions that activation of cortical regions during sleep loss may be task specific (Drummond, Brown et al., 2000). An increase in prefrontal activation while performing on a learning task following one night without sleep was evident, relative to a baseline measure following one night with sleep. A relationship between increased sleepiness levels and increased prefrontal activation was reported to exist.

Taken together, these studies support the hypothesis that the prefrontal cortex plays an integral role in neurocognitive functioning, and that changes in its activation may underlie the changes in performance observed during periods of sleep loss.

In an attempt to quantify the magnitude of cognitive impairment associated with sleep loss, recent experiments have compared the cognitive effects of sleep loss to those of alcohol intoxication. These experiments have demonstrated that remaining awake for as little as one night (i.e., 24 hour) can degrade cognitive performance to levels comparable to those found for

TABLE 18.1
Cognitive Performance Effects of Sleep Deprivation

Response time slows.
Attention-intensive performance is unstable with increased errors of omission and commission.
Cognitive slowing occurs in subject-paced tasks, while time pressure increases cognitive errors.
Both short-term recall and working memory performances decline.
Reduced learning (acquisition) of cognitive tasks.
Response suppression errors increase in tasks primarily subserved by prefrontal cortex.
Response perseveration on ineffective solutions is more likely.
There is growing neglect of activities judged to be nonessential (loss of situational awareness).
Involuntary microsleep attacks begin to occur.
Tasks may be begun well, but performance deteriorates with increasing rapidity.
Increased compensatory effort is required to remain behaviorally effective.

0.10% blood alcohol concentration—that is, over the blood alcohol concentration legally allowed to operate a motor vehicle (Dawson, Lamond et al., 1998; Dawson & Reid, 1997; Lamond & Dawson, 1999; Powell, Schechtman et al., 2001; Williamson & Feyer, 2000; williamson, Feyer et al., 2001).

The cognitive effects listed in Table 18. 1 have also been observed during chronic partial sleep deprivation when daily time in bed allowed for sleep is reduced from 8 hr/night to 5 hr, 6 hr, or 7 hr/night (Dinges, Pack et al., 1997; Kuo, Carlin et al., 1988; Rowland and 1997). Whereas subjects are able to maintain cognitive performance at acceptable levels across a 2-week period when allowed 8 hours of sleep per night, a reduction in sleep opportunity to 6 hours produces profound decrements in neurobehavioural performance across days, including reduced learning of cognitive tasks. Increases in lapsing on a psychomotor vigilance task, decreased memory, and decreased cognitive throughput are evident following even one night of reduced sleep (Dinges, Maislin et al., 2003).

The neurobiological bases of the wake-promoting and sleep-promoting systems are increasingly being delineated. Although the picture is still far from complete, there is considerable evidence to suggest that monoaminergically mediated midbrain and brain stem nuclei (i.e., tubero mamillary nucleus, dorsal raphe, and locus coeruleus) provide a waking drive to the cortex—possibly via the orexin/hypocretin system—thereby maintaining a stable basis for cortical and cognitive functioning of the kind valued in intelligence tests (Saper, Chou et al. 2001).

Individual Differences in Cognitive Response to Sleep Loss and Night Work

Biologically based interindividual differences exist in a number of physiological and behavioral systems in humans. For example, there is evidence for substantial interindividual differences in the phase relationship of the internal circadian timing system to environmental time; in the amount of sleep required per day to maintain optimal cognitive capability; and in the rate and magnitude of impairment per hour of sleep loss.

Although most individuals maintain a balance between their internal timing system and the external environmental timing system, some people experience a discrepancy between the two. For example, individuals can be classified as morning-types (larks) or evening-types (owls). The circadian system of larks typically "runs early" relative to normally entrained individuals, with the circadian nadir (measured using core body temperature) occurring at an earlier time, and sleep onset and offset also occurring earlier. In contrast, the circadian system of owls typically "runs late," with the circadian nadir delayed, and sleep onset and offset occurring at later times relative to normal. These points are illustrated by findings from constant routine experiments, that have demonstrated a difference of more than 2 hours in the phase positions of the endogenous circadian systems of extreme morning-types and evening-types, as measured by core body temperature. Further, via an interaction with the sleep home-ostatic system, this results in a difference of at least 4 hours in the timing of peak alertness between morning-types and evening-types (Kerkhof & Van Dongen, 1996). Cognitively speaking, morning-types appear to have a relative advantage on morning shifts, whereas evening-types are better able to tolerate night work (Akerstedt & Torsvall, 1985; Alward, 1988; Costa, Lievore et al., 1989).

Interindividual differences in sleep need (i.e., naturally short sleepers vs. naturally long sleepers have been studied using the waking electroencephalogram (EEG) as a physiological marker of sleep homeostasis. Naturally short sleepers were reported to tolerate a higher homeostatic pressure for sleep relative to naturally long sleepers (Aeschbach, Postolache et al., 2001). Although there may be a genetic basis for this variability in natural sleep need, not everybody who subjectively reports being a naturally short sleeper actually is so "natu-rally" (Monk, Buysse et al., 2001). Rather, many individuals are able to sustain living on a short sleep schedule for a period of time, but eventually accumulate a significant sleep debt, which then results in cognitive deficits. This point can be illustrated by workers who are required to work long hours and commute a considerable distance to work, thereby reducing the amount of time available for and allocated to sleep. Walsleben, Norman et al. (1999) reported a reduction in sleep duration in rail commuters who had a long commute to work rel-ative to those who had a short commute time. Associated with this reduction in sleep time, 50% of commuters reported difficulty with their waking functions, and one third reported experiencing excessive daytime sleepiness. In an earlier study, (McCartt, Ribner et al. (1996) reported that 55% of 1,000 New York drivers surveyed reported feeling drowsy while driving, and 24% of drivers reported having fallen asleep at the wheel. These subjective feelings of sleepiness and awareness of decreases in neurobehavioral function reflect the increase in homeostatic sleep pressure due to chronically restricted sleep.

Individuals who sleep comparable amounts each night, with comparable circadian phases, and who are comparable cognitively and neurobehaviorally when not sleep deprived, are nev-ertheless observed to be differentially affected—by as much as an order of magnitude—in their cognitive capability when exposed to sleep deprivation (Dinges & Kribbs, 1991; Doran, Van Dongen et al., 2001). These interindividual differences in vulnerability to the cognitive effects of sleep loss appear to have a high level of intrasubject consistency, reflecting greater cognitive sensitivity of some subjects to sleep loss. A recent study in our laboratory quanti-fied the intrasubject stability of interindividual differences in cognitive responses to sleep loss. In this study 58% of the variance in vigilance performance deficits was found to be stable, (Van Dongen, Maislin et al. 1999), suggesting that individuals have a traitlike predis-position to a certain level of cognitive vulnerability during sleep loss (i.e., differential vulner-ability to cognitive incapacitation from sleep loss and circadian misalignment).

This finding of trait-like differential vulnerability to acute sleep loss was recently extended to an investigation of chronic sleep restriction, which produces a cumulative sleep debt and escalating cognitive deficits (Van Dongen, Maislin et al., 2001). Thus, there is mounting evi-dence that interindividual differences in vulnerability to cognitive impairment from sleep loss are stable over time. Whether these differential vulnerabilities have any relationship to intel-ligence remains unknown, but it is currently being evaluated. Even if they share no variance with intelligence tests, it means that at least some subjects who are presumed to be cognitively capable based on intelligence scores may nevertheless be differentially vulnerable to cognitive deficits when sleep and/or circadian parameters are altered even moderately.

TIME AND INTELLIGENCE: BIOLOGY VERSUS INDUSTRIALIZATION

The fact that sleep need and circadian regulation are fundamental to human cognitive capability is orthogonal to the debate about the nature of human intelligence (e.g., g vs. g's). However, when the enhancement of human intelligence is considered (or the converse—the degradation of human intelligence), biological time and the social use of time become relevant. With the advent of the industrial revolution, which brought the world, among other things, cheap energy for artificial light, shift work, global transportation, real-time worldwide communication (and of course, intelligence tests), there has been a systematic encroachment of complex human behavior into the night. This has translated into the potential for widespread induction of cognitive deficits for tens of millions of people by way of sleep deprivation and circadian displacement. The latter is evident in many areas, including the following examples:

- The proliferation of around-the-clock/ 24-hour industries (e.g., banking, transportation, health care, telecommunications);
- The widespread use of nonstop automated systems on a grand scale (e.g., a wide range of manufacturing, petrochemical, and energy industries);
- The increased exposure of large segments of the population to night-shift work (e.g., 10% of blue collar workers in the United States work nights periodically);
- The growing trend toward prolonged work hours (e.g., recent federal concern in the United States over abuse of prolonged work hours);
- Overnight and just-in-time delivery (e.g., freight hauling, mail and package delivery, perishable items such as food and flowers, gasoline);
- Emergency operations (e.g., forest fires, floods, hurricanes, blizzards, military operations).
- The production and deployment large numbers of jet airplanes for commercial aviation (e.g., an estimated 75 million travelers a year move across time zones);
- Late-night entertainment and shopping (e.g., television and the Internet are available 24/7);
- Earlier school start times coupled with later bed times (e.g., many adolescents go to bed around midnight and awaken for school around 6:30 a.m.);
- Lifestyle-induced chronic sleep restriction (e.g., in a recent poll by the National Sleep Foundation, 18% of Americans reported obtaining 6 or fewer hours of sleep per day, and 19% reported having dozed off while driving).

The continued development of societal systems that operate 24 hours a day, 7 days a week (i.e., 24/7) appears to have its origin in the human desire to control time. The cortical ability to conceive of and create technologies that are not entirely subject to the temporal or spatial limits imposed by Earth's orbital mechanics have permitted our species to step beyond the influence of daily light–dark and seasonal environmental forces that have provided the most pervasive evolutionary pressure for appropriately timed behavior in complex animals. In this sense, human intelligence has created a lifestyle for millions that can be, paradoxically, cognitively incapacitating.

Enhancement of Cognitive Performance in a 24/7 World

The response to the dilemma posed by the human use of time that is in conflict with the bio-logically programmed, temporally dynamic nature of human cognitive capabilities has been the accelerated invention and deployment of preventative and operational "countermeasures" in recent decades, to overcome the neurobehavioral deficits from a 24/7 world. These enhancements to cognitive capability include behavioral, pharmacological, and technological strategies that are rapidly and almost invisibly integrated into industrialized societies. The more effective these enhancements become in promoting or sustaining cognitive capabilities in all persons, regardless of individual differences in cognitive abilities, the more they challenge our concept of intelligence as a predetermined and predetermining force. The emerging efforts to use pharmacological, behavioral, and technological strategies to maintain optimal cognitive functions and behavioral capability by society as a whole, and specifically in 24/7 human endeavors, has begun to refocus the debate of aptitude away from a concern with individual characteristics or traits (e.g., intelligence) and toward pragmatic goals. Thus, countermeasure deployment to enhance cognitive capability in everyone is largely undertaken without theoretical or operational distinctions among analytic, creative, practical, or any other putative intelligences. Achievement of broader behavioral goals is typically the ultimate criterion for effectiveness of these countermeasures in a 24/7 world. In the following we briefly provide examples of three types of countermeasures currently being studied and used to maintain cognitive capability.

Behavioral Countermeasures: Prophylactic (Power) Napping as a Case Example

Behavioral countermeasures for the cognitive impairments induced by fatigue due to 24/7 operations include education, training, exercise, work–rest schedules, and limited sleep opportunities (i.e., naps) in the workplace. Whereas the first three are popular in the workplace, there is little evidence that they mitigate the cognitive effects of sleep loss or night work—although education and training might make one more aware of the neurobehavioral deficits to be experienced. The fourth one—scheduling—is often the most contentious, being at the nexus of individual desires, company demands, and for federally regulated industries, enforcement, and litigation. In contrast to the first four, naps as a workplace countermeasure offer a putative physiological mechanism (i.e., sleep) for enhancing cognition.

There has been a long-standing scientific search for ways to use briefer periods of sleep (i.e., naps) to enhance cognitive capability. Naps are often alleged to be refreshing disproportionate to their length, and there are apocryphal tales of many "geniuses" and otherwise famous individuals who reputedly survived for years solely on nap sleep (e.g., Leonardo daVinci, Napoleon Bonaparte, Thomas Edison, Winston Churchill). Although no one has ever been documented to live solely by napping, research has demonstrated that naps can have very important benefits, depending on the sleep need and work–rest schedule of the individual. Whereas napping behavior has been a theoretically important issue in sleep research (Dinges & Brougton, 1989), it has also been of practical concern. In many of the 24/7 activities listed previously, especially transportation modes, training of medical doctors, and sustained military operations, napping behavior has been studied for its effectiveness in maintaining optimal cognitive functioning during activities in which flexibility of sleep time is essential. Naps involving physiological sleep durations between 20 minutes and 2 hours have been extensively studied scientifically for their effects on alertness and cognitive performance (Dinges & Broughton, 1989; Stampi, 1992). More recently, naps of only 10 minutes duration have been demonstrated to produce both increased objective performance and subjective assessments of sleepiness following one night of restricted sleep (Tietzel & Lack, 2001). Brief prophylactic or power naps have been shown to be preventive countermeasures against the cognitive deficits associated with sleep loss, especially when taken in advance of night work or prolonged sleep loss (Dinges, Orne et al., 1987; Dinges, Whitehouse et al., 1988). Recent evidence suggests that the benefit of naps is derived from the exponential relationship between sleep duration and recovery of neurobehavioral performance functions, such that a greater recovery of cognitive function occurs in the first few hours of sleep than in the final hours of sleep (Jewett, Dijk et al., 1999).

In non-sleep-deprived subjects, enhanced cognitive performance was observed between 1.5 hours and 10 hours following a prophylactic nap (20-min to 2-hr duration) (Carskadon & Dement, 1987; Gillberg, 1984; Godbout & Montplaisir, 1986). In sleep-deprived subjects (up to 52 hours of continuous wakefulness), the beneficial effects of a prophylactic nap on cognitive performance were evident within an hour after awakening and were sustained for between 6 and 30 hours after the nap, depending on the placement of the nap in the course of sleep deprivation (Bonnet, 1991, Dinges, Orne et al., 1987). The practical countermeasure benefits of prophylactic or "power" naps (as they have come to be called) as brief as 24 minutes, have also been demonstrated in long-haul commercial airline pilots flying B747 commercial aircraft on transmeridian Pacific routes (Rosekind, Graeber et al., 1994).

The results of studies on prophylactic napping were unexpected because a prophylactic nap taken in advance of prolonged work appears to yield greater cognitive benefits (probably by reversing wake state instability (see Doran, Van Dongen et al., 2001) than naps taken after sleep pressure has been allowed to accumulate due to prolonged wakefulness, despite the earlier prophylactic nap containing less consolidated sleep. It appears that the prophylactic nap reduces the potential for later sleepiness and cognitive deficits. For this reason prophylactic napping is now viewed as a viable countermeasure to performance impairment accompanying many modern sustained work scenarios. Some international long-haul commercial aviation carriers now permit brief cockpit naps, and nearly all airlines offer bunks for flight crews to take naps (ranging in duration from 1–4 hours) on long-haul aircraft. In recent years, fully reclining seats have become available in the first and business class sections of many international carriers, in an effort to offer optimal sleeping conditions, and hence physiological sleep to customers that spend more on their flights. Commercial trucking and railroads have also embraced sleeper berths and napping as countermeasures for the adverse cognitive effects of their 24/7 operations. There are signs that other 24/7 industries are also exploiting the cognitive benefits of naps.

Prophylactic napping to maintain cognitive proficiency also has a negative consequence, however, called "sleep inertia." Sleep inertia manifests as rather severe cognitive impairment following abrupt awakening from sleep, especially deep slow wave sleep (Dinges, 1990). Sleep inertia can last for up to an hour or more (Jewett, Wyatt et al., 1999) before cognitive functions recover and are further enhanced by nap sleep. Consequently, sleep inertia poses a significant problem in situations where high-level cognitive proficiency is required soon after awakening from a nap (e.g., a medical doctor who is on call for emergencies, or a fighter pilot who must be airborne within minutes of an alert). In a recent study in our laboratory, it was discovered that the cognitive impairment of sleep inertia following naps of 2-hours duration, during an 88-hour period of sustained wakefulness, could be effectively blocked by administration of sustained low-dose caffeine (Van Dongen, Price et al., 2001). This unexpected finding led to the conclusion that a combination of naps and sustained caffeine provided the optimal countermeasure pairing during a 4-day simulated operation with sustained cognitive demands.

Pharmacological Countermeasures: Caffeine and Modafinil as Case Examples

Caffeine is the most widely used, unregulated central nervous system stimulant in the world. Its use as a cognitive enhancing agent appears to have increased in the past decade, as sleep loss, night work, and drug availability have increased. Caffeine is most commonly consumed as coffee, which next to oil is the second-most traded commodity in the world. Fully 80% of adult Americans are regular or occasional coffee drinkers, with an average daily consumption of 3.3 cups (i.e., approximately 250 to 450 mg/day). As an example of the popularity of caffeine, coffee retailer Starbucks, which was founded in Seattle in 1971, grew from 90 locations in 1990 to 4,435 stores in the United States and 21 countries by 2001. Caffeine consumption has also spread into adolescent and preadolescent populations with the growing number and popularity of soft drinks that contain 30 to 60 mg of caffeine. There is little doubt that caffeine has become a socially acceptable way to manipulate alertness and cognitive functions in modern industrialized societies.

The ability of caffeine to enhance cognitive functioning with or without sleep loss has been the focus of hundreds of experimental reports. In one of the more extensive reviews of this literature, the U.S. Committee on Military Nutrition Research for the Institute of Medicine of the National Academy of Sciences (2001) concluded that caffeine at levels ranging from 100 to 600 mg/day has been shown to enhance cognitive functions including speed of reaction time (without affecting accuracy), performance on visual and auditory vigilance tasks, and long-term memory recall. These effects on cognitive performance were most evident when cognitive functions were impaired or suboptimal. Space precludes a review of caffeine's full pharmacological and physiological effects. Although caffeine is popular and has limited effectiveness in enhancing certain psychomotor aspects of cognitive performance, it also has a number of negative features, including mild addiction, the development of tolerance, and a long half-life that can result in disturbed sleep. Nevertheless, the widespread use of caffeine to "stay alert and focused" shows no sign of abating.

The search for pharmacological countermeasures more potent than caffeine that safely and effectively promote cognitive capabilities, especially in times of national crisis (e.g., war) spans much of the past century. Traditionally, dopaminergic agonists (e.g., amphetamines) have been the only option available, but these FDA-regulated substances have many serious risks associated with their repeated use. With the advent of sleep disorders medicine in the 1970s and the recognition of patients suffering from disorders of severe and debilitating sleepiness during waking periods (e.g., narcolepsy), a renewed effort was made to find safe and effective pharmacological agents.

Modafinil was classified by the U.S. Food and Drug Administration as a "wake promoting therapeutic," and approved as a treatment of the excessive sleepiness associated with narcolepsy (Lafon, 1988)—a genetically based CNS disorder the symptoms of which include excessive daytime sleepiness, cataplexy, and nocturnal sleep disturbance. Although the exact mechanism of action for modafinil is not yet fully elucidated, it appears to be a novel wake-promoting compound, chemically and pharmacologically different from previous CNS psychostimulants (e.g., amphetamine), with the absence of the more serious adverse effects of these drugs (e.g. locomotor agitation). Using a randomized double-blind, placebo-controlled, crossover study, Warot, Corruble et al. (1993) reported that the subjective effects of modafinil (300 mg) were similar to those of caffeine (300 mg), and markedly different from those of dextroamphetamine (15 mg).

When modafinil (200 mg) was administered to rested, non-sleep-deprived subjects in the morning, an increase in EEG-recorded vigilance, daytime sleep latency, concentration, complex reactions, subjective alertness, and performance on search and memory tests was observed (for review see Lyons & French, 1991). In addition, numerous studies have examined the efficacy of modafinil administration in maintaining neurobehavioral functioning and alertness levels during exposure to excessive sleepiness, due to pathological disorders (e.g., narcolepsy), and sleep deprivation (e.g., as experienced by shiftworkers). For example, Pigeau, Naitoh et al. (1995) compared the effects of modafinil (300 mg) to d-amphetamine (20 mg) and placebo in a double-blind crossover trial. Both modafinil and d-amphetamine reduced subjective feelings of sleepiness and fatigue and improved a range of performance measures, including reaction time, logical reasoning, and short-term memory. Comparison of sleep polysomnography (PSG) before and after administration of the drugs and sleep deprivation, demonstrated fewer sleep disturbances associated with administration of modafinil relative to amphetamine. Following modafinil administration, subjects were better able to sleep compared to subjects who ingested amphetamine, and their sleep structure more closely resembled the sleep of subjects receiving placebo (Buguet et al., 1995). Additionally, subjects administered modafinil appeared to require a reduced duration of sleep for recovery following the 64 hours of sleep deprivation. This latter finding is consistent with results from work in rodents by (Edgar & Siedel, 1997) demonstrating a reduction in rebound sleepiness and apparent reduction in the requirement for recovery sleep following modafinil administration, compared to other psychostimulants studied. Modafinil has also been reported to improve the residual daytime sleepiness in patients suffering from obstructive sleep apnea and treated with mechanical airway splints (CPAP) (Pack, Black et al., 2001).

In a randomized, double-blind, placebo-controlled study examining the effects of modafinil on sleepiness and cognitive functioning during four 24-hour periods of simulated night shiftwork (subjects slept during the day and were awake and performing across the night), modafinil (200 mg) improved nocturnal neurobehavioral performance on a range of computerized cognitive performance tasks, including psychomotor vigilance, cognitive throughput, and subjective assessments of sleepiness and alertness, without disturbing the subsequent daytime sleep periods (Hughes, Van Dongen et al., 2001).

Although it may seem irrelevant to describe the results of experiments on the effects of a novel, FDA-regulated drug currently only approved for excessive sleepiness due to certain sleep disorders, the example is a reminder that modafinil is likely to be the first of other new wake-promoting, and possibly even cognitive-enhancing, drugs, some of which may ultimately become available in this century for off label or over the counter use by segments of the population charged with maintaining cognitive proficiency in safety-sensitive activities.

The administration of pharmacological compounds as a means of increasing performance or increasing intelligence is not a new one. Primarily these compounds have been administered to ageing populations, for the treatment of declining cognitive functions associated with both clinical states, such as Alzheimer's disease, and with normal ageing (for review see Riedel & Jolles, 1996). Although several classes of drugs exist that may be administered in an attempt to improve cognitive abilities in these populations (e.g., nootropic agents, cholinergic agents, monoaminergic agents, methlxanthines, and thiamine) no one drug or class of drugs exists that has yet provided a breakthrough in the treatment of these populations.

Technological Countermeasures: Operator-Centered Technologies as Case Examples

Technological countermeasures for human alertness and cognitive capability are ubiquitous but also often invisible and relatively low tech (e.g., shoulder rumble strips along highways provide a vibrotactile warning that a driver is departing the roadway). In the past 50 years, since the development of microelectronics, many technological advances for decreasing human cognitive errors have involved the widespread deployment of automation, which in many instances has reduced human workload from high cognitive demand to very low cognitive demand (e.g., flying at cruise altitude in a "glass cockpit" commercial jet). Automation has, however, resulted in a high requirement for vigilance and detection of salient, albeit infrequent, signals. In a 24/7 world, it is sustained attention and vigilance that are among the cognitive functions most severely affected by sleep loss, night work, and jet lag. In an effort to detect hypovigilance in human operators, a number of technological countermeasure approaches have begun to be pursued. An area that amply illustrates these developments is in the transportation industry, where there are a variety of countermeasure initiatives underway owing to the prevalence and seriousness of fatigue-related crashes, the unreliability of subjective estimates of cognitive impairment, the potential of drowsiness-detection technologies as a component in alternatives to federally mandated proscriptive hours of service, and the fact that technological advances have made the goal of on-line drowsiness detection feasible (Dinges & Mallis, 1998).

Nearly all of the technologies currently being proposed to assess or monitor cognitive capability in a transportation operator are in the prototypical development, validation testing, or early implementation stages. Technologies can be arbitrarily grouped by different criteria, but at least three broad categories of fatigue-related technologies (for detection and/or prevention) include: operator-centered technologies, system-centered technologies, and environmentally oriented technologies (Dinges, 1997). Operator-centered technologies will be the focus here.

Most operator-centered technologies explicitly claim or imply detection of some aspect of either a heightened risk of operator cognitive error or outright cognitive impairment through one or more of the following hypothetical constructs: operator vigilance, operator attention/inattention, operator alertness/drowsiness, operator microsleeps, operator hypovigilancce, operator performance variability, or operator vulnerability to error. It remains a matter for scientific inquiry as to what extent these constructs overlap empirically. Generic categories of operator-centered technologies currently being developed or marketed include, but are not limited to, the following four classes.

Readiness-to-Perform and Fitness-for-Duty Technologies.   Fitness-for-duty or readiness-to-perform approaches can involve sampling aspects of performance capability or physiological responses. Because these tests are increasingly becoming briefer and more portable, the developers are seeking to extend their use beyond prediction of functional capability at the start of a given work cycle (i.e., prediction of relative risk over many hours) to prediction of capability in shorter time frames (e.g., whether it is safe for an individual to extend their work time at the end of a shift or duty period). As such these technologies are intended to provide some behavioral or biological estimate of an operator's cognitive capability for work yet to be performed, relative to a standard, such as the operator's idiosyncratic function when unimpaired, or relative to a group norm (Gilliland & Schlegel, 1993). Although some biologically based (primarily ocular) technologies for fitness for duty are currently available, most of the technologies in this area are performance based (Gilliland & Schlegel, 1993; Daecher, 1996). There are a large number of cognitive performance test batteries touted as candidates for readiness-to-perform and/or fitness-for-duty testing. Unfortunately, many of them are aptitude- and language-skill sensitive, and many have rather dramatic learning curves, making them less than ideal candidates for repeated usage in diverse populations. In addition, many have not been validated to be sensitive to cognitive impairment, and do not provide criteria by which to determine when someone is dysfunctional.

Mathematical Models of Alertness Dynamics Joined With Ambulatory Technologies. These technologies involve application of mathematical models that predict operator alertness/performance at different times based on interactions of sleep, circadian, and related temporal antecedents of fatigue. This is the subclass of operator-centered technologies that includes those devices that seek to monitor sources of fatigue, such as how much sleep an operator has obtained (e.g., via wrist actigraphy), and combine this information with a mathematical model that is designed to predict cognitive performance capability over a period of time as a function of the interaction of sleep homeostasis and the circadian pacemaker. However, like the other categories of technologies, precision and validation are critical criteria that must be met. A mathematical model that misestimates a cumulative performance decrement by only a few percentage points can lead to a gross miscalculation of alertness and cognitive performance capability over a work week. This is clearly a promising area, but much more work is needed (Dinges & Achermann, 1999; Diwges, 2004).

Vehicle-Based Performance Technologies.   These technologies are directed at measuring the behavior of the transportation hardware systems under the control of the operator, such as truck lane deviation, or steering or speed variability, or, in a pilot, interaction with the avionics, which are hypothesized to reflect identifiable behavioral alterations when an operator is fatigued. The technologies are challenging to develop and implement owing to the diversity of operator behaviors under different conditions and the complexity of vehicle behavior relative to environmental conditions. They are less concerned with the condition of the operator than with the status of the vehicle. In addition to their face validity, they have many advantages (e.g., no wires, devices, or monitors on or aimed at an operator), but as with all technologies for preventing, or at least detecting, cognitive decreases in operators, their scientific validity and cost effectiveness remain to be demonstrated.

In-Vehicle, On-Line, Operator Status Monitoring Technologies. This category of fatigue-monitoring technologies includes a broad array of approaches, techniques, and algorithms. Technologies in this category seek to record some biobehavioral dimension(s) of an operator, such as a feature of the eyes, face, head, heart, brain electrical activity (EEG), and the like, on-line (i.e., continuously, during driving). These are the most common and diverse of the monitoring technologies.

If operator-centered monitoring technology development continues and is proposed as a way to "manage" cognitive capability in a 24/7 world, then technologies that allege to be effective must be shown to meet or exceed a range of criteria involving scientific, practical, and legal/ethical standards (Dinges, 1995; Dinges, 1996; Dinger, 1997; Dinges, Mallis et al., 1998; Dinges & Mallis, 1998; Mallis, Maislin et al., 1999). Even if a device is valid and reliable, to be practically useful, it must meet additional standards of high sensitivity and high specificity. Thus, the device must detect all (or nearly all) operator deficits (i.e., high sensitivity standard), without too many false alarms (i.e., high specificity standard). In an effort to obtain measures of the scientific validity of a number of fatigue-detection technologies, we completed a double-blind controlled laboratory validation experiment examining six on-line, operator status-monitoring technologies (Dinges, Mallis et al., 1998). Each technology was time-locked to vigilance performance to test coherence between vigilance lapses and each technology's specific hypovigilance metric. Algorithms were applied to technology results by the respective vendors, who remained blind both to the lapse data and to time (i.e., the specific hour of continuous wakefulness at which each data file was acquired). These procedures were used to eliminate possible bias in drowsiness scores derived from the vendors. This trial revealed that although nearly all of the technologies were found to accurately predict lapses in at least one subject or a subset of subjects, only one technology consistently correlated at a high level with performance lapses within and between different subjects (Dinges, Mallis et al., 1998). Meeting the validation criterion both through high intrasubject and high intersubject coherence is an important and highly promising outcome, as one of the more serious problems plaguing fatigue-detection and prevention is the large intersubject differences in vulnerability to fatigue.

Finally, just as with cognitive enhancement by way of sleep in the workplace (i.e., naps) and pharmacological manipulation, there are substantive legal and policy questions associated with deployment of operator-centered technologies (Dinges & Mallis, 1998). These issues range from control over the detection technology, to the privacy rights of the individual being monitored, to the confidentiality issues of the information acquired. Related to the confidentiality question are issues of enforcement and use of punitive contingencies when impairment is detected but no appropriate operator action is taken.

It appears that within the not-too-distant future some technologies will be deployed to prevent or limit certain types of cognitive errors from leading to catastrophic outcomes. Such a development raises provocative questions about the standards for cognitive capability and whether it is meaningful to regard intelligence as a predictor of cognitive capability in a 24/7 world in which cognitive functions can be maintained or enhanced using behaviors, pharmocology or technology.

ACKNOWLEDGMENTS

Supported by grant NR-04281 and RR00040 from the National Institutes of Health, U.S. Public Health Service; by NASA grant NAG9-1161, NASA cooperative agreement NCC 2-1077, and NASA cooperative agreement NCC 9-58 with the National Space Biomedical Research Institute; by grants F49620–95-1-0388 and F49620-00-1-0266 from the U.S. Air Force Office of Scientific Research; and by unrestricted grant support from Cephalon, Inc. We thank Hans P.A. Van Dongen, PhD for help in developing specific sections of the chapter.

REFERENCES

Aeschbach, D., Postolache, T.T., Sher L., Matthews, J. R., Jackson, M. A., Wehr, T. A. (2001). Evidence from the waking electroencephalogram that short sleepers live under higher homeostatic sleep pressure than long sleepers. *Neuroscience. 102*(3), 493–502.

Belenky G., Wesensten N.J., Thorne D.R., Thomas M.L., Sing H.C., Redmond D.P., Russo M.B., Balkin T.J. (2003). Patterns of performance degradation and restoration during sleep restriction and subsequent recovery: a sleep dose-response study. *Journal of Sleep Research. 12*(1):1–12.

Buguet A., Montmayeur A., Pigeau R., Naitoh P. (1995). Modafinil, d-amphetamine and placebo during 64 hours of sustained mental work. II. Effects on two nights of recovery sleep. *Journal of Sleep Research. 4*(4), 229–241.

Costa G., Lievore F., Casaletti G., Gaffuri E., Folkard S. (1989). Circadian characteristics influencing interindividual differences in tolerance and adjustment to shiftwork. *Ergonomics. 32*(4):373–385.

Dagher A., Owen A.M., Boecker H., Brooks D.J. (1999). Mapping the network for planning: A correlational PET activation study with the Tower of London task. *Brain. 122*(10), 1973–1987.

Dawson, D., Lamond, N., Donkin, K., Reid, K. (1998). Quantitative similarity between the cognitive psychomotor performance decrement associated with sustained wakefulness and alcohol intoxication. In L. Hartley (Ed.)., *Managing fatigue in transportation* (pp. 231–255). Oxford, England: Pergamon.

Dijk D.J., Duffy J.F., Czeisler C.A. (1992). Circadian and sleep/wake dependent aspects of subjective alertness and cognitive performance. *Journal of Sleep Research.* 1(2), 112–117.

Dinges, D. F.: Critical research issues in development of biomathematical models of fatigue and performance. Aviation, Space and Envionement Medicine *75* (3): A181-A191, 2004.

Dinges D.F., Orne M.T., Whitehouse W.G., Orne E.C. (1987). Temporal placement of a nap for alertness: Contributions of circadian phase and prior wakefulness. *Sleep. 10*(4), 313–329.

Dinges D.F., Pack F., Williams K., Gillen K.A., Powell J.W., Ott G.E., Aptowicz C., Pack A.I. (1997). Cumulative sleepiness, mood disturbance, and psychomotor vigilance performance decrements during a week of sleep restricted to 4-5 hours per night. *Sleep. 20*(4):267–277.

Dinges, D.F., Whitehouse, W.G., Orne, E.C., Orne, M.T. (1988). The benefits of a nap during prolonged work and wakefulness. *Work and Stress.* 2(2)139–153.

Dinges, D.F., Mallis, M., Maislin, G., Powell, J.W. (1998). *Evaluation of techniques for ocular measurement as an index of fatigue and the basis for alertness management.* U.S. Department of Transportation, National Highway Traffic Safety Administration, Contract No. DTNH22-93-D-07007. pp. 1–113.

Dinges, D.F., Maislin, G., Kuo, A., Carlin, M.M., Powell, J.W., Van Dongen, H., Mullington, J. (1999). Chronic sleep restriction: Neurobehavioral effects of 4hr, 6hr, and 8hr TIB. *Sleep, 22*(Suppl. 1), S115.

Dinges, D.F. (2004). Critical research issues in development of biomathematical models of fatigue and performance. *Aviation, Space and Environmental Medicine, 75*(3), A181–A191.

Diwadkar V.A., Carpenter P.A., Just M.A. (2000). Collaborative activity between parietal and dorsolateral prefrontal cortex in dynamic spatial working memory revealed by fMRI. *Neuroimage. 12*(1):85–99.

Doran S.M., Van Dongen H.P., Dinges D.F. (2001). Sustained attention performance during sleep deprivation: evidence of state instability. *Archives Italiennes deBiologie. 139*(3):253–67.

Drummond S.P., Brown G.G., Gillin J.C., Stricker J.L., Wong E.C., Buxton R.B. (2000). Altered brain response to verbal learning following sleep deprivation. *Nature, 403*(6770), 655–657.

Drummond S.P., Brown G.G., Stricker J.L., Buxton R.B., Wong E.C., Gillin J.C. (1999). Sleep deprivation-induced reduction in cortical functional response to serial subtraction. *Neuroreport. 10*(18), 3745–3748.

Edgar D.M., Dement W.C., Fuller C.A. (1993). Effect of SCN lesions on sleep in squirrel monkeys: evidence for opponent processes in sleep-wake regulation. *Journal of Neuroscience. 13*(3), 1065–1079.

Folkard S., Marks M., Minors D.S., Waterhouse J.M. (1985). Circadian rhythms in human performance and affective state. *Acta Psychiatrica Belgica. 85*(5):568–581.

Gilliland, K. & Schlegel, R.E. (1993). *Readiness to perform testing: A critical analysis of the concept and current practices,* Final report, DTFA-02-92P23499, Office of Aviation Medicine, Federal Aviation Administration, Civil Aeromedical Institute, Oklahoma City, Oklahoma.

Hughes, R.J., Van Dongen, H.P.A., Dinges, D.F., Rogers, N., Wright, K.P., Edgar, D.F., Czeisler, C.A. (2001). Modafinil improves alertness and performance during simulated night work. *Sleep, 24*(Suppl. 1), A200.

Jewett M.E., Dijk D.J., Kronauer R.E., Dinges D.F. (1999). Dose-response relationship between sleep duration and human psychomotor vigilance and subjective alertness. *Sleep. 22*(2), 171–179.

Jewett M.E., Wyatt J.K., Ritz-De Cecco A., Khalsa S.B., Dijk D.J., Czeisler C.A. (1999). Time course of sleep inertia dissipation in human performance and alertness. *Journal of Sleep Research. 8*(1):1–8.

Kroger J.K., Sabb F.W., Fales C.L., Bookheimer S.Y., Cohen M.S., Holyoak K.J. (2002). Recruitment of anterior dorsolateral prefrontal cortex in human reasoning: a parametric study of relational complexity. *Cerebral Cortex. 12*(5):477–485.

Mallis, M., Maislin, G., Konowal, N., Byrne, V., Bierman, D., Davis, R., Grace, R., Dinges, D.F. (1999). *Biobehavioral responses to drowsy driving alarms and alerting stimuli. Final report to develop, test and evaluate a drowsy driver detection and warning system for commercial motor vehicle drivers.* U.S. Department of Transportation, National Highway Traffic Safety Administration, Federal Highway Administration, Office of Motor Carriers. Contract No. DTNH22-93-D-07007. pp. 1–127.

Mallis, M., Mejdal, S., Nguyen, T.T., Dinges, D.F. (2004). Summary of the key features of seven biomathematical models of human fatigue and performance. *Aviation, Space and Environmental Medicine,* 75(3), A4–A14.

McCartt A.T., Ribner S.A., Pack A.I., Hammer M.C. (1996). The scope and nature of the drowsy driving problem in New York State. *Accident Analysis & Prevention,* 28(4):511–517.

Miller J.D., Morin L.P., Schwartz W.J., Moore R.Y. (1996). New insights into the mammalian circadian clock. *Sleep,* 19(8):641–67.

Monk T.H., Buysse D.J., Reynolds C.F., Berga S.L., Jarrett D.B., Begley A.E., Kupfer D.J. (1997). Circadian rhythms in human performance and mood under constant conditions. *Journal of Sleep Research.* 6(1), 9–18.

Monk T.H., Buysse D.J., Welsh D.K., Kennedy K.S., Rose L.R. (2001). A sleep diary and questionnaire study of naturally short sleepers. *Journal of Sleep Research.* 10(3), 173–179.

Mottaghy F.M., Gangitano M., Sparing R., Krause B.J., Pascual-Leone A. (2002). Segregation of areas related to visual working memory in the prefrontal cortex revealed by rTMS. *Cerebral Cortex.* 12(4), 369–375.

Pack A.I., Black J.E., Schwartz J.R., Matheson J.K. (2001). Modafinil as adjunct therapy for daytime sleepiness in obstructive sleep apnea. *American Journal of Respiratory & Critical Care Medicine.* 164(9), 1675–1681.

Pigeau R., Naitoh P., Buguet A., McCann C., Baranski J., Taylor M., Thompson M., MacK I. I. (1995). Modafinil, d-amphetamine and placebo during 64 hours of sustained mental work. I. Effects on mood, fatigue, cognitive performance and body temperature. *Journal of Sleep Research,* 4(4), 212–228.

Powell N.B., Schechtman K.B., Riley R.W., Li K., Troell R., Guilleminault C. (2001). The road to danger: the comparative risks of driving while sleepy. *Laryngoscope.* 111(5), 887–893.

Reid K.J., Zeldow M., Teplin L.A., McClelland G.M., Abram K.A., Zee P.C. (2002). Sleep habits of juvenile detainees in the Chicago area. *Sleep,.* 25(Abstract Suppl.), A433–A434.

Rosekind, M.R., Graeber, R.C., Dinges, D.F., Connell, L.J., Rountree, M.S., Spinweber, C.L., and Gillen, K.A. (1994) *Crew Factors in Flight Operations: IX. Effects of Planned Cockpit Rest on Crew Performance and Alertness in Long-haul Operations.* NASA Technical Memorandum #108839. Moffett Field, CA: NASA Ames Research Center. 1–82.

Saper C.B., Chou T.C., Scammell T.E. (2001). The sleep switch: hypothalamic control of sleep and wakefulness. *Trends in Neuroscience.* 24(12), 726–731.

Thomas M., Sing H., Belenky G., Holcomb H., Mayberg H., Dannals R., Wagner H., Thorne D., Popp K., Rowland L., Welsh A., Balwinski S., Redmond D. (2000). Neural basis of alertness and cognitive performance impairments during sleepiness. I. Effects of 24 h of sleep deprivation on waking human regional brain activity. *Journal of Sleep Research.* 9(4), 335–52.

Thomas M., Sing H., Belenky G., Holcomb H., Dannals R., Wagner H., Peller P., Mayberg H., Wright J., Thorne D., Popp K., Redmond D., Zurer J., Balwinski S. (1993). Cerebral glucose utilization during task performance and prolonged sleep loss. *Journal of Cerebral Blood Flow and Metabolism,* 13(Abstract Suppl.), S531.

U.S. Committee on Military Nutrition Research. (2001). Caffeine for the sustainment of mental task performance: Formulations for military operations. Institute of Medicine, National Academy Press, Washington, D.C.

Van Dongen, H., Maislin, G., Dinges, D. (1999). Chronic partial sleep deprivation: Neurobehavioral response and sleep architecture. *Sleep Research Online,* 2(Suppl. 1), 735.

Van Dougen H.P., Price N.J., Mullington J.M., Szuba M.P., Kapoor S.C., Dinges D.F. (2001). Caffeine eliminates psychomotor vigilance deficits from sleep inertia. *Sleep,* 24(7), 813–819.

Van Dongen H.P.A., Maislin G., Hachadoorian B., Dinges D.F. (2001). A mixed regression model of cumulative sleep debt in chronic sleep restriction. *Sleep-Wake Research in the Netherlands,* 12, 31–32.

Van Dongen, H.P.A., Maislin, G., Mullington, J.M., Dinges, D.F. (2003). The cumulative cost of additional wakefulness: Dose-response effects on neurobehavioral functions and sleep physiology from chronic sleep restriction and total sleep deprivation. *Sleep, 26*(2), 117–126.

Walsleben J.A., Norman R.G., Novak R.D., O'Malley E.B., Rapoport D.M., Strohl K.P. (1999). Sleep habits of Long Island Rail Road commuters. *Sleep, 22*(6), 728–734.

Warot, D., Corruble, E., Payan, C., Weil, J.S., Puech, A.J. (1993). Subjective effects of modafinil, a new central adrenergic stimulant in healthy volunteers: A comparison with amphetamine, caffeine and placebo. *European Psychiatry, 8*, 201–208.

Williams H.L., Lubin A. (1959). Impaired performance with acute sleep loss. *Psychological Monographs: General and Applied, 73*, 1–26.

Williamson A.M., Feyer A.M., Mattick R.P., Friswell R., Finlay-Brown S. (2001). Developing measures of fatigue using an alcohol comparison to validate the effects of fatigue on performance. *Accident Analysis and Prevention, 33*(3), 313–326.

Wyatt J.K., Ritz-De Cecco A., Czeisler C.A., Dijk D.J. (1999). Circadian temperature and melatonin rhythms, sleep, and neurobehavioral function in humans living on a 20-h day. *American Journal of Physiology, 277*(4 Pt. 2), R1152–63.

Zysset S., Huber O., Ferstl E., von Cramon D.Y. (2002). The anterior frontomedian cortex and evaluative judgment: an fMRI study. *Neuroimage, 15*(4):983–991.

CONCLUSIONS

VII

CONCLUSIONS

Extending Intelligence: Conclusions and Future Directions

Richard D. Roberts,
Lazar Stankov,
Ralf Schulze,
Patrick C. Kyllonen[1]
Educational Testing Service

We begin this concluding commentary with a somewhat contentious statement that supports us compiling this current edited volume. The main topics covered in this book—enhancement and new constructs—appear as recurring themes in 21st century education, psychology, and more recently, economic theory and practice. The contributors to this volume argue mostly from the vantage point of education, cognitive, and/or differential psychology, though there are also chapters that cover biological agents, technological aids, and temporal conditions that allow for enhancement of human abilities, as well. The populations covered by the contributors are expansive. The targets of intervention approaches include children starting school, children in the school system, college students, and special populations, such as the gifted and elderly. The contributors' combined reflection on lifelong capabilities for enhancement and for exploring the status of new psychological constructs is nonincidental; we contend that the principal positive message to come out of this volume is that enhancement is something that is possible at all stages of life, though the "what" that can be enhanced may well vary.

Before reviewing the specific contributions of the chapter authors, a comment on the importance of *both* enhancement and new constructs to education, psychology, and economics appears in order. Consider the following. In education, countries now place considerable emphasis on OECD Programme for International Student Assessment (PISA) scores. The importance of enhancement derives from the realization that these scores are not what they should be, either in some domain relative to some other nation or across specific subgroups within a country (see OECD PISA, 2005). The importance of new constructs rests, for example, in the realization that academic ability, although important, is not the only predictor of educational success, of sticking to school, or of indicating conduct problems (e.g., Neisser et al., 1996). In psychology, both enhancement and new constructs blend naturally in various positive psychology

---

[1]The ideas expressed in this paper are those of the authors and not necessarily of the Educational Testing Service.

movements, which seek to create greater opportunities for future holistic growth of the individual that will, in turn, impact on society (e.g., Seligman, 2002). In economics, these two topics again combine with the realization that humans are not merely motivated by capital and dollar value, but rather by issues of happiness, personal satisfaction, and well being, and, ultimately, how to quantify and/or intervene in these less-well understood domains and how this might ultimately prove of benefit to the global economy (e.g., Layard, 2005).

Each discipline grappling with such issues is forced to ask itself some vexing questions, which ultimately play into the very concerns of the other. To enhance education levels, do we need simply to provide better schools, better teachers, better curricula, or better economic policies? Should one simply target academics—reading and math—as has been mandated in the United States by No Child Left Behind (NCLB) legislation? What of the very areas that both psychologists and economists are giving greater emphasis; should not the teaching of social and emotional learning, for example, be as much part and parcel of the educational experience as learning basic academics? And even if we began to exhaust the available "stock" of concepts and constructs, should there not always be specialists whose agenda is to find new domains of human individual differences that might add still further value to prediction, intervention, and policies central to the various applied domains affecting everyday life?

The preceding are complex questions that cannot be answered in one volume or, we suspect, in the near future. Nor was it the intention of any of the contributors to address these issues specifically. However, we believe that the flavor of this book is that enhancement is important, as is the way that new constructs (especially those representing emotional intelligence, practical intelligence, critical thinking, creativity, and the like) are assessed. Evidence presented by the contributors makes these issues take on scientific credibility, though also important is how this evidence feeds into a recursive cycle of programmatic research aimed at finding the right questions for scientists to address in the future. Thus, in this concluding chapter, we attempt a synthesis of the various perspectives offered throughout this volume, while offering a series of comments on future directions that researchers might profitably explore.

FRAMES OF REFERENCE

By and large, in this volume, enhancement refers to an increase in performance on objective tests of cognitive abilities. We note, however, that there are also chapters that address new constructs, and their enhancement. Indeed, the main title of the book—Extending Intelligence—reflects each of several, related meanings: Can we extend (the domain of) intelligence by including new constructs, can we extend (i.e., improve) intelligence and, indeed, extend (i.e., enhance) new constructs? By new constructs is generally meant concepts, procedures, or assessment vehicles that have not necessarily been the focus of a large body of systematic, previous research in psychology or education. The extent that a construct is actually new is equivocal. We can find within the history of differential psychology, for example, concepts such as social intelligence, which share overlaps with several new concepts covered in the book (e.g., emotional intelligence, practical intelligence) (see Landy, 2005). In such cases, there have often been new paradigms, approaches, methodological or technological advances, and/or a critical piece of scientific evidence that gives these new constructs currency at the present point of time.

We wish to mention a sample of additional themes that cut across many of the chapters of this edited volume. One of these themes is discussion about the nature of intelligence (or perhaps more correctly cognitive abilities). For some of the authors, intelligence is a single unitary dimension, much as Spearman first considered it at the beginning of the 1900s (Brody, chap. 5). Others view it as a hierarchical construct that may or may not include this general factor. In such instances, the efficacy of enhancement is made more complex. Hunt (chap. 2), for example, suggests that it is crystallized (Gc), rather than fluid (Gf), intelligence that is predominantly responsive to educational influences that lead to enhancement; Gustafsson (chap. 4) settles on a different set of higher order factors. Still other authors view a focus on cognitive forms of intelligence as delimiting; this is the flavor of many of the chapters describing new constructs. And to provide still further perspectives on the nature of intelligence, it is worth noting too that several of the chapter authors are entirely agnostic on this point (e.g., Dinges & Rogers, chap. 18).

A second theme cutting across many of the chapters is a methodological one. It concerns the use of factor analytic techniques in both intelligence research and investigations of new constructs. The research community has witnessed a shift in the use of factor analytic techniques in the past few decades. Whereas the *establishment* of models of intelligence and other constructs was dominated by the use of exploratory factor analysis (EFA), the new standard seems to be confirmatory factor analysis (CFA) (see Schulze, 2005). CFA allows for tests of critical assumptions about the nature of new constructs *and* the enhancement of latent variable scores. In terms of the latter, these assumptions pertain to the question of whether factorial invariance is tenable when examining group differences with multigroup CFA (MGCFA) (see Dolan & Molenaar, 1994; Lubke, Dolan, Kelderman, & Mellenbergh, 2003). At the heart of every examination of a construct's of enhancement lies the assumption that what is enhanced with an intervention of any type, are latent variable scores and *not* the properties of the measurement instrument. MGCFA is a technique that allows for the disentanglement of such effects and may therefore be considered highly relevant for application in enhancement studies. We note that many of the issues raised by contributors might be resolved, or propositions otherwise weakly stated given greater force, with application of this methodology.

COGNITIVE ENHANCEMENT: ISSUES, PROSPECTS, AND LIMITATIONS

We structure these passages in the following way. First, we provide a synthesis of empirical evidence for enhancement provided by the contributors. Our purpose is to evaluate whether cognitive performance can be improved. We attempt to be balanced in this approach, as the available evidence is mixed. Next, we address the issue of what is being enhanced. We address the issue of whether this is something central to intelligence, something peripheral to it, or perhaps some nonintellective factor (or factors)? We also address the impact of intervention; if there is even a small effect size this may be justification enough to suggest that research should be directed toward further exploring the issue. Inside this section, we also discuss some studies that the contributors do not necessarily consider. Throughout we include suggestions for future directions, particularly empirical studies that might more definitively address issues raised by the contributors.

Empirical Evidence for Enhancement

The evidence as it has been presented throughout the current volume needs to be considered relative to a host of relevant psychological, sociological, and demographic variables. The most salient appear to be the age at which potentially enhancing interventions are administered, the nature of intervention as it relates to different aspects of cognitive function, and its subsequent impact on cognitive ability. It is natural to assume that interventions that take place early in life may be the most important as they are likely to provide for a greater accrual over the life span and therefore be most beneficial to the individual. Thus, we give consideration to the effects of early intervention first.

Campbell's (chap. 4) report on the follow-up of participants in the Abecedarian Project, when these participants reached 21 years of age, is an important contribution to the literature on the effects of early intervention. Campbell's exposition focuses on three main findings. First, the randomized controlled design employed in the Abecedarian Project suggests that altering educational stimulation within the environment of young children at risk can enhance intellectual development in a lasting way. Second, the unadjusted IQ score difference between treated and control groups, by available standards, is impressive. Third, there are important academic gains and real life benefits at age 21 that can be ascribed to early educational intervention with African American children at risk.

Findings of lasting WAIS-R differences of about 4.5 IQ points can, on cursory inspection, be interpreted as modest. However, consider the following scenario: Let a cut-point of IQ = 120 serve for admission to a special student support program (as is done in some countries in programs for the gifted). Enhancing the IQ of a subpopulation with mean IQ = 100 and SD = 15 would result in all those having an IQ between 115.5 and 119.9 before enhancement being granted admission after enhancement. Assuming scores are normally distributed, this means that 6% of the population would now move beyond the cutoff. Depending on the size of the subpopulation, this could impact on the lives of hundreds or thousands of students now benefiting from the program. Coupled with the findings of much stronger effects on real life outcomes such as achievement scores on verbal and math tests, greater attendance at college, and later age of having the first child, it is easy to see the importance of Campbell's (chap. 4) findings for social policy decisions and for theories about the nature of cognitive abilities and their malleability.

Three chapters in this volume report on findings targeting interventions with students of high school age. They all have a different focus. Hunt's (chap. 2) treatment is perhaps the closest to the kind employed by Campbell, in that a particular procedure was developed in an effort to enhance performance in subjects taught in school (e.g., a course on physics). Principles employed by the DIAGNOSER are clearly successful in demonstrating improved performance on tests of physics. Again, experimental manipulation by Hunt and his associates augur well for demonstrating the positive effects of enhancement.

In his chapter, Hunt referred to the hypothesis that, at the lower ability levels, the g factor is stronger than it is at high-ability levels. In other words, he referred to the "Law of Diminishing Returns" (LDR; Spearman, 1927). The use of the term "law" in LDR suggests that there is a substantial empirical research base invariably supporting such a hypothesis so that it can be assigned the status of a law. This is, however, not the case. In fact, there is conflicting evidence (cf., Deary & Pagliari, 1991; Detterman & Daniel, 1989; Fogarty & Stankov, 1995; Hartmann & Teasdale, 2004; Jensen, 2003; Legree, Pifer, & Grafton, 1996) calling for a quantitative research synthesis (i.e., a metaanalysis) of these data.[2] Nevertheless, Hunt (chap. 2) uses the purported status of the LDR to argue that at low-ability levels the distinction between Gf and Gc disappears and therefore training in Gc areas (e.g., literacy) can affect Gf as well. Given the present status of the LDR and potential alternative explanations for Hunt's interesting observation, it is unclear whether his explanations are entirely correct.

---

[2]In addition to the unexplained heterogenetiy of findings on the LDR, one of the desiderata to be addressed in future studies is the issue of factorial invariance mentioned previously. Applied to established the lawfulness of LDR, this issue concerns the question of whether the measurement instruments used for different age groups or ability levels do indeed measure the same abilities.

Nevertheless, these suggestions certainly warrant further consideration, perhaps using more stringent methods like MGCFA.

The two other chapters examining performance of high school students do not employ systematic experimental manipulations. Gustafsson (chap. 3) dealt with the effects of different streams of schooling on a general cognitive factor (g) and broad abilities of fluid (Gf), crystallized (Gc), and spatial/visualization ability (Gv). His conclusion is quite different from that of Hunt, as his findings indicate that participation in an academic track at high school has the strongest effect on g and Gf, and a much weaker effect on Gc. Also, academic tracks with an orientation toward technology and science affect performance on tasks measuring Gv positively. His estimate of the effects of schooling on IQ is approximately 2.5 IQ points per year. Clearly, following a particular academic track can influence (enhance) one's performance on the general factor of intelligence and its components. Interestingly, Table 3. 5 in Gustafsson's chapter shows that Gc is better predicted by school marks from an earlier grade level than either the general factor or Gf. In concert with Hunt (chap. 2), Gustafsson suggested that Gc is most affected by schooling, although Gustafsson also suggested the involvement of Gf and Gv to a larger extent than what follows from Hunt's work.

Lubinski and Bleske-Rechek (Chapter 7) reviewed the findings with intellectually talented populations. Their report is similar to Gustafsson's in the sense that they linked the pattern of performance to lines of study people choose to follow in their academic careers. It is not surprising that people whose SAT Math scores are higher than SAT Verbal scores tend to choose careers in Science/Technology and those with the opposite sign of the difference between the components tend to move into Humanities. It is worth noting that Ackerman and colleagues reported similar findings under the so-called PPIK theory (process, personality, interests, knowledge) with samples drawn from the general population (see e.g., Ackerman, 1996; Ackerman & Heggestad, 1997).

In the chapter by Lubinski and Bleske-Rechek it is also demonstrated that adolescent scores on spatial abilities, in addition to verbal and mathematical abilities, can predict career paths of intellectually talented adults. This result stands out because there is a general belief that predictive validity of everything else but measures of g is insignificant. These authors are also in agreement with Comer (chap. 6) in pointing out that commitment to work and the actual amount of work is unusually high among the intellectually talented. But is there evidence for enhancement in their chapter? Not, it seems, as measured by cognitive ability tests. But how much enhancement can one expect from a population that is already within the top .05% in ability? It is the extraordinary achievement in their chosen careers that matters and there is a considerable evidence for enhanced performance in the body of research reviewed by Lubinski and Bleske-Rechek.

McArdle (chap. 8) reported on the findings with a special group of university students, in particular, those that have been selected to higher education predominantly for their athletic, rather than academic, prowess. The chapter examines longitudinal changes in academic performance as a result of the introduction of more rigorous academic standards for these students. The findings show positive effects of a selection process on academic achievement of students–athletes. However, due to the design of the study, firm conclusions about the enhancement of cognitive abilities are not warranted. For example, most of the effects reported in this chapter could be attributed to out-migration due to an improved selection process, not to enhancement within the individual. Potential threats to internal validity, not ruled out by research design or statistical controls, limit major insights into the efficacy of enhancement in this instance.

Kliegl and Philipp (chap. 11) pointed out that cognitive deficits and cognitive expertise appear to be at the opposite end of a continuum of cognitive skill. However, strategies identified in cognitive expertise research could be used to overcome cognitive deficits. As an example, old adults' complaints about poor person memory proved to be quite resistant to memory training. In the expertise-based approach Kliegl and Philipp labeled as cognitive engineering, a sample of participants overcame the deficit in a training program that assembled the required components of skill and provided a tailored-learning environment and opportunities for deliberate practice. As in the acquisition of any other cognitive expertise (such as becoming a chess master), a high level of commitment of time was required, converting the deficit to a special area of interest in everyday life.

Horn (chap. 10) focused on expertise, not as a way to overcome deficiencies, but rather as an important aspect of intelligence. Expertise is defined as high-level ability to deal successfully with complex problems in which the solutions require advanced, deep understanding of a knowledge domain. Components of intelligence such as the ability to retrieve information from the store of knowledge, as well as the amount of knowledge, tend to increase over adult development (see also Hunt, chap. 2). Tests of Gc that measure knowledge acquired throughout development tap only surface knowledge, not depth of knowledge. Studies of experts in chess, GO, medical diagnosis, and financial planning, reported by Horn, indicate that superior performance of experts is characterized by a form of long-term working memory (LTWM). This type of memory relies on deductive reasoning processes that utilize a complex store of information to effectively anticipate, predict, evaluate, check, analyze, and monitor problem solving within the knowledge domain. Years of intensive, well-structured learning and regular practice are needed to develop and maintain a high level of expertise. Under these conditions, level of expertise is found to increase with age.

In summary, apart from McArdle (chap. 8), who as we suggest cannot speak directly to the issues covered in these passages, the research reviewed in a large number of chapters comprising this volume reveals evidence for enhancement in cognitive performance and in real life accomplishments. The amount of enhancement achieved through different interventions varies. It depends on the nature (and intensity) of treatment, the age when the treatment is administered, temporal factors (in fields of expertise, many thousands of hours of practice), and on noncognitive factors like persistence, interests, and motivation to work and study.

What Can Be Enhanced and by How Much?

Leaving aside new constructs and new interventions, there are two different answers to questions concerning the qualities enhanced and the quantity of enhancement in the current volume that we address in this section. In particular, Flynn (chap. 12) provided an account of IQ gains that have been documented in much of his previous work. His account is expressed largely in terms of environmental/demographic/sociological factors. By contrast, Brody (chap. 5) restricted himself to educational interventions and, despite the evidence summarized here, reached the conclusion that the effects are minimal and therefore of minor social importance.

Flynn (chap. 12) focused on American IQ gains in pre-1950 and post-1950 periods. The former are attributed primarily to increased years and quality of formal schooling. The latter are attributed to a variety of factors: the decline of the 1930s depression, reduced family size, more leisure and new leisure-time activities, jobs emphasizing manipulation of symbols or abstractions, and greater on-the-spot problem solving. He also contended that collectively these influences represent an attitude shift toward taking "nonpractical" problems more seriously. The key to the magnitude of transgenerational IQ gains appears social multipliers, that is, reciprocal causality between various cognitive skills and the relevant environments. In a later section, we discuss both additional and emerging societal factors that may play a salient role in this relationship.

However, there is also debate about the very nature of the Flynn effect that pertains to the issue of factorial invariance of the measurement instruments used to investigate the effect. Wicherts et al. (2004) have reanalyzed several data sets from different countries and shown that factorial invariance is not tenable across cohorts. This means that increases in latent variable scores are not the sole cause for observed gains in the data sets that were used by Wicherts et al. Hence, there is evidence to suggest that future studies examining the Flynn effect might in particular address the issue of factorial invariance.

Brody (chap. 5) asked whether education influences intelligence and concluded that there is no evidence that variation in educational experiences have enduring and substantial effects on intelligence. Part of his conclusion derives from the definition of intelligence. To him, only Gf is intelligence and therefore Hunt's findings that Gc can be enhanced should be discarded. The problem with such a claim is that many measures often considered the avatar of g (e.g., vocabulary tests, verbal analogies) (see, e.g., Stauffer, Reet Casette, 1996) would be rendered relatively trivial according to this argument. We take up the issue of definitions of intelligence, and how they play into gauging the effects of educational interventions, in a later section of the current chapter.

In maintaining his position, Brody acknowledged that both Gustafsson and Campbell showed enhancement of intelligence but renders these as limited because of problems in their study designs. What are the problems? In Gustafsson's case, one is the lack of control for self-selection on variables like intellectual interests. Whereas this is likely to have some impact, we question whether these can account for all of the observed effects; note also that in the absence of data the tenability of this argument is uncertain. The second problem has to do with the fact that there is no evidence that the effects are long lasting. To illustrate this point, Brody cited unpublished research purportedly showing that highly educated people differ from less educated more on WAIS subtests that have low g saturation than on those with high g saturation. Without having all the details of that study, it is worth noting that WAIS data are generally collected on adult samples, Gustafsson's work is with high school students; throughout the volume we see that different age cohorts may be differentially sensitive to intervention rendering any comparison problematic. Moreover, the amount of education appears a gross measure in the study based on WAIS subtests—Gustafsson showed the effects of different streams of education on measures of ability. The second set of unpublished data Brody (chap. 5) cites show that the amount of educational exposure is positively correlated with verbal ability and negatively correlated with the general factor (i.e., g) and Gf. These data appear again to be based on adults, rendering comparisons equivocal.

In Campbell's case, the problem that Brody singled out is easily identified. In short, the gap between treatment and control group at age 21 is smaller than at earlier ages and it can be speculated by extrapolation that it will eventually disappear. However, we do not really know what may happen after the age of 21. The gap of 4.5 IQ points may remain for the rest of the participants' lives. Indeed, this is plausible given that other "real-life" outcome measures (i.e., college attendance and higher verbal and math achievement scores) point to a significant difference in favor of the treatment group. Intellectual activities implied by these outcome measures may retain the gap in IQ at the same level. In short, we know that the difference remains at 21 years of age but we cannot be as certain as Brody that this difference will disappear completely.

It is pertinent to mention here the work carried out in two high schools by the Yugoslavian psychologist Kvashchev over the 25-year period from the early 1960s until the mid-1980s. This research was based largely on the early notion of schemas, of the kind described in Hunt's (chap. 2) exposition, along with similar ideas expressed by Halpern (chap. 15) in this volume. One of his projects has been described extensively elsewhere (see Stankov, 1986; Stankov & Chen, 1988a, 1988b), although there exist four additional monographs (published in Serbocroatian, perhaps explaining why they are not so well known) that produced essentially the same outcomes.[3] In Kvashchev's experiments, students in one school in a small city were exposed to a treatment and the other school was used as a control. At the beginning of the experiment, all participants were given a battery of tests of fluid and crystallized intelligence and the same battery was given at the end of the treatment period and twice in the final year (at the beginning and the end of the school year) of high school. The treatment lasted for 3 years, schema-based exercises were developed not only for physics but also for some three to five additional school subjects, and the training was intensive. The outcome of this work was a statistically significant increase in scores of the treated group over and above the control group. On the average, the increase of between 3 and 12 IQ points for individual tests was evident for both Gf and Gc and some of the individual measures showed an even larger improvement. This body of work clearly shows enhancement in cognitive performance.

Effect Size and Enhancement: "Half-Full," "Half-Empty"?

But the real reason Brody (chap. 5) appears to so steadfastly hold to the notion that enhancement is not pronounced, or important, perhaps derives from issues raised in the concluding section of his critique. In particular, he argued that the enhancement effects are small relative to the role of prenatal factors such as mother's education or, indeed, genetics. If we were to attach a rough estimate of the effect size due to educational interventions summarized throughout this volume, we agree with Brody—it is about 8 IQ points or 6% in terms of variance in IQ and these figures somehow look small on first blush. To arrive at a judgment about whether this is an important, or negligible, effect, we have to think about the potential implications of such an effect for valued outcomes. We have already provided an example of how an intervention effect of 4.5 IQ points might turn out to be important in terms of affecting a sizable proportion of the targeted population; we comment further in the following, on the issue of effect size.

In essence, an evaluation of the importance of effects is a question of framing. Effect size measures like variance explained are known to be misleading and it has been repeatedly argued in the methodological literature that a translation of such effect sizes has to be done to make a judgment about the "real" size of such effects (Abelson, 1985, 1995; D'Andrade & Dart, 1990; Rosenthal, Rosnow, & Rubin, 2000). A possible means of translating relatively abstract effect size figures, like incremental variance explained, into real-world units that are more easily amenable to judgments about their importance, is utility analysis (see, e.g., Schulze & Holling, 2005). There is considerable evidence from industrial-organizational psychology that a small effect size can translate into significant monetary gains for companies (e.g., Cascio, 2000) and from medicine that these can result in substantial changes to

---

[3]Data from Kvashchev's experiment are available on the University of Virginia web site: http://kiptron.psyc virginia.edu/ngcs2000/LongitudinalData/KvashchevStudy/Kvashchev.html

health policy (e.g., D'Andrade & Dart, 1990). In summary, we question Brody's judgments about the importance of effects of educational intervention and suggest careful interpretation of effect sizes in terms of implications that are of obvious benefit to the wider society.

Educational Malleability of Intelligence

There is also a theoretical angle to the assessment of the impact of education on intelligence. Hunt (chap. 2), for example, stated: "the study of intelligence should be the study of individual differences in human competence to perform cognitive tasks. That competence is determined by a biological capability to move information around in the head and by social conditions that facilitate the acquisition of information to be moved". This can be supplemented by the position long held by Horn (chap. 10) concerning distinctions between fluid and crystallized intelligence. According to Horn, both Gf and Gc are affected by learning: incidental learning for Gf and formally sanctioned learning for Gc. This is not commonly appreciated by some who assume that Cattell's investment theory accounts for relations between Gf and Gc. Horn is not denying the role of genetics, although his estimates of its impact tend to be on the low end. From this point of view, it is not surprising that Gustafsson found enhanced effects on Gf as well as Gc.

We agree with the foregoing but wish to move a step further. The construct of intelligence is imprecisely defined in the absence of a clear definition of the domain of behavior under consideration. Proponents of single factor models of intelligence (e.g., Jensen, 1998) often define this domain by exclusion; that is, cognitive acts such as those underlying sensory processes do not belong to this domain. As argued by Stankov (2005), it is often difficult and arbitrary to make this distinction because the difference between lower and higher order processes is blurred. We may, therefore, follow the lead of Burt (1940) and equate the domain of cognition with intelligence. Every cognitive act taps some aspect, however small, of intelligence. This way of understanding intelligence expands it beyond Gf and Gc and at the very least explicitly incorporates other broad ability (or second-stratum) factors, including those of verbal production, perception, memory, and speed (Carroll, 1993). Jensen-like definitions also blur the distinction between intelligence and many outcome measures, including achievement. Performances on achievement tests are also cognitive acts. Under this definition, both improvement on verbal and math scores reported by Campbell (chap. 4) as well as superior performance of talented students who invest considerable time into certain activities that are reported by Lubinski and Bleske-Rechek (chap. 7) count as enhancements of cognitive performance and, therefore, of intelligence.

Societal Factors Influencing Intelligence

In his largely autobiographical account, Comer (chap. 6) forcefully argued for the need to take into account early childhood experiences and home environment as a catalyst for the expression of intelligence. Comer's is almost a literary contribution that demonstrates the importance of noncognitive constructs, both external and internal to the individual, that can help disadvantaged African Americans move out of the circle that leads to the achievement gap. Indeed, the adoption of many school districts of the Comer School Development Program[4] and his own career accomplishments stands as testament to Comer's conviction that social change must start from within the individual.

---

[4]For more information on this program, see: http://info.med.yale.edu/comer/

Another chapter that points to societal influences is by Grigorenko, Jarvin, Niu, and Preiss (chap. 9). In particular, they considered assessments in diverse educational systems across the globe. Its import derives from the trends that have been set in place by international bodies, which we commented briefly on in our introduction to this chapter. Over the past decade, cross-national comparisons of performance (e.g., Program for International Student Assessment [PISA], Trends in International Mathematics and Science study [TIMMS]) have become a common occurrence. As a result, it is likely that there will be greater homogeneity across the educational systems in terms of syllabi and assessments because countries will attempt to emulate those that produce higher achievement scores. The effect of this trend on conventional measures of intelligence is yet to be seen.

NEW CONSTRUCTS, AND NEW MEANS FOR ENHANCEMENT

New constructs that are considered in this book are diverse. Many represent an extension of intelligence, with some empirical/quantitative evidence attesting to the success of certain interventions. In total, three chapters explicitly argue for the need to extend the study of intelligence in a way that lays emphasis on constructs that are not well represented in contemporary theories of intelligence. We also subsume in this section efforts aimed at enhancement of psychological constructs using new technologies or new knowledge of existing biological phenomena. Specifically, in this part of our concluding chapter, we comment on the evidence provided by our expert contributors for the effects of nutrition, augmented intelligence agents, and sleep on a range of psychological factors, many of which also impinge (either directly or indirectly) on cognitive performance.

Evidence for New Constructs

Sternberg (chap. 13) reviewed the findings from seven studies in which the choice of instructional programs designed to enhance cognitive performance was guided by his triarchic theory of successful intelligence. We consider its main focus to be new constructs, because in addition to traditional intelligence, both practical intelligence and creativity are key components of this model. Altogether, findings from seven instructional studies designed to improve these three constructs are summarized in this chapter. The samples involved 13 to 15 year-old children from Africa and the United States, middle school, high school, and college students, as well as adults of working age. These studies varied in terms of the type of training and include strategy training (spatial/verbal) in problem solving, knowledge acquisition, insight training, practical intelligence and metacognitive processing, insightful learning, and reading skills. As might be expected, the magnitudes of effects of these different instructional procedures varied, but, overall, there was evidence for enhancement. Sternberg thus appears to have successfully applied his instructional procedures to enhance aspects of both traditional intelligence measures and the new constructs he has postulated.

In another effort to extend the domain of intelligence through new constructs, Halpern (chap. 15) argued that intelligence should be redefined in terms of critical thinking. Halpern's goal is to arrive at a definition of intelligence, and corresponding tests, that more closely resemble an ability to solve, and make judgments about, current and suspected future real-world problems.[5]

---

[5]Critical thinking is sometimes contrasted with problem solving in that critical involves "reasoning in an open-ended manner, with an unlimited number of solutions" (U.S. Department of Education, Office of Educational Research and Improvement, 1995), but this is not a universally on distinction.[5]

Notably, current theories of intelligence do not include a critical thinking factor or similar abilities among constructs comprising structural models of human abilities in particular (see, e.g., Carroll, 1993). Halpern's definition of critical thinking is a synthesis of reasoning, problem solving, judgment, and decision making, and a personality trait reflecting the tendency to engage in cognitively demanding endeavors. The incorporation of need for cognition—or similarly named traits like openness from the Five-Factor model (see, e.g., Digman, 1990) and typical intellectual engagement (Goff & Ackerman, 1992)—is certainly interesting, because it provides a link to research in social psychology especially in relationship to the effectiveness of persuasion (Cacioppo, Petty, Feinstein, & Jarvis, 1996). Viewed from this perspective, critical thinking appears as a new construct composed of vastly different, synthesized parts. It is easily comprehensible that such an agglomerate of constructs is not operationalized without difficulty, an issue that is elaborated considerably in Halpern's chapter.

In their chapter, Mayer, Salovey, and Caruso (chap. 14) provided an account of recent findings with yet another new construct: emotional intelligence (EI). This latter construct has been the subject of considerable debate over the past decade (see Matthews, Zeidner, & Roberts, 2004; Matthews, Zeidner, & Roberts, 2002). The authors brought to light additional evidence that is favorable to their position, including discussion of predictive validity evidence. Indeed, between the authors completing this chapter and this book going to press, evidence for relations between skills underlying social interactions and relationships (Engelberg & Sjöberg, 2005), organizational commitment (Abraham, 2005), the ability to cope with stress (Zeidner, Matthews & Roberts, 2006), and a range of educational outcomes (Zins, Weissberg, Wang, & Walberg, 2004) have been demonstrated for EI, or other closely related measures of affective processes. Although these are subject to replication and not without attendant caveats (see Roberts, Schulze, Matthews, & Zeidner, 2006), they are suggestive of the importance of this new domain of psychological inquiry.

Nevertheless, many issues surrounding the scientific status of EI remain unresolved. One critical issue is that of measurement. Mayer et al. (chap. 14) addressed this issue and defended their procedures for measurement, including consensual scoring of EI items. Indeed, the justification for consensual scoring seems further buttressed by a fascinating popular account, which has at its heart a complex model related to games theory (Surowiecki, 2004; see also Legree, Psotka, Tremble, & Bourne 2006). Because the susceptibility of these measures to coaching and fakability is undetermined, studies addressing these issues are required, as are alternative scoring (e.g., veridically based) techniques.

New Technologies for Enhancement

An interesting new area related to intelligence enhancement is the effort to provide humans with technological devices that help them become smarter. Rhodes (chap. 17) placed this research into an historical background, acquainted the reader with this emerging science's terminology (and certain problems that need to be resolved), and provided a preview of many domains where wearable intelligence is starting to make its mark.[6] The field of intelligence augmentation certainly provides conditions that might allow certain component processes underlying intelligence to be available in near-equal measure to all individuals. Its potential in special education, in particular, is thus undoubted. Even so, intelligence augmentation raises some ethical concerns, which we discuss later in this section.

---

[6]Advances are made so rapidly in this domain that we cannot necessarily assume that a reader out there is not currently processing this chapter using wearable technology!

Notwithstanding Rhodes' (chap. 17) intriguing exposition, there are further developments in technology and artificial intelligence that also impact on several of the new constructs addressed in the current volume. Leaders in the cognitive revolution, among them Simon, Norman, and Neisser, always envisaged better representation of affect in their models (Picard et al., 2004). Over the past decade, however, there appears to have been a significant impetus toward heeding this early call, giving rise to the field of affective computing. Picard (1997), a pioneer of this field, defined affective computing as "computing that relates to, arises from, or deliberately influences emotions ... (and includes) giving a computer the ability to recognize and express emotions, developing its ability to recognize and express emotions, and enabling it to regulate and utilize its emotions" (p. 3).

Despite being a relatively new field, affective computing boasts an impressive array of applications in the research and/or development phase (see Roberts et al., 2005). These include technologies for assisting those with autism and those without effective speech communication and technologies for improving consumer feedback (Picard, 1997; Trappl, Petta, & Payr, 2002). Affective computing interventions are also being developed to improve student learning, including those based on intelligent tutors that impact (e.g., through the use of avatars) or otherwise adapt (e.g., through monitoring interest level) to the learner and her or his environment (Picard et al., 2004). Research at the MIT Media Lab also appears directed towards a variety of new measurements of affective state. For example, Picard et al. reported promising correlates of teacher's ratings of student affect from measures of chair pressure patterns (assessed with a device that records how postures shift during learning), upper facial features (captured using a sophisticated video camera and analyzed with a proprietary algorithm), and a skin-conductivity sensing glove that communicates wirelessly with the computer. Plausibly then, some of these methodologies may be used minimally to validate new constructs previously discussed (in particular, though not limited to, emotional intelligence).

New Knowledge of Biology for Enhancement

Biological approaches to enhancement are also covered in this book, though we limit them to a relatively small set of possible influences. Indeed, we might have chosen to have contributors discuss the effects of hormones, various neurochemicals and neurotoxicins, so-called enhancement drugs, various physical diseases known to influence cognition, genetics, and so forth. Instead, we chose internationally renowned scholars to discuss biological influences that are notable both for their pervasiveness and the ease with which interventions are possible: the effects of nutrition (Benton, chap. 16) and the sleep-wake cycle (Dinges & Rogers, chap. 18) on cognitive performance.

Benton (chap. 16) led the reader through a diverse literature detailing the effects of various vitamins, diet, fatty acids, duration of breast-feeding, and perinatal diet constituency, to name a few, overarching his focus on nutrition. He also tackled the issue of how aspects of nutrition and diet play out across the life span. Whereas there is considerable evidence to suggest that poor diet will limit the intellectual development of the young child, the evidence for more subtle effects, particularly among school-aged children and adults who live in industrialized nations, is scant. Surprisingly perhaps, this seems an area in need of more systematic programs of research and, in certain instances, metaanalytic investigations.

Dinges and Rogers (chap. 18) began their discussion of circadian rhythms with the basic premise that human cognitive abilities have allowed us to create a 24/7 world. In something of a cruel twist, however, biology demands that we conform to a sleep–wake cycle, which if distorted too much, can actually disrupt cognitive performance. Indeed, the dynamics of the sleep drive and circadian clock may impinge greatly on cognitive performance, with circadian effects demonstrably variable across individuals. Dinges and Rogers then considered a range of countermeasures that effectively constitute enhancement aids given the constraints imposed by the biological clock. Among those that they give considerable attention are prophylactic (power) naps, caffeine, modafinil, and technological aids. The evidence for the efficacy of these interventions is compelling. This is no doubt a function of the fact that the circadian system can be modeled effectively in all living organisms such that its biological mechanisms are much better understood than cognitive ability constructs. Moreover, it should be mentioned that many of the effects Dinges and Rogers discussed, although often couched in terms of a single circadian cycle (or in the case of sleep deprivation, several days), may have considerable effects if multiplied over the course of a lifetime.

A Cautionary Note

As is often the case, new developments in science that point to biological and technological means of changing the human condition do raise ethical concerns. For example, in a recent issue of *Lancet*, Butcher (2003) asked questions about the use of cognitive enhancing drugs and forms of neurotechnology. Interventions discussed include the use of methylphenidate by university students to enhance the ability to focus and study, the use of brain–computer interfaces for enhancement purposes, and cognitive enhancing drugs to counter age-related memory loss. Significantly, these exemplars might easily have been replaced with forms of enhancement that the contributors discussed in the current volume. Clearly, these various interventions may impinge on social justice and equality, run the risk of creating population homogeneity (with an attendant loss of diversity), and cause individuals to distort the perception of self (see also Sententia, 2004). Butcher suggested that these ethical concerns are sufficient for those interested in enhancement to consider the implications of their research and to take responsibility for its applications. We concur with this set of recommendations; as with any science having this much potential impact on the human condition an iterative procedure is required among programmatic research, policy, and ethical-legal implications associated with enhancement aids.

CONCLUSIONS

In summary, the chapters in this book point to:

1   The possibility of achieving enhancement in cognitive performance using biological, instructional, technological, and societal interventions;
2   New areas that expand the traditional notion of cognitive performance beyond those covered by the construct of intelligence; and
3   The possibility of enhancing at least a subset of these new constructs.

The message, we believe, is an optimistic one for educational endeavors: Cognitive performance is not totally immutable as is sometimes claimed by those prone to uncritical interpretation of behavioral genetic data. It is also optimistic for those looking for new frontiers in intelligence research; there are areas both within, and broaching, the disciplines of education, psychology, biology, artificial intelligence, economics, and policy that are worthy of further investigation.

This volume presents only a sample of recent work on enhancement and new constructs by internationally acclaimed experts in different fields. We believe that the effects of enhancement procedures reviewed here are moderate, yet they are also socially important. We do not know if future interventions may lead to stronger effects. We believe that the work on new constructs should proceed with increased vigor. Future efforts may include the development of emerging "new" constructs in psychology (e.g., metacognition, social attitudes, values, and norms) as they impinge on cognitive performance as well as technological and biological innovations of the kind mentioned throughout. It is to be hoped that the experimental designs and statistical techniques used to analyze these effects will also increase in sophistication. Indeed, some upcoming Spearman Seminar will likely revisit many or all of these topics.[7]

REFERENCES

Abelson, R. P. (1985). A variance explanation paradox: When a little is a lot. *Psychological Bulletin, 97,* 129–133.

Abelson, R. P. (1995). *Statistics as principled argument.* Hillsdale, NJ: Lawrence Erlbaum Associates.

Abraham, R. (2005). Emotional intelligence in the workplace: A review and synthesis. In R. Schulze & R. D. Roberts (Eds.), *Emotional intelligence: An international handbook.* Cambridge, MA: Hogrefe & Huber.

Ackerman, P. L. (1996). A theory of adult intellectual development: Process, personality, interests, and knowledge. *Intelligence, 22,* 227–257.

Ackerman, P. L., & Heggestad, E. D. (1997). Intelligence, personality, and interest: Evidence for overlapping traits. *Psychological Bulletin, 121,* 219–245.

Burt, C. (1940). *The factors of the mind: An introduction to factor analysis in psychology.* London: University of London Press.

Butcher, J. (2003). Cognitive enhancement raises ethical concerns. *Lancet, 362,* 132–133.

Cacioppo, J. T., Petty, R. E., Feinstein, J. A., & Jarvis, W. B. G. (1996). Dispositional differences in cognitive motivation: The life and times of individuals varying in need for cognition. *Psychological Bulletin, 119,* 197–253.

Carroll, J. B. (1993). *Human cognitive abilities: A survey of factor-analytic studies.* New York: Cambridge University Press.

Cascio, W. F. (2000). *Costing human resources: The financial impact of behavior in organizations* (4th ed.). Cincinnati, OH: South-Western Publishing.

D'Andrade, R., & Dart, J. (1990). The interpretation of r versus r² or why percent of variance explained accounted for is a poor measure of size of effect. *Journal of Quantitative Anthropology, 2,* 47–59.

Deary, I. J., & Pagliari, C. (1991). The strength of g at different levels of ability: Have Detterman and Daniel rediscovered Spearman's "Law of Diminishing Returns"? *Intelligence, 15,* 247–250.

Detterman, D. K., & Daniel, M. H. (1989). Correlates of mental tests with each other and with cognitive variables are highest for low IQ groups. *Intelligence, 13,* 349–359.

Digman, J. M. (1990). Personality structure: Emergence of the five-factor model. *Annual Review of Psychology, 41,* 417–440.

Dolan, C. V., & Molenaar, P. C. M. (1994). Testing specific hypotheses concerning latent group differences in multi-group covariance structure analysis with structured means. *Multivariate Behavioral Research, 29,* 203–222.

Engelberg, E., & Sjöberg, L. (2005). Emotional intelligence and interpersonal skills. In R. Schulze & R. D. Roberts (Eds.), *Emotional intelligence: An international handbook.* Cambridge, MA: Hogrefe & Huber.

---

[7]As mentioned in the introductory chapter to this book, the tradition is to have a different theme for each of the Spearman Seminars. The next topic, with hopefully a follow-on book, is "Diagnostics for Education: Theory. Measurement, and Applications."

Fogarty, G. J., & Stankov, L. (1995). Challenging the "law of diminishing returns." *Intelligence, 21,* 157–174.

Goff, M., & Ackerman, P. A. (1992). Personality-intelligence relations: Assessment of typical intellectual engagement. *Journal of Educational Psychology, 84,* 537–552.

Hartmann, P., & Teasdale, T. W. (2004). A test of Spearman's "Law of Diminishing Returns" in two large samples of Danish military draftees. *Intelligence, 32,* 499–508.

Jensen, A. R. (1998). *The g factor: The science of mental ability.* Westport, CT: Praeger.

Jensen, A. R. (2003). Regularities in Spearman's law of diminishing returns. *Intelligence, 31,* 95–105.

Landy, F. J. (2005) Some historical and scientific issues related to research on emotional intelligence *Journal of Organization Behavior,* 26, 411–424, 2005.

Layard, R. (2005). *Happiness: Lessons from a new science.* New York: Penguin.

Legree, P. J., Pifer, M. E., & Grafton, F. C. (1996). Correlations among cognitive abilities are lower for higher ability groups. *Intelligence, 23,* 45–57.

Legree, P., Psotka, J., Tremble, T., & Bourne, D. R. (2005). Using consensus based measurement to assess emotional intelligence. In R. Schulze & R. D. Roberts (Eds.), *Emotional intelligence: An international handbook.* Cambridge, MA: Hogrefe & Huber.

Lubke, G. H., Dolan, C. V., Kelderman, H., & Mellenbergh, G. J. (2003). On the relationship between sources of within- and between-group differences and measurement invariance in the common factor model. *Intelligence, 31,* 543–566.

Matthews, G., Zeidner, M., & Roberts, R. D. (2002). *Emotional intelligence: Science and myth.* Boston: MIT Press.

Matthews, G., Zeidner, M., & Roberts, R. D. (2004). Seven myths about emotional intelligence. *Psychological Inquiry, 15,* 179–196.

Neisser, U., Boodoo, G., Bouchard, Jr., T. J., Boykin, A. W., Brody, N., Ceci, S. J., et al. (1996). Intelligence: Knowns and unknowns. *American Psychologist, 51,* 77–101.

OECD Programme for International Student Assessment. (2005). *Introduction.* Retrieved March 20, 2005 at http://www.pisa.oecd.org/pages/

Picard, R. W. (1997). *Affective computing.* Cambridge, MA: MIT Press.

Picard, R. W., Papert, S., Bender, W., Blumberg, B., Breazel, C., Cavallo, D., Machover, T., Resnick, M., Roy, D., & Strohecker, C. (2004). Affective learning: A manifesto. *BT Technology Journal, 22,* 253–269.

Roberts, R. D., Schulze, R., Matthews, G., & Zeidner, M. (2005). Understanding, measuring, and applying emotional intelligence: What have we learned? What have we missed? In R. Schulze & R. D. Roberts (Eds.), *International handbook of emotional intelligence.* Cambridge, MA: Hogrefe & Huber.

Rosenthal, R., Rosnow, R. L., & Rubin, D. B. (2000). *Contrasts and effect sizes in behavioral research: A correlational approach.* New York: Cambridge University Press.

Schulze, R. (2005). Modeling structures of intelligence. In O. Wilhelm & R. W. Engle (Eds.), *Handbook of understanding and measuring intelligence* (pp. 241–263). Thousand Oaks, CA: Sage.

Schulze, R., & Holling, H. (2005). Assessing the monetary benefits of selection procedures with utility analysis. In A. Beauducel, B. Biehl, M. Bosnjak, W. Conrad, G. Schönberger, & D. Wagener (Eds.), *Multivariate research strategies: Festschrift in honor of Werner W. Wittmann* (pp. 303–328). Aachen, Germany: Shaker.

Seligman, M. E. P. (2002). *Authentic happiness: Using the new positive psychology to realize your potential for lasting fulfillment.* New York: Free Press/Simon & Schuster.

Sententia, W. (2004). Neuroethical considerations: Cognitive liberty and converging technologies for improving human cognition. In C. D. Montemagno & M. C. Roco (Eds.), *The coevolution of human potential and converging technologies* (pp. 221–228). New York: New York Academy of Sciences.

Spearman, C. E. (1927). *The abilities of man.* London: Macmillan.

Stankov, L. (1986). Kvashchev's experiment: Can we boost intelligence? *Intelligence, 10,* 209–230.

Stankov, L. (2005). "g" factor: Issues of design and interpretation. In O. Wilhelm & R. Engle (Eds.), *Understanding and measuring intelligence* (pp. 279–294). Thousand Oaks, CA: Sage.

Stankov, L., & Chen, K. (1988a). Training and changes in fluid and crystallized intelligence. *Contemporary Educational Psychology, 13,* 382–396.

Stankov, L., & Chen, K. (1988b). Can we boost fluid and crystallized intelligence? A structural modeling approach. *Australian Journal of Psychology, 40,* 363–376.

Stauffer, J. M., Ree, M. J., & Carretta, T. R. (1996). Cognitive-components tests are not much more than g: An extension of Kyllonen's analyses. *The Journal of General Psychology, 123,* 193–205.

Surowiecki, J. (2004). *The wisdom of crowds: Why the many are smarter than the few and how collective wisdom shapes business, economies, societies and nations.* Garden city, NY: Doubleday.

Trappl, R., Petta, P., & Payr, S. (Eds.). (2002). *Emotions in humans and artifacts.* Cambridge, MA: MIT Press.

U.S. Department of Education, Office of Educational Research and Improvement. (1995). *National assessment of college student learning: Identifying college graduates' essential skills in writing, speech and listening, and critical thinking* (NCES Publication No. 95–001). Washington, DC: U.S. Government Printing Office.

Wicherts, J. M., Dolan, C. V., Hessen, D. J., Oosterveld, P., van Baal, G. C. M., Boomsma, D. I., et al. (2004). Are intelligence tests measurement invariant over time? Investigating the nature of the Flynn effect. *Intelligence, 32,* 509–537.

Zeidner, M., Matthews, B., & Roberts, R .D. (2006). Emotional intelligence, adaptztion, and coping. In J. Ciarrochi, J. Forgas, & J. D. Mayer (Eds), Emotional intelligence in everyday life: A scientific inquing (second edition). (pp. 100–125). Philadelphiz, PA: Psychology Press.

Zins, J. E., Weissberg, R. P., Wang, M. C., & Walberg, H. J. (Eds.). (2004). *Building school success through social and emotional learning: Implications for practice and research.* New York: Teachers College Press.

Author Index

Subject Index

Printed in the United States
by Baker & Taylor Publisher Services